COLLINS
GEM
ENCYCLOPEDIA

VOLUME 2
L-Z

COLLINS GEM
ENCYCLOPEDIA

VOLUME 2
L-Z

Collins
London & Glasgow

First Published 1979
Revised Impression 1980
© 1979 William Collins Sons & Co. Ltd.

ISBN: 0 00 458755 3

Typeset by C.R. Barber & Partners, Wrotham, Kent

Printed in Great Britain by
William Collins Sons & Co. Ltd.

Collins Gem Encyclopedia
is based on and abridged from
Collins Concise Encyclopedia

PREFACE

The *Gem Encyclopedia* is a completely up-to-date, easy to use reference guide to all fields of human activity and knowledge. *The Encyclopedia* has been arranged into two compact volumes, containing over 14,000 articles. The entries have been listed alphabetically so that the reader can locate the information required as quickly and easily as possible.

The coverage of the *Gem Encyclopedia* ranges from the birth of civilization in Sumeria to the furthest reaches of space exploration, from ancient Greek tragedy to pop art. Both text and selection strive for impartiality and wherever possible stick to facts rather than opinions. Finally, although the *Encyclopedia* aims at world-wide coverage, it has been particularly tailored to the needs of the English-speaking world.

Ian Crofton

EDITORIAL STAFF

Editor
Ian Crofton

Editorial Assistants
Irene Chapman
Danielle McGrath
Kay Macpherson
Nancy Marshall

ABBREVIATIONS USED IN THE ENCYCLOPEDIA

AD	anno domini	Dec.	December
admin.	administration, administrated	dept.	department
		dist.	district
agric.	agricultural, agriculture	E	east
		eg	for example
alt.	altitude	Eng.	English
anc.	ancient	esp.	especially
anon.	anonymous	est.	estimated
Arab.	Arabic	estab.	established
at. no.	atomic number	*etc*	and so on
at. wt.	atomic weight	excl.	excludes, excluding
Aug.	August		
autobiog.	autobiography	Feb.	February
auton.	autonomous, autonomy	Finn.	Finnish
		fl	flourished
av.	average	Flem.	Flemish
b.	born	Fr.	French
BC	before Christ	ft	foot, feet
biog.	biography	Ger.	German
bor.	borough	Gk.	Greek
C	central	gm	gram
c	about	govt.	government
cap.	capital	ha.	hectare, hectares
cent.	century	Heb.	Hebrew
cm	centimetre, centimetres	h.e.p.	hydro-electric power
co.	county, company	hist.	historical
co. bor.	county borough	hr	hour
coll.	college	hq	headquarters
co. town	county town	Hung.	Hungarian
d.	died	*ie*	that is

in.	inch, inches	penin.	peninsula
incl.	include, including, included	PM	Prime Minister
		Pol.	Polish
indust.	industrial, industry	pop.	population
isl.	island	Port.	Portuguese
Ital.	Italian	prehist.	prehistoric
Jan.	January	prob.	probably
Jap.	Japanese	protect.	protectorate
jct.	junction	prov.	province
kg	kilogram	pseud.	pseudonym
km	kilometre, kilometres	pub.	published
		R.	River
kmh	kilometres per hour	RC	Roman Catholic
		Russ.	Russian
L.	Lake	S	south
lat.	latitude	sec	second
lb	pound (unit of weight)	Sept.	September
		Span.	Spanish
long.	longitude	sq km	square kilometres
max.	maximum	sq mi	square miles
mfg.	manuacture, manufacturing	St	Saint
		St.	Street
mi	mile, miles	str.	strait
min.	minimum, minute	Swed.	Swedish
mm	millimetre	territ.	territory
MP	Member of Parliament	Turk.	Turkish
		TV	television
mph	miles per hour	UK	United Kingdom
Mt.	Mount	UN	United Nations
Mts.	Mountains	univ.	university
mun. bor.	municipal borough	US	United States
N	north	v	against
Nov.	November	vol.	volume
NT	New Testament	WW	World War
Oct.	October	W	west
orig.	originally	yd	yard, yards
OT	Old Testament		

L

labelled compound, compound in which radioactive isotope of an element replaces normal stable atom. Used to trace paths of compound through mechanical or biological systems.

Labiatae, family of flowering plants. Characterized by square stem, hairy leaves, grouping of flowers on stem, hooded petals, *eg* lavender, thyme, sage, MINT.

Labor Day, in US, Canada, 1st Monday in September, legal holiday in honour of labour.

labour, in economics, factor of PRODUCTION. In perfect competition, price of labour (wages) is elastic and depends on demand.

labour, division of, *see* DIVISION OF LABOUR.

Labour Party, in UK, political party organized to implement socialist policies, as advocated by Fabian Society, on evolutionary basis, supported by most of trade union movement. Formed (1906), adopted socialist programme (1918) and set up local branches, admitting individual members. Rose rapidly in elections, sharing major party status with Conservatives from 1922. Prominent figures incl. MacDonald, Attlee, Bevan, Wilson. Elsewhere, grouping of socialists and trade unions characterize labour parties, *eg* N Europe, Australia, New Zealand. Labour links with Euro-

pean SOCIAL DEMOCRACY reflect similar policies and means of implementation.

labour relations, *see* INDUSTRIAL RELATIONS ACT.

Labrador, mainland territ. of Newfoundland, E Canada. Area 292,000 sq km (*c* 113,000 sq mi). Separated from Newfoundland Isl. by Str. of Belle Isle. Tundra in N; forests in S. Cod fishing, iron ore industs. H.e.p. supplies from Churchill R. Inhabited by Eskimos in N. British gained control (1763); joined Newfoundland 1809.

Labrador Current, cold ocean current of W Atlantic. Flows S past W Greenland, E Canada, meets Gulf Stream off Newfoundland. Frequent fogs where currents meet.

La Bruyère, Jean de (1645-96), French writer. Known for misanthropic social satire, esp. *Les Caractères* (1688), combining portraits of types, individuals with general maxims, after model of Theophrastus.

laburnum, genus of deciduous trees of Leguminosae family. Native to S and C Europe, widely grown in US. Clusters of yellow flowers followed by pods of poisonous seeds.

Laccadive, Minicoy and Amindivi Islands, union territ. of India, comprising group of 27 isls. in Arabian Sea off coast of Kerala state. Area 32 sq km (12 sq mi); pop.

c 32,000; cap. Kavaratti Isl. Territ. renamed Lakshadweep (1973).

lace, openwork fabric woven in ornamental designs. Finest lace is made from linen. Lace became fashionable in 16th cent. and reached height of production in Flanders in 18th cent. Machine-made lace first appeared *c* 1760. Chief manufacturing centres are France, Belgium, England, Ireland and Italy.

Lachlan, river of S New South Wales, Australia. Flows *c* 1480 km (920 mi) from Great Dividing Range via Wyangala Dam to Murrumbidgee R. Provides irrigation.

Laclos, Pierre [Ambroise François] Choderlos de (1741-1803), French artillery officer, author. Known for epistolary novel, *Les Liaisons dangereuses* (1782), dealing with power of evil to corrupt innocence.

lacquer, solution of film-forming substances dissolved in volatile solvents, applied to decorate or protect surfaces. Commonest forms use cellulose esters. Lacquer work was highly developed in art of China and Japan.

lacrosse, ten-a-side outdoor sport played with ball and netted stick. Originated by North American Indians, it was named by French settlers; 1st games played by white men date from 1840s. Adopted as Canada's national sport 1867.

lactic acid, see LACTOSE.

lactose, white crystalline sugar found in mammalian milk; less sweet than cane sugar. Bacterial fermentation of lactose in milk produces lactic acid. Lactic acid also formed by splitting of glucose in animal cells, with consequent release of useful body energy.

Ladakh, region of NE Kashmir, India, bordering on Tibet. Incl. highest of Karakoram Mts.; traversed by upper reaches of Indus. Claimed by Chinese, who occupied parts in 1962.

Ladoga, Lake, largest lake in Europe, in USSR, NW European RSFSR. Area *c* 18,200 sq km (7000 sq mi). Outlet is R. Neva, flowing to Gulf of Finland. Originally divided between Finland and USSR; passed into Soviet control (1940).

ladybird or **ladybug,** any of Coccinellidae family of small beetles; red or yellow with black spots. Larvae and adults feed on aphids.

Lady Day, see ANNUNCIATION, FEAST OF THE.

Lady of the Lake, see ARTHURIAN LEGEND.

Ladysmith, town of W Natal, South Africa. Pop. 33,000. Railway jct., engineering, textiles. Besieged 1899-1900 by Boers, relieved by British force under Buller.

lady's slipper, any of various plants of ORCHID family whose flowers resemble a slipper, esp. of genus *Cypripedium* native to Americas.

Lae, town of Papua New Guinea, E New Guinea isl. Pop. 32,000. Transportation centre.

Laënnec, René Théophile Hyacinthe (1781-1826), French physician. Invented stethoscope, which he used to diagnose disorders of the chest. Authority on tuberculosis and heart disease.

La Fayette, Comtesse de, née Marie Madeleine Pioche de la

Vergne (1634-92), French novelist. Known for psychological novel, *La Princesse de Clèves* (1678).

Lafayette, Marie Joseph Paul Yves Roch Gilbert du Motier, Marquis de (1757-1834), French soldier. Went to America in 1777 to fight for the colonists. Elected to the French National Assembly (1789) and commanded the French National Guard (1789-92), but his moderate views antagonized the Jacobins and he fled the country. Imprisoned by the Austrians, he was released by Napoleon. Led moderates in the July Revolution (1830).

La Follette, Robert Marion (1855-1925), American statesman. As governor of Wisconsin (1901-6), introduced progressive reforms known as Wisconsin Idea. As a senator (1906-25), he opposed US entry into WWI. Progressive Party presidential nominee (1924).

La Fontaine, Jean de (1621-95), French author. Known for *Fables choisies* (1668-94), adaptations of ancient fables affectionately ridiculing human folly. Also wrote *Contes et nouvelles* (1664-74) derived from tales of Ariosto, Boccaccio and others.

Laforgue, Jules (1860-87), French poet. Associated with symbolists. Works, *eg Les Complaintes* (1885), *Le Concile féerique* (1886), influenced T.S. Eliot's early poetry in form, subject matter.

lager, a light beer, stored for several months for ageing. Most beers in Europe, many in America are lagers.

Lagerkvist, Pär Fabian (1891-1974), Swedish author. Known for novels, *eg The Dwarf* (1944), *Barabbas* (1950). Also wrote poetry,

experimental dramas *eg Let Man Live* (1951). Nobel Prize for Literature (1951).

Lagos, cap. of Nigeria, on Bight of Benin. Pop. 1,477,000. Built on several isls. and mainland, linked by bridges. Admin., indust. centre; railway terminus and port, exports palm produce, groundnuts, cocoa; univ. (1962). Formerly notorious slave market; ceded (1861) to UK, became colony (1886) until merged with Southern Nigeria (1906).

Lagrange, Joseph Louis, Comte (1736-1813), French mathematician. Famed for *Mécanique analytique* (1788), purely analytic study of mechanics; contributed to calculus of variations. Advocated adoption of metric system in France.

La Guardia, Fiorello Henrico (1882-1947), American politician. Mayor of New York (1934-45), instituted major welfare programme and reduced political corruption.

Lahore, city of N Pakistan. Pop. 2,148,000. Indust., transport centre; railway engineering. Cap. of Mogul, then Sikh empires; captured by British (1846). Has Shah Jehan's Shalamar gardens (1637), tomb of Sikh ruler Ranjit Singh; univ. (1882).

Laibach, *see* LJUBLJANA, Yugoslavia.

Laing, Ronald David (1927-), Scottish psychiatrist. Work, notably *Sanity, Madness and the Family* (1964), assumes mental illness does not exist clinically.

laisser-faire or **laissez-faire,** in economics, doctrine that economic system functions best without govt. interference and that, unregulated by artificial means, natural economic order tends to favour maximum good of individual and community as a whole. First formulated by PHYSIOCRATS in reaction to MERCANTILISM, later adapted by Adam Smith, Bentham and Mill. Basis of Western economic activity in 19th cent., but development of monopolies led to govt. regulation in 20th cent.

lake (Scot. *loch*, Irish, *lough*), body of water surrounded by land. May form naturally in depression caused by glacial, volcanic or tectonic action, or artificially by damming. Normally freshwater; high evaporation causes salt lakes (sometimes, if large, called seas, eg Caspian, Dead Sea). Some lakes disappear in dry season, eg L. Eyre, Australia.

Lake District, Cumbria, NW England. National Park (area 2242 sq km/866 sq mi) of lakes (incl. Windermere, Coniston Water, Ullswater, Derwent Water) and mountains (incl. Scafell Pike, Helvellyn, Skiddaw). Literary connections eg Wordsworth, Coleridge, Southey ('Lake Poets').

lake dwelling, in archaeology, habitation built on artificial platform, usually supported by piles driven into lake bottom. Examples incl. one at Glastonbury, England, important for information about Iron Age in Britain, also Neolithic and Bronze Age sites in Switzerland, Germany. *See also* CRANNOG.

Lakshadweep, *see* LACCADIVE, MINICOY AND AMINDIVI ISLANDS.

lalique, art nouveau style of glassware, decorated with figures in relief. Introduced by René Lalique (1860-1945), French jeweller.

Lalo, [Victor Antoine] Edouard (1823-92), French composer. Works

incl. *Symphonie espagnole* for violin and orchestra, opera *Le Roi d'Ys.*

Lamaism, form of Buddhism practised in Tibet, Bhutan and Mongolia. Derived from Mahayana Buddhism but incorporating erotic mysticism, many animistic elements. Introduced into Tibet in 8th cent. Monastery estab. near Lhasa (c 750). Spiritual head, DALAI LAMA, ruled in Tibet until 1959.

Lamarck, Jean Baptiste, Chevalier de (1744-1829), French naturalist. Proposed evolutionary theory (Lamarckism) that modifications induced in an individual by the environment are transmitted to individual's descendants. His *Histoire naturelle des animaux sans vertèbres* (1815-22) founded modern invertebrate zoology.

Lamartine, Alphonse Marie Louis de (1790-1869), French poet, statesman. Major Romantic. Wrote *Les Méditations poétiques* (1820) incl. 'Le Lac'. Other works incl. narrative poem *La Chute d'un ange* (1838), *Histoire des Girondins* (1847). One-time Royalist politician, led provisional govt. of Revolution (1848).

Lamas, Carlos Saavedra, *see* SAAVEDRA LAMAS.

Lamb, Caroline, *see* MELBOURNE, WILLIAM LAMB, 2ND VISCOUNT.

Lamb, Charles (1775-1834), English essayist. Works incl. *Specimens of English Dramatic Poets* (1808), collection *Essays of Elia* (1823) incl. 'A Dissertation on Roast Pig'. Children's books incl. *Tales from Shakespeare* (with sister, 1807), *Beauty and the Beast* (1811). Friend of Coleridge and other Romantics.

Lambert, Constant (1905-51), English composer. Known for his concert work *The Rio Grande*, and for his book *Music Ho!* (1934), a penetrating yet idiosyncratic evaluation of music of the time.

Lambert, John (1619-83), English soldier. Led the parliamentary cavalry at Marston Moor (1644) and was second-in-command to Cromwell in Scotland (1650-1). Though he supported Cromwell as protector, he opposed attempts to extend his powers. At Restoration, was arrested and banished.

Lambeth, bor. of SC Greater London, England. Pop. 303,000. Created 1965 from met. bor., incl. part of Wandsworth. Has 5 Thames bridges; Old Vic Theatre, Royal Festival Hall; Lambeth Palace (residence of Archbishop of Canterbury).

Lamentations, prophetic book of OT, traditionally attributed to Jeremiah but written after fall of Jerusalem (c 586 BC). Consists of 5 poems mourning the fall of the city. Stanzas in Chapters 1-4 form Hebrew alphabetical acrostic.

lammergeier, *Gypaetus barbatus,* bird of vulture family, found in remote mountain ranges of Europe and Asia. Also called bearded vulture.

Lammermuir Hills, range of SE Scotland, runs SW-NE through Lothian, Borders regions. Rise to 533 m (1749 ft) at Meikle Says Law.

lamprey, primitive marine or freshwater CYCLOSTOME. Atlantic lamprey, *Petromyzon marinus,* has penetrated Great Lakes, becoming serious pest of fishing.

Lanarkshire, former county of SC Scotland, now in Strathclyde region. Lowther Hills in S (sheep); low-

lying, fertile in C (market gardening); heavy industs. based on iron, coal deposits in N. Chief city Glasgow. Co. town was Lanark, former royal burgh on R. Clyde. Pop. 9000. Market town; textiles mfg. Owen's New Lanark model town (1784) nearby.

Lancashire, county of NW England. Area 3043 sq km (1175 sq mi); pop. 1,363,000; co. town Preston. Pennine moors in N, E; fertile lowlands in C, SW. Coal mining; textile indust. (once famous for cotton); engineering. County palatine from 1351.

Lancaster, city of Lancashire, NW England, former co. town on R. Lune. Pop. 50,000. Textiles, furniture mfg. Has univ. (1964); 13th cent. castle on site of Roman camp.

Lancaster, House of, English royal family. Founded by Edmund ('Crouchback'), son of Henry III, who was granted title of earl of Lancaster in 1267. John of Gaunt became duke (1362) through marriage into Lancaster family and his son became 1st Lancastrian king as Henry IV. Others were Henry V and Henry VI. Rivalry with House of York led to Wars of the Roses.

Lancelot, *see* ARTHURIAN LEGEND.

lancers, originally light cavalry regiments armed with lances, survived until WWI, after which they were mechanized, becoming mainly armoured car units.

Lanchow, cap. of Kansu prov., NC China. Pop. 1,500,000. On Hwang Ho. Major oil refinery, plutonium processing plant. Hist. and modern transport hub. Petrochemical, plastic and fertilizer industs.

Landes, coastal region of SW

France, between Médoc and R. Adour. Formerly wasteland of dunes, lagoons, moorland; pine forests now yield lumber, resins etc.

Land League, Irish organization, formed 1879 under leadership of PARNELL and Michael Davitt, which sought to improve conditions of land ownership for Catholics and to fight evictions. By operation of boycott, influenced passage of Gladstone's Land Act (1881), which fixed fair rents and secured tenure.

Landor, Walter Savage (1775-1864), English poet. Works, eg Gebir (1798), Hellenics (1847), draw on Classical, Arabic material. Also wrote prose Imaginary Conversations of Literary Men and Statesmen (1824-8).

Landseer, Sir Edwin Henry (1802-73), English painter. Specialized in sentimental paintings of animals, esp. dogs displaying human characteristics. Modelled the group of lions at base of Nelson's Column in Trafalgar Square, London. Works incl. The Monarch of the Glen.

Land's End, granite headland of Cornwall, SW England. Most W point of England.

landslide, mass movement of earth and rock down a slope. Normally occurs along definite interface, when water-saturated material detaches from impermeable material underneath. Also caused by earth tremors, undercutting of cliff face, etc.

Landsteiner, Karl (1868-1943), American pathologist, b. Austria. Identified 4 main human blood groups whose incompatibility is important in transfusions; awarded Nobel Prize for Physiology and Medicine (1930). Co-discoverer (1940) of Rh (Rhesus) blood factor.

Lanfranc (d. 1089), Italian churchman and scholar. Quarrelled with tutor, Berenger of Tours. Archbishop of Canterbury (1070-89), instituted many church reforms incl. replacing English bishops with Normans, subjugating archbishop of York to Canterbury.

Lang, Cosmo Gordon (1864-1945), English churchman, b. Scotland. Archbishop of Canterbury (1928-42). Influential in abdication of Edward VIII.

Lang, Fritz (1890-1976), American film director-producer, b. Vienna. Known for expressionist silent films made in Germany, eg Nibelung Saga (1923-4), Metropolis (1926), and esp. M (1931), study of child molester. Went to US (1934), fleeing Nazis, to make more conventional melodramas, eg Fury (1936), The Big Heat (1953).

Langevin, Paul (1872-1946), French physicist. Developed electron theory of paramagnetism and diamagnetism. Studied ultrasonic sound to facilitate submarine detection, basis of modern sonar.

Langland, William (c 1331-c 1400), English poet. Probable author of Piers Plowman, Middle English religious allegory; long, ambitious poem exploring human predicament in relation to God.

Langton, Stephen (d. 1228), English churchman, theologian. Elected archbishop of Canterbury, in defiance of King John, through influence of Pope Innocent III (1207). Assumed see (1213) after John submitted to papal authority.

Supported barons in struggle leading to Magna Carta.

Langtry, Emilie Charlotte ('Lillie') (1853-1929), English actress, known as 'Jersey Lily'. Famous for beauty, friendship with Prince of Wales (later Edward VII).

language, systematically differentiated sounds used in significant sequences as means of communication. May be represented by further system of written signs (see ALPHABET). Considered a defining attribute of mankind. See LINGUISTICS.

langue and parole, see SAUSSURE, FERDINAND DE.

Languedoc, region and former prov. of S France, hist. cap. Toulouse. Cévennes in E; fertile Garonne plain in W. Agric., vineyards. Under medieval counts of Toulouse until incorporated (1271) into France. Name derived from *Langue d'oc* (medieval Provençal dialect).

Lanier, Sidney (1842-81), American poet. Works, eg 'The Symphony' (1875), 'The Marshes of Glynn' (1878), attempt to combine techniques of music with those of poetry. Also wrote novel, *Tiger-Lilies* (1867), criticism, eg *The Science of English Verse* (1880).

Lansbury, George (1859-1940), English politician. Helped found *Daily Herald* newspaper (1912) and edited it until 1922. Led parliamentary Labour Party (1931-5) but resigned leadership because of pacifist views.

Lansdowne, Henry Charles Keith Petty-Fitzmaurice, 5th Marquis of (1845-1927), British statesman. Governor-general of Canada (1883-8). As foreign secretary (1900-6), he negotiated alliances with Japan (1902) and France (1904), thus abandoning British isolationist policy.

Lansing, cap. of Michigan, US; on jct. of Grand and Cedar rivers. Pop. 132,000. Railway centre; has important motor car indust. Cap. from 1847.

lantern fish, any of Myctophidae family of deep-sea fish, with light-producing organs on body and head.

lanthanides or rare earths, group of rare metallic elements with atomic numbers from 57 to 71 inclusive. Have similar chemical properties and are difficult to separate.

lanthanum (La), metallic element of lanthanide series; at. no. 57, at. wt. 138.91. Discovered (1839) by Mosander.

Laocoön, in Greek legend, Trojan priest of Apollo. He warned against admitting the Greek wooden horse within the city walls. Angered Apollo (Athena in some versions) who sent sea serpents to strangle him and his 2 sons. Death represented in famous 1st cent. BC statue (now in Vatican).

Laodicea, ancient city of Asia Minor, now in SW Turkey near Denizli. Early Christian centre, it was one of the Seven Churches in Asia. Roman ruins incl. theatres and aqueduct.

Laoighis or Leix, county of Leinster prov., C Irish Republic. Area 1720 sq km (664 sq mi); pop. 45,000; co. town Port Laoighise. Mainly flat, with Slieve Bloom Mts. in N. Agric., dairying. Formerly called Queen's County.

Laos, republic of SE Asia. Area 236,800 sq km (91,500 sq mi); pop. 3,383,000; cap. Vientiane. Languages: Laotian, French. Religion: Buddhism. Forested (teak), mountainous terrain apart from Mekong valley; principal crop rice; maize, tobacco, coffee grown. French protect. 1893-1949. Communist Vietminh forces invaded, withdrew with French 1954. Civil war from 1960; neutral govt. estab. 1962; fighting resumed 1967 with involvement of North Vietnamese forces. Ceasefire (1973). Monarchy abolished 1975 and Communist control estab.

Lao-tze or **Lao-tzu** (fl 6th cent. BC), Chinese philosopher. Traditionally held to be founder of Taoism and author of Tao. Te Ching.

La Paz, admin. cap. of Bolivia, cap. of La Paz dept.; near L. Titicaca. Pop. 562,000. Seat of govt. Has airport at 3960 m (c 13,000 ft). Tanning, brewing, flour milling; textile, chemical mfg. Founded by Spanish (1548).

lapis lazuli, silicate mineral, a semi-precious gemstone. Opaque, azure blue in colour; consists mainly of lazurite (sodium aluminium silicate). Used in production of vases, bowls, beads, etc. Major sources in Afghanistan, Chile, US.

Laplace, Pierre Simon, Marquis de (1749-1827), French mathematician and astronomer. His Mécanique céleste (1799-1825) demonstrated stability of solar system and confirmed Newton's theory of gravitation. Formulated nebular hypothesis of origin of solar system (planets formed by shrinkage of gaseous nebula surrounding Sun).

Lapland, region of Arctic Europe, in N Norway, Sweden, Finland, NW USSR. Forest in S, tundra in N. Nomadic Lapps form indigenous pop.; reindeer herding, fishing, hunting. Area has rich mineral resources, esp. iron ore at Kiruna, Gällivare (Sweden).

La Plata, city of E Argentina, cap. of Buenos Aires prov. Pop. 408,000. Exports agric. produce from pampas region through its port, Ensenada. Meat packing, oil refining. Called Eva Perón (1952-5).

Lapps, N Scandinavian people, concentrated largely in Norway (called Finns there). Semi-nomadic reindeer herdsmen, hunters, some fishers. Origins believed to be C Asian, then pushed N. Speak Finno-Ugric language. Pop. c 30,000.

Laptev Sea, part of Arctic Ocean, lying N of Siberia. Bounded by Severnaya Zemlya in W, New Siberian isls. in E. Receives R. Lena.

lapwing, Vanellus vanellus, large greenish-black and white plover of Europe and C Asia, noted for erratic flight during breeding season. Also called peewit.

Laramie, town of SE Wyoming, US; on Laramie R. Pop. 23,000. Commercial, transport centre in livestock rearing region.

larceny, in law, unlawful taking away of another's property without his consent, with intention of depriving person of it. In UK, replaced by Theft Act (1968). In US, it remains, with division into 'grand' and 'petty' (abandoned in UK 1827).

larch, any of genus Larix of tall deciduous coniferous trees of pine family. Found mainly in N hemisphere. European L. decidua is

American *L. occidentalis* are used in building.

lares and penates, Roman gods of the home. Lares represented ancestral spirits and were associated with fields, boundaries and crossroads. Penates were guardians of the store-cupboard.

Largo Caballero, Francisco (1869-1946), Spanish politician. Led propaganda campaign against rightist govt. from 1933. Premier of Loyalist govt. (1936-7), presided at outbreak of Spanish Civil War. Died in exile in France.

Largs, town of Strathclyde region, W Scotland, on Firth of Clyde. Pop. 10,000. Tourist resort. Scene of battle (1263) in which Alexander III of Scotland defeated Haakon IV of Norway.

Larisa or **Larissa,** town of E Greece, on R. Peneus, cap. of Larisa admin. dist. Pop. 56,000. Railway jct., agric. market. Cap. of ancient Thessaly.

lark, any of Alaudidae family of mainly Old World songbirds. Skylark, *Alauda arvensis*, noted for song as it hovers or ascends.

Larkin, Philip Arthur (1922-), English poet. Known for collections, *eg The Less Deceived* (1955), estab. 'new poetry' as reaction against romanticism, political enthusiasms, *The Whitsun Weddings* (1964), *High Windows* (1975).

larkspur, *see* DELPHINIUM.

Larne, port of E Northern Ireland. Pop. 18,000. In former Co. Antrim. Bauxite refining; linen mfg.; has ferry service to Stranraer (Scotland).

La Rochefoucauld, François, Duc de (1613-80), French author. Known for *Maximes* (1665), bitter epigrams illustrating belief that self-interest is main human motivation.

La Rochelle, town of W France, on Bay of Biscay, cap. of Charente-Maritime dept. Pop. 76,000. Port, fishing, shipbuilding. Huguenot stronghold in 16th-17th cent., successfully besieged (1627-8) by Richelieu. Medieval buildings, 18th cent. cathedral.

Larousse, Pierre Athanase (1817-75), French grammarian and lexicographer. Best known for his *Grand dictionnaire universel du XIXe siècle* (1866-76) which continues in revised form.

larva, free-living form of animal emerging from egg, usually distinct from adult and incapable of sexual reproduction. Undergoes metamorphosis into adult, *eg* tadpole into frog or caterpillar into butterfly.

larvae, *see* LEMURES.

larynx, organ of speech at entrance to windpipe (trachea); contains vocal cords; visible on outside as Adam's apple. Composed mainly of cartilage and muscle. Inflammation of lining causes laryngitis; accompanied by hoarseness, coughing and sore throat.

La Salle, René Robert Cavelier, Sieur de (1643-87), French explorer. Went to New France (1666); built forts and developed fur trade. Claimed Mississippi valley. for France after journeying down river (1682); later attempt to reach its mouth from sea ended in mutiny and murder by his own men.

Lascaux, site of caves in SW France decorated with animal paintings of Upper Palaeolithic Age, dating from *c* 20,000-14,000 BC. Discovered

1940, cave had to be closed following deterioration of paintings.

laser (light amplification by stimulated emission of radiation), source of intense narrow beam of coherent light. Atoms of gas or crystalline solid (eg ruby) are stimulated into excited states by light beams. They return to ground state with emission of pulses or continuous beams of highly coherent light. Used in cutting and welding metals, in surgery and holography.

Laski, Harold Joseph (1893-1950), British political scientist. Influential Fabian, he taught at London School of Economics from 1920. Chairman of Labour Party (1945-6). Works incl. *Liberty in the Modern State* (1930), *Democracy in Crisis* (1933), *The American Democracy* (1948).

Las Palmas, see PALMAS, LAS Spain.

La Spezia, see SPEZIA, LA, Italy.

Lassa fever, acute virus disease endemic to W Africa. Symptoms incl. high fever, pains in the back and ulcers in the throat; frequently fatal. Transmitted by rodents.

Lassalle, Ferdinand (1825-64), German socialist and writer. Influenced by Marx, he advocated form of state socialism in series of speeches and pamphlets. Founded General German Workers' Union (1863), forerunner of Social Democratic party. Died after a duel.

Lassus, Orlandus or **Orlando di Lasso** (c 1530-94), Flemish composer. Produced over 2000 vocal works, both secular and religious, in high polyphonic style. Choirmaster at St John Lateran in Rome (1553-4), settled in Munich after travelling widely in Europe.

Last Supper, see EUCHARIST.

Las Vegas, resort of S Nevada, US. Pop. 126,000; state's largest town. In ranching area; entertainment centre with famous gambling casinos. First settled by Mormons.

Latakia (*El Ladhiqiya*), port of NW Syria, on Mediterranean. Pop. 126,000. Exports famous tobacco, cotton. Prospered under Romans and Crusaders, but declined 16th cent. Revived with tobacco trade.

La Tène, shallows at E end of L. Neuchâtel, Switzerland. Site of discovery of Iron Age remains of Celtic people; name now given to European Iron Age (2nd period), c 5th cent. BC-1st cent. AD.

latent heat, heat required to change state of a substance from solid to liquid, or from liquid to gas, without increase in its temperature. During a change of state the addition of heat causes no rise in temperature until the change of state is complete.

Lateran Treaty, agreement signed (1929) between Church and state in Italy. Confined papal sovereignty to independent Vatican City and specified extra-territorial buildings. Recognized Roman Catholicism as state religion and guaranteed religious teaching in schools.

laterite, reddish soil composed mainly of hydrated iron oxide. Formed by decomposition of underlying rocks, eg granite, basalt, in areas with distinct wet and dry seasons. Used as building material, source of iron. Found in India, Malaya, tropical Africa.

latex, milky fluid found in several plants, eg rubber tree, poppy. Consists of an emulsion of various resins and proteins. Latex of Pará rubber tree is worked into various types of rubber.

Latimer, Hugh (c 1485-1555), English churchman. Supported Cranmer's rejection of papal authority under Henry VIII. Appointed bishop of Winchester (1535); resigned over Act of Six Articles (1539). Under Edward VI, preached against corruption among clergy. With Ridley, burned at stake for heresy under Mary I.

Latin, language in Italic branch of Indo-European family. Standard language of Roman empire. Divided into Classical Latin and Vulgar (vernacular) Latin. Latter gave rise to Romance languages. Now dead, but Classical form still used in Roman Catholic church, and read as vehicle of great literature. Was European lingua franca till c 18th cent.

Latin America, term denoting countries of Central and South America, S of US-Mexico border; excl. British West Indies. Refers esp. to Spanish, Portuguese-speaking countries.

Latin American Free Trade Association (LAFTA), economic organization formed (1961) by Argentina, Brazil, Chile, Colombia, Ecuador, Mexico, Paraguay, Peru, Uruguay. Venezuela joined later in 1960s. Elimination of tariffs eventual goal. 1967 Punta del Este conference agreed to work towards joining LAFTA with Central American Common Market to create Latin American Common Market.

Latini, Brunetto (c 1220-94), Italian writer. May have been Dante's teacher. Known for *Trésor* (written in French, c 1265), 1st vernacular encyclopedia.

latitude, in geography, angular distance north or south of the Equator of any point on Earth's surface, measured from Earth's centre. Parallels are lines of latitude encircling the Earth parallel to the Equator (0°).

Latium (*Lazio*), region of C Italy, cap. Rome. Coastal plain in W, Apennine foothills in E; much reclaimed marshland, *eg* Pontine Marshes. Agric., fishing, tourism, h.e.p. Ancient Latium fell to Romans 3rd cent. BC.

La Tour, Georges de (1593-1652), French painter. Worked all his life in Lorraine. Specialized in nocturnal religious and genre scenes dramatically illuminated by concealed source of light. Works incl. *St Sebastian mourned by St Irene*.

La Trappe, see TRAPPISTS.

Latter Day Saints, see MORMONS.

Latvian Soviet Socialist Republic, constituent republic of W USSR. Area c 66,600 sq km (25,600 sq mi); pop. 2,365,000; cap. Riga. Mainly low-lying plain with extensive forests; dairy products, timber, textiles produced. Hist. controlled by Sweden, Poland and Russia (from 1721); independent (1918-40) until annexed by USSR.

Laud, William (1573-1645), English churchman, archbishop of Canterbury (1633-45). Supported Charles I in struggle with Parliament. Attempted to eradicate Puritanism, favouring instead High Church ritual and doctrine. Attempt to impose the Prayer Book on Scotland (1638) was resisted by force.

Impeached by Parliament (1640), imprisoned and executed.

Lauder, Sir Hugh MacLennan ('Harry') (1870-1950), Scottish music-hall singer. Known for comic or sentimental Scots songs, eg 'Roamin' in the Gloamin'.

Laue, Max Theodor Felix von (1879-1960), German physicist. Awarded Nobel Prize for Physics (1914) for prediction that atomic lattice of a crystal would act as diffraction grating for X-rays.

laughing gas, see NITROUS OXIDE.

laughing jackass, see KOOKA-BURRA.

Laughton, Charles (1899-1962), British film actor. Known for roles in, eg, *The Private Life of Henry VIII* (1933), *Mutiny on the Bounty* (1935), *Advise and Consent* (1962).

Launceston, city of N Tasmania, Australia, at head of Tamar estuary. Pop. 35,000. Port, exports agric. produce; timber; textile mfg.

laurel, any of genus *Laurus* of evergreen trees or shrubs; esp. bay laurel, *L. nobilis,* with greenish flowers, black berries, glossy leaves used as flavouring (as bay leaves) and in wreaths. Name also applied to certain similar trees and shrubs, eg cherry laurel, *Prunus laurocerasus,* spurge laurel, *Daphne laureola,* and American trees of Rhododendron and Magnolia families and Australian shrubs of *Anopterus* genus.

Laurel and Hardy, American comedians, known for numerous short films in which everything they do ends in chaos. They were Stan Laurel (1890-1965) and Oliver Hardy (1892-1957).

Laurens, Henri (1885-1954), French sculptor. Influenced by cubist painters, he created geometric compositions based on natural forms. Later work, based on female figure, was more naturalistic.

Laurentian Plateau, mainly in N Ontario, C Canada. Oldest rock formation of North America with dotted lake pattern formed by glacial action. Tundra in N; forested areas in S. Has rich mineral, timber, fur resources.

Laurier, Sir Wilfrid (1841-1919), Canadian statesman. First French-Canadian PM of Canada (1896-1911); influential in defining Liberal Party policy. Estab. principle of choosing regionally representative cabinet. Supported imperial preference.

Lausanne, city of SW Switzerland, on L. Geneva, cap. of Vaud canton. Pop. 137,000. Printing, woodworking, leather, tourism. Cathedral (12th cent.); coll. (1537) became univ. (1890).

Lausanne Conference, peace treaty (1922-3) between Allies and Turkey resolving problems raised by Treaty of SÈVRES, which had not been recognized by new Turkish govt. under Ataturk. Status of Dardanelles was decided and E Thrace recovered by Turkey.

lava, molten rock from interior of Earth which has reached surface through volcanic vents and fissures. 'Acid lavas', with high silica content, are thick and slow moving; 'basic lavas', with low silica content, are very fluid. Rock froth formed on surface of lava flow is called pumice.

Laval, François Xavier de (1623-1708), French churchman in Canada. First bishop of Québec (1674-88), he gave Church a strong base in colony. Opposed royal governors and traders whom he considered to be corrupting the Indians.

Laval, Pierre (1883-1945), French politician. Premier and foreign minister (1931-2, 1935-6). Created vice-premier of Pétain's Vichy govt. (1940) and all-powerful premier (1942). Collaborated with Germans, sending French workers to Germany. Executed for treason after summary trial following liberation.

La Vallière, Louise de (1644-1710), French noblewoman. Mistress of Louis XIV, she gave birth to 4 children before he transferred his affections to Mme de Montespan. Entered a Carmelite convent in 1674.

lavender, any of genus *Lavandula* of fragrant European plants of mint family, esp. *L. officinalis*, with spikes of pale purple flowers used in making perfumes.

Laver, Rod[ney] (1938-), Australian tennis player. Winner of 'grand slam' (British, US, Australian, French open titles) as an amateur (1962) and as a professional (1969).

Lavoisier, Antoine Laurent (1743-94), French chemist. A founder of modern chemistry, he introduced rational nomenclature, distinguished between elements and compounds, and made quantitative investigations of reactions. Explained role of oxygen in combustion and respiration, thus invalidating phlogiston theory. Estab. composition of water.

Law, Andrew Bonar (1858-1923), British statesman, b. Canada. Elected leader of Conservative Party (1911), he served in coalitions under Lloyd George (1915-21). PM (1922-3) after withdrawing from coalition; resigned because of poor health.

Law, John (1671-1729), Scottish financier. Founded Banque générale (1716) in Paris, which became royal bank (1718), issued paper currency. He acquired (1717) monopoly of trade in Louisiana, estab. vast stock company, merging it with bank (1720). Excessive speculation led to frenzied selling and ruin of thousands, incl. Law.

Law, William (1686-1761), English clergyman, writer. Known for devotional *A Serious Call to a Devout and Holy Life* (1728), which influenced the Wesleys and promoted evangelical revival.

law court, see COURT.

lawn tennis, see TENNIS.

Lawrence, D[avid] H[erbert] (1885-1930), English novelist, poet. Works reflect belief in sex, primitive subconscious, and nature as cures for destructive effects of modern indust. society. Novels incl. semi-autobiog. *Sons and Lovers* (1913), *Women in Love* (1920), *Lady Chatterley's Lover* (1928). Also wrote short stories, plays, art criticism.

Lawrence, Sir Thomas (1769-1830), English painter. Succeeded Reynolds as painter to the king (1792); leading portraitist of his time. Commissioned to paint portraits of heads of state and military leaders concerned in the defeat of Napoleon (1818).

Lawrence, T[homas] E[dward] (1888-1935), British soldier, scholar, b. Wales. Known as 'Lawrence of Arabia'. Joined Arab revolt against Turks (1916), secured Arab cooperation for Allenby's campaign. As colonial adviser on Arab affairs, failed to realize his pro-Arab objectives and withdrew into obscurity. His experiences are recalled in *Seven Pillars of Wisdom* (1926).

lawrencium (Lr), transuranic element of actinide series; atomic no. 103, mass no. of most stable isotope 256. Lawrencium 257 first prepared (1961) by bombarding californium with boron nuclei.

Layamon (fl c 1200), English poet. Known for long verse-chronicle *Brut*, on early British history. First prominent Middle English poet.

Lazarists, popular name for the Congregation of Priests of the Mission, an RC teaching order founded by St Vincent de Paul (1626). Named from its 1st priory, St Lazare, Paris.

Lazio, see LATIUM, Italy.

Leacock, Stephen Butler (1869-1944), Canadian humorist, b. England. Works, eg *Literary Lapses* (1910), *Sunshine Sketches of a Little Town* (1912), draw out everyday problems with perverse logic.

lead (Pb), soft metallic element; at. no. 82, at. wt. 207.19. Occurs as galena (PbS); obtained by roasting this ore. Used in accumulators, alloys, plumbing and roofing, and as shield against radiation; compounds used in paint. Lead tetraethyl used in petrol to prevent knocking.

leaf, outgrowth of stem of plant. Usually consists of broad blade, petiole (stalk), and stipules. Functions incl. food mfg. through assimilation of carbon dioxide and absorption of light, see PHOTOSYNTHESIS, releasing water to atmosphere, see TRANSPIRATION. Chloro-

phyll gives green colour. Evergreen leaves are termed persistent, those which fall annually, deciduous.

leaf insect, tropical insect of same family (Phasmidae) as stick insect. Wings shaped and coloured to resemble leaves among which it lives.

League of Nations, first major organization of world's countries dedicated to preservation of peace and international cooperation; hq. Geneva. Founded (1920) as part of TREATY OF VERSAILLES, largely on initiative of Woodrow Wilson. Members incl. (at some time) all major nations except US; Germany and Japan withdrew 1933. Although successful in humanitarian actions, it failed to act against aggression by some of its members, eg Japan (1931), Italy (1935). Dissolved itself (1946) and transferred services and property to UN.

Leakey, Louis Seymour Bazett (1903-72), British anthropologist, b. Kenya. Discovered fossil remains in East Africa, incl. those of *Zinjanthropus*, proto-man c 1,750,000 years old, estab. man to have existed earlier than previously supposed. Works incl. *Unveiling Man's Origins* (1969).

Leamington Spa, Royal, mun. bor. of Warwickshire, C England. Pop. 45,000. Engineering; saline springs, popular health resort from 18th cent. Visited by Queen Victoria (1838).

Leander, see HERO.

Lear, Edward (1812-88), English humorist, artist. Famous for nonsense verse, esp. limericks, sometimes reflecting alienation and melancholy, eg 'The Jumblies', *A*

Book of Nonsense (1846), The Owl and the Pussycat (1871), illustrated by himself.

leather, durable material prepared from hide or skin of animals by removal of flesh and hair and subsequent tanning. Tanning helps prevent decay and gives leather flexibility and toughness.

leatherjacket, see CRANEFLY.

Leavis, F[rank] R[aymond] (1895-1978), English literary critic. Editor of influential periodical Scrutiny (1932-53). Works, eg The Great Tradition (1948), The Common Pursuit (1952), reflect belief that literature should have moral value and meet standards of intellectual elite.

Lebanon, republic of SW Asia, E Mediterranean. Area c 10,000 sq km (3860 sq mi); pop. 2,961,000; cap. Beirut. Language: Arabic. Religions: Islam, Maronite Christian. Fertile Beqa valley (grain, fruit) lies between Lebanon Mts. and Anti-Lebanon. Centre of ancient Phoenician empire; part of Syria under Romans, Byzantines, Turks until French mandate (1920); independent 1945. Destructive religious and civil strife in mid-1970s.

Leblanc, Nicolas (1742-1806), French chemist. Invented Leblanc process for large scale production of soda from salt; important in 19th cent. indust.

Lebrun, Albert (1871-1950), French statesman. Last president of Third Republic (1932-40), he was deprived of power by Pétain after armistice with Germany.

Lebrun, Charles (1619-90), French painter. Studied with Poussin in Rome; became court painter to Louis XIV and director of reorganized Gobelins tapestry works. One of leaders in foundation of French Academy of Painting and Sculpture (1648), later became its director. Responsible for much of decoration at Versailles palaces.

Lech, river of C Europe. Flows 282 km (175 mi) from Vorarlberg (W Austria) past Augsburg to R. Danube at Donauwörth (West Germany).

Leconte de Lisle, Charles Marie René (1818-94), French poet. Leading PARNASSIEN. Wrote austere, pessimistic poetry, eg Poèmes antiques (1852), Poèmes tragiques (1884), verse drama L'Apollonide (1888).

Le Corbusier, see CORBUSIER, LE.

Leda, in Greek myth, wife of Tyndareus. Seduced by Zeus who visited her in form of a swan. She bore 2 eggs; one contained DIOSCURI, other Helen and Clytemnestra.

Le Duc Tho (c 1912-), Vietnamese political leader. Shared Nobel Peace Prize (1973) with Kissinger for negotiating 1973 ceasefire. Rejected award.

Lee, Robert E[dward] (1807-70), American army officer, commander of the Confederate forces in the Civil War. Frustrated McClellan's campaign in the Seven Days battles (June-July, 1862). Won 2nd battle of Bull Run (1862) and Chancellorsville (1863), but was defeated at Gettysburg (July, 1863) and ultimately outnumbered, surrendered to Grant (April, 1865). Became a symbol of Southern resistance.

leech, any of Hirudinea class of annelids. Body segmented, with sucker at each end; most species suck blood, using anticoagulant (hirudin) to keep blood liquid. Lives in water or wet earth. *Hirudo medicinalis* once used medicinally to bleed patients.

Leeds, city of West Yorkshire met. county, N England, on R. Aire. Pop. 495,000. Textiles; engineering industs. Has univ. (1904). Woollen indust. from 14th cent.; St John's Church (17th cent.).

leek, *Allium porrum,* biennial plant of same genus as ONION. Cylindrical stem and flat leaves. Used as vegetable and in soups. National emblem of Wales.

Lee Kuan Yew (1923-), Singapore statesman. Became 1st PM of Singapore (1959). Withdrew country from Federation of Malaysia (1965) which it had joined in 1963. Expanded economic base of country.

Leeuwenhoek, Antony van (1632-1723), Dutch naturalist. Developed single lens microscope, which enabled him to discover protozoa, spermatozoa and bacteria and study red blood cells.

Leeward Islands, archipelago of E West Indies, N Lesser Antilles. Extend SE from Puerto Rico to Windward Isls. Incl. Virgin Isls. (US); ex-British colonies Antigua, St Kitts-Nevis-Anguilla, Montserrat, British Virgin Isls.; Guadeloupe (French); St Eustatius (Dutch), St Martin. Isls. discovered by Columbus (1493). Disputed by Britain and France; ownership resolved 1815.

Le Fanu, Joseph Sheridan (1814-73), Irish novelist. Known for mystery and occult suspense stories, eg *The House by the Churchyard*

(1863), *Uncle Silas* (1864), *In a Glass Darkly* (1872).

Léger, Fernand (1881-1955), French painter. Associated with cubism, he later created a style employing machine-like forms and flat bands of pure colour. Designed ballet sets and decorative murals.

Leghorn (*Livorno*), town of Tuscany, NW Italy, on Ligurian Sea. Cap. of Livorno prov. Pop. 78,000. Port, exports wine, olive oil, marble; resort; naval academy. Created free port 1590. Many buildings, eg cathedral, destroyed in WWII.

legion, fighting unit of Roman army varying from 3000 to 4000 foot soldiers (divided into 10 cohorts) with additional cavalrymen. Organization attributed to Marcus Camillus (d. c365 BC). Tended to be vulnerable to cavalry, archers and guerrilla tactics.

legislature, in politics, that part of govt. empowered to make laws for a country or state, usually comprising elected representatives. British Parliament and US Congress were important in development of legislatures as check on judiciary and executive. Also *see* SEPARATION OF POWERS.

Leguminosae, family of flowering plants and trees. Characterized by having seed pods and nitrogenous nodules on roots which allow NITROGEN FIXATION in soil. Incl. laburnum, gorse, CLOVER. Many species have tendrils which twine around supports, eg PEA.

Lehár, Franz (1870-1948), Hungarian composer. Works, mostly operettas, incl. *The Merry Widow* (1905).

Le Havre, city of N France, at

mouth of R. Seine. Pop. 200,000. Major port with passenger and cargo traffic. Oil refining, pipeline to Paris. Founded in 1576 by Francis I. Heavily bombed in WWII.

Leibnitz, Gottfried Wilhelm, Baron von (1646-1716), German philosopher, mathematician. In *Monadology* (1714) posited universe of units (monads) which cannot act independently but which follow a harmony estab. by God. Thus this becomes the 'best of all possible worlds'. Devised form of calculus independently of Newton.

Leicester, Robert Dudley, Earl of (*c* 1532-88), English courtier. Favourite of Elizabeth I, he was once considered her most likely choice of husband. From *c* 1564 advocated strong measures against Catholics and Spain. Led unsuccessful expedition to assist revolt of United Provinces against Spanish rule in Netherlands (1585-7).

Leicestershire, county of EC England. Area 2553 sq km (986 sq mi); pop. 824,000. Mainly low-lying; uplands in E. Dairying (Stilton cheese); coal mining in W. Co. town Leicester, co. bor. on R. Soar. Pop. 287,000. Hosiery, shoe mfg. Has univ. (1957); Roman *Ratae*, remains incl. Jewry Wall; Norman castle (12th cent.); cathedral (1926).

Leichhardt, [Friedrich Wilhelm] Ludwig (1813-48), German explorer, scientist. Explored N and E Australia; journeyed from SE Queensland to Port Essington, Northern Territ. (1844-5), gaining useful knowledge of region. Disappeared on trans-continental expedition (1848).

Leiden or **Leyden,** city of WC Netherlands, on R. Old Rhine. Pop. 100,000. Produces textiles, machinery. Univ. (1575) was centre of learning in 17th and 18th cents. Survived Spanish siege (1574) by cutting dykes, flooding surrounding land. Birthplace of Rembrandt.

Leif Ericsson (*fl c* 1000), Norse explorer, son of Eric the Red. Thought to have reached North America; the 'Vinland' he discovered has not been precisely delimited, perhaps New England or Newfoundland.

Leigh, Vivien, née Hartley (1913-67), British actress. Famous in film roles incl. *The Skin of Our Teeth, A Streetcar Named Desire, Anna Karenina.* Also played on stage, esp. in *Antony and Cleopatra* with husband, Sir Laurence Olivier.

Leinster, prov. of E Irish Republic. Area 20,331 sq km (7850 sq mi); pop. 1,495,000. Comprises cos. Carlow, Dublin, Kildare, Kilkenny, Laoighis, Longford, Louth, Meath, Offaly, Westmeath, Wexford, Wicklow. Ancient kingdom, former cap. Naas.

Leipzig, city of S East Germany, at confluence of Pleisse, White Elster. Pop. 581,000. Indust. centre, annual trade fair; centre of German fur trade and publishing until WWII. Univ. (1409). Medieval town, has tavern featured in Goethe's *Faust.* Badly damaged in Thirty Years War and WWII; scene of Napoleon's defeat (1813) in Battle of the Nations.

Leith, town of Lothian region, E Scotland, on Firth of Forth. Part of Edinburgh from 1920. Major Scottish seaport; fishing, whisky distilling.

Leitrim, county of Connacht prov., NW Irish Republic. Area 1526 sq km

(589 sq mi); pop. 28,000; co. town Carrick-on-Shannon. Many lakes; hilly in N. Poor soil, climate. Cattle, dairying.

Leix, see LAOIGHIS, Irish Republic.

Léman, Lac, see GENEVA, LAKE, Switzerland.

Le Mans, city of NW France, on R. Sarthe, cap. of Sarthe dept. Pop. 143,000. Railway jct., agric. market, engineering. Annual 24-hour motor race. Hist. cap. of Maine. Site of final French defeat by Prussia (1871). Cathedral (11th cent.).

Lemberg, see LVOV.

lemming, small thick-furred rodent, resembling vole, of Arctic and subarctic regions. Norwegian lemming, *Lemmus lemmus,* noted for mass migration during times of overpopulation and food scarcity.

Lemnos (*Limnos*), isl. of Greece, in N Aegean Sea. Area 482 sq km (186 sq mi); main town Kastron. Fertile valleys; fruit, cereals. Traditionally sacred to Hephaestus.

lemon, *Citrus limon,* evergreen tree bearing bitter yellow fruit. Grown in Mediterranean regions, S US and South Africa. Juice used in cooking, rind in candied peel.

lemon balm, see BALM.

lemon sole, *Microstomus kitt,* edible flatfish of eastern N Atlantic.

lemur, primitive arboreal primate, found mainly in Madagascar. Usually nocturnal, with large eyes and long non-prehensile tail. Diet of insects, fruit. Species incl. ring-tailed lemur, *Lemur catta.*

lemures or larvae, in Roman religion, malevolent ghosts of the dead. Propitiated in Lemuria rites.

Lena, longest river of USSR. Rises in Baikal Mts. W of L. Baikal, flows NE

c 4250 km (2650 mi) through EC Siberian RSFSR to Laptev Sea. Gold and other minerals obtained along its course.

Le Nain, Antoine (*c* 1588-1648), **Louis** (*c* 1593-1648), and **Mathieu** (1607-77), family of French painters, all brothers. Series of paintings are attributed to them, esp. realistic genre scenes of peasant life, painted in greyish tones.

Lend-Lease Act, legislation passed (1941) by US Congress, empowering president to sell, lend or lease US war supplies[4] to countries whose defence was considered vital to defence of US. Countries such as Britain provided reciprocal programmes.

Lenin, Vladimir Ilyich, orig. Ulyanov (1870-1924), Russian revolutionary. Exiled twice for anti-govt. activity, engineered split (1903) between BOLSHEVIKS and Mensheviks in Social Democrats. Returned to Russia after outbreak of RUSSIAN REVOLUTION to overthrow Kerensky's govt. (Nov. 1917), estab. Council of People's Commissars. Civil war (1918-20) ended with founding of the Soviet Union. Exercised dictatorial powers as chairman of the council and chairman of the Communist Party. Instrumental in creation of COMINTERN world socialist movement. Differed from orthodox MARXISM in his actions and writings, *eg What is to be done?* (1902), advocating violent revolution, instigated by disciplined professional revolutionaries.

Leningrad, city of USSR, W European RSFSR; at mouth of R. Neva. Pop. 4,066,000. Major port;

cultural and indust. centre; shipbuilding, exports timber. Founded (1703) as St Petersburg by Peter the Great. Intersected by numerous canals; spaciously planned, buildings incl. Winter Palace and cathedral; has Hermitage art gallery and univ. (1819). Scene of revolutions (1905, 1917). Replaced as cap. by Moscow (1918). Called Petrograd (1914-24).

Lenôtre, André (1613-1700), French landscape gardener. Designed parks and gardens for Louis XIV, in particular those at Versailles. His formal designs were highly influential until the growth of more naturalistic approach in 18th cent.

lens, portion of transparent medium, eg glass, bounded by curved or plane surfaces, which causes light rays to converge or diverge on passing through it. Convex lens causes parallel beam of light to converge and produce real image, concave lens causes divergence of light and produces virtual image. ABERRATION is defect of lens.

Lent, Christian period of 40 days of penance and fasting before Easter (Ash Wednesday to Easter Sunday). Observance dates from 4th cent.

lentil, *Lens culinaris,* small branching plant of Leguminosae family. Cultivated for its round flat seeds which are dried and used in cooking. Native to Old World.

Lenz, Siegfried (1926-), German writer. Works, often set in N Germany, incl. symbolic short stories *Das Feuerschiff* (1960), novel *Deutschstunde* (1968) based on life of painter Nolde.

Leo I, St (c 400-461), Italian churchman, pope (440-61). Estab. authority over bishops. Author of *Tome of Leo* defining the 2 natures of Christ. Dissuaded (452) Attila from sacking Rome.

Leo III, St (d. 816), Italian churchman, pope (795-816). Crowned Charlemagne emperor (800) marking start of Holy Roman Empire and estab. papal right to consecrate emperor.

Leo IX, St (1002-54), Alsatian churchman, pope (1049-54). Related to Emperor Conrad II. Reformed clerical abuses. Excommunicated (1054) Michaël Cerularius, patriarch of Constantinople, initiating split of Church into East and West.

Leo X, orig. Giovanni de' Medici (1475-1521), Italian churchman, pope (1513-21). Patron of Raphael, continued rebuilding of St Peter's, Rome. Excommunicated Luther (1521).

Leo XIII, orig. Gioacchino Vincenzo Pecci (1810-1903), Italian churchman, pope (1878-1903). Issued important encyclicals, moulding RC beliefs to the conditions of secular democratic states, eg *Rerum novarum* (1891). Declared Thomism official philosophy of Church and encouraged wide-ranging scholarship.

Leo, see ZODIAC.

León, city of C Mexico, in Guanajuato state; alt. 1700 m (c 5600 ft). Pop. 454,000. Agric., mining centre; shoe, textiles, cement mfg. Founded 1576.

León, city of W Nicaragua. Pop. 91,000. Cultural, agric. and trade centre. National cap. until 1855. Destroyed by earthquake, moved to present site (1610). Has part of National Univ.

León, region and former kingdom of NW Spain. Chief cities Salamanca, Valladolid. Cantabrian Mts. in N, elsewhere plateau; drained by R. Douro. Agric., stock raising, mining, forests. Formed, with Asturias, Christian kingdom from 866; united with Castile 1230. Hist. cap. León, pop. 105,000, cap. of modern León prov. Agric., commercial centre. Gothic cathedral (13th cent.).

Leonardo da Vinci (1452-1519), Italian artist, scientist, engineer. Regarded as epitome of Renaissance creativity, his extant works are few and often unfinished. Paintings incl. *Adoration of the Magi, Last Supper* fresco, *Mona Lisa, Virgin of the Rocks.* His commission to decorate the Council Chamber of Florence was abandoned after 2 years work. Served as military engineer to Cesare Borgia (c 1500); last years were spent in service of Francis I of France. Produced notebooks covering problems in hydraulics, mechanics, anatomy, *etc.*

Leoncavallo, Ruggiero (1858-1919), Italian operatic composer. Known for *I Pagliacci* (1892), but his other operas have not survived in the repertory.

Leonidas (d. 480 BC), Spartan king. Although heavily outnumbered, he and his Spartan troops defended pass of Thermopylae (480 BC) against Persians under Xerxes; defeated and killed.

leopard or **panther,** *Panthera pardus,* mammal of cat family, found in Africa and Asia. Yellow-buff coat, with black markings.

Leopardi, Giacomo, Conte (1798-1837), Italian poet. Belief that cosmos is inevitably hostile reflected in melancholic lyrics, *eg Versi* (1826), *Canti* (1836), philosophical essay *Le Operette Morali* (1824), aphorisms *Pensieri* (1834-7).

Leopold I (1640-1705), Holy Roman emperor (1658-1705). Reign was marked by almost continual conflict with Louis XIV of France; opposed French territ. ambitions in Low Countries, Germany and Spain in series of wars. Campaigns against Turks incl. relief of siege of Vienna (1683) and victory at Zenta (1697).

Leopold II (1747-92), Holy Roman emperor (1790-2). Succeeded his brother Joseph II. Allied with Prussia to restore Louis XVI to French throne, but died before French Revolutionary Wars broke out.

Leopold I (1790-1865), king of Belgium. Having refused Greek throne (1830), he was elected king of Belgium on its separation from Netherlands (1831). Known as the 'Uncle of Europe'.

Leopold II (1835-1909), king of Belgium (1865-1909). Financed Stanley's explorations (1879-84) in the Congo, leading to formation of Congo Free State (1885) which Leopold ruled personally. His ruthless exploitation of the territ., by which he amassed a fortune, drew much hostility.

Leopold III (1901-), king of Belgium (1934-51). Led Belgian resistance to the German occupation in WWII. Surrendered unconditionally in 1940; imprisoned until 1945. Accused of cooperating with the Germans, he remained in exile until 1950; abdicated in favour of his son Baudouin.

Léopoldville, *see* KINSHASA, Zaïre.

Lepanto, see NAUPAKTOS, Greece.

Lepidoptera, order of insects, comprising moths and butterflies, with c 150,000 species.

Lepidus, Marcus Aemilius (d. c 12 BC), Roman politician. Formed 2nd Triumvirate with Antony and Octavian. Attempt to take Sicily led to his being deprived of office by Octavian.

leprosy, chronic infectious disease of the skin and nerves, caused by bacterium *Mycobacterium leprae*. Lepromatous form causes ulcerous blotches on face; tuberculoid form causes loss of sensation in skin. Advanced leprosy may result in loss of fingers, toes. Most prevalent in tropical regions. Treated with sulphone drugs.

leptons, elementary particles which do not experience strong nuclear interaction. At present, those known are electron, muon, 2 types of neutrino and corresponding antiparticles.

Le Puy (en Velay), town of SC France, cap. of Haute-Loire dept. Pop. 30,000. Liqueur mfg., hist. lace indust. Medieval pilgrimage centre. Romanesque cathedral (12th cent.).

Lermontov, Mikhail Yurevich (1814-41), Russian author. Wrote lyric poetry influenced by Byron, *eg The Demon* (1829-41), classic novel of 'superfluous man' *A Hero of Our Time* (1840), anticipating work of 19th cent. realists.

Lerwick, port of Shetland, N Scotland, on Mainland isl. Pop. 6000. Fishing, knitwear, offshore oil industs.

Le Sage, Alain René (1668-1747), French author. Best known for picaresque novel of manners, *Gil Blas* (1715-35). Also wrote many farces, comedies.

lesbianism, see HOMOSEXUALITY.

Lesbos or Mytilene, isl. of Greece, in E Aegean Sea. Area 1632 sq km (630 sq mi); cap. Mytilene. Wheat, olives, fruits. Cultural centre c 6th cent. BC, home of Aristotle, poets Sappho, Alcaeus, Member of Delian League.

Lesina, see HVAR, Yugoslavia.

Leslie, Alexander, 1st Earl of Leven (c 1580-1661), Scottish army officer. Fought in the Swedish army and was made field · marshal. Returning to Scotland (1639), he organized the Covenanting army which he commanded in N England (1644) and against the Royalists in the Civil War. Accepted Charles I's surrender at Newark (1646).

Lesotho, kingdom of S Africa, surrounded by Republic of South Africa. Area 30,300 sq km (11,700 sq mi); pop. 1,214,000, mainly Basuto tribe; cap. Maseru. Languages: Sesotho, English. Religions: native, Christian. Drakensberg Mts. in E, elsewhere tableland; main rivers Orange, Caledon. Main occupation stock rearing; exports wool, mohair, diamonds. Many Basuto tribesmen work in South African mines. British Protect. of Basutoland from 1868, independent from 1966. Member of British Commonwealth.

Lesseps, Ferdinand Marie, Vicomte de (1805-94), French diplomat, engineer. Negotiated concession for Suez Canal and supervised its construction (1859-69). Began work on Panama Canal (1881), but company went bankrupt.

Lessing, Doris May, née Taylor (1919-), English author, b. Persia.

Known for semi-autobiog. 'Children of Violence' novel sequence incl. *Martha Quest* (1952), *A Proper Marriage* (1954), *The Four Gated City* (1969), dealing with her African childhood, political activism, psychological development; also wrote *The Golden Notebook* (1962).

Lessing, Gotthold Ephraim (1729-81), German aesthetician, dramatist. Known for theoretical works, *eg Laokoön* (1766) demarcating subject matter of painting, poetry, *Hamburg Dramaturgy* (1767-8) attacking neo-classical formalism, *Education of the Human Race* (1780) taking rationalist view of theology. Best-known dramas incl. *Emilia Galotti* (1772), *Nathan the Wise* (1779).

Lethbridge, town of S Alberta, Canada; on Oldham R. Pop. 41,000. In coal mining, agric. (esp. cattle, wheat) region. Founded in 1870s as Coalbanks; renamed 1885.

Lethe, in Greek myth, one of rivers of HADES. Water drunk by the dead to gain forgetfulness of previous existence.

lettuce, *Lactuca sativa,* vegetable widely grown for its crisp leaves used raw in salads. Varieties incl. asparagus lettuce (*angustana*), cabbage lettuce (*capitata*) and Cos (*longifolia*).

leucotomy, alternative term for LOBOTOMY.

leukaemia, cancer-like disease of white blood cells resulting from disorder of bone marrow and other blood-forming tissue. Accompanied by anaemia and enlargement of lymph nodes, liver, spleen. Generally fatal, though has been cured in

children; may be relieved or controlled by X-rays and drugs.

Levant, name given to coastlands of E Mediterranean in Turkey, Syria, Lebanon and Israel.

Levellers, extreme republican and democratic party in English Civil War period. Advocated religious and social equality, sovereign House of Commons elected by universal manhood suffrage. Gained some support in army rank and file from 1647; suppressed by Cromwell (1649) after fomenting several mutinies.

Leven, Loch, two lochs of Scotland. **1,** in Highland region, extends 14 km (9 mi) E from Loch Linnhe to Kinlochleven. **2,** in Fife region, with isl. castle in which Mary Queen of Scots was imprisoned (1567-8).

Leverhulme, William Hesketh Lever, 1st Viscount (1851-1925), English industrialist. Founded Lever Bros. Ltd. (1886), international soap manufacturers, which later became Unilever. Estab. (1888) model village, Port Sunlight, as part of benefits to employees.

Leverrier, Urbain Jean Joseph (1811-77), French astronomer and mathematician. Independently of Adams, he explained irregularities in motion of Uranus by existence of previously unknown planet Neptune. Galle identified Neptune (1846) in position predicted by Leverrier.

Lévesque, René (1922-), Canadian politician. Left Liberal Party to found Parti Québecois (1967) with aim of Québec's secession from Canada. Became premier of Québec (1976) after party's election victory.

Lévi-Strauss, Claude (1908-),

French anthropologist, b. Belgium. Founded 'structural' method of analyzing cultures. Works incl. *Totemism* (1962), *The Raw and the Cooked* (1969).

Levites, in OT, descendants of Levi, son of Jacob and Leah. Hereditary religious caste, bearers of the Ark of the Covenant.

Leviticus, in OT, third book of Pentateuch, detailing duties and ceremonies of priests and Levites.

Lewes, George Henry (1817-78), English miscellaneous writer. Wrote on philosophy, introducing Comte's positivism to England. Works incl. *Life and Works of Goethe* (1855), *Problems of Life and Mind* (1874-9). Lived with Mary Ann Evans (George Eliot) after 1854.

Lewes, mun. bor. and co. town of East Sussex, SE England. Pop. 14,000. Has ruined 11th cent. priory, Norman castle. Scene of defeat of Henry III by Simon de Montfort (1264).

Lewis, C[ecil] Day, *see* DAY-LEWIS, C[ECIL].

Lewis, C[live] S[taples] (1898-1963), English author, b. Ireland. Known for criticism, *eg The Allegory of Love* (1936) on medieval literature, allegorical fantasy fiction, *eg Out of the Silent Planet* (1938), Christian apologetics, esp. *The Screwtape Letters* (1942), children's books, *eg The Lion, the Witch, and the Wardrobe* (1950).

Lewis, [Harry] Sinclair (1885-1951), American novelist. Known for satires of American life, *eg Main Street* (1920), *Babbitt* (1922), *Arrowsmith* (1925), *Elmer Gantry* (1927). *It Can't Happen Here* (1935) speculates about possibilities of fascist dictatorship in US. Nobel Prize for Literature (1930).

Lewis, John L[lewellyn] (1880-1969), American labour leader. President of United Mine Workers of America (1920-60). Helped found and headed (1935-40) Congress of Industrial Organizations, which aimed to unionize large mass production industs.

Lewis, Meriwether (1774-1809), American soldier, explorer. Secretary to President Jefferson (1801-3). With William Clark, led successful expedition (1803-6) in search of route across Rocky Mts. to the Pacific. Governor of Louisiana (1807-9).

Lewis, [Percy] Wyndham (1884-1957), English painter, author, b. US. Leader of vorticist painting movement. Edited magazine *Blast* (1914-15) with Ezra Pound. Wrote novels, *eg The Apes of God* (1930), attacking cultural fashions of 1920s, *The Childermass* (1928).

Lewis, *see* LEWIS WITH HARRIS, Scotland.

Lewis and Clark Expedition, exploring expedition (1803-6) across North America led by Meriwether Lewis and William Clark. They followed Missouri R. to its source, crossed continental divide, and explored Columbia R. from its source to Pacific.

Lewisham, bor. of SE Greater London, England. Pop. 265,000. Created 1965 from former met. bor. and Deptford. Incl. Blackheath, where Tyler (1381), Cade (1450) mustered rebel peasant forces.

Lewis with Harris, largest isl. of Outer Hebrides, NW Scotland, in WESTERN ISLES. Area 2137 sq km

(825 sq mi); main town Stornoway. Mainly peat bog, moorland. Crofting, fishing industs.; Harris Tweed mfg.

Lexington, *see* BOSTON, Massachusetts.

Leyden, *see* LEIDEN, Netherlands.

Lhasa, cap. of Tibet auton. region, SW China. Pop. 175,000. Alt. 3600 m (11,800 ft). Trade, religious centre; Lamaist temple, monasteries, palace of Dalai Lama.

Liaoning, maritime prov. of NE China. Area *c* 230,500 sq km (89,000 sq mi); pop. 28,000,000; cap. Shenyang. Heavily industrialized; major coal, iron ore, paper producer. Soya beans major crop. Incl. hist. disputed LU-TA at end of Liaotung penin.

Libby, Willard Frank (1908-), American chemist. Developed technique to find age of carbon-containing materials by measuring content of radioactive carbon 14. Awarded Nobel Prize for Chemistry (1960).

libel, in law, one of two types of defamation (exposure to hatred, contempt, ridicule or material loss), other being slander. Libel must take permanent form, *eg* writing, picture, tape, film, whereas slander consists in utterance (by speech, gesture, *etc*) of defamatory statement. Both, to be actionable, must affect living individual (*eg* relative of defamed deceased). Slander is a civil offence, libel may be criminal, *eg* if likely to cause breach of the peace. Defences incl. truth, fair comment, qualified privilege.

liberalism, philosophy or movement advocating individual freedom. Theory based on LOCKE's doctrine involving freedom from restraint on life, health, liberty, property. In politics, manifested in parties pressing for democratic govt. and gradual reform of social institutions. Influence of utilitarians (esp. Bentham, Mill) enabled movement to promote state-controlled social measures in early 19th cent. Economic policies founded on opposition to state regulation. In UK, **Liberal Party** developed from WHIG PARTY after Reform Bill (1832), declining in 20th cent. with rise of Labour Party. Prominent leaders incl. Palmerston, Gladstone, Lloyd George. Liberalism in W Europe associated with nationalist movements in 19th cent. In British Commonwealth, Liberal parties achieved major party status, often forming govts., *eg* Canada (formed in 1850s) and Australia (founded 1944).

Liberia, republic of W Africa. Area 111,300 sq km (43,000 sq mi); pop. 1,751,000; cap. Monrovia. Languages: tribal, English. Religions: native, Islam. Coastal plain, inland plateaux; extensive rain forest. Main food crop rice; exports iron ore, gold, diamonds. Major rubber-producing indust. from 1925; large merchant fleet using 'flag of convenience'. Founded (1822) as colony for freed American slaves; independent republic from 1847.

Liberty, Statue of, landmark dominating harbour of New York City in form of colossal female figure holding up torch. Stands on Liberty Island. Presented by Franco-American Union to commemorate alliance during American Revolution, it was constructed in 1884.

Designed by F.A. Bartholdi; 46 m (152 ft) high.

libido, in psychology, term used by Freud to denote energy of sexual and creative instincts, as opposed to death instinct, destructive drive.

Libra, *see* ZODIAC.

library, organized collection of books and other written material. Earliest known library was collection of clay tablets in Babylonia (21st cent. BC). Noted ancient examples incl. that of Assurbanipal (d. *c* 626 BC) at Nineveh and those at Alexandria and Pergamum. Public libraries estab. in Greece (330 BC) and at Rome. Oldest existing public library of Europe is that of Vatican (15th cent.) with many univ. libraries estab. earlier, *eg* Sorbonne (1257). Modern libraries incl. Bodleian (Oxford), Bibliothèque Nationale (Paris), British Library (London), LIBRARY OF CONGRESS.

Library of Congress, public, national library of US, at Washington DC, estab. 1800. Act of 1870 provided that a copy of any book copyrighted in US must be deposited in it. Library of Congress catalogue number is given to every book published in US.

Libreville, cap. of Gabon, on estuary of R. Gabon. Pop. 73,000. Port, exports timber, palm oil; commercial, admin. centre. Founded (1848) by freed slaves.

Libya, republic of N Africa. Area 1,759,500 sq km (679,350 sq mi); pop. 2,444,000; cap. Tripoli. Language: Arabic. Religion: Islam. Fertile coastal strip; interior mainly desert (Libyan, Sahara) with some oases. Grain, fruit growing; major producer of oil, natural gas. Under Turkish rule from 16th cent.; taken by Italy 1912. Scene of heavy fighting in WWII; under Franco-British military govt., then UN rule, 1943-51. Federal kingdom of Libya estab. 1951, comprising Cyrenaica, Fezzan, Tripolitania provs.; unitary state from 1963. Republic proclaimed (1969) after military coup.

lichee, *see* LITCHI.

lichen, any of large group (Lichenes) of dual plants composed of a particular alga (blue-green or green) and particular fungus growing in SYMBIOSIS. The algal cells manufacture food sugars while the fungus forms a protective shell. Typically greyish-green, grows on rocks or trees from Arctic to tropical regions.

Lichtenstein, Roy (1923-), American painter, sculptor. A leading exponent of pop art, uses subjects of commercial art and its techniques, *eg* magnification of coarsely screened picture to bring out round dots and primary colours. Works incl. *Whaam!*, based on comic strips.

licorice, *see* LIQUORICE.

Liddell Hart, Sir Basil Henry (1895-1970), British military historian and strategist. Wrote official training manuals and histories of WWI and II. He was an early advocate of air power and mechanized warfare, greatly influencing German planning. before WWII.

Lidice, village of W Czechoslovakia. Wholly destroyed in Nazi massacre after assassination of local Nazi leader (1942). Rebuilt after war.

Lie, Trygve Halvdan (1896-1968), Norwegian statesman. First secretary-general of the UN (1946-53).

Denounced by Communist bloc for supporting UN action in Korea.

Liebig, Justus von (1803-73), German chemist. Developed methods of quantitative organic analysis. Pioneer of chemical methods in physiology and agric., he experimented in use of artificial fertilizers.

Liebknecht, Wilhelm (1826-1900), German politician. In exile in England (1849-62), where he was influenced by Marx. Founded (with August Bebel) German Social Democratic Labour Party (1869). His son, Karl Liebknecht (1871-1919), formed communist Spartacus party (1916). Imprisoned for anti-war demonstrations (1916-18); on release led, with Rosa LUXEMBURG, Spartacist insurrection against Social Democratic govt. Killed after arrest by army officers.

Liechtenstein, independent principality of WC Europe, in Rhaetian Alps. Area 166 sq km (64 sq mi); pop. 22,000; cap. Vaduz. Language: German. Religion: RC. Cereals, wine; tourism. Created 1719 from union of Vaduz, Schellenberg countships; independent 1866; joined Swiss customs union 1923.

Liège (Flem. *Luik*), city of E Belgium, on R. Meuse and Albert Canal, cap. of Liège prov. Pop. 150,000. Coal region; machinery, arms mfg.; univ. (1817). Centre of Walloon culture.

Lifar, Serge (1905-), Russian ballet dancer. Joined Diaghilev's Ballets Russes (1923); created title role in Prokofiev's *Prodigal Son* and choreographed Stravinsky's *Renard* (1929). Principal dancer and ballet-master at Paris Opéra (1947-58); had important influence on French ballet.

Liffey, river of E Irish Republic, flows 80 km (50 mi) from Wicklow Mountains via Dublin to Dublin Bay; 3 power stations on river.

Lifford, co. town of Donegal, N Irish Republic, on R. Foyle. Pop. 1000.

ligament, short band of tough fibrous tissue connecting 2 bones at a joint, or holding an organ, *eg* liver, spleen, in position.

light, electromagnetic radiation which is detectable by the eye; variation in its wavelength produces sensation of colour. According to quantum theory, light consists of discrete bundles of energy (photons) and the energy of each photon is proportional to frequency of the light. In this theory, light exhibits both wave-like and particle-like properties.

lighthouse, structure in or adjacent to navigable waters, equipped to give optical or, more recently, radio-electrical guidance to ships (*see* RADIO RANGE). Identified by characteristic light flashes, fog sirens, radio signals. Now largely automatic. First lighthouse was Pharos of Alexandria (*c* 280 BC); first British was Eddystone (1698).

lightning, electrical discharge in the atmosphere. May be from one part of cloud to another, from cloud to cloud, or from cloud to Earth. Types incl. forked, sheet lightning; both are accompanied by thunder. Much rarer ball lightning sometimes seen as moving luminous ball, which may disintegrate explosively.

light year, distance travelled by light in 1 year; equals c 9.46 × 10^{12}

km (5.88 × 10^{12} mi). Measure of distance in astronomy.

lignite or brown coal, soft, brownish-black fossil· fuel intermediate between peat and COAL. Has low carbon content, burns with smoky flame and has low heat-producing capacity. Dates mainly from Carboniferous period and later.

lignum vitae, hard wood of tropical American evergreen trees of genus *Guaiacum*. Used for pulleys, chopping boards; contains resin used medicinally.

Liguria, region of NW Italy, cap. Genoa. Alps in W, Apennines in E, Italian Riviera in S. Olives, vines, fruit, flowers; shipbuilding, chemicals. Celtic inhabitants conquered by Romans 2nd cent. BC; dominated by Genoa in Middle Ages; annexed by Sardinia 1815.

Ligurian Sea, arm of Mediterranean Sea, between Liguria, Tuscany, and Corsica. Incl. Gulf of Genoa; Italian Riviera on N shores.

lilac, any of genus *Syringa* of trees or shrubs of olive family, esp. *S. vulgaris* native to Europe and Asia. Has cone-shaped clusters of blue, pink or white fragrant flowers and very hard wood.

Lilith, Jewish female demon, prob. derived from Babylonian fertility goddess Ninlil. In some traditions, 1st wife of Adam; later folklore makes her a vampire child-killer.

Lille, city of N France, cap. of Nord dept. Pop. 191,000. Forms conurbation with Roubaix, Tourcoing; major textile mfg., engineering centre; coalfield nearby. Cap. of French Flanders from 1668. Citadel, 17th cent. Bourse, art gallery, univ. (1808). Birthplace of De Gaulle.

Lillehammer, town of SE Norway, on L. Mjøsa. Pop. 20,000. Tourist and commercial centre for Gudbrandsdal. Open-air museum.

Lilly, John, *see* LYLY, JOHN.

Lilongwe, cap. of Malawi. Pop. 20,000. Admin. centre, agric. coll. Founded 1947; has replaced Zomba as cap.

lily, any of genus *Lilium* of perennial, bulbous plants. Native to N temperate zones. Showy, trumpet-shaped flowers. Species incl. white madonna lily, *L. candidum*. Name also used for many unrelated lily-like flowers esp. of AMARYLLIS genus.

lily of the valley, *Convallaria majalis*, perennial plant of lily family. Native to Europe, N Asia and US. Dark green leaves with bell-shaped, fragrant, white flowers.

Lima, cap. of Peru, with Pacific port at Callao. Pop. 2,416,000. Commercial, indust. centre; oil refining, textile mfg. Founded by Pizarro (1535), centre of Spanish colonial power in South America until 19th cent. Has numerous churches, cathedral, colonial buildings; San Marcos Univ., founded 1551, is oldest univ. on continent.

Limbo, in some Christian theologies, region bordering on hell, where unbaptized children and righteous people who lived before Jesus dwell after death.

Limbourg, Pol de (active c 1400 - c 1416), Franco-Flemish miniature painter. With his 2 brothers, worked for Duke of Berri, for whom they produced famous manuscript *Très Riches Heures du Duc de Berri* in International Gothic style.

lime or linden, any of genus *Tilia* of tall deciduous trees native to N temperate regions. Heart-shaped leaves, white fragrant flowers. Common lime, *T. europaea*, yields whitewood used in furniture. Also, small, thorny, semitropical tree, *Citrus aurantifolia*, bearing small, lemon-shaped, greenish-yellow citrus fruit rich in vitamin C.

lime, quicklime or **calcium oxide** (CaO), white solid made by heating calcium carbonate (limestone). Combines with water to form calcium hydroxide (slaked lime). Used to make mortar, cement and to neutralize acidic soil.

Limerick (*Luimneach*), county of Munster prov., SW Irish Republic. Area 2686 sq km (1037 sq mi); pop. 140,000. Galty Mountains in SE; has part of fertile Golden Vale. Agric., salmon fishing. Co. town Limerick, on Shannon estuary. Pop. 57,000. Port, shipbuilding; tanning, curing industs. Once cap. of Munster kingdom. Norman castle; Protestant, RC cathedrals; site of Treaty (1691) after siege by William III of England.

limerick, humorous, usually epigrammatic poem of 5 lines of mixed iambic and anapestic metre with rhyme scheme aabba. Popularized by Edward Lear.

limestone, sedimentary rock composed wholly or mainly of calcium carbonate. Formed from remains of marine organisms, *eg* shells, skeletons, by chemical precipitation, or by mechanical deposition. Varieties incl. chalk, dolomite, marble; used as building stone, in lime and cement mfg.

Limoges, city of C France, on R. Vienne, cap. of Haute-Vienne dept. Pop. .133,000. Enamelling indust.

(estab. 13th cent.); porcelain mfg. (estab. 18th cent.) using local kaolin. Hist. cap. of Limousin. Sacked (1370) by Black Prince. Cathedral (13th cent.); ceramics museum, univ.

limonite, iron ore mineral, any of several mixtures of iron oxides and iron hydroxides. Normally brownish with yellow streak; formed by weathering of iron-rich minerals. Types incl. gossan, bog iron ore, ochre. Used as source of ochre pigment, iron.

limpet, marine gastropod mollusc with flattened cone-shaped shell. Uses fleshy foot to adhere to rocks. Used for bait and food.

Limpopo or **Crocodile**, river of SE Africa. Flows *c* 1600 km (1000 mi) from Transvaal, South Africa to Indian Ocean in SE Mozambique. Forms part of South Africa-Botswana border, all of South Africa-Rhodesia border.

Linacre, Thomas (*c* 1460-1524), English humanist, physician. Founder of Royal College of Physicians (1518); instituted lectureships at Oxford and Cambridge. Translated works of Greek physician Galen into Latin.

Lincoln, Abraham (1809-65), American statesman, president (1861-5). Gained prominence in campaign for senatorship for Illinois during debates with STEPHEN DOUGLAS on slavery issue. Elected president shortly before secession of Southern states and outbreak of CIVIL WAR. Tenure marked by conflicts over policies, but he eventually acquired almost dictatorial control. Morally justified Union cause with EMANCIPATION PROCLAMATION freeing slaves and GETTYSBURG ADDRESS

(1863). After re-election (1864), opposed by Republican radicals for policy seeming to favour leniency towards the South. Assassinated (April, 1865) by John Wilkes Booth.

Lincoln, cap. of Nebraska, US. Pop. 150,000. In prairie region; indusits. incl. food processing, flour milling. Important insurance centre. Became cap. 1867.

Lincolnshire, county of E England. Area 5885 sq km (2272 sq mi); pop. 513,000. Wolds in S; Fens in S; elsewhere fertile lowland. Agric., livestock; fishing; iron, steel indusits. Co. town Lincoln, on R. Witham. Pop. 74,000. Agric. processing, machinery. Was Roman *Lindum*; 11th cent. cathedral with 'Great Tom' bell.

Lincoln's Inn, see INNS OF COURT.

Lindbergh, Charles Augustus (1902-74), American aviator. Made 1st solo transatlantic, non-stop flight (1927). His son died (1932) in prominent kidnapping. Criticized for isolationist speeches before US entry into WWII.

linden, see LIME.

Lindisfarne or Holy Island, off Northumberland, NE England. Causeway to mainland. Monastery estab. 635 by St Aidan; priory (1083); Lindisfarne Gospels (7th cent.) now in British Museum.

Lindsay, [Nicholas] Vachel (1879-1931), American poet. Attempted to find distinctively American rhythm drawing on folk tales, ballads. Works incl. *General William Booth Enters into Heaven* (1913), *The Congo* (1914), 'In Praise of Johnny Appleseed' (1921).

Lindsey, Parts of, former admin.

county of Lincolnshire, E England. Co. town was Lincoln.

Linear B, see VENTRIS, MICHAEL.

Line Islands, group of coral isls. in C Pacific Ocean. Christmas, Fanning, Washington isls. part of Gilbert and Ellice Isls. colony. Kingman Reef, Jarvis, Palmyra isls. admin. by US. Remainder disputed by US, UK.

linen, fabric made from fibre of FLAX plant. Uneven texture, durable and crisp. Introduced to N Europe by Romans, widely used in Middle Ages. Ireland is chief producer of fabric; Belgium produces finest fibre.

ling, large edible fish of cod family. Common blue, *Molva molva*, found in European waters. Name also applied to burbot.

lingam, phallic symbol used in worship of Hindu god Siva. See YONI.

lingua franca, spoken language allowing communication between people of mutually unintelligible languages. Originally applied to hybrid language (incl. Turkish, French, Spanish, Arabic elements) used by traders in E Mediterranean. Modern examples incl. use of Latin in RC church and French by diplomats.

linguistics, science of LANGUAGE, concerned both with its structure (synchronic analysis) and its hist. development (diachronic). In 19th cent., comparative philology estab. generic relations between languages, *eg* Indo-European family SAUSSURE developed structural, synchronic approach to language which has subsequently predominated. See CHOMSKY, PHONETICS, SEMANTICS.

Linklater, Eric Robert Russell (1899-1974), Scottish novelist.

Works incl. picaresque *Juan in America* (1931), *Ripeness is All* (1935), short stories, *Sealskin Trousers* (1947).

Linköping, town of SE Sweden. Pop. 77,000. Railway jct., engineering; textiles; tobacco. Romanesque-Gothic cathedral (13th cent.).

Linlithgow, town of Lothian region, EC Scotland. Pop. 6000. Former royal burgh and co. town of West Lothian. Paper mfg., whisky distilling. Has ruined palace, birthplace of Mary Queen of Scots.

Linnaeus, Carolus, orig. Karl von Linné (1707-78), Swedish taxonomist. Estab. binomial nomenclature principle of botanical classification in *Species plantarum* (1753). *Systema naturae* (1758) extends system to animals.

linnet, *Acanthis cannabina,* small songbird of finch family, found in open countryside of Europe and W Asia.

linotype, typesetting machine, patented (1884) by Ottmar Mergenthaler (1854-99). Operated by keyboard, it composes an entire line of type in one metal bar or slug.

Lin Piao (1908-71), Chinese military and political leader. Became defence minister (1959). Ranked second to Mao Tse-tung in Communist Party hierarchy; considered Mao's political successor. Said to have died in mysterious plane crash in Mongolia; may have been removed in party purge.

linseed, seed of common FLAX plant which yields an oil used in paint, varnish and linoleum. After oil extraction, residue is used in cattle feed as linseed cake.

Linz, city of N Austria, on R.

Danube, cap. of Upper Austria prov. Pop. 203,000. River port; produces iron, steel, machinery. Roman *Lentia;* prov. cap. in Holy Roman Empire. Neo-Gothic cathedral (1924).

lion, *Panthera leo,* large carnivore of cat family; once widespread, now found in Africa S of Sahara and NW India. Yellow to brown in colour; male usually has black or tawny mane. Social, lives in group called pride. Hunts zebras, wildebeeste, *etc;* old or wounded animals may attack man.

Lions, Gulf of (*Golfe du Lion*), bay of Mediterranean Sea, extending from NE Spain to Toulon (S France).

Lipari Islands or **Aeolian Islands,** isl. group of SW Italy, in Tyrrhenian Sea. Incl. active volcanoes (Stromboli, Vulcano). Exports pumice stone, wine. Traditional home of Aeolus, the wind god.

Lippe, river of NW West Germany. Flows *c* 240 km (150 mi) via Hamm to R. Rhine at Wesel. Agric. region with deciduous forests.

Lippi, Fra Filippo (*c* 1406-69), Italian painter. Master of colour and line, as shown in *Coronation of the Virgin;* masterpiece is fresco series in the choir of Prato Cathedral (1452-*c* 1465). His son, Filippino Lippi (*c* 1457-1504), was also a Florentine painter. Work incl. frescoes in Florence and Rome.

liquefaction of gases, process of changing gases to liquid state. Gases can be liquefied by application of pressure provided, their CRITICAL TEMPERATURE is not exceeded. Methods of cooling gas incl. Joule-Thomson effect, in which gas loses temperature by expanding through porous plug.

liquid, state of matter intermediate between gas and solid. In a liquid, molecules are free to move with respect to each other but are restricted by cohesive forces from unlimited expansion as in a gas.

liquorice or licorice, dried root of leguminous plant, *Glycyrrhiza glabra,* of Europe and Asia. Used in confectionery and medicine.

Lisbon (*Lisboa*), cap. of Portugal, at mouth of R. Tagus. Pop. 1,034,000. Indust., commercial centre; port, exports wine, olive oil, cork. Taken from Moors 1147; cap. from 1260. Rebuilt after 1755 earthquake; floods 1967. Univ. (1290), Hieronymite monastery; Salazar suspension bridge (1966).

Lisburn, town of W Northern Ireland, on R. Lagan. Pop. 29,000. In former Co. Antrim. Linen mfg. Has 17th cent. Protestant cathedral. Lisburn, district; area 447 sq km (172 sq mi); pop. 73,000. Created 1973, formerly part of Cos. Antrim, Down.

Lismore, isl. of Strathclyde region, W Scotland, at mouth of Loch Linnhe. Has restored 13th cent. cathedral. Gaelic poetry collection made here 16th cent.

Lister, Joseph, 1st Baron Lister (1827-1912), English surgeon. Founded antiseptic surgery; used carbolic acid (1865) and heat to sterilize instruments to prevent septic infection of wounds. Introduced many surgical techniques, incl. absorbable ligature and drainage tube.

Liszt, Fránz (1811-86), Hungarian pianist, composer. Foremost pianist of his time; protégés incl. Wagner, who married his daughter Cosima. His music is highly romantic and incl. many virtuoso piano pieces, *eg* 'Hungarian Rhapsodies', as well as songs, choral and orchestral music (esp. symphonic poems). Took minor religious orders (1865), becoming known as Abbé Liszt.

Li Tai Po or Li Po (*c* 700-62), Chinese poet. Wrote great number of poems (mostly lost) celebrating natural beauty, wisdom found in drunkenness, rejection of duty, preferment. According to tradition died trying to embrace reflection of moon in river.

litchi, lychee or lichee, *Litchi chinensis,* Chinese tree, now grown in Florida and California. Cultivated for pulpy fruit enclosed in thin, brittle shell.

literature, all writings in prose or verse, esp. those of imaginative or critical character, often distinguished from scientific writing, news reporting, *etc.* Sometimes denotes only such writings considered to be of permanent value, but use can be extended to incl. printed matter of any kind, *eg* campaign leaflets, promotional material, or to writings in particular subject area, *eg* medical literature. Historically chief vehicle for transmitting and conserving culture of society, enabling much more complex and complete records to be kept than society relying on oral, pictorial transmission. CHINESE LITERATURE prob. 1st in world. In West literature founded on writings of Greeks, Romans.

lithium (Li), soft metallic element, lightest metal known; at. no. 3, at.

wt. 6.94. Chemically similar to sodium, but less active. Used in alloys; compounds used in nuclear research.

lithography, process of printing from a flat stone or metallic plate. Design is applied to surface with greasy material and surface is then wetted. Greasy ink is applied and is absorbed by greasy parts of surface but repelled by wet parts. Prints are then taken from the surface. Most modern lithography is offset, design being transferred from metal plate to rubber-covered cylinder, then to the paper. Technique invented by Aloys Senefelder (1796).

Lithuanian Soviet Socialist Republic, constituent republic of W USSR. Area c 65,200 sq km (25,200 sq mi); pop. 3,129,000; cap. Vilnius. Largely flatland, drained by R. Neman; formerly mainly agric., indust. development from 1940. In 13th cent. was grand duchy formed to oppose Teutonic knights; became powerful and expanded in 14th cent. Merged with Poland (1569); passed to Russia after Polish partition (1795). Independent (1918-40) until incorporated into USSR.

litmus, colouring matter obtained from various lichens. Used as acid-base indicator in chemical analysis; acids turn it red, bases blue.

litre, unit of liquid capacity in metric system. Originally defined as volume occupied by 1 kilogram of water at 4° C; now defined as 1000 cubic cm; 1 litre = c 1.76 pints.

Little Belt, see BELT, GREAT and LITTLE, Denmark.

Little Bighorn, see BIGHORN.

Little Rock, cap. of Arkansas, US; on Arkansas R. Pop. 132,000.

Commercial centre; cotton, bauxite, coal trade centre; clothing mfg. Federal troops enforced school integration (1957) during race riots.

Liu Shao-chi (c 1898-c 1974), Chinese political leader. Chairman of Chinese People's Republic (1959-68), he was heavily criticized for revisionism during Cultural Revolution (1966-9) and removed from all political offices in 1968.

liver, large gland of vertebrates. In man, opens off beginning of small intestine. Functions incl. formation and secretion of bile, storage of glucose in form of glycogen, synthesis of blood proteins, storage of iron, and breakdown of haemoglobin from worn-out red blood cells.

Liverpool, Robert Banks Jenkinson, 2nd Earl of (1770-1828), British statesman, PM (1812-27). Early years of his Tory admin. were marked by introduction of Corn Laws and repressive measures against unrest (1815-20). Later took more liberal line, repealing anti-trade union laws. Abolished sinecures, took moderate line on Catholic Emancipation issue.

Liverpool, city of Merseyside met. county, NW England, on R. Mersey. Pop. 607,000. Major seaport; indust. centre; road tunnel to Birkenhead. Has Anglican, RC cathedrals; univ. (1903).

liverwort, any plant of class Hepaticae of flowerless, moss-like plants. Grows on moist ground or tree-trunks. *Marchantia* and *Riccia* are 2 common genera. Name is also applied to unrelated flowering plants of buttercup family of genus *Hepatica*.

Livingstone, David (1813-73),

Scottish missionary and explorer. Journeyed extensively in C and S Africa; believed in ending slave trade by estab. Christianity and legitimate commerce in its place. Reached L. Ngami (1849), R. Zambezi (1851); led 3 expeditions, discovering Victoria Falls (1855), L. Nyasa (1859). Set out (1866) to seek Nile's source; met by H.M. Stanley at Ujiji (1871). Wrote *Missionary Travels* (1857).

Livingstone, town of S Zambia, on R. Zambezi near Victoria Falls. Pop. 52,000. Tourist, commercial and trade centre. Cap. of Northern Rhodesia 1911-35. Livingstone-Rhodes museum. Renamed Maramba 1972.

Livonia, region of NE Europe, comprising modern Estonian SSR and N Latvian SSR. Conquered by Livonian Brothers of the Sword in 13th cent., later disputed by Sweden, Russia and Poland; ceded to Russia in 1721.

Livorno, *see* LEGHORN, Italy.

Livy, full name Titus Livius (59 BC-AD 17), Roman historian. Wrote *History of Rome* in 142 volumes, covering period from arrival of Aeneas to death of Drusus (9 BC). Only 35 volumes survive, with summaries of others. Sacrificed accuracy for patriotic effect, but works are noted for style.

lizard, reptile of suborder Lacertilia, incl. gecko, iguana, monitor. Scaly skin, long body and tail; usually 4-legged, but some species legless, *eg* snake-like slow-worm.

Lizard Point, headland of Cornwall, SW England. Most S point in England.

Ljubljana (Ger. *Laibach*), city of NW Yugoslavia, on R. Sava, cap. of Slovenia. Pop. 174,000. Cultural, indust. centre; univ. (1595). Under Habsburgs from 1277; cap. of Austrian Illyria 1816-49, of Carniola until 1918.

llama, *Lama peruana*, South American hoofed mammal of camel family. Humpless, stands *c* 1.2 m/4 ft high at shoulder. Used as pack animal and for wool, meat. Vicuña and guanaco are related species..

Llandudno, urban dist. of Gwynedd, N Wales. Pop. 19,000. Seaside resort.

Llanelli, mun. bor. of Dyfed, S Wales, on Carmarthen Bay. Pop. 26,000. Exports coal; indust. centre, esp. tinplate mfg.

Llanos, prairie of C Venezuela and E Colombia, in Orinoco basin. In famous cattle-raising region.

Llewelyn ap Gruffydd (d. 1281), prince of North Wales. Succeeded his uncle as ruler (1246). Recovered much of South and North Wales during Barons' War in England; recognized as prince of Wales (1267). Lost most of his lands in invasion of Edward I (1277).

Lleyn Peninsula, penin. of Gwynedd, NW Wales, W of Snowdonia. Main town Pwllheli. Pastoral region; fishing.

Lloyd, Harold (1893-1971), American silent film comedian. Famous as timid, bespectacled victim of accidents, hair-raising stunts in many two-reelers. Full-length films incl. *The Freshman* (1925).

Lloyd, Marie, pseud. of Matilda Alice Victoria Wood (1870-1922), English music-hall entertainer. Popularized songs 'Oh, Mr Porter!', 'My Old Man Said Follow the Van'.

Lloyd George, David, 1st Earl Lloyd-George of Dwyfor (1863-1945), British statesman, PM (1916-22). Liberal chancellor of the exchequer (1908-15). Rejection by House of Lords of his 1909 budget, seeking to finance old-age pensions, led to Parliament Act (1911) curtailing power of Lords; also introduced health and unemployment insurance (*see* NATIONAL INSURANCE ACT). As PM of wartime coalition, unified Allied war command; worked with Clemenceau and Wilson to draw up TREATY OF VERSAILLES (1919). Achieved victory in 1918 election, but reliance on Conservatives led to disintegration of his support. Remained in Parliament until 1944.

Lloyd's, association of English insurance underwriters; originally covering marine risks only, now issuing many types of insurance policy. Name derived from the coffee house, kept by Edward Lloyd in 18th cent., used as meeting place. *Lloyd's Register of Shipping* is annual publication detailing information on world shipping.

loach, any of Cobitidae family of small freshwater fish with several barbels around mouth. Found in Europe, Asia, N Africa. Species incl. stone loach, *Nemacheilus barbatula*.

loam, type of soil, composed of sand, silt, clay and humus. Porous, retains moisture well, has good air circulation. Easily worked and fertile.

Lobachevski, Nikolai Ivanovich (1793-1856), Russian mathematician. Independently of Gauss and Bolyai, discovered a form of non-Euclidean geometry. Works incl. *Pangéométrie* (1855).

lobelia, genus of annual or perennial plants of bellflower family. Native to temperate regions. Small, rounded leaves with blue, red, yellow or white irregular flowers.

Lobito, town of W Angola, on Atlantic Ocean. Pop. 98,000. Port, built mainly on reclaimed land, exports minerals, coffee, maize. Terminus of trans-African railway from Mozambique, completed 1929.

lobotomy, surgical operation to treat certain severe psychoses. Consists of severing fibres between prefrontal lobes and rest of brain. Devised by Portuguese physician Egas Moniz (1874-1955) who shared Nobel Prize for Physiology and Medicine (1949).

lobster, edible marine crustacean of Homaridae family with 5 pairs of jointed legs, 1st pair having pincerlike jaws. Greenish or grey when alive, turns red when boiled. Species incl. common European lobster, *Homarus vulgaris*.

Locarno, town of S Switzerland, on L. Maggiore. Pop. 14,000. Tourism. Locarno Conference (1925) guaranteed post-WWI territ. boundaries.

Locarno Pact, series of treaties concluded among European nations (1925) at Locarno, Switzerland, guaranteeing German borders in W, as designated by Treaty of Versailles (1919). Germany also agreed to demilitarize Rhineland and was promised League of Nations membership. Chief architects of Pact were Stresemann, Briand and Austen Chamberlain.

Locke, John (1632-1704), English philosopher. Leading empiricist, wrote *Essay concerning Human Understanding* (1690), holding knowledge to be based on sense experience, not innate ideas. Opposed Hobbes in belief in equality of men and happiness of original natural state. Two *Treatises on Government* (1689) influenced framers of US Constitution.

Lockhart, John Gibson (1794-1854), Scottish editor, biographer. Editor of *Quarterly Review* (1825-53), noted contributor to *Blackwood's Magazine*. Known for vicious reviews of Keats's work, uncritical lives of Burns (1828) and father-in-law Scott (1837).

lockjaw, see TETANUS.

lockout, refusal by employers to allow employees to come in to work until they agree to employers' terms. Famous example is lockout of British coalminers by mine owners which provoked General Strike (1926).

Lockyer, Sir Joseph Norman (1836-1920), English astronomer. Pioneer of spectroscopic analysis of solar prominences and sunspots. Discovered helium in Sun (1868) before its discovery on Earth.

locomotive, powered vehicle designed to push or pull railway train. First practical example built by Trevithick (1804); other early models incl. Stephenson's *Rocket* (1829), Cooper's *Tom Thumb* (1830), all with steam as driving force. Electric locomotives (introduced c 1895) obtain power from 3rd rail or overhead wire. Diesel electric locomotives (c 1925), in which electric generator is driven by diesel engine, have extensively replaced steam locomotives.

locust, insect of short-horned grasshopper family (Acrididae). Often migrates in swarms, devastating large areas of crops. Species incl. migratory locust, *Locusta migratoria*, of Africa and S Asia.

lodestone, see MAGNETITE.

Lodge, Henry Cabot (1850-1924), American politician. Republican senator for Massachusetts (1893-1924), he led opposition to America's joining the League of Nations.

Łódź, city of C Poland, cap. of Łódź prov. Pop. 764,000. Major textile centre; electrical, metal industs.; univ. (1945). Village until c 1830; rapid growth based on weaving indust. Under Russian rule 1815-1919.

loess, fine-grained, yellowish soil transported and deposited by wind. Originates as dust from arid areas or margins of ice-sheets; forms porous, well-graded, very fertile soils. Major deposits in N China, C Europe, C US. With high humus content, forms BLACK EARTH soils of USSR.

Lofoten Islands, isl. group of NW Norway, incl. Vesteralen Isls. Within Arctic Circle; chief town Svolvaer. Rich cod, herring fisheries.

Logan, Mount, in St Elias Mts., SW Yukon, Canada. Highest mountain in Canada rising to 6050 m (19,850 ft).

loganberry, hybrid BLACKBERRY, *Rubus loganobaccus,* developed from American blackberry and raspberry. Acid, purplish-red fruit.

logarithm, power to which a given number (base of logarithm) must be raised to produce that number; thus if $b^n = c$, n is said to be logarithm of c to base b, written $\log_b c$. Tables of logarithms used extensively to reduce problems in multiplication and division to easier problems in addition and subtraction; base of common logarithms is 10. Invented by John Napier.

loggerhead, *Caretta caretta,* large-headed carnivorous sea turtle.

logic, the science of correct reasoning. Aristotle founded systematic logic using SYLLOGISM and deductive method (reasoning from general to particular). His system still finds general acceptance, although attacked by medieval nominalists who argued that logic merely reflects structure of mind, not reality. Formal logic is not to be confused with truth as it requires no reference to content. More recent developments have been made by *eg* Boole, Russell, Wittgenstein.

logical positivism, modern school of philosophy which believes that the work of the philosopher is to clarify concepts rather than to make metaphysical speculations. Holds that for a proposition to be meaningful, it must be scientifically testable. Originated in Vienna Circle of 1920s. Exponents incl. Carnap, WITTGENSTEIN. See POSITIVISM.

logistics, branch of military operations concerned with supply and maintenance of equipment. Strategic implications involve personnel movement, evacuation and hospitalization.

logos (Gk.,=word), in Greek philosophy, any immanent ordering principle in universe. In Christian theology, the link between God and man manifested in God's word becoming flesh in Jesus. Specifically stated in St John's Gospel.

Lohengrin, in medieval German legend, knight of HOLY GRAIL who is led by a swan to save Princess Elsa from an unwanted suitor. Story is basis of Wagner's opera (1850).

Loire, longest river of France. Flows *c* 1005 km (625 mi) from Cévennes Mts. via Orléans, Tours, Nantes to Bay of Biscay at St Nazaire. With tributaries, incl. Allier, Cher, Vienne, drains much of France; limited navigation, seasonal flooding. Loire valley famous for wines and hist. châteaux.

Loki, in Norse myth, personification of evil and trickery. Constantly warred against gods of Asgard. It was prophesied he would cause their final downfall.

Lollards, followers of JOHN WYCLIFFE. Sect in England who anticipated some Reformation doctrines, *eg* the individual's direct responsibility to God, use of vernacular Bible as only reliable guide to faith. Attacked ecclesiastical wealth and monasticism; denied transubstantiation. Their persecution led to a minor rebellion in 1414, but movement had declined by 16th cent.

Lombardo, Pietro (*c* 1435-1515), Italian artist. He and his 2 sons were leading sculptors and architects in Venice. Executed many tombs, incl. that of Doge Pietro Mocenigo and Dante's tomb in Ravenna. Also responsible for church of Santa Maria dei Miracoli.

Lombards, Germanic people who originally inhabited lower basin of the Elbe. Under Alboin, invaded N Italy (568) and estab. kingdom of Lombardy. After threatening the power of the popes, they were conquered by Charlemagne, who took control of Italy.

Lombardy, region of N Italy, cap. Milan. Mountains, lakes, Alpine passes in N; tourism, h.e.p. Lombard Plain (Po basin) in S; irrigated agric. esp. maize, wheat, rice, flax; dairying. Italy's main indust. area, esp. textiles, chemicals, iron and steel. Taken by Romans 3rd cent. BC, by Charlemagne 774. Cities formed Lombard League in 12th cent., defeated Frederick I at Legnano (1176). Later ruled by Spain, France, Austria; annexed 1859 by Sardinia.

Lomé, cap. of Togo, on Bight of Benin. Pop. 193,000. Port, exports cocoa, coffee, copra; univ. of Benin (1970).

Lomond, Loch, largest lake of Scotland, between Central, Strathclyde regions. Length 35 km (22 mi); tourist and recreation area.

London, Jack, pseud. of John Griffith London (1876-1916), American author. Known for adventure novels incl. *The Call of the Wild* (1903), *White Fang* (1906), reflecting Darwinian view of natural laws. Also wrote anti-Utopia, *The Iron Heel* (1907).

London, cap. city of England and UK, on R. Thames. Greater London area 1579 sq km (610 sq mi); pop. 7,349,000. Major admin., commercial, indust., cultural centre; has univ. (1836). Governed from 1965 by Greater London Council; comprises City of London (pop. 5000), 32 bors.; incl. Middlesex, parts of Kent, Essex, Surrey, Hertfordshire. Roman *Londinium*; chief English city from reign of Alfred. Buildings incl. Tower of London, Westminster Abbey, St Paul's Cathedral (1710), Buckingham Palace (1852), Houses of Parliament (1852), GPO Tower

(1964). Extensively rebuilt after Great Plague, Fire (1665-6); damaged in WWII air raids.

London, town of S Ontario; on Thames R. Pop. 223,000. Railway jct.; indust. and commercial centre; food produce, textile mfg. Settled 1826. Seat of Univ. of Western Ontario.

Londonderry or **Derry,** former county of N Northern Ireland. Hilly in S incl. Sperrin Mts.; rivers incl. Foyle, Bann. Agric., distilling, fishing. Co. town was Londonderry, on R. Foyle. Pop. 52,000. Port; shipbuilding; clothing mfg. Has Protestant, RC cathedrals. Withstood siege (1688-9) by James II. Scene of religious conflict from 1969.

Long, Huey Pierce (1893-1935), American politician. As governor of Louisiana (1928-31), he dominated state politics, using corruption and force to achieve his ends. As senator (1932-5), gained national following as potential presidential candidate advocating 'share-the-wealth' policy. Assassinated.

Long Beach, port of S California, US. Pop. 359,000. Major oil, defence industs. Tourist resort; liner *Queen Mary* is an attraction.

long-eared bat, *Plecotus auritus,* common European bat with ears almost as long as its body. Found in lofts and belfries.

Longfellow, Henry Wadsworth (1807-82), American poet. Known for sentimental lyrics, narrative poems, *eg* 'The Village Blacksmith', *Evangeline* (1847), *Song of Hiawatha* (1855), *The Courtship of Miles Standish* (1858).

Longford, county of Leinster prov., C Irish Republic. Area 1044 sq km

(403 sq mi); pop. 28,000. Low-lying, peat bogs. Cattle, dairying. Co. town **Longford**, pop. 3000. Castle (17th cent.), RC cathedral.

Long Island, SE New York, US, separated from mainland by Long Isl. Sound. Length 190 km (118 mi); width 19-32 km (12-20 mi). Extends E from New York City (incl. Brooklyn, Queen bors., Coney Isl. resort). Mainly residential and resort area, esp. in E. Has Kennedy, La Guardia airports.

longitude, in geography, angular distance east or west of prime meridian at any point on Earth's surface, measured from Earth's centre. By international agreement, prime meridian (0°) runs through Greenwich, England.

Long March, journey from Kiangsi prov. to Shensi prov., c 9600 km (6000 mi), made (1934-5) by c 90,000 Chinese Communist soldiers, women and children. Under constant threat of attack from Nationalist forces, less than half of them survived. Mao Tse-tung estab. himself as Communist leader during march.

Long Parliament, name given to English Parliament (1640-60) whose opposition to Charles I led to Civil War. After expulsion of Presbyterian members (Pride's Purge, 1648), was known as Rump Parliament. Dissolved (1653) by Cromwell; reassembled (1659) and finally dissolved at Restoration (1660).

long sight, see HYPERMETROPIA.

loofah, skeleton of dishcloth gourd of genus *Luffa*. Used as bath sponge.

loom, frame machine used for weaving cloth. Power loom was introduced (1785-7) by Cartwright. An attachment invented by J. M. Jacquard (1804), using punched cards and needles, made it possible to weave intricate patterns.

loon, see DIVER.

Lope de Vega, see VEGA [CARPIO], LOPE [FELIX] DE.

loquat, *Eriobotrya japonica*, small evergreen tree of rose family, native to China and Japan. Yellow fruit known as Japanese plum.

Lorca, Federico Garcia, see GARCÍA LORCA.

Lords, House of, see HOUSE OF LORDS.

Lord's Prayer or **Pater Noster**, most widely known and used Christian prayer. Taught by Jesus to his disciples; part of Sermon on the Mount (Matthew 6: 9-13).

Lord's Supper, see EUCHARIST.

Lorelei, rock on E bank of Rhine, West Germany, midway between Bingen and Koblenz. In legend, home of a siren who lured sailors onto reef below.

Lorenz, Konrad (1903-), Austrian zoologist. Estab. science of ethology, *ie* study of group behaviour patterns in animals. Works incl. *On Agression* (1966). Nobel Prize for Physiology and Medicine (1973).

Lorenzetti, Ambrogio (active 1319-48), and his brother **Pietro** (active 1320-48). Italian painters of Sienese school. Influenced by Duccio and Giovanni Pisano, they continued movement towards naturalism. Pietro's work incl. *Birth of the Virgin* at Siena; Ambrogio is known for allegorical fresco of *Good and Bad Government* at Siena.

Lorient, town of Brittany, NW

France, on Bay of Biscay. Pop. 69,000. Port, fishing indust. Founded 1664 by French East India Co.; naval base estab. by Napoleon I. German submarine base in WWII, heavily bombed.

loris, tailless arboreal mammal of lemur group, found in SE Asia, India and Sri Lanka. Nocturnal, with large eyes and furry body. Species incl. slender loris, *Loris tardigradus*, and slow loris, *Nycticebus coucang*.

Lorraine, Claude, *see* CLAUDE LORRAINE.

Lorraine (Ger. *Lothringen*), region and former prov. of E France, hist. cap. Nancy. Low plateau, rising to Vosges Mts. in E. Main rivers Meuse, Moselle. Rich iron ore deposits; coalmining in Saar basin. French prov. from 1766. Ceded with Alsace to Germany (1871), returned (1918). Again annexed during WWII.

lory or **lorikeet**, small brightly coloured parrot of Australasia with brush-tipped tongue used to gather nectar.

Los Alamos, *see* SANTA FE.

Los Angeles, Victoria de (1923–), Spanish soprano. Active in opera and on the concert platform. Has done much to popularize Spanish songs, *eg* those of Falla.

Los Angeles, city of S California, US; near Pacific. Pop. 2,810,000; state's largest city with extensive suburbs. Shipping, communications centre; agric. trade, business centre; defence, film industs. Founded by Spanish Franciscan monks (1781). Became cap. of Mexican California (1845); captured by US forces (1846). Growth boosted with railway development and oil discovery. Has part of Univ. of California (1919).

Losey, Joseph (1909–), American film director, British resident from 1952. Films incl. *The Servant* (1963), *Accident* (1967), *The Go-Between* (1971).

Lot, river of S France. Flows *c* 480 km (300 mi) from Cévennes via Cahors to R. Garonne. Fertile valley; vineyards.

Lothair I (795-855), Holy Roman emperor (840-55). From 817 ruled as joint emperor with his father, Louis I, on whose death empire was divided between Lothair and his brothers, Charles and Louis the German. Lothair's attempts to re-unite empire were resisted by his brothers.

Lothian, region of EC Scotland. Area 1753 sq km (677 sq mi); pop. 742,000; chief city Edinburgh. Created 1975, incl. former East Lothian, Midlothian, West Lothian.

Lotto, Lorenzo (*c* 1480-1556), Italian artist. Influenced by Giovanni Bellini and Titian, his best work combines Venetian colour and northern sentiment. Painted portraits, altarpieces, frescoes.

lotus, various tropical African and Asiatic water or pond lilies. Species incl. Egyptian lotus, *Nymphaea lotus*, with white flowers and American lotus, *Nelumbo lutea*, with yellow flowers, and Indian lotus, *Nelumbo nucifera*. Blossom symbolic in Indian art and religion.

Loughborough, mun. bor. of Leicestershire, EC England. Pop. 46,000. Engineering; hosiery; bell foundry. Technological univ. (1964); teachers' coll.

Louis [I] the Pious (778-840), Holy Roman emperor (814-40). Succeeded father, Charlemagne. Reign marked by conflict between his sons (Pepin, Lothair, Louis the German, Charles the Bald) over his attempts to divide the empire between them.

Louis VII (c 1120-80), king of France (1137-80). Led disastrous 2nd Crusade (1147-9). Annulled marriage to wife, Eleanor of Aquitaine, whose subsequent marriage to Henry II of England provoked continual warfare for her possessions.

Louis [IX], St (1214-70), king of France (1226-70). Led 7th Crusade to Egypt, but was captured (1250) and did not return to France until 1254. Reign noted for bringing of peace and prosperity, building of great Gothic churches, *eg* Chartres, Sainte Chapelle.

Louis XI (1423-83), king of France (1461-83). Successfully curtailed power of great nobles, led by Charles the Bold of Burgundy, by mixture of cunning and force. Gained Burgundian dominions in France by Treaty of Arras (1482).

Louis XIII (1601-43), king of France (1610-43). Assumed power in 1617 following regency of mother, Marie de' Medici. Policy controlled by her protégé, Richelieu, from 1624; exiled mother (1630) after she had attempted to dismiss Richelieu.

Louis XIV (1638-1715), king of France (1643-1715). During his minority, France was ruled by Mazarin. Known as the 'Sun King', Louis assumed absolute control after 1661; rule, epitomized by remark, *L'état, c'est moi,* marked by territ. expansion with development of army and economic reform until death of Colbert. Louis' ambitions in Europe led to numerous wars

(1683-1715), esp. with Spain, Holland and England. War of Spanish Succession (1701-14), by which he secured Spanish throne for his grandson, led to military weakness and huge debts. Under his patronage, arts and sciences flourished; had magnificent palace built at Versailles.

Louis XV (1710-74), king of France (1715-74). During minority, left govt. to duke of Orléans (d. 1723) and Cardinal Fleury. After Fleury's death (1743), attempted to rule alone but was dominated by mistresses such as Mme de Pompadour, whose influence proved disastrous. Lost possessions in Canada and India after Seven Years War (1756-63). Personal extravagance and expenditure on war left France on verge of bankruptcy.

Louis XVI (1754-93), king of France (1774-92). Dismissed 2 ablest ministers, Turgot and Necker, who had tried to reorganize country's disastrous finances. Dominated by wife, Marie Antoinette, and his court. Forced to recall Estates-General (1789), opening way for French Revolution. At first still popular with the people, weakened his position by attempting to flee country (1791); recaptured at Varennes; agreed to become constitutional monarch. Deposed (Sept. 1792) after failures in war against Austria; tried for treason and guillotined.

Louis XVII (1785-c 1795), titular king of France. Son of Louis XVI, he was imprisoned from 1792 until his death. Proclaimed king by royalist exiles.

Louis XVIII (1755-1824), king of

France (1814-24). Lived in exile (1791-1814); assumed royal title on death of Louis XVII. On fall of Napoleon (1814), ascended throne through influence of Talleyrand; expelled (1815) during Hundred Days. Restored by allies (June, 1815). Ruled moderately until 1820, after which he fell under control of reactionary ultra-royalists.

Louis, Joe, orig. Joseph Louis Barrow (1914-), American boxer. World heavyweight champion (1937-49), he made record 25 successful defences of his title. Retired 1949; defeated in comeback attempt (1950, 1951).

Louisiade Archipelago, volcanic isl. group in SW Pacific, SE of New Guinea isl.; part of Papua New Guinea.

Louisiana, state of S US, on Gulf of Mexico. Area 125,675 sq km (48,523 sq mi); pop. 3,643,000; cap. Baton Rouge; chief city New Orleans. Coastal plain dominated by Mississippi delta (subject to floods). Forestry; agric. incl. cotton, rice, sugar cane; salt, petroleum, sulphur mining. Claimed by France in 17th cent.; part of Louisiana Purchase by US in 1803. Admitted as 18th state (1812).

Louisiana Purchase, land bought from France by US in 1803 for 15 million dollars. Extended from Mississippi to Rocky Mts., and from Gulf of Mexico to Canada.

Louis Napoleon, see NAPOLEON III.

Louis Philippe (1773-1850), king of France (1830-48), known as the Citizen King. Lived in exile (1793-1814) after serving in French Revolutionary army. As Duc d'Orléans, supported deposition of Charles X (1830) and was chosen king. Reign, known as 'July Monarchy', characterized by middle-class ideals. Increasing opposition turned him from liberalism to absolutism. Reform movements forced abdication after Revolution of 1848. Fled to England.

Louisville, city of N Kentucky, US; on Ohio R. Pop. 362,000. Tobacco, whisky processing; meat packing, chemical mfg. Supplied with h.e.p. from falls on Ohio R. Has annual Kentucky Derby horse race. Nearby is Fort Knox (US gold bullion stores).

Lourdes, town of SW France, at foot of Pyrenees. Pop. 18,000. Site of St Bernadette's vision of the Virgin (1858); now major pilgrimage centre.

Lourenço Marques, see MAPUTO, Mozambique.

louse, small wingless insect with sucking mouthparts. Divided into 2 orders: Anoplura, blood-sucking lice, parasitic on most mammals; Mallophaga, biting lice, parasitic mainly on birds. Species incl. *Pediculus capitis*, human head louse.

Louth, county of Leinster prov., NE Irish Republic. Area 821 sq km (317 sq mi); pop. 75,000; co. town Dundalk. Smallest Irish county; flat, low-lying. Dairying, fishing.

Louvain (Flem. *Leuven*), town of C Belgium, on R. Dyle. Pop. 32,000. Brewing, lace mfg. Medieval cloth centre, cap. of Brabant 11th-15th cents. RC univ. (1426), library.

Louvre, former French royal palace in Paris, opened to the public as an art museum in 1793. Contains one of the finest collections in world, incl. *Venus de Milo*, particularly strong in Italian Renaissance paintings incl. da Vinci's *Mona Lisa*.

love bird, small Old World parrot, esp. African genus *Agapornis*. Frequently kept as cage bird.

love-in-a-mist, *Nigella damascena*, annual garden plant of buttercup family. Feathery leaves, blue or white flowers.

Lovelace, Richard (1618-58), English poet. Known for Cavalier lyrics, esp. 'To Lucasta, Going to the Wars', 'To Althea, from Prison'.

Lovell, Sir [Alfred Charles] Bernard (1913-), English astronomer. Helped in development of radar. Director of Jodrell Bank Observatory, site of radio telescope, after 1951.

Low, Sir David (1891-1963), British political cartoonist, b. New Zealand. Created 'Colonel Blimp', caricature of conservative Englishman, TUC horse, among other characters.

Low Countries, region of NW Europe. Incl. NETHERLANDS, BELGIUM, LUXEMBOURG; *also see* BRABANT, FLANDERS, HOLLAND.

Lowell, prominent American family of New England. **Francis Cabot Lowell** (1775-1817), pioneered cotton mfg., building factory which processed raw cotton to cloth. His nephew, **James Russell Lowell** (1819-91), was a poet. Wrote *Biglow Papers* (1848) in Yankee dialect, *The Vision of Sir Launfal* (1848), *A Fable for Critics* (1848) satirizing his contemporaries. Also wrote criticism, eg *Among My Books* (1870, 1876). **Percival Lowell** (1855-1916) was an astronomer. Founded Lowell Observatory, Arizona (1894) to study planet Mars; contended that 'canals' seen on Mars were waterways constructed by intelligent life.

Predicted existence of planet Pluto, discovered 1930. His sister, **Amy [Lawrence] Lowell** (1874-1925), was a poet, a member of the IMAGISTS. Works incl. *Sword Blades and Poppy Seed* (1914), *Pictures of the Floating World* (1919), *What O'Clock?* (1925).

Lowell, Robert [Traill Spence] (1917-77), American poet. Works incl. *Lord Weary's Castle* (1946), *The Mills of the Kavanaughs* (1951), verse, prose autobiog. *Life Studies* (1959).

Lower California, *see* BAJA CALIFORNIA.

Lower Hutt, city and indust. centre of SW North Isl., New Zealand, on Port Nicholson. Pop. 59,000. Engineering, food processing, car assembly; fruit, vegetable growing in nearby Hutt R. valley.

Lowestoft, mun. bor. of Suffolk, E England. Pop. 52,000. Port, resort on North Sea. Fishing, yachting.

Lowry, [Clarence] Malcolm (1909-57), English author. Best known for *Under the Volcano* (1947) portraying the disintegration of personality through alcoholic delirium. Other works incl. *Ultramarine* (1933), *Hear Us O Lord from Heaven Thy Dwelling Place* (1961).

Lowry, Laurence Stephen (1887-1976), English artist. Known for his paintings of the industrial landscape and its inhabitants; employed seemingly naive style, depicting people almost as matchsticks.

Loyalists, in American Revolution, those who supported British cause. Many emigrated to Canada, where they became known as United Empire Loyalists.

Loyalty Islands (Fr. *Iles Loyauté*),

isl. group of SW Pacific Ocean, dependency of New Caledonia. Area: *c* 2070 sq km (800 sq mi); main isls. Lifu, Maré, Uvéa. Chief crops copra, rubber, sugar cane.

Loyola, St Ignatius of, see IGNATIUS OF LOYOLA, ST.

LSD, see LYSERGIC ACID DIETHYLAMIDE.

Luanda, São Paulo de, cap. of Angola, on Atlantic Ocean. Pop. 475,000. Admin., commercial centre; port, exports coffee, cotton, minerals; oil refining. Founded 1575, former slave trade centre.

Lübeck, city of N West Germany, on R. Trave. Pop. 240,000. Linked by canal (1900) to R. Elbe; port, shipbuilding, food processing. Chief city of Hanseatic League (1241-1630). Medieval buildings incl. cathedral, town hall.

Lubitsch, Ernst (1892-1947), German film director. Known for sophisticated sex comedies, with the 'Lubitsch touch', made in Hollywood from 1922, eg *The Love Parade* (1929), *Ninotchka* (1939), *Heaven Can Wait* (1943).

Lublin, city of SE Poland, cap. of Lublin prov. Pop. 239,000. Railway jct., agric. machinery, textile mfg.; univ. (1944). Under Russian rule 1815-1919; seat of provisional govts. 1919, 1944.

lubricants, substances used to reduce friction between moving surfaces. May be liquid (oil), semisolid (grease), solid, eg colloidal graphite in water (aquadag) or oil (oildag). Since 19th cent. mostly derived from mineral oil but adapted to many specialist uses. Recently gas at pressure has been used in high speed machinery.

Lubumbashi, city of SE Zaïre, cap. of Shaba region. Pop. 357,000. Mineral refining centre in Katanga mining dist.; food processing, RC cathedral. Founded (1910) as Elisabethville, renamed 1966. Scene of heavy fighting during Katanga secession (1960-3).

Lucan, full name Marcus Annaeus Lucanus (AD 39-65), Roman poet, b. Spain. Enjoyed patronage of Nero, but was forced to commit suicide after unsuccessful republican plot against latter. His epic *Bellum Civile* (or *Pharsalia*) deals with war between Caesar and Pompey.

Lucas van Leyden (1494-1533), Dutch painter, engraver. Influenced by Dürer in woodcuts and engravings, he was a brilliant draughtsman; paintings reflect beginnings of Dutch genre art.

Lucerne (Ger. *Luzern*), town of C Switzerland, on L. Lucerne, cap. of Lucerne canton. Pop. 70,000. Tourism, printing, machinery. Lion of Lucerne monument to Swiss Guard. Joined Swiss Confederation 1332.

Lucerne, Lake (Ger. *Vierwaldstättersee*), in C Switzerland, bordering on the four forest cantons. Area 111 sq km (43 sq mi). Tourism.

lucerne, see ALFALFA.

Lucian (fl 2nd cent.), Greek prose writer. Wrote scathing indictments of contemporary conditions, beliefs. Of *c* 80 works, best known are dialogues, eg *Dialogues of the Dead*, *Dialogues of Courtesans*.

Lucifer, in OT book of Isaiah, figurative reference to king of Babylon, misconstrued to mean fallen angel; hence became a term for Satan. Also Roman name for Venus as morning star.

Lucknow, cap. of Uttar Pradesh, NC India. Pop. 826,000. Railway engineering; paper, carpet mfg. Cap. of Oudh kingdom (1775-1856). British besieged city for 5 months during Indian Mutiny until relieved in Nov. 1857.

Lucretius, full name Titus Lucretius Carus (c 95-c 55 BC), Roman poet. Known for *De rerum natura* expounding Epicurean philosophy. Concerned with nature of physical world, arguing against supernatural origin of universe, and with liberating mankind from fear of gods and death.

Lucullus, Lucius Licinius (c 110-56 BC), Roman statesman, soldier. Appointed consul (74); fought successfully against Mithradates (73-72) in Asia. Mutinies later in his Asian campaigns led to his recall (66). Famous for luxurious living in his retirement.

Luddites, in English history, name given to those taking part in machine-wrecking riots (1811-16). Rioters were protesting against low wages and unemployment attributed to introduction of textile-making machines. Named after mythical Ned Ludd.

Ludendorff, Erich (1865-1937), German general. Chief of staff in WWI, ably supporting Hindenburg's military successes. Backed Hitler's 'beer-hall putsch' (1923).

Ludwig I (1786-1868), king of Bavaria (1825-48). Made Munich great artistic centre. Initially a liberal, but later reactionary policies and scandalous affair with Lola Montez led to enforced abdiction.

Ludwig II (1845-86), king of Bavaria (1864-86). A liberal romantic, he lavished a fortune on the composer Wagner and the building of fairy-tale castles. His growing insanity led to confinement in one of these; he drowned himself nearby.

Ludwigshafen, city of W West Germany, on R. Rhine, opposite Mannheim. Pop. 176,000. River port, major chemical indust., dyes, plastics.

Lugano, town of S Switzerland, on L. Lugano, near Italian border. Pop. 22,000. Tourist centre.

Lugansk, see VOROSHILOVGRAD.

lugworm or **lobworm,** tube-dwelling annelid worm with bristly appendages on body; burrows into mud and sand. Used as bait. Species incl. common European *Arenicola marina.*

Lu Hsun, pseud. of Chou Shujen (1881-1936), Chinese author. Leader in movement to overthrow Ch'ing government. Short stories collected in *Ah Q and others* (1941).

Luik, see LIÈGE, Belgium.

Lukács, Georg or **György** (1885-1971), Hungarian literary theorist. Leading Marxist aesthetician. *History and the Class Consciousness* (1923) links artistic creativity with social struggle. Other works incl. *The Destruction of Reason* (1954), *The Historical Novel* (1955).

Luke, St (fl AD 1st cent.), Gentile physician, friend of St Mark and St Paul. Credited with authorship of 3rd Gospel of NT and Acts of the Apostles.

Luke, Gospel according to St, third of NT Gospels, attributed to St Luke. Longest and historically most detailed of the Gospels.

Luleå, town of NE Sweden, on Gulf of Bothnia at mouth of R. Lule. Pop.

37,000. Exports iron ore from Kiruna and Gällivare; timber, reindeer hides.

Lully, Jean Baptiste (1632-87), French composer, b. Italy. Court composer to Louis XIV. Pioneered introduction of opera in France; operas incl. *Alceste* and *Cadmus et Hermione*. Also helped to estab. ballet in his comedy-ballets, in association with Molière.

Luluabourg, see KANANGA, Zaïre.

lumbago, pain in the small of the back, often associated with pain down the leg. May be caused by back strain or pressure on nerves by a 'slipped disc'.

Lumière, Louis Jean (1864-1948), French cinema pioneer. With his brother, **Auguste Marie Louis Nicholas Lumière** (1862-1954), invented cinematograph in 1895, 1st device to project moving pictures onto screen.

luminosity, in astronomy, measure of actual quantity of light emitted by a star, irrespective of its distance from Earth. See MAGNITUDE.

luminous paint, paint containing a phosphorescent sulphide, usually of barium or calcium. After exposure to light it appears luminous in dark. The type used on watch faces is excited radioactively and does not need exposure to light.

Lumumba, Patrice Emergy (1925-61), Congolese politician. Became premier at independence of Congo. Involved in power struggle with KASAVUBU; each dismissed the other during civil war. Arrested by MOBUTU and taken to Katanga, where he was murdered.

lunacy, see INSANITY.

Lund, town of SW Sweden. Pop. 52,000. Paper, furniture mfg.; printing, publishing. Cathedral (12th cent.) with medieval astronomical clock. Univ. (1668).

Lüneburg Heath (*Lüneburger Heide*), sandy heath of NE West Germany, between Elbe and Aller rivers. Sheep grazing, potato growing. Site of German surrender (1945).

lungfish, any of various fish which have lungs as well as gills. Six freshwater species known, considered living fossils. Australian lungfish, *Neoceratodus forsteri*, found in Queensland, uses lungs during droughts. Other species in S America, Africa.

lungs, respiratory organs in air-breathing vertebrates. In humans, occupy most of thorax and are separated by heart. Carbon dioxide in blood is exchanged for oxygen as blood circulates through the air sacs (alveoli) of the lungs.

Lupercalia, ancient Roman fertility festival held on 15 Feb. in honour of Faunus. Goats were sacrificed and 2 male youths ran through the city slapping passers-by with lashes of the goatskin. Persisted into 6th cent.

lupin, any of genus *Lupinus* of plants of Leguminosae family. Native to Mediterranean region and North America. Flowers, borne on long spike, may be a variety of colours. Russell lupin is popular garden hybrid.

Lurgan, town of E Northern Ireland. Pop. 24,000. In former Co. Antrim. Linen, nylon mfg.

Lusaka, cap. of Zambia. Pop. 348,000. Admin., commercial, communications centre; agric. market; univ. of Zambia (1966). Replaced Livingstone as cap. of Northern Rhodesia (1935).

Lushun, see LU-TA.

Lusitania, British liner sunk without warning off Irish coast by German submarine on 7th May, 1915. Almost 1200 people were killed, over 100 of them American. This act aroused considerable American hostility to Germany and helped bring US into WWI.

Lu-ta or **Lushun-Tallen,** municipality of Liaoning prov., NW China comprising Lushun (formerly Port Arthur) and Talien. Pop. 4,000,000. Soya bean, grain, coal exports; oil refining. Important naval base and ice-free port at end of Liaotung penin. Part of Kwanfung lease (1898-1945) under Japanese; finally reintegrated into China 1955.

lute, string instrument shaped like half pear, with fretted finger-board; the strings, usually 6 in number, are plucked. Popular domestic instrument (15th-17th cents.), both as a solo instrument and for accompanying singers.

lutetium (Lu), metallic element of lanthanide series; at. no. 71, at. wt. 174.97. Discovered (1907) in sample of ytterbium.

Luther, Martin (1483-1546), German religious leader. Augustinian friar, teacher at Univ. of Wittenberg. Campaigned against sale of indulgences; nailed 95 theses to Wittenberg church door (regarded as start of Protestant Reformation). Initially sought reform within Church but excommunicated in 1521. Fled to Wartburg after refusing to retract statements at Diet of Worms. Translated NT into German. Endorsed Melanchthon's Augsburg Confession (1530), basis of Lutheranism.

Lutheranism, Protestant doctrine founded on teachings of MARTIN LUTHER and formulated in confessional Book of Concord (1580). Regards the Bible as only necessary guide to faith; holds the individual to be directly responsible to God and salvation to come through faith alone. Rejects transubstantiation and has no unified liturgical order. Flourishes primarily in Germany, Scandinavia and US.

Luthuli, Albert John (1899-1967), South African political leader. Openly opposed *apartheid*, advocating non-violent resistance. Kept under restriction after 1952; arrested for treason (1956) but acquitted (1959). Awarded Nobel Peace Prize (1960).

Luton, mun. bor. of Bedfordshire, C England, on R. Lea. Pop. 161,000. Engineering, esp. car indust.; airport. Former centre of strawplaiting.

Lutosławski, Witold (1913-), Polish composer. Has written music in wide range of styles, incl. symphonies, songs, choral works. Compositions incl. *Concerto for Orchestra.*

Lutyens, Sir Edwin Landseer (1869-1944), English architect. Leading English architect of early 20th cent. Employing eclectic style, designed country houses, churches, office blocks *etc.* Works incl. Cenotaph, Whitehall (1922), imperial capital of India at New Delhi (1915-30).

Luxembourg, grand duchy of NW Europe. Area 2587 sq km (999 sq mi); pop. 358,000. Language: Letzeburgesch (Ger. dialect). Religion: RC. Agric., cattle; iron mining. Duchy from 1354 (Habsburg from 15th cent.); grand duchy within Netherlands from 1815; independent

1890. Occupied by Germans in both WWs. In Benelux customs union from 1948; member of EEC. Cap. **Luxembourg**, on R. Alzette. Pop. 76,000. Cultural centre. Iron, steel indust. Hq. of ECSC, European Court of Justice. Palace (16th cent.); cathedral.

Luxembourg, Palais du, Renaissance palace in Paris, France; constructed 1615-20 for Marie de' Medici, it was enlarged in 19th cent. Surrounded by famous gardens.

Luxemburg, Rosa (1870-1919), German revolutionary, b. Poland. A Marxist, she founded the Spartacus League (1916) with Karl LIEBKNECHT. Arrested and killed after leading Spartacist insurrection.

Luxor, town of C Egypt, on R. Nile. Pop. 30,000. Occupies part of site of ancient city of THEBES.

Luzern, see LUCERNE, Switzerland.

Luzon, largest isl. of Philippines. Area c 105,000 sq km (40,400 sq mi). Largely mountainous, rising to 2928 m (9606 ft) at Mt. Pulog. Rich agric. areas produce rice, sugar cane, hemp; minerals incl. chromite, nickel, copper. Cap. is Quezon City, chief city Manila. Scene of heavy fighting in WWII.

Lvov, Prince Georgi Evgenyevich (1861-1925), Russian statesman. Led provisional govt. (Feb.–July, 1917) after February uprising. Succeeded by Kerensky.

Lvov (Ger. *Lemberg*), city of USSR, W Ukrainian SSR. Pop. 579,000. Indust. centre; oil refining, machinery mfg. Taken by Poles (1349), became cap. of Austrian Galicia (1772-1919). Returned to Poland, ceded to USSR (1945).

lycanthropy, originally, in folklore, the transformation of humans into wolves or other carnivorous animals. Common to many cultures, described by Vergil, Pliny. Used now by psychologists to denote mental disorder through which patient believes he is an animal. Subject of study by Freud.

lyceum, originally, the grove in Athens where Aristotle taught, so-called from neighbouring temple of *Apollón Lykeios*. Now public hall for lectures, performances of music, *etc*, or an organization providing such services.

lychee, see LITCHI.

Lydgate, John (c 1370-c 1452), English poet, monk. Very famous in own time but now eclipsed by his friend Chaucer. Prolific writer, works incl. *The Fall of Princes*.

Lydia, see SARDIS.

Lyell, Sir Charles (1797-1875), Scottish geologist. Author of standard text *The Principles of Geology* (1830-3), expounding uniformitarianism theory of James HUTTON.

Lyly or **Lilly, John** (c 1554-1606), English author. Known for *Euphues, the Anatomy of Wit* (1578), *Euphues and His England* (1580) written in elaborately rhetorical style known as 'euphuistic' when taken up by school of prose-romancers. Also wrote courtly entertainments, *eg Alexander and Campaspe* (1584).

lymph, colourless fluid derived from blood plasma which has filtered through the capillary walls. Carried by lymphatic vessels to various parts of body where it distributes nutrients and oxygen to the tissues. Lymph nodes are organs in lymphatic vessels which collect bacteria from lymph; also produce lymphocytes, class of white blood cells important in formation of antibodies.

Lynch, John ('Jack') (1917-), Irish politician. Was finance minister in Fianna Fáil cabinet before succeeding Sean Lemass as PM (1966-73); re-elected PM (1977).

lynching, murder of accused person by mob action, without lawful trial. Term possibly derives from Captain William Lynch (1742-1820), member of vigilante group in Virginia (1780). Practice of pioneers in US before rule of law as penalty for, *eg*, horse-stealing, rape. Common in S US after Civil War.

Lynn, town of E Massachusetts, US; N of Boston. Pop. 90,000. Important shoe mfg. Settled by Pilgrims in 1629.

Lynn (Regis), see KING'S LYNN, England.

lynx, any of genus *Lynx* of wildcats with short tail, tufted ears. European lynx, *L. lynx*, found in N Europe and Siberia, now rare. Largest North American variety is Canadian lynx, *L. canadensis*. See BOBCAT.

Lyons, Joseph Aloysius (1879-1939), Australian statesman, PM (1932-9). Helped estab. United Australia party (1931), headed coalition govt.

Lyons (Lyon), city of EC France, at confluence of Rhône and Saône, cap. of Rhône dept. Pop. 528,000. River port, transport jct.; banking centre, major textile indust. (esp. silk, rayon), univ. (1808). Roman *Lugdunum*, founded *c* 43 BC; hist. cap. of Lyonnais. Cathedral (12th cent.), stock exchange (1506).

lyre, ancient Greek stringed musical instrument, like a small portable harp but played with a plectrum. Also known in other ancient civilizations, incl. Assyria and Egypt, and in medieval Europe.

lyrebird, brightly coloured Australian bird, genus *Menura*. Male displays lyre-shaped tail during courtship dance, performed on specially built mound. Renowned mimics.

Lysander (d. 395 BC), Spartan general. Commanded fleet which inflicted final defeat on Athens at Aegospotamos (405); captured Athens (404).

Lysenko, Trofim Denisovich (1898-1976), Russian agronomist. Leading exponent of theory that characteristics acquired through influences of environment can be inherited; his genetic views became official Soviet policy in 1948 but were repudiated after Stalin's death.

lysergic acid diethylamide or **LSD**, alkaloid synthesized from lysergic acid, which is found in the fungus ergot. Powerful hallucinogenic drug, capable of inducing delusions resembling those occurring in psychotic state.

Lysippus (4th cent. BC), Greek sculptor. Leader of Sicyon school, he was prolific worker in bronze. Made many portraits of Alexander the Great. Prob. introduced new scheme of proportions for human figures.

Lytton, 1st Baron, see BULWER-LYTTON, EDWARD GEORGE EARLE LYTTON.

M

Maas, see MEUSE.

Maastricht, city of SE Netherlands, on R. Maas, cap. of Limburg prov. Pop. 112,000. Railway, canal jct.; produces textiles, ceramics. Pop. massacred by Spanish 1579. Site of oldest Dutch church (6th cent.).

Mabinogion, collection of medieval Welsh prose tales, from *mabinogi* (youth, tale of youth). Some contain ancient mythological material, show evidence of oral transmission, others much more literary. Three on parts of ARTHURIAN LEGEND.

Mabuse, Jan, orig. Jan Gossaert (*c* 1478–*c* 1533), Flemish painter. Following visit to Italy in 1508, he adopted style based on Italian Renaissance forms; introduced classical subjects with nude figures into Flemish art.

McAdam, John Loudon (1756–1836), Scottish engineer. Introduced (*c* 1815) improved roads made of crushed stone; known as 'macadam' roads.

MacAlpin, Kenneth (d. *c* 860), king of the Scots. Succeeded father in 832 or 834. United kingdoms of Scots and Picts *c* 844. Said to be first to call his kingdom Scotland.

Macao, Portuguese colony of SE Asia on Chukiang (Pearl) estuary. Area 15 sq km (6 sq mi); pop. *c* 275,000. Chief town Macao is largely coextensive with colony. Free port; trade, tourism centre; textile indust., gambling casinos. Leased by Portuguese (1557), *fl* as trade post until rise of neighbouring Hong Kong.

macaque, monkey of genus *Macaca* found mainly in India and SE Asia. Species incl. barbary ape of Gibraltar and rhesus monkey.

macaroni, preparation of glutinous wheat (semolina) and eggs originating in Italy. Other forms of same material are spaghetti and vermicelli.

MacArthur, Douglas (1880–1964), American general. Chief of general staff (1930–5). Commanded US and Allied forces in SE Asia during WWII. Directed post-war occupation of Japan. Recalled (1951) from post as UN commander in Korea for public disagreement with President Truman over strategy.

Macarthur, John (1767–1834), Australian farmer, merchant, b. England. Leader in estab. New South Wales wool indust. through use of better breeds of sheep. Also introduced viniculture.

Macaulay, Thomas Babington, Baron Macaulay of Rothley (1800–59), English historian. Known for Whig interpretation of history in *The History of England from the Accession of James the Second* (1849–61). Also wrote poetry, *Lays of Ancient Rome* (1842) and numerous essays, notably one on Milton (1825).

MACAW

macaw, brightly coloured long-tailed parrot of tropical Central and South America. Species incl. scarlet macaw, *Ara macao.*

Macbeth (d. 1057), king of Scotland. Killed Duncan I and took crown (1040). Defeated and killed by Duncan's son, Malcolm III. Principal character of Shakespeare's *Macbeth.*

MacBride, Sean (1904-), Irish diplomat, b. South Africa. Secretary-general of International Commission of Jurists (1963-70). UN Commissioner for Namibia from 1974. Shared Nobel Peace Prize (1974).

Maccabees, Jewish family (fl 2nd cent. BC) founded by priest Mattathias (d. 166 BC). With sons, led opposition against Syrians. Judas Maccabeus (d. 161 BC) reoccupied Jerusalem, rededicated the Temple. Simon Maccabeus (d. 135 BC) estab. peace in Palestine.

Maccabees, last two books of OT Apocrypha. Covers history of MACCABEES family.

McCarthy, Eugene Joseph (1916-), American politician, academic. Democratic candidate for presidency (1972), defeated by Nixon. Liberal Independent candidate for presidency (1976), defeated by Carter.

McCarthy, Joseph Raymond (1909-57), American politician. As Republican senator for Wisconsin (1947-57), he claimed (1950) that state dept. had been infiltrated by Communists. Held Senate investigations of people suspected of subversion, accused many of Communist sympathies. Censured by Senate (1954).

McCarthy, Mary (1912-), American writer. Best known for novel *The Group* (1963), sharply-observed, coldly witty view of contemporary social and sexual mores. Other works incl. autobiog. *Memories of a Catholic Girlhood* (1957).

Macclesfield, mun. bor. of Cheshire, W England. Pop. 44,000. Textiles mfg., esp. silk.

McCullers, Carson, neé Smith (1917-67), American novelist. Works, *eg The Heart is a Lonely Hunter* (1940), short stories *The Ballad of the Sad Café* (1951), deal with spiritual isolation in Southern US setting.

McCulloch v Maryland (1819), case decided by US Supreme Court in dispute between federal and state authority over control of currency. Decision upheld federal govt.'s supremacy over states.

McDiarmid, Hugh, pseud. of Christopher Murray Grieve (1892-1978), Scottish poet. Attempted to create a contemporary Scots poetic in *A Drunk Man Looks at the Thistle* (1926). 'Hymns to Lenin' (1931, 1935) reflect Marxist views.

Macdonald, Flora (1722-90), Scottish heroine. After Jacobite defeat at Culloden (1746), she aided Prince Charles Edward Stuart's escape to France by disguising him as her Irish maidservant and escorting him to Skye. Briefly imprisoned afterwards.

Macdonald, Sir John Alexander (1815-91), Canadian statesman, b. Scotland, PM (1867-73, 1878-91). Premier of Upper Canada (1857), he was leading figure in promoting Canadian Confederation; became 1st PM of Dominion of Canada. Scandal over contract for Canadian Pacific Railway forced resignation of his Conservative govt. (1873).

MacDonald, [James] Ramsay (1866-1937), British statesman, PM (1924, 1929-35). Leader of parliamentary Labour Party (1911-14) until removed over pacifist stand at outbreak of WWI. First Labour PM (1924), lost ensuing election after publication of ZINOVIEV letter. PM of minority govt. (1929), split in cabinet led to formation of Conservative-dominated National govt. (1931) with MacDonald as nominal head.

Macdonnell Ranges, mountain system of S Northern Territory, Australia. Highest peak Mt. Zeil (1510 m/4955 ft). Cut by many gorges; Alice Springs built near gap in E mountains.

mace, see NUTMEG.

Macedonia, region of SE Europe, in Greece, Yugoslavia, Bulgaria. Mainly mountainous, rising to over 2450 m (8000 ft). Sheep, goats; wheat, tobacco. Ancient Macedon reached imperial zenith under Philip II, Alexander the Great (4th-3rd cent. BC). Later held by Romans, Slavs, Turks until 1912. Hist. cap. of Greek Macedonia is Salonika. Yugoslav Macedonia is autonomous republic, cap. Skopje.

Maceló, Atlantic port of NE Brazil, cap. of Alagôas state. Pop. 264,000. Sugar, cotton processing; textile, soap mfg. Has old colonial buildings and lighthouse near town centre.

Macgillicuddy's Reeks, range of Co. Kerry, SW Irish Republic, near Lakes of Killarney. Incl. CARRANTUOHILL.

McGonagall, William (1830-1902), Scottish poet. Known for doggerel verse displaying unconsciously ludicrous rhyme, disregard for rhythm, unintentional bathos.

Work collected in *Poetic Gems* (1890).

Mach, Ernst (1838-1916), Austrian physicist and philosopher. Emphasized that scientific laws are generalizations of numerous observations, not *a priori* truths. Rejected ideas of absolute space and time implicit in Newtonian mechanics; his views were vindicated by Einstein's theory of relativity.

Machel, Samora (1933-), Mozambican politician. A founder of Mozambique Liberation Front (FRELIMO), dedicated to freedom from Portugal by armed struggle. Returned to Mozambique (1975) after 13 years exile to become 1st president of independent country.

Machiavelli, Niccolò (1467-1527), Italian writer, statesman. Prominent figure in Florentine republic from 1498, he learnt much of politics in several diplomatic missions. Ruined by restoration of the Medici (1512). Retired to country estate where he wrote *The Prince* (c 1517), an objective analysis of means to achieve power; had enormous influence.

machine gun, firearm with mechanism allowing rapid and continuous fire. R.J. Gatling developed multibarrel type in US (1862) but earliest in general use was belt-fed, recoil-powered Maxim (1884) issued to British army in Boer War. In WWI, Lewis light machine gun was a standard infantry weapon, while specialized machine gun tasks were allotted to the medium, water-cooled Vickers. Lewis still in use in WWII, although superseded by the Bren.

machine tools, term for large power-driven tools esp. lathe, drill, planer. Operate by removing material from object being machined, *eg* in turning (shaping cylindrical external contours), milling (shaping flat surfaces), drilling, boring, threading (cutting external screw thread) and tapping (cutting internal screw thread).

Mach number, ratio of speed of a body in some medium (*eg* air) to speed of sound in same medium. Mach number greater than 1 indicates supersonic speed.

Machu Picchu, ruined Inca city, *c* 80 km (50 mi) NW of Cuzco, Peru. Discovered 1911; terraced slopes descend to Urubamba R.; major tourist attraction.

Macias Nguema Biyoga, isl. of Equatorial Guinea, in Gulf of Guinea. Area 2020 sq km (780 sq mi); cap. Rey Malabo. Of volcanic origin, rises to 3007 m (9870 ft). Hot, wet climate; produces cocoa. Formerly called Fernando Póo.

Macintosh, Charles (1766-1843), Scottish chemist. Developed waterproof fabric ('mackintosh') and improved bleaching powder.

Macintyre, Duncan Bàn (1724-1812), Scottish Gaelic poet. Poems, often dealing with wildness of nature and habits of deer, employ rich vocabulary and great descriptive power. His greatest poem is *Moladh Beinn Dobhrain* ('The Praise of Ben Dorain').

Macke, August (1887-1914), German painter. Influenced by Delaunay and futurism, his work is noted for colour and prismatic patterns, although remaining figurative. Associated with Marc and Kandinsky in Blaue Reiter group.

Mackenzie, Sir Alexander (*c* 1755-1820), Scottish explorer, fur trader. Journeyed in Canada from Great Slave L. via Mackenzie R. to Arctic Ocean (1789). Became 1st European to cross continent N of Mexico (1793).

Mackenzie, Alexander (1822-92), Canadian statesman, b. Scotland. First Liberal PM (1873-8) of Canada.

Mackenzie, Sir Compton, orig. Edward Montague Compton (1883-1972), British author. Works incl. *Sinister Street* (1913), comic novel *Whisky Galore* (1947), autobiog. *My Life and Times* in 8 'octaves' (1963-9).

Mackenzie, William Lyon (1795-1861), Canadian journalist, b. Scotland. Organized short-lived Rebellion of 1837, failing in attempt to seize Toronto. Fled to US, where he set up provisional govt. on isl. in Niagara R., thus provoking international incident between US and Canada. Imprisoned for violating neutrality laws; returned to Canada (1849).

Mackenzie, admin. dist. of W mainland Northwest Territs., Canada. Area 1,366,200 sq km (527,490 sq mi); chief city Yellowknife. Mackenzie Mts. in W; drained by Mackenzie R., Great Bear and Great Slave lakes. Indian, Eskimo pop. Mineral resources (esp. oil, gold); fishing, fur trapping. Large areas are wildlife reserves.

Mackenzie, river of Mackenzie Dist., Northwest Territs., Canada. Flows NW from Great Slave L. 1800 km (1120 mi) to Beaufort Sea. Tributaries incl. Liard, Athabasca, Peace, Slave. With Slave, Peace, Finlay rivers, forms the longest river system in Canada. Natural gas fields in delta region. Explored (1789) by Alexander Mackenzie.

mackerel, *Scomber scombrus,* food fish of N Atlantic and Mediterranean. Swims in large schools near surface, often inshore.

McKinley, William (1843-1901), American statesman, president (1897-1901). Elected (1896) on gold-standard platform. Republican admin. dominated by expansionist policy; Philippines acquired after Spanish-American War (1898) and Hawaii annexed. Shot by anarchist in Buffalo.

McKinley, Mount, mountain of SC Alaska, US; in Alaska Range and Mt. McKinley National Park. Height 6194 m (20,320 ft). Highest peak in North America.

Mackintosh, Charles Rennie (1868-1928), Scottish artist, architect, furniture designer. Influenced by Celtic art, he was a major exponent of art nouveau. Buildings, noted for their lack of ornament and bold geometry, incl. Glasgow School of Art and Hill House, Helensburgh.

MacLean, John (1879-1923), Scottish political activist. Frequently imprisoned for opposition to WWI and for advocating Scottish workers' republic.

McLuhan, [Herbert] Marshall (1911-), Canadian writer, academic. Known for controversial communication theories, *eg* 'the medium is the message'. Works incl. *The Gutenberg Galaxy* (1962), *Understanding Media* (1964).

MacMahon, Marie Edmé Patrice Maurice de (1808-93), French army officer, statesman. Defeated Austrians at Magenta (1859). Defeated and captured by Prussians at Sedan (1870); on release, suppressed Paris Commune (1871). A monarchist, chosen president of the republic (1873); forced to resign through antagonism of republicans (1879).

McMillan, Edwin Mattison (1907-), American physicist. Shared Nobel Prize for Chemistry (1951) with Seaborg for discovery of transuranic elements neptunium and plutonium. Made improvements in particle accelerators.

Macmillan, [Maurice] Harold (1894-), British statesman, PM (1957-63). Foreign secretary (1955), chancellor of the exchequer (1955-7); headed Conservative govt. after Eden's resignation. Famous for slogan 'You've never had it so good' in 1959 election campaign. Period of office marked by recognition of many colonies as independent states, failure of attempt to join EEC. Resigned soon after PROFUMO affair.

McNamara, Robert Strange (1916-), American politician, diplomat. Secretary of defence (1961-8), reorganized Defence Dept. using modern management techniques; resigned over handling of Vietnam War. President of World Bank (1968-).

MacNeice, Louis (1907-63), English poet, b. Ireland. Works incl. *Blind Fireworks* (1929), *Solstices* (1961), allegorical radio play *The Dark Tower* (1947). Also translated Aeschylus, Horace, Goethe.

Mâcon, town of Burgundy, EC France, on R. Saône. Cap. of Saône-et-Loire dept. Pop. 35,000. Burgundy wine trade. Huguenot stronghold in 16th cent.

Macon, town of C Georgia, US; on Ocmulgee R. Pop. 122,000. Transport jct.; cotton, clay products.

Macpherson, James (1736-96), Scottish poet. Known for *The Works of Ossian* (1765), which he claimed were translations from 3rd cent. bard. His sources were never produced but work considerably influenced Romantic movement in Britain, Germany.

Macquarie, Lachlan (1761-1824), British colonial administrator, governor (1809-21) of British colonies in Australia. Reduced corruption, estab. humane admin.

Macquarie Island, volcanic isl. of Australia, in SW Pacific Ocean *c* 1600 km (1000 mi) SE of Tasmania. Uninhabited except for meteorological station.

Madagascar, isl. republic of W Indian Ocean, separated from Africa by Mozambique Channel. Area 587,000 sq km (226,600 sq mi); pop. 8,266,000; cap. Tananarive. Languages: Malagasy, French. Religions: Christian, native. Pop. divided into Indonesian and black African ethnic groups. Main isl. Madagascar, also incl. Nossi-Bé, Sainte-Marie Isls. Narrow coastal strip; mainly C highland, now largely deforested. Unique flora and fauna. Crops incl. sugar, coffee, rice; cattle raising. French colony from 1896 until independence in 1960. Member of French Community. Known as Malagasy Republic till 1976.

madder, any of genus *Rubia* of perennial herbs, esp. Eurasian vine, *R. tinctorum,* cultivated for red madder dye extracted from root.

Madeira, river of W Brazil, formed by jct. of Beni and Mamoré rivers, near Bolivian border. Flows NE 1450 km (c 900 mi) to join Amazon R. E of Manáus.

Madeira Islands, archipelago of N Atlantic, forming Funchal dist. of Portugal. Area 790 sq km (305 sq mi); cap. Funchal. Only 2 inhabited isls.: Madeira, Porto Santo. Largest isl. is Madeira, rising to 1860 m (6106 ft). Health, tourist resort. Madeira wine, fruit, fishing.

Madeira wine, dark brown fortified wine produced on isl. of Madeira. Four main types: sercial, a dry wine, and verdelho, bual and malmsey, all dessert wines. Matured for several years.

Madero, Francisco Indalecio (1873-1913), Mexican statesman. An advocate of democracy and social reform, he led successful revolution against Diaz (1910-11). As president (1911-13), failed to achieve significant reform. Shot after insurrection led by Huerta.

Madhya Pradesh, state of C India. Area *c* 443,400 sq km (171,200 sq mi); pop. 41,650,000; cap. Bhopal. Mainly on N Deccan plateau; monsoon climate aids largely agric. economy; dense forests provide teak. Coalmining; major source of manganese.

Madison, James (1751-1836), American statesman, president (1809-17). Leading figure in drafting US Constitution (1787), promoting its adoption through *The Federalist Papers* (1787-8). Democratic-Republican secretary of state (1801-9). War of 1812 main event of his presidency.

Madison, cap. of Wisconsin, US; on isthmus between Monona and

Mendota lakes. Pop. 172,000. Centre of farming region. Founded as territ. cap. (1836). Has Univ. of Wisconsin (1848).

Madras, cap. of TAMIL NADU, SE India. Pop. 2,470,000. Major seaport, exports cotton, hides. Textile, clothing mfg. Founded as Fort St George by British (1639). Nearby is traditional site of martyrdom of St Thomas. University (1857).

Madrid, cap. of Spain and Madrid prov., on R. Manzanares. Pop. 3,146,000. Admin., indust., transport centre on the Castile plateau. Fortress, taken from Moors by Castile (1083); cap. from 1561. Besieged 1936-9 by Nationalists in Civil War. Buildings incl. Bourbon palace, Prado art gallery; univ. (1508).

madrigal, musical composition written for two or more singers and usually performed unaccompanied. First flourished in Italy in 14th cent., and then again in Italy and England in more elaborate form in 16th and 17th cents.

Madurai, city of Tamil Nadu, S India. Pop. 548,000. Textile, brassware mfg. Dates from 5th cent. BC. Ceded to British (1801). Has many temples, famous for festivals.

Maecenas, Gaius (d. 8 BC), Roman patron of writers. Adviser and friend of Augustus, encouraged Horace, Vergil, Propertius. Name now synonym for wealthy patron of arts.

Maelström, channel off NW Norway, in S Lofoten Isls. Area of whirlpools, dangerous currents. Term now applied to all whirlpools.

Maeterlinck, Maurice, Count (1862-1949), Belgian author. Known for anti-naturalistic dramas, eg

Pelléas et Mélisande (1892), *L'oiseau bleu* (1909). Also wrote dream-like verse incl. *Serres chaudes* (1889), studies of plant, animal life, eg *La vie des abeilles* (1901). Nobel Prize for Literature (1911).

Mafeking, town of NE Cape Prov., South Africa. Pop. 8000. Agric. trade centre. Scene of 7-month siege of British by Boers 1899-1900. Extra-territ. cap. of Bechuanaland until 1965.

Mafia, originally, name given to secret groups in Sicily and S Italy, opposed to landowners and process of law. Esp. powerful 19th-early 20th cent., suppressed by Fascist govt. in 1920s, turned to industry, commerce after WWII. Brought to US by immigrants, long suspected of controlling illegal operations. Also known as 'Cosa, Nostra'.

Magadha, ancient Indian kingdom, situated in modern Bihar state. Prominent in 7th cent., BC, came under Mauryan empire *c* 320 BC; recovered importance in 5th cent. AD under Gupta dynasty. Scene of development of Buddhism and Jainism.

Magdalena, river of Colombia. Rises in W Andes, flows N 1600 km (*c* 1000 mi) to Caribbean near Barranquilla. Important trade route, navigable to Neiva. Large oilfield in middle valley.

Magdalene, see MARY MAGDALENE.

Magdalenian, in archaeology, final phase of Upper Palaeolithic age, centred on SW France; lasted from *c* 15,000 to 10,000 BC. Magdalenians are known for their cave art (*eg* that at Altamira) and refined tools, weapons.

Magdeburg, city of WC East

MAGELLAN

Germany, on R. Elbe. Pop. 272,000. Railway jct., canal link with R. Weser; industs. incl. sugar refining, textiles, glass, chemicals. Former Hanseatic League member, with town law code widely copied in middle ages. Badly damaged in Thirty Years War, WWII.

Magellan, Ferdinand, English form of Fernão de Magelhães (c 1480-1521), Portuguese navigator. In service of Spain, sailed W (1519) to find S passage to Pacific. Explored Río de la Plata estuary; rounded South America via Str. of Magellan (1520). Killed by natives in Philippines. One of ships, under del Cano, completed 1st global circumnavigation (1522).

Magellan Strait, narrow channel of extreme S Chile, between island and Tierra del Fuego. Connects Atlantic and Pacific. Discovered by Magellan (1520).

Magenta, town of Lombardy, N Italy. Pop. 18,000. Scene of battle (1859) in which French and Sardinians defeated Austrians.

Maggiore, Lake, Lombardy, NW Italy, N tip in Switzerland. Area 212 sq km (82 sq mi); incl. Borromean Isls. In mountainous region; vines, olives. Resorts incl. Locarno, Stresa.

maggot, legless worm-like larva of certain insects; *eg* house fly.

Maghreb or **Maghrib,** Arabic term for NW Africa. Incl. N areas of Morocco, Algeria, Tunisia and, sometimes, Libya. During Moorish occupation incl. Spain.

Magi, priestly caste in ancient Media and Persia, reputed to possess supernatural powers. ZOROASTER was prob. a Magus. Term also refers

to Wise Men of the East in NT who brought gifts to newborn Jesus.

magic (from MAGI), attempt to manipulate world by supernatural means. Practice depends on theory of underlying, unseen forces. Concept occurs in many cultures, incl. fetishism, totemism, necromancy. Malevolent magic called 'black' magic.

Maginot Line, a fortification system built in 1930s along French frontier, begun by André Maginot (1877-1932), minister of war. It failed to deter German flanking action (1940) in WWII.

magma, molten material beneath the solid crust of the Earth. Solidifies when cooled to form IGNEOUS ROCKS, occasionally reaching surface as lava.

Magna Carta, charter signed by King John of England (1215) in face of demands by barons. Secured feudal rights and estab. areas over which king had no jurisdiction. Interpreted throughout English history as guaranteeing certain political and civil liberties.

magnesium (Mg), light silver-white metallic element; at. no. 12, at. wt. 24.31. Burns with intense white flame. Occurs in magnesite, dolomite and sea water. Used in lightweight alloys, photographic flash bulbs; compounds used in medicine.

magnetic pole, either of 2 points on a magnet where its magnetism appears to be concentrated and from which magnetic lines of force emanate. Magnetic poles exist only in pairs (north and south poles); freely suspended magnet turns so that its south pole points N (principle used in compass). Like poles repel each other, unlike poles attract. Force acting between poles is inversely proportional to the square of the distance between them.

magnetic poles, in geography, 2 points on Earth's surface corresponding to poles of a magnet, towards which needle of magnetic compass points and where magnetic force is vertically downwards. N and S magnetic poles do not coincide with geographical poles; positions vary, following circular paths.

magnetic tape, thin plastic ribbon coated with ferromagnetic particles (usually an oxide of iron or chromium). In TAPE RECORDER particles are aligned in varying degrees according to amplitude and frequency of signal. Also used to store information in computers.

magnetism, branch of physics dealing with magnets and magnetic phenomena. Magnetic force results from electricity in motion. Magnetic properties of materials such as iron result from unbalanced electron spin in the atom, giving rise to magnetic moment of atom. Overall magnetism follows when individual magnetic moments of atoms are aligned together.

magnetite (Fe_3O_4), iron ore mineral. Hard, black in colour; consists of magnetic iron oxide (variety called lodestone is natural magnet). Major sources in Sweden, USSR, US.

Magnitogorsk, town of USSR, W Siberian RSFSR. Pop. 373,000. Major metallurgical centre based on magnetite ore; iron and steel, coke, chemical mfg. Built 1929-31.

magnitude, in astronomy, measure of star's apparent brightness. Stars of any one magnitude are 2.512 times brighter than stars of next magnitude; thus stars of 1st magnitude are brightest and are 2.512 times brighter than those of 2nd. Faintest stars visible are approximately 6th magnitude.

magnolia, genus of trees and shrubs with showy, fragrant flowers. Native to North America and Asia. Species incl. southern magnolia or bull bay, *Magnolia grandiflora*, with large white flowers, and umbrella tree, *M. tripetala*, with white flowers grouped in umbrella forms at end of branches.

Magog, see GOG AND MAGOG.

magpie, long-tailed, black and white bird of crow family, genus *Pica*. Common magpie *P. pica* found in North America, Europe.

Magritte, René (1898-1967), Belgian surrealist painter. His work examines nature of reality, often depicting familiar objects in disturbing juxtapositions or unfamiliar settings. Work incl. *Time Transfixed* (1930).

Magyars, people constituting main ethnic group of Hungary. Originally nomadic, migrated from Urals to Caucasia (5th cent.). Forced W, settled in Hungary in 9th cent. Magyar language belongs to Finno-Ugrian group.

Mahábhárata, great Sanskrit epic of India, compiled *c* 400 BC-AD 200. Main story is struggle for succession to kingdom of Bháratas. Incl. BHAGAVAD-GITA and an abridgment of RAMAYANA. Rest of book contains mix of folklore, myth, philosophy.

Maharashtra, state of W India. Area *c* 307,000 sq km (118,500 sq mi); pop. 50,335,000; cap. Bombay. Mainly on Deccan plateau, with coastal plain on Arabian Sea. Mainly agric. economy; cotton, rice, groundnuts. Textile mfg.

Mahayana, branch of BUDDHISM which arose in NW India before 6th cent. Stresses disinterested love, salvation of others as route to the individual's own salvation. Developed extensive pantheon and changed concept of NIRVANA to denote salvation or damnation in afterlife resulting from nature of one's actions. *See* BODHISATTVA.

Mahdi, leader and prophet expected by Moslems to appear on earth before the world ends to restore justice. In Sunnite Islam he is a descendant of Mohammed's daughter Fatima. In Shiite Islam he is a hidden IMAM. There have been many claimants, notably **Mohammed Ahmed** (1848-85), who led rebellion against Egyptian rule in Sudan. Died after capturing Khartoum. His followers, the Mahdists, were defeated (1898) by British.

Mahler, Gustav (1860-1911), Austrian composer. Wrote music often classic in form but highly romantic and expressive in style. Works incl. 9 symphonies, song cycle *Das Lied von der Erde.* Also renowned as a conductor, esp. in Vienna and New York.

mahogany, any of genus *Swietenia* of tropical trees. Dark, heavy wood valued for furniture, esp. that of *S. mahogani* of tropical America. Name also applied to various similar woods, *eg* African mahogany of genus *Khaya,* Australian red mahogany of genus *Eucalyptus.*

Mahrattas or **Marathas,** people of WC India who speak Marathi language. Supplanted Moguls in

18th cent., controlling the Deccan and much of S India. Lost most of their territ. to the British by 1818.

Maiden Castle, well-preserved site of Iron Age hill fort near Dorchester, Dorset, England. Occupied from 3rd cent. BC, it became stronghold of Durotriges, a Belgic tribe. Captured by Romans under Vespasian (AD 43).

maidenhair, any of genus *Adiantum* of ferns native to tropical and warm temperate regions. Delicate, green fronds. Cultivated as pot-plant.

maidenhair tree, *see* GINKGO.

Maidenhead, mun. bor. of Berkshire, SC England, on R. Thames. Pop. 45,000. Boating centre; electronic equipment mfg.

Maidstone, mun. bor. and co. town of Kent, SE England, on R. Medway. Pop. 71,000. Hops market, brewing. Has All Saints' Church (14th cent.).

Mailer, Norman (1923-), American author. Novels incl. *The Naked and the Dead* (1948) in WWII setting, *An American Dream* (1964). Also wrote political essays, *eg The Presidential Papers* (1963). Concerned with moral and political analysis, using unconventional prose, of contemporary US.

Main, river of C West Germany. Flows *c* 500 km (310 mi) from N Bavaria via Würzburg, Frankfurt to R. Rhine at Mainz. Navigable for *c* 355 km (220 mi); canal link to R. Danube.

Maine, region and former prov. of NW France, cap. Le Mans. Agric., stock raising. County from 10th cent., united with Anjou (1126). Returned to French crown (1584).

Maine, state of extreme NE US.

Area 86,027 'sq km (33,215 sq mi); pop. 994,000; cap. Augusta; chief town Portland. Forested lakeland; hilly in W; crossed by many rivers esp. St John, Kennebec, Penobscot. Main occupations lumbering, farming, fishing (esp. lobsters); some mining (stone, clay). Part of Massachusetts colony in 17th-18th cent. Admitted to. Union as 23rd state (1820).

Maintenon, Françoise d'Aubigné, Marquise de (1635-1719), second wife of Louis XIV. Married Louis XIV secretly (*c* 1685). A convert to Catholicism, she had considerable influence over him in matters of morality.

Mainz (Fr. *Mayence*), city of WC West Germany, at confluence of Rhine and Main, cap. of Rhineland-Palatinate. Pop. 179,000. River port, chemicals, engineering; major wine centre. Roman camp; 1st German archbishopric (747). Early printing centre, home of Gutenberg. Univ. (1477-1798, 1946).

maize or **Indian corn**, *Zea mays*, cultivated American cereal plant of grass family. Grain borne on cobs enclosed in husks. Naturalized in S Africa, India, China, .S Europe and Australia. Cobs may. be roasted or boiled. When coarsely milled, called hominy or polenta; with gluten removed becomes cornflour.

majolica or **maiolica**, variety of pottery which grew to prominence in 15th cent. Italy, after being introduced from Spain. Produced by applying tin enamel to earthenware; on firing it forms white opaque surface, on which design is painted. Object is then glazed and fired again.

Majorca (*Mallorca*), largest of Balearic Isls., Spain. Area 3639 sq km (1405 sq mi); cap. and chief port Palma. Mountainous in NW. Tourism, fruit growing, wine mfg., fishing. Kingdom from 1276, united with Aragón 1343.

Majuba Hill, mountain of NW Natal, South Africa, in Drakensberg Mts. Height 1980 m (6500 ft). Scene of Boer victory (1881) over British.

Makarios III, orig. Michael Christedoulos Mouskos (1913-77), Cypriot churchman, political leader. Leader of Greek Cypriot movement for union with Greece (Enosis); exiled by British (1956-7). Elected president on estab. of republic (1959). Deposed by Greek-inspired coup (1974) but took up presidency again after Turkish invasion.

Makassar, *see* UJUNG PANDANG.

Malabar Coast, coastal region of SW India extending from Goa to Cape Comorin. Now mainly in Kerala state.

Malabo, cap. of Equatorial Guinea, on Macias Nguema Biyoga isl. Pop. 37,000. Commercial, admin. centre; port, exports cacao, coffee; fish processing. Formerly called Santa Isabel.

Malacca, cap. of Malacca state, SW West Malaysia. Pop. 86,000. Seaport on Str. of Malacca. Trade declined after rise of Singapore. Held by Portuguese, then Dutch, until ceded to Britain (1824).

Malachi, prophetic book of OT, sometimes attributed to Ezra. Castigates priests and the people for their laxity. Foretells judgment and coming of a Messiah.

malachite, copper ore mineral. Soft, green in colour; consists of basic copper carbonate. Found in oxidized zones of copper deposits, sometimes as cement in sandstones. Used as gem, source of pigment. Major sources in US, Chile, USSR.

Málaga, city of S Spain, on Mediterranean Sea, cap. of Málaga prov. Pop. 374,000. Resort; port, exports wine, fruit. Founded 12th cent. BC by Phoenicians; chief port of Moorish Granada, taken by Spain 1487. Moorish citadel, 16th cent. cathedral. Birthplace of Picasso.

Malagasy Republic, see Madagascar.

Malamud, Bernard (1914-), American novelist. Known for novels incl. *The Natural* (1952), *The Fixer* (1966), short story collections, eg *Idiots First* (1963), dealing with Jewish themes.

Malan, Daniel François (1874-1959), South African politician, PM (1948-54). Leader of Nationalist Party (1933-54), advocated white supremacy and republicanism. His govt. enacted 1st *apartheid* laws.

malaria, infectious disease caused by parasitic protozoon, genus *Plasmodium*, which feeds on red blood cells. Transmitted by bite of female mosquito of *Anopheles* group. Characterized by intermittent attacks of fever and shivering. Formerly treated by quinine, now by synthetic drugs.

Malawi, republic of EC Africa. Area c 118,000 sq km (45,250 sq mi); pop. 5,175,000; cap. Lilongwe. Languages: Bantu dialects, English. Religions: native, Christian. Great Rift Valley runs N-S, filled by L. Malawi; elsewhere plateau, incl. Shiré Highlands (SW). Produces tea, cotton, tobacco, sugar cane, groundnuts. Area of L. Malawi visited by Livingstone (1859); British protect. estab. 1891; called Nyasaland (1907-64). Formed federation with Rhodesia (1953-62); independent 1964, republic 1966. Member of British Commonwealth.

Malawi, Lake, lake of EC Africa, between Malawi, Tanzania, Mozambique. Length c 580 km (360 mi); part of Great Rift Valley. Drained to S by R. Shiré into Zambezi. Major trade artery. Explored (1859) by Livingstone; called L. Nyasa until Malawi's independence (1964).

Malay, major language in MALAYO-POLYNESIAN family, with c 10 million speakers in Malaya and Straits settlements.

Malaya, region of SE Asia, comprising former British colonies of Malay penin.; corresponds to West Malaysia. Area c 131,400 sq km (51,000 sq mi). Mountainous interior flanked by plains; densely forested. Equatorial climate. World's leading rubber, tin producer. Called Federation of Malaya (1948-63); independence from Britain 1957.

Malay Archipelago, group of isls. between SE Asia and Australia. Incl. Indonesia, Philippines.

Malayo-Polynesian, widespread family of languages, covering vast area of Pacific incl. Madagascar, Taiwan, Papua and New Guinea, Hawaii, *etc.*

Malaysia, federated state of SE Asia in British Commonwealth. Area c 332,650 sq km (128,500 sq mi); pop. 12,300,000; cap. Kuala Lumpur. Language: Malayan. Religion: Islam. Formed (1963) from MALAYA (West Malaysia) and SABAH, SARAWAK (East Malaysia). Singapore seceded in 1965.

Malcolm I, king of Scots (943-954). Gained Strathclyde by treaty of alliance with English king Edmund (945).

Malcolm II, king of Scotland (1005-34). Frequently invaded England; by battle of Carham (c 1016 or 1018) finally secured area between Forth and Tweed for Scotland. Succeeded by Duncan I.

Malcolm III [Canmore] (d. 1093), king of Scotland (1057-93). Defeated and succeeded MACBETH (1057). Married (1070) St Margaret of Scotland, by whose influence Celtic culture of Scotland was gradually replaced by English ways. Killed while invading England.

Malcolm IV (1142-65), king of Scotland (1153-65). Grandson of David I. Treaty of 1157 with Henry II fixed Anglo-Scottish border at Tweed and Solway. Succeeded by brother William the Lion.

Malcolm X, orig. Malcolm Little (1925-65), American Negro leader. Became a Black Muslim (1952); suspended from movement by Elijah Muhammad (1963). Founded Organization of Afro-American Unity (1964), dedicated to black nationalism. Assassinated.

Maldive Islands, republic in N Indian Ocean, SW of Sri Lanka; comprises c 2000 coral isls. Area 298 sq km (115 sq mi); pop. 122,000; cap. Malé. Language: Divehi. Religion: Islam. Agric. economy based on coconuts, fruit. British protect. from 1887, independent in 1965; became republic (1968).

Malenkov, Georgi Maksimilianovich (1902-), Soviet political leader. Succeeded Stalin as premier (1953-5). Forced to resign over failure of agric. policy. Succeeded by Khrushchev. Expelled from Communist Party (1961).

Malevich, Casimir (1878-1935), Russian artist. Founder of suprematist movement, which stressed absolute geometric abstraction. His *White on White,* white square on a white background, summed up the movement.

Mali, republic of W Africa. Area 1,240,000 sq km (478,000 sq mi); pop. 5,844,000; cap. Bamako. Languages: French, various African. Religions: Islam, native. Desert in N, elsewhere semidesert; main rivers Senegal, Niger. Swamp, marsh SW of Timbuktu; irrigation at Ségu. Main crops groundnuts, cotton, rice, maize; cattle raising. Economy severely affected by drought in early 1970s. Occupied by French in late-19th cent.; became colony (1904), called French Sudan from 1920. Part of Mali Federation (1959-60) with Senegal; independent 1960.

Malines, see MECHELEN, Belgium.

Malinowski, Bronislaw (1884-1942), British social anthropologist, b. Poland. Estab. 'participant observer' technique of examining culture, esp. writings on Trobriand isls. One of founders of functionalist sociology.

mallard, *Anas platyrhynchos,* wild duck of N hemisphere, from which most domestic ducks are descended. Male has green head and white band around neck.

Mallarmé, Stéphane (1842-98), French poet. Formulated theories of SYMBOLISTS. Works incl. *Hérodiade* (1869), *L'Après-midi d'un faune* (1876) which inspired Debussy's orchestral piece.

Mallorca, see MAJORCA, Spain.

mallow, any of genus *Malva* of herbs native to N temperate regions. Large dissected leaves, purple, pink or white flowers.

Malmö, city of SW Sweden, on Öresund. Pop. 265,000. Port, exports timber, grain, dairy produce; shipbuilding. Ferry to Copenhagen. Church (14th cent.), Malmöhus castle (15th cent.). Held by Denmark until 1658.

malnutrition, deficiency of essential component of diet. May be caused by inadequate food or insufficient vitamins in food. May also be caused by failure to assimilate food during illness.

Malory, Sir Thomas (d. 1471), English writer. Known for *Le Morte d'Arthur* (c 1469), last medieval English treatment of the ARTHURIAN LEGEND. Still read for vivid characterization, vigorous prose, varied stories.

Malplaquet, village of Nord, N France. Scene of battle (1709) in which Marlborough defeated French in War of Spanish Succession.

Malraux, André (1901-76), French author, politician. Novels, incl. *La Condition humaine* (1933), *L'Espoir* (1937), deal with struggle for meaning in political setting. Also wrote *The Psychology of Art* (1947-50), depicting history of man's search for the absolute.

malt, grain, chiefly barley, which has been partially germinated and then dried in kilns. Used in brewing. Contains nutritional carbohydrates and protein.

Malta, republic of S Europe, in Mediterranean Sea S of Sicily, comprising isls. of Malta, Gozo,

Comino. Area 316 sq km (122 sq mi); pop. 304,000; cap. Valletta. Languages: Maltese, English. Religion: RC. Tourist resort; agric. incl. cereals, potatoes, fruit. Taken by Norman Sicily 1090; given to Knights Hospitallers 1530. Annexed by Britain 1814; independent from 1964. Formerly major naval base; heavily bombed during WWII. Member of British Commonwealth, UN.

Malthus, Thomas Robert (1766-1834), English economist, churchman. Suggested in *An Essay on the Principle of Population* (1798) that poverty is inevitable as population increases geometrically while food supply increases arithmetically. Theory influenced Ricardo.

Maluku, see MOLUCCAS.

Malvern, urban dist. of Hereford and Worcester, W England, on E slopes of Malvern Hills. Pop. 29,000. Resort, spa; has annual drama festival associated with Shaw's plays.

Malvinas, Islas, see FALKLAND ISLANDS.

mamba, large arboreal snake, genus *Dendraspis*, of C and S Africa. Aggressive, with large fangs; venom can be fatal. Species incl. green mamba, *D. viridis*, and black mamba, *D. angusticeps*.

Mamelukes, members of military caste, originally made up of slaves, used as soldiers of caliphate. Mameluke sultanate was estab. in Egypt (1250) and dominated Middle East until absorbed into Ottoman empire (1517). Mamelukes retained actual control of Egypt until 1811.

mammals (Mammalia), class of warm-blooded vertebrates with hair on body, lungs for respiration, 4-

chambered heart. Offspring fed on milk secreted by female mammary glands. Divided into 3 subclasses: primitive egg-laying monotremes, pouch-bearing marsupials and more advanced. placentals.

mammoth, extinct large elephant of Eurasia and North America, with hairy skin and long upward-curving tusks. Known from fossil remains of Pleistocene period, frozen corpses in Siberia and cave paintings.

Mammoth Cave National Park, in S Kentucky, US. Has one of world's largest caves (area 20,783 ha./51,354 acres); limestone formations.

man, *Homo sapiens,* sole surviving member of the hominid family. Precise evolution of modern man from more primitive forms, eg AUSTRALOPITHECUS and HOMO ERECTUS, is unclear and subject to controversy. NEANDERTHAL and CROMAGNON man are considered early forms of *H. sapiens.*

Man, Isle of, isl. of UK, in Irish Sea. Area 588 sq km (227 sq mi); pop. 56,000; cap. Douglas. Hilly (Snaefell, 620 m/2034 ft); mild climate. Crops, livestock; tourism. Hist. dependency of Norway, Scotland; passed to UK 1828. Parliament ('Tynwald'); Manx language now little used.

Manado or **Menado,** cap. of N Sulawesi prov. (Celebes), Indonesia. Pop. 170,000. Seaport in extreme NE of isls.; exports coffee, copra.

Managua, cap. of Nicaragua, on L. Managua. Pop. 374,000. Admin., indust., trade centre; textiles, cement, cigarette mfg. Became cap. 1855. Evacuated 1972 after severe earthquake.

manatee, herbivorous aquatic mammal, genus *Trichechus,* with rounded tail and 2 front flippers. Found in shallow coastal waters of West Indies, South America, W Africa. Numbers reduced by over-hunting.

Manáus, inland port of NC Brazil, cap. of Amazonas state; on Negro R. near jct. with Amazon. Pop. 312,000. Timber, rubber, nuts exports; jute milling, oil refining. Grew during early 20th cent. rubber boom. Buildings incl. opera house; famous botanical gardens.

Mancha, La, arid treeless plateau of S New Castile, Spain. Made famous by Cervantes in *Don Quixote de la Mancha.*

Manche, La, *see* ENGLISH CHANNEL.

Manchester, city of Greater Manchester met. county, NW England. Met. county pop. 2,730,000; city 541,000. Linked to sea by Ship Canal (1894); major seaport. Textiles (hist. cotton mfg.), chemicals mfg. Has grammar school (1519), univ. (1880). Roman *Mancunium;* medieval wool trade. Scene of Peterloo massacre (1819).

Manchester Ship Canal, NW England, canal for ocean-going vessels, 56 km (35 mi) long. Links Manchester with Mersey estuary, Irish Sea. Opened 1894.

Manchu, Chinese imperial dynasty (1644-1912). Strong rulers up till end of 18th cent. expanded empire, adding Turkestan, Mongolia, Manchuria. Later reigns marked by numerous rebellions and increased pressure of European powers for profitable trading terms. Dynasty overthrown by revolution led by Sun Yat-sen.

Manchukuo, puppet state set up in

Manchuria (1932) by the Japanese after their occupation of country (1931). Ruled by Pu-yi, last emperor of all China. Manchukuo returned to China after WWII.

Manchuria, region of NE China. Comprises Liaoning, Kirin, Heilungkiang provs. Mountains surround fertile C plain, drained by Liao, Sungari rivers; major agric. and mfg. centre of China. Important timber and mineral resources. Occupied by Japanese 1931-45.

Mandaeans, ancient Gnostic sect still extant in Iran and S Iraq. Beliefs drawn from Babylonian astrology and cults of the Magi. Principal rite is frequent baptism based on concern for ritual cleanliness and belief in water as life principle. Scripture, the *Ginza Rba* is fragmentary collection of legend, astrological and cosmogonical lore.

Mandalay, city of C Burma, on the Irrawaddy. Pop. 401,000. Transport and commercial centre. Old walled city largely destroyed by Japanese (1942); numerous pagodas.

Mandarin, see CHINESE.

Mandeville, Sir John (fl 14th cent.), English author. Wrote *The Travels of Sir John Mandeville* (c 1356), part genuine, but vividly imagined, record of travels in Near and Far East. Authorship disputed.

mandoline or **mandolin,** musical instrument of lute family, with 4 or 5 pairs of strings, each pair tuned to same note. Played with a plectrum.

mandrake, *Mandragora officinarum,* poisonous plant of nightshade family. Short stem, purple flowers. Fleshy, forked root thought to resemble a human form, long believed to have supernatural properties. Used as narcotic in Middle Ages.

mandrill, *Mandrillus sphinx,* large fierce baboon of W Africa with red nose, blue cheeks. Drill, *M. leucophaeus,* less colourful.

manes, in Roman religion, deified souls of the dead. Associated with LARES AND PENATES and LEMURES.

Manet, Edouard (1832-83), French painter. Influenced by Spanish art and Hals, his portrayal of commonplace scenes, using light and dark shadows, pioneered a new style; he greatly influenced the impressionists. In 1870s, adopted a lighter, more colourful manner. Works incl. *Déjeuner sur l'herbe,* which created a scandal on exhibition, and *Bar at the Folies-Bergère.*

manganese (Mn), hard brittle metallic element; at. no. 25, at. wt. 54.94. Occurs as pyrolusite (MnO_2), from which it is obtained by reduction with aluminium. Used in making alloys, esp. very hard manganese steel. Manganese dioxide is used in dry cells, in glass manufacture and as an oxidizing agent.

mango, *Mangifera indica,* tree bearing fleshy yellowish-red fruit, native to Malaya and West Indies. Eaten ripe, preserved or pickled.

mangold or **mangel-wurzel,** *Beta vulgaris,* variety of beet, native to Europe. Formerly cultivated as cattle food.

mangrove, any of genus *Rhizophora* of tropical evergreen trees found in swampy areas and on river banks. American mangrove, *R. mangle,* common in Florida, is important in land reclamation.

Manhattan, see NEW YORK CITY.

manic-depressive psychosis, form of severe mental disturbance, characterized by alternate bouts of mania and depression. Patient is abnormally excited in manic phase, lethargic and withdrawn in depressive. Treatment incl. shock therapy for depression, lithium compounds for mania.

Manichaeism, dualist religious philosophy (fl 3rd cent.-7th cent.) based on teachings of Mani (b. Persia, c 216-76). Combined elements of Zoroastrianism, Gnostic Christianity and Platonism. Persecuted by orthodox Zoroastrians. Term came to be used in medieval Church for all dualist heresies.

Manila, chief seaport of Philippines, SW Luzon isl. Pop. 1,436,000. Exports hemp, sugar; cigarette, textile mfg. Founded 1571; national cap. until 1948. Divided by R. Pasig into old Spanish walled city (Intramuros) and modern section. Has Univ. of St Thomas (1611). Spanish fleet destroyed by US under Dewey (1898) in Manila Bay.

Manila hemp, strong cord-like fibre obtained from abacá (Manila hemp plant); used to make rope, paper, clothing.

manioc, see CASSAVA.

Manipur, state of NE India. Area c 22,300 sq km (8600 sq mi); pop. 1,070,000; cap. Imphal. Bounded on E by Burma; largely mountainous. Forests provide teak.

Manitoba, Prairie prov. of WC Canada. Area 638,466 sq km (246,512 sq mi); pop. 988,000; cap. Winnipeg. Tundra in N (Laurentian Shield); lakes in C; farmland in S watered by Red, Assiniboine rivers. Mainly agric. (esp. wheat, oats,

barley growing); timber; mining (gold, copper, zinc). Meat packing, flour milling industs. Chartered 1670 to Hudson's Bay Co.; British control from 1763; became prov. 1870 after purchase by Canada.

Manitoba, Lake, SW Manitoba, Canada. Area 4076 sq km (1817 sq mi). N end is connected to L. Winnipegosis; drained by Dauphin R. into L. Winnipeg.

Manitoulin Islands, chain of Canada-US, in N L. Huron. Most are in Canada, incl. Manitoulin Isl., the world's largest lake isl. Summer tourist resorts on most isls.

Manley, Norman Washington (1893-1969), Jamaican politician, PM (1959-62). Founded socialist People's National Party (1938), leader while Jamaica was in West Indies Federation (1958-62). His son, **Michael Norman Manley** (1924-), was PM from 1972. Programme incl. widespread socialist reform, closer ties with other Third World states, esp. Cuba.

Manlius Capitolinus, Marcus (d. c 384 BC), Roman politician. According to legend, on being aroused by sacred geese, he repulsed the invading Gauls (c 389) from the Capitol. Later accused of seeking kingly power, he was executed for treason.

Mann, Thomas (1875-1955), German author. Preoccupied with duality of artistic and practical life. Novels incl. Buddenbrooks (1901), Death in Venice (1913), The Magic Mountain (1924), Dr Faustus (1948). Settled in US (1939). Nobel Prize for Literature (1929). His brother, **Heinrich Mann** (1871-1950) wrote Professor Unrat (1905), basis of von

Sternberg's film *The Blue Angel.*
Also wrote *Man of ·Straw* (1918).

Mann, · Tom (1856-1941), English
labour· leader. Organized London
dock·strike (1889)·with John·Burns.
Helped organize Australian Labor
Party. A founder of British Communist Party (1920)·.

manna, in OT, food·provided by God
for the Israelites in the wilderness.
Various natural explanations proposed, *eg* edible lichen, *Lecanora
esculenta*.

**Mannerheim, Carl Gustav Emil,
Baron** (1867-1951), Finnish field
marshal, statesman. Led Finnish
forces which drove Bolsheviks from
Finland (1918); ·regent (1918-19).
Headed army in;·war with ·Soviet
Union (1939-44). President·of Finland (1944-6).

mannerism, in art·and architecture,
16th cent. style,·originating in Italy
as reaction against classical perfection of high Renaissance style of
Raphael, *etc.* Painting characterized
by contorted figures, lack of
classical balance, vivid colour.
Exponents incl. Parmigianino, Tintoretto, Pontormo.

Mannheim, Karl (1893-1947), Hungarian sociologist. In Germany,
developed from Marxist theory a
'sociology of knowledge', stated in
Ideology and Utopia (1929).

Mannheim, city of WC West
Germany, at confluence of Rhine
and Neckar, opposite Ludwigshafen.
Pop. 331,000. Vehicles, machinery
mfg. Seat of Electors Palatine from
1720, became centre of music,
theatre (*eg* Mannheim orchestra).
Has baroque buildings, palace.

Manning, Henry Edward (1808-92), English churchman. At first

Anglican, was converted (1851) to
RC faith through influence of
OXFORD MOVEMENT. Archbishop of
Westminster from 1865; created
cardinal 1875. Worked for social
reform, settled London dock strike
of 1889.

manometer, instrument used to
measure pressure of gases. Simplest
type consists of U-shaped tube
.partially filled with liquid.

manor, *see* FEUDALISM.

Mans, Le, *see* LE MANS, France.

Mansard or **Mansart, François**
(1598-1666), French architect. Considered outstanding exponent of
French 17th cent. Classicism. His
Hôtel de la Vrillière served as model
for Parisian·town house for many
years; surviving work incl. château
of ·Maisons Lafitte. Type of roof
designed to give higher interior
space named after him.

Mansfield, Katherine, pseud. of
Kathleen· Mansfield Beauchamp
(1888-1923), British author, b. New
Zealand. Known for short stories
with New Zealand setting, *eg Bliss*
(1920), *The· Garden Party* (1922).
Married Middleton MURRY.

manslaughter, unlawful killing of
human being, distinguished from
murder in ·being without premeditated malice. Usually divided
into voluntary (intentional killing
but done in heat, *eg* in sudden affray)
and involuntary ·(unintentional;
resulting from culpable negligence,
eg reckless driving).

Mansūra, city of N Egypt, on Nile
delta. Pop. 212,000. Cotton mfg.
centre, railway jct. Scene of Mamelukes' victory (1250) over Crusaders
under St Louis.

Mantegna, Andrea (c 1431-1506),

Italian painter. Influenced by Donatello, his figures have sculptural quality and display extreme foreshortening. Paintings reflect intense interest in classical antiquity, derived from archaeological studies. Works incl. frescoes in Mantua in honour of Gonzaga family.

mantis or **mantid**, any of Mantidae family of elongated slender insects. Seizes insect prey with pincer-like forelegs, often held up together as if praying.

Mantua (*Mantova*), town of Lombardy, N Italy, cap. of Mantova prov. Pop. 67,000. Renaissance cultural centre under Gonzaga family; ducal palace (14th cent.). Birthplace of Vergil nearby.

Manu, in Hindu myth, survivor of great flood and ancestor of mankind. Traditional author of *Laws of Manu* (prob. written c AD 100), detailing the codes of ritual and daily life for Brahman caste. Used by Warren Hastings in formulating laws for India.

Manutius, Aldus, see ALDUS MANUTIUS.

Manx, see GAELIC.

Manx cat, short-haired tailless variety of domestic cat.

Manzala or **Menzaleh, Lake**, coastal lagoon of N Egypt. Area 1710 sq km (660 sq mi); extends from Damietta to Suez Canal.

Manzoni, Alessandro (1785-1873), Italian author. Known for romantic historical novel, *The Betrothed* (1827), depicting divine intervention in everyday life. His death inspired Verdi's *Requiem*.

Maori, aboriginal inhabitants of New Zealand, of Polynesian stock. Traditional economy based on agric., fishing, hunting, gathering. Originally divided into tribes, with frequent intertribal wars. On British colonists' attempts to settle large tracts of land, began Maori Wars (1861-71). Now comprise 10% of pop., with 4 Maori electorates sending representatives to Parliament.

Mao Tse-tung (1893-1976), Chinese political leader. Helped found Chinese Communist Party; after Communist split with KUOMINTANG (1927), organized Red Army and consolidated authority during LONG MARCH (1934-5). Prolonged civil war of 1930s and 1940s ended in triumph over Chiang Kai-shek's Nationalists and estab. of People's Republic of China (1949) with Mao as chairman of govt. council (1949-59). Retained post as Party chairman, instigating CULTURAL REVOLUTION in 1966, purging leadership in effort to recreate revolutionary spirit. Widely influential, esp. in his writings, as exponent of revolution and guerrilla warfare.

map, two-dimensional representation of the Earth's surface or part of it. Sphere cannot be represented on flat surface without some distortion of shape, area or direction. Various map projections may be used to preserve one of these qualities at expense of others; types incl. conic, cylindrical, azimuthal. Also see CARTOGRAPHY.

maple, any of genus *Acer* of deciduous trees or shrubs, native to N temperate regions. Various species cultivated as ornamentals, for timber or for sap which is source of maple syrup. Leaf is emblem of Canada. Also see SYCAMORE.

Maputo, cap. of Mozambique, on Delagoa Bay. Pop. 355,000. Admin., commercial centre; port, exports hardwoods, cotton, sugar, tobacco, mineral ores; transit trade, rail links with South Africa, Rhodesia (closed 1976), Swaziland; univ. (1962). Cap. from 1907; formerly called Lourenço Marques, renamed after Mozambique's independence (1975).

maquis (Ital. *macchia,* Span. *matorral*), term applied to robber bands widespread in Corsica until early 20th cent., later to French underground resistance movement during German occupation of WWII. Originally word for droughtresistant scrub vegetation of W Mediterranean region.

marabou, *Leptoptilus crumeniferus,* large-billed stork of Africa, SE Asia. Green back plumage, bald head; tail feathers highly prized. Also called adjutant stork.

Maracaibo, port of NW Venezuela, on outlet of L. Maracaibo. Pop. 666,000. Coffee exports; major oil refining industs. Founded 1571, grew with exploitation of oil resources after 1917.

Maracaibo, Lake, NW Venezuela, connected by waterway with Gulf of Venezuela. Area 13,210 sq km (*c* 5100 sq mi). Major oil deposits (discovered 1917), led to deepening of channel to Caribbean.

Maracay, town of Venezuela, at NE end of L. Valencia. Pop. 193,000. Textile mfg. Has military training centre. Town modernized 1909-35, when opera house, bull ring were built.

Marajó, isl. of N Brazil, in Amazon delta. Length 240 km (*c* 150 mi). Swampy rain forest in W (timber, rubber products); grassland in E (cattle rearing). Prehist. pottery found here.

Maramba, see LIVINGSTONE.

Marañon, river of Peru, headstream of Amazon R. Rises in C Andes, flows NE 1600 km (*c* 1000 mi) joining Ucayali R. to form Amazon headstream.

Marat, Jean Paul (1743-93), French revolutionary, b. Switzerland. Founded and edited journal *L'Ami du peuple* (1789), in which he denounced those in power. Elected to National Convention (1792), he led campaign against Girondists. Stabbed to death while in his bath by Charlotte Corday, a Girondist sympathizer.

Marathon, village of SE Greece, on Plain of Marathon. Here Athenians defeated (490 BC) Persians under Darius. Soldier's run to Athens with news of victory commemorated in Olympic marathon race.

marathon race, long distance race derived from run of Pheidippides from Marathon to Athens to announce defeat of Persians (490 BC). Olympic event since 1896; distance standardized to 42.18 km (26 mi 385 yd).

marble, crystallized variety of LIMESTONE. Formed by metamorphism under heat and pressure; colour varies due to different impurities. Can take on high polish; used in building and sculpture. Major sources in Italy, Greece, Ireland.

Marc, Franz (1880-1916), German painter. Leading member of the Blaue Reiter group; attempted to describe a mystical animal world in an expressionist style employing distortion and colour symbolism. Work incl. *Blue Horses*.

Marceau, Marcel (1923-), French mime. Known as creator of clown Bip. Films incl. *Un jardin public* (1955).

Marches, The (*Marche*), region of EC Italy, cap. Ancona. Apennines in W (h.e.p.); cereals, vines, livestock in river valleys, coastal plain. Name derives from frontier (march) fiefs estab. here (10th cent.) by Holy Roman Empire.

Marciano, Rocky, orig. Rocco Francis Marchegiano (1924-69), American boxer. Became world heavyweight champion 1952; retired 1956.

Marcionites, first heretical Christian group, founded by Marcion of Sinope (*fl* 2nd cent.). Posited 2 gods: creator and lawgiver of OT, and merciful, loving God of NT. Rejected OT and much of Gospels. Position forced Church to show fulfilment of the OT law in NT and to promulgate a canonical Gospel.

Marconi, Guglielmo, Marchese (1874-1937), Italian physicist. Famous for development of wireless telegraphy; made use of an aerial to improve transmission. Transmitted long-wave signals (1895), transatlantic signals (1901). Shared Nobel Prize for Physics (1909).

Marcos, Ferdinand Edralin (1917-), Philippine political leader. President of Philippines from 1965. Suppressed political opposition; declared martial law (1972) in face of alleged Communist subversion.

Marcus Aurelius Antoninus, orig. Marcus Annius Verus (AD 121-80), Roman emperor (161-80), Stoic philosopher. Defended empire against Parthians and Germans. Persecuted Christians as enemies of empire. Wrote *Meditations*, an expression of his Stoic philosophy.

Marcuse, Herbert (1898-1979), American philosopher, b. Berlin. Has applied theories of Marx and Freud to analyze modern indust. society, holding that new revolutionary elite will be drawn from skilled technical workers. Works incl. *Eros and Civilization* (1955), *One Dimensional Man* (1964).

Mar del Plata, resort of E Argentina, on Atlantic coast. Pop. 317,000. Tourist industs.; fish canning, meat packing.

Mardi Gras, French name for SHROVE TUESDAY. Last day before fasting of Lent, hence celebrated in festivals, notably in New Orleans, Rio de Janeiro, Nice.

Marduk, chief god of Babylonian pantheon. Creator of mankind, god of fertility. Identified with Bel in OT.

Marengo, village of Piedmont, NW Italy, near Alessandria. Scene of battle (1800) in which French under Napoleon defeated Austrians.

mare's tail, *Hippuris vulgaris,* aquatic perennial herb with erect stem, whorls of slender leaves and minute green flowers. Native to Europe, Asia and N Africa.

Margaret, St (c 1045-93), Scottish queen. Grand-daughter of Edmund Ironside, went to Scotland after Norman conquest. Through her influence, Roman form of Christianity replaced earlier Celtic rites in Scotland. Helped introduce English ways into Scotland.

Margaret (1353-1412), queen of Denmark, Norway and Sweden. Married Haakon VI of Norway

(1363). Became regent of Denmark (1375-87) and Norway (1380-7) for son Olaf, taking control of both kingdoms on his death (1387). Invaded Sweden (1389) and deposed Albert of Mecklenburg. United (1397) the 3 nations, ruling through grand-nephew, Eric of Pomerania.

Margaret, Maid of Norway (1283-90), queen of Scotland. Daughter of Eric II of Norway, inherited throne on death (1285) of her grandfather Alexander III. Marriage was arranged between her and Edward, prince of Wales. Died on crossing to Scotland, provoking war over succession.

Margaret of Anjou (c 1430-82), queen consort of England. Married Henry VI (1445); when Henry became insane, she opposed the protector, Richard, duke of York. Strengthened her position with birth of son Edward (1453), whose cause she supported during conflict between houses of York and Lancaster (beginning 1455). Captured (1471) at Tewkesbury; returned to France.

Margaret of Navarre or **Angoulême** (1492-1549), queen of Navarre, sister of Francis I of France. Influenced political life, religion and letters, patronizing Marot, Rabelais. Wrote French Renaissance classic *Heptaméron*, version of Boccaccio's *Decameron*.

Margaret of Valois (1553-1615), queen of Navarre and France. Wife of Henry of Navarre, later Henry IV of France. Notorious for promiscuity. Centre of literary circle during enforced retirement at Usson (1587-1605). Marriage annulled (1599).

Margaret [Rose], Countess of Snowdon (1930-   ), British princess. Second daughter of George VI. Married (1960) Antony Armstrong-Jones. 2 children, David (1961-   ) and Sarah (1964-   ). Divorced (1978).

margarine, butter substitute prepared from hydrogenated vegetable oils and skim milk; vitamins A and D are usually added. Developed in France in 1860s using animal fats.

Margate, mun. bor. of Isle of Thanet, Kent, SE England. Pop. 50,000. Seaside resort.

marguerite, several cultivated flowers of genus *Chrysanthemum* of composite family, esp. *C. frutescens* (Paris daisy) with single flower of white petals surrounding yellow centre.

Mari, auton. republic of EC European RSFSR, USSR; in middle Volga valley. Area c 23,000 sq km (8960 sq mi); pop. 685,000; cap. Yoshkar-Ola. Extensively forested; main indust. lumbering, wood product mfg. The Mari, a Finno-Ugrian people, were conquered by Ivan the Terrible in 16th cent.

Mariana Islands, isl. group of W Pacific Ocean. Main isls. GUAM, Saipan, Tinian; all except Guam part of US trust territ. of the Pacific Isls. Produce copra, sugar cane. Discovered (1521) by Magellan; all except Guam, which was ceded to US, sold by Spain to Germany (1899). Japanese from WWI, taken by US (1944).

Mariana Trench, deepest known depression on Earth's surface (11,033 m/36,198 ft), in W Pacific. Lies to E of Mariana Isls. Bottom has been reached by bathyscaphe.

Maria Theresa (1717-80), Austrian empress. Ruled (1745-65) through husband, Emperor Francis I, and (1765-80) through son, Joseph II. Succeeded (1740) to Habsburg lands by terms of PRAGMATIC SANCTION. Right to do so was opposed by European alliance in War of Austrian Succession (1740-8); lost Silesia to Prussia. Alliance with France to regain Silesia led to SEVEN YEARS WAR.

Marie Antoinette (1755-93), Austrian princess, queen consort of Louis XVI of France. Her Austrian origin, extravagance, involvement in scandal, attempts to influence policy in favour of Austria, opposition to economic reform, all made her unpopular. Sought Austrian military intervention (1792) in French Revolution. Convicted of treason, guillotined.

Marie Byrd Land or Byrd Land, region of Antarctica, E of Ross Sea and S of Amundsen Sea. Claimed for US by R.E. Byrd (1929).

Marie de' Medici, see MEDICI.

Marie Louise (1791-1847), Austrian princess. Married (1810) Napoleon I, after he had divorced Josephine. She bore him a son (1811) before returning to Austria after his 1st abdication (1814).

marigold, several plants of genus *Calendula* with orange or yellow flowers. *C. officinalis* is pot marigold. So-called African marigold, *Tagetes erecta,* is unrelated species, native to Mexico.

marijuana, see HEMP.

marimba, musical instrument, resembling a xylophone, but with larger resonators and usually made of metal. Played with soft-headed mallets. Of African origin, it is popular in South America.

Marin, John (1870-1953), American painter. Known for his seascapes and city scenes, painted in watercolour and employing the broken planes of cubism. Works incl. *Maine Islands* and *Lower Manhattan*.

marines, troops trained and organized for service at sea or on land. In UK, Royal Marines (founded 1664) constitute main commando force of army, as do Marine Corps (1775) in US. Traditional roles incl. spearheading beach attacks.

Marinetti, Filippo Tommaso (1876-1944), Italian author. Known as formulator of FUTURISM in *Manifeste du Futurisme* (1909).

Marini, Marino (1901-), Italian sculptor. Influenced by primitive art, he is best known for works in bronze on *Horse and Rider* theme.

Maritimes, region in E Canada. Comprise Atlantic provs. of New Brunswick, Nova Scotia, Prince Edward Isl.

Maritzburg, see PIETERMARITZBURG, South Africa.

Mariupol, see ZHDANOV.

Marius, Gaius (c 155-86 BC), Roman soldier, politician. His rivalry with Sulla over the command against Mithradates led to civil war (88). Forced by Sulla to flee Rome, he later seized the city (87) with help of Cinna during Sulla's absence and ruthlessly destroyed his enemies.

Marivaux, Pierre Carlet de Chamblain de (1688-1763), French dramatist. Known for stylized comedies of love, eg *Le Jeu de l'amour et du hasard* (1730), *Les Fausses Confidences* (1737). Also wrote fanciful mythological plays, novels.

marjoram, several plants of mint

MARK

family of genera *Origanum* or *Marjorana*, esp. *M. hortensis* (sweet marjoram), grown for its aromatic leaves used in cooking.

Mark, St, orig. John Mark (*fl* 1st cent. AD), disciple of Jesus, friend of St Peter and St Paul. Traditional author of 2nd Gospel and 1st bishop of Alexandria. Patron saint of Venice.

Mark, Gospel according to St, second of NT Gospels, attributed to St Mark; written *c* AD 70. Shortest of Gospels, recounts life of Jesus. Only Gospel in which every passage is paralleled in another Gospel.

Mark Antony, *see* ANTONY, MARK.

Markiewicz, Constance Georgine, Countess, née Gore-Booth (*c* 1868-1927), Irish patriot. Active in Easter Rebellion (1916), she was sentenced to death; released (1917) after sentence commuted. First woman elected to British Parliament (1918), but did not take her seat.

marl, calcareous mudstone, consisting of clay with calcium carbonate. Sedimentary, laid down by fresh or sea water. Crumbles easily; 'marling' is spreading marl on poor soils to reduce acidity, promote nitrification.

Marlborough, John Churchill, 1st Duke of (1650-1722), English army officer, statesman. Second-in-command of James II's army which crushed Monmouth's rebellion (1685). Supported William of Orange in deposing James. Gained power through influence of his wife, Sarah Jennings (1660-1744), over Queen Anne. Famed for victories at Blenheim (1704), Ramillies (1706) and Malplaquet (1709). Dismissed from office (1711) after wife's quarrel with Anne and return of Tories to power. Reinstated on George I's accession.

Marlborough, region of NE South Isl., New Zealand. Area 10,930 sq km (4220 sq mi); pop. 32,000; main town Blenheim. Largely mountainous; sheep rearing, dairying, wheat and barley growing, tourism.

marlin, large oceanic gamefish with spear-like snout. Species incl. blue marlin, *Makaira nigricans*, and white marlin, *Tetrapturus albidus*, of American Atlantic coast.

Marlowe, Christopher (1564-93), English dramatist, poet. Powerful plays, eg *Tamburlaine the Great*, *The Jew of Malta*, *Dr Faustus*, *Edward II*, estab. blank verse as Elizabethan dramatic form. Lyrics incl. famous 'Come live with me and be my love'. Life ended mysteriously in tavern brawl.

Marmara or **Marmora, Sea of** (anc. *Propontis*), sea between European and Asiatic Turkey. Links Black Sea (by Bosporus) to Aegean Sea (by Dardanelles).

marmoset, small squirrel-like social monkey of Callithricidae or Hapalidae family, found in Central and South America. Non-prehensile tail, claws on fingers and toes. Species incl. pygmy marmoset, *Cebuella pygmaea*, smallest monkey.

marmot, any of genus *Marmota* of squirrel-like rodents found in mountainous areas of temperate N hemisphere. Short legs, coarse thick fur; lives in burrows. Species incl. Alpine marmot, *M. marmota*, and North American woodchuck, *M. monax*.

Marne, river of NE France. Flows *c* 525 km (325 mi) from Langres

Plateau via Châlons, Epernay to R. Seine near Paris. Linked by canals to many rivers, incl. Aisne, Rhine. Scene of unsuccessful German WWI offensives (1914, 1918).

Maronites, Christian sect chiefly in Lebanon, with patriarch recognized by the pope. Distinct community since 7th cent. when they adopted MONOTHELETISM; re-entered Roman communion in 12th cent.

Marprelate controversy, 16th cent. English religious argument. Seven Puritan-inspired pamphlets, pub. (1588-9) under pseudonym of Martin Marprelate, scurrilously attacked authoritarianism of Church of England.

Marquesas Islands, archipelago of C Pacific Ocean, part of French Polynesia. Comprise N group (Washington Isls.) and S group (Mendaña Isls.); main isl. Hiva Oa. Mountainous; fertile, produce fruit, copra, cotton. Acquired by France (1842).

Marquet, Albert (1875-1947), French painter. Exhibited with the fauves in 1905; evolved a quiet clear style of depicting landscapes and port and harbour scenes.

marquetry, decorative technique in which ornamental woods, bone, metal, tortoiseshell, *etc*, are inlaid in veneer and then fixed to surface of furniture. Characteristic of work of A.C. Boulle.

Marquette, Jacques (1637-75), French Jesuit missionary. Accompanied Louis Jolliet on voyage from L. Michigan to the Mississippi, by way of Wisconsin R. (1673). Wrote journal of expedition (pub. 1681).

Marquis, Don[ald Robert Perry] (1878-1937), American author. Known for humorous works, eg

satire of Greenwich Village, *Hermione and Her Little Group of Serious Thinkers* (1916), archy and mehitabel (1927).

Marrakesh (Fr. *Marrakech*), city of C Morocco, in foothills of Atlas Mts. Pop. 330,000. Commercial centre, agric. market; carpets, leather goods mfg.; tourist indust. Founded 1062, fl in Middle Ages as terminus of Saharan caravan routes. Has Koutoubiya mosque and tower (1195).

marram grass, coarse perennial grass of genus *Ammophila* grown on sandy shores to bind sand. Species incl. American *A. arenaria* and European *A. baltica*.

Marranos, Spanish term for Jews who (after 1391) had been forced to profess Christianity to escape death or persecution. They were suspected of secretly practising Judaism and were targets of the Spanish Inquisition.

marriage, union, sanctioned by custom and religion, of persons of the opposite sex as husband and wife. In most societies, sanctified by rite or sacrament. Normally limitations are placed on choice of mate, eg exogamy (marriage outside group), or endogamy (marriage within group). Exchange of property is often a concomitant of marriage. *See* POLYGAMY.

marrow, soft pulp in interior cavities of bones. Red marrow, in which blood cells originate, fills all bones at birth. Replaced in long bones of adults by yellow marrow, containing mainly fat.

Marryat, Frederick (1792-1848), English author. Wrote sea adventure novels, eg *Mr Midshipman Easy* (1836), children's historical novel,

The Children of the New Forest (1847).

Mars, in Roman religion, god of war, identified with Greek Ares. Father of Romulus and greatest god after Jupiter. Represented as fully-armed warrior. Honoured in several festivals in March, named after him.

Mars, planet 4th in distance from Sun; mean distance from Sun *c* 227.9 × 10⁶ km; diameter 6790 km; mass *c* 11% that of Earth. Solar orbit takes 687 days; period of axial rotation 24 hrs 37 mins. Thin atmosphere composed mainly of carbon dioxide; temperature varies from -70° C to 30° C during day. Viking space mission (1976) showed polar caps were ice but found no evidence of life.

Marsala (anc. *Lilybaeum*), town of W Sicily, Italy. Pop. 79,000. Fishing; Marsala wine. Major Carthaginian fortress from 4th cent. BC; Roman naval base. Garibaldi began Sicilian campaign here (1860).

Marseillaise, La, French national anthem. Words and music written by Rouget de Lisle (1792). Name was gained when troops from Marseilles sang the anthem on entering Paris later the same year.

Marseilles (Fr. *Marseille*, anc. *Massilia*), city of Provence, SE France, on Gulf of Lions. Cap. of Bouches-du-Rhône dept. Pop. 889,000. Major port and naval base, linked to Rhône by tunnel; soap, margarine mfg., chemicals, oil refining. Founded *c* 600 BC by Greeks; free city until passing to France in 1481.

Marsh, Ngaio Edith (1899-), New Zealand author. Known for detective stories incl. *A Man lay Dead* (1934), *Enter a Murderer* (1935), *Death in a White Tie* (1938).

Marshall, Alfred (1842-1924), English economist. Updated formulations of classical economists, developed marginal utility theory. Chief work, *Principles of Economics* (1890).

Marshall, George Catlett (1880-1959), American army officer, statesman. Army chief of staff (1939-45). As secretary of state (1947-9), he initiated (1947) European Recovery Program (Marshall Plan) giving economic aid to European countries. Awarded Nobel Peace Prize (1953).

Marshall, John (1755-1835), American jurist. Chief Justice of Supreme Court (1801-35), helping to define its role and interpret its constitution. Important decisions, incl. McCULLOCH v MARYLAND, set precedents on Supreme Court's right to review constitutionality of legislation in appeal cases.

Marshall Islands, archipelago of W Pacific Ocean, part of US trust territ. of the Pacific Isls. Area 180 sq km (70 sq mi); comprise Ralik (W), Ratak (E) chains; main town Jaluit. Produce coffee, copra, sugar cane. German from 1885; occupied by Japanese from WWI. Taken (1944) by US; BIKINI ATOLL site of US atomic bomb tests.

Marshall Plan, see MARSHALL, GEORGE CATLETT.

marsh gas, see METHANE.

marsh mallow, *Althaea officinalis*, perennial herb with pink flowers, native to Europe, Asia and N Africa. Found in marshes. Root yields mucilage used in confectionery.

marsh marigold, *Caltha palustris*, perennial herb of buttercup family with yellow flowers and round leaves. Native to Europe, Asia and North America.

Marsilius of Padua (d. *c* 1342), Italian political theorist. Author of controversial *Defensor pacis*, written (1324) on behalf of Emperor Louis IV who was in dispute with Pope John XXII. Its advocacy of secular power against ecclesiastical was condemned by papacy.

Marston, John (1576-1634), English dramatist, satirist. Known for *The Malcontent* (1604), *The Dutch Courtesan* (1605).

Marston Moor, Yorkshire, England. Scene of battle (1644) in which Parliamentarians defeated Royalists in Civil War.

marsupial mole, *Notoryctes typhlops*, mole-like Australian marsupial with silky golden hair. Lives underground, burrowing for insects.

marsupials (Marsupialia), subclass of primitive mammals incl. kangaroo, wombat, found mainly in Australasia but with species, *eg* opossum, in America. Young, born small and underdeveloped, are nourished by mammary glands in female's pouch.

martello towers, circular forts, modelled on one at Mortella in Corsica, built around S and E coasts of England as defence against Napoleon's projected invasion.

marten, any of genus *Martes* of weasel-like arboreal carnivores with long body, short legs and valuable fur. Pine marten, *M. martes*, is European variety, with dark brown coat.

Martha's Vineyard, isl. off SE Massachusetts, US. Area 260 sq km (*c* 100 sq mi). Atlantic summer resort. Settled 1643; hist. important whaling, fishing industs.

Martial, full name Marcus Valerius Martialis (*c* AD 40-*c* 104), Roman poet, b. Spain. Known for epigrams, modern concept of which derives from his. Based works on sharply observed contemporary society.

Martin, St (*c* 316-397), bishop of Tours, b. Illyria. Originally a soldier, traditionally left army giving his cloak to a beggar. Evangelized Gaul, estab. many monastic communities.

Martin V (1368-1431), Roman churchman, pope (1417-31). His election during Council of Constance ended GREAT SCHISM (1378-1417). Worked to restore Church unity and rebuild Rome.

Martin, John (1789-1854), English painter. Known for his enormous paintings of visionary, usually overdramatized, religious scenes and landscapes, which brought him short-lived international fame. Works incl. *Belshazzar's Feast*.

Martin, [Basil] Kingsley (1897-1969), English journalist. Edited *New Statesman* (1931-60). Also wrote *The Press the Public Wants* (1947), *The Crown and the Establishment* (1962).

martin, small bird of swallow family that feeds on insects caught in flight. Species incl. house martin, *Delechon urbica*, which builds mud nest under eaves, and sand martin, *Riparia riparia*.

Martini, Simone (*c* 1284-1344), Italian painter of Sienese school. Pupil of Duccio, he developed his decorative linear style and colour harmonies. Works incl. mural *The Virgin in Majesty* in Siena and equestrian portrait of Guidoriccio da Fogliano.

Martinique, overseas dept. of France; isl. of SE West Indies; in Windward Isls. Area 1100 sq km (425 sq mi); pop. 369,000; cap. Fort-de-France (pop. 99,000). Mountainous (Mont Pelée); of volcanic origin. Agric. incl. sugar cane, coffee; rum mfg. Colonized by French 1635; overseas dept. from 1946.

Martinů, Bohuslav (1890-1959), Czech composer. Prolific writer, sometimes employing extreme dissonance. Works incl. 13 operas, 6 symphonies, chamber music. Lived mainly in France and US after 1932.

martyr (Gk.,=witness), in Christian church, one who chooses to die rather than give up the Christian faith; 1st recorded Christian martyr is St Stephen (Acts 6: 7).

Marvell, Andrew (1621-78), English poet. Known for metaphysical lyrics incl. 'To his Coy Mistress', 'The Garden', 'The Definition of Love', 'The Nymph Complaining for the Death of her Fawn'. Also wrote political pamphlets.

Marx, Karl Heinrich (1818-83), German philosopher. Journalist and radical leader; with ENGELS, pub. *Communist Manifesto* (1848). After Revolution of 1848, spent much of his life in London and helped found (1864) association which became First INTERNATIONAL. In his theory of social change adapted Hegel's thesis to produce DIALECTICAL MATERIALISM, involving conflict of economic classes, first expressed in *The German Ideology* (1846). Major work, *Das Kapital* (1867; vols. II, III edited by Engels 1885-94), was basis for much subsequent doctrine of modern COMMUNISM and SOCIALISM. Also see MARXISM, SOCIAL DEMOCRACY.

Marx Brothers, American comedians, originally in vaudeville, but best known for films. They were Leonard ('Chico') (1891-1961), Adolph ('Harpo') (1893-1964), Julius ('Groucho') (1895-1977), and Herbert ('Zeppo') (1901-), who left after 1st 5 films. Anarchic, wisecracking films incl. *Duck Soup* (1933), *A Night at the Opera* (1936), *A Day at the Races* (1937).

Marxism, political and economic system of thought, developed from philosophy of Karl MARX; also known as economic determinism. Method of analysis is DIALECTICAL MATERIALISM, from which was derived assertion that social change results from class struggle over control of means of production with the working class (proletariat) ultimately triumphing and leading to classless society. Marxism spread in late 19th cent. Europe through INTERNATIONALS and socialist parties (see SOCIAL DEMOCRACY), eventually dividing between those who believed struggle would be evolutionary and those led by Lenin advocating violent revolution if necessary. Success of Russian Revolution (1917) made permanent split between Socialists and Communists (see COMMUNISM, MODERN). Orthodox Marxism subsequently esp. influential in Third World countries with mainly agrarian workers.

Mary, the Virgin (1st cent. BC-1st cent. AD), mother of Jesus, wife of Joseph of Nazareth. RC, Orthodox and Anglican churches teach doctrine of her perpetual virginity. In

RC church she is regarded, with Christ, as co-redeemer of mankind.

Mary I (1516-58), queen of England (1553-8). Daughter of Henry VIII and Catherine of Aragon; accession was resisted by NORTHUMBERLAND. Restored papal supremacy in England and married Philip II of Spain (1554). Sanctioned persecution of Protestants, incl. Cranmer, Latimer, Ridley, thus earning nickname 'Bloody Mary'.

Mary II (1662-94), queen of England (1689-94). Daughter of James II, she married (1677) William of Orange (William III of England). After 'Glorious Revolution' (1688), they ruled jointly until her death from smallpox.

Mary, town of USSR, Turkmen SSR; in oasis of Kara Kum desert. Pop. 61,000. Cotton grown by irrigation. Formerly known as Merv. Nearby old city of Merv, centre of medieval Moslem culture under Arab rule. In Hindu and Arab tradition, believed to be source of Aryan race.

Maryland, state of E US, on Atlantic. Area 27,394 sq km (10,577 sq mi); pop. 3,922,000; cap. Annapolis; chief city Baltimore. Almost divided by Chesapeake Bay; rolling upland in interior. Agric. (esp. poultry rearing; food processing, metals, shipbuilding industs.; fishing in Chesapeake Bay. Settled early 17th cent.; one of original 13 colonies of US.

Marylebone Cricket Club (MCC), London cricket club, founded 1787; responsible for original rules of game. Located at Lord's ground.

Mary Magdalene or Magdalen (1st cent. AD), Christian saint. In NT, demoniac healed by Jesus; present at Crucifixion and one of those who found the tomb empty and to whom the risen Christ appeared. Traditionally identified with the repentant prostitute who anointed Jesus' feet in Luke's Gospel.

Mary of Burgundy (1457-82), Burgundian noblewoman. Daughter of Charles the Bold, she married (1477) Maximilian of Austria, thus adding the Low Countries to the Habsburg empire. This alliance was opposed by the French.

Mary Queen of Scots (1542-87), queen of Scotland (1542-67). Daughter of James V, she was brought up in France. Married Francis II of France; returned to Scotland (1561) after his death. Married her cousin DARNLEY (1565), who was murdered (1567). Mary then married BOTHWELL, suspected of being Darnley's murderer. Ensuing civil war forced her abdication in favour of son by Darnley, James VI. Fled to England after defeat at Langside (1568); imprisoned by Elizabeth. Involved in several Catholic plots to place her on English throne. Executed for implication in Babington's plot.

Masaccio, orig. Tommaso Guidi (1401-c 1428), Italian painter. His revolutionary handling of perspective and use of light to define forms profoundly influenced subsequent painters of the Renaissance. His major extant work is fresco series in Brancacci Chapel, Florence.

Masai, nomadic E Africa people, of Hamitic origin. Mainly in Kenya and Tanzania. Noted for physical courage. Livelihood depends largely on cattle rearing.

Masaryk, Thomas Garrigue (1850-1937), Czech statesman, philosopher. As member of parliament, strongly opposed Austrian policy. At outbreak of WWI, travelled widely making propaganda for Czech independence from Austria. Became president (1918) of new republic; resigned 1935, succeeded by Beneš. His son, Jan Masaryk (1886-1948), was foreign minister (1945-8). Said to have committed suicide after Soviet-organized coup of 1948.

Mascagni, Pietro (1863-1945), Italian composer, conductor. Known for *Cavalleria Rusticana*, which won an opera competition in 1889. Wrote several other operas, but none achieved its fame.

Mascarene Islands, group of isls. in W Indian Ocean, E of Madagascar. Incl. Réunion, Mauritius, Rodriguez.

Masefield, John [Edward] (1878-1967), English poet, playwright. Works incl. *Salt Water Ballads* (1902), containing 'Sea Fever', 'Cargoes', narrative poems, *eg The Everlasting Mercy* (1911), *Dauber* (1913). Also wrote verse dramas, sea adventure stories. Poet laureate (1930-67).

maser (microwave amplification by stimulated emission of radiation), device for creation of intense, narrow beam of high frequency radio waves; waves produced have same frequency and are in phase. Depends on excitation of atoms of a crystal or gas by incoming radiation. Hydrogen maser is basis of highly accurate atomic clock. ·LASER is maser operating at optical frequencies.

Maseru, cap: of Lesotho, on ·R.

Caledon. Pop. 29,000. Admin. centre; railway links with South Africa.

Mashhad or **Meshed**, city of NE Iran, cap. of Khurasan prov. Pop. 562,000. Site of tomb of Imam Riza and pilgrimage centre for Shiite Moslems. Cap. of Persia in 18th cent.

Mashonaland, region of NE Rhodesia. Fertile plain and tableland, inhabited mainly by Mashona tribe; chief city Salisbury. Part of Southern Rhodesia from 1923.

Mason, A[lfred] E[dward] W[oodley] (1865-1948), English novelist. Works incl. *Four Feathers* (1902), *The Broken Road* (1907) with Eastern settings, and detective novels, *eg At the Villa Rose* (1910), featuring hero Hanaud of the Sûreté.

Mason-Dixon Line, boundary between Maryland and Pennsylvania, US, fixed (1763-7) by Charles Mason and Jeremiah Dixon to resolve border disputes. Regarded, before Civil War, as separating free states from slave states and now North from South.

Masons, see FREEMASONRY.

Masorah, collection of Jewish annotations concerning the correct Hebrew text of the Holy Scriptures. Involved the creation of system of vowels for pronunciation of text (Hebrew alphabet has only consonants). Compilation ceased in 15th cent.

masque, form of dramatic entertainment in which spectacle, music are emphasized, usually based on mythological, allegorical theme. Reached height with court masques contrived by partnership of Ben Jonson, Inigo Jones for James I.

Mass, liturgical service of RC church, incl. celebration of EUCHA-

RIST. Low Mass is spoken; High Mass is more elaborate ritual, chanted and sung. Term also used by Anglo-Catholics; in Eastern churches the terms 'Holy Liturgy' or 'Offering' are used for a similar service. Formerly RCs used medieval Latin liturgy; vernacular adopted since 2nd Vatican Council.

mass, in physics, the quantity of matter in a body. More precisely, inertial mass of body is determined by acceleration produced in it by applied force. Mass is distinct from weight, which is measure of gravitational force of attraction on body. By theory of relativity, inertial mass increases as velocity increases, so that a given force produces smaller acceleration with increasing velocity (only appreciable at velocities approaching that of light). Einstein's equation $E = mc^2$ shows that mass and energy are equivalent (where c = speed of light).

Massachusetts, New England state of US. Area 21,386 sq km (8257 sq mi); pop. 5,689,000; cap. Boston. Berkshire Hills in W; Atlantic resort area (Cape Cod, Martha's Vineyard, Nantucket). Agric., livestock rearing, fisheries. Main industs. shipbuilding, machinery, textile, paper mfg. Education, research centre. Pilgrim Fathers landed at Plymouth Rock in *Mayflower* (1620); Puritan theocracy estab. Focus of pre-Revolution protest (1776). One of original 13 colonies of US.

Massachusetts Institute of Technology (MIT), Cambridge, Massachusetts, US, scientific and technical school, coeducational, chartered 1861. Famous for re-

search, facilities incl. 70 special laboratories.

Masséna, André (1756-1817), French marshal. Noted for tactical abilities, victorious in Napoleon's Austrian campaigns (1800-9). Failed to dislodge Wellington in Peninsular War, recalled (1811) by Napoleon.

Massenet, Jules Emile Frédéric (1842-1912), French composer. Best known for lyrical operas, esp. *Manon* (1884) and *Thaïs* (1894). Also wrote oratorios, orchestral suites.

Massey, Vincent (1887-1967), Canadian statesman, diplomat. Canadian high commissioner to Britain (1936-46). First Canadian-born governor-general of Canada (1952-9). Brother of actor, Raymond Massey.

Massey, William Ferguson (1856-1925), New Zealand statesman, b. Ireland, PM (1912-25). Estab. 'Reform Party' (1903), offshoot of Conservative Party supported mainly by farmers. Headed WWI coalition govt.

Massif Central, large plateau region of SC France. Area *c* 85,000 sq km (33,000 sq mi); highest peak Puy de Sancy (1885 m/6187 ft). Incl. volcanic Auvergne, limestone Cévennes. Stock rearing; coal, kaolin mining. Source of many rivers, incl. Allier, Dordogne, Loire.

Massine, Léonide (1896-1979), American ballet dancer, choreographer, b. Russia. Worked with Diaghilev. Staged *The Three-cornered Hat*, *La Boutique fantasque*.

Massinger, Philip (1583-1640), English dramatist. Associate of Fletcher, Dekker. Works incl. comedies *The City Madam* (1632), *A New Way to Pay Old Debts* (1625).

mass number, in chemistry, number of protons plus neutrons in atomic nucleus.

Masson, André (1896-   ), French painter. Member of surrealist group, his later work influenced American abstract expressionist painters. Evolved landscape style under influence of Chinese art.

mass spectrometer, instrument which uses electric and magnetic fields to arrange streams of ionized particles into order depending on their charge to mass ratio. Used to determine atomic weights of individual isotopes of an element and to find relative abundance of isotopes in sample of an element.

Massys or **Matsys, Quentin** (*c* 1466-1530), Flemish painter. Influenced by the Italian Renaissance, he is known for his genre pictures of bankers and merchants, *eg Banker and his Wife.* His many portraits incl. that of Erasmus.

Masters, Edgar Lee (1869-1950), American poet. Known for *Spoon River Anthology* (1915), a cycle of 'epitaphs' spoken by dead of mid-Western town. Also wrote novels, hostile life of Lincoln.

mastiff, large powerful smooth-coated dog, used as watchdog. Stands *c* 76 cm/30 in. at shoulder.

mastodon, extinct elephant-like mammal that flourished from Oligocene epoch onwards. Differed from elephant in larger size and in structure of teeth; had 4 tusks. Term used in US for American 2-tusked mastodon of Pleistocene epoch.

Masurian Lakes, group of *c* 2700 lakes, Mazury region, NE Poland. Formerly part of East Prussia, passed to Poland 1945. Scene of Russian defeats in WWI (1914, 1915).

Matabeleland, region of SW Rhodesia. Inhabited mainly by Matabele tribe; chief city Bulawayo. Rich gold deposits. Part of Southern Rhodesia from 1923.

Mata Hari, orig. Margaretha Geertruida Zelle (1876-1917), Dutch-Indonesian dancer. Joined German secret service (1907). Betrayed Allied secrets to Germans in WWI. Executed by French.

Matapan, Cape, headland of Greece, S extremity of Peloponnese. Scene of British naval victory (1941) over Italians.

match, small strip of wood, cardboard, *etc,* tipped with composition which catches fire by friction. Modern match-heads contain phosphorus sulphide and oxidizing agent. Safety match-head contains antimony trisulphide and potassium chlorate; striking surface contains red phosphorus.

maté or **Paraguay tea,** dried leaves of South American evergreen tree, *Ilex paraguariensis.* Popular bitter beverage, drunk from special calabashes, is made from it.

materialism, in philosophy, system of thought which takes matter as only reality. Early materialist philosophies incl. Democritus' atomistic theory, Epicureanism, Stoicism. Subsequent exponents incl. Hobbes, Mill, Marx. Often widely held in times of scientific achievement.

mathematics, study of numbers, spatial relations and axiomatic systems. Branches of mathematics under early investigation incl. arithmetic, geometry (esp. by Greeks) and algebra. Seventeenth cent. saw beginning of standard algebraic methods and introduction of calculus, prob. most frequently applied mathematical method. Axiomatic development of mathematics began in 19th cent., which also saw perfection of techniques to solve classical problems. Twentieth cent. has seen greater subdivision of major areas of research, eg geometry now divided into topology, differential geometry, algebraic geometry, etc, as well as development of abstract mathematical systems, originally arising out of specific problems, but now studied in their own right, eg group theory.

Mathura or Muttra, town of Uttar Pradesh, N India, on R. Jumna. Pop. 140,000. Cotton, paper mfg. Hindu religious centre, revered as birthplace of Krishna.

Matilda or Maud (1102-67), queen of England. Daughter of HENRY I; married Emperor Henry V, and, after his death Geoffrey Plantagenet. Her cousin, Stephen, seized throne (1135) but was challenged (1139) by Matilda. Captured Stephen (1141) and was elected 'lady of the English'. Later withdrew claim to throne in favour of son, Henry II.

Matisse, Henri (1869-1954), French painter, sculptor. Leader of fauves, he developed bright, often stylized decorative design. His characteristic decorative works, influenced by Near Eastern art, juxtaposed brilliant colours and employed distorted perspectives. He painted long series of odalisques and still lifes, incl. *The Pink Nude.*

Mato Grosso, forested area of WC Brazil. Heavy rainfall, cattle raising in SW upland; mineral resources unexploited (manganese mining near Corumba). Region mainly in Mato Grosso state. Indian pop. in Amazon basin.

matriarchy, form of social organization in which the mother is head of family or group, descent and kinship being traced through mother rather than father. Often associated with polyandry (see POLYGAMY). Found in South Sea Isls. and among certain North American Indians.

matrimony, see MARRIAGE.

matrix, in mathematics, rectangular array of numbers, arranged into rows and columns. Matrix is said to be square if it has same number of rows and columns. Used in all branches of mathematics, esp. in solution of systems of linear equations.

Matterhorn (Fr. *Mont Cervin,* Ital. *Monte Cervino*), peak of Pennine Alps, on Swiss-Italian border. Height 4475 m (14,690 ft). First climbed 1865 by Whymper.

Matthew, St (fl 1st cent. AD), tax gatherer of Capernaum, one of Twelve Disciples. First Gospel usually attributed to him. Traditionally said to have been martyred.

Matthew, Gospel according to St, first of NT Gospels, traditionally attributed to St Matthew since 2nd cent. Gives account of Jesus' life stressing that he was Messiah as foretold in OT.

Matthews, Sir Stanley (1915-), English footballer. Renowned dribbler, he played 54 full international games for England as a winger. Played last first-class game at age of 50.

Matthias Corvinus (c 1440-90),

king of Hungary (1458-90). At instigation of Pope Pius II, fought against Bohemian regent George of Podebrad.. Annexed Moravia, Silesia; proclaimed king of Bohemia (1469) but later forced to recognize Ladislaus as rightful king. Annexed parts of Austria (1482-5). Patron of learning and science; estab. fine library at Budapest.

Maudling, Reginald (1917-79), British politician. Posts in Conservative govts. incl. chancellor of the exchequer (1962-4), home secretary (1970-2). Resigned amidst allegations of corruption.

Maugham, W[illiam] Somerset (1874-1965), English author, b. France. Novels incl. autobiog. *Of Human Bondage* (1915), *The Moon and Sixpence* (1919), *Cakes and Ale* (1930), *The Razor's Edge* (1944). Also wrote masterly short stories, plays, often using tropical setting to explore its effect on white colonialists.

Mau Mau, secret terrorist organization, active 1952-60, whose members, drawn from Kikuyu tribe, took oath to drive white settlers from Kenya. Also attacked Africans who opposed Mau Mau. Finally offered free pardon by Kenya govt. (1963).

Maundy Thursday, Thursday before Easter, historically, when British sovereign distributes Maundy money to the poor. Relic of ceremony commemorating Jesus' washing Apostles' feet.

Maupassant, Guy de (1850-93), French author. Known for naturalistic short stories depicting ironies of life, *eg* 'Boule de Suif', 'La Parure'. Also wrote novels

incl. *Une Vie* (1883), *Pierre et Jean* (1888).

Mauretania, ancient region of N Africa, incl. present-day N Morocco, W Algeria. Kingdom under Numidian control in 2nd cent. BC; became Roman prov., divided (AD 42) into 2 provs. by Claudius. Overrun by Vandals in 5th cent.

Mauriac, François Charles (1885-1970), French novelist. Preoccupied with sin, salvation. Novels incl. *Thérèse Desqueyroux* (1927), *Vipers' Tangle* (1932). Nobel Prize for Literature (1952).

Mauritania, republic of NW Africa. Area 1,031,000 sq km (398,000 sq mi); pop. 1,481,000; cap. Nouakchott. Languages: Arabic, French. Religion: Islam. Mainly in Sahara, pop. mostly nomadic herdsmen; limited agric. (maize, millet) in S along R. Senegal. Exports iron ore, copper ore, gum arabic, dried and salted fish. French protect. from 1903; became colony (1920), admin. from St Louis (Senegal) until 1957. Independent from 1960.

Mauritius, isl. state of W Indian Ocean, part of Mascarene Isls. Has 3 dependencies incl. Rodriguez isl. Total area 1860 sq km (720 sq mi); pop. 895,000; cap. Port Louis. Languages: English, French. Religions: Hinduism, Christianity. Majority of pop. of Indian descent. Hilly, largely volcanic; economy dominated by sugar cane. Discovered (1505) by Portuguese; held by Dutch (1598-1710), by French (1715-1810), by British from 1815. Independent from 1968. Member of British Commonwealth.

Maurois, André, pseud. of Emile Herzog (1885-1967), French author.

Known for biographies, *eg Ariel* (1923) on Shelley, *Don Juan* (1930) on Byron. Also wrote humorous novels, *Les Silences du Colonel Bramble* (1918).

Maurras, Charles (1868–1952), French writer. Ardent royalist, edited daily *L'Action Française*. Imprisoned (1945–52) for collaboration with Germans in WWII.

Mavor, Osborne Henry, *see* BRIDIE, JAMES.

Maxim, Sir Hiram Stevens (1840–1916), British inventor, munitions maker, b. US. Developed Maxim machine gun (1884) and a smokeless powder.

Maximilian I (1459–1519), Holy Roman emperor (1493–1519). Acquired Low Countries by marriage to Mary of Burgundy (1477). Involved in wars to defend his new territ. against French. Opposed French expansion in Italy but lost Milan to French (1516).

Maximilian [Joseph Ferdinand] (1832–67), emperor of Mexico (1864–7). Younger brother of Francis Joseph of Austria; accepted crown offered (1863) by French-dominated Mexican assembly. After French military support was withdrawn through American pressure, he lost power. Refused to leave country; was captured and shot.

Maxwell, James Clerk (1831–79), Scottish physicist. His 4 equations concerning electric and magnetic fields described interaction between electricity and magnetism and unified all previous observations about the 2 phenomena. Deduced that light is electromagnetic in nature and predicted existence of electromagnetic (radio) waves, detected by Hertz. Contributed to kinetic theory of gases.

Maya, pre-Columbian South American civilization of Yucatán Penin., S Mexico, Guatemala and Honduras. Relics of Classic period (*c* AD 317–889) incl. pyramidal temples. Hieroglyphic inscriptions and calendars indicate knowledge of mathematics, abstract astronomy. Culture declined after 9th cent. with Spanish conquest (1546) completing its destruction.

Maya, in Hindu religion, term for goddess Devi, consort of SIVA. Also used as term for illusory world of the senses, often personified as a woman.

Mayakovski, Vladimir Vladimirovich (1893–1930), Russian poet. Leading futurist. Works incl. propagandist *Ode to the Revolution* (1918), *150,000,000* (1920). Also wrote satirical plays incl. *Mystery-bouffe* (1918), *The Bedbug* (1928).

May Day, first day of May. Important European festival, originating from pre-Christian fertility ceremonies. Traditions incl. maypoles, election of May king or queen. In Scotland, Ireland, day is called Beltane, celebrated with bonfires. May Day designated (1889) by Second Socialist International as international labour holiday.

Mayence, *see* MAINZ, West Germany.

Mayer, Louis B[urt] (1885–1957), American film executive. Formed Metro-Goldwyn-Mayer (1924) with Sam GOLDWYN. Known for flamboyant use of power over Hollywood.

Mayfair, fashionable dist. of City of WESTMINSTER, London, England.

Named after fair held every May until 1809.

Mayflower, ship which carried the Pilgrims from England to America (1620). Colony was estab. at Plymouth, Mass. Agreement for govt. of colony was known as Mayflower Compact.

mayflower, name applied to several spring-blooming plants, *eg* in America the trailing arbutus, *Epigaea repens,* a trailing evergreen shrub with pink or white fragrant flowers. In Britain name given to blossoms of HAWTHORN.

mayfly, any of order Ephemeroptera of insects with 4 gauzy wings and 3 long tail filaments. Larvae live several years in ponds, streams, eventually changing into dull brown winged insect (subimago). Subimago moults rapidly to form shiny adult; adult dies within a few hours, being unable to feed.

Mayhew, Henry (1812-87), English author. Founded *Punch* (1841). Known for surveys of social conditions esp. *London Labour and the London Poor* (1849-62).

Maynooth, town of Co. Kildare, E Irish Republic. Pop. 1000. St Patrick's Coll. (1795), RC seminary.

Mayo, county of Connacht prov., NW Irish Republic. Area 5398 sq km (2084 sq mi); pop. 109,000; co. town Castlebar. Rugged terrain in W; more fertile E has agric., livestock.

Mazarin, Jules, orig. Giulio Mazarini (1602-61), French statesman, b. Italy. Created cardinal (1641), he succeeded his patron, Richelieu, as chief minister of France (1642). Exercised great power during Louis XIV's minority. Negotiated end of Thirty Years War at Westphalia

(1648). Autocratic rule, taxation policies provoked Fronde revolt (1648-53).

mazurka, lively folk dance in 3/4 time. Originally from Poland, it spread to the ballrooms of W Europe and North America in 19th cent. Estab. as musical form by Chopin, who composed over 50 mazurkas.

Mazzini, Giuseppe (1805-72), Italian nationalist. Worked, primarily while in exile, to unify Italy under republican govt. by revolutionary action. Founded secret society 'Young Italy' (1830) dedicated to these aims. Headed shortlived republic in Rome (1849).

Mbabane, cap. of Swaziland. Pop. 14,000. Admin., commercial centre; railway to Mozambique. Tin, iron mining nearby.

Mdina, *see* CITTÀ VECCHIA, Malta.

Mead, Margaret (1901-78), American anthropologist. Extended scope of anthropology by relating culture to personality. Works incl. *Coming of Age in Samoa* (1928), *Sex and Temperament in Three Primitive Societies* (1935).

mead, alcoholic beverage made from fermented honey and water flavoured with spices. Mead drinking was an important social activity in Anglo-Saxon communities.

meadow grass, *see* BLUEGRASS.

meadow saffron or **autumn crocus,** *Colchicum autumnale,* native to Europe and N Africa. Widely cultivated for purple crocus-like flowers in autumn. Corms yield the alkaloid colchicine used in genetic experiments and as treatment for gout.

meadowsweet, any of genus *Filipendula,* esp. *F. ulmaria,* perennial herb of rose family, native to Europe and Asia, with pink or white flowers. Name also used for several species of genus *Spiraea*.

mealybug, insect of Coccidae family, whose body is covered with waxy secretion. Some species injurious to trees and plants.

mean, in mathematics, number between smallest and largest values of some set of numbers, obtained by some prescribed method. Usually refers to arithmetic mean, *ie* sum of numbers in a group divided by number of members in the group; geometric mean of *n* positive numbers is *n*-th root of their product.

meander, curve in course of a river winding from side to side over flat land. By erosion, river may cut off its own meanders, forming ox-bow or mort lakes. Term derived from ancient R. Maeander (now Büyük Menderes) in Turkey.

Meany, George (1894-), American labour leader. Secretary-treasurer of American Federation of Labor (AFL) (1939-52) and later its president (1952-5). President of new federation formed by merger of AFL and Congress of Industrial Organizations (1955-).

Mearns, The, *see* KINCARDINESHIRE, Scotland.

measles, infectious viral disease spread by airborne droplets. Most common in childhood. Characterized by blotchy body rash preceded by. running nose, watery eyes, fever. Incubation period 10-14 days.

meat, flesh of animals, esp. sheep, pigs and cattle, used as food. Composed mainly of muscle and connective tissue. Contains fat, vitamin B, minerals such as iron, and large amounts of protein. Cooking meat helps coagulate blood and albumen, improve flavour, soften and sterilize it. Meat packing industry concerned with slaughtering of animals and preparing their meat for marketing. Modern form dates from 1870s in US when frozen meat was transported by train; shipping of frozen meat to Europe began·in 1875.

Meath, county of Leinster prov., E Irish Republic. Area 2339 sq km (903 sq mi); pop. 72,000; co. town Trim. Undulating terrain, drained by R. Boyne. Agric., livestock. Ancient kingdom (larger than present county); antiquities (*eg* at Kells, Tara).

Mecca (*Makkah*), cap. of Hejaz region, W Saudi Arabia. Pop. 250,000. Birthplace of Mohammed. Islam's holiest city and pilgrimage centre. Goal of pilgrimage is the Kaaba, cubical stone building, contained in Great Mosque. Kaaba contains sacred Black Stone, kissed by pilgrims.

mechanical engineering, branch of ENGINEERING dealing with machines, engines and power plants. Divided into heat utilization (in engines, *etc*) and machine design.

mechanics, branch of physics dealing with effect of forces acting on bodies. Usually divided into statics and dynamics.

Mechelen (Fr. *Malines*), town of NC Belgium, on R. Dyle. Pop. 66,000. Railway jct., industs. incl. furniture, textiles, vehicles. Once famous for lace mfg. Cathedral (14th cent.), metropolitan see.

Mecklenburg, region of N East Germany. Large, low-lying fertile plain with lakes, forests. Crops incl. rye, potatoes, sugar beet. Hist. cap. Schwerin; chief ports Rostock, Wismar, Stralsund. Imperial duchy from 1348, divided into 2 duchies 1621; both joined German empire 1871. Reunited as state 1934.

medals, *see* DECORATIONS.

Medan, city of Indonesia, cap. of North Sumatra prov. Pop. 636,000. Trade centre, dealing in tobacco, rubber; tourism.

Medawar, Sir Peter Brian (1915-), English biologist, b. Brazil. With Sir Macfarlane Burnet was awarded Nobel Prize for Physiology and Medicine (1960) for showing that animals can be induced to overcome their tendency to reject transplanted tissue or organs.

Medea, in Greek myth, sorceress who helped JASON obtain Golden Fleece. When Jason wished to marry Creusa, Medea sent her a poisoned wedding dress which burned her to death. Killed her own children by Jason and married King Aegeus.

Medellín, city of NW Colombia, in Andes; alt. 1520 m (c 5000 ft). Pop. 1,040,000. Important textile industs., coffee exports; gold mining. Founded 1675.

Medes, ancient people of W Asia, in area now NW Iran. Subjects of Assyria in 9th cent. BC, they gained their independence in 7th cent. BC. Defeated by Cyrus the Great c 550 BC, after which they merged with Persians.

Medicaid and **Medicare,** *see* HEALTH INSURANCE.

Medici, Italian family of merchants and bankers, who ruled Florence (15th-18th cent.) and were famous patrons of the arts during the Renaissance. **Cosimo de' Medici** (1389-1464) was first of family to rule Florence. Greatly extended family's banking interests; encouraged study of Greek. Patron of Donatello, Brunelleschi. His grandson, **Lorenzo de' Medici** (1449-92), called 'Il Magnifico', was a lavish patron of Greek and Latin learning, art and literature. Averted plot by Pazzi family (encouraged by Pope Sixtus IV) to overthrow Medici rule in Florence (1478). His son, Giovanni de' Medici, became pope as LEO X. Giulio de' Medici became pope as CLEMENT VII. Alessandro de' Medici (1510-37) was created hereditary duke of Florence after period of exile. His tyrannical rule ended in his assassination. Succeeded by Cosimo de' Medici (1519-74), who became grand duke of Tuscany. Catherine de' Medici (1519-89), consort of Henry II of France, was regent for her son Charles IX (1560-74); instigated St Bartholomew's Day massacre of French Protestants (1572). Marie de' Medici (1573-1642), was queen of Henry IV of France. Acted as regent for her son, Louis XIII, after Henry's death (1610); ultimately exiled by Louis when Richelieu became his chief minister (1630).

medicine, art and science of diagnosis, treatment, curing and prevention of disease. Hippocrates (c 400 BC) estab. rational basis of observation in medicine, rejecting superstition and magic. Galen's anatomical writings (AD 2nd cent.), preserved by Moslem physicians in Middle Ages, dominated medical thought until more accurate studies of Vesalius appeared in 16th cent.

Harvey's discovery of circulation of blood (1628) was also important. Medicine revolutionized in 19th cent. by use of antiseptics, anaesthetics and by Pasteur's findings on microbes. Advances in 20th cent. incl. use of antibiotics, inoculation with vaccine, blood transfusion, organ transplants.

Medicine Hat, indust. town of SE Alberta, Canada; on S Saskatchewan R. Pop. 27,000. In natural gas, coal mining, farming region.

Medina, city of Hejaz region, W Saudi Arabia. Pop. 80,000. Mosque contains Mohammed's tomb, pilgrimage centre. Mohammed fled here from Mecca in 622.

Mediterranean Sea (anc. *Mare Internum*), inland sea bounded by S Europe (N), W Asia (E), and N Africa (S). Area *c* 2,512,300 sq km (970,000 sq mi). Linked to Atlantic by Str. of Gibraltar; to Black Sea by Dardanelles; to Red Sea by Suez Canal. Main isls. Balearics, Corsica, Sardinia, Sicily, Crete, Cyprus. Focus of ancient and classical civilizations. Declined from 15th cent. until Suez Canal opened (1869). Strategic, commerical importance; tourism.

medium, see SPIRITUALISM.

medlar, *Mespilus germanica,* deciduous, sometimes thorny tree of rose family, native to Europe and Asia. Small, apple-shaped fruit eaten when partly decayed.

Médoc, region of SW France, between Bay of Biscay and Gironde. Famous vineyards, *eg* Château Latour, Château Margaux.

Medusa, see GORGONS.

medusa, free-swimming generation of coelenterates, resembling bell or umbrella. Usually produced asexually by budding of polyps, itself reproducing sexually to form polyps. In class Scyphozoa, incl. common jellyfish, medusa stage is dominant.

Medway, river of SE England, flows 113 km (70 mi) from Surrey, Sussex through Kent to Thames estuary. Medway conurbation incl. Chatham, Gillingham, Rochester. Dutch fleet destroyed much shipping here (1667).

meerkat, see MONGOOSE.

meerschaum, soft, white clay-like mineral, consisting of hydrous magnesium silicate. Absorbent, heat-resistant; used for tobacco pipes, cigar-holders, *etc.* Major source in Asia Minor. Also called sepiolite.

megalithic, form of building using large stones, common in tomb construction in Neolithic and early Bronze Age periods. Megalithic structures incl. menhirs and stone circles, *eg* those at Avebury and Stonehenge.

Mehemet Ali, see MOHAMMED ALI.

Meighen, Arthur (1874-1960), Canadian statesman, PM (1920-1, 1926) as leader of Conservative Party.

meiosis, in biology, method of nuclear division in formation of gametes (sex cells) in animals and spores of most plants, by which number of chromosomes is reduced by half. Usually consists of 2 successive divisions, each resembling MITOSIS.

Meir, Golda (1898-1978), Israeli political leader, b. Russia. Settled in Palestine (1921) having previously emigrated to US. Premier (1969-74), she resigned in aftermath of 4th Arab-Israeli war.

Meissen, town of SE East Germany, on R. Elbe. Pop. 51,000. From 1710 'Dresden' china made here, from local kaolin. Castle (15th cent.).

Meistersinger (Master singers), members of German guild of poets or musicians (14th-16th cents.). Drawn from craftsmen and traders, they aimed to preserve traditions of medieval MINNESINGER.

Meknès, city of N Morocco. Pop. 245,000. Trade centre in agric. region; carpets, leather goods, pottery mfg. Former cap. of Morocco, has famous 17th cent. palace.

Mekong, river of SE Asia. Rises in SC China (Tsinghai prov.), flows c 4180 km (2600 mi) SE along Laos border into Cambodia and forms large (c 194,000 sq km/75,000 sq mi) rice-growing delta in South Vietnam.

Melanchthon, orig. Philip Schwarzerd (1497-1560), German humanist scholar. Friend and follower of Luther, explained Reformation principles in *Loci communes* (1521); wrote Augsburg Confession (1530). After Luther's death, was influenced by Calvin. Helped create German school system.

Melanesia, one of three divisions of Pacific isls., S of equator. Incl. Admiralty Isls., Bismarck Archipelago, Solomon Isls., New Hebrides, New Caledonia and Fiji. Also see MICRONESIA, POLYNESIA.

Melanesians, peoples of S and SW Pacific isls., of Australoid stock. Language is Malayo-Polynesian. Main groups are the Papuans and taller, finer featured 'true' Melanesians.

melanin, dark brown pigment found in skin, hair and other tissues.

Protects body from harmful ultra-violet solar radiation.

Melba, Dame Nellie, orig. Helen Porter Mitchell (1859-1931), Australian soprano. Went to Europe in 1886 and achieved great fame in her lyrical and coloratura roles in opera. Name survives in sweet 'peach melba' created in her honour by Escoffier.

Melbourne, William Lamb, 2nd Viscount (1779-1848), British statesman, PM (1834, 1835-41). Second Whig admin. marked by Chartist agitation, trouble in Ireland. Acted as trusted adviser to young Queen Victoria. His wife, Lady Caroline Lamb (1785-1828), is chiefly remembered for tempestuous love affair with Byron.

Melbourne, city of SE Australia, on Yarra R., cap. of Victoria. Pop. 2,498,000. Admin., commercial, indust. centre; exports (via Port Melbourne) minerals, agric. produce, wool; 3 univs. First settled 1835; cap. of Victoria from 1851, of Australia 1901-27. Site of 1956 Olympics. Mint, Victorian arts centre.

Melchites, Arabic-speaking Christians of Egypt, Israel and Syria. Members of part of Eastern Orthodox Church which reunited with Rome. Their head (under the pope) is patriarch of Antioch.

Meleager, in Greek myth, son of King Oeneus of Calydon and Althaea. Led hunt against boar sent by Artemis to ravage Calydon. Killed Althaea's brothers when they tried to steal hide. The Fates had told Althaea that Meleager would live while a certain log remained unburnt. She took revenge by burning log and he died. Was also one of Argonauts.

Melilla, Spanish enclave in N Morocco, on Mediterranean Sea. Pop. 65,000. Port, exports iron ore; fishing. Spanish from 1470; held despite many assaults incl. Rif revolt 1921-6.

melodrama, originally sensational drama with musical accompaniment. Now any play which exaggerates emotions, conflicts, at cost of psychological depth or development of characters.

melody, a sequence of notes having a distinctive musical shape. May form the tune of a song or short instrumental piece, or serve as a theme from which a longer work is developed.

melon, *Cucumis melo*, sweet juicy, edible fruit of gourd family, native to S Asia but widely cultivated in tropical and subtropical countries. Varieties incl. musk melon, honeydew and cantaloupe, a hard-shelled Mediterranean variety. *See* WATERMELON.

Melos or **Milos**, isl. of S Greece, in the Cyclades. Area 158 sq km (61 sq mi). Venus de Milo statue found here 1820.

Melrose, town of Borders region, SE Scotland, on R. Tweed. Pop. 2000. Has ruins of Cistercian abbey (1136). Scott's estate, Abbotsford, is nearby.

Melville, Herman (1819-91), American author. Known for symbolic adventure novel on whaling, *Moby Dick* (1851). Also wrote *Billy Budd* (pub. 1924), short stories, poetry.

Melville Island, isl. of Northern Territ., Australia, separated from mainland by Clarence Str. Area *c* 5700 sq km (2200 sq mi); mainly

wooded hills, mangrove swamp. Aboriginal reserve in N; lumbering, pearling, fishing.

Melville Island, W Franklin Dist., Northwest Territs., Canada; largest of Parry Isls. Area 42,500 sq km (*c* 16,400 sq mi). Separated from Victoria isl. by Viscount Melville Sound. Discovered 1819.

membrane, pliable sheetlike material; may be artificial or natural. Semi-permeable membrane forms barrier in OSMOSIS. Mucous membrane is form of animal tissue that lines internal passages and acts as connective tissue.

Memling or **Memlinc, Hans** (*c* 1430-94), Flemish painter, b. Germany. Influenced by van der Weyden, he painted pious religious subjects, lacking in dramatic intensity. Works incl. *Shrine of St Ursula* in Bruges.

memory, in psychology, term for capacity to retain and consciously recall past experience, therefore underlying all learning. Most accurate when individual is interested in subject of memory. Early childhood memories can often only be recalled in psychoanalysis, as they have been repressed.

Memphis, ancient city of N Egypt, on R. Nile. Traditionally founded by 1st pharaoh, Menes; cap. (*c* 3100-*c* 2250 BC) of united Egypt. Ruins incl. temple of Ptah, palaces, pyramids; nearby is SAKKARA.

Memphis, city of SW Tennessee, US; on Mississippi R. Pop. 624,000; state's largest city. Port, railway jct. Cotton, timber, livestock market. Settled *c* 1820, boomed as river port.

Menai Strait, channel (24 km/15 mi long) between NW Wales coast and Anglesey. Spanned by road bridge built by Telford (1826), rail bridge by Stephenson (1850).

Menander (c 342-291 BC), Greek comic poet. Known mainly through Latin adaptations of his plays by Plautus and Terence, through which they influenced modern European literature. Only complete play in existence is *Misanthrope*, discovered 1958.

Mencius, Latin form of Meng-tse (c 371-c 288 BC), Chinese scholar. Taught that man is innately compassionate and that only poor material conditions drive him to be self-seeking. Thus urged rulers to follow doctrines of Confucius to ensure the happiness of their subjects. Writings became fundamental in Chinese education.

Mencken, H[enry] L[ouis] (1880-1956), American journalist. Attacked America's complacent bourgeois mores as co-editor (with George Jean Nathan) of *Smart Set*, (1914-23) and as founder-editor of *American Mercury* (1924-33). Compiled *The American Language* (1919, often revised).

Mendel, Gregor Johann (1822-84), Austrian monk and botanist. Pioneer of modern genetics; his experiments in cross-breeding peas led to theory of organic inheritance determined by dominant and recessive traits.

Mendeleev or **Mendelejeff, Dmitri Ivanovich** (1834-1907), Russian chemist. Developed periodic classification of elements by atomic weight (now atomic number is used); predicted existence and properties of then unknown ele-

ments scandium, gallium and germanium.

mendelevium (Md), transuranic element; at. no. 101, mass no. of most stable isotope 258. First prepared (1955) by bombarding einsteinium with alpha particles.

Mendelssohn, Moses (1729-86), German scholar. Friend of Lessing. Advocated religious toleration and separation of religion and state in *Jerusalem* (1783). Translated Pentateuch and Psalms into German. His grandson, **[Jakob Ludwig] Felix Mendelssohn [-Bartholdy]** (1809-47), was a composer. Romantic in style but often classical in form, his music has great charm and lyricism. Works incl. overture to *A Midsummer Night's Dream*, oratorio *Elijah*, chamber music, violin concerto, 5 symphonies. Revived interest in Bach's music.

Menderes, Adnan (1899-1961), Turkish statesman. Premier (1950-60), overthrown after an army coup against his repressive measures and unsuccessful economic policies. Executed.

Mendès-France, Pierre (1907-), French political leader. Radical Socialist premier (1954-5), he negotiated French withdrawal from Indo-China. Defeated over N African policy. Anti-Gaullist leader during 1960s.

Mendicant Orders, name for 4 orders of RC church which subsist mainly on alms, ie Augustinian Hermits, Carmelites, Dominicans, Franciscans.

Mendip Hills, limestone range of Somerset, SW England. Extend c 37 km (23 mi), rising to 325 m (1068 ft) in Blackdown. Cheddar Gorge; caves with prehist. remains.

Mendoza, Antonio de (1490-1552), first viceroy of New Spain (Mexico) (1535-50). Introduced printing to colony (1536); encouraged education and conversion of the Indians. Promoted exploration of N Mexico. Appointed viceroy of Peru (1551).

Menelaus, in Greek myth, king of Sparta, husband of Helen. Abduction of Helen by Paris instigated Trojan War. Reconciled with Helen after fall of Troy.

Menelik II (1844-1913), emperor of Ethiopia (1889-1913). Gained throne with aid of Italy. Signed treaty with Italy which he renounced after discovering Italy claimed whole country as protect. Thwarted Italian invasion (1895-6), thus ensuring Ethiopian independence.

Menes (*fl* 3200 BC), founder of 1st dynasty of ancient Egypt. Traditionally, united Upper and Lower Egypt and founded Memphis.

Menger, Karl (1840-1921), Austrian economist. Using empirical methods, explained phenomena of distribution and price in terms of social value. Author of *Principles of Economics* (1871).

Mengs, Anton Raffael (1728-79), German painter. Leading exponent of neo-Classicism, his best-known work is ceiling painting *Parnassus* in Rome. Court painter to Charles III of Spain, he decorated the royal palaces.

Meng-tse, *see* MENCIUS.

menhir, tall upright standing stone, found singly or in groups. Famous examples found at Carnac, Brittany.

Some believed to have importance in prehist. astronomical calculations.

meningitis, inflammation of meninges, membranes surrounding brain and spinal cord. Results from infection by viruses or bacteria. Symptoms incl. fever, severe headache, muscular spasms in neck or back.

Mennonites, fundamentalist, pacifist Protestant sect. Originally Swiss, developed under influence of teachings of Anabaptist Menno Simons (c 1496-1561). Now found chiefly in Canada, US. Amish and Herrite churches are conservative branches of Mennonites.

menopause, permanent cessation of menstruation, commonly occurring between ages of 40 and 50. Results from changes in pituitary and ovarian hormones. Also called change of life or climacteric.

Menorca, *see* MINORCA, Spain.

Menshevism, *see* BOLSHEVISM.

menstruation, discharge of cells and blood from the uterus through the vaginal opening. Occurs approximately every 4 weeks when lining of uterus is shed and regenerated. Begins in puberty and ends at menopause.

mental retardation, lack since birth of certain mental functions present in normal individual. Terms idiot (mental age of 2 or less), imbecile (3 to 6), moron (7 to 9) describe severity of retardation. Caused by infection of foetus during pregnancy, birth injury, hormone disturbance, *etc.*

menthol, white crystalline solid with characteristic smell. Found in oil of peppermint; used in medicine, cosmetics.

Menton (Ital. *Mentone*), town of SE France, on Côte d'Azur. Pop. 25,000. Resort. Part of Monaco until 1848, then independent republic until ceded to France in 1860.

Menuhin, Yehudi (1916-), American violinist. Debut made at age seven. Famed for interpretations of Elgar and Beethoven concertos.

Menzaleh, *see* MANZALA, LAKE, Egypt.

Menzies, Sir Robert Gordon (1894-1978), Australian statesman. Attorney-General (1934-9); PM (1939-41, 1949-66). In 1944 initiated formation of Australian Liberal Party. Lord Warden of Cinque Ports (1965-78).

Mephistopheles, in German legend, personification of the Devil to whom FAUST sold his soul.

mercantilism, economic policy founded on principle that national wealth and power are best served by accumulating large reserves of bullion. Aim achieved by encouraging export and levying high duties on imports. Predominated during period (16th-18th cents.) of W European warfare with need to maintain armies. Supplanted during Industrial Revolution by LAISSER-FAIRE theories.

Mercator, Gerardus, Latinized form of Gerhard Kremer (1512-94), Flemish cartographer, mathematician. Developed map projection (1569) named after him: modified cylindrical, all lines of latitude and longitude being straight. Produced world atlas (3 vols., 1585-94).

Merckx, Eddy (1945-), Belgian road-race cyclist. Most successful rider ever, has won numerous one-day races and tours. Has equalled record of 4 successive wins in Tour de France.

Mercury, in Roman religion, god of commerce. Usually identified with Greek HERMES.

Mercury, planet nearest to Sun and smallest in Solar System. Mean distance from Sun 57.91×10^6 km; diameter 4840 km. Solar orbit takes 88 days; period of axial rotation 59 days. Almost no atmosphere; daytime temperatures reach c 430° C.

mercury or **quicksilver** (Hg), metallic element, only common metal liquid at room temperature; at. no. 80, at. wt. 200.59. Occurs as cinnabar (HgS); prepared by roasting ore in air. Used in thermometers, barometers and other scientific instruments and in mercury vapour light; alloys (amalgams) used in dentistry. Compounds, which are extremely poisonous, used in medicine, as detonators, *etc.*

Meredith, George (1828-1909), English author. Known for novels incl. *The Ordeal of Richard Feverel* (1859), *The Egoist* (1879). Also wrote poetry, *eg Modern Love* (1862).

merganser, diving sea duck of N hemisphere, with thin hooked beak. Species incl. common merganser or goosander, *Mergus merganser*, of Europe, North America, and red-breasted merganser, *M. serrator*.

meridian, line of LONGITUDE. All meridians converge at the poles, cutting Equator at right-angles.

Mérimée, Prosper (1803-70), French author. Known for short novels esp. *Carmen* (1845) which inspired Bizet's opera. Also wrote literary hoaxes, *eg Théâtre de Clara*

Gazul (1825) 'translated' from imaginary Spanish actress' works.

merino, breed of sheep, originally from Spain, noted for fine silky wool. Comprises 70% of Australian sheep population. Rams have wide horns.

Merionethshire, former county of NW Wales, now in Gwynedd. On Cardigan Bay, drained by R. Dee. Mainly mountainous, many lakes *eg* Bala. Livestock rearing; slate quarrying. Co. town was Dolgellau.

Merlin, see ARTHURIAN LEGEND.

merlin, *Falco columbarius,* small falcon of N hemisphere. Male slate-blue above with reddish striped underparts. Called pigeon hawk in America.

mermaid, in folklore, sea creature with head and upper body of a beautiful woman and tail of a fish. Often represented as luring sailors to their death.

Merovingians, Frankish dynasty (5th-8th cents.). First important member was CLOVIS (c 466-511), who estab. Frankish monarchy (481). Kingdom divided at his death. Childeric III, last Merovingian king, deposed (751) by PEPIN THE SHORT.

Mersey, river of NW England. Flows 113 km (70 mi) to Irish Sea. Estuary 26 km (16 mi) long, incl. ocean ports of Liverpool, Birkenhead; Ship Canal to Manchester.

Merseyside, met. county of W England. Area 652 sq km (252 sq mi); pop. 1,621,000. Created 1974, comprises Liverpool and suburbs; incl. N Wirral penin.

Merthyr Tydfil, co. bor. of Glamorgan, S Wales, on R. Taff. Pop. 55,000. Coalmining, light industs. former iron, steel centre.

Merton, bor. of S Greater London, England. Pop. 177,000. Created 1965 from residential N Surrey; incl. Wimbledon (tennis championships). Has ruined 12th cent. priory.

Merv, see MARY, town of USSR.

mesa (Span., = table), flat-topped, tableland area with steep sides. Formed by hard-capped, horizontal strata resisting denudation. Over time, erosion of sides of mesa produces a butte. Both are common in SW US.

mescal or **peyote,** *Lophophora williamsii,* species of cactus native of N Mexico and SW US. Button-like tops are source of hallucinogenic drug mescaline.

Meshed, see MASHHAD.

Mesmer, Friedrich Anton (1734-1815), German physician. Developed theory of animal magnetism (mesmerism) for curing disease. His cures of psychosomatic ailments by suggestion caused brief sensation, but were soon discredited.

Mesolithic, transitional period between Palaeolithic and Neolithic, beginning with withdrawal of ice sheets c 10,000 years ago. Nomadic hunting and collecting economy was replaced by localized, specialized methods. Lasted longest in N Europe.

mesons, group of unstable elementary particles with mass intermediate between that of electron and proton. Existence predicted by Yukawa to explain forces holding atomic nucleus together; first observed in cosmic rays (1947), several different types are now known.

Mesopotamia, region of SW Asia, between R. Tigris and R. Euphrates;

mainly in modern Iraq. Cradle of several ancient civilizations esp. at Ur, Babylon, Nineveh.

Mesozoic or Secondary era, geological era intermediate between Palaeozoic and Cenozoic eras. Duration c 160 million years. Comprises Triassic, Jurassic, Cretaceous periods. Extensive deposition of limestone and chalk; fauna incl. molluscs, ammonites, brachiopods, giant reptiles; 1st mammals and birds. Also see GEOLOGICAL TABLE.

mesquite, any of genus *Prosopis* of thorny shrubs of Leguminosae family. Native to SW US and Mexico. Roots may reach depth of 20 m/70 ft. Seed pods used as animal fodder.

Messiaen, Oliver (1908-), French composer. Works, sometimes based on bird song, Oriental percussion or Indian music, are often expressive of his religious mysticism. Works incl. *Turangalila* symphony, *Vingt Regards sur l'enfant Jésus* for piano.

Messiah (Heb.,=the anointed), in Judaism, the leader promised by God to restore the kingdom of David. Christians regard Jesus as Messiah.

Messina (anc. *Zancle*), town of NE Sicily, Italy, on Str. of Messina. Cap. of Messina prov. Pop. 262,000. Port, exports olive oil, wine, fruit; univ. (1549). Greek colony founded 8th cent. BC. Badly damaged by earthquakes 1783, 1908.

Messina, Strait of, channel between Italy and Sicily, linking Tyrrhenian and Ionian Seas. Length c 32 km (20 mi). Currents, whirlpools gave rise in ancient times to legends of Scylla and Charybdis.

metabolism, chemical processes associated with living organisms, largely controlled by enzymes. Divided into 2 parts: catabolism, breaking down of complex substances into simpler ones or waste matter, with release of energy for vital processes; anabolism, building up of complex substances from simpler material, with storage of energy.

metallurgy, science of metals, incl. their extraction from ores and purification, formation of alloys, and study of their properties and behaviour.

metamorphic rocks, igneous or sedimentary rocks transformed in character and appearance by any of the processes of METAMORPHISM. Examples incl. granite into gneiss, limestone into marble, shale into slate.

metamorphism, in geology, processes causing change in character and appearance of rocks in Earth's crust. Caused by heat, pressure, or chemically active fluids. Commonest types of metamorphism are thermal (heat only), dynamic (pressure only), regional (heat and pressure, always associated with mountain-building).

metamorphosis, period of transformation of animal from larval to adult form. Insects placed in 2 divisions according to type of metamorphosis: Endopterygota, those undergoing complete metamorphosis with pupal stage, and Exopterygota, without pupal stage. See NYMPH.

metaphor, figure of speech in which word or phrase ordinarily denoting one thing is made to stand for another, *eg* 'My love is a red, red rose', whereas **simile** states the comparison explicitly by using 'like' or 'as', *eg* 'My love is like a red, red rose'.

metaphysical poetry, term first applied by Dr Johnson to early 17th cent. English verse genre, marked by complexity, compression, use of puns, paradox, unusual imagery and syntax. Poets incl. John DONNE, Richard CRASHAW, George HERBERT, Andrew MARVELL.

metaphysics, branch of philosophy which deals with first principles and seeks to explain the nature of being (ontology). Epistemology (the study of the nature of knowledge) is a major part of most metaphysical systems. The foundations were laid by Plato, Aristotle, with one of the most complete structures being estab. by St-Thomas Aquinas. Since Comte many have regarded metaphysical problems as insoluble. *See* POSITIVISM, LOGICAL POSITIVISM.

Metaxas, Joannis (1871-1941), Greek army officer, statesman. Active in restoration of monarchy (1935), he was premier from 1936; exercised dictatorial powers. Led successful resistance against Italian invasion (1940).

metempsychosis, *see* REINCARNATION.

meteor, small body which enters Earth's atmosphere from outer space; becomes incandescent (shooting star) through friction with air, leaving bright streak as it passes. Most are consumed but some, called meteorites, consisting of metal or stone, reach Earth's surface.

Meteor Crater, hole *c* 1280 m (4200 ft) wide and 180 m (600 ft) deep, in Arizona, US; formed by meteorite impact.

meteorology, study of phenomena in all levels of atmosphere. Incl. WEATHER, one branch of meteorology confined to lower levels. Earliest work is Aristotle's *Meteorologica* (*c* 340 BC); later inventions *eg* thermometer, barometer increased accuracy of observations. Advances incl. V. and J. Bjerknes' polar front theory (1917), and use of satellites.

methane (CH_4), colourless inflammable gas, 1st hydrocarbon of paraffin series. Given off by decaying vegetable matter (marsh gas); found in coal mines (firedamp). Occurs in natural gas and coal gas.

methanol or **methyl alcohol** (CH_3OH), colourless liquid, originally obtained by destructive distillation of wood. Used as a solvent, in organic synthesis; as it is poisonous, used to denature ethyl alcohol.

Methodism, Protestant religious denomination. Originated as part of Church of England revival (*c* 1729) led by John WESLEY. Doctrines, influenced by those of ARMINIUS, stress repentance, salvation for all and thus evangelism and lay preaching. Separated from Church of England (1791); now has *c* 13 million followers, mainly in UK and US.

Methodius, St, *see* CYRIL, ST.

Methuselah, in OT, an antediluvian patriarch credited with having lived 969 years.

metre, SI unit of length; 1 metre = *c* 39.37 in., 1000 metres = 1 kilometre = *c* 0.62 miles.

metric system, decimal system of weights and measures in which kilogram, metre and litre are basic units of weight, length and liquid capacity, respectively. Devised in France during revolutionary period (1791-5).

metronome, mechanism used to indicate the exact pace of music, indicated in beats per minute. Consists of a pendulum driven by clockwork and carrying a sliding weight that is set to the required pace. Electronic metronomes also exist.

Metropolitan Museum of Art, civic museum of New York. Founded 1870, it is supported by private endowment and membership fees. Contains European and American paintings and sculpture, also Greek, Egyptian, Oriental and medieval works of art.

Metropolitan Opera House, principal American opera house, in New York City. Opened in 1883 and rehoused in Lincoln Center in 1966.

Metsu, Gabriel (1629-67), Dutch painter. Specialized in interiors and genre scenes, depicting middle-class life. Works incl. *Mother and Sick Child.*

Metternich [-Winneburg], Clemens Wenzel Lothar, Fürst von (1773-1859), Austrian statesman, b. Germany. Foreign minister (1809-48), negotiated Napoleon's marriage to Marie Louise of Austria (1810); kept Austria out of Franco-Russian war (1812-13). Later formed alliance with Prussia and Russia against France. Chief figure at Congress of VIENNA (1814-15); advocated maintenance of 'balance of power' in Europe. Repressive measures within Austria led to

enforced abdication during Revolution of 1848.

Metz, city of NE France, on R. Moselle, cap. of Moselle dept. Pop. 108,000. Centre of Lorraine iron mining; metals, textiles industs. Important city of Roman Gaul; powerful medieval bishopric. Annexed by France in 1552; part of Germany (1871-1918). Gothic cathedral (13th cent.).

Meuse (Flem. *Maas*), river of NE France, S Belgium, and Netherlands. Flows 933 km (580 mi) from Langres Plateau via Namur, Liège, Maastricht to join Rhine delta. Heavy traffic on lower course.

Mexicali, town of NW Mexico, cap. of Baja California state; on US border. Pop. 390,000. Commercial centre in agric. region producing cotton, dates, alfalfa, wine. Border resort.

Mexican War, conflict (1846-8) between US and Mexico. Immediate cause was annexation of Texas by US (1845); war declared when Mexico declined to negotiate over border dispute and American claims in California. Taylor defeated Mexicans under Santa Anna at Buena Vista (1847). Mexico City captured by Scott after march from Veracruz. Settlement reached under Treaty of GUADALUPE HIDALGO.

Mexico (Span. *Mejico*), federal republic of SW North America. Area 1,972,544 sq km (761,600 sq mi); pop. 62,329,000; cap. Mexico City. Languages: Spanish, Indian dialects. Religion: RC. Pacific and Gulf of Mexico coastlines rise to high C plateau dominated by Sierra Madre range. Varied climate. Limited agric. concentrated in irrigated region

(many of foodstuffs imported).
Mineral wealth incl. silver, lead,
iron, coal; tourism. Had ancient
Maya, Toltec, Aztec civilizations;
Spanish conquest (1519) under
Cortés. Independence struggle
(1810-21); in Texas revolt (1836) and
war with US (1846-8), Mexico ceded
all land N of Rio Grande to US.
Revolution (1910); civil war estab.
new constitution (1917).

Mexico, Gulf of, extensive arm of
Atlantic, bounded by US, Mexico.
Connected to Atlantic by Str. of
Florida, and to Caribbean by
Yucatán Channel. Receives Mis-
sissippi, Grande rivers.

Mexico City, cap. of Mexico and
Federal Dist.; on C plateau, alt. 2380
m (c 7800 ft). Pop. 3,026,000.
Transport, financial, cultural,
indust. centre. Textile, glass mfg.;
automobile indust.; gold, silver
refining. Built on site of ancient
Aztec cap. Tenochtitlán (1521). Has
Central Plaza, Palace, National
Univ. (1551), cathedral (1573);
famous bull ring. Nearby shrine of
Our Lady at Guadalupe Hidalgo is
pilgrimage centre; also ancient site
of Teotihuacán, with famous pyramids and temples. Held Olympic
Games in 1968.

Miami, city of SE Florida, US; on
Biscayne Bay. Pop. 335,000. Famous
tourist and holiday resort. Suburbs
incl. Coral Gables, Miami Beach.
Has international airport. Grew with
1920s land boom.

mica, group of minerals consisting
of silicates of aluminium and
potassium. Crystallize into thin
plates; flexible and heat resistant.
Types incl. muscovite (colourless),

phlogopite (yellow to brown); used
in insulators, paints, tiles.

Micah, prophetic book of OT,
attributed to prophet Micah (8th
cent. BC). Denounces social injustice and hypocrisy but foretells
Messianic deliverance.

Michael (1596-1645), tsar of Russia,
founder of Romanov dynasty. Election as tsar (1613) ended confusion
in finding successor to Boris
Godunov caused by series of
usurpers (false Dmitris).

Michael I (1921-), king of Romania (1927-30, 1940-7). Ruled
(1927-30) under regency until replaced by his father, Carol II. When
Carol abdicated, regained throne.
Overthrew dictatorship of Atonescu
(1944) and concluded armistice with
Allies. Abdicated in favour of
Communist republic (1947).

Michael, archangel in Jewish, Christian and Islamic tradition, guardian
of Israel. His feast (Michaelmas) is
celebrated on 29th September.

Michaelmas daisy, see ASTER.

Michaelangelo (Buonarroti)
(1475-1564), Italian artist, architect
and poet, a major figure of the
Renaissance. First great sculptures
incl. *Pietà* (St Peter's, Rome), *David*
(Florence). His tomb of Pope Julius
II was much delayed and a greatly
reduced version was substituted;
only colossal *Moses* was completed.
Painted fresco cycle on Old Testament themes (1508-12) and *Last
Judgment* (1536-41) in Sistine
Chapel, Rome. Also did frescoes
Conversion of St Paul and *Crucifixion of St Peter* for Pauline
Chapel in the Vatican, and designed
sepulchral chapel of Medici in

Florence. Architect of St Peter's from 1546.

Michelozzo di Bartolommeo (1396-1472), Italian architect, sculptor. One of the founders of the Renaissance architectural style; built Medici-Riccardi palace for Cosimo de' Medici in Florence. Worked with Donatello and Ghiberti.

Michigan, state of NC US. Area 150,779 sq km (58,216 sq mi); pop. 8,875,000; cap. Lansing; chief city Detroit. Upper and Lower penins. separated by L. Michigan. Agric., dairying and livestock raising, lumbering in S; iron ore, copper, peat, bromine exploitation in N. Leading motor vehicles mfg., machinery, heavy industs. French settlement in 17th cent.; ceded to British 1763; passed to US 1783; became separate territ. 1805. Admitted to Union as 26th state (1837).

Michigan, Lake, third largest of Great Lakes, entirely within NC US. Area 57,441 sq km (22,178 sq mi). Chief ports Chicago, Milwaukee. Main cargoes incl. coal, grain, iron ore.

microbe, microscopic organism, esp. any of the bacteria which cause disease.

microfilm, film on which documents, printed pages, *etc*, are photographed in a reduced size for convenience in storage. Enlarged prints may be made or film may be projected on ground glass screen in special viewer. A microfiche is a sheet of microfilm (10 cm × 15 cm) on which several pages may be recorded.

micrometer, scientific instrument for making very accurate measurement of distances and angles.

Micronesia, one of three divisions of Pacific isls., N of equator. Incl. Caroline, Mariana, Marshall and Gilbert isls. and Nauru. Also *see* MELANESIA, POLYNESIA.

Micronesians, peoples of Pacific isls. N of Melanesia. Of Australoid stock, language is Malayo-Polynesian.

microphone, device for converting sound waves into an electrical signal. Type used in telephone consists of diaphragm in close contact with loosely packed carbon grains; sound waves cause diaphragm to vibrate and compress grains. Motion of grains causes variation in current flow through associated electric circuit.

microprocessor, in electronics, a single CHIP or complex of chips assembled to perform specific functions; used esp. as central processing unit in calculators and computers. Has led to increased automation.

microscope, optical instrument used to obtain enlarged images of small objects. Simple microscope uses single convex lens to produce virtual image; compound microscope uses 2 convex lenses (objective and eyepiece) mounted at opposite ends of tube. See ELECTRON MICROSCOPE.

microwave heating, form of high-frequency radiation which may be used in very high speed cooking. Heat is immediately generated throughout an object rather than passing in from surface by conduction. Also used in pasteurization, insect destruction.

microwaves, electromagnetic radiation with wavelength between 1 mm and 30 cm. Ranges from short radio waves almost to infrared rays.

Midas, in Greek myth, king of Phrygia. Dionysus gave him power of turning everything he touched to gold. Begged relief of this power when even his food turned to gold. In another legend, given ass's ears as punishment for preferring Pan's music to Apollo's.

Middle Ages, period in W European history considered to have begun with fall of Roman Empire (5th cent.) and ended with early Renaissance in 15th cent. Period marked by unity of W Europe within RC church and prevalence of feudal system.

Middle English, see ENGLISH.

Middlesbrough, co. town of Cleveland, NE England. Port; iron, steel indust.; chemicals mfg. From 1968 part of co. bor. of TEESSIDE.

Middlesex, former county of SE England. Mainly absorbed by Greater London 1965, small parts joined to Surrey, Hertfordshire.

Middle Temple, see INNS OF COURT.

Middleton, Thomas (1580-1627), English dramatist. Works incl. comedies, eg *The Roaring Girl* (1611, with Dekker), tragedies, eg *The Changeling* (c 1623, with T. Rowley), *Women Beware Women* (c 1625).

Midgard, in Norse myth, region between the lands of dwarfs and giants. Incl. Mannheim, the world of men. Said to be encircled by the serpent Jormungard.

midge, small 2-winged insect of Ceratopogonidae family with sucking mouthparts. Some species bloodsuckers, eg *Culicoides impunctatus.*

Mid Glamorgan, see GLAMORGAN, Wales.

Midlands, term used for central counties of England, incl. Derby, Nottingham, Leicester, Northampton, Warwick, Stafford.

Midlothian, former county of E Scotland, now in Lothian region. Previously called Edinburghshire. Moorfoot Hills (SE), Pentland Hills (SW); low-lying in N. Chief city Edinburgh. Sheep, dairy farming; market gardening; coalmining; fishing.

midnight sun, feature of high latitude regions where, during midsummer period, Sun remains visible above horizon throughout 24 hours. Caused by tilting of Earth's axis.

Midrash, collection of rabbinical commentaries and explanatory notes on the Scriptures. Compiled between c 400 BC and c AD 1200.

midsummer, the summer solstice, ie in N hemisphere c 21 June. Midsummer day is 24 June, feast of St John the Baptist. Night before has been occasion for solar ceremonies since ancient times, with vestiges (eg bonfires, merrymaking, association with love, lovers) remaining in Europe to present day.

Midway Islands, two isls. of NC Pacific Ocean, admin. by US Dept. of Interior. Area 5 sq km (2 sq mi); pop. 2,000; comprise Eastern, Sand Isls. Discovered by US (1859), annexed (1867). Naval air base estab. 1941; site of US victory (1942) over Japan.

Midwest or Middle West, C region of US. Incl. prairie states of Illinois, Indiana, Ohio, Iowa, Kansas, Nebraska, Minnesota, Wisconsin, North and South Dakota, and E Montana. Mainly agric. esp. grain production. Large indust. cities concentrated in Great Lakes area.

midwife toad, *Alytes obstetricans,* small dark European toad. After female spawns, male twists strands of eggs round his hind legs, carrying them until tadpoles hatch.

Mies van der Rohe, Ludwig (1886-1969), German architect. Produced designs for all-glass skyscrapers (1921); his German pavilion for 1929 Barcelona exhibition was influential example of pure geometric architecture. Director of Bauhaus (1930-3), later worked in US. Designed Seagram Building, New York.

mignonette, any of genus *Reseda* of annual or perennial herbs native to Mediterranean and E Africa. Garden variety *R. odorata* has small spikes of fragrant, whitish flowers.

migraine, extremely severe prolonged headache, often affecting only one side of head. May be accompanied by nausea and disturbed vision. Believed to be caused by excessive expansion and contraction of blood vessels of brain.

migration, movement of animals from one place to another for breeding or finding new food supplies. Some animals, *eg* lemmings, undertake spontaneous migrations resulting from overpopulation. Certain birds and fish migrate seasonally.

Mikoyan, Anastas Ivanovich (1895-1978), Soviet political leader. Supported Khrushchev in power struggle after Stalin's death. Deputy premier (1955-7, 1958-64), president (1964-5). Retired from public office 1974.

Milan (*Milano*), city of N Italy, cap. of Lombardy and of Milan prov. Pop. 1,725,000. Indust., commercial cen-

tre, major railway jct., agric. market. Roman *Mediolanum;* member of Lombard League (12th cent.), later medieval duchy under Visconti and Sforza families. Under Habsburgs 1713-1861, passed to Sardinia. Cathedral (1386), La Scala opera house (1778), many art galleries. Badly damaged in WWII.

mildew, any fungus, esp. of families Peronosporaceae and Erysiphaceae that attacks various plants or appears on organic matter, *eg* leather, fabrics, *etc,* when exposed to damp. Characterized by whitish, powdery coating on surface.

mile, unit of linear measure, equal to 1760 yds or 1.609 km.

Miletus, ancient port of Asia Minor, in W Turkey on R. Menderes (Maeander). Most important of 12 Ionian Cities; major trade city and centre of learning. Led revolt against Persia (499 BC). Prosperity declined when harbour silted up in early Christian times.

milfoil, see YARROW.

Milford Haven, Louis Alexander, 1st Marquess of, orig. Prince Louis of Battenberg (1854-1921), British naval officer, b. Germany. Director of naval intelligence (1902); 1st sea lord (1912). Resigned at outset of war because of anti-German public feeling.

Milford Haven, urban dist. of Dyfed, SW Wales. Pop. 14,000. Fishing port; oil importing and refining.

Milhaud, Darius (1892-1974), French composer. Member of 'les Six' group. Numerous works, often lighthearted in style, were variously influenced by jazz, Latin American rhythms, *etc.* Compositions incl.

ballet *La Création du monde*, Scaramouche for 2 pianos.

militia, an organized military force of civilians called upon in national emergency. Known in Europe before formation of regular armies; again raised in Britain when Napoleonic invasions threatened, it later merged with the TERRITORIAL ARMY; in US it merged with the NATIONAL GUARD.

milk, fluid secreted by mammary glands of female mammals for nourishment of young. Almost a complete food, containing fat, carbohydrates, lactose sugar, vitamins A, B, D. Source of calcium and phosphorus.

milkwort, any of genus *Polygala* of herbs native to Europe and North America. Common European milkwort, *P. vulgaris*, with small blue flowers was supposed to increase milk production of cows. American milkwort, *P. senega*, was reputed cure for snakebite.

Milky Way, belt of faint stars encircling the heavens, seen as an arch across sky at night. Now known to be a galaxy containing *c* 10^{11} stars, incl. the Sun.

Mill, James (1773-1836), English philosopher. An associate of Bentham, and advocate of UTILITARIANISM. Also wrote *History of India* (1817). His son, **John Stuart Mill** (1806-73), was also a philosopher. Introduced more humanitarian ideas into utilitarian theory, favouring democracy and social reform. Emphasized importance of quality, as well as quantity, of pleasure as motivating force in life. Works incl. *Essay on Liberty* (1859), *Utilitarianism* (1863), *Autobiography* (1873).

Millais, Sir John Everett (1829-96), English painter. Founder member of the Pre-Raphaelite Brotherhood with Hunt and Rossetti; early work was richly coloured and detailed. Later painted trivial genre scenes and fashionable portraits. Works incl. *Christ in the House of his Parents.*

Miller, Arthur (1915-), American playwright. Known for committedly liberal plays, eg *Death of a Salesman* (1947), *The Crucible* (1953) using 17th cent. Salem witch hunt as metaphor for McCarthy investigations, *The Price* (1968). Also autobiog. *After the Fall* (1964), perhaps portraying second wife, Marilyn Monroe.

Miller, Henry (1891-), American author. Many works mainly fictionalized autobiog. incl. *Tropic of Cancer* (1934), *Nexus* (1960). Also many essays on literature, painting.

miller's thumb, see BULLHEAD.

Millet, Jean François (1814-75), French painter. Worked at Barbizon after 1849, where he specialized in painting peasant life and rustic scenes. Works incl. *The Gleaners* (1857) and *The Angelus* (1859).

millet, name for several cereal and forage grasses, eg common millet, *Panicum miliaceum*, grown in Asia, N Africa and S Europe as food crop. North American foxtail millet, *Setaria italica*, is used for fodder.

millipede, any of class Diplopoda of many-legged arthropods. Cylindrical, segmented body; herbivorous. Differs from centipede in having 2 pairs of legs on each segment and no poisonous bite.

Milne, A[lan] A[lexander] (1882-1956), English author. Known for children's books originally written for son, Christopher Robin, incl. *Winnie-the-Pooh* (1926) and verse collection, *When We Were Very Young* (1924). Also wrote plays, detective story *The Red House Mystery* (1922).

Milos, see MELOS, Greece.

Milosh [Obrenovich] (1780-1860), Serbian ruler. Led Serbian rebellion against Turks (1815-17). Prob. had his rival KARAGEORGE murdered. Assumed title of prince (1817); recognized by sultan (1830). Despotic ruler, forced to abdicate (1839) in favour of son; reinstated 1858.

Miltiades (d. 489 BC), Athenian army commander. Defeated Persians at Marathon (490 BC), then marched his troops to Athens and defended city against naval attack.

Milton, John (1608-74), English poet. Early works incl. 'L'Allegro', 'Il Penseroso', masque *Comus* (1634), pastoral elegy *Lycidas* (1637). Blind after 1652, wrote his masterpiece, blank verse epic *Paradise Lost* (1667), attempting to 'justify the ways of God to men'. Also wrote classical drama, *Samson Agonistes* (1671), prose pamphlets, eg *Areopagitica* (1644) on censorship, *Of Education* (1644). Latin secretary to Commonwealth (1649-60).

Milton Keynes, area of Buckinghamshire, SC England, designated new town. Present pop. 46,000; planned 250,000. Site of Open University.

Milwaukee, port of SE Wisconsin, US; on L. Michigan. Pop. 717,000; state's largest city. Shipping centre; important brewing, meat packing industs.; heavy machinery, electrical equipment mfg. Trade post estab.

1795; grew after German refugee influx (1848).

mimicry, in zoology, protective resemblance of one species to another. In Batesian mimicry, harmless animal resembles poisonous or dangerous animal and thus gains protection from predators; in Müllerian mimicry, 2 harmful or distasteful species resemble each other and each gains protection from other's predators.

mimosa, genus of trees, shrubs and herbs of Leguminosae family, mostly native to tropical and subtropical America. Several species respond to light and touch, eg *Mimosa pudica*, the sensitive plant. Related species incl. ACACIA of Africa and Australia.

minaret, slender tower attached to corner of Islamic mosque from which muezzin calls the faithful to prayer 5 times a day. Oldest minarets were 4 Greek watchtowers at corners of ancient temple which became Great Mosque at Damascus.

Minch, channel off NW Scotland, separating Outer Hebrides from mainland. Little Minch to S separates Inner and Outer Hebrides.

mind, presumed seat of consciousness. In philosophy, the concept has been interpreted in various ways. Materialists explaining it in terms of matter, dualists holding that the mind exists independently alongside matter, idealists that the mind is the only reality and apparent matter the creation of the imagination.

Mindanao, isl. of S Philippines. Area *c* 94,600 sq km (36,500 sq mi). Mountainous, rising to 2954 m (9690 ft) at Mt. Apo; heavily forested. Produces pineapples, hemp, rice, coffee; gold mined. Underwent rapid population growth in 1960s; scene of fighting against terrorists belonging to large Moslem minority in 1970s.

Mindoro, isl. of Philippines, S of Luzon. Area 9740 sq km (3760 sq mi). Mountainous, with little arable land. Timber produced.

Mindszenty, Jozsef (1892-1975), Hungarian churchman. Primate of Hungary (1945-74); arrested (1948), sentenced to life imprisonment for opposing Communist rule. Released during 1956 rising; took refuge in US legation, Budapest, after rising suppressed. Moved to Rome (1971). Removed from primacy (1974).

mine, originally explosive-filled tunnel dug under an enemy position, used in static situations as in WWI. Later, took form of buried canister, detonated by pressure or remote control, laid in systematic patterns as defence against armoured fighting vehicles. Anti-personnel version scatters shrapnel. Naval mine is larger container of explosive detonated by contact, magnetically or by remote control.

mineral, naturally occurring inorganic solid of homogeneous structure and definite composition expressible as a chemical formula. ROCKS are usually a mixture of minerals.

mineralogy, branch of geology dealing with the study of minerals. Early works incl. Theophrastus' *On Stones* (c 315 BC), Pliny's *Natural History* (c AD 77); advances in classification made by Agricola (16th cent.). Emphasis in 19th-20th cent. on chemical composition and crystallographic features.

mineral water, water naturally impregnated with metallic salts or gases, often held to have medicinal value. Sulphates, phosphates, carbonates of such metals as iron, magnesium, sodium, barium, or gases such as carbon dioxide or hydrogen sulphide, occur in mineral waters. Famous spas incl. Bath, Vichy, Aachen.

Minerva, in Roman religion, goddess of arts, craftsmen and wisdom. Identified with Greek ATHENA. Worshipped with Jupiter and Juno.

Ming, Chinese dynasty (1368-1644), founded by Chu Yuan-chang. Empire extended from Korea to Burma at its height. First contacts with Europeans, esp. missionaries, began in Ming period. Noted for literary excellence, fine porcelain. Supplanted by Manchu dynasty.

miniature, very small painting, usually a portrait, executed in gouache or watercolour. Early miniatures on card or vellum developed from medieval manuscript illumination; form fl in 16th and 17th cent. in hands of such practitioners as Holbein, Hilliard and Cooper.

mining, process of extracting metallic ores and minerals from Earth's crust. When mineral deposits lie near surface, opencast (open cut) and strip mining are used. Subterranean system of shafts and galleries is used to extract minerals which lie deeper.

mink, semi-aquatic carnivore of weasel family, genus *Mustela*. Species incl. European mink, *M. lutreola* and larger North American, *M. vison*, bred for its soft, thick fur.

Minneapolis, city of E Minnesota, US; contiguous with St Paul ('Twin Cities'), on Mississippi R. Pop.

432,000, state's largest city. Financial, commercial, indust. centre of agric. region; processes grain and dairy produce, clothing mfg. Seat of Univ. of Minnesota (1851).

Minnesinger, poet and musician of Germany in 12th-13th cents. who sang of courtly love; incl. Walther von der Vogelweide, Wolfram von Eschenbach. Corresponded to TROUBADOURS. See MEISTERSINGER.

Minnesota, state of N US. Area 217,736 sq km (84,068 sq mi); pop. 3,805,000; cap. St Paul; largest city Minneapolis. N borders with Canada; prairies in S (grain, dairy farming esp. butter production); iron ore, granite mining in Mesabi Range. Drained by Hudson, St Lawrence, Mississippi river systems. Region ceded to British by French (1763); obtained by US from British (1783) and French (1803). Admitted to Union as 32nd state (1858).

minnow, Phoxinus phoxinus, smallest fish of carp family, common in European fresh. water. Males brightly coloured at spawning time.

Minoan civilization, Bronze Age civilization of Crete revealed by excavations of ARTHUR EVANS. During Middle Minoan period (c 2000-1600 BC), great palaces were built at Knossos, Phaistos, Mallia, urbanization began and metalworking reached high point. Two pictographic scripts, Linear A and later Linear B (deciphered 1952), were used. Destruction of Knossos c 1400 BC marks decline of civilization and growth of Mycenaean power.

Minorca (Menorca), second largest of Balearic Isls., Spain. Area 702 sq km (271 sq mi); main town and port

Mahón. Mainly low-lying. Tourism, cereals, fruit growing, livestock.

Minos, in Greek myth, king of Crete, son of Zeus and Europa. Had Labyrinth built to house the monstrous Minotaur (man with bull's head), offspring of wife Pasiphaë by a bull. Minotaur was slain by THESEUS. Minos became a judge in Hades after his death.

Minotaur, see MINOS.

Minsk, city of USSR, cap. of Byelorussian SSR. Pop. 996,000. Indust. and cultural centre; tractor, automobile, textile mfg. Passed from Poland to Russia (1793). Large Jewish community (40% of pop.) decimated during German occupation (1941-4).

mint, any of genus Mentha of aromatic herbs native to Mediterranean area but now widespread. Species incl. garden mint, M. rotundifolia, used for sauces; peppermint, M. piperita, used in confectionery and medicines and spearmint, M. spicata, used in chewing gum and sauces.

Minton, Thomas (1765-1836), English potter. Estab. small pottery at Stoke-on-Trent (1789). Created celebrated Willow Pattern ware and produced good bone china. His son, Herbert Minton (1793-1858), developed pottery, estab. reputation of company.

minuet, French dance in triple time. Originally rustic, became fashionable court dance in 18th cent. Used by Haydn, Mozart in sonatas.

Miocene epoch, fourth geological epoch of Tertiary period. Alpine mountain building continued; withdrawal of seas, formation of extensive plains. Mammals still dominant. Decrease in temperature continued from Oligocene. Also *see* GEOLOGICAL TABLE.

Miquelon, *see* ST PIERRE AND MIQUELON.

Mirabeau, Honoré Gabriel Riqueti, Comte de (1749-91), French statesman. A leader in National Assembly (1789), he sought to create constitutional monarchy on lines of British one. Aimed to become chief minister of the king and began to advise him in secret. This role was not discovered until after his death.

miracle, event which apparently transcends laws of nature and is thus thought to be due to supernatural intervention, esp. that of God. Concept only occurs where natural laws and divine will have been clearly distinguished, *eg* in the 3 major monotheistic religions. Many miracles of Jesus recorded in Gospels. In RC church, attestation of miracles required in process of canonization.

miracle play or mystery play, medieval religious drama. Began as simple dramatization of religious stories, later presented with contemporary social realism, humour. Developed into full cycles, performed on feast-days by town guilds on movable wagons. French, German, English works extant.

mirage, optical illusion in the atmosphere. Caused by refraction and reflection of light rays in layers of air of different temperature and density. Occurs most often in deserts, polar seas.

Mirandola, *see* PICO DELLA MIRANDOLA.

Miró, Joan (1893-), Spanish painter. Joined surrealist group in 1925; work has become more abstract and is noted for its use of amoeba-like shapes and bright colours. Executed murals in UNESCO building, Paris.

miscarriage, in medicine, *see* ABORTION.

misdemeanour, minor crime, distinguished from FELONY. In UK, distinction no longer maintained. In US, penalty is summary fine and imprisonment for less than year.

Mishima, Yukio, pseud. of Kimitake Hiraoka (1925-70), Japanese author. Works, *eg Confessions of a Mask* (1949), *Sound of Waves* (1954), *The Sailor Who Fell from Grace with the Sea* (1963) celebrate the beauty and violence of traditional Japanese life. Committed ritual suicide after haranguing a demonstration.

Mishnah, *see* TALMUD.

Miskolc, city of NE Hungary, on R. Sajó. Pop. 186,000. Iron, steel indust., railway engineering. Cattle, wine, tobacco market. Medieval church, buildings. Univ. (1949).

missile, *see* GUIDED MISSILE.

missions, organizations with aim of spreading religious knowledge. Early dissemination of Christianity undertaken by missionaries, *eg* St Paul; in early Middle Ages by St Patrick, St Augustine, St Boniface. Further wave of activity (esp. by Jesuits) with opening up of New World. Protestant missions incl. Society for Promoting Christian Knowledge (1698), Baptist Missionary Society (1792). Since 19th cent., missions have emphasized medical care and education.

Mississippi, state of SE US. Area

123,584 sq km (47,716 sq mi); pop. 2,217,000; cap. Jackson; other major town Meridian. W border formed by Mississippi R.; mainly on Gulf of Mexico coastal plain. Cotton, soya beans, poultry, livestock farming. Some oil resources, fishing, lumbering. Taken by British from French (1763); gained by US after Revolution. Admitted to Union as 20th state (1817).

Mississippi, river of C US. Rises in N Minnesota, flows S 3780 km (c 2350 mi) forming many natural state boundaries. Enters Gulf of Mexico forming delta in SE Louisiana. Tributaries incl. Ohio, Missouri, Arkansas rivers; main ports St Louis, New Orleans. Region explored by French in 17th cent.; US control after Louisiana Purchase 1803; important in 19th cent. W expansion.

Mississippian period, earlier of 2 subdivisions of Carboniferous period in North America. Began c 345 million years ago, lasted 20 million years. Time of large shallow seas, deposition of limestones. sandstones, shales. Typified by brachiopods, crinoids, corals; increasing amphibians, fish, insects; mosses, ferns. See GEOLOGICAL TABLE.

Missolonghi (*Mesolóngion*), town of WC Greece, on Gulf of Patras. Pop. 11,000. Fish, tobacco trade. Greek stronghold in independence struggle against Turks (1822-6), Byron died here (1824).

Missouri, state of C US, on W bank of Mississippi R. Area 180,487 sq km (69,686 sq mi); pop. 4,677,000; cap. Jefferson City; other major city St Louis. Mainly rolling prairie, crossed by Missouri R. Livestock, grain,

dairy farming; lead, barytes mining. Explored by French in 17th cent.; bought by US as part of Louisiana Purchase (1803). Admitted to Union as 24th state (1821). Slave state, remained in Union in Civil War.

Missouri, river of WC US; longest in North America. Rises in SW Montana (Rocky Mts.); flows E 4130 km (c 2565 mi), then SE across C plains through North and South Dakota, Missouri to join Mississippi near St Louis. Hist. fur trade route until railway boom. Provides h.e.p., irrigation.

Missouri Compromise, legislation (1820-1) passed by US Congress, providing for Missouri's entry into Union as a slave state but prohibiting slavery in rest of Louisiana Purchase N of Missouri's S boundary. See KANSAS-NEBRASKA BILL.

mistletoe, *Viscum album,* European evergreen plant. Parasitic on trees, has yellowish flowers and white, poisonous berries. Traditional Christmas decoration. Name also used for similar and related plants of genera *Phoradendron* of North America and *Loranthus* of Africa.

mistral, cold, dry, often strong N or NW wind which blows in S France, esp. Rhône valley and delta, in winter.

Mitchell, John Newton (1913-), American govt. official. Attorney-general (1969-72). Headed committee to re-elect Nixon (1972). Involvement in 'Watergate affair' led to conviction (1975) for conspiracy and obstruction of justice.

Mitchell, Margaret (1900-49), American novelist. Known for only book, best-selling romantic novel about Georgia during Civil War, *Gone with the Wind* (1936); made into one of most successful films ever (1939).

mite, tiny arachnid of order Acarina, with 4 pairs of legs and rounded body. Often parasitic on animals or destructive of food. Species incl. itch mite, *Sarcoptes scabiei*, which lays eggs under skin surface, causing scabies.

Mitford, Nancy Freeman (1904-73), Known for ironic, satirical novels of upper-class manners, eg *The Pursuit of Love* (1945). With Professor Alan Ross edited comic study of social distinctions, *Noblesse Oblige* (1956), coining terms 'U', 'non-U'. Her sister, *Jessica Mitford* (1917-), wrote autobiog. *Hons and Rebels* (1960), *The American Way of Death* (1963).

Mithra, originally, in ancient Zoroastrian myth, god of light and wisdom; by 5th cent. BC principal Persian god. Cult spread into Europe; by 2nd cent. AD major religion of Roman Empire. Mithras (Latin form) worshipped by legions as ideal comrade and soldier. Cult involved rigorous ethics and secret ritual; declined in 3rd cent.

Mithradates [VI] the Great (c 132-63 BC), king of Pontus. Expansion of his empire over Asia Minor and into Greece led to series of 3 wars with Rome (88-84, 83-81, 74-63). In last war, defeated by Lucullus and driven into Armenia. Later recovered Pontus but was defeated by Pompey (66).

mitosis, in biology, method of division of nucleus of body cells, prior to division into 2 new cells. Chromosomes are formed in nucleus and, when nuclear membrane breaks up, they migrate to equator of cell and divide lengthways. The 2 halves move to opposite ends of the cell where 2 new nuclei are assembled around them.

Mitterrand, François Maurice Marie (1916-), French politician. Head of Socialist Party from 1971. Narrowly defeated in presidential elections (1965 against De Gaulle, 1974 against Giscard d'Estaing) as candidate of Combined Left.

moa, any of Dinornithidae family of extinct flightless birds of New Zealand, hunted by Maoris c 500 years ago. Resembled ostrich, reaching heights of 3.7 m/12 ft.

Moab, ancient country of Jordan, in uplands E of Dead Sea. Moabite stone is 9th cent. BC record, in language similar to Biblical Hebrew, of successful revolt against Israel. Discovered 1868, now in Louvre.

Mobile, seaport of SW Alabama, US, on Mobile Bay. Pop. 190,000. Shipbuilding indust.; exports cotton, timber. Founded by French (1710). Seized from Spanish by US (1813).

mobile, form of moving abstract sculpture invented by Alexander Calder (1932). Consists of series of thin metal or wood shapes connected by wire or rods, and set in motion by air currents.

Mobutu, Joseph Désiré (1930-), Zairian army officer, politician. Led army coup against 1st Congolese govt. (1960); arrested Lumumba, who was later murdered by Mobutu's troops. In 2nd coup (1965), deposed Kasavubu and Tshombe, becoming head of state. Changed name to Mobutu Sese Seko (1972).

Moçambique, see MOZAMBIQUE.

mock heroic, satirical poem in which insignificant people and events are treated in an epic framework, eg Pope's *The Rape of the Lock.*

mockingbird, *Mimus polyglottos,* American bird noted for melodious song and mimicry of other birds.

Model Parliament, parliament summoned (1295) by Edward I of England, so called because it estab. general type of future parliaments. First attempt to be representative, as it drew on all 3 estates.

Modena (anc. *Mutina*), city of Emilia-Romagna, NC Italy, cap. of Modena prov. Pop. 173,000. Agric. machinery, vehicles; univ. (1678). Ruled by Este family 13th-19th cent. Medieval cathedral, ducal palace.

moderator, in physics, substance, eg graphite or heavy water, used to slow down high energy neutrons produced during fission in nuclear reactor, thus making them more likely to cause further fission.

modern art, term used loosely to describe painting and sculpture of late 19th and 20th cent., esp. abstract work.

modernism, in religion, term for movement in late 19th and 20th cents. which tries to redefine Christian teachings in light of modern science, historical research. In RC Church referred to specific movement condemned by Pius X in 1907 when its adherents denied divine sanction of the sacraments.

Modigliani, Amedeo (1884-1920), Italian painter, sculptor. Influenced by African sculpture, cubism and Italian masters such as Botticelli, he was a superb draughtsman. His distinctive elongated portraits incl. *The Little Peasant.*

modulation, in physics, alteration of characteristics, eg frequency or amplitude, of a wave in accordance with characteristics of another wave. Amplitude modulation, in which amplitude of radio wave is changed in accordance with signal to be broadcast, is principal mode of radio transmission. Frequency modulation provides radio transmission with reduced noise and outside interference.

Mogadishu (Ital. *Mogadiscio*), cap. of Somalia, on Indian Ocean. Pop. 230,000. Admin., commercial centre; port, exports livestock, bananas. Founded 9th cent. by Arabs. Taken by sultan of Zanzibar (1871); sold to Italy (1905), became cap. of Italian Somaliland.

Mogul, dynasty of Moslem emperors of India. Founded (1526) by BABER. Achieved greatest power under AKBAR. Weakened by wars against MAHRATTAS in 18th cent., later emperors were under control of the British, who dissolved empire in 1857.

Mohács, town of S Hungary, on R. Danube. Pop. 20,000. Scene of defeat of Hungary by Turkey (1526) and of defeat of Turks by Charles of Lorraine (1687).

Mohammed (c 570-632), Arab prophet, founder of ISLAM. A rich merchant, b. in Mecca, where he had vision (c 610) calling on him to found a monotheistic religion. Word of God revealed to him by angel Gabriel became text of KORAN. Plot to kill him led to flight (HEGIRA) to Medina (622), where he estab. Islamic theocracy. Conquered Mecca (630), estab. basis for Mohammedan empire.

Mohammed Ahmed, see MAHDI.

Mohammed Ali or **Mehemet Ali** (c 1769-1849), pasha of Egypt, b. Albania. Suppressed power of MAMELUKES in Egypt (1811). Intervened successfully in Greek war of independence until defeated by European allies at Navarino (1827). Invaded Syria (1831) after Ottoman sultan Mahmud II denied him its governorship. Revolted against sultan in Asia Minor (1839), but European intervention prevented sultan's overthrow. Granted hereditary rights to governorship of Egypt, founding royal line.

Mohammedanism, see ISLAM.

Mohammed II (1429-81), Ottoman sultan (1451-81), founder of Ottoman empire. After 50 day siege, captured Constantinople (1453), which he made his cap. Conquered Greece, Serbia, Albania and the Crimea. Noted linguist and patron of arts and learning.

Mohammed V (1844-1918), Ottoman sultan (1909-18). Dominated by ENVER PASHA, reign saw loss of Tripoli to Italy (1911-12), loss of most European territ. in Balkan Wars (1912-13) and defeat in WWI.

Mohammed VI (1861-1926), Ottoman sultan (1918-22). After Turkey's defeat in WWI, he retained power with Allied support through Treaty of Sèvres. Deposed and exiled by ATATURK.

Mohawk, see IROQUOIS.

Mohegan or **Mohican,** North American Indian tribe of Algonquian linguistic stock. In SW Connecticut, broke away from Pequot tribe. Supported by British became one of most powerful tribes in S New England. Increase of white settlement led to virtual extinction by 19th cent.

Mohenjo-Daro, one of two centres of INDUS VALLEY CIVILIZATION.

Mohican, see MOHEGAN.

Mohl, Hugo von (1805-72), German botanist. Working in plant physiology and histology, discovered and named protoplasm. Expert on microscopy.

Moholy-Nagy, László (1895-1946), Hungarian artist. Influenced by constructivism, he experimented with kinetic art and photography, and made use of new materials such as plexiglass. Founded (1937) Institute of Design in Chicago.

Mohorovičić Discontinuity or **Moho,** boundary line between Earth's crust and mantle, av. depth below land surface c 35 km (22 mi). Discovered by Andrija Mohorovičić (1857-1936), Croatian geologist, during his investigation of earthquakes.

Mojave or **Mohave,** desert of S California, US; S of Sierra Nevada. Area 38,850 sq km (c 15,000 sq mi). Death Valley in N, Mojave R. in S. Arid region with wide valleys and mountain ranges.

molasses, syrup obtained from drainings of raw sugar cane or from sugar during refining (latter syrup being called treacle in Britain). Used in making rum, confectionery and as cattle feed.

Mold, urban dist. and co. town of Clwyd, N Wales. Pop. 8000. Livestock market; coal mining.

Moldau (*Vltava*), river of Czechoslovakia. Flows c 435 km (270 mi) from Böhmerwald via Prague to R. Elbe. H.e.p.

Moldavia (*Moldova*), region of NE Romania,' fertile plain between rivers Prut, Siret. Principality founded 14th cent., formerly incl. Bukovina, Bessarabia. United with Walachia to form Romania (1859).

Moldavian Soviet Socialist Republic, constituent republic of W USSR, bounded by Ukrainian SSR and Romania. Area c 33,800 sq km (13,000 sq mi); pop. 3,572,000; cap. Kishinev. Largely flat, with fertile black-earth soil; extensive vineyards. Created (1940) by merger of former Moldavian ASSR with parts of Bessarabia ceded by Romania.

mole, small burrowing insectivore of Talpidae family, with small weak eyes, pointed snout, clawed feet. European common mole, *Talpa europaea*, has black velvety fur, eats mainly earthworms. *Scalopus aquaticus* is North American variety.

mole (= gram-molecule), in chemistry, quantity containing same number of molecules as number of atoms in 0.012 kg of carbon 12 isotope.

molecular weight, sum of atomic weights of all atoms in a molecule of a substance.

molecule, smallest portion of a substance able to exist independently and retain properties of original substance.

Molière, pseud. of Jean Baptiste Poquelin (1622-73), French dramatist. Known for comedies of manners involving caricatures of human folly, pretentiousness, eg *Tartuffe* (1664), *Le Misanthrope* (1666), *Le Bourgeois Gentilhomme* (1670), *Les Femmes savantes* (1672), *Le Malade imaginaire* (1673).

Founded Illustre Théâtre company in 1643.

Mollusca (**molluscs**), phylum of soft-bodied unsegmented animals often with hard shell. Usually move by means of single muscular foot. Incl. snail, slug, octopus (no shell), squid (small internal shell).

Moloch, pagan Semitic god of fire. Practice of sacrificing first-born children to him condemned by OT prophets.

moloch, *Moloch horridus*, agamid lizard of Australian deserts. Brown body covered with spines; feeds on ants. Also called spiny lizard or thorny devil.

Molotov, Vyacheslav Mikhailovich, orig. Skriabin (1890-), Soviet political leader. As foreign minister (1939-49, 1953-6), he negotiated Non-aggression Pact with Germany (1939). Influence declined during Khrushchev's rise, which he opposed. Expelled from party (1964).

Moltke, Helmuth Bernhard, Graf von (1800-91), Prussian army officer. As chief of staff (1858-88) reorganized Prussian army, facilitating victories against Denmark (1864), Austria (1866), France (1870). His nephew, **Helmuth Johannes Ludwig von Moltke** (1848-1916), became chief of staff (1906) but was relieved of his post after the loss of the battle of the Marne (1914).

Moluccas, group of isls., forming Maluku prov. of Indonesia. Area c 84,000 sq km (32,000 sq mi). Incl. Amboina, Ceram, Halmahera, Aru and Tanimbar Isls. Formerly called Spice Isls., nutmeg and cloves originated here. Under Dutch control from 1667 to WWII.

molybdenum (Mo), metallic element; at. no. 42, at. wt. 95.94. Occurs as molybdenite (MoS₂); obtained by reducing oxide with carbon. Used to harden steel; molybdenum disulphide used as a lubricant.

Mombasa, city of E Kenya, on Indian Ocean. Pop. 255,000. Port at Kilindini to SW exports coffee, sisal, hides, tea; handles major part of Kenya, Uganda, Tanzania's trade. Oil refining, cement, glass mfg. Arab trade centre from 11th cent.; held by Portugal 16th-17th cent. Ceded to UK by Zanzibar 1887. Oriental influence still evident; mosques, bazaars.

moment of force, measure of tendency of a force to cause rotation of a body about a point or axis. Measured as product of magnitude of force and perpendicular distance from its line of action to axis of rotation.

momentum, in physics, the product of mass and velocity of a body. In Newtonian mechanics, total momentum of system of bodies on which no external forces act is constant.

Monaco, independent principality of S Europe, enclave within SE France. Area 149 ha. (368 acres); pop. 25,000; cap. Monaco. Commercial centre La Condamine; tourism in MONTE CARLO. Ruled by Genoese Grimaldi family from 13th cent. Part of France (1793-1814), Sardinia (1815-61). Constitutional monarchy from 1911-59 (restored 1962). Customs union with France.

Monadhliath Mountains, range of NC Scotland, in Highland region; rise to 941 m (3087 ft).

Monaghan, county of Ulster prov., NE Irish Republic. Area 1290 sq mi (498 sq mi); pop. 46,000. Undulating terrain; oats, livestock. Co. town Monaghan, on Ulster Canal. Pop. 5000. RC cathedral.

monasticism, system of organized community life for those who have retired from world under religious vows. Vows of celibacy, poverty and obedience are typical. Feature of Christianity, Buddhism, Jainism and Islam. Middle Ages in Europe saw rise of great monastic orders, eg Benedictines, Cistercians, Carthusians.

Mönchen-Gladbach, city of W West Germany. Pop. 151,000. Centre of cotton indust., also produces paper. Grew around abbey founded 972. Badly damaged in WWII. Called München-Gladbach till 1963.

Monck or **Monk, George, 1st Duke of Albemarle** (1608-70), English soldier. Fought for Charles I in Scotland, captured at the battle of Nantwich (1644) and in 1646 turned parliamentarian. In the unrest which followed Cromwell's death, he intervened with an army from Scotland and engineered Charles II's restoration (1660) by inducing him to make Declaration of Breda.

Moncton, town of SE New Brunswick, Canada, on Petitcodiac R. Pop. 48,000. Railway jct.; engineering indust., clothes mfg. Tidal bore is feature of river.

Mond, Ludwig (1839-1909), British chemist, b. Germany. Perfected Solvay process for manufacture of alkali. Devised method for extraction of nickel from its ores using carbon monoxide (Mond process). His son, Alfred Moritz Mond, 1st Baron Melchett (1868-1930), was an industrialist. Merged (1926) Brunner-Mond with other companies to form Imperial Chemical Industries (ICI).

Mondale, Walter Frederick (1928-), American politician, vice-president (1977-). Senator from Minnesota (1964-77), successful Democratic vice-presidential candidate in 1976 election.

Mondrian, Piet (1872-1944), Dutch painter. Chief exponent of neo-plasticism, a strict form of geometric abstraction. Works are characterized by use of straight line grids and rectangles of primary colours. *Broadway Boogie-woogie* was in more vibrant style.

Monet, Claude (1840-1926), French painter. Leading member of the impressionists, he evolved a broken-colour technique to catch the changing effects of light. In later work, he ceased painting directly from nature; series of waterlily paintings culminated in almost abstract vision of nature. Works incl. *Impression, Sunrise* (1872) and *Rouen Cathedral* series.

money, in economics, unit of value or means of payment. Cattle often used as unit of value in ancient societies with more convenient objects as means of payment. Subsequently both these roles merged in durable, intrinsically valuable metals. State coinage prob. originated in Lydia (7th cent. BC), thus allowing govt. to use currency of higher face value than its commodity value. Paper currency (widely in use since 17th cent.) usually backed by a precious metal until 1930s (*see* FIDUCIARY ISSUE).

Mongolia, republic of C Asia, formerly Outer Mongolia. Area c 1,566,000 sq km (605,000 sq mi); pop. 1,488,000; cap. Ulan Bator. Language: Mongolian. Religion: Lamaist Buddhism. Mainly grazing plateau land (*see* GOBI DESERT) with extremes of climate. Trade in wool, hides, cloth; mineral extraction. Economy based on stock rearing. Nomadic Mongols conquered region under Genghis Khan (c 1205). Communism estab. 1924 after break with China.

mongolism or **Down's syndrome**, congenital disease caused by fault in formation of ovum. Characterized by mental retardation and broad face, slanting eyes.

Mongols, nomadic Asiatic tribe who, under GENGHIS KHAN and his sons, conquered much of Asia, incl. China. Also invaded Europe, penetrating as far as Hungary and Poland. Power waned towards end of 14th cent.; Mongol rule in China ended 1368.

mongoose, small Old World carnivore of Viverridae family. Feeds on small mammals, birds' eggs, *etc*; often kept for killing snakes. Species incl. Indian mongoose, *Herpestes edwardsi*. Meerkat, *Suricata suricata*, is South African species.

monism, in philosophy, doctrine that there is only one ultimate substance or principle, whether matter (materialism) or mind (idealism) or some third thing which unifies both.

monitor, any of Varanidae family of large carnivorous lizards of Africa, Asia, Australia. Elongated snout, long neck and extensible forked tongue. Largest species is KOMODO DRAGON.

monitor, a class of warship designed for coastal bombardment, named after the Union turret-ship *Monitor* in the American Civil War. British monitors were used off German-occupied Channel ports in WWI.

Moniz, Egas, see LOBOTOMY.

Monk, George, see MONCK, GEORGE, 1ST DUKE OF ALBEMARLE.

monkey, group of long-tailed primates; divided into platyrrhines (New World monkeys) of South America and catarrhines (Old World monkeys) of African and Asian tropics. Incl. capuchin, marmoset, macaque.

monkey puzzle or Chile pine, *Araucaria araucana*, coniferous tree, native to Chile. Stiff pointed leaves, contorted appearances; grown as ornamental.

monkshood or aconite, any of genus *Aconitum* of perennial herbs of buttercup family, esp. *A. napellus*, native to N temperate regions, with hoodshaped flowers. All species are poisonous.

Monmouth, James Scott, Duke of (1649-1685), claimant to English throne. Illegitimate son of Charles II by Lucy Walter, he became figurehead for Whig supporters of Protestant succession in opposition to Catholic duke of York. Fled to Holland after RYE HOUSE PLOT (1683). On accession of James II (1685), returned to England and raised rebellion against him. Defeated at Sedgemoor and executed.

Monmouthshire, former county of SE Wales, on English border, now called Gwent. Hilly in W, incl. part of S Wales coalfield. Main town Newport. Coalmining; iron, steel works; light industs. Co. town was **Monmouth**, mun. bor. at confluence of Wye and Monnow. Pop. 7000. Has remains of town walls; 12th cent. castle.

Monnet, Jean (1888-1979), French economist. Produced Monnet Plan for revival of French indust. and agric. (1947). President of European Coal and Steel Community (1952-5). Leading advocate of European unity.

Monod, Jacques (1910-), French molecular biologist. Shared Nobel Prize for Physiology and Medicine (1965) with François Jacob and André Lwoff for work on the way in which body cells synthesize protein. Writings incl. *Chance and Necessity* (1971).

Monophysitism, Christian heresy of 5th and 6th cents. Taught that Jesus had only one nature (divine), opposed at Council of Chalcedon (451). Adhered to by Coptic, Jacobite and Armenian churches.

monopoly, in economics, virtual control of supply of commodity or service by one producer, enabling producer to fix price at which consumer must purchase product. Legislation places restraints on monopolistic tendencies; in US began with Sherman Anti-Trust Act (1890), subsequently reinforced; in UK, Monopolies Commission set up 1948. Govt. monopolies (eg postal system) operated to facilitate public services. Socialist doctrine extends monopoly principle to all basic industries, eg nationalization of steel by British Labour govt. See OLIGOPOLY.

monorail, railway with single rail. Usually the rail is elevated with cars suspended from it or running above it. Driving wheels may rotate horizontally making contact with side of rail.

monosodium glutamate, white soluble crystalline salt extracted from grains or beets. Intensifies flavours, used widely in tinned food.

monotheism, belief that there is only one god, as in Judaism, Christianity and Islam.

Monotheletism, Christian heresy of 7th cent. Taught that Christ operated with one will although he had 2 natures. Arose as compromise between MONOPHYSITISM and orthodoxy. Adopted (622) by Emperor Heraclius I as official form of Christianity in Byzantine Empire. Died out except among MARONITES.

monotremes (Monotremata), subclass of primitive egg-laying mammals showing many reptilian features. Echidna and duckbilled platypus only living species, found in Australia and New Guinea.

monotype, typesetting machine which produces separate letters. Consists of composing machine, operated by a keyboard, which perforates a paper roll. The roll is fed into and used to operate a casting machine which casts each letter and assembles the type.

Monroe, James (1758-1831), American statesman, president (1817-25). Negotiated Louisiana Purchase (1803). His 2-term admin. marked by acquisition of Florida from Spain (1819), entry of Missouri into Union as slave state (1821). Promulgated Monroe Doctrine (1823), opposing European attempts to interfere in affairs of American countries or to recolonize recently independent American colonies; provided basis for much subsequent American foreign policy.

Monroe, Marilyn, orig. Norma Jean Baker or Mortenson (1926-62), American film actress. Known for sex goddess image which frustrated her real talent for comedy, revealed in, eg *Gentlemen Prefer Blondes* (1953), *The Seven-Year Itch* (1955), *Some Like It Hot* (1959). Committed suicide.

Monroe Doctrine, see MONROE, JAMES.

Monrovia; cap. of Liberia, near mouth of R. St Paul. Pop. 110,000. Admin., commercial centre; port, exports rubber, iron ore. Founded (1822) for freed American slaves.

Mons (Flem. *Bergen*), town of SW Belgium, cap. of Hainaut prov. Pop. 28,000. Coalmining, textiles, chemicals. Battleground in both WWs. Town hall (15th cent.), cathedral (16th cent.).

Monsarrat, Nicholas (1910-79), English author. Known for novels of war at sea, eg *The Cruel Sea* (1951), *The Ship That Died of Shame* (1959). Also wrote war reminiscences, *Corvette Command* (1944).

monsoon, wind system involving seasonal reversal of prevailing wind direction. Found most often within tropics, esp. SE Asia. In India, winter monsoon (Nov.-April) is cold, dry N wind; summer monsoon (May-Sept.) is warm, wet SW wind.

Montagu, Lady Mary Wortley, née Pierrepont (1689-1762), English letter-writer. Member of circle of Pope, Addison. Known for lively descriptions of Turkish life from viewpoint as wife of British ambassador. Introduced inoculation to England from Turkey.

Montaigne, Michel Eyquem, Seigneur de (1533-92), French writer. Creator of modern essay form. *Essais* (complete edition, 1595) reflect personal scepticism, philosophical interests. Greatly influenced European thought.

Montale, Eugenio (1896-), Italian poet. Known for pessimistic 'hermetic' poetry, *eg Ossi di seppia* (1925), *Le occasioni* (1940). Awarded Nobel Prize for Literature (1975).

Montana, state of NW US, in Rocky Mts. Area 381,087 sq km (147,138 sq mi); pop. 694,000; cap. Helena. Bounded in N by Canada; Bitterroot Range in W; plains in E. Main occupations cattle, grain farming; lumbering; copper, zinc, silver, gold mining. Explored by fur traders in 18th, 19th cents.; developed with gold, silver, copper strikes. Admitted to Union as 41st state (1889).

Montanism, movement in Christian church (2nd cent.). Arose in Phrygia under leadership of Montanus. Followers believed in imminent Judgment Day; encouraged ecstatic prophecy. Survived in isolated pockets in Phrygia until 7th cent.

Mont Blanc, peak of Savoy Alps, SE France. Highest in Alps (4808 m/15,781 ft). Part of Mont Blanc massif extending into Italy, Switzerland; incl. several peaks, glaciers (*eg* Mer de Glace). First ascended 1786. Road tunnel (11.3 km/7 mi long) opened 1965, links France with Italy.

montbretia, any of genus *Tritonia* of flowering plants native to S Africa. European garden varieties incl. *T. crocosmiflora* with orange-crimson flowers.

Montcalm, Louis-Joseph de Montcalm-Gozon, Marquis de (1712-59), French general. Commanded French forces in Canada after 1756, capturing Fort William and defending Ticonderoga (1758). Killed in defeat at Québec by British forces under Wolfe.

Monte Carlo, town of Monaco, on Riviera. Resort, gambling casino. Annual car rally and motor racing grand prix.

Monte Cassino, see CASSINO, Italy.

Monte Cervino, see MATTERHORN.

Monte Cristo, isl. of Italy, in Tyrrhenian Sea, made famous by Alexandre Dumas' *The Count of Monte Cristo*.

Montenegro (*Crna Gora*), autonomous republic of SW Yugoslavia. Area 13,838 sq km (5343 sq mi); cap. Titograd. Mountainous, except around L. Scutari; sheep, goats. Mineral resources. Medieval prov. of Zeta, within Serbia; independent after 1389, resisted Turks 14th-19th cent. Yugoslav prov. from 1918, republic from 1946.

Monte Rosa, mountain group of SW Switzerland and N Italy, in Pennine Alps. Highest is Dufourspitze (4636 m/15,217 ft), first climbed 1855.

Monterrey, city of NE Mexico, cap. of Nuevo León state. Pop. 1,180,000. Indust. and rail centre; lead, iron, steel, textile, glass mfg. Founded 1579. Has notable 18th cent. cathedral.

Montesquieu, Charles Louis de Secondat, Baron de la Brède et de (1689-1755), French political theorist. Wrote ironic *Lettres persanes* (1721), satirizing French contemporary life and institutions.

His comparative analysis of govt. in *L'Esprit des Lois* (1748) influenced formulation of American Constitution.

Montessori, Maria (1870-1952), Italian educator, doctor. Developed Montessori Method, emphasizing importance for children of 3-6 years of freedom of choice and action and use of exercises and games in growth of coordination, perceptual skills.

Monteux, Pierre (1875-1964), French conductor. Conductor of Diaghilev's Ballets Russes, with which he premiered Stravinsky's *Rite of Spring* and Ravel's *Daphnis and Chloe*. Later, conducted several major orchestras, incl. London Symphony.

Monteverdi, Claudio Giovanni Antonio (1567-1643), Italian composer. Leading figure in early development of opera with such works as *Orfeo* (1607). Wrote 9 books of madrigals and much church music, incl. 2 sets of Vespers.

Montevideo, cap. of Uruguay, on Río de la Plata estuary. Pop. 1,280,000. Major seaport, handles most of Uruguay's trade. Wool, hides, meat exports. Meat packing, tanning, flour milling indusrs. Founded 1726. Became cap. 1828. Has National Univ. (1849). Tourism, in scenic area.

Montez, Lola, real name Maria Gilbert (1818-61), Irish adventuress. Great beauty and would-be Spanish dancer, she became mistress of Ludwig I of Bavaria. Greatly influenced his policy until banished (1848). After travelling widely, died in US.

Montezuma II (c 1480-1520), Aztec emperor of Mexico (1502-20). Captured by Cortés (1519) during Spanish conquest and held hostage in Mexico City (Tenochtitlán). Persuaded by Cortés to quell an Aztec uprising, he was killed by his own subjects.

Montfort, Simon de, Earl of Leicester (c 1208-65), English statesman. Led baronial opposition to Henry III, securing Provisions of Oxford (1258), which set up council of 15 to advise the king. Led baronial side in Barons' War (1263-7). Victory at Lewes (1264) followed by the Great Parliament estab. precedent of representation in England. Defeated and killed at Evesham.

Montgolfier, Joseph Michel (1740-1810), French inventor. With his brother, Jacques Etienne Montgolfier (1745-99), invented 1st practical hot-air balloon, in which they made 1st manned flight (1783).

Montgomery, Bernard Law, 1st Viscount Montgomery of Alamein (1887-1976), British field marshal. Given command of British 8th Army in N Africa in 1942, restored morale after German successes and won the victory of El Alamein, followed by successful penetration into Tunisia and final defeat of Axis forces. Commanded land forces in Normandy invasion (1944) and was made chief of Imperial General Staff after war.

Montgomery, cap. of Alabama, US; on Alabama R. Pop. 133,000. Railway jct.; cotton, livestock produce. First cap. of Confederacy (1861).

Montgomeryshire, former county of C Wales, now in Powys. Mountainous, moorland; fertile valleys in E. Sheep rearing, oats; slate, stone quarrying. Co. town was Montgomery, mun. bor. Pop. 1000. Agric. market.

Monthierlant, Henry de Millon (1896-1972), French author. Known for novels celebrating masculine 'superiority', eg Les bestiaires (1926), Les célibataires (1934), Les jeunes filles (1936). Also wrote plays, eg La reine morte (1942).

Montluçon, town of C France, on R. Cher. Pop. 60,000. Indust. centre, esp. steel, chemicals; Commentry coalfield nearby. Many 15th-16th cent. houses.

Montmartre, see PARIS, France.

Montpelier, cap. of Vermont, US; on Winooski R. Pop. 9000. Agric. market. Cap. from 1805.

Montpellier, city of Languedoc, S France, cap. of Hérault dept. Pop. 162,000. Resort, wine trade, chemicals mfg. Purchased (1349) from Aragón; former Huguenot stronghold. Botanic gardens (1593); univ. (1289).

Montréal or **Montreal,** largest city of Canada, in SE Québec; on isl. at confluence of St Lawrence, Ottawa rivers, at foot of Mt. Royal. Pop. 1,214,000; mainly French-speaking. Major seaport, commercial, transport, financial centre. Leading grain exports; railway equipment mfg.; iron and steel industs.; fur trade centre. Settled by French (1642); surrendered to British (1760). Seat of McGill Univ. (1821), Montréal Univ. (1876). Site of Expo 1967 fair, 1976 Olympic Games.

Montreux, town of SW Switzerland, on L. Geneva. Pop. 20,000. Tourism; woodworking; mountain railway. Castle of CHILLON nearby.

Montrose, town of Tayside region, E Scotland. Pop. 10,000. On penin. between North Sea and Montrose Basin (lagoon). Port, tourist resort; fishing; flax, jute mills.

Montrose, James Graham, Marquess of (1612-50), Scottish soldier. Leader of Covenanters in Bishops' War (1639-40). Changed sides in Civil War and successfully led Highland army for Charles I against Presbyterians. Defeated by Leslie at Philiphaugh (1645) and fled abroad. On return, hanged after attempt to raise rebellion.

Montserrat, isl. of E West Indies, in Leeward Isls. Area 98 sq km (38 sq mi); pop. 13,000; cap. Plymouth. Cotton, fruit exports. Discovered by Columbus (1493). British colony from 17th cent. Volcanic and rugged; subject to earth tremors.

Montserrat or **Monserrat,** mountain of Catalonia, NE Spain. Height 1235 m (4054 ft). On ledge is Benedictine Monastery and church containing shrine of black Virgin.

Mont-St-Michel, rocky isl. of NW France, in Bay of Mont-St-Michel. Tourist centre, linked to mainland by causeway. Abbey (founded 708), used as prison in 19th cent.

Monza, city of Lombardy, NW Italy. Pop. 116,000. Textiles, carpets, hats. Cathedral contains iron crown of Lombardy. Scene of assassination (1900) of Umberto I. Motor racing track.

Moon, only natural satellite of Earth; diameter 3476 km (2160 mi). Revolves around Earth at mean distance of 384,000 km once in c 27¼ days (with reference to stars) or c 29½ days (with respect to Sun). Shines by reflected light from Sun;

said to be full when opposite · Sun and new when between Earth and Sun and partly visible. Without atmosphere or water; first visited by American spacemen July, 1969.

moonstone, semi-precious gemstone. Blue-white, translucent; a variety of feldspar. Major sources in Sri Lanka, Burma.

moonwort, *see* HONESTY.

Moore, George (1852-1933), Irish author. Novels, *eg Esther Waters* (1894), reflect influence of French naturalism. Also wrote several volumes of autobiog., plays, art criticism championing impressionism.

Moore, G[eorge] E[dward] (1873-1958). English philosopher. Known mainly as rigorous expounder of philosophical problems rather than deviser of a system. Concerned with language, epistemology. Works incl. *Principia Ethica* (1903).

Moore, Henry (1898-), English sculptor. Advocate of direct carving, his work is based on natural forms expressed in stone, wood or bronze. Themes incl. mother and child, reclining figures; drawings incl. studies of underground air raid shelters.

Moore, Sir John (1761-1809), British army officer, b. Scotland. Commander of expedition sent by Wellington (1808) to assist Spanish army in dislodging Napoleon, was mortally wounded at battle of Corunna, which he had won though greatly outnumbered.

Moore, Marianne [Craig] (1887-1972), American poet. Witty, meticulous verse incl. *What Are Years?* (1941), *Collected Poems* (1951),

translation of La Fontaine's *Fables* (1954).

moorhen, *Gallinula chloropus*, olive green water bird of Europe and North America, found near ponds, marshes. Called gallinule in America.

Moors, nomadic people of N Africa of mixed Arab and Berber descent. Became Moslem in 8th cent., conquered Spain (711) but were defeated in France by Charles Martel (732). Founded caliphate in Spain famed for learning and architectural splendour. Gradually expelled from Spain by Christians, their last stronghold, Granada, falling in 1492.

moose, *Alces americanus*, largest of deer family, found in Alaska, Canada, N US. Huge branching antlers spanning up to 1.8 m/6 ft. Elk is related European species.

moraine, accumulation of ungraded debris, ranging from clay to boulders, transported and deposited by glacier. Types incl. lateral, medial, ground and terminal moraines, classification being dependent on which part of glacier laid them down.

morality plays, didactic late medieval, early Renaissance verse dramas. Developed from MIRACLE PLAYS, Biblical characters of which gave place to personifications of vice, virtues, as in EVERYMAN.

Moral Re-Armament or **MRA,** movement started (1938) by F. Buchman. Followers believe in national spiritual reconstruction starting with the individual. They base evangelical work on informal meetings, group confessions.

Moravia, Alberto, pseud. of Alberto Pincherle (1907-), Italian novelist. Known for realistic novels, eg *The Time of Indifference* (1929), *Mistaken Ambitions* (1935), *Two Women* (1957).

Moravia (*Morava*), region of Czechoslovakia, between Bohemia (W) and Slovakia (E). Main towns Brno, Ostrava. Drained by R. Morava. Agric., coalmining. Habsburg domain until 1918, became prov. of Czechoslovakia. Combined with Silesia (1927); abolished as political unit (1949).

Moravian Church, evangelical Protestant episcopal sect, founded in Bohemia (1457) among followers of JAN HUS. Persecuted and driven out of Bohemia; revived in Saxony (18th cent.). Active in all Americas; missionary work continues.

Moraviantown, Battle of, encounter (Oct. 1813) near Thames R., S Ontario, during War of 1812. American forces defeated retreating British and Indian troops. Indian leader, Tecumseh, was killed. Also known as Battle of the Thames.

Moray, James Stuart, 1st Earl of, see MURRAY.

moray eel, any of Muraenidae family of widely distributed marine eels. Aggressive carnivore, laterally compressed, often brightly coloured; hides in rock crevices. *Muraena helena* found in Mediterranean and E Atlantic.

Morayshire, former county of NE Scotland, now in Grampian region. Previously called Elginshire. Cromdale Hills in S; low-lying, fertile in N. Livestock rearing, salmon fishing, whisky distilling. Co. town was Elgin. **Moray Firth**, inlet of North Sea, between former Morayshire, Nairnshire and Ross and Cromarty.

mordant, substance used in dyeing to fix colouring matter. Usually consists of basic metal hydroxide (eg aluminium hydroxide), which combines with dye to form insoluble coloured compound (lake) in fibres of fabric.

Mordvinia, auton. republic of E European RSFSR, USSR. Area c 26,160 sq km (10,100 sq mi); pop. 1,030,000; cap. Saransk. Forested steppe; agric., lumbering and wood product mfg. Mordvinians, a Finno-Ugrian people, were conquered by Russians in 16th cent.

More, Henry (1614-87), English philosopher. Leading Cambridge Platonist. Attempted to reconcile rational and mystical. Works incl. *The Mystery of Godliness* (1660), *Divine Dialogues* (1668).

More, Sir Thomas (1478-1535), English statesman, scholar. Friend of Erasmus, who exerted strong influence on More's humanist ideas. Succeeded Wolsey as lord chancellor (1529-32); resigned over Henry VIII's divorce from Catherine of Aragon. Refused (1534) to recognize Henry as head of Church; executed for treason. Most famous work, *Utopia* (1516), depicts ideal state ordered by reason.

Moreau, Gustave (1826-98), French painter. Painted religious and mythological fantasies in an ornate detailed style. Taught at Ecole des Beaux-Arts, Paris, where his pupils incl. Matisse and Rouault.

Morecambe (and Heysham), mun. bor. of Lancashire, NW England, on Morecambe Bay. Pop. 42,000. Resort; port, ferry to Belfast; oil refinery.

morel, any of genus *Morchella* of edible mushrooms resembling a sponge on a stalk. *M. esculenta*, the commonest, is found in deciduous woods and pastures of Europe and North America. Used in soups and sauces.

Morgan, Sir Henry (*c* 1635-88), Welsh buccaneer. Led pirates in West Indies against Spaniards; made daring march across Panama isthmus to capture Panama City (1671). Called to England to answer charges of piracy, he gained royal favour and was later made governor of Jamaica.

Morgan, Junius Spencer (1813-90), American financier. Head of international banking enterprise handling British funds in US. Made notable loan to French govt. during Franco-Prussian War. His son, J[ohn] Pierpont Morgan (1837-1913), enlarged family fortunes, esp. in railway holdings; formed (1901) US Steel Corporation. Became a symbol of wealth, renowned philanthropist. His son, J[ohn] Pierpont Morgan (1867-1943), helped raise Allied funds during WWI.

Morgan, Thomas Hunt (1866-1945), American biologist. Awarded Nobel Prize for Physiology and Medicine (1933) for genetic research on laws and mechanism of heredity, following studies of fruit fly *Drosophila*.

morganatic marriage, form of marriage in which man of royalty marries a woman of inferior social status with provision that although children of the marriage will be legitimate, neither they nor the wife may lay claim to his rank or property.

Moriscos, name given to Spanish Moslems who accepted Christian baptism. Edict of 1568 demanded abandonment of all remaining Moorish customs; led to revolt and persecution of Moriscos. Finally expelled from Spain in 1609.

Morland, George (1763-1804), English painter. Painted numerous landscapes and genre scenes, esp. of cottage interiors and taverns. Works were much popularized by engravings.

Morley, Thomas (1557-1603), English composer. Organist at St Paul's Cathedral. Wrote *A Plaine and Easie Introduction to Practicall Musicke* (1597) on composition. Works incl. madrigals, consort pieces.

Mormons or **Church of Jesus Christ of Latter-Day Saints**, evangelical religious sect founded in US (1830) after JOSEPH SMITH after divine revelations. Settled in communities in W Missouri but came into conflict with their neighbours. After death of Smith, BRIGHAM YOUNG became leader and transferred centre of movement to Salt Lake City, Utah. Now worldwide membership of *c* 3 million as result of extensive proselytizing.

morning glory, common name for various twining vines of convolvulus family esp. of genus *Ipomoea*; incl. American *I. purpurea*, widely cultivated for its purple flowers. Seeds of some varieties contain hallucinogens.

Morocco (Arab. *Al-Mamlaka al-Maghrebia*), kingdom of NW Africa. Area 447,000 sq km (172,500 sq mi); pop. 17,828,000; cap. Rabat. Language: Arabic. Religion: Islam. Largely desert; Atlas Mts. in SW-NE; fertile coast. Produces cereals, fruit, olives, cattle. Minerals incl.

phosphates, petroleum, iron ore. Part of Roman MAURETANIA: Arabs brought Islam 7th cent., *fl* under Berber dynasties 11th-14th cents. Settled by Portuguese (1415-1769); became Barbary pirate base. Disputed in 19th cent.; French, Spanish protects. estab. 1912, Tangier internationalized (1923). Independent 1956, constitutional monarchy from 1962.

Moroni, Giovanni Battista (*c* 1525-78), Italian painter. Best known for his portraits, which combine realism of Holbein with Venetian style. Works incl. *The Tailor* (London).

Morpheus, in Greek and Roman myth, shaper of dreams.

morphine, white crystalline alkaloid derived from opium. Used in medicine to relieve pain; continued use leads to addiction.

Morris, William (1834-96), English artist, writer, decorator, printer. Founded firm of Morris and Company to produce stained glass, tapestry, furniture, in an attempt to raise standard of Victorian design. Founded Kelmscott Press (1890) to revive possibility of printing. Believed in possibility of improving quality of working life through craftsmanship (*see* ARTS AND CRAFTS MOVEMENT); his socialist beliefs are reflected in writings such as *Dream of John Ball* (1888).

Morris, William Richard, *see* NUFFIELD, WILLIAM RICHARD MORRIS, VISCOUNT.

Morris Jesup, Cape, *see* PEARY LAND.

Morrison, Herbert Stanley, Baron Morrison of Lambeth (1888-1965), British statesman.

Leader of London County Council (1934-40). Home secretary in National govt. (1940-5). Defeated by Gaitskell in vote for Labour Party leadership (1955).

Morse, Samuel Finley Breese (1791-1872), American inventor, painter. Devised one form of electric telegraph and system of communication, Morse Code, using short and long taps to represent letters of alphabet.

mortar, short-barrelled, large-bore cannon, used in early siege warfare for lobbing missiles over city walls at short range. In WWI and II modern version projected 2 or 3 in. finned bombs (explosive or smoke) as infantry support.

Mortimer, Roger de, 1st Earl of March (*c* 1287-1330), English nobleman. Opposed EDWARD II in baronial wars (1321-2) but was captured (1322); escaped to France (1324) where Edward's wife, ISABELLA, became his mistress. Together they invaded England, forced Edward's abdication (1326). Ruled England until Edward III had him executed.

mosaic, surface ornamentation by laying small pieces of stone, tile, metal or glass on a bed of cement. Used principally for decoration of floors and walls. Art was first developed by the Romans and perfected by Byzantines (6th cent.); revived by the Italians in 13th cent., it declined with introduction of fresco.

Mosaic Law, laws by which the Jewish people were governed, contained mainly in Pentateuch and stated in Ten Commandments given to Moses on Mt. Sinai.

moschatel, *see* MUSK.

Moscow (*Moskva*), cap. of USSR and RSFSR; on R. Moskva. Pop. 7,300,000. Indust., cultural and political centre; metal goods, textile mfg. Founded 12th cent.; became national cap. (1547) under 1st tsar Ivan the Terrible; remained so until 1712. Burned during occupation by Napoleon (1812). Cap. again after Revolution (1918). Kremlin (fortified citadel) contains 15th cent. Uspenski and 16th cent. Arkhangelski cathedrals, Grand Palace. Lenin's tomb and 16th cent. St Basil's Cathedral in Red Square. Theatres incl. Moscow Arts, Bolshoi.

Moseley, Henry Gwyn-Jeffreys (1887-1915), English physicist. His work on frequencies of atomic spectra led him to equate charge on atomic nucleus with atomic number; this resolved problems in Mendeleev's periodic table.

Moselle (Ger. *Mosel*), river of NE France and NW West Germany. Flows *c* 550 km (340 mi) from Vosges via Metz, Thionville to R. Rhine at Koblenz. Canalized for much of course. Vineyards below Trier produce Moselle wines.

Moses (*fl c* 13th cent. BC), Jewish lawgiver, OT prophet. Led Jews out of captivity in Egypt (Exodus); received Ten Commandments on Mt. Sinai. Estab. organized Jewish religion. Traditional author of Pentateuch.

Moses, Anna Mary Robertson ('Grandma') (1860-1961), American painter. A modern primitive, she is remembered for her popular scenes of rural life, which evoke nostalgia for old world simplicity.

Moslem League, political organization estab. (1906) to safe-guard rights of Moslems in India. Under leadership of Jinnah, demanded creation of separate Moslem state in 1940s; achieved its founding (1947) of Pakistan.

Moslem religion, see ISLAM.

Mosley, Sir Oswald (1896-), British politician. Held office in Labour govt. of 1929; resigned over economic policy. Organized (1932) British Union of Fascists; led agitation against Jews. Detained 1940-3, attempted to revive movement after WW II.

mosque, building for Moslem worship. Main features are: *qibla* wall, with its central *mihrab* or prayer niche which indicates direction of Mecca; a *dikka* (platform for services); a minaret. Early mosques were adaptations of Christian basilicas, *eg* Great Mosque at Damascus. Domed mosques incl. Hagia Sophia in Istanbul.

mosquito, any of Culicidae family of 2-winged insects. Female uses skin-piercing mouthparts to suck blood of animals, often transmitting diseases through its saliva, *eg Anopheles* carries malaria parasite.

Mosquito Coast, belt of land on Caribbean coast, in NE Honduras and E Nicaragua. Sparse pop.; lumbering, banana industs. British protect. (1678-1860), S part annexed by Nicaragua (1894).

Moss, Stirling (1929-), British racing driver. British National Champion (1950-2, 1954-9); winner of European Grand Prix (1961). Twice second in world championship. Retired after serious crash in 1962.

moss, any of class *Musci* of small primitive plants. Worldwide distribution. Grows in tufts on moist ground, tree trunks. Important as pioneers of rock surfaces, holding moisture and producing humus, mosses allow seeds of other plants to germinate.

Mossadegh, Mohammed (1880-1967), Iranian statesman. Premier (1951-3), nationalized (1951) British-owned oil indust.; dispute led to breaking-off of diplomatic relations between Iran and Britain. Imprisoned after attempt to overthrow shah.

Mössbauer, Rudolf Ludwig (1929-), German physicist. Awarded Nobel Prize for Physics (1961) for discovery of Mössbauer effect in which gamma rays emitted by certain radioactive isotopes maintain unvarying wavelength if radiating nuclei are held in crystal form. Effect has been widely used.

Mosul (*Al Mawsil*), city of N Iraq, on R. Tigris. Pop. 293,000. Agric. trade centre; rich oilfields indust. Near ruins of Nineveh. A centre of Nestorian Christianity.

motet, relatively short, freely contrapuntal piece of vocal music, usually unaccompanied, with Biblical or similar prose text. Early motets were based on plainsong.

moth, insect of order Lepidoptera. Distinguished from butterfly by different antennae, wing arrangement, and night flight.

mother-of-pearl, hard iridescent lining of certain marine shells, eg pearl oyster, abalone. Used for decoration, jewellery.

Motherwell, Robert (1915-), American painter, theorist. Proponent of abstract expressionism, his work is characterized by

undefined shapes painted in strong colours.

Motherwell (and Wishaw), town of Strathclyde region, C Scotland. Pop. 74,000. Towns united 1920. Coalmining; iron, steel industs.

motion pictures, *see* CINEMA.

motion sickness, nausea and vomiting caused by effect of motion on balance organ of inner ear; experienced on ships, motor vehicles, aircraft, *etc.* Relieved by drugs, eg hyoscine, which often cause drowsiness.

motor, *see* ELECTRIC MOTOR.

motor car, *see* AUTOMOBILE.

motorcycle, two-wheeled vehicle propelled by an internal combustion engine. Prob. first built by Gottlieb Daimler (c 1885). Engines are usually air-cooled, often 2-stroke (cycle) and generally range from 50-1000 cc. Their popularity has revived greatly since 1960s through technical innovations of Japanese manufacturers.

motorcycle racing, sport dating from introduction of reliable motorcycles in early 1900s. Events incl. annual TT races held in Isle of Man since 1907 and American National Jack Pine 500 mi (805 km) championships.

motor racing, competitive sport for motor cars, introduced in France (1894). Present-day international Formula One championship is decided on results of Grand Prix races in over 10 countries. Other events incl. Indianapolis 500 (805 km) in US and Le Mans 24-hr race.

motorway [UK], road designed to link major centres of pop.; restrictions of use facilitate speed and obviate congestion. Modelled on

Italian autostrada, German autobahn. US equivalent is turnpike, networked to form Interstate Highway System.

mould, name for various minute fungi forming furry coating mostly on dead organic matter. Common forms incl. black bread mould, *Rhizopus nigricans.* The blue mould often found on cheese is of *Penicillium* genus, source of penicillin.

Moulmein (*Maulamyaing*), seaport of S Burma, near mouth of R. Salween. Pop. 175,000. Exports rice, teak.

mountain, natural elevation of Earth's surface, raised relative to surrounding area to height over 305 m/1000 ft. Distinguished from plateau by summit being small in proportion to base. Formed by volcanic action, differential erosion of high land, earth movements, esp. folding and faulting, or combination of all factors. A major mountain-building period is called an orogeny (*see* GEOLOGICAL TABLE).

mountain ash or **rowan,** any of genus *Sorbus* of small trees and shrubs of rose family. Native to N temperate regions. Compound leaves, white flowers followed by red berries. Common European species is *S. aucuparia.*

mountaineering, sport of climbing mountains. Modern form dates from 1850s when British climbers scaled most of the Alpine peaks; Alpine Club founded in London (1857) did much to popularize sport. Ten highest mountains in world had been climbed by 1964.

Mountbatten, Louis Francis Albert Victor Nicholas, 1st Earl

Mountbatten of Burma (1900–   ), British admiral. In WWII, supreme Allied commander in SE Asia (1943–6). Last viceroy of India (1947), governor-general (1947–8) after partition. Admiral of fleet (1955–9) and chief of defence staff (1959–65).

Mount Vernon, Virginia, home of George Washington from 1747 until his death in 1799. Preserved as US national monument.

Mourne Mountains, range of SE Northern Ireland. Highest peak Slieve Donard (852 m/2796 ft). Scenic area.

mouse, small omnivorous rodent of same family (Muridae) as rat, vole. Species incl. house mouse, *Mus musculus,* found worldwide near human habitation, and wood or field mouse, *Apodemus sylvaticus,* of W European countryside.

mouse deer, *see* CHEVROTAIN.

mouth, in anatomy, front opening of the alimentary canal. Roof is formed of hard palate, muscular tongue rests on floor; lined with mucous membrane. Process of digestion is begun in mouth by enzyme in saliva which helps convert starch to sugar.

mouth organ, *see* HARMONICA.

Mozambique or **Moçambique,** republic of SE Africa. Area 783,000 sq km (302,300 sq mi); pop. 9,444,000; cap. Maputo. Languages: Bantu, Portuguese. Religions: native, Christianity. Coastal lowlands; mountains in interior, N and W; main rivers Limpopo, Zambezi. Produces sugar cane, cashew nuts, tea, copra, sisal; h.e.p. at Cabora Bassa. Transit trade with C, S Africa. Reached (1498) by Vasco da Gama; Portuguese settlement followed 15th-19th cent. Became Portuguese East Africa colony (1907). Overseas prov. from 1951. Intense guerrilla warfare by 'Frelimo' nationalists from mid-1960s and fall of govt. in Portugal (1974) resulted in independence (1975).

Mozart, Wolfgang Amadeus (1756-91), Austrian composer. Began to perform in public and compose at age of six. Prolific composer, raised classical music to great heights in his elegance of style and beauty of form. Died in poverty. Over 600 compositions incl. 41 symphonies, 21 piano concertos, string quartets, operas, *eg Marriage of Figaro, Don Giovanni, Cosi fan tutte, The Magic Flute.*

mucous membrane, skin-like layer lining alimentary canal and air passages. Secretes mucus, which has protective and lubricating function.

mudpuppy, aquatic North American salamander, genus *Necturus.* Retains certain larval characteristics, *eg* external gills, underdeveloped legs.

mudskipper, fish of goby family, genus *Periophthalmus* or *Boleophthalmus,* found in tropics. Lives in mud of mangrove swamps, using pectoral fins to hop over mud surface or climb mangrove roots.

Muhammad, alternative spelling of MOHAMMED.

Mühlheim-an-der-Ruhr, city of W West Germany, in Ruhr. Pop. 193,000. Coalmining, iron and steel mfg., textiles. Coal research institute.

Muir, Edwin (1887-1959), Scottish poet. Works, *eg* in *Collected Poems*

(1952), draw on dream imagery, archetypal myth. Also translated Kafka into English, wrote prose *Autobiography* (1954).

Mujibur Rahman (1920-75), Bangladeshi political leader. Leader of Awami League in East Pakistan (later Bangladesh) which sought independence from Pakistan; imprisoned in West Pakistan (1971) after electoral victory. Returned (1972) as 1st PM of independent Bangladesh following Indian intervention in civil war. Killed in army coup.

Mukden, see SHENYANG.

mulberry, any of genus *Morus* of deciduous trees and shrubs, native to N temperate and subtropical regions. Fruit resembles raspberry. Leaves of *M. alba,* white mulberry, and *M. nigra,* black mulberry, used for feeding silkworms.

Muldoon, Robert David (1921-), New Zealand statesman, PM (1975-). Headed National Party elected on pledges to reduce inflation, deal with problems in indust. relations.

mule, see ASS.

Mulhouse (Ger. *Mülhausen*), city of Alsace, E France, on R. Ill and Rhine-Rhône canal. Pop. 116,000. Textile mfg., chemicals (potash deposits nearby), engineering. Part of Swiss Confederation (1515-1798), voted to join France. Held by Germany (1871-1918).

Mull, isl. of Inner Hebrides, W Scotland, in Strathclyde region. Area 909 sq km (351 sq mi), main town Tobermory. Crofting, fishing, tourism.

mullein, any of genus *Verbascum* of biennial herbs of figwort family.

Found in Europe and Asia. *V. thapsus* has woolly leaves and spike of yellow flowers. *V. phoenicium* is purple mullein.

Müller, Paul Herman (1899-1965), Swiss chemist. Discovered (1939) DDT's use as insecticide; its large-scale production was begun in WWII. Awarded Nobel Prize for Physiology and Medicine (1948).

mullet, any of Mugilidae family of grey edible freshwater or marine fish. Feeds on debris in shallow water. Unrelated red mullet or goat fish of Mullidae family is important food fish.

Mullingar, co. town of Westmeath, C Irish Republic. Pop. 6000. Agric. market, tanning. RC cathedral.

multinational corporation, company or group of commonly-owned companies operating in a number of countries, usually involving extensive financial and indust. interests. As policy decisions are made in international context, they often conflict with local interests in countries where particular operations take place. Thus demands have been made for legislation to enable national interests to prevail, both in West and Third World.

multiple sclerosis, chronic disease of nervous system, resulting in degeneration of nerve sheaths of brain and spinal cord. Symptoms incl. speech disorder, loss of muscular coordination; cause unknown.

Mumford, Lewis (1895-), American writer. Concerned with man and his environment; has written on history of technology, architecture, town planning. Works incl. *The Golden Day* (1926), *Technics and Civilization* (1934), *The City in History* (1961).

mummy, dead body preserved by embalming, esp. associated with ancient Egypt. Usual method was removal of internal organs, drying of body with natron and wrapping in linen bandages. Human mummies often placed in human-form coffins.

mumps, infectious disease caused by airborne viruses. Symptoms incl. fever and painful swelling of parotid salivary glands. Usually childhood disease; may cause sterility in adult men. Incubation period 2-4 weeks.

Munch, Edvard (1863-1944), Norwegian painter, graphic artist. Forerunner of expressionism; his neurotic works, characterized by distortion and vivid colour, depict anguish and themes of love and death. Works incl. *The Scream*, *The Sick Child* and numerous woodcuts, lithographs, *etc.*

München, *see* MUNICH, West Germany.

München-Gladbach, *see* MÖN-CHEN-GLADBACH.

Münchhausen, Karl Friedrich Hieronymus, Baron von (1720-97), German soldier. Fought for Russians against Turks. Best known as hero of many fantastic adventures, collected and pub. in 1785 by Rudolf Erich Raspe and subsequently expanded by others.

Mungo, St. (d. c 612), Scottish churchman, also called St. Kentigern. Missionary in Cumbria; said to have founded church at Glasgow.

Munich (*München*), city of S West Germany, on R. Isar, cap. of Bavaria. Pop. 1,338,000. Cultural, indust. centre; publishing, brewing industs. Tourism, annual *Oktoberfest*. Under

Wittelsbachs from 1255, cap. of Bavaria from 1506. Nazi hq. from 1919; scene of Hitler's *Putsch* (1923), Munich Pact (1938). Has museums, art galleries, English Garden (1832), univ. (moved from Landshut 1826). Site of Olympics 1972.

Munich Pact, agreement (Sept. 1939) signed by Germany, Italy, Britain and France, sanctioning Hitler's annexation of Sudetenland, Czechoslovakia. Represented height of Western appeasement policy towards Nazi Germany; agreement thought then to have averted world war.

Munro, H[ector] H[ugh], see SAKI.

Munster, prov. of SW Irish Republic. Area 24,126 sq km (9315 sq mi); pop. 880,000. Comprises cos. Clare, Cork, Kerry, Limerick, Tipperary, Waterford. Ancient kingdom, former cap. Cashel.

Münster, city of NW West Germany, on Dortmund-Ems canal. Pop. 198,000. Metal goods, brewing; univ. (1773). Hanseatic League member; scene of experimental Anabaptist govt. (1533-5) under John of Leiden. Treaty of Westphalia (1648) signed here. Medieval appearance destroyed in WWII.

muntjac, small deer with short antlers, genus *Muntiacus,* found in forests of India and SE Asia. Also called barking deer.

muon or **mu-meson,** elementary particle of lepton family with mass 207 times that of electron and either positive or negative charge. Decays rapidly into electron, neutrino and anti-neutrino.

mural painting, decoration of walls

or ceilings by oil paint, ceramics, tempera, fresco, encaustic wax, *etc.*

Murat, Joachim (1767-1815), French marshal, king of Naples (1808-15). Grew to favour with Napoleon as leader of cavalry; married Napoleon's sister, Caroline (1800). Made king of Naples (1808). Joined Allies (1814) in attempt to retain throne, but fought for Napoleon during Hundred Days; defeated by Austrians. Shot after unsuccessful invasion to recover Naples.

Murcia, city of SE Spain, on R. Segura, cap. of Murcia prov. Pop. 244,000. Textiles (hist. silk mfg.), food processing; univ. (1915). From 11th cent. cap. of Moorish kingdom of Murcia, conquered by Castile 1266. Gothic cathedral (14th cent.).

murder, unlawful killing of human being, distinguished from MAN-SLAUGHTER in that it is malicious, premeditated; also, any killing done while committing another serious crime, *eg* rape, robbery. In some countries, premeditated murder still receives CAPITAL PUNISHMENT. In US, some statutes grade seriousness of murder, *eg* 1st degree receives harshest penalty.

Murdoch, [Jean] Iris (1919-), English author, b. Ireland. Known for sensitive, intricate, intellectual novels, *eg Under the Net* (1954), *The Bell* (1958), *The Unicorn* (1963). Also wrote *Sartre, Romantic Rationalist* (1953).

Murdock, William (1754-1839), Scottish engineer. Discovered and demonstrated use of coal gas in lighting (1792).

Murillo, Bartolomé Estéban (1617-82), Spanish painter. Known for his idealized religious paintings, *eg The Immaculate Conception*, and sentimental genre scenes; his work was enormously popular into the 19th cent.

Murmansk, city of USSR, N European RSFSR; on Barents coast of Kola penin. Pop. 329,000. Ice-free port; exports timber; fisheries. Founded 1915, important base in WWII.

Murray, [George] Gilbert [Aimé] (1866-1957), British scholar, b. Australia. Known for verse translations of Aristophanes, Sophocles, Euripides, Aeschylus. Also wrote *Four Stages of Greek Religion* (1912) giving picture of religious, social background to plays.

Murray or Moray, James Stuart, 1st Earl of (c 1531-70), Scottish nobleman. One of leaders in Scottish Reformation. Adviser to half-sister, Mary Queen of Scots, on her return to Scotland; appointed regent after her abdication (1567). Assassinated.

Murray, chief river of Australia, flows c 2575 km (1600 mi) from Snowy Mts. via Albury, Murray Bridge to Indian Ocean at L. Alexandrina. Main tributaries Darling, Goulburn, Murrumbidgee. Forms most of Victoria-New South Wales border. Provides extensive irrigation, h.e.p.

Murrumbidgee, river of S New South Wales, Australia. Flows c 1600 km (1000 mi) W from Snowy Mts. to Murray R. Main tributary Lachlan. Murrumbidgee Irrigation Area (MIA) permits high-yield fruit, rice, livestock farming.

Murry, [John] Middleton (1889-1957), English author. Known for biographical literary criticism, *eg Keats and Shakespeare* (1925), *Son of Woman, the Story of D.H. Lawrence* (1931), *William Blake* (1933). Also wrote *Life of Jesus* (1926) reflecting his Christian Marxism. Married to Katherine Mansfield.

Muscat, cap. of Oman. Pop. 25,000. Port on Gulf of Oman. Exports dates, dried fish, mother-of-pearl.

Muscat and Oman, *see* OMAN.

muscle, body tissue consisting of bundles of cells in the form of fibre which contract or expand under suitable stimulation. Three types of muscle exist: striated or voluntary muscle, which forms flesh and is under conscious control; smooth or involuntary, which is found in walls of alimentary canal, blood vessels, *etc*, and is under control of nervous system; cardiac or heart muscle.

muscovite, *see* MICA.

muscular dystrophy, condition which produces progressive wasting of the muscles, esp. in males. Cause unknown; no method of treatment or cure.

Muses, in Greek myth, nine daughters of Zeus and Mnemosyne, goddesses of the arts and literature. Worshipped at Pieria in Thessaly and Mt. Helicon in Boeotia.

mushroom, fleshy, edible fungi esp. those of family Agaricaceae. Species incl. field mushroom *Agaricus campestris*, horse mushroom, *A. arvensis*, and wood mushroom, *A. silvicola*.

music, art of combining sounds made by musical instruments or human voice. In Europe up to 17th cent., vocal music was dominant form (*see* PLAINSONG; POLYPHONY). In 17th cent., instrumental music developed independent style and

OPERA emerged. CONCERTO form
dates from early 18th cent.; beginnings of classical SYMPHONY were
estab. by STAMITZ and form
developed to great heights by
Haydn, Mozart and Beethoven.
Music of 20th cent. has moved away
from conventional harmony and
tonality, under influence of such
innovators as SCHOENBERG. Musical
instruments can be divided into 6
main groups: string, wind (woodwind, brass), percussion, keyboard,
electric, electronic. Recent developments incl. use of chance and
electronic methods.

music, electronic, music produced
by electronic circuits. In electronic
instruments, *eg* electronic organ and
synthesizer, signals are produced by
such devices as oscillators, amplified and then fed into loudspeakers. Keyboard of electronic
instrument serves as group of
switches. Electronic music can be
performed 'live' or may be
prerecorded on tape, processed in
the studio, and replayed at any time.

musicology, academic study of
music, *eg* history, analysis, acous-
tics, music appreciation and music
education.

Musil, Robert [Edler von] (1880-
1942), Austrian novelist. Chiefly
known for monumental masterpiece
Der Mann ohne Eigenschaften (1930-
43; *The Man Without Qualities* 1953-
60), examining cultural collapse
through story of year in life of
brilliant intellectual.

musk, various plants with musky
scent esp. *Mimulus moschatus* of
figwort family, with yellow flowers,
and moschatel, *Adoxa mos-
chatellina,* with greenish flowers.

musk deer, *Moschus moschiferus,*
small solitary deer from highlands of
C Asia. Hunted for glandular
secretion (musk) from abdomen of
male, used in perfumery.

muskellunge, *Esox masquinongy,*
large North American game fish
related to pike, found esp. in Great
Lakes. Reaches lengths of 1.8 m/6 ft.

musket, muzzle-loading handgun
with matchlock action used by
infantry from late 15th cent., later
(from *c* 1680) with flintlock, esp.
'Brown Bess' musket. Superseded
by breech-loading magazine rifle in
19th cent.

musk ox, *Ovibos moschatus,* hoofed
ruminant intermediate between ox
and sheep, found in tundra of
Canada and Greenland. Long coarse
hair, downward curving horns,
musky smell.

muskrat or **musquash,** *Ondatra
zibethica,* North American aquatic
rodent with musky odour. Cultivated for glossy brown fur;
introduced *c* 1905 into Europe,
proved to be pest.

musk turtle, North American freshwater turtle, genus *Sternotherus,*
with strong musky odour.

Muslim religion, *see* ISLAM.

muslin, group of plain woven cotton
fabrics, believed to be named after
Mosul, Iraq. Introduced into England in late 17th cent.

musquash, *see* MUSKRAT.

mussel, marine or freshwater bivalve mollusc. Marine mussels,
usually of Mytilidae family, attach
themselves to rocks, *etc,* by thread-
like secretions. Freshwater mussels
of Unionidae family sometimes
source of mother-of-pearl and
pearls. Species incl. edible common

mussel, *Mytilus edulis*, of N Atlantic coasts, and freshwater pearl mussel, *Unio margaritiferus*.

Musselburgh, town of Lothian region, EC Scotland; a suburb of Edinburgh. Pop. 17,000. Paper, rope mfg.

Musset, [Louis Charles] Alfred de (1810-57), French poet. Known for introspective love lyrics, *Les nuits* (1835-40). Also wrote comedies of manners, eg *On ne badine pas avec l'amour* (1834), novels. Lover of George Sand.

Mussolini, Benito (1883-1945), Italian dictator. Originally a Socialist, he founded (1919) *Fasci di Combattimento*, dedicated to aggressive nationalism and suppression of Socialism and Communism. Organized Fascism into political party (1921). Directed march on Rome (Oct. 1922) which led to his appointment as premier. Assumed dictatorial powers by 1926; reformed govt. according to Fascist principles. Conquered Ethiopia (1935-6), annexed Albania (1939). Entered WW II (1940) in Axis alliance with Hitler. Resigned 1943 after Allied invasion of Italy; rescued from custody by German paratroopers. Shot by partisans.

Mussorgsky, Modest Petrovich (1839-81), Russian composer. Member of 'the Five'. Musical output was restricted by alcoholism. Famed for opera *Boris Godunov* (revised by Rimsky-Korsakov), and piano work *Pictures at an Exhibition* (orchestrated by Ravel).

Mustafa Kemal, see ATATÜRK.

mustard, various annual plants of genus *Brassica* with yellow flowers and slender seed pods. Native to Europe and W Asia. Main types are black mustard, *B. nigra*, and white mustard, *B. hirta*, both used in condiment mustard.

mutation, in heredity, sudden change in number or chemical composition of chromosomes. Mutation in gametes can produce inherited change in characteristics of organisms which develop from them and is basis of evolution. Mutations occur naturally at slow rate but can be accelerated, eg by exposure to radiation.

mute swan, see SWAN.

Muttra, see MATHURA.

Muzorewa, Abel Tendekayi (1925-), Zimbabwe-Rhodesian political leader, churchman. PM in first 'black majority' govt. (1979-).

Mycenae, ancient city of Greece, in NE Peloponnese, near modern Mikinai. Centre of MYCENAEAN CIVILIZATION.

Mycenaean civilization, late Bronze Age Greek civilization with its centre at Mycenae, which fl 1600-1200 BC. Deriving their culture in part from the Minoans of Crete, Mycenaeans gained ascendancy over Crete by 1450 BC and achieved commercial and cultural dominance in Greece (1600-1200 BC). Built strongly-walled cities at Mycenae, Tiryns, Pylos, and noted beehive tombs. Overthrown by Dorian invaders.

My Lai, small village of South Vietnam, scene of massacre (1968) of over 300 civilians by US troops, who alleged that it was a Viet Cong base. Incident contributed to growing disillusionment over US involvement in Vietnam War.

mynah, Asiatic starling found mainly in India and Sri Lanka. Hill mynah, *Gracula religiosa*, noted for mimicking human speech, has black plumage; often kept as pet.

myopia or **short sight**, condition in which images are focused in front of retina, so that distant objects are seen unclearly. Caused because lens of eye is too long or its refractive power too great. Corrected by glasses with concave lenses. Called near sight in US.

Myrdal, Gunnar (1898-), Swedish economist. Wrote *Asian Drama* (1968) analyzing how social and economic factors affect govt. in Asia. Expert on economic problems of developing countries. Shared Nobel Prize for Economics with Friedrich von Hayek (1974).

Myrmidons, ancient Greek warrior tribe of Thessaly. In legend, descendants of ants changed by Zeus into fighting men. In Homer, warriors of Achilles.

myrrh, aromatic gum resin extracted from small tree, *Commiphora myrrha*, native to Arabia and Ethiopia.

myrtle, any of genus *Myrtus* of evergreen shrubs native to Asia. Common Mediterranean myrtle, *M. communis*, has oval leaves, white flowers, purple berries. Yields extract used in perfumery.

Mysore, city of Karnataka state, SW India. Pop. 356,000. Silk and cotton goods mfg. Former state cap. Has maharajah's palace with notable throne.

mysteries, in Greek and Roman religion, various secret cults. Most important among the Greeks were the Eleusinian (*see* ELEUSIS) and Orphic. Esp. important from 5th cent. BC. Several Asiatic cults were incorporated by the Romans, *eg* those of Isis and Mithras. Possibly many of the cults derived from earlier fertility rituals.

mystery plays, *see* MIRACLE PLAYS.

mysticism, belief that person can intuitively understand spiritual truths beyond the comprehension of the intellect, *eg* that individual can form a direct relationship with God. Has incl. such movements as neoplatonism, Gnosticism; influenced Quakers.

myth, traditional story of unknown authorship, usually relating supernatural events, actions of gods. May be associated with religious ceremony or offer explanations of natural phenomena, customs, origin of a people, *etc.* Modern myth interpretation regarded as beginning with Max Müller, who took linguistic approach; Sir James Frazer's *The Golden Bough* (1890) linked myth with birth, death, resurrection cycle in nature. Today anthropologists tend to reject interpretations of the concept of myth and concentrate on the various myths of a given people.

Mytilene (*Mitilini*), cap. of Lesbos isl., Greece. Pop. 26,000. Port; fruit, olive trade.

myxomatosis, infectious virus disease of rabbits spread by mosquitoes and fleas. Characterized by growth of soft tumours in connective tissue. Artificially introduced into Britain and Australia to reduce rabbit population.

N

Naas, co. town of Kildare, EC Irish Republic. Pop. 5000. Hunting, horse-racing. Former cap. of Leinster.

Nabis, les, name taken by group of French artists, incl. Bonnard, Vuillard and Denis, during 1890s. Influenced by Gauguin, work is characterized by flat areas of pure colour and heavy outlines.

Nabokov, Vladimir, pseud. of Vladimir Sirin (1899-1977), American author, b. Russia. Works, incl. *Laughter in the Dark* (1938), *The Real Life of Sebastian Knight* (1941), *Lolita* (1958), *Pale Fire* (1962), use idiosyncratic verbal games.

nacre, see PEARL.

nadir, in astronomy, point on celestial sphere directly opposite ZENITH and directly below observer.

Nagaland, state of NE India on Burma border. Area 16,500 sq km (6400 sq mi); pop. 515,600; cap. Kohima. Wild, forested region inhabited by Nagas, headhunters until recently. Formed in 1962 following nationalist agitation; ceasefire followed in 1964, but armed separatist activity continued sporadically.

Nagasaki, major port of Japan, W Kyushu isl. Pop. 421,000. Shipbuilding and engineering indust.; fisheries. Opened to foreign trade in 16th cent.; kept open to Dutch (1641-1858) when rest of Japan closed to foreigners. Devastated by 2nd atomic bomb (9 Aug. 1945), with loss of 25,000 lives.

Nagoya, major port of Japan, SC Honshu isl. Pop. 2,036,000. Engineering, chemical and textile mfg.; produces pottery and porcelain. Has Atsuta Shinto shrine (2nd cent.), Buddhist temple (1692) and castle (1612).

Nagpur, city of Maharashtra state, C India. Pop. 866,000. Railway jct.; cotton goods, hosiery mfg. Former cap. of Nagpur Mahratta kingdom; passed to British (1853).

Nagy, Imre (1896-1958), Hungarian political leader. As Communist premier (1953-5), he introduced reforms to hard-line Stalinist Communism. Critical of Soviet influence in Hungary, removed from office. Recalled to lead new govt. after revolution (1956). Executed after Soviet military occupation.

Nahum, prophetic book of OT, written *c* 650 BC; of unknown authorship. Foretells fall of Nineveh (612 BC).

Naiads, in Greek myth, NYMPHS of springs, lakes and rivers.

nail, in anatomy, horny outgrowth of the outer layer of skin (epidermis) growing at tips of fingers and toes. Grows from fold in skin at base of nail; composed of keratin.

Naipaul, V[idiadhar] S[uraj-prasad] (1932-), English novelist, b. Trinidad. Known for comic novels with Caribbean setting, *eg The Mystic Masseur* (1957), *A House for Mr Biswas* (1961). His brother, Shiva Naipaul, is known for novel *Fireflies* (1971).

Nairnshire, former county of NE Scotland, now in Highland region. Hilly in S; low-lying, fertile in N. Agric., livestock rearing; fishing. Co. town was Nairn, former royal burgh on Moray Firth. Pop. 8000. Fishing port, tourist resort.

Nairobi, cap. of Kenya, in E African highlands. Pop. 535,000. Admin., commercial, tourist centre on Uganda-Mombasa railway; exports coffee, sisal, hides; has coil., part of Univ. of E Africa. Nairobi National Park (game reserve) nearby. Founded 1899.

Nalchik, city of USSR, cap. of Kabardino-Balkar auton. republic, S European RSFSR. Pop. 171,000. Food-processing, furniture, oilfield equipment mfg. Health resort on N slope of Greater Caucasus.

Namaqualand, coastal desert of South West Africa and Cape Prov., South Africa; divided by R. Orange. Source of copper, tungsten, alluvial diamonds. Pop. mainly Nama Hottentots.

Namibia, see SOUTH WEST AFRICA.

Namur (Flem. *Namen*), town of SE Belgium, at confluence of Meuse and Sambre, cap. of Namur prov. Pop. 33,000. Leather goods, cutlery, glass mfg. Battleground in many wars; badly damaged in WWII. Cathedral (18th cent.).

Nanchang, cap. of Kiangsi prov., SE China. Pop. 900,000. Transport, indust. centre in R. Kan; tractor mfg., engineering, large silk complex. First Chinese soviet estab. here briefly (1927).

Nancy, city of NE France, on R. Meurthe and Marne-Rhine canal, cap. of Meurthe-et-Moselle dept. Pop. 123,000. Iron and steel mfg., engineering; univ. (1768). Cap. of duchy of Lorraine from 12th cent.; model of 18th cent. planning under Stanislas I.

Nanga Parbat, Himalayan peak in N India, near Kashmir-Pakistan border; height 8126 m (26,660 ft). First climbed 1953.

Nanking, cap. of Kiangsu prov., E China. Pop. 2,000,000. Rail jct. on Yangtze; textiles, oil refining, iron and steel mfg. Treaty of Nanking (1842) opened China to foreign trade. Cultural centre; Ming imperial tombs. Cap. of Nationalist govt. (1928-37), until captured by Japanese.

Nansen, Fridtjof (1861-1930), Norwegian explorer, scientist and statesman. Crossed Greenland icefields (1888); attempted to reach North Pole by drifting in ship *Fram* (1893-5), further N than anyone before. Awarded Nobel Peace Prize (1922) for work with post-WWI refugees.

Nantes, city of Brittany, NW France, on R. Loire. Cap. of Loire-Atlantique dept. Pop. 259,000. Outport at St Nazaire; oil refining, food processing. Seat of dukes of Brittany (10th-16th cent.). Edict of Nantes (1598), giving Huguenots freedom, signed here. Ducal castle, cathedral; univ. (1460).

Nantes, Edict of, decree issued (1598) by Henry IV of France granting religious freedom and civil rights to Huguenots (French Protestants). Its terms were gradually nullified in 17th cent.; revoked 1685.

Nantucket, isl. off SE Massachusetts, US; separated from Cape Cod by Nantucket Sound. Atlantic summer resort. Settled 1659. Hist. whaling centre.

napalm, incendiary material made from petrol or oil and a thickening agent (soap or polymer). Used in warfare as it sticks to target while burning.

naphtha, mixture of light hydrocarbons obtained by distillation of petroleum, coal tar, *etc.* Inflammable and volatile; used as cleaning solvent and in making varnish.

naphthalene ($C_{10}H_8$), white crystalline solid with penetrating smell. Obtained from distillation of coal tar. Used in moth balls and manufacture of dyes.

Napier, Sir Charles James (1782-1853), British army officer. Sent to India (1841) to subdue the emirs of Sind, whom he finally defeated at Hyderabad (1843) after which he was made governor. Returned to England (1847) after disagreements with govt.

Napier, John (1550-1617), Scottish mathematician. First to publish table of logarithms (1614); introduced calculating rods ('Napier's bones') to facilitate arithmetic computations. Also produced religious writings.

Napier, city of E North Isl., New Zealand, on Hawke's Bay. Pop. 40,000. Major wool trade centre; textile, tobacco, food processing industs. Founded 1855; rebuilt after 1931 earthquake.

Naples (*Napoli,* anc. *Neapolis*), city of S Italy, on Bay of Naples. Cap. of Campania and of Napoli prov. Pop. 1,259,000. Major port, indust. centre; tourism. Greek colony founded 6th cent. BC, Roman resort. Under Normans from 1139; cap. of Kingdom of Naples (1282-1860). Univ. (1224), cathedral, castles, museum (has relics of Herculaneum, Pompeii). Damaged in WWII.

Napoleon I, full name Napoleon Bonaparte or Buonaparte (1769-1821), French military and political leader, emperor (1804-14), b. Corsica. Revitalized Revolutionary Army in Italian campaign (1796-7), driving out Austrians. Invaded Egypt (1798) as part of plan to take India; campaign became hopeless after Nelson's naval victory at Aboukir. Coup d'état (1799) estab. Napoleon as first consul, effectively dictator. Reorganized state, codified laws in Code Napoléon. Had himself created emperor. In Napoleonic Wars, thwarted European alliance against him by defeating Austria at Austerlitz (1805), Prussia at Jena (1806), Russia at Friedland (1807); ruled virtually entire continent after peace treaty of Tilsit, placing members of his family on several thrones (*see* BONAPARTE). Defeated by Nelson at Trafalgar (1805); failed in attempts to prevent trade with Britain by CONTINENTAL SYSTEM (1806-12). Decline set in with failure of PENINSULAR campaign in Spain and disastrous invasion of Russia (1812), ending in retreat and loss of most of army. Defeated at Leipzig by new European alliance. Abdicated 1814, exiled to Elba. Returned to France, but Hundred Days rule ended in defeat at Waterloo (1815). Exiled to St Helena, where he died.

Napoleon III, orig. Louis Napoleon Bonaparte (1808-73), French political leader, emperor (1852-70). Nephew of Napoleon I, he spent youth in exile. Plotted 2 unsuccessful coups (Strasbourg, 1836; Boulogne, 1840). Elected president of republic after Revolution of 1848. After coup d'état (1851), dissolved legislature and assumed dictatorial powers; proclaimed emperor (1852). Rule marked by military intervention in Crimea, Mexico, Italy; annexed Nice, Savoy. Manoeuvred by Bismarck into war with Prussia (1870); defeated, taken prisoner at Sedan. Exiled to England, where he died.

Napoli, *see* NAPLES, Italy.

Nara, town of Japan, SC Honshu isl. Pop. 208,000. Cultural and religious centre; 1st permanent cap. of Japan 709-84. Has many Buddhist temples, one with colossal bronze statue of Buddha. Nearby is Mt. Kasuga, revered as home of gods.

Narbonne (anc. *Narbo Martius*), town of Languedoc, S France. Wine trade, brandy distilling, sulphur processing. Pop. 40,000. First Roman colony in transalpine Gaul, estab. 118 BC; *fl* in Middle Ages until harbour silted up (14th cent.). Palace, cathedral (both 13th cent.).

narcissism, in psychology, extreme self-love, term deriving from Greek myth of Narcissus. Regarded by psychoanalysts as early stage in normal psychosexual development, at which sexual object is self.

Narcissus, in Greek myth, beautiful youth who rejected love of others. Caused by Aphrodite to become enamoured of his own image in a mountain pool. Pined away and was changed into a flower.

narcissus, genus of bulbous perennial herbs of amaryllis family. Found in Europe, Asia and North America. Erect linear leaves; yellow, white or bicolour flowers, often with trumpet-shaped corolla. Species incl. jonquil, *Narcissus jonquilla,* and DAFFODIL.

narcotic, substance which has depressant effect on nervous system. Used medicinally in small doses to relieve pain, induce sleep, *etc.* Main narcotics are opium and its derivatives (morphine, heroin). Usually addictive; overdoses may cause coma and death.

Narva, town of USSR, NE Estonian SSR. Pop. 31,000. Port on R. Narva. Textile centre. Founded 1223 by Danes; member of Hanseatic League. Scene of Charles XII of Sweden's victory (1700) over Peter the Great, who later took town (1704).

Narvik, town of NW Norway, on Ofot Fjord. Pop. 13,000. Ice-free port, railway terminus; exports Swedish iron ore. Scene of heavy fighting (1940).

narwhal, *Monodon monoceros,* medium-sized arctic whale. Male has long spiral tusk, up to 2.4 m/8 ft long, extending from upper jaw. Hunted for oil.

NASA, *see* NATIONAL AERONAUTICS AND SPACE ADMINISTRATION.

Naseby, village of Northamptonshire, C England. Site of Royalists' defeat by Cromwell's Parliamentarians (1645).

Nash, John (1752-1835), English architect, town planner. Achieved most noted effects in elegant classicism of his developments in

London for George IV, eg Regent Street and Regent's Park.

Nash, Ogden (1902-71), American poet. Known for humorous verse pub. in *New Yorker*. Collections incl. *I'm a Stranger Here Myself* (1938), *Everyone But Thee and Me* (1962).

Nash, Paul (1889-1946), English artist. Official war artist in both World Wars; poetic vision, influenced by surrealism, is revealed in his landscapes. Works incl. *Totes Meer*, painted during WWII. His brother, **John Nash** (1893-1977), is best known for English landscapes, less visionary than Paul's.

Nash, Sir Walter (1882-1968), New Zealand statesman, b. England. Labour Party leader and PM (1957-60).

Nashe, Thomas (1567-1601), English author. Wrote anti-Puritan pamphlets in Marprelate controversy. Known for picaresque novel, *The Unfortunate Traveller* (1594), satirical masque *Summer's Last Will and Testament* (1592) containing famous lyric, 'Adieu, . farewell, earth's bliss'.

Nashville, cap. of Tennessee, US; on Cumberland R. Pop. 448,000. Road, railway jct.; cotton trade, printing and publishing industs.; centre of recording indust. Seat of Vanderbilt Univ. (1873).

Nasmyth, Alexander (1758-1840), Scottish painter. Pupil of Allan Ramsay. Specialized in topographical landscapes incl. series of 16 views of places mentioned in Scott's *Waverley* Novels.

Nassau, former duchy of WC West Germany, cap. Wiesbaden. Forested and hilly; agric., wine production, spas (eg Bad Homburg). Duchy from 1806; part of Prussian prov. of Hesse-Nassau from 1866, of Hesse from 1945. Branches of Orange-Nassau family rule Luxembourg, Netherlands.

Nassau, cap. and port of Bahamas, on New Providence Isl. Pop. 102,000. Famous holiday resort. Exports pulpwood, salt, crayfish.

Nasser, Gamal Abdel (1918-70), Egyptian political leader. Joined Mohammed Neguib in military coup which estab. 1952 republic; became premier (1954), president (1956). Nationalized Suez Canal (1956) and withstood Anglo-French invasion to recover it. Aggressive anti-Israel policy led to war (1967); resignation after defeat was rejected by legislature. Promoted building of Aswan dam (completed 1970).

Nasser, Lake, see ASWAN, Egypt.

nasturtium, any of genus *Tropaeolum* of plants, native to South America. Common garden variety is *T. majus* with orange spurred flowers. Leaves sometimes used in salads. Also name of genus of WATERCRESS.

Natal, smallest prov. of South Africa, in E. Area 91,400 sq km (35,300 sq mi); pop. 2,193,000; cap. Pietermaritzburg. Coastal strip, interior plateau with Drakensberg foothills in W. Sugar, cereals, fruit growing; coalmining. Sighted 1497 and named by da Gama. Boer republic founded 1838; annexed by Britain 1843, became UK colony 1856. Absorbed Zululand 1897; prov. of Union of South Africa 1910.

Natal, port of NE Brazil, cap. of Rio Grande do Norte state; near mouth of Potengi R. Pop. 265,000. Exports sugar, cotton, salt; textile **mfg.** International airport nearby.

Natchez, North American Indian tribe of Hokan-Siouan linguistic stock. Sedentary farmers of SW Mississippi from 17th cent. Scattered during wars with French.

National Aeronautics and Space Administration (NASA), US govt. agency (estab. 1958) responsible for space exploration. Supervises construction of equipment and research on flights within and without Earth's atmosphere.

national anthem, patriotic hymn sung on ceremonial occasions. Some countries have had compositions created specifically to serve as anthems.

National Assembly, name adopted by Estates-General of France in 1789, marking its defiance of Louis XVI.

National Association for the Advancement of Colored People (NAACP), organization formed (1910) to end racial discrimination and segregation in US. Early campaigns were directed against lynching of blacks. Now advocates non-violent opposition to discrimination rather than methods of black power extremists.

national debt or **public debt,** indebtedness of govt. expressed in monetary terms. Calculated in many different ways, variously incl. public borrowing from individuals (eg loan stocks, bonds, treasury notes) or from foreign govts. or international organizations.

National Gallery, London, art gallery in Trafalgar Square containing British national picture collection. Founded 1824 with purchase of the Angerstein collection, present building was opened 1838. Holding of Italian art is esp. strong.

National Gallery of Art, Washington DC, part of the Smithsonian Institution; estab. 1937, it was opened in 1941. Fine collections of French, Italian and American paintings.

National Guard, in US, body estab. (1903) to replace state militias. Subject to state jurisdiction in peacetime. Responsible to president in national emergency.

National Health Insurance Act (1946), in UK, legislation providing for estab. of National Health Service (1948), most comprehensive medical care scheme of its time. Under it, free medical attention can be obtained from any doctor participating in service. Funded by national govt. and local taxation.

National Insurance Act (1911), in UK, legislation devised by LLOYD GEORGE, providing for estab. of compulsory national schemes in areas of old age pensions, sickness and disability insurance, and unemployment. *See* SOCIAL SECURITY.

nationalism, social and political creed expressing common heritage and culture through unification of an ethnic group, manifested either, in estab. nations, as doctrine that national welfare should prevail over international considerations, or, as basis for achieving independence as advocated by separatist groups (eg Spanish Basques). Nationalism was driving force behind expansionist nation-building in 19th cent. Europe, and in 20th cent. Asia and Africa.

Extreme forms linked with FASCISM, as in Nazi Germany.

nationalization, transference of ownership or control of land, resources, industs., *etc.,* to national govt. Associated with socialist, communist regimes, *eg* USSR after 1918, UK and France (1945-50). Also refers to acquisition by state of foreign-owned assets, *eg* Suez Canal by Egypt (1956).

national liberation front, revolutionary political front, or party, working for national independence. Originated with FLN (Front de Libération Nationale) in Algeria, where independence was achieved under Ben Bella after guerrilla campaign (1955-62); only recognized party under Algerian constitution. Influenced FLQ whose terrorist activities in Québec in 1960s led Canada's PM Trudeau to impose War Measures Act, (1970). Formation of such a front in South Vietnam (1961) helped Communists infiltrate villages, leading ultimately to victory over US-supported forces in early 1970s.

national park, area of scenic beauty and scientific interest, protected from development. Main purposes are conservation of flora and fauna, and human recreation. Since estab. at Yellowstone, US (1872), many countries, *eg* Canada, South Africa, UK, Tanzania, have designated national parks.

National Socialism or **Nazism,** ideology of National Socialist German Workers' Party (Nazi Party). Formulated in part by Hitler in *Mein Kampf* (1923) and by ROSENBERG. Founded on principles of racial purity, (Aryans representing 'master race'), allegiance to *Führer* (leader), reversal of terms of Versailles Treaty, German territ. expansion, esp. into Slav lands, and eradication of Communists and Jews, who were said to have betrayed Germany in WWI. As sole legal party after Hitler's rise to power, acted with brutality in consolidating power within Germany and forced outbreak of WWII through aggressive external policies.

National Theatre Company, repertory theatre company opened (1963) in Old Vic Theatre, London, under direction of Sir Laurence Olivier. New theatre complex opened 1976 on South Bank of Thames.

National Trust, in UK, nonprofitmaking organization chartered (1895) by Parliament. Aims to promote preservation for the people of lands and buildings of historic or aesthetic value. Has power to acquire land, issue protective orders on private property.

native cat, carnivorous arboreal Australian marsupial of Dasyuridae family. Species incl. Eastern native cat, *Dasyurus viverrinus,* with white spots on body.

NATO *see* NORTH ATLANTIC TREATY ORGANIZATION.

natterjack, *Bufo calamita,* small toad of W Europe. Brownish yellow in colour; short hind legs make it poor jumper.

natural gas, mixture of gaseous hydrocarbons, esp. methane, occurring naturally as deposits in porous rock, often in association with petroleum. Used as domestic fuel.

natural selection, in evolution, process by which those individuals of a species best-fitted to their specific environment tend to leave more offspring, which inherit those characteristics in which this fitness lies, whereas those less fitted tend to leave less offspring and die out. Thus there is progressive tendency towards greater degree of adaptation. Basis of Darwin's theory of evolution described by him and A.R. Wallace (1859).

Naucratis, ancient city of N Egypt, on R. Nile, SE of Alexandria. First Greek colony in Egypt, founded 7th cent. BC. Remains incl. temples, pottery.

Naupaktos (Ital. *Lepanto*), town of WC Greece, on Gulf of Corinth. Pop. 7000. Athenian naval base in Peloponnesian War. Scene of destruction of Turkish fleet by Holy League in battle of Lepanto (1571).

Nauplia (*Návplion*), town of Greece, in E Peloponnese, cap. of Argolis admin. dist. Pop. 9000. Port; tobacco, fruit trade. First cap. of independent Greece (1830-4).

Nauru, isl. republic of SW Pacific Ocean. Area 20 sq km (8 sq mi); pop. 8000. Extensive phosphate deposits. Discovered (1798), named Pleasant Isl.; admin. by Australia from 1947 until independence (1968). Member of British Commonwealth.

nausea, feeling of a desire to vomit. May be caused by irritation of stomach, unpleasant smells, *etc.*

Nausicaä, in Greek myth, daughter of Alcinoüs of Phaeacia. Welcomed Odysseus when shipwrecked during his wanderings after Trojan War.

nautical mile, unit of distance used in sea and air travel; equivalent to 1 minute of arc of a great circle of Earth. International nautical mile equals · 1852 m (*c* 1.15 mi); UK nautical mile is slightly larger, equalling 6080 ft (1853.18 m).

nautilus, cephalopod mollusc of Indian and Pacific oceans. External coiled shell divided into chambers, animal living in outermost chamber; other chambers filled with gas, giving shell buoyancy.

Navaho or **Navajo,** North American Indian tribe of Nadene linguistic stock. Inhabited NE Arizona in 17th cent. Nomadic hunters, farmers, shepherds. Raided Pueblo and Spanish settlements in New Mexico. Settled on reservations in SW US. Largest surviving tribe.

Navarino, *see* PYLOS, Greece.

Navarre, region and former kingdom of N Spain and SW France, hist. cap. Pamplona. Mountainous, incl. pass of Roncesvalles; drained by R. Ebro. Pop. mainly Basque. Cereals, livestock, h.e.p. Founded 9th cent.; S part annexed to Spain (1515), N part to France (1589).

nave, in architecture, central aisle of a church. Term once meant the area from the altar to main door, incl. side aisles, intended for use of the laity.

navel or **umbilicus,** scar, usually in form of depression in middle of the abdomen, marking place where the umbilical cord was joined to the foetus.

Navigation Acts, English legislation designed to restrict carrying of goods from abroad only to English-owned ships or to ships of country producing the goods. Acts of 1651 were designed to combat Dutch competition in trade with English possessions. Finally repealed 1849.

navy, branch of armed services

equipped for maritime warfare. Originated among ancient nations bordering on Mediterranean. In Britain, expanded 16th-17th cents., becoming in Charles II's reign disciplined and efficient. British naval dominance challenged in early 20th cent. esp. by Germany, Japan, leading to estab. of US as a major naval power. With development of air and submarine warfare in 20th cent., size of vessels has given place to speed and mobility, the only large warships being aircraft carriers. By early 1970s most powerful navies were those of USSR and US.

Naxos, isl. of Greece, in Aegean Sea, largest of Cyclades. Area 438 sq km (169 sq mi). Fruits, wine. Ancient centre for worship of Dionysus. In legend, here Theseus abandoned Ariadne.

Nazareth, town of N Israel. Pop. c 23,000. Associated with early life of Jesus. Pilgrimage centre.

Nazism, see NATIONAL SOCIALISM.

Nazi-Soviet Non-aggression Pact, see NON-AGGRESSION PACT.

Ndjamena, cap. of Chad, at confluence of Logone, Shari rivers. Pop. 179,000. Admin. centre, market for salt, dates, livestock. Founded 1900, known as Fort Lamy until ·1973.

Ndola, city of NC Zambia. Pop. 201,000. Indust., commercial, railway centre in copperbelt region. Scene of aircrash (1961) in which Dag Hammarskjold died.

Neagh, Lough, C Northern Ireland. Largest freshwater lake in British Isles: length 29 km (18 mi); width 18 km (11 mi).

Neanderthal man, early form of man, usually considered a representative of *Homo sapiens.* Lived between 100,000 and 40,000 years ago. Had prominent brow ridges, receding chin, sloping forehead but brain similar in size to modern man's. Remains 1st discovered (1856) in Neanderthal valley, Germany.

Nebraska, state of C US; on W bank of Missouri R. Area 200,000 sq km (77,230 sq mi); pop. 1,484,000; cap. Lincoln; chief city Omaha. Mainly prairies; tableland in W. Maize, wheat, sorghum, livestock farming. Agric. related industs. Exploration by Spanish in 16th cent. Region developed after Louisiana Purchase by US (1803). Admitted to Union as 37th state (1867).

Nebuchadnezzar II (d. 562 BC), king of Babylonia (c 605-562 BC). Quelled revolt in Judah (597), taking many Jews into exile in Babylon. Destroyed Jerusalem (586) after 2nd revolt. Rebuilt Babylon, constructing temples, palaces and city walls.

nebula, luminous cloud-like patch seen in night sky, consisting of masses of rarefied gas and dust. Name was formerly applied to extragalactic systems of stars.

neck, part of man or animal joining the head to the body. In man, column of 7 cervical vertebrae form bones of neck; they are surrounded by systems of muscles which move and support them.

Neckar, river of SW West Germany. Flows c 370 km (230 mi) from Black Forest to R. Rhine at Mannheim. Navigable to Stuttgart; canal link to Danube. Vineyards, h.e.p., tourism.

Necker, Jacques (1732-1804), French statesman, b. Switzerland. Succeeded TURGOT as finance minister (1776) and attempted fiscal reform to restore financial stability; dismissed (1781) by Louis XVI. Recalled 1788, he advised summoning of Estates-General. Subsequent dismissal led to storming of Bastille (14 July, 1789) and reinstatement. Resigned 1790.

necrosis, in medicine, death of a particular area of tissue. May be caused by cessation of blood supply, bacterial poisoning, *etc.*

nectar, *see* AMBROSIA.

nectarine, *see* PEACH.

Needles, The, three chalk stacks off W Isle of Wight, S England. Has lighthouse.

Nefertiti or **Nefretete** (*fl* 14th cent. BC), Egyptian queen, wife of Ikhnaton. Her beauty is suggested by famous portrait bust found (1912) at Amarna (now in Berlin).

Negev or **Negeb,** semi-desert of S Israel, between Mediterranean and Aqaba. Area *c* 13,310 sq km (5140 sq mi). Minerals, natural gas. Settled by immigrants on cooperative farms (*kibbutzim*).

Negro, river of NW Brazil. Rises in E Colombia, forming part of Colombia-Venezuela border. Flows SE 2250 km (*c* 1400 mi) to join Amazon near Manáus.

Negros, isl. of Philippines, NW of Mindanao. Area *c* 12,700 sq km (4900 sq mi). Mountainous, with extensively cultivated lowland. Major sugar producer.

Nehemiah, historical book of OT. Relates story of Nehemiah, cupbearer to King Artaxerxes I of Persia. Later governed Jerusalem (from 445 BC). Rebuilt city walls and reformed temple worship.

Nehru, Jawaharlal (1889-1964), Indian statesman and writer, PM

(1947-64). Influenced by Gandhi, devoted himself to obtaining Indian independence from Britain. President of Indian National Congress 4 times. Frequently in jail for civil disobedience campaigns of 1930s. First PM of independent Indian state. Maintained influential neutral stand in foreign affairs.

Neill, Alexander Sutherland (1883-1973), British educator. Known for views on progressive, child-centred education; founded Summerhill, school run according to his views, in Suffolk. Books incl. *Summerhill* (1962).

Neisse (*Nysa*), two rivers of E Europe. **Glatzer** or Silesian **Neisse** flows *c* 195 km (120 mi) NE from SW Poland to R. Oder near Brzeg. **Görlitzer** or Lusatian **Neisse** flows *c* 225 km (140 mi) N from NW Czechoslovakia via Görlitz to R. Oder near Gubin (Poland); forms part of Poland-East Germany border.

Nekrasov, Nikolai Alekseyevich (1821-77), Russian poet, editor. Published early work of Dostoyevski, Tolstoy, Turgenev. Wrote verse reflecting social concern, *eg Frost the Rednosed* (1863).

Nelson, Horatio, Viscount Nelson (1758-1805), English admiral. Aided Jervis off Cape St Vincent and ended Napoleon's Egyptian campaign by destroying the French fleet at Aboukir Bay (1798). At Naples he put down a Jacobin revolt and formed a liaison with EMMA HAMILTON, wife of the British ambassador. In 1801 he destroyed the Danish fleet at Copenhagen, and in 1805 died of wounds at the moment of victory over a combined

French and Spanish fleet at Trafalgar.

Nelson, region of NW South Isl., New Zealand. Area 17,900 sq km (6910 sq mi); pop. 69,000. Mainly mountainous; lowlands around Tasman Bay. Forestry; sheep, cattle raising; fruit, hops, tobacco growing. Main town **Nelson,** on Tasman Bay. Pop. 29,000. Port with ferry service to North Isl.; fruit, vegetables, tobacco exports; food processing, sawmilling, textile mfg. Has marble Anglican cathedral.

Nematoda (nematodes), phylum of unsegmented roundworms, *eg* threadworms, eelworms. Incl. soil-dwellers, free-swimming forms, and parasites, *eg* hookworm.

Nemean lion, in Greek myth, monstrous lion, offspring of Typhon and Echidna. Invulnerable to weapons but strangled by Heracles (1st labour).

Nemertea (nemerteans), phylum of mainly marine worms with unsegmented body and protrusible proboscis used to catch prey. Variable length, reaching 18 m/60 ft. Also called ribbon worms.

Nemesis, in Greek myth, personification of retribution, esp. in cases of human presumption towards the gods.

Nennius (*fl* 796), Welsh chronicler. *Historia Britonum* attributed to him, on early British history and legends, incl. ARTHURIAN LEGEND.

neo-Classicism, artistic style of 2nd half of 18th cent. which began as reaction to Baroque and rococo styles. Inspired by antique buildings and archaeological finds, its principal theorist was Winckelmann. Noted practitioners incl. Adam brothers in architecture, Mengs in painting.

neodymium (Nd), metallic element of the lanthanide series; at. no. 60, at. wt. 144.24. Compounds used to colour glass.

Neolithic, last period of STONE AGE in which domestication of animals, farming began. Started in SW Asia 8000-6000 BC; ended at different times in different areas, *eg* c 3500 BC in Mesopotamia but later in Europe.

neon (Ne), inert gaseous element; at. no. 10, at. wt. 20.18. Found in traces in atmosphere; obtained by fractional distillation of liquid air. Produces bright reddish-orange glow when electric current is passed through it; used in neon signs.

neon fish, *Paracheirodon innesi,* small brightly coloured fish discovered in Amazon R. (1936). Popular aquarium fish.

neo-plasticism, *see* MONDRIAN, De STIJL.

neoplatonism, philosophy loosely derived from doctrines of Plato, expounded (3rd cent.) by Plotinus. Held that all existence, material and spiritual, emanates from transcendent One through the divine mind (*see* LOGOS) and world soul. Freedom from sin gained by the individual soul seeking reintegration with the One. Exponents incl. Porphyry and Iamblichus. Banned by Justinian I (529) but influence continued through Middle Ages, affected 17th-19th cent. writers, poets.

Neoptolemus, in Greek legend, son of Achilles. Summoned to Trojan War after death of Achilles; killed Priam and was awarded Andromache, Hector's widow, as captive.

Married Hermione, daughter of Menelaus and Helen.

Nepal, kingdom of SC Asia. Area *c* 140,000 sq km (54,600 sq mi); pop. 12,904,000; cap. Katmandu. Language: Nepali. Religions: Hindu, Buddhism. Formerly remote region in Himalayas, bordered by India and Tibet; rice and grain grown in Nepal valley. Under Gurkha control from 1768; sovereignty recognized by British in 1923.

nephritis, inflammation of the kidneys, often caused by bacterial infection. Form known as acute glomerulonephritis usually follows infection by streptococci; characterized by swelling under skin due to leakage of water. Chronic form involves deterioration of kidneys.

Neptune, planet 8th in distance from Sun; mean distance from Sun *c* 4500 × 10⁶ km; diameter 44,800 km; mass *c* 17 times that of Earth. Solar orbit takes *c* 165 years. Discovered (1846) by Galle following predictions of Leverrier and Adams.

Neptune, in Roman religion, god of water. Possibly derived from an indigenous fertility god; sometimes identified with Greek POSEIDON, whose attributes he assimilated.

neptunium (Np), transuranic element; at. no. 93, mass no. of most stable isotope 237. First transuranic element, discovered (1940) by McMillan and Abelson during neutron bombardment of uranium.

Nereids, in Greek myth, daughters of Nereus; NYMPHS of the Aegean Sea.

Nereus, in Greek myth, wise and kindly sea deity. Had attributes of prophecy and shape-changing.

Nero [Claudius Caesar Drusus

Germanicus] (AD 37-68), Roman emperor (AD 54-68). Adopted as heir to Claudius I through intrigues of his mother Agrippina. After accession, arranged deaths of rightful heir Britannicus, Agrippina, wives Octavia and Poppaea, his adviser Seneca and many others. Suspected of starting great fire of Rome (64), began persecution of Christians, whom he accused of the crime. Committed suicide during revolt.

Neruda, Pablo, pseud. of Neftalí Ricardo Reyes (1904-73), Chilean poet. Best-known works incl. *Crepusculario* (1923), *Residencia en la tierra* (1933). Also wrote play, *The Splendour and Death of Joaquin Murieta* (1967). Nobel Prize for Literature (1971).

Nerval, Gérard de, pseud. of Gérard Labrunie (1808-55), French author. Wrote short stories, *eg* in *Les Filles du feu* (1854), sonnet series, *Les Chimères,* translation of Goethe's *Faust* (1828), spiritual autobiog. *Aurélia.*

Nervi, Pier Luigi (1891-1979), Italian architectural engineer. Known for his masterful use of reinforced concrete to create complicated new structures. Works incl. Giovanni Berta stadium in Florence (1929-32) and Turin exhibition hall (1948-9).

nervous system, network of nerves and nerve tissue in animals which conducts impulses to other parts of animal to coordinate actions and activities. Basic unit is nerve cell or neuron, consisting of nerve cell body and various thread-like processes (usually single long axon and several short dendrites). Impulses are transmitted from axons to dendrites at junctions called SYNAPSES. Certain impulses are communicated to brain and spinal cord from receptors (sensory organs inside or outside body), other impulses are communicated to effectors, *eg* muscles or glands.

Nesbit, E[dith] (1858-1924), English author. Known for anti-romantic children's fiction, *eg The Railway Children* (1906), *Five Children and It* (1902), which attempted to break with conventional middle-class mode.

Ness, Loch, lake of Highland region, N Scotland. Length 39 km (24 mi), forms part of Caledonian Canal. Home of reputed 'monster'.

Nessus, in Greek myth, centaur slain by Heracles for attempt to violate his wife, Deianira. The blood of Nessus, smeared on a robe by Deianira to regain Heracles' love, caused his death.

nest, structure prepared by animals for laying of eggs or giving birth to young. Many birds and certain reptiles, insects, fish and mammals build nests. Structure of bird's nest varies greatly, with most elaborate nests built by smallest birds. Some birds do not build nests, laying eggs on ground, *eg* ostrich.

Nestor, in Greek myth, son of Neleus and king of Pylos. In old age went with Greeks to Trojan War and was respected warrior and counsellor.

Nestorians, Christian followers of Nestorius (d. *c* 451). Driven into Persia after Council of Ephesus (431), they suffered much persecution. Modern Nestorian Church (mainly in Iraq) upholds Nestorius'

doctrines only in denying Virgin Mary name 'Mother of God'.

netball, seven-a-side game for women played mainly in English-speaking countries. Introduced into England (1897) from US as form of BASKETBALL; 1st rules date from 1901.

Netherlands (*Nederland*), kingdom of NW Europe. Area 41,344 sq km (15,963 sq mi); pop. 13,710,000; cap. Amsterdam, seat of govt. The Hague. Language: Dutch. Religions: Protestant, RC. Low-lying, 25% below sea level; large reclaimed areas. Dairying, bulbs, fishing. Extensive canal system links main rivers (Scheldt, Maas, Rhine), important transit trade. Industs. centred in Amsterdam, Rotterdam (Europe's leading port), Utrecht. Member of EEC. Part of Low Countries until 16th cent.; rebelled against Spanish rule after religious repression. N provinces declared independence 1579. Estab. overseas empire 17th cent. Union with former Austrian Netherlands (Belgium) (1814-30). German occupation in WWII.

Netherlands Antilles, autonomous Dutch isl. groups in Caribbean. Area 394 sq km (1020 sq mi); pop. 241,000; cap. Willemstad. Language: Dutch. N group in Leeward Isls. incl. Saba, St Eustatius, S part of St Martin; S group off Venezuela, incl. Curaçao, Aruba, Bonaire. Economy depends on refining of Venezuelan oil on Curaçao and Aruba. Dutch territ. from 17th cent. (known as Curaçao until 1949; granted full autonomy (1954).

Netherlands New Guinea, see IRIAN JAYA.

nettle, any of genus *Urtica* of plants with stinging hairs on leaves which cause a rash (urticaria) by injecting histamine into the skin. Common stinging nettle, *U. dioica*, found in Europe and North America.

nettle rash, see URTICARIA.

Neuchâtel, (Ger. *Neuenburg*), city of W Switzerland, on L. Neuchâtel, cap. of Neuchâtel canton. Pop. 39,000. Watch mfg.; chocolate, condensed milk. Academy (1838) now univ.

neuralgia, pain felt along the course of a nerve. Trigeminal neuralgia is severe pain along the branches of the trigeminal nerve in the face.

neuritis, inflammation of a nerve or group of nerves. May be caused by viral infection (eg shingles) or by bacteria (eg leprosy), etc.

neuron, see NERVOUS SYSTEM.

neurosis, form of mental disturbance merging normal behaviour with genuine derangement. Characterized by one or more of following: anxiety, depression, phobias, compulsions and obsessions, etc.

Neusiedler, Lake (Hung. *Fertő Tó*), on Austria-Hungary border. Area 337 sq km (130 sq mi). Reeds supply cellulose indust.; fishing. Prehist. remains.

neutrality, condition of a state abstaining from participation in a war between other states, and maintaining an impartial attitude in dealing with belligerent states.

neutralization, in chemistry, interaction of acid and base to form a salt and water. Solution is said to be neutral when there are equal numbers of hydrogen and hydroxyl ions present.

Neutral Territory, see KUWAIT.

neutrino, uncharged elementary particle with zero rest mass. Existence predicted by Pauli in connection with beta-decay. First detected 1956; 2 different types exist, corresponding to electron and to muon.

neutron, uncharged elementary particle, with mass slightly greater than that of proton, found in nucleus of atom (except that of hydrogen). Outside nucleus, neutron decays into proton, electron and antineutrino (half-life c 13 mins.). Discovered by Chadwick (1932); neutrons play important role in nuclear fission.

neutron star, hypothetical state of sufficiently massive star which undergoes GRAVITATIONAL COLLAPSE. Gravitational forces within star would be sufficient to compress the matter composing star into immensely dense ball of neutrons a few kilometres wide. Pulsars are believed to be rapidly rotating neutron stars.

Nevada, state of W US. Area 286,299 sq km (110,540 sq mi); pop. 489,000; cap. Carson City. Mainly within arid Great Basin region; Sierra Nevada on W border. Livestock rearing esp. cattle, sheep; important mining (iron ore, copper, gold). Resort towns incl. Las Vegas, Reno (famous for gambling casinos). Ceded to US by Mexico (1848); developed with Comstock gold, silver strikes. Admitted to Union as 36th state (1864).

Nevis, isl. of E West Indies, in Leeward Isls. Area 130 sq km (50 sq mi); pop. 46,000 (with St Kitts); chief town Charlestown. Cotton, sugar cane growing. Former British colony with St Kitts, Anguilla; became associate state 1967.

Nevis, Ben, mountain of Highland region, W Scotland, near Fort William. Highest in British Isles, 1342 m (4406 ft).

Newark, city of NE New Jersey, US; on Newark Bay and Passaic R. Pop. 382,000; state's largest city. Commercial, indust., shipping centre. Varied mfg. industs. Founded by Connecticut Puritans (1666). Photographic film first made here.

New Bedford, port of SE Massachusetts, US; on Buzzard's Bay. Pop. 102,000. Resort, fishing, varied mfg. industs. Hist. important whaling in 18th, 19th cents. Settled 1652.

New Britain, isl. in Bismarck Archipelago; part of Papua New Guinea. Area c 36,600 sq km (14,100 sq mi); chief town Rabaul. Mountainous, with active volcanoes. Exports copra, timber.

New Brunswick, Maritime prov. of SE Canada. Area 72,481 sq km (27,985 sq mi); pop. 635,000; cap. Fredericton; chief city St John. Mainly low-lying; major river St John. Timber, coal, gas, h.e.p. resources. Agric. esp. dairy farming. Fishing in Gulf of St Lawrence, Bay of Fundy. French settlement (1604); passed to English (1714); separated from Nova Scotia (1784). Became one of 4 original provs. of Canada (1867).

Newbury, mun. bor. of Berkshire, S England. Pop. 24,000. Market town; brewing, flour milling. Has famous racecourse; Cloth Hall (16th cent.)

now museum. Two battles of Civil War fought here (1643, 1644).

New Caledonia, overseas territ. of France, in SW Pacific Ocean. Comprises New Caledonia, Loyalty, and other isls. Area 18,700 sq km (7200 sq mi); pop. 135,000; cap. Nouméa. Produces copra, coffee, cotton; deposits of nickel, iron ore, chromium. Discovered (1774) by Cook; French from 1853, used initially as penal colony.

Newcastle, Thomas Pelham-Holles, Duke of (1693-1768), British politician, PM (1754-6, 1757-62). Secretary of state (1724-54). Headed Whig admin. dominated by William PITT during Seven Years War.

Newcastle, city of E New South Wales, Australia, at mouth of Hunter R. Pop. 250,000. Major coalmining, iron and steel mfg. centre; port, exports coal, wheat, wool. Has cultural centre, cathedral, univ.

Newcastle-under-Lyme, mun. bor. of Staffordshire, WC England. Pop. 77,000. In the Potteries; tile mfg. Keele Univ. (1962) nearby.

Newcastle upon Tyne, city of Tyne and Wear met. county, NE England, on R. Tyne. Pop. 222,000. Major indust. centre; coal, shipbuilding indust., chemicals mfg.; port. Has univ. (1963). Linked by tunnel, 5 bridges to Gateshead. On Hadrian's Wall; has castle (12th cent.); St Nicholas Cathedral (14th cent.).

New Church or Church of the New Jerusalem, religious body estab. by followers of SWEDENBORG. First public service held in London (1788). Each congregation administers itself but with annual conventions.

Newcomen, Thomas (1663-1729), English inventor. In partnership with Thomas Savery (c 1650-1715), devised steam engine (1705) used to pump water from mines.

New Deal, US domestic reform programme enacted (1933) during admin. of F.D. Roosevelt. Sought recovery from Depression by centralizing under federal govt. extensive economic and social reform and public works projects. Estab. numerous emergency organizations (eg National Recovery Administration), passed Social Security Act. Long-term projects incl. Tennessee Valley Authority.

New Delhi, see DELHI.

New Democratic Party (NDP), Canadian political party, founded (1961) as union of Co-operative Commonwealth Federation (CCF) and Canadian Labour Congress (CLC). CCF estab. (1932) to represent agrarian, labour and socialist aims, formed Saskatchewan govt. (1944-64). NDP attempted to widen programme. Strongest in W, winning (early 1970s) provincial govts. in Manitoba, Saskatchewan, British Columbia.

New Economic Policy (NEP), official economic policy (1921-8) of USSR. Introduced by Lenin to counter unrest. Abolished compulsory labour service, requisition of grain. Provided open market with fixed prices and limited private enterprise. Replaced by FIVE YEAR PLAN.

New England, region of NE US, incl. Maine, New Hampshire, Vermont, Massachusetts, Rhode Isl.,

Connecticut. Centre of pre-American Revolution activity.

New English Art Club, society of artists founded in 1886 to oppose conventionalism of the Royal Academy and to promote naturalism in the French manner. Members incl. Steer, Sargent, Sickert, Augustus John.

New Forest, woodland heath of Hampshire, S England. National park, area 376 sq km (145 sq mi). Agric.; livestock, ponies. Royal hunting forest of Saxons; William II killed here (1100).

Newfoundland, isl. and prov. of E Canada. Area 404,519 sq km (156,185 sq mi); pop. 522,000; cap. St John's. Prov. comprises isl. (area 106,810 sq km /42,734 sq mi) and mainland Labrador which are separated by Str. of Belle Isle. Timber, iron ore, h.e.p. resources. Fisheries (esp. cod) on Grand Banks. Discovered by John Cabot (1497); British sovereignty estab. 1714; jurisdiction over Labrador 1809. Voted to join Canada as 10th prov. (1949).

Newfoundland dog, breed of large powerful dog, developed in Newfoundland. Coat dense and oily; noted for swimming prowess. Stands c 71 cm/28 in. high at shoulder.

New Guinea, isl. of SW Pacific, N of Australia. Area c 830,000 sq km (320,000 sq mi). Mountainous, rising to over 5000 m (16,500 ft); tropical rain forests. Agric. economy, minerals largely unexploited. Divided into IRIAN JAYA (West Irian) and mainland of PAPUA NEW GUINEA.

Newham, bor. of E Greater London, England. Pop. 236,000. Created 1965

from East Ham, West Ham co. bors., parts of Barking, Woolwich.

New Hampshire, New England state of US. Area 24,097 sq km (9304 sq mi); pop. 738,000; cap. Concord; largest town Manchester. White Mts. in N.; many lakes, woods. Poultry, dairy farming; granite quarrying; timber, h.e.p. resources. Mfg. industs. concentrated in S. First colonized in 1620s. Under Massachusetts jurisdiction until 1679. One of original 13 colonies of US.

New Haven, port of S Connecticut, US; on Long Island Sound. Pop. 138,000. Varied mfg. industs. Settled as Puritan theocracy. Joint cap. with Hartford (1701-1875). Seat of Yale Univ. (1701).

New Hebrides, archipelago of SW Pacific Ocean, jointly admin. by UK and France. Area *c* 14,760 sq km (5700 sq mi); pop. 97,000; cap. Vila. Produces copra, tuna fish, manganese ore. Discovered (1606) by Portuguese; UK-French condominium estab. 1906.

New Ireland, isl. in Bismarck Archipelago; part of Papua New Guinea. Area *c* 8600 sq km (3300 sq mi). Mountainous. Coconuts chief crop.

New Jersey, state of NE US; on Atlantic. Area 20,295 sq km (7836 sq mi); pop. 7,168,000; cap. Trenton; chief cities Newark, Jersey City. Indust. concentrated in N; farmlands, resorts in S. Shipbuilding, oil refining; machinery, textiles, chemicals mfg. First settled by Dutch, Swedish colonists. English gained control 1664. One of original 13 colonies of US.

Newman, John Henry (1801-90), English churchman. Anglican vicar, joined KEBLE in writing *Tracts for the Times* (1833), inspiring OXFORD MOVEMENT. Became RC in 1845; created cardinal in 1879. Writings, noted for lucid prose style, incl. spiritual autobiog. *Apolologia pro Vita Sua* (1865), begun as defence against attacks by Charles Kingsley.

Newmarket, urban dist. of Suffolk, E England. Pop. 13,000. Horse racing, training centre from 17th cent.; hq. of Jockey Club.

New Mexico, state of SW US. Area 315,115 sq km (121,606 sq mi); pop. 1,016,000; cap. Santa Fé; largest city Albuquerque. Arid plateau crossed by Rio Grande, Pecos R. Agric., incl. cattle, sheep, grain farming; important mining (copper, petroleum, uranium, potash). Spanish colonies opposed by Apache, Pueblo Indians. US control estab. after Mexican War (1846-8); developed with Santa Fé Trail and railway. Admitted to Union as 47th state (1912).

New Orleans, port of SE Louisiana, US; on Mississippi R. Pop. 593,000. Major commercial, trade centre. Sugar, oil refining; petroleum, timber, iron and steel exports. Founded by French (1718); French-Creole cultural influence still remains. Hist. cotton, slave trade. Andrew Jackson defeated British here (1815). Seat of Tulane Univ. (1884). Has annual Mardi Gras festival; traditional home of jazz.

Newport, mun. bor and co. town of Isle of Wight, S England. Pop. 22,000. Market town. Has Parkhurst prison; Carisbrooke Castle nearby.

Newport, resort and naval base of SE Rhode Isl., US. Pop. 35,000. Settled 1639; hist. shipbuilding, molasses trade. Joint cap. with Providence until 1900. Has many fashionable 19th cent. mansions.

Newport, co. bor. and co. town of Gwent, SE Wales, on R. Usk. Pop. 112,000. Extensive docks (exports coal); iron, steel indust. Old church became cathedral in 1921.

Newport News, seaport of SE Virginia, US; on Hampton Roads (James R.). Pop. 138,000. Has shipyards, drydocks. Coal, petroleum, tobacco exports. Settled by Irish colonists (1621).

Newry, port of S Northern Ireland. Pop. 11,000. In former Co. Down. Linen, rope mfg.

news agency, see NEWSPAPER.

New Siberian Islands, archipelago of USSR, between Laptev and East Siberian seas. Incl. Kotelny, Faddeyevsky and Novaya Sibir. Remains of mammoths found here; site of meteorological stations.

New South Wales, state of SE Australia. Area 801,300 sq km (309,400 sq mi); pop. 4,590,000; cap. Sydney. Incl. Lord Howe Isl. dependency. Comprises narrow coastal lowlands; tablelands and mountains of Great Dividing Range; W slopes and plains, incl. Murray-Darling basin. Mainly pastoral, agric. incl. dairying, wheat. Indust. centred in Newcastle, Wollongong, Sydney; h.e.p. in Snowy Mts. Australian E coast called New South Wales by Cook (1770); first colonized 1788. Became federal state (1901); ceded Australian Capital Territ. (1911), Jervis Bay (1915) to federal govt.

newspaper, publication usually intended to convey news, issued regularly, eg daily or weekly. Developed in 17th cent. with spread of printing. In late 19th cent. achieved mass appeal with growth of literacy, better printing techniques, and newspapers attempting literary merit were joined by sensationalist 'tabloids'. Increased interest in international news gave rise to news agencies, eg Associated Press, Reuters. Leading newspapers incl. British *The Times* and US *New York Times*.

newt, small lizard-like amphibian of salamander family, found in Europe, North America, Asia. Crested newt, *Triturus cristatus*, is largest European species.

New Testament, second part of the Christian Bible which deals with life and teachings of Jesus Christ (4 Gospels); growth of the Church (Acts of the Apostles); letters to individuals and newly-formed Christian communities (Epistles); vision of the struggle between the Church and its enemies (Revelation). Recorded in Greek in early Christian period.

Newton, Sir Isaac (1642-1727), English physicist, mathematician. Author of *Principia* (1687), in which he enunciated 'inverse square law' of gravitation and 3 laws of motion; application of these laws enabled him to explain planetary motion for 1st time. Made discoveries in optics, incl. fact that white light is composed of colours of spectrum; invented reflecting telescope. Developed differential and integral calculus, independently of Leibnitz, as tool for studies of motion.

newton, SI unit of force; defined as force required to impart an acceleration of 1 m/sec^2 in mass of 1 kilogram.

Newtonian mechanics, mechanics described by Newton's 3 laws of motion. Its predictions prove extremely successful for describing motion of bodies at ordinary velocities but must be modified to take account of relativistic effects for velocities close to that of light.

new town, planned urban community in UK, estab. under New Towns Act of 1946. Created, like GARDEN CITIES, to reduce congestion in major conurbations eg Greater London, Clydeside; some completely new, some extend existing towns. Examples incl. Basildon, England and Cwmbran, Wales.

Newtownabbey, town of EC Northern Ireland. Pop. 58,000. In former Co. Antrim; suburb of Belfast.

Newtownards, town of EC Northern Ireland, on Strangford Lough. Pop. 15,000. Linen, hosiery mfg. Has 13th cent. monastery.

New Westminster, seaport of SW British Columbia, Canada; on Fraser R. Pop. 43,000. Fishing, food processing industs. Founded 1859; was colonial cap. until 1866.

New World, name used for the continent of America, ie North, Central and South America.

New York, state of NE US, incl. Long Isl. in SE. Area 128,402 sq km (49,576 sq mi); pop. 18,241,000; cap. Albany; chief cities Buffalo, New York, Rochester. Appalachian Mts. in C; St Lawrence valley in N; crossed by Erie Canal, Mohawk, Hudson rivers. Agric. esp. dairy farming, fruit, cereal growing. Food produce, clothing, machinery mfg., printing and publishing. Indust., shipping concentrated in New York City. E region explored by Hudson (1609), settled by Dutch as New Amsterdam; taken by English (1664). Battleground during Revolution. One of original 13 colonies of US.

New York City, in SE New York state; major port on Hudson R. Pop. 7,896,000; largest city in US. Comprises bors. Bronx, Brooklyn, Manhattan, Queen's, Richmond (Staten Isl.). Rail, air, shipping terminal. Varied mfg. industs. esp. consumer goods. Financial centre (Wall Street); major US trade centre. Manhattan Isl. settled by Dutch (1625); seized by English (1664); state cap. until 1797. Harbour dominated by Statue of Liberty; has UN hq., Empire State Building. Notable areas Chinatown, Greenwich Village, Harlem. Seat of 5 univs. incl. Columbia (1754).

New Zealand, country in SW Pacific Ocean. Area 268,100 sq km (103,500 sq mi); pop. 3,140,000; cap. Wellington. Comprises North, South, Stewart, and several smaller isls. Mountain ranges run NE - SW, rising to Mt. Cook in Southern Alps; many fertile valleys, coastal lowlands, eg Canterbury Plains. Economy based on sheep farming, dairying; timber indust., h.e.p.; food processing, engineering in towns. Ancestors of Maoris arrived 10th cent.; Tasman was 1st white man to reach New Zealand (1642). Under UK rule from 1840; Maori freedom guaranteed by Waitangi Treaty, but land disputes led to series of wars after 1843. Gold discoveries from 1861 accelerated settlement. Dominion from 1907; independent 1931. Member of British Commonwealth.

Ney, Michel (1769?-1815), French army officer. Won victory of Elchingen (1805), commanded rearguard in retreat from Moscow (1812). He supported Louis XVIII after Napoleon's abdication but changed side again to lead Old Guard at Waterloo (1815). Condemned as traitor and shot.

Niagara Falls, resort of NW New York state, US; on Niagara R. Pop. 86,000. Indust. based on h.e.p. from Falls. Town burned by British in war of 1812.

Niagara Falls, famous waterfalls on Canada-US boundary; on Niagara R. Forms part of border between Ontario and New York State. Goat Isl. separates Canadian-(Horseshoe) Falls and American Falls. Popular tourist area. H.e.p. supplies. Circumvented by Welland Ship Canal.

Niamey, cap. of Niger, on R. Niger. Pop. 102,000. Admin., commercial centre; trade in livestock, hides, groundnuts; bricks, cement mfg. Terminus of trans-Sahara motor route.

Nibelungenlied (The Lay of the Nibelungs), medieval German heroic epic written c 1200 from older sources. First part tells legend of Siegfried, his love for Kriemhild, wooing of Brunhild on behalf of Burgundian king Gunther, and death at hands of Hagen; second part deals with historical encounter between Burgundians (Nibelungs) and Huns. Wagner used first part for opera *Ring of the Nibelung*.

Nicaea (modern *Isnik*), ancient city of Asia Minor, in NW Turkey. Founded in 4th cent. BC as Antigonia, was Roman trade centre.

Scene of ecumenical council of AD 325 called by Constantine I.

Nicaragua, republic of Central America. Area 128,410 sq km (49,579 sq mi); pop. 2,233,000; cap. Managua. Language: Spanish. Religion: RC. Mountain ranges and interior plateaus flanked by Pacific, Caribbean coasts. Main crops incl. cotton, coffee, sugar; exports timber, gold. Under Spanish rule (1522-1821); member of Central American Federation (1825-38). Earthquake damage (1972).

Nicaragua, Lake, in SW Nicaragua, largest lake in Central America. Area 8000· sq km (3089 sq mi). Commercial, sporting fisheries (esp. tuna, shark).

Nice (Ital. *Nizza*), city of Provence, SE France, on Côte d'Azur, cap. of Alpes-Maritimes dept. Pop. 322,000. Port, resort, perfume and soap mfg., fruit and flowers (has 'battle of flowers' festival). Greek colony of *Nikaia*, founded 3rd cent. BC. Ceded by Sardinia to France in 1860. Cathedral, observatory. Birthplace of Garibaldi.

Nicene Creed, statement formulated by Council of Nicaea (325); modified by 1st Council of Constantinople (381) giving orthodox doctrine of the Trinity. *See* CREED.

Nicholas, St (*fl* 4th cent.), Lycian churchman, bishop of Myra. Popular saint in Eastern churches, patron of children, mariners, pawnbrokers (his emblem is 3 golden balls). Origin of Santa Claus.

Nicholas I (1796-1855), tsar of Russia (1825-55). Crushed Decembrist revolt (1825) which arose over his succession. Ruled autocratically, suppressing dissent; introduced secret police. Militarist policies helped precipitate Crimean War (1853).

Nicholas II (1868-1918), tsar of Russia (1894-1917). Suppressed Revolution of 1905 which followed defeat in Russo-Japanese war; later came under influence of RASPUTIN. Maintained autocratic rule of predecessors. Forced to abdicate after failures in WWI and held captive during Russian Revolution. He and his family said to have been shot at Ekaterinburg.

Nicholson, Jack (1937-), American film actor, director. Best known as actor, esp. for *One Flew Over the Cuckoo's Nest* (1976); also directed and appeared in *Five Easy Pieces* (1970).

Nicholson, Sir William (1872-1949), English painter. Collaborated with James Pryde in designing posters under name of 'The Beggarstaff Brothers'; known for woodcuts and still lifes. His son, Ben Nicholson (1894-), was influenced by cubism and Mondrian. Works are characterized by austere geometric designs and restricted colour range.

nickel (Ni), magnetic metallic element; at. no. 28, at. wt. 58.71. Extremely resistant to corrosion; used in numerous alloys, as a catalyst, in electro-plating, *etc*.

Nicklaus, Jack William (1940-), American golfer. Has won more major championships than any other golfer; titles incl. 2 US Amateurs, 3 US Opens, 3 British Opens, 5 Masters and 4 PGAs.

Nicobar Islands, *see* ANDAMAN.

Nicosia (Gk. *Levkosia*, Turk. *Lefkosha*), cap. of Cyprus. Pop. 117,000. Commercial centre, agric. market.

Produces leather, textiles, cigarettes. Has 16th cent. walls built by Venetians. Scene of fighting in 1960 and during Turkish invasion (1974).

nicotine, colourless water soluble alkaloid found in leaves of TOBACCO plant. Extremely poisonous, used as basis of insecticides.

Nielsen, Carl August (1865-1931), Danish composer. Works characterized by progressive tonality, esp. in his 6 symphonies. Other compositions incl. opera *Saul and David*, concertos, chamber music.

Niemeyer, Oscar (1907-), Brazilian architect. Worked with Le Corbusier on building of Ministry of Education in Rio de Janeiro (1937-43). Directed planning of Brasilia (1950-60).

Nietzsche, Friedrich Wilhelm (1844-1900), German philosopher. Most influential work, *Thus Spake Zarathustra* (1883), characterized by passionate individualism, calls for race of 'supermen' to replace 'slave morality' of Christianity. Other works incl. *The Birth of Tragedy* (1872), *Beyond Good and Evil* (1886).

Niger, republic of W Africa. Area 1,267,000 sq km (489,000 sq mi); pop. 4,727,000; cap. Niamey. Language: French. Religion: Islam. Sahara desert, Aïr Mts. in N, semidesert in S; drained by R. Niger. Produces groundnuts, cotton, animal products, uranium ore. Territ. of French West Africa from 1904, became independent 1960.

Niger, river of W Africa. Flows c 4180 km (2600 mi) from Guinea via Mali, Niger, entering Gulf of Guinea by large delta in S Nigeria. Main tributary is R. Benue. Irrigation, h.e.p., *eg* Kainji Dam, N of Jebba, opened 1969.

Niger-Congo, vast branch of Niger-Kordofanian language family. Languages within it spoken throughout S, C Africa and most of W Africa south of Sahara. Subdivided into W Atlantic, Mande, Gur or Voltaic, Kwa, Benue-Congo and Andamawa-Eastern groups.

Nigeria, federal republic of W Africa, on Gulf of Guinea. Area 925,000 sq km (357,000 sq mi); pop. 64,750,000; cap. Lagos; site near Abuja, C Nigeria, designated for new cap. Main languages: Hausa, Ibo, Yoruba, English. Main religions: Islam, Christianity, animism. Chief tribes Fulani, Hausa, Ibo, Yoruba. Flat semi-desert in N, savannah plateaux in C, tropical forest in S; main rivers Niger, Benue. Agric. products incl. palm oil, cocoa, groundnuts, cotton, rubber. Major petroleum exporter, found in Niger delta and offshore. Colony and protect. estab. (1914) by merging of Northern and Southern Nigeria and Lagos. Four regions created (1954); independent 1960, republic 1963. Military govt. imposed (1965); 12 states replaced regions (1967), 7 new states added 1976. Secession of Eastern Region (mainly Ibo) as Biafra caused civil war (1967-70). Member of British Commonwealth, UN.

Nightingale, Florence (1820-1910), English nurse, hospital administrator. Took 38 nurses to Crimea (1854); estab. hospital units at Scutari and Balaklava. Greatly reduced death rate among army casualties by imposing high standards of hygiene and care. Founded (1860) nurses' training institution at St Thomas's Hospital, London.

nightingale, *Luscinia megarhynchos,* small migratory songbird of thrush family, with brown upperparts, whitish brown under-parts. Found in woods of Europe, Asia, N Africa. Male noted for singing at night.

nightjar or goatsucker, any of Caprimulgidae family of small nocturnal birds. Short bill and wide mouth; feeds on insects captured in air. European nightjar, *Caprimulgus europaeus,* brown with white marks on tail. Nighthawks form New World subfamily Chordeilinae.

nightshade, any plant of genera *Solanum* and *Atropa* mainly native to South America and subtropical regions. Black nightshade, *S. nigrum,* has white flowers followed by black berries. Woody nightshade (bittersweet), *S. dulcamara,* has red berries. Extremely poisonous deadly nightshade, *A. belladonna,* has black berries and yields the alkaloid atropine which reduces action of parasympathetic nerves. Formerly used cosmetically to dilate pupils of eyes.

nihilism, in political history, 19th cent. Russian revolutionary movement. Rejected all estab. institutions, took terrorist action, *eg* arson, assassination; culminated in tsar's murder (1881). Term (from Latin, *nihil* = nothing) coined by Turgenev in *Fathers and Sons.* In philosophy, denial of any basis for knowledge or truth; rejection of beliefs in morality, religion, *etc.*

Nijinsky, Vaslav (1890-1950), Russian ballet dancer. One of most famous of Diaghilev's dancers, created leading roles in *L'Après-midi d'un faune*, *Spectre de la rose*. Famed for graceful athleticism; career cut short by insanity.

Nijmegen (Ger. *Nimwegen*, Fr. *Nimègue*), city of E Netherlands, on R. Waal. Pop. 150,000. Inland port, with canal link to R. Maas; engineering, chemicals. RC univ. (1923). Scene of Treaty of Nijmegen (1678) formed between Dutch wars. Remains of Charlemagne's palace (777) in Valkhof park.

Nike, in Greek myth, goddess of victory, daughter of Pallas and Styx. Usually represented as winged, carrying wreath or palm branch. Presided over all contests, athletic and military; esp. popular after Persian Wars. Identified by Romans with Victoria.

Nile, world's longest river, in NE Africa. Flows *c* 6690 km (4160 mi) from farthest headstream, R. Luvironza (Burundi), to Mediterranean Sea. Nile proper (c 3015 km/1875 mi long) formed at Khartoum by union of Blue Nile (rises in Ethiopian Highlands) and White Nile (formed at L. No, Sudan, by jct. of Bahr-el-Ghazal and Bahr-el-Jebel). Drops 285 m (935 ft) in 6 cataracts between Khartoum and Aswan; joined by R. Atbara. Below Cairo enters wide delta, reaches sea via Rosetta (W), Damietta (E) channels. Seasonal flooding, due to Blue Nile, used for irrigation from c 4000 BC; irrigation, h.e.p. developed 20th cent. by series of dams (eg Aswan, Sennar, Jebel Aulia) and barrages. Nile valley was focus of ancient Egyptian civilization; its source legendary until 19th cent. explorations by Bruce, Speke, Stanley.

Nilo-Saharan, African language family, second to Niger-Kordofanian in size. Divided into 6 branches: Songhai (Mali); Saharan; Maban (E of Lake Chad); Furian (Sudan); Coman (Ethiopia and Sudan); Chari-Nile (Sudan, Zaïre, Uganda, Cameroon, Chad, Central African Empire, Kenya, Tanzania, Ethiopia).

Nîmes (anc. *Nemausus*), city of Languedoc, S France, cap. of Gard dept. Pop. 123,000. Tourist centre; wine, fruit, grain trade. Founded by Greek colonists; important Roman remains incl. arena, temples, nearby Pont du Gard aqueduct.

Nimrud, remains of ancient town on N bank of Tigris, S of Mosul, Iraq. Founded 13th cent. BC, became Assyrian cap. under Assurnasirpal II (883-859 BC). Destroyed by Medes (612 BC). Excavated by Sir Austen Layard in 19th cent.; identified with biblical Calah.

Nineveh, ruins of N Iraq, on R. Tigris. Cap. of ancient Assyrian empire (*fl* 9th-7th cent. BC).

Ninghsia-Hui, auton. region of NC China. Area *c* 276,000 sq km (106,000 sq mi); pop. (est.) 2,000,000; cap. Yinchuan. Mainly desert, rough grazing on Inner Mongolian plateau; agric. in SE near Hwang Ho. Largely pop. by Mongols.

Ninian, St (c 360–c 432), Scottish missionary. Made pilgrimage to Rome, later named bishop of S Picts. Founded church at Whithorn, Galloway Region, Scotland (397).

Niobe, in Greek myth, queen of Thebes and daughter of Tantalus. Boasted about her many children compared to Leto, whereupon Artemis and Apollo (the only 2 children of Leto), killed them all. Turned by

Zeus into a stone column which wept perpetually.

niobium or columbium (Nb), rare metallic element; at. no. 41, at. wt. 92.91. Used in alloys which are resistant to high temperatures.

Nippur, ancient Sumerian city in Mesopotamia; religious centre for worship of god Enlil. Excavations revealed cuneiform tablets which are major source of information on Sumerian culture.

nirvana, in Buddhism and some forms of Hinduism, state of annihilation of the worldly self and thus of being free of the cycle of rebirth.

Niš (anc. *Naïssus*), city of Serbia, SE Yugoslavia, on R. Nišava. Pop. 133,000. Major railway centre, engineering, tobacco. Held by Turks 1386-1878. Medieval fortress. Birthplace of Constantine the Great.

Niterói, residential town of SE Brazil, cap. of Rio de Janeiro state; on E shore of Guanabara Bay. Pop. 324,000. Shipbuilding, textile mfg. Popular tourist resort. Has ferry link with Rio de Janeiro.

nitrates, salts or esters of nitric acid, the salts being soluble in water. Nitrates in soil are source of nitrogen, needed by plants for growth; produced from nitrogen by bacteria. Metallic nitrates used to make explosives, as fertilizers and in chemical synthesis.

nitric acid (HNO₃), colourless corrosive liquid; powerful oxidizing agent. Obtained by catalytic oxidation of ammonia. Used in manufacture of fertilizers, explosives and in organic synthesis.

nitrocellulose or cellulose nitrate, any of various esters of nitric acid and cellulose, formed by action

of mixture of nitric and sulphuric acids on cellulose. Used to make explosives (guncotton), plastics and lacquers.

nitrogen (N), colourless gaseous element, chemically inactive; at. no. 7, at. wt. 14.01. Forms c 4/5 of atmosphere; occurs in Chile saltpetre (sodium nitrate) and saltpetre deposits. Essential constituent of living organisms, occurring in proteins and nucleic acids. Used in manufacture of ammonia (Haber process).

nitrogen cycle, cycle of natural processes by which nitrogen is made available to living organisms. Inorganic nitrogen compounds in soil are absorbed by plants and converted to proteins and nucleic acids; animals absorb proteins by eating plants. Nitrogen compounds re-enter soil by plant decay or as animal excreta; they can be broken down by bacteria in soil into form suitable for plant utilization.

nitrogen fixation, conversion of atmospheric nitrogen into nitrates, which can be used by plants, by action of bacteria or blue-green algae. Bacteria are found in soil or in nodules of certain leguminous plants (peas, clover, *etc*). Part of NITROGEN CYCLE.

nitroglycerin[e], thick pale yellow oily liquid, prepared by action of concentrated sulphuric and nitric acids on glycerol. Explodes when struck; used to make DYNAMITE, cordite, *etc*.

nitrous oxide or laughing gas (N₂O), colourless sweet-tasting gas, used as light anaesthetic in dentistry. Obtained by heating ammonium nitrate.

Nixon, Richard Milhous (1913-
), American statesman, president
(1969-74). Republican vice-president
(1953-61) under Eisenhower. Narrowly lost 1960 election to Kennedy.
Retired from politics after failure to
win governorship of California
(1962). Comeback culminated in
successful bid for presidency (1968).
Terms marked by US withdrawal
from Vietnam, rapprochement with
China, economic recession. Investigations into 'Watergate affair'
after 1972 revealed widespread govt.
corruption in which Nixon was
involved. Threatened with impeachment, he resigned; pardoned by
successor, President Ford.

Nizhni Novgorod, see GORKY.

Nkomo, Joshua (1917-), Zimbabwe-Rhodesian politician. President of Zimbabwe African People's
Union (1961-). Imprisoned (1963-4).
Placed under restriction (1964-74).
On release, entered into constitutional negotiations with Ian
Smith. After breakdown of talks,
headed Patriotic Front guerilla war
against Smith's 'Internal Settlement'.
Talks resumed 1979.

Nkrumah, Kwame (1909-72),
Ghanaian political leader. PM of
Ghana (formerly Gold Coast) at its
independence (1957), became 1st
president (1960) of republic. Rule
marked by extravagance and self-
glorification. Overthrown by army
coup (1966).

no or **noh play,** highly stylized form
of Japanese theatre. Plays mostly
written in 15th cent., c 800 extant.
Characteristic features incl. use of
chorus, wooden masks, elaborate
costumes, many symbolic allusions,
formal acting style using dance to
express emotion, and the 'freezing'
of characters in elaborate tableaux.

Noah, in OT, builder of the ark
which saved human and animal life
from the Flood. His sons Shem, Ham
and Japheth became the eponymous
ancestors of the biblical races of
mankind.

Nobel, Alfred Bernhard (1833-
96), Swedish chemist, philanthropist. Invented dynamite (1866) and
perfected other explosives. Be-
queathed fund from which annual
prizes were to be awarded for work
in physics, chemistry, physiology
and medicine, literature, and for
work in cause of peace. Awards
made annually since 1901.

nobelium (No), transuranic element; at. no. 102, mass no. of most
stable isotope 255. Discovered
(1957) at Nobel Institute, Stockholm, by nuclear bombardment of
curium.

noble gases, see INERT GASES.

noble metals, metals such as gold,
platinum or silver which resist
corrosion and are chemically inactive.

nocturne, short lyrical piece usually
for piano; introduced by JOHN FIELD
and much used by Chopin.

Nolan, Sidney (1917-), Australian artist. Known for his paintings of
the Australian scene in deliberately
naive style; esp. concerned with
myth surrounding Ned Kelly, whom
he depicted clad in home-made
armour in outback landscapes.

Nolde, Emil, orig. Hansen (1867-
1956), German expressionist
painter. Painting is characterized by
violent colour, simplified form and
influence of primitive art; finest

works are landscapes and religious subjects.

nomad, member of a tribe of people having no permanent home, moving about constantly in search of food, pasture *etc.* Characteristic of C Asian herdsmen, Australian aborigines, African bushmen, Eskimos, some North American Indian tribes, Lapps, Bedouins, Tuaregs.

nominalism, in philosophy, doctrine first current in medieval SCHOLASTICISM that universal concepts (*eg* the concept of 'table' rather than a particular table) have no general reality and are merely conveniences of classification. Concomitant of most empiricist and materialist philosophies. Opposed to REALISM.

Non-aggression Pact (Aug. 1939), secret agreement between USSR and Germany to divide Poland and E Europe into spheres of Soviet and German influence, and to foil Anglo-French moves to involve USSR in containing German aggression. Ended with German attack on USSR in 1941.

nonconformist, *see* DISSENTER.

non-Euclidean geometry, branch of geometry based on postulates different from those of Euclid. Usually Euclid's 5th or parallel postulate is rejected (that through any point only 1 line can be drawn parallel to another line). Invented independently by Lobachevski, Bolyai and Gauss.

Nonjurors, English and Scottish clergymen who, after Revolution of 1688, refused to take oath of allegiance to William and Mary. Incl. archbishop of Canterbury, 7 bishops and many others.

Nordenskjöld, Nils Adolf Erik, Baron (1832-1901), Swedish explorer and geologist, b. Finland. Navigated Northeast Passage (1878-80) in ship *Vega*; made several expeditions to Spitsbergen and Greenland, mapping large areas.

Nördlingen, town of SC West Germany. Pop. 14,000. Scene of major battles in 1634 (Imperial victory) and 1645 (French victory) in Thirty Years' War.

Norfolk, Dukes of, *see* HOWARD, THOMAS.

Norfolk, county of E England. Area 5355 sq km (2068 sq mi); pop. 624,000; co. town Norwich. Flat, low-lying; fertile soils; rich agric., fishing. In E, Norfolk Broads, area of shallow lakes, rivers; yachting.

Norfolk, seaport of SE Virginia, US; on Hampton Roads (Elizabeth R.). Pop. 308,000. Naval base (Atlantic fleet hq.), shipyards; coal, tobacco exports. Founded 1682.

Norfolk Island, territ. of Australia, in S Pacific Ocean *c* 1600 km (1000 mi) NE of Sydney. Area 34 sq km (13 sq mi); pop. 2,000. Tourist resort; whaling; exports fruit. Discovered (1774) by Cook; penal colony until 1855. Transferred from New South Wales to federal govt. 1913.

Norman architecture, form of Romanesque developed in Normandy and England (11th-12th cents.). Characterized by massive construction, semi-circular arches, barrel vaults. Keep (White Tower) of Tower of London and Durham Cathedral (1st to use rib vaulting) are examples.

Normandy (*Normandie*), region and former prov. of N France, hist.

cap. Rouen. Low-lying, drained by Seine, Eure, Orne: incl. Cotentin penin. Main towns Rouen, Le Havre, Cherbourg. Agric. (cattle, dairying, apples), fishing, tourism. Name derives from Norsemen who invaded area in 9th cent.; Normandy conquered England (1066), colonized S Italy (11th-12th cent.). Part · of France from 1450. Scene of Allied invasion in 1944.

Normans, descendants of Viking settlers who conquered N France (Normandy) in 9th cent. Under Duke William, conquered England (1066), displaced Anglo-Saxon nobility, reformed law and social system. Also conquered S Italy and Sicily (11th cent.), on pretext of expelling Byzantine Greeks and Arabs.

Norns, FATES of Norse myth; determined destiny of gods and men. Usually represented as Urth (past), Verthandi (present), Skuld (future), who spun and wove web of life.

Norris, Frank (1870-1902), American novelist. Known for naturalistic novels incl. *McTeague* (1899) and 2 vols. of projected trilogy on wheat trade, *The Octopus* (1901), *The Pit* (1903).

Norrköping, town of SE Sweden, on inlet of Baltic Sea. Pop. 91,000. Port; textile centre; paper mfg.; h.e.p.

Norse, see GERMANIC LANGUAGES, OLD NORSE LITERATURE.

Norsemen, see VIKINGS.

Norse mythology, see TEUTONIC MYTHOLOGY.

North, Frederick North, 8th Baron (1732-92), British politician, PM (1770-82). Premiership was dominated by influence of George III; carried out taxation policies which led to American Revolution

(1776). Resigned after British surrender.

North, Sir Thomas (c 1535-c 1601), English translator. Best known for translation of Plutarch's *Lives* (1579, from French version by Amyot) used as source by Shakespeare.

North Africa campaign, conflict (1940-3) during WWII along Egypt-Libya coastal area for control of Mediterranean and Suez Canal. Began with Italian attempts to capture Egypt. German forces under Rommel (Afrikakorps) drove British back into Egypt; advance was halted by British victory under Montgomery at El Alamein (1942). Germans retreated into Tunisia and eventually surrendered to Allies (May, 1943).

Northallerton, urban dist. and co. town of North Yorkshire, N England. Pop. 7000. Agric. market. Nearby is site of Battle of the Standard where English defeated Scots (1138).

North America, third largest continent; in W hemisphere; comprises US (incl. Alaska), Canada, Mexico. Area c 24,346,000 sq km (9,400,000 sq mi); pop. 327,000,000. Central plain separates E mountain ranges (Laurentian, Appalachian) from W Rocky systems incl. Mississippi, St Lawrence-Great Lakes. Highest point Mt. McKinley. Climate varies from Arctic in N to subtropical in S. Varied agric., pastoral in plains; extensive mineral resources. Indigenous Indian pop.; Spanish settlers followed by French, British and some Germans. Thirteen British colonies gained independence after American Revolution

(1776-83). Mexico gained independence from Spain in 1821. Canada settled by traders, ceded to Britain by France (1763); confederation formed 1867. Pop. now mainly of European descent with Negro, Indian minorities.

Northamptonshire, county of C England. Area 2367 sq km (914 sq mi); pop. 488,000. Wheat growing, cattle, sheep rearing; iron ore; fox hunting. Co. town **Northampton,** on R. Nene. Pop. 128,000. Footwear mfg. Has round church (12th cent.).

North Atlantic Drift, warm ocean current of N Atlantic Ocean. Continuation of Gulf Stream, flows NE from off Newfoundland. Ameliorates W European winters.

North Atlantic Treaty Organization (NATO), defence force estab. 1952 as result of pact (1949) between US, Britain, Canada, France, Benelux, Denmark, Norway, Iceland, Italy and Portugal. Later additions were Greece (1952), Turkey (1952), West Germany (1954).

North Bay, town of SE Ontario, Canada; on L. Nipissing. Pop. 49,000. Railway jct., lumber industs.

North Borneo, *see* SABAH.

North Brabant, prov. of S Netherlands. Area 4929 sq km (1903 sq mi); cap. 's Hertogenbosch. Textiles, electrical industs. Hist. links with N Belgium (*see* BRABANT).

North Cape (*Nordkapp*), headland of Norway, on Mageröy Isl. Popularly taken as most N point of Europe, lat. 71° 10' N.

North Carolina, state of E US; on Atlantic. Area 136,200 sq km (52,590 sq mi); pop. 5,082,000; cap. Raleigh; largest city Charlotte. Coastal swamp rises to Piedmont and Appalachians in W (Mt. Mitchell, highest mountain in E US). Tobacco, cotton, peanut growing, mica quarrying. Settled 1650 by Virginia colonists. One of original 13 colonies of US. Joined South during Civil War.

Northcliffe, Alfred Charles William Harmsworth, Viscount (1865-1922), British journalist, publisher. With his brother Harold, later Lord ROTHERMERE, estab. world's largest newspaper enterprise, the Amalgamated Press. He founded the *Daily Mail* (1896), and *Daily Mirror* (1903), innovating use of attractive lay-out, esp. through pictures. Acquired and revived *The Times* (1908). Influential in politics, esp. in WWI.

North Dakota, state of NC US; on Canada border. Area 183,000 sq km (70,670 sq mi); pop. 618,000; cap. Bismarck. Mainly plains crossed by Missouri R. Barley, wheat, livestock farming; quarrying. Explored by French; acquired by US in Louisiana Purchase (1803). Admitted to Union, jointly with South Dakota, as 39th state (1889).

Northeast Frontier Agency, *see* ASSAM.

Northeast Passage, passage from North Sea to Pacific, along N coast of Europe and Asia. Explored 16th-18th cent.; first navigated 1878-9 by Swede Nils Nordenskjöld. Soviet shipping route, kept open by icebreakers.

Northern Ireland, constituent part of UK. Area 14,146 sq km (5462 sq mi); pop. 1,525,000; cap. Belfast. Comprises former Cos. Antrim, Armagh, Down, Fermanagh, Londonderry, Tyrone (most of ancient ULSTER); divided into 26 dists. (1973). Agric. (cereal, potatoes, livestock); fishing; industs. incl. shipbuilding, textiles (esp. linen). Estab. 1921 after IRELAND partitioned; continuing Protestant-RC conflict led to suspension of Stormont govt. 1972. 'Powersharing' attempted (1973-4) but direct rule from Westminster restored.

Northern Rhodesia, see ZAMBIA.

Northern Territory, territ. of N Australia. Area 1,349,000 sq km (521,000 sq mi); pop. 86,000, incl. c 21,000 aborigines; territ. cap. Darwin. Plains, basins in N, mountain ranges in S; tropical monsoon climate in N, arid in S. Beef cattle raising; mining, esp. copper, manganese, bauxite, iron, lead. Fifteen aboriginal reservations, largest of which is Arnhem Land. Became federal territ. 1911; divided into Central and Northern Australia 1926-31.

North Holland, see HOLLAND.

North Island, one of main isls. of New Zealand, separated from South Isl. by Cook Str. Area 114,690 sq km (44,280 sq mi); pop. 2,051,000; main cities Wellington, Auckland. C plateau has active volcanoes, hot springs, geysers, and L. TAUPO. Dairy cattle and sheep in fertile valleys, coastal lowlands.

North Korea, see KOREA.

North Ossetia, auton. republic of S European RSFSR, USSR; on N slopes of Caucasus. Area c 8030 sq km (3090 sq mi); pop. 552,000; cap. Ordzhonikidze. Mountainous; fruit, grain, cotton grown in valleys. Metal ore (lead, zinc) and oil deposits.

Region annexed by Russia by 1806. South Ossetia is auton. region of Georgian SSR on S slopes of Caucasus.

North Pole, northern end of Earth's axis; first reached (1909) by Peary. Distinct from north magnetic pole, position towards which needle of magnetic compass points and location of which varies with time.

North Rhine-Westphalia (*Nordrhein-Westfalen*), state of W West Germany. Area c 33,930 sq km (13,100 sq mi); cap. Düsseldorf. Highly indust. region (incl. RUHR), main products iron, steel, chemicals, textiles. Formed 1946 from Westphalia, part of Rhine prov., Lippe state.

North Riding, see YORKSHIRE, England.

North Sea, between Great Britain and NW Europe, c 965 km (600 mi) long N-S, up to 645 km (400 mi) wide. Shallows incl. DOGGER BANK. Fishing grounds; natural gas, oil deposits off Norway, Scotland. Major ports on coasts eg Rotterdam.

North Star, see POLARIS.

Northumberland, John Dudley, Duke of (c 1502-53), English statesman. As chief minister to Edward VI, he tried to alter succession in favour of his daughter-in-law, Lady Jane Grey, a Protestant, thus excluding Mary Tudor, a Catholic. His plot, lacking popular support, failed; executed for treason.

Northumberland, county of NE England. Area 5033 sq km (1943 sq mi); pop. 283,000; co. town Newcastle. Cheviot Hills (N), Pennines (W). Sheep farming; coal, shipbuilding, engineering industs. on Tyneside. Northumberland National

Park (1031 sq km/398 sq mi) incl. Hadrian's Wall.

North Vietnam, see VIETNAM.

North West Company, organization of Montréal merchants and fur traders formed (1783) to compete with Hudson's Bay Co. Its employees, incl. Thompson and Mackenzie, made pioneering explorations of W Canada. Merged with Hudson's Bay Co. (1821) following period of bitter rivalry.

Northwest Frontier Province, former province of British India on Afghanistan border, created 1901. Became part of Pakistan in 1947. Mountainous region; passes, incl. Khyber, were strategically important.

Northwest Passage, sea route linking Atlantic, Pacific oceans round N America. Long-sought as possible short route to Orient.. Frobisher, Davis, Franklin failed to discover it. First navigated by. Amundsen (1903-6).

Northwest Territories, admin. region of N Canada; incl. 3 dists.: MACKENZIE (SW), FRANKLIN (N), KEEWATIN (SE). Area 3,379,699 sq km (1,304,903 sq mi); pop. 35,000, mainly Eskimo, · Indian; admin. centre Yellowknife. Drained in W by Mackenzie R.; has many lakes incl. Great Bear, Great Slave. Fur trading; mineral resources in Mackenzie Dist. Exploration, trade sponsored by Hudson's Bay Co. (estab. 1670); known as Rupert's Land (incl. Prairies) until ceded to Canada (1869).

North Yorkshire, county of N England. Area 8317 sq km (3211 sq mi); pop. 645,000; co. town Northallerton. Created 1974, comprising mainly former N, W Ridings of Yorkshire.

Norway (*Norge*), kingdom of NW Europe, in W Scandinavia. Area 324,250 sq km (125,200 sq mi); pop. 4,027,000; cap. Oslo. Language: Norwegian. Religion: Lutheran. Nomadic Lapps in N. Deeply indented coast (ice-free due to N Atlantic Drift), mountainous; partly within Arctic Circle. Important North Sea fishing, forestry, minerals, h.e.p., limited agric.; offshore oil resources developed in 1970s. United with Denmark, Sweden 1397, ceded to Sweden 1814; independent from 1905. Occupied by Germans 1940-5.

Norwegian, N Germanic Indo-European language. Spoken in Norway and parts of US. Descended from Old Norse. Two official forms: formal *bokmål*, found in south and east, and *nynorsk* found in west and north; may be melded to form *samnorsk*, one common tongue.

Norwegian Antarctic Territory, all isls. and mainland S of 60°S and between 20°E and 45°W. Incl. Queen Maud, Princess Astrid, Princess Ragnhild, Prince Harald, Crown Prince Olav, Crown Princess Martha lands and part of Coats Land.

Norwich, city and co. town of Norfolk, E England, on R. Wensum. Pop. 122,000. Agric. market; food processing; footwear mfg. Has Univ. of East Anglia (1963). Medieval ecclesiastical centre; Norman cathedral (1096).

nose, facial organ containing openings of respiratory passages and organ of smell. Internal cavity is divided by cartilaginous septum into 2 halves which unite in nasal part of PHARYNX.

Nostradamus, Latin name of Michel de Nostredame (1503-66), French astrologer, physician. Wrote *Centuries* (1555), rhymed quatrains of obscure prophecies, long popular.

notochord, skeletal rod, composed of cells, lying between digestive tract and central nervous system in most primitive members of phylum Chordata. Present in embryonic stages of vertebrates, it is later surrounded and replaced by the vertebral column.

Notre Dame de Paris, cathedral church of Paris; on Ile de la Cité, isl. in R. Seine. Masterpiece of early French Gothic, begun in 1163; W front is esp. fine.

Nottinghamshire, county of C England. Area 2164 sq km (836 sq mi); pop. 982,000. Low-lying in Trent Valley, hilly in SW. Cereals, root crops, cattle; coal mining in W. Incl. remains of Sherwood Forest. Co. town Nottingham, city on R. Trent. Pop. 300,000. Hosiery, bicycles; Danish town (9th cent.); hist. silk, lace mfg. Has univ. (1948); RC cathedral.

Nouakchott, cap. of Mauritania. Pop. 55,000. Admin., commercial centre on caravan routes; harbour nearby on Atlantic coast. Grew rapidly after selection (1957) as future cap.

nova, in astronomy, star whose brightness suddenly increases by several thousand times and then slowly fades to its original intensity. Believed to be caused when star blows off part of its outer layer.

Novalis, pseud. of Friedrich Leopold von Hardenberg (1772-1801), German poet. Leading Romantic, *Hymns to the Night* (1800) express yearning for mystical unity in death. Also wrote unfinished novel *Heinrich von Ofterdingen* (1802).

Novara, city of Piedmont, NW Italy, cap. of Novara prov. Pop. 103,000. Textiles, rice-milling, map-making. Scene of Austrian victory (1849) over Piedmontese under Charles Albert.

Nova Scotia, Maritime prov. of SE Canada, incl. CAPE BRETON Island. Area 55,491 sq km (21,425 sq mi); pop. 788,960; cap. Halifax. Rugged coastline has many natural harbours. Fishing (esp. cod), timber, agric. (dairy farming, fruit); coal, metals, salt mining. Settled as ACADIA by French; British gained possession (1714); joined with Cape Breton (1820). One of 4 original provs. of Canada (1867).

Novaya Zemlya, 2 isls. of USSR, between Barents and Kara seas. Area c 83,000 sq km (32,000 sq mi). N island permanently ice covered, tundra in S.

novel, long fictional prose narrative. Although antecedents exist in Classical Greece, Rome, medieval Italy, 1st true examples with realistic treatment of psychology incl. Cervantes' *Don Quixote*, Richardson's *Pamela*, Fielding's *Tom Jones*. Influential exponents incl. Jane Austen (domestic novel of manners), Melville, Flaubert, Dostoyevski, Zola (naturalism), Proust, Joyce, Robbe-Grillet.

Novello, Ivor, pseud. of Ivor Novello Davies (1893-1951), Welsh actor-manager, composer. Known for songs, esp. 'Keep the Home Fires Burning', plays, *eg The Dancing Years* (1939), *Perchance to Dream* (1945).

Novgorod, city of ·USSR, W European RSFSR; on R. Volkhov. Pop. 135,000. One of oldest Russian cities; estab. of Rurik as Prince of Novgorod (862) regarded as foundation of Russia. Cap. of powerful trading state in 13th and 14th cent., rivalling Moscow in power. Subjugated by Ivan III and devastated by Ivan the Terrible (1570). Its kremlin has 11th cent. Cathedral of St Sophia.

Novi Sad (Ger. *Neusatz*), city of NE Yugoslavia, on R. Danube, cap. of Vojvodina. Pop. 142,000. River port; commercial, indust. centre. Serbian cultural, religious centre until WWI.

Novokuznetsk, city of USSR, SC Siberian RSFSR. Pop. 508,000. Metallurgical centre in Kuznetsk Basin; iron and steel, aluminium mfg. Developed as Stalinsk following amalgamation of old city of Kuznetsk and new indust. town (1932); renamed 1961.

Novosibirsk, city of USSR, SC Siberian RSFSR; jct. of Trans-Siberian railway on R. Ob. Pop. 1,200,000. Founded 1896, grew as indust. centre based on proximity of Kuznetsk Basin; agric. machinery, textile mfg.

Noyes, Alfred (1880-1958), English poet, critic. Known for ballads, *eg* 'The Highwayman', 'Come to Kew in Lilac-time', verse epic *Drake* (1908). Criticism incl. fiercely anti-modernist *Some Aspects of Modern Poetry* (1924).

Nubia, ancient region of NE Africa. Extended from Aswan (Egypt) to Khartoum (Sudan), boundaries poorly defined. Conquered Egypt (7th cent. BC) after being subject to it for cents.; powerful Christian kingdom 6th-14th cent. Conquered by Egypt in 19th cent. Incl. **Nubian Desert,** barren sandstone plateau of NE Sudan, between Nile valley and Red Sea; rises to over 2135 m/7000 ft near coast.

Nubian, language group within Chari-Nile branch of Nilo-Saharan language family. Remarkable among modern indigenous African languages in that it was used as written language, with extant texts, during medieval period. Spoken in Sudan.

nuclear energy, energy released from atomic nucleus during nuclear reactions, esp. FISSION or FUSION. Results from conversion of matter into energy.

nuclear fission, see FISSION.

nuclear forces, forces which hold together neutrons and protons in the atomic nucleus. Their range is less than 10^{-13} cm but they are immensely strong. Yukawa suggested that these forces arise from interchange of mesons between protons and neutrons

nuclear fusion, see FUSION.

nuclear physics, branch of physics dealing with structure of atomic nuclei, subatomic particles, fission process, radioactive decay, *etc.*

nuclear reactor, structure in which nuclear fission chain reaction is initiated and controlled to produce energy or further fissionable material. Metal rods are used to absorb neutrons produced during fission and so control rate at which reaction proceeds.

nuclear warfare, hostilities involving use of nuclear warheads, envisaging total destruction of enemy's war potential before retaliation is possible. Strategic emphasis is therefore on methods of delivery, which incl. low-level bombers and long range GUIDED MISSILES. Tactical weapons carrying small amounts of nuclear material have also been tested.

nucleic acids, see DNA, RNA.

nucleus, in biology, central body present in most plant and animal cells, enclosed by membrane which separates it from protoplasm of rest of cell. Contains hereditary material in form of chromosomes, which control reproduction, growth, etc.

nucleus, in physics, central part of the atom, consisting of protons and neutrons (except for hydrogen nucleus, which consists of single proton). Mass of atom is concentrated in nucleus, which bears a positive charge.

Nuffield, William Richard Morris, Viscount (1877-1963), English industrialist, philanthropist. Beginning in 1912, developed Morris Motors Ltd. into major mass-producer of motor cars. His benefactions incl. founding of Nuffield College, Oxford, and Nuffield Foundation for research (1943).

Nullarbor Plain, arid limestone tableland of South and Western Australia. Extends c 400 km (250 mi) inland from Great Australian Bight. No surface water or trees (hence name); many subterranean caves, passages. Sheep pasture on margins; crossed by Trans-Australian Railway.

nullification, political doctrine, advocated by exponents of STATES' RIGHTS in US, that state is not bound to enforce federal legislation. Leading advocate, John Calhoun, encouraged South Carolina to nullify

federal tariff acts (1832), but state rescinded (1833) after President Jackson had been empowered to use army to enforce tariffs.

numbat, Myrmecobius fasciatus, small rat-sized Australian marsupial anteater. Long snout and bushy tail; catches ants, termites with sticky tongue. Brown with distinctive white stripes.

Numbers, in OT, fourth book of Pentateuch. Contains two censuses of Israelites and continues history of Exodus and journey to Promised Land with rise of Joshua and Caleb as leaders.

Numidia, ancient kingdom of NW Africa, corresponding nearly to modern Algeria. United as Roman prov. after defeat (201 BC) of Carthage; fl 3rd-1st cent. BC. Main cities were Cirta (now Constantine), Hippo Regius (now Annaba).

numismatics, study of coins and medals. Invention of coinage is attributed to Chinese; in West, first coins were struck by Lydians of Asia Minor in electrum (mixture of gold and silver) c 750 BC.

nun, member of a religious community of women, esp. one living under monastic vows. See MONASTICISM.

Nuremberg (Nürnberg), city of SC West Germany, on R. Pegnitz. Pop. 480,000. Toys, precision instruments, clocks (first pocket watch made here c 1500). Medieval commercial centre; centre of German Renaissance. Religious Peace of Nuremberg agreed here (1532). Scene of annual Nazi rallies from 1933, and war crimes trials (1945-6). Birthplace of Albrecht Dürer.

Nuremberg Trials, trial of Nazi leaders and military commanders after WWII by Allied Tribunal under charter agreed upon by US, UK, USSR and France. Charges incl. crimes against peace and humanity, war crimes. Those sentenced to death or long terms of imprisonment incl. Goering, Ribbentrop, Speer, Hess and Dönitz. Trial estab. principle of individual responsibility not to carry out criminal orders.

Nureyev, Rudolf (1939–), Russian ballet dancer. Lived in West after 1961. Internationally known for appearances with Dame Margot Fonteyn and others.

Nurmi, Paavo (1897-1973), Finnish athlete. Won 6 Olympic titles in running at 1500-10,000 m distances and 3 more in cross-country events. Set 20 world records (1920-31). Famous for timing himself with stopwatch while running.

nursery rhymes, short poems for children, stressing rhythm, rhyme; usually traditional. Many thought to have basis in ancient rites, eg 'Here we go round the mulberry bush', or more recent historical events.

nursing, care of the sick. Practised by various religious orders in the Middle Ages, it was revitalized in 17th cent. by the founding of the Sisters of Charity by St Vincent de Paul. First hospital training school was estab. at Kaiserswerth, Germany by Theodor Fliedner (1836). School estab. (1860) at St Thomas's Hospital by Florence Nightingale became model for such schools everywhere.

Nusa Tenggara, see SUNDAS.

Nut, Egyptian mother goddess. Personified sky by day. Mother of Osiris, Isis.

nut, dry, one-seeded fruit of various trees and shrubs. Consists of kernel (often edible) in a hard woody shell which is separable from the seed itself, eg walnut, hazelnut.

nutcracker, *Nucifraga caryocatactes,* bird of crow family, found in coniferous forests of Europe and Asia. Brown with white speckles.

nuthatch, small sharp-beaked tree-climbing bird of Sittidae family. Nests in holes in trees; diet of insects, nuts. Species incl. European nuthatch *Sitta europaea* and North American white-breasted nuthatch *S. carolinensis.*

nutmeg, hard aromatic seed of East Indian tree, *Myristica fragrans.* Grated and used as spice, while outer covering yields the spice mace. Oil derived from seed and covering used in medicine and cosmetics.

nux vomica, poisonous disc-shaped seed of Asiatic deciduous tree, *Strychnos nux-vomica,* of logania family. Contains various alkaloids, incl. strychnine.

Nyasa, Lake, see MALAWI, LAKE.

Nyasaland, see MALAWI.

Nyerere, Julius Kambarage (1921–), Tanzanian statesman. Became PM at independence (1961) of Tanganyika, then president upon estab. of republic (1962). Pursued socialist policies, with Chinese aid. Negotiated union with Zanzibar which created Tanzania, becoming president (1964).

nylon, name given to group of synthetic long-chain polymeric amides, made into fibres, yarn, moulded plastics, *etc.* Fibre, characterized by strength, elasticity and low absorbency of moisture, is used in mfg. of hosiery and textiles.

nymph, larva of insect undergoing

incomplete metamorphosis (without pupal stage). Resembles adult, but without wings and sexually immature. Winged adult emerges after series of moults.

nymphs, in Greek myth, generic name for large number of minor female deities associated with natural objects. Usually represented as young, beautiful and amorous, *eg* NAIADS, NEREIDS, DRYADS, OREADS.

O

Oahu, volcanic isl. of Hawaii, US. Area 1540 sq km (595 sq mi); main city HONOLULU. Tourism; extinct volcanoes.

oak, any of genus *Quercus* of hardwood trees and shrubs of beech family bearing nuts called ACORNS. Widely distributed in N temperate regions. Wood used in furniture. Bark of cork oak, *Q. suber,* is used commercially as source of cork.

Oakland, port of W California, US; on San Francisco Bay. Pop. 362,000. Naval base; electrical equipment, chemicals, shipbuilding. Incl. residential areas overlooking Bay. Connected by bridge with San Francisco.

oarfish or **king-of-the-herring,** marine fish, genus *Regalecus,* with long ribbon-like body and mane-like crest behind head. Reaches lengths of 6.1 m/20 ft or more.

oasis, fertile area in a desert, caused by presence of water. May be natural spring or made by sinking artesian well. Date palm is commonest vegetation. Some oases very extensive, *eg* Kufra Oasis, Libya.

oat, *Avena sativa,* hardy, widely grown cereal grass, native to Asia. Cultivated as food for man, *eg* oatmeal, and for horses.

Oates, Titus (1649-1705), English Protestant conspirator. Fabricated and testified to 'Popish Plot' (1678), said to involve murder of Charles II,

burning of London, and reintroduction of Catholicism. Resulting panic caused judicial murder and persecution of many Catholics. Imprisoned for perjury (1685); pardoned (1688).

Ob, river of USSR. Formed by union of Biya and Katun rivers, flows *c* 3500 km (2200 mi) N and NW through W Siberian RSFSR to Gulf of Ob. Middle course extensively flooded during spring thaw. Trade route in summer; h.e.p. near Novosibirsk.

Obadiah or **Abdias,** shortest prophetic book of OT. Foretells triumph of Israel over Edom. Prob. written before 550 BC.

Oban, town of Strathclyde region, W Scotland. Pop. 7000. Port, tourist resort; fishing industs. Ferry services to Inner Hebrides.

obbligato, musical term originally denoting essential part of composition, usually a particular instrumental line, as opposed to an optional part. Mainly found in baroque music. Subsequent misunderstanding has reversed meaning.

Obeid, El, town of C Sudan. Pop. 66,000. Railway terminus, road jct., trade in gum arabic, cereals, cattle. Scene of Mahdi's victory (1883) over Egyptians.

obelisk, in ancient Egypt, four-sided monolithic slender shaft, tapering

towards top, with pyramidical apex. Dedicated to the sun god, they were often placed in pairs about temples. Examples have been removed to London, New York, Paris. London and New York examples called Cleopatra's Needles.

Oberammergau, town of S West Germany, on R. Ammer, in Bavarian Alps. Pop. 5000. Woodcarving, tourism, winter sports. Passion Play performed every 10 years (begun 1634) is thanksgiving for deliverance from plague.

Oberhausen, city of W West Germany, on Rhine-Herne canal, in Ruhr. Pop. 245,000. Coalmining, oil refining, zinc smelting. Founded 19th cent.

obesity, excess of body fat. Usually results from over-eating of carbohydrate foods. Obesity can usually be reduced by eating less sugar and starch and taking more exercise.

oboe, woodwind instrument with double reed and conical bore, developed from medieval shawm or pommer. Attained its present form in France in c 1650. Cor anglais or English horn is similar, but a fifth lower in pitch.

Obote, [Apollo] Milton (1924-), Ugandan political leader, PM (1962-6). Seized presidency (1966); while absent abroad, deposed by Amin (1971).

O'Brien, Conor Cruise (1917-), Irish statesman, writer. Represented UN in Katanga, during province's secession from Congo (1961). Labour member of Irish parliament from 1969; minister of posts and telegraphs 1973-1977. Sought to restrict IRA activities in the re-

public. Editor of *Observer* newspaper (1978-).

observatory, building designed for observation of astronomical or meteorological phenomena, *eg* Mt. Palomar and Mt. Wilson observatories in California.

obsidian, hard, usually black, volcanic glass. Formed by viscous acid lava cooling too quickly for minerals to crystallize. Used esp. in prehist. times for weapons, ornaments. Major sources in Mediterranean isls., Iceland, Mexico, US.

obstetrics, branch of medicine concerned with childbirth and treatment of mother before and after delivery.

O'Casey, Sean (1880-1964), Irish dramatist. Works, reflecting early life in Dublin slums, incl. tragicomedies *Juno and the Paycock* (1924), *The Plough and the Stars* (1926). Also wrote expressionist anti-WWI drama, *The Silver Tassie* (1929).

occasionalism, see GEULINCX.

occultism, belief in hidden powers and forces, esp. supernatural. Designates alleged mystic arts, *eg* alchemy, astrology, magic, spiritualism.

ocean, large expanse of salt water on Earth's surface. Five usually distinguished: Antarctic or Southern, Arctic, Atlantic, Indian and Pacific, the largest. Together, oceans cover 71% of Earth's surface.

Oceania, general term for isls. of Pacific belonging to Melanesia, Micronesia and Polynesia groups, and sometimes those of Australasia.

Oceanus, in Greek myth, the great outer stream which encircled the earth. Personified as a TITAN who was father of river gods and **sea** nymphs (Oceanids).

ocelot, *Felis pardalis*, wild cat of Central and South America; body length *c* 76 cm/30 in. Yellow or grey coat with black spots. Valued for its fur.

Ochil Hills, range of C Scotland, in Central, Tayside, Fife Regions. Rise to 720 m (2360 ft).

ochre or **ocher**, natural earth, mixture of hydrated iron oxide and clay. Ranges in colour from yellow to brown and red. Used as pigment in paints. Major sources in US, France, Italy.

O'Connell, Daniel (1775-1847), Irish nationalist leader. Founded (1823) Catholic Association to further Catholic emancipation. Elected **to** Parliament (1828), although unable to take oaths necessary to assume seat; Catholic Emancipation Act (1829) was passed as a result. After 1841, worked for repeal of union with Britain but his conservative ways lost him popular support.

Octavian, see AUGUSTUS.

octopus, cephalopod mollusc with rounded sac-like body, no shell and 8 sucker-bearing arms. Lives mainly on sea bottom, ejecting inky fluid for protection. Species incl. common octopus, *Octopus vulgaris*, of Atlantic and Mediterranean.

ode, originally Greek poem sung to musical accompaniment. Either for single voices, *eg* those of Sappho, Alcaeus, Anacreon; or choral, *eg* Pindar. In modern period, revived in 16th cent. France by Ronsard; 17th cent. English poets influenced chiefly by Horace, also by Pindar, *eg* Milton, Cowley, Dryden.

Odense, city of Fyn Isl., Denmark. Pop. 137,000. Port, exports dairy produce; shipbuilding; textiles. Founded 10th cent., cathedral (rebuilt in 13th cent.). Birthplace of Hans Christian Andersen.

Oder (Czech and Pol. *Odra*), river of E Europe. Flows 900 km (560 ml) from NC Czechoslovakia through Poland to Baltic Sea at Szczecin. Forms N Part of Polish-East German border. Navigable below Raciborz, canals to Katowice indust. region.

Odessa, city of USSR, SW Ukrainian SSR; on Black Sea. Pop. 941,000. Port; exports grain, timber; indust. centre. Taken in 1789 from Turks by Russia. Scene of workers' revolution led by mutineers from *Potemkin* (1905). Under Romanian occupation (1941-3); large Jewish pop. decimated.

Odets, Clifford (1906-63), American playwright. Known for committedly socialist plays, *eg Waiting for Lefty* (1935), *Awake and Sing!* (1935), *Golden Boy* (1937).

Odin, in Norse myth, the supreme god, creator of earth, sky and mankind. Associated with war and learning. Sometimes identified with Roman Mercury.

Odovacar or **Odoacer** (*c* 435-93), German chieftain, 1st barbarian ruler of Rome. Proclaimed king by the German mercenaries he led in service of Rome, he deposed the emperor Romulus Augustulus (476), thus ending Western Roman Empire. Defeated by invading Ostrogoths under Theodoric and treacherously murdered at latter's instigation.

Odysseus, in Greek myth, king of Ithaca. A leader of Greeks in TROJAN

WAR, noted for his cunning. Devised Wooden Horse scheme. Hero of Homer's ODYSSEY. Known as Ulysses by Romans.

Odyssey, Greek epic in 24 books attributed to Homer. Tells story of ODYSSEUS. After fall of Troy, attempted to return to kingdom Ithaca, but incurred curse of Poseidon which led to 10 years of wandering before homecoming, having lost all companions; rid palace of wife Penelope's suitors with aid of son Telemachus before estab. rule again.

OECD, see ORGANIZATION FOR ECONOMIC COOPERATION AND DEVELOPMENT.

oedema or **dropsy,** abnormal accumulation of fluid in body tissues, resulting in swelling. Caused by heart failure, obstruction of lymphatic vessels, kidney disease, etc.

Oedipus, in Greek myth, son of Thebes. Abandoned on Mt. Cithaeron when it was prophesied that he would kill his father Laius and marry his mother Jocasta. Brought up in Corinth ignorant of his true parentage; fled upon learning of prophecy from Delphic oracle. Killed Laius in chance encounter on way to Thebes and married Jocasta after saving kingdom by answering riddle of the Sphinx. Later learned truth, blinded himself; Jocasta committed suicide. Succeeded by Creon and died at Colonus. Children were POLYNICES, Eteocles, ANTIGONE and Ismene. Hero of Sophocles' *Oedipus Rex, Oedipus at Colonus.*

Oedipus complex, in psychoanalytic theory, sexual desire of son for mother and conflict with father.

May be openly expressed at age 4-5 years, later repressed as son realizes sanctions against incest, but persists in unconscious. Concept developed by Freud, using the Greek legend, and was fundamental not only to psychoanalysis but to his theory of culture and religion. Daughter's desire for father called Electra complex.

Oersted, Hans Christian (1777-1851), Danish scientist. Estab. relationship between electricity and magnetism (1819) by discovery that magnet takes up right-angled position to direction of electric current.

oesophagus or **gullet,** part of alimentary canal connecting the PHARYNX with the stomach. Carries food to stomach by muscular contraction of its walls.

oestrogen, any of group of female hormones, produced synthetically or secreted in ovaries of mammals. Responsible for development of female secondary sexual characteristics and stimulation of ovulation.

oestrus, period of heat (maximum sexual receptivity) in female mammals.

Offa (d. 796), Anglo-Saxon chieftain, king of Mercia (757-96). Estab. Mercian supremacy over most of England S of the Humber. Had defensive earthwork, Offa's Dyke, built on Welsh border. Recognized as an equal by Charlemagne, with whom he drew up a trading treaty (796).

Offaly, county of Leinster prov., C Irish Republic. Area 1997 sq km (771 sq mi); pop. 52,000; co. town Tullamore. Flat, low-lying, has part of Bog of Allen; Slieve Bloom Mts. in

SE. Agric., cattle; peat. Formerly called King's County.

Offa's Dyke, ancient earthworks between England and Wales, from R. Dee to R. Severn. Built (8th cent.) by Offa, king of Mercia; parts still form border.

Offenbach, Jacques (1819-80), French composer, b. Germany. Wrote popular light operas, eg *Orpheus in the Underworld,* and serious *Tales of Hoffmann.*

O'Flaherty, Liam (1897-), Irish novelist. Works incl. *Thy Neighbour's Wife* (1923) set in Aran Islands, *The Informer* (1925) depicting Republican terrorism.

ogam or **ogham,** alphabetic system of writing developed in Ireland in 5th cent. AD. Letters are represented by combinations of lines and notches carved along edges of memorial stones.

Ogbomosho, city of SW Nigeria. Pop. 387,000. Trade centre for agric. region, esp. cotton, yams, cassava.

Ogden, C[harles] K[ay] (1889-1957), English psychologist, linguist. With I. A. Richards originated BASIC ENGLISH, collaborated in *The Meaning of Meaning* (1923).

ogham, *see* OGAM.

Oglethorpe, James Edward (1696-1785), English army officer, philanthropist. Estab. (1733) colony of Georgia as refuge for imprisoned debtors. Accompanied 1st colonists, founded Savannah; organized defence against Spaniards.

O'Higgins, Bernardo (1776-1842), Chilean revolutionary. Led opposition to Spanish rule from 1810; defeated at Rancagua (1814), fled to Argentina. Returned with San Martin's army, became ruler after victory at Chacabuco (1817). Exiled to Peru after overthrow (1823).

Ohio, state of N US. Area 106,765 sq km (41,222 sq mi); pop. 10,652,000; cap. Columbus; chief cities Cleveland, Cincinnati. Mainly flat with L. Erie in NE, Ohio R. in S, Allegheny Mts. in E, prairies in W. Important agric. esp. wheat, livestock; mining incl. coal, oil; indust. concentrated in iron and steel, machinery, rubber, motor car, paper mfg. Control of fur trade estab. by British (1763); ceded to US after Revolution (1783). Admitted to Union as 17th state (1803).

Ohio, river of NC US. Flows from W Pennsylvania SW 1579 km (981 mi) to Mississippi R. Forms 5 state borders; drains indust. region of Pittsburgh, Cincinnati, Louisville. Navigable from Pittsburgh; subject to flooding.

Ohm, Georg Simon (1787-1854), German physicist. His work on electrical circuits led him to formulate Ohm's law: potential difference between ends of a conductor is proportional to current flowing. Unit of electrical RESISTANCE named after him.

oils, group of liquids divided into 3 main classes: (1) fatty oils, consisting of mixtures of glycerides of fatty acids, found in animals and plants; (2) mineral oils, consisting of mixtures of hydrocarbons, obtained from petroleum, shale or coal; (3) ESSENTIAL OILS.

Oise, river of N France. Flows c 305 km (190 mi) from Belgian Ardennes via Compiègne to R. Seine NW of Paris. Heavy river traffic, canal links with Sambre, Somme, Escaut (Scheldt).

Ojos del Salado, peak in Chilean Andes, on Argentina-Chile border. Height 6870 m (22,539 ft); 2nd highest peak in Andes.

Ojukwu, Chukwuemeka Odumegwu (1933-), Nigerian general. Leader of Biafra secessionist govt. (1967-70) in Nigerian civil war. Escaped into exile after defeat.

okapi, *Okapia johnstoni*, rare mammal of giraffe family, from Congo forests. Stands *c* 1.5 m/5 ft at shoulder; red-brown in colour, white bands on legs.

Okhotsk, Sea of, arm of NW Pacific, on E Siberian RSFSR. Enclosed by Kamchatka penin., Kuril and Sakhalin isls.

Okinawa, largest of Ryuku Isls., W Pacific. Area 1176 sq km (454 sq mi); cap. Naha. Sugar cane, rice, sweet potatoes grown. Scene of intense fighting between Japan and US (1945). Placed under US military control until returned to Japan in 1972.

Oklahoma, state of SC US. Area 181,090 sq km (69,919 sq mi); pop. 2,559,000; cap. Oklahoma City; other major city Tulsa. Mainly prairie, mountainous in E; chief rivers Red on S border, Arkansas and tributaries. Main occupations wheat growing, livestock rearing esp. cattle; oil, natural gas resources. First explored by Spanish; part of Louisiana Purchase (1803); reserved for Indians, redistributed (1889) for white settlers. Admitted to Union as 46th state (1907).

Oklahoma City, cap. of Oklahoma, US; on North Canadian R. Pop. 369,000. Indust., commercial centre in agric., oil producing region; related industs. incl. oil refining,

food processing. Founded 1889; became cap. 1910.

okra or **gumbo,** *Hibiscus esculentus*, aromatic bean of mallow family, native to Africa. Grown extensively in US, India. Used as vegetable and in soups.

Olaf II [Haraldsson] (c 995-1030), king of Norway (1015-28). Attempted to convert Norway to Christianity and unify country under his rule. Exiled after rebellion in favour of CANUTE (1028). Killed during invasion to regain crown. Patron saint of Norway.

Olaf V (1903-), king of Norway (1957-). Succeeded his father, Haakon VII. His son, Harald, is heir to throne.

Oland Island, Baltic isl. of SE Sweden, separated from mainland by Kalmar Sund. Area 1347 sq km (520 sq mi); main town Borgholm. Agric.; limestone quarrying; tourism.

Olbers, Heinrich Wilhelm (1758-1840), German astronomer. Known for Olbers' paradox: night sky should be uniformly bright if there are infinitely many stars evenly distributed in space. Paradox now explained by expansion of universe causing red shift of light emitted by stars.

Old Bailey, street in City of London. Name used popularly for Central Criminal Court, sited there.

Old Catholics, Christian church estab. by German clergy who rejected decrees of the 1870 Vatican Council, esp. dogma of papal infallibility. Priests are allowed to marry; confession is optional. Survives in Germany, Netherlands, US.

Oldenburg, Claes (1929-), American sculptor, b. Sweden. Works, derived from advertising and display techniques, are usually classed as pop art; most famous are large, soft renditions of everyday objects.

Old English, *see* ENGLISH.

Oldham, bor. of Greater Manchester met. county, NW England. Pop. 106,000. Textile indust., esp. cotton spinning.

Old Moore's Almanac, annual British publication containing predictions of events of coming year. First published (1700) as *Vox Stellarum* by Francis Moore (1657-*c* 1715) as vehicle to advertise his patent medicines.

Old Norse literature, literature of Northmen, or Norsemen, *c* 850-*c* 1350. Little survives outside ICELANDIC LITERATURE, which incl. Edda, ancient lays on gods, goddesses; Scaldic poetry, subjective songs of love, sorrow, triumph; sagas, heroic prose narratives; also noteworthy hist. writing, eg by SNORRI STURLUSON.

Old Testament, Christian term for Hebrew part of the Bible. Relates story of the Jews from time of Moses to (with APOCRYPHA) cent. before birth of Jesus. Largely based on 3rd cent. BC translation into Greek (SEPTUAGINT). W Churches adopted the Latin version (VULGATE).

Olduvai Gorge, archaeological site in Tanzania where remains of toolmaking precursors of man, *c* 1.8 million years old, were discovered by the LEAKEYS in 1959. Other fossil hominids have since been found there.

Old Vic, London theatre. Opened (1818) as Coburg. Renamed (1880) as Royal Victoria Hall (hence 'Old Vic'). Famous for productions of Shakespeare (1914-39) under management of Lilian Baylis. Became home of National Theatre Company (1963-76).

Old World, name used for the continents of Europe, Asia and Africa.

oleander, *Nerium oleander,* poisonous evergreen shrub native to Mediterranean region. Lance-shaped leathery leaves, large pink flowers.

oleaster, common name for plants of genus *Elaeagnus;* incl. *E. angustifolia,* ornamental shrub, native to S Europe and W Asia. Yellow flowers and olive-like fruit.

Oligocene epoch, third geological epoch of Tertiary period. Alpine mountain building continued. Mammals dominant; rise of true carnivores, erect primates. Decrease in temperature from Eocene epoch. Also *see* GEOLOGICAL TABLE.

oligopoly, in economics, virtual control of supply of commodity or service by a few producers. While privately-controlled MONOPOLY is rare, oligopoly is relatively usual in form of CARTEL or interlocking directorates. Also *see* MULTI-NATIONAL CORPORATION.

Oliphant, Sir Marcus Laurence Elwin ('Mark') (1901-   ), Australian physicist. Studied nuclear disintegration of lithium; designed Australian proton synchrotron.

olive, *Olea europaea,* European evergreen tree, native to Asia Minor. Cultivated since ancient times for fruit, eaten either unripe (green) or ripe (black), or used as source of oil. Wood prized for ornamental work.

Oliver, Isaac (*c* 1565-1617), English painter. Worked under Hilliard; continued art of miniature painting, but portraits are in more naturalistic style.

Olives, Mount of or **Olivet**, ridge E of Jerusalem visited many times by Jesus. Garden of Gethsemane on W slope.

Olivier, Laurence [Kerr], Baron Olivier of Brighton (1907-), English actor, director. Famous for appearances at Old Vic and in films, *eg Rebecca, Richard III, Hamlet.* Director of UK's National Theatre (1962-73).

Olomouc (Ger. *Olmütz*), town of C Czechoslavakia, on R. Morava. Pop. 80,000. Food processing. Former cap. of Moravia. Cathedral (14th cent.); town hall (15th cent.) with astronomical clock. Univ. (1573).

Olympia, ancient city of Greece, in W Peloponnese. Founded c 1000 BC; centre for worship of Zeus, temple had Phidias' statue of Zeus. OLYMPIC GAMES first held here.

Olympia, cap. and port of Washington, US; at end of Puget Sound. Pop. 23,000. Exports fish, timber. Tourism in Olympic Mts. to N. Founded 1850; became territ. cap. 1853.

Olympian gods, in Greek myth, the twelve major gods who lived on Mt. Olympus. Succeeded the TITANS as rulers of universe. Headed by Zeus and his sister and wife, Hera.

Olympic games, ancient Greek festival consisting of contests in athletics, poetry and music held every 4 years at Olympia. First records kept from 776 BC; abolished AD 393. Games were revived (1896) by Pierre de Coubertin; women participated from 1912. Winter Olympics estab. 1924.

Olympus (*Olimbos*), mountain range of NE Greece, near Aegean coast. Rises to 2915 m (9570 ft), highest point in Greece. Legendary home of ancient gods.

Omagh, town of WC Northern Ireland. Pop. 12,000. Former co. town of Tyrone. Agric. market; dairy produce.

Omaha, city of E Nebraska, US; on Missouri R. Pop. 347,000; state's largest city. Railway, insurance centre. Livestock market, meat packing, machinery mfg. Supply base for mid-19th cent. W expansion. Founded 1854; territ. cap. 1855-67.

Oman, independent sultanate of SW Asia, SE Arabian penin., along Gulf of Oman. Area *c* 212,000 sq km (82,000 sq mi); pop. 791,000; cap. Muscat. Coastal plain (dates) backed by mountains, arid plateau. Linked by treaty with Britain. Called Muscat and Oman until 1970.

Omar (*c* 581-644), Arab ruler. One of Mohammed's ablest advisers, he succeeded Abu Bakr (634) as 2nd caliph. Greatly extended Islamic empire with victories in Persia, Syria, Egypt.

Omar Khayyam (*fl* 11th cent.), Persian poet, mathematician. Famous in West for *Rubáiyát* through Edward Fitzgerald's English translation (1859); series of independent epigrammatic stanzas. Famous in East as astronomer and mathematician, assisted calendar reform.

Omayyads, Arab dynasty of caliphs. Founded 661 by Muawiya, whose cap. was Damascus. Overthrown by Abbasids (750), who massacred Omayyad family. A survivor escaped to Spain, where he founded emirate of Córdoba (756-929) later a caliphate (929-1031).

ombudsman, public official appointed to investigate citizens' complaints against local or national govt. agencies for infringement of rights of individual. Introduced into Sweden (1809). Appointed in New Zealand (1962), UK (1966), Hawaii (1969).

Omdurman, city of C Sudan, on White Nile opposite Khartoum. Pop. 230,000. Noted for native markets, trade in livestock, hides, cotton goods. Mahdi's cap. 1884, site of his tomb. Scene of Kitchener's victory (1898) over Khalifa's forces.

Omsk, city of USSR, W Siberian RSFSR; at confluence of Om and Irtysh. Pop. 876,000. Automobile, agric. machinery mfg; oil refining. Founded 1716 as fort.

onager, *Equus hemionus onager,* wild ass of India and Persia.

Onassis, Aristotle · Socrates (1906-75), Greek shipping magnate, b. Turkey. Known as 'the Golden Greek', amassed vast fortune in shipping, real estate. Married Jacqueline Bouvier Kennedy (1968).

Onega, Lake, second largest lake of Europe, in USSR, NW European RSFSR. Area c 9840 sq km (3800 sq mi). Outlet is R. Svir, flowing into L. Ladoga. Important fisheries.

O'Neill, Eugene [Gladstone] (1888-1953), American dramatist. Experimented with technique, combining myth, symbolism, expressionism. Plays incl. trilogy *Mourning Becomes Electra* (1931), *The Iceman Cometh* (1946), *Long Day's Journey into Night* (pub. 1956). Nobel Prize for Literature (1936).

onion, *Allium cepa,* biennial plant of

OPAL

lily family, native to SW Asia. Widely cultivated for edible bulb with pungent smell and flavour. Used as vegetable since ancient times.

Ontario, prov. of C Canada. Area 1,068 587 sq km (412,582 sq mi); pop. 7,703,000; cap. Toronto; other major cities Ottawa, Hamilton. Forests, lakes in N (Laurentian Plateau) with nickel, uranium, iron, copper resources. Indust., agric., pop. concentrated in S around Great Lakes (trade, transport focus of Canada). French fur traders settled region in 17th cent., British control from 1763; area named Upper Canada (1791); became one of 4 original provs. of Canada (1867).

Ontario, Lake, smallest of Great Lakes, EC Canada-US. Connects L. Erie with St Lawrence Seaway. Area 19,529 sq km (7540 sq mi); chief port Toronto. Important trade link; commercial fishing (affected by recent pollution).

onyx, semi-precious form of CHAL-CEDONY. Differs from agate only in having straight, parallel, regular bands of colour. Used by Romans for cups, vases, *etc,* now in cameos, ornaments.

oolite, sedimentary rock composed of spherical nuclei surrounded by concentric layers, normally of calcium carbonate. Oolitic LIMESTONE is chemically precipitated; term formerly applied to upper Jurassic period in Europe.

Oostende, see OSTEND, Belgium.

opal, hydrated amorphous form of silica. Impurities determine colour; gem opals pearly and translucent, with red, green and blue tints. Major sources of gem opals in Australia, Mexico.

op or **optical art,** style of abstract painting developed in 1960s which uses geometric patterns to create optical illusions of movement. Exponents incl. Bridget Riley, and Vasarely.

OPEC, see ORGANIZATION OF PETROLEUM EXPORTING COUNTRIES.

Open University, Milton Keynes, UK, estab. 1969 to provide tuition for non-qualified part-time adult students through correspondence courses integrated with radio, TV broadcasts, summer schools, and counselling and tutorial system. Has over 50,000 students.

opera, stage drama in which singing largely or totally takes place of speech. Developed in West as Italian court entertainment from c 1600 (MONTEVERDI being earliest master of form). Rigidity of resulting conventions led to reaction in favour of dramatic expression c 1750. In 19th cent., grand opera, spectacular and serious, contrasted with entertaining light operas. Most operas of 20th cent. retain earlier musical forms, but are often more subtle or symbolic in content.

operetta, short light OPERA, usually with some spoken dialogue, esp. works of Offenbach, Johann Strauss, Gilbert and Sullivan.

Ophion, in Greek myth, serpent who ruled world before Cronus.

opium, narcotic drug obtained from unripe seed capsules of OPIUM POPPY. Derivatives incl. morphine, heroin, codeine, used medicinally as sedative, but strictly controlled as they are addictive.

opium poppy, *Papaver som-*

niferum, annual plant native to Asia and Asia Minor. Cultivated as source of OPIUM.

Opium Wars (1839-42, 1856-8), wars between China and Britain, resulting from Chinese refusal to allow importation of opium from India. Hong Kong ceded by China after British victory (1842). British-French victory in 2nd war estab. free trade in Chinese ports and legalization of opium trade.

Oporto (*Pôrto*), city of W Portugal, on R. Douro. Pop. 693,000. Seaport, exports port wine; artificial harbour for large ships at nearby Leixões; textiles, pottery mfg. Univ. (1911); Torre dos Clerigos is famed landmark (75 m/246 ft high); 2-storey bridge (1887). Roman *Portus Cale,* gave name to Portugal.

opossum, any of Didelphidae family of mainly arboreal American marsupials with long prehensile tails. Noted for habit of feigning death when in danger - 'playing possum'. Species incl. nocturnal rat-like Virginia opossum *Didelphis virginiana* found from Argentina to N US. Name also applied to Australian HONEY MOUSE.

Oppenheimer, J[ohn] Robert (1904-67), American physicist. Directed research at Los Alamos (1942-5) leading to production of 1st atomic bomb; opposed decision to develop hydrogen bomb. Considered security risk, he was deprived of membership of US Atomic Energy Commission (1953).

Ops, in Roman religion, wife of Saturn; mother of Jupiter and Juno. Goddess of the harvest. Identified with Greek Rhea.

optical fibres, see FIBRE OPTICS.

optics, science of light and principles underlying phenomena of light and vision, divided into physical and geometrical optics. Former studies nature of light and its wave properties, latter treats reflection, refraction, *etc*, by ray aspect of light.

oracle, in Greek religion, answer given by particular gods, usually through priest or priestess, to human questioner. Name also applied to shrine where such responses were given. Most famous were those of Zeus at Dodona and of Apollo at Delphi. Apart from Sibylline Books, oracles at Rome were much less important than those in Greece.

Oran, city of NW Algeria, on Gulf of Oran. Pop. 328,000. Port, exports wine, wheat, wool; food processing. Founded 10th cent.; alternated between Spain, Turkey after 1509, taken by France (1831). Severely damaged by earthquake (1791). Scene of British destruction of French fleet (1940), to prevent capture by Germans.

Orange, House of, ruling family of the Netherlands. Name derives from principality in SE France inherited (1544) by William the Silent, of house of Nassau. His successors were stadholders of Dutch republic. William VI, prince of Orange, became 1st king of Netherlands in 1815.

Orange, town of Provence, SE France. Pop. 26,000. Tourist centre. Hist. cap. of Orange principality, rulers united (16th cent.) with House of Nassau; descendants form Dutch royal family. Roman remains incl. arch, amphitheatre.

Orange, river of S Africa. Flows *c* 2100 km (1300 mi) W from N

Lesotho via South Africa to Atlantic Ocean at Alexander Bay. Forms part of South Africa-South West Africa border. Large irrigation, h.e.p. scheme; alluvial diamond deposits.

orange, evergreen tree of genus *Citrus*, bearing round, reddish-yellow fruit. Native to China but widely cultivated. Species incl. *C. sinensis*, common sweet orange used esp. in production of orange juice, and *C. aurantium*, bitter or Seville orange used in marmalade.

Orange Free State, prov. of EC South Africa. Area 129,250 sq km (49,900 sq mi); pop. 1,652,000; cap. Bloemfontein. Mainly plateau, bounded by R. Orange (S), R. Vaal (N). Sheep rearing, fruit, cereal growing; mines produce gold, diamonds, coal. Settled after 1836 Trek by Boers; republic created 1854. Annexed by Britain in Boer War, became Orange River Colony 1900. Prov. of Union of South Africa from 1910.

orange hawkweed, same as DEVIL'S-PAINTBRUSH.

Orange Society, militant Irish Protestant organization; named after William of Orange, whose victory at battle of Boyne (1690) estab. Protestant succession. Formed (1795) to maintain Protestant supremacy over Catholics.

orangutan, *Pongo pygmaeus,* large anthropoid ape of forests of Borneo and Sumatra. Long arms, short legs and reddish-brown hair; male up to 1.5 m/5 ft tall. Mainly arboreal; vegetarian diet.

oratorio, musical setting of text (usually religious) for soloists, chorus and orchestra, first introduced by St Philip Neri at his

Oratory in Rome *c* 1550. Examples are Handel's *Messiah* and Bach's *Christmas Oratorio*.

oratory, art of eloquence. Originated in ancient Greece and Rome as branch of rhetoric concerned with effective delivery of speeches. Noted classical exponents incl. Demosthenes and Cicero; Aristotle and Quintilian wrote on theory of oratory. Classical models influenced medieval sermons, and with rising importance of parliaments, 18th cent. political speakers.

orbit, in astronomy, path described by one body (*eg* planet, spacecraft) round a heavenly body (*eg* star, planet). In physics, path of electron round atomic nucleus. In anatomy, eye socket in vertebrate animals.

Orcagna, orig. Andrea di Cione (*c* 1308-68), Italian painter, sculptor, architect. Leading Florentine artist after Giotto, his style represents reversion to monumental Byzantine figure type. Few extant works incl. frescoes and marble tabernacle at Orsanmichele, Florence.

orchestra, large group of players of musical instruments, usually under direction of a conductor. Developed in West from *c* 1600. Modern symphony orchestra evolved in course of 18th and early 19th cents. and consists of 4 sections: strings, brass, woodwind and percussion. Except in string section, where several players play same part to increase volume, players have separate parts to play.

orchid, any of family Orchidaceae of perennial plants. Worldwide distribution but most of *c* 450 genera native to humid tropical regions. Some species are epiphytic. Flowers usually showy and of all colours, esp. genus *Cattleya* of tropical America, used in decoration.

Orczy, Emmuska, Baroness (1865-1947), English author, b. Hungary. Remembered for romantic adventure story of French Revolution, *The Scarlet Pimpernel* (1905), and many sequels.

ordeal, ancient method of trial. Accused exposed to physical dangers, *eg* fire. If he survived, was thought to have done so through divine intervention and therefore was innocent.

order in council, in UK, govt. decree of the sovereign issued with advice of the Privy Council. Survival of sovereign's sole power to govern. Used by Victoria to abolish (1870) purchase of army commissions, thereby avoiding opposition of House of Lords. Still used as subordinate legislation to issue new constitution for overseas territ.

orders of architecture, several classical styles of structure distinguished chiefly by the type of column (incl. base, shaft, and capital) and entablature. The 5 orders are IONIC, DORIC and CORINTHIAN, developed in Greece, and Tuscan and Composite, developed in Italy.

Ordnance Survey, official UK mapping agency. Estab. 1791 under Board of Ordnance, produced 1st map 1801. Also *see* CARTOGRAPHY.

Ordovician period, second geological period of Palaeozoic era; began *c* 500 million years ago, lasted *c* 65 million years. Extensive seas; beginning of Caledonian mountain building period. Typified by graptolites, trilobites, crinoids, corals;

earliest vertebrates (fish) in North America. Also see GEOLOGICAL TABLE.

ore, mineral or rock from which one or more metals may be profitably extracted.

Oreads, in Greek myth, NYMPHS of the mountains.

Orebro, town of SC Sweden, at W end of Lake Hjalmaren. Pop. 87,000. Railway jct.; shoe mfg. 15l. castle scene of many hist. diets *eg* when Bernadotte chosen king of Sweden (1810).

Oregon, state of NW US, on Pacific. Area 251,181 sq mi (96,981 sq mi); pop. 2,091,000; cap. Salem; largest city Portland. Columbia R. forms N border, Willamette R. divides W Coast and Cascade ranges. Important timber production, industs. Agric. in valleys (wheat, fruit, vegetables, livestock). Contested by Britain, US until 1846; territ. 1848, settlement began in 1840s via Oregon Trail. Admitted to Union as 33rd state (1859).

Orel or **Oryol**, city of USSR, SW European RSFSR; on R. Oka. Pop. 247,000. Market centre; textile machinery mfg. Founded 1564 as outpost against Tartars. Birthplace of Turgenev.

Orestes, in Greek myth, only son of AGAMEMNON and Clytemnestra. Avenged father's murder by killing Clytemnestra and her lover, Aegisthus, with aid of sister Electra. Pursued by Eumenides to Athens. Acquitted of matricide by the Areopagus. Married Hermione, daughter of Menelaus and Helen. Story is treated by Aeschylus, Sophocles and Euripides.

Öresund (Eng. The Sound), str.

between Denmark and Sweden, links Kattegat with Baltic Sea. Minimum width 5 km (2 mi).

Orff, Carl (1895-   ), German composer. Known for his highly rhythmic compositions, frequently for the stage. Works incl. *Carmina Burana* (1937), based on medieval Latin and Middle High German verse.

organ, keyboard instrument, sound of which is produced by air forced through a pipe or past a metal reed (*see* HARMONIUM). Modern instruments generally have 2 or 3 keyboards (great, swell and choir) controlling different sets or ranks of pipes, and a set of foot pedals. The electronic organ contains electrical circuits that create electric signals when the keys are pressed; signals are amplified and fed to a loudspeaker to produce sound.

Organization for Economic Co-operation and Development (OECD), body of 24 nations, founded 1961; hq. in Paris. Aims incl. promotion of economic growth among its member countries, expansion of world trade, coordination and improvement of development aid.

Organization of African Unity (OAU), group of 30 African states estab. 1963 in Addis Ababa. Aims incl. African solidarity, elimination of colonialism, coordination of economic, cultural, health, defence policy. Now has over 40 member states.

Organization of American States (OAS), body of 24 American countries, estab. 1948; hq. in Washington. Aims incl. promotion of peace and economic development.

Expelled Cuba (1962) and began trade boycott against it; some member countries have resumed trade with Cuba.

Organization of Petroleum Exporting Countries (OPEC), body of 11 countries which export large quantities of crude oil. Founded 1960 in Baghdad; aims to unify petroleum policies of member countries, which incl. Saudi Arabia, Iran, Libya, Algeria. Imposed threefold increase in price of oil in 1974.

Orientale, region of N Zaïre, main town Kisangani. Goldmining; cotton, coffee growing. Secession attempted after independence of Congo, became centre of rebel forces (1960-3). Renamed Haut-Zaïre 1972.

orienteering, sport combining cross-country running with navigation by map and compass. Introduced (1918) in Sweden, it is most popular in Scandinavia.

Origen [Adamantius] (c 185-c 254), Egyptian theologian. Head of catechetical school of Alexandria. Compiled parallel text of 6 Hebrew and 2 Greek versions of Bible. Wrote defence of Christianity, *Contra Celsum*.

original sin, in Christian theology, tendency to sin considered innate in mankind as a result of Adam's sin of rebellion. Thus salvation can only be obtained through divine GRACE.

Orinoco, river of Venezuela. Rises in Guiana Highlands, flows NW to Colombia, then NE across Venezuela into Atlantic creating wide delta. Length 2735 km (1700 mi). Navigable for 435 km (c 270 mi) as far as Ciudad Bolívar.

oriole, any of Oriolidae family of brightly coloured songbirds of Europe and Asia. Species incl. golden oriole, *Oriolus oriolus*; male yellow with black wings. Name also applied in US to genus *Icterus*, incl. BALTIMORE ORIOLE.

Orion, in Greek myth, giant and hunter of Boeotia loved by Artemis. She accidentally killed him and in grief placed him in heavens as a constellation.

Orion, in astronomy, constellation located at celestial equator, containing bright stars Rigel and Betelgeuse. Incl. gaseous Orion nebula, visible to unaided eye as faint patch of light.

Orissa, maritime state of E India. Area c 156,000 sq km (60,000 sq mi); pop. 21,935,000; cap. Bhubaneswar. Mainly hilly with fertile coastal strip; agric. economy based on rice. Iron and manganese ore, coalmining. Under British control (1803).

Orizaba, resort town of EC Mexico. Pop. 93,000. Agric. industs., major textile mfg. centre. To N is volcanic **Orizaba**, highest mountain in Mexico. Height 5700 m (18,700 ft). Tourist resort, with magnificent scenery.

Orkney, isl. authority of N Scotland, comprising Orkney Isls. Area 975 sq km (376 sq mi); pop. 17,000; main town Kirkwall. Only 20 of c 70 isls. inhabited, incl. Mainland, South Ronaldsay, Hoy. Low-lying, treeless. Dairy, poultry farming; fishing. Have prehist. remains. Isls. passed from Norway to Scotland 1471.

Orléans, Charles, Duc d' (1391-1465), French nobleman and poet. Taken prisoner at Agincourt (1415) and held in captivity in England for 25 years until ransomed. Devoted himself to poetry on return to France. His son became Louis XII.

Orléans, Philippe, Duc d' (1674-1723), French nobleman. Acted as regent for Louis XV after annulling terms of Louis XIV's will. Rule was noted for corruption; notorious for his profligacy. Encouraged financial methods of John Law. His great-grandson, Louis Philippe Joseph, Duc d'Orléans (1747-93), known as Philippe Egalité, achieved prominence as liberal during French Revolution. Guillotined after eldest son (later LOUIS PHILIPPE) deserted French army.

Orléans, town of Orléanais, NC France, on R. Loire, cap. of Loiret dept. Pop. 96,000. Road and railway jct., wine and grain trade, textile mfg., univ. (1312). From 10th cent. second residence after Paris of French kings; duchy from 1344. Besieged by English (1428-9), saved by Joan of Arc; again by Catholics (1563) as Huguenot stronghold. Gothic cathedral.

Ormandy, Eugene (1899-), American conductor, b. Hungary. Succeeded Stokowski as conductor of Philadelphia Orchestra (1936), a position he still holds. Known for interpretation of 19th cent. classics.

ormer, *see* ABALONE.

ormolu, copper and zinc alloy used in imitation of gold. Much used in France in 18th cent. to decorate furniture and clocks.

Ormonde, James Butler, 1st Duke of (1610-88), Irish soldier. Appointed lieutenant-general of troops in Ireland (1640), he fought against Irish rebels. As lord lieutenant of Ireland, came to terms with rebels (1647). Left for France

after Cromwell's conquest of Ireland (1649). Lord lieutenant twice more; finally removed from office (1684) by intrigue.

Ormuz, *see* HORMUZ.

ornithology, branch of zoology dealing with birds.

orogenesis, process of mountain building, resulting in formation of mountain ranges. *See* also MOUNTAIN.

Orpheus, in Greek myth, poet and musician, son of muse Calliope by Apollo. His music charmed animals, trees and rivers. After wife Eurydice's death, went to Hades to recover her. The gods, persuaded by his music, released her on condition that he should not look at her until they reached upper world. He could not resist and she vanished. He was later torn to pieces by Thracian women; head floated, still singing, down R. Hebrus and reached Lesbos.

Orphic mysteries, religious cult of ancient Greece, traditionally founded by Orpheus. Followers believed in dual nature of man; Dionysian (divine) and Titanic (evil). Stressed strict ethical code.

Orr, John Boyd, *see* BOYD ORR, JOHN, 1ST BARON.

orris root or **orrice**, root of *Iris florentina*, a European IRIS. Powdered and used in perfumery, dentifrices.

Ortega y Gasset, José (1883-1955), Spanish essayist, philosopher. Author of *Revolt of the Masses* (1930), demonstrating decay of art under mob control.

Orthodox Church, *see* EASTERN ORTHODOX CHURCH.

orthopaedic surgery, branch of surgery concerned with diagnosis and treatment of injuries, deformities and diseases of bones, joints, muscles, etc.

Orvieto, town of Umbria, WC Italy. Pop. 25,000. Market town, wine, pottery. Cathedral (13th cent.) with marble facade, palace has Etruscan relics.

Orwell, George, pseud. of Eric Arthur Blair (1903-50), English author, b. India. Known for novels reflecting independent socialist commitment, esp. allegory of Russian Revolution *Animal Farm* (1946), anti-Utopia *1984* (1949). Also wrote many important literary, political essays.

Oryol, see OREL.

oryx, any of genus *Oryx* of long-horned African and Asian antelopes, inhabiting semi-desert areas. Species incl. Arabian oryx, *O. leucoryx*, nearing extinction, and *O. gazella* of Kalahari.

Osaka, major seaport of Japan, on Osaka Bay, SW Honshu isl. Pop. 2,980,000. Indust. and commercial centre; exports cotton goods, machinery. Textiles, chemical and steel mfg. Has rebuilt 16th cent. castle, Buddhist and Shinto temples. Univ. (1931).

Osborne, John [James] (1929-   ), English playwright. Plays incl. *Look Back in Anger* (1956), creating archetype of the 'angry young man', *The Entertainer* (1957).

'Oscar', see ACADEMY AWARDS.

oscillograph, instrument for displaying or recording, in form of curve, waveforms of alternating currents and high frequency oscillations, eg sound waves. Oscilloscope is type of oscillograph which displays waveforms on fluorescent screen of cathode ray tube.

Oshawa, port of SE Ontario, Canada; on N shore of L. Ontario. Pop. 92,000. Car mfg., leather goods, plastics industs.

osier, see WILLOW.

Osiris, ancient Egyptian god of underworld; husband and brother of Isis. Treacherously slain by brother, Set. Associated with fertility and immortality; represented as wearing mummy wrappings.

Oslo, cap. of Norway, on Oslo Fjord. Pop. 477,000. Admin., commercial centre; ice-free port; timber, electrical, clothing industs., ship-building. Founded 1048, medieval Hanseatic town. Rebuilt after fire (1624), called Christiania 1624-1925. Seat of Nobel Institute. Buildings incl. Storting (parliament), Akershus fortress (13th cent.).

Osman or **Othman I** (1259-1326), Turkish sultan, founder of Ottoman dynasty. Asserted his independence from Seljuk Turks by estab. own sultanate (c 1299). Conquered NW Asia Minor.

osmium (Os), hard metallic element; at. no. 76, at. wt. 190.2. Densest substance known; occurs in natural alloy osmiridium with iridium. Forms hard alloys with platinum and iridium, used in pen points.

osmosis, tendency of solvent to pass through a semi-permeable membrane (permeable to solvent but not to dissolved substance) into solutions of higher concentrations. Makes possible absorption of water by plant roots and cells of animal bodies.

osprey, *Pandion haliaetus,* large bird of hawk family of Europe, Asia,

North America. Dark plumage with white underparts. Found near water; feeds on fish.

Ossetia, see NORTH OSSETIA.

Ossian or **Oisin**, semi-legendary Irish bard of 3rd cent. Supposedly son of Finn MacCumhaill who lived to tell tales of his father to St Patrick. See MACPHERSON, JAMES.

Ossietzky, Carl von (1889-1938), German pacifist. Imprisoned (1932) for writings exposing German rearmament. Placed in concentration camp (1933-6). Award of 1935 Nobel Peace Prize to him prompted Hitler to forbid acceptance of any further Nobel Prizes by Germans.

Ossining, village of SE New York, US; on Hudson R. Pop. 22,000. Originally named Sing Sing; renamed 1901. Site of Sing Sing state prison, once noted for severe discipline procedures.

Ostend (Flem. *Oostende*), town of W Belgium, on North Sea. Pop. 58,000. Resort; port, ferry to Dover, canal to Bruges, Ghent. Fishing, fish processing, shipbuilding.

osteoarthritis, see ARTHRITIS.

osteomyelitis, infection of bone, with formation of pus in the marrow. Usually caused by bacteria carried in the bloodstream; treated by antibiotics.

osteopathy, medical practice based on theory that ailments result from 'structural derangements' of bones and muscles, which can be corrected by manipulation. Pioneered by Andrew Still (1828-1917).

Ostia, ancient city of WC Italy. Once port for Rome, at mouth of Tiber, *fl c* AD 100-300. Now 5 km (3 mi) from sea. Extensive ruins excavated from 1854.

Ostrava or **Moravská Ostrava**, city of E Czechoslovakia, on Moravian side of R. Ostravice. Iron, steel indust., railway engineering. Opposite is Slezská Ostrava, on Silesian side, coalmining centre. Combined pop. 279,000.

ostrich, *Struthio camelus*, fast-running flightless bird of Africa and Arabia. Long sparsely-feathered neck, long legs with 2 toes on each foot; largest of all birds, *c* 2.4 m/ 8 ft tall. Male is black with white wing and tail feathers.

Ostrogoths, branch of GOTHS who were conquered by the Huns *c* 370. Gained their independence *c* 450 and settled in Pannonia (modern Hungary). Under Theodoric, invaded and conquered Italy (488-93). Lost their separate identity after defeat by Byzantine forces of Justinian (552).

Oswald, Lee Harvey (1939-63), American accused of assassination (Nov. 1963) of President J.F. Kennedy. Shot while under arrest in Dallas by Jack Ruby. Held to be responsible for crime by Warren Commission (1964).

Oswego tea, see BERGAMOT.

Oswiecim (Ger. *Auschwitz*), town of S Poland. Pop. 39,000. Railway jct.; agric. machinery, chemical indust. Site of Nazi concentration camp in WWII, where *c* 4 million people died.

Otago, region of S South Isl., New Zealand. Area 66,120 sq km (25,530 sq mi); pop. 294,000; chief city Dunedin. Southern Alps, glacial lakes, fjords in W; valleys, coastal lowlands in E. Sheep, dairy farming, tourism, h.e.p. Pop. rose rapidly during gold rush of 1860s.

Othman I, see OSMAN I.

Otranto (anc. *Hydruntum*), town of Apulia, SE Italy, on Str. of Otranto. Pop. 5000. Roman port; destroyed 1480 by Turks, never recovered.

Ottawa, cap. of Canada, in SE Ontario; on Ottawa R. Pop. 302,000. Connected to L. Ontario by Rideau Canal. Political, social, cultural centre. Important lumber indust.; major pulp and paper mills. Founded 1827 as Bytown, renamed 1854; chosen as cap. by Queen Victoria (1858). Has Parliament buildings, National Gallery, Ottawa Univ. (1866), Carleton Univ. (1942).

Ottawa, river of EC Canada. Flows from W Québec, SE 1130 km (*c* 700 mi) to St Lawrence R. near Montréal. Forms extensive part of S Québec-Ontario border. Many lakes, rapids along its course. Connected with L. Ontario by Rideau Canal.

otter, any of genus *Lutra* of aquatic carnivorous mammals, of worldwide distribution. Long flattened tail, webbed feet used for swimming. Usually lives beside fresh water, feeding on fish; SEA OTTER is marine variety. Species incl L. *lutra*, European otter, and American L. *canadensis*.

Otto [I] the Great (912-73), king of Germany (936-73) and Holy Roman emperor (962-73). Succeeded his father Henry the Fowler. Extended realm over much of Germany and Lombardy. Defeated Magyars at Lechfeld (955). Crowned emperor by Pope John XII (962). Deposed John (963) and had his own choice elected pope.

Otto, Nikolaus August (1832-91), German engineer. Developed 4-stroke (or Otto) cycle (1876), widely used in INTERNAL COMBUSTION ENGINE.

Ottoman Empire, Islamic empire estab. in Asia Minor by OSMAN I and his descendants following collapse of Seljuk Turk empire. Under Mohammed II, Constantinople captured (1453). Under Suleiman the Magnificent, empire reached its peak, incl. Turkey, Syria, Hungary, Egypt, Persia, most of Greece and Balkans. After unsuccessful siege of Vienna (1683), its European power declined. Gradually dismembered by Russia and European powers (19th-early 20th cent.).

Otway, Thomas (1652-85), English playwright. Wrote Restoration tragedies, *eg The Orphan* (1680), *Venice Preserved* (1682).

Ouagadougou, cap. of Upper Volta. Pop. 125,000. Admin., commercial centre. Railway to Abidjan (Ivory Coast); trade in groundnuts, millet, livestock. In Ivory Coast (1933-47).

Oudenaarde (Fr. *Audenarde*), village of W Belgium, on R. Scheldt. Scene of French defeat (1708) by British and Austrians in War of Spanish Succession.

Oudh, former province of British India, now part of Uttar Pradesh. Annexation by Britain (1856) **a** cause of Indian Mutiny (1857-8).

Oudjda, *see* OUJDA, Morocco.

Ouessant, *see* USHANT, France.

Ouija (from French, *oui*, German, *ja*, both = 'yes'), trademark for device consisting of a planchette and a board inscribed with the alphabet. Used in spiritualist séances to convey messages supposedly from spirits.

Oujda or **Oudjda,** city of NE

Morocco. Pop. 156,000. Railway jct., agric. trade centre for E Morocco, W Algeria. Occupied by French 1907-56.

Oulu (Swed. *Uleåborg*), town of W Finland, on Gulf of Bothnia. Pop. 85,000. Port, exports timber products; shipbuilding. Univ. (1958), cathedral.

ounce, *see* SNOW LEOPARD.

Our Father, *see* LORD'S PRAYER.

Ouse, rivers of England. **1,** in Yorkshire, flows 97 km (60 mi) to R. Trent, forming Humber estuary. **2,** in Sussex, flows 48 km (30 mi) through S Downs to English Channel at Newhaven. **3,** Great Ouse, flows 257 km (160 mi) from Northamptonshire across the Fens to the Wash.

Outer Hebrides, *see* HEBRIDES, Scotland.

Outer Mongolia, *see* MONGOLIA.

outlawry, originally deprivation by law of person's legal rights, property, protection, as punishment for crime. Killing of outlaw was not an offence.

ouzel, name applied to birds of DIPPER family and RING OUZEL.

ovary, in zoology, either of 2 female reproductive organs (ductless glands) which produce germ cells or ova, and, in vertebrates, sex hormones.

ovenbird, *Seiurus aurocapillus,* North American bird of wood warbler family, that builds oven-shaped grass nest on ground. Name also applied to birds of Furnariidae family from Central and South America that build similar clay nests, incl. spinetails, canasteros.

overture, prelude for orchestra before opera or choral work, or independent orchestral work in similar style, eg Brahms' *Tragic Overture.*

Ovid, full name Publius Ovidius Naso (43 BC–c AD 18), Roman poet. Known for erotic *Ars Amatoria,* and *Metamorphoses,* series of tales from ancient mythology. Latter profoundly influenced European literature from medieval times on. Later wrote poems of exile, *Tristia,* after banishment.

ovum · or **egg,** in biology, female gamete or reproductive cell. Once fertilized by male sperm, develops into new member of same species.

Owen, Robert (1771-1858), British social reformer. Estab. model indust. community for mill workers at New Lanark, Scotland. Improved housing and working conditions, opened schools and shops. Similar scheme at New Harmony, Indiana, unsuccessful. In 1830s, advocated that trade unions should run industs. along cooperative lines.

Owen, Wilfred (1893-1918), English poet. Known for *Poems* (1920, collected by Sassoon) expressing horror of war. Killed in WWI.

Owen Falls, waterfall of SE Uganda, on Victoria Nile near Victoria Nyanza. Site of dam (1954) which controls floods, ' supplies h.e.p. to Uganda and Kenya.

Owens, John Cleveland ('Jesse') (1913-), American athlete. Only man to win 4 track and field gold medals (100m, 200m, long jump, 4 × 100m relay) in single Olympics (1936). In an athletics meeting in 1935 he broke 6 world records within 45 mins.

owl, any of order Strigiformes of widely distributed nocturnal birds of prey. Broad head and forward-facing eyes surrounded by disc of stiff feathers; short hooked beak. Feeds on rodents and small birds, regurgitating pellets of fur and feathers.

ox, name for several members of Bovidae family. Name specifically applies to castrated bull of domesticated breeds, esp. *Bos taurus*.

oxalic acid, white crystalline poisonous solid occurring in small quantities in sorrel and rhubarb leaves. Used in ink manufacture, dyeing and bleaching.

oxalis or **wood sorrel**, any of genus *Oxalis* of creeping plants with five-parted flowers, clover-like leaves. European wood sorrel, *O. acetosella*, contains oxalic acid.

ox bow lake, see MEANDER.

Oxenstierna, Count Axel Gustafsson (1583-1654), Swedish statesman. Appointed chancellor (1612), administered country during Gustavus Adolphus' absence at war. Continued Swedish involvement in Thirty Years War after Gustavus' death; made alliance with France after defeat at Nördlingen (1634). Virtual ruler of Sweden during minority of Queen Christina.

Oxfam, British organization, estab. 1942 to raise funds for relief of poverty, suffering in Third World or disaster-hit areas. Name originally Oxford Committee for Famine Relief, changed in 1965.

Oxford, Provisions of, programme of political reform, drawn up (1258) by Simon de Montfort and forced upon Henry III of England. Provided for advisory council of 15 and attempted to limit king's taxation powers. Repudiation by Henry (1261) precipitated Barons' War (1263-7).

Oxford Movement, term for movement (from 1833) to revive Church of England through a return to practices of early Christianity. Held Anglicanism to be middle ground between Roman Catholicism and évangelicalism. First led by NEWMAN who, with Keble and Pusey, *Tracts for the Times* (1833-41). Controversial in its emphasis on ritual. Movement lost ground with entry of Newman and others into RC church. Also called Tractarianism, Anglo-Catholicism.

Oxfordshire, county of SC England. Area 2611 sq km (1008 sq mi); pop. 530,000. Cotswolds in W, Chilterns in SE; elsewhere fertile clay vale. Cereals, livestock. Co. town Oxford, on R. Thames (Isis). Pop. 114,000. Cars, electrical goods industs. Univ. grew as medieval centre of learning from 1249. Buildings incl. Bodleian Library, Ashmolean Museum. Scene of several medieval parliaments, esp. 1258 (Provisions of Oxford). Royalist hq. in Civil War.

Oxford University, oldest univ. in UK, estab. in early 12th cent. Has grown to comprise 28 undergraduate colleges, 5 of which are women's. Centre of medieval learning, has more recently led in classics, theology, political science.

Incl. Ashmolean Museum and BODLEIAN LIBRARY.

oxidation, in chemistry, originally, process by which oxygen combines with or hydrogen is removed from a substance. More generally, process in which electrons are removed from atoms or ions.

oxlip, *Primula elatior*, perennial plant of primrose family. Yellow flowers in spring.

Oxus, *see* AMU DARYA.

oxyacetylene welding, form of metal welding using mixture of oxygen and ACETYLENE. Gases are sent through high-pressure system and burn with extremely hot flame.

oxygen (O), gaseous element; at. no. 8, at. wt. 16.00. Forms *c* 1/5 of atmosphere; most abundant of all elements on Earth. Chemically active, it combines with most elements. Necessary in respiration and combustion. Obtained by fractional distillation of liquid air; used in welding flames; liquid oxygen used as rocket propellant.

oyster, edible marine bivalve mollusc, esp. of genera *Ostrea* and *Crassostrea*. Shell made of 2 unequal halves with rough outer surface. Lives on sea bed or adheres to rocks in shallow water. May be cultivated as food or for pearls in artificial beds.

oyster catcher, any of Haematopodidae family of wading birds of Europe, and the Americas. Lives on sea shores, feeding on limpets, oysters, *etc.* Species incl. *Haematopus ostralegus*, with black and white plumage, red legs and beak.

Ozark Mountains, plateau of SC US; mainly in S Missouri and NW Arkansas. Average height 610 m (2000 ft). Important lead, barytes deposits; many mineral springs. Tourist area.

ozone (O_3), unstable allotropic form of oxygen, with 3 atoms in molecule rather than usual 2. Pale blue gas with penetrating odour; powerful oxidizing agent. Formed by silent electrical discharge through oxygen or, naturally, by action of ultraviolet light; used as bleaching agent and germicide.

ozonosphere, layer of upper atmosphere, between 15 and 30 km above Earth's surface, in which there is an appreciable concentration of ozone. It absorbs much of Sun's ultraviolet radiation, which would be harmful to animal life.

P

Paarl, town of SW Cape Prov., South Africa. Pop. 49,000. Wine-making centre. Settled (1690) by Huguenots.

pacemaker, electronic device connected to the wall of the heart which provides small regular electronic shocks to restore normal heartbeat.

Pacific, War of the, war (1879-84) between Chile and Bolivia, allied to Peru. Precipitated by rescinding of Chilean mining contract in Bolivian prov. of Atacama. War declared after Chile took port of Antofagasta. Separate treaties with Peru (1883) and Bolivia (1904) gave victorious Chile provs. of Tacna, Arica and Atacama.

Pacific Islands, Trust Territory of, the, isls. of Pacific Ocean, held from 1947 by US under trusteeship from UN. Incl. Caroline, Mariana (except Guam), Marshall isls. Area c 1800 sq km (700 sq mi); pop. 114,000; cap. Saipan (Marianas).

Pacific Ocean, world's largest and deepest ocean; stretches from Asia-Australia (W) to the Americas (E), from Antarctica to the Bering Strait. Area c 180,000,000 sq km (70,-000,000 sq mi). Reaches depth of 11,033 m (36,198 ft) in Mariana Trench. Many volcanic and coral isls. in S and W, esp. Polynesia, Melanesia and Micronesia. Ocean currents circulating in Pacific incl. Equatorial, Kuroshio, East Australia, Humboldt, California.

Pacific scandal (1873), Canadian political issue which hastened fall of Conservative govt. of Sir John Macdonald. Charge was made that Macdonald accepted campaign funds for awarding Hugh Allan's syndicate a contract to build Canadian Pacific Railway.

pacifism, individual or collective opposition to the use of armed force, esp. between nations; more generally, opposition to any violence. Religious reasons for pacifism found in Christianity, Buddhism, Confucianism, *etc.* Noted exponents incl. Gandhi, Bertrand Russell.

pack rat, North American rodent, genus *Neotoma,* often with bushy tail. Noted for habit of collecting shiny objects to decorate nest.

Paddington, *see* WESTMINSTER, CITY OF, England.

paddy or **padi field,** intensively irrigated or lightly flooded area of land in which rice is cultivated. Common throughout India, China, SE Asia. Derived from *padi,* Malay term for unhusked rice.

Paderewski, Ignacy Jan (1860-1941), Polish pianist, statesman. Famed performer, esp. of Chopin. Best-known composition is *Minuet in G.* Active in cause for Polish independence, became premier for 10 months in 1919.

Padua (*Padova*), city of Venetia, NE Italy, cap. of Padova prov. Pop. 238,000. Indust., transport centre. Roman *Patavium; fl* in Middle Ages under Carrara family and Venice. Galileo taught *c* 1600 at univ. (1222), basilica (13th cent.), botanical gardens (1545). Birthplace of Livy.

Páez, José Antonio (1790-1873), Venezuelan revolutionary. Led guerrilla band against Spaniards from 1810. Assisted Bolívar in victories (1821, 1823) which drove out Spaniards. Secured separation of Venezuela from Greater Columbia (1830). President (1831-5, 1839-43); dictator (1861-3).

Paganini, Niccolò (1782-1840), Italian violinist, composer. His virtuoso playing revolutionized violin technique. Compositions feature brilliant effects that he discovered; incl. 4 violin concertos, *Perpetual Motion*, and 24 caprices for solo violin.

Page, Sir Earle Christmas Grafton (1880-1961), Australian statesman, PM (1939). Leader of Country Party (1920-39). Minister for health (1937-9, 1949-55), estab. national health scheme (1953).

pagoda, Buddhist temple in form of pyramidal tower, built in superimposed storeys tapering towards top. Common in India and China, they were imitated in 18th cent. European architecture.

Pahlavi, Mohammad Reza (1919-   ), shah of Iran (1941-   ). Succeeded on abdication of father. Followed policy of rapid westernization, inspiring widespread opposition. Forced into exile (1979).

pain, sensation arising from excessive stimulation of sensory nerve ends and conveyed by nerve fibres to the brain, where it is perceived. Relieved by analgesics, narcotics, *etc.*

Paine, Thomas (1737-1809), American writer, b. England. Argued for immediate independence of American colonies in pamphlet *Common Sense* (1775); promoted patriot cause in series of pamphlets *The American Crisis*. Defended French Revolution in *The Rights of Man* (1791-2). Accused of treason in England, fled to France (1792).

paint, pigment in suspension with oil, water or other medium (often with additional thinners) used to decorate or protect a surface. After application, dries to adhesive film by evaporation of thinner or oxidation of medium. One of commonest media is linseed oil with turpentine as thinner, but many specialized synthetic paints increasingly used.

painted lady, *Vanessa cardui*, widely distributed butterfly with brownish-black and orange wings.

painting, one of the fine arts, practised from earliest times. Examples of palaeolithic animal paintings survive at Lascaux. Frescoes were important in art of ancient Egypt and Rome. Oil colour, portraiture and use of perspective were developed in 15th cent., landscape in 16th and 17th cents. Abstract painting began in early 20th cent.

Paisley, town of Strathclyde region, WC Scotland. Pop. 95,000. Textiles industs. esp. thread; once famous for Paisley shawls. Has 12th cent. abbey.

Paiute or **Piute**, North American Indian tribes of Uto-Aztecan linguistic family. N group of Idaho and

Nevada opposed white settlers of 1860s. S group of Great Basin, Nevada were sedentary root gatherers. Originators of GHOST DANCE religion.

Pakistan, republic of SC Asia, on NW India boundary. Area c 804,000 sq km (311,000 sq mi); pop. 72,368,000; cap. Islamabad. Language: Urdu. Religion: Islam. Mountains in N and W; population concentrated in plains watered by Indus and its tributaries; desert in SW. Agric. economy (esp. grains, rice, cotton). Major cities Karachi, Lahore. Divided into 4 provs. (Baluchistan, Punjab, Sind, North-west Frontier). Created 1947 out of India following Moslem agitation led by Jinnah; became republic 1956. Long-standing dispute with India over possession of Kashmir led to fighting (1965). East Pakistan became independent republic of BANGLADESH (1972) following civil war and Indian military intervention.

Palaeocene epoch, first geological epoch of Tertiary period. Beginning of Alpine mountain building. Replacement of dinosaurs by primitive mammals, ancestors of cat, dog, horse, elephant; modern vegetation eg seed-bearing plants. Also see GEOLOGICAL TABLE.

palaeography or **paleography**, study of ancient writing. Concerned with deciphering, describing and dating of scripts.

Palaeolithic or **Old Stone Age**, prehist. period beginning c 1.8 million years ago during which modern man, Homo sapiens, evolved from 1st tool-making predecessors, eg AUSTRALOPITHECUS. Usually subdivided into Lower,

Middle and Upper periods. Lower period, earliest division, saw development of simple stone tools, eg hand axes. Middle period, represented by culture of Neanderthal man, saw introduction of flint tools. In Upper period, H. sapiens emerged, and specialized tools, eg burins, were developed.

Palaeologus, last dynasty to rule Byzantine Empire (1260-1453). First of dynasty was Michael VIII (d. 1282), last was Constantine XI who died defending Constantinople against Turks.

palaeontology, branch of geology dealing with the study of prehist. life, based on fossil remains. Incl. palaeobotany, palaeozoology; yields information on evolution, adaptation of organisms to changing environment. Early works incl. Agricola's De natura fossilium (1558); foundations laid in 19th cent. by Cuvier, Darwin, Smith, Osborne.

Palaeozoic or **Primary era**, geological era intermediate between Precambrian and Mesozoic eras. Duration c 350 million years. Cambrian, Ordovician, Silurian periods form Lower Palaeozoic; time of trilobites, graptolites, brachiopods, earliest fish. Devonian, Carboniferous, Permian periods form Upper Palaeozoic; time of amphibians, reptiles, corals, crinoids, earliest terrestrial flora. Also see GEOLOGICAL TABLE.

palate, term for roof of human mouth. Front portion, hard palate, joins tooth ridge; back portion, soft palate, is fibrous muscular arch which closes back of nose during swallowing. Uvula projects from centre of arch.

Palatinate (*Pfalz*), two regions of West Germany, hist. linked under Wittelsbach family (1214-1918). **Lower** or **Rhenish Palatinate** (*Rheinpfalz*), lies between R. Rhine and French border; now part of Rhineland-Palatinate state. Fertile, produces wines; main towns Neustadt, Kaiserslautern. **Upper Palatinate** (*Oberpfalz*), now part of Bavaria prov. Agric., cattle raising. Counts Palatine were imperial electors from 1356; territ. called Electoral Palatinate (*Kurpfalz*).

Palau Islands, isl. group of W Pacific Ocean, part of Caroline Isls. Japanese base in WWII, taken (1944) by US.

Palawan, isl. of W Philippines. Area *c* 11,800 sq km (4550 sq mi). Little arable land; produces timber, chromite.

pale, hist. term for restricted region within a country, where different system of law and govt. prevailed. In Irish history, denotes region around Dublin where English rule was enforced (12th-17th cent.).

Palembang, city of Indonesia, cap. of South Sumatra prov., port on R. Musi. Pop. 583,000. Trade centre for nearby oilfields; exports petroleum products, rubber. Cap. of sultanate until abolished by Dutch in 1825.

Palermo (anc. *Panormus*), town of N Sicily, Italy, on Tyrrhenian Sea. Cap. of Sicily and Palermo prov. Pop. 657,000. Port, exports fruit, wine, olive oil; indust. centre; univ. (1805). Founded by Phoenicians, later held by Carthage, Rome, Byzantium. *Fl* under Arabs, Normans (esp. 12th-13th cents.). Cathedral (12th cent.).

Palestine, see ISRAEL.

Palestrina, Giovanni Pierluigi da (*c* 1525-94), Italian composer. Director of Julian Chapel choir in St Peter's, Rome. Wrote mainly sacred works for unaccompanied voices, incl. over 100 Mass settings. Considered master of counterpoint and polyphony.

Pali, vernacular dialect of classical SANSKRIT. The language of S Buddhist scriptures, has become religious language of Buddhism.

Palladio, Andrea (1508-80), Italian architect. Known for theoretical writings on harmonic proportion in architecture, esp. Roman, as exemplified by *Quattro Libri dell'Architettura* (1570). Designed many villas in or near Vicenza, *eg* Villa Rotonda, which display classical temple front. Greatly influenced neo-Classical work of 17th and 18th cents. throughout Europe.

palladium (Pd), white metallic element; at. no. 46, at. wt. 106.4. Occurs with platinum and iridium. Used as catalyst in hydrogenization and in alloys with gold, platinum, silver.

Pallas, one of the minor planets, or asteroids, revolving about the Sun between Mars and Jupiter. Discovered (1802) by Olbers.

Pallas Athena, see ATHENA.

palm, any of family Palmae of tropical and subtropical trees or shrubs. Woody, branchless trunk, large evergreen feather-like or fan-shaped leaves growing in bunch at top. Economically important species incl. date, coconut, raffia and sago palms.

Palma (de Mallorca), cap. of Majorca and Baleares prov., Spain, on Bay of Palma. Pop. 234,000. Chief city and port of Balearic Isls., exports agric. produce; tourist resort. Roman colony; held by Moors 8th-13th cent. Moorish palace, 13th cent. cathedral; Lonja exchange.

Palmas, Las, city of Grand Canary, Canary Isls., Spain, cap. of Las Palmas prov. Pop. 287,000. Tourist resort, in fertile valley noted for palms; outport at Puerto de la Luz, exports fruit, wine; fishing. Cathedral (18th cent.).

Palme, [Sven] Olof [Joachim] (1927–), Swedish politician, premier (1969-76). Succeeded Erlander as Social Democratic leader and premier. Defeat in 1976 election marked end of 44 years of Social Democrat rule in Sweden.

Palmer, Arnold (1929–), American golfer. Winner of 4 US Masters, 1 US Open, 2 British Open championships. His exciting play helped make golf a major spectator sport.

Palmer, Samuel (1805-81), English painter. Influenced by Blake, he is remembered for the visionary landscapes of his 'Shoreham Period' (1826-35).

Palmerston, Henry John Temple, 3rd Viscount (1784-1865), English statesman, PM (1855-8, 1859-65). As Whig foreign secretary (1830-41, 1846-51), secured Belgian independence and supported Turkish territ. integrity against plans of Russia and France to take control of Bosporus and Egypt. As PM, continued Crimean War, supported Italian nationalism, put down Sepoy revolt in India (1857-8).

Palmerston North, city of S North Isl., New Zealand, on Manawatu R. Pop. 57,000. Market town and railway jct. for dairying, sheep farming region; woollen mills; timber indust.

palm oil, fatty, orange-red oil obtained from fruit of many palms, incl. oil palm *Elaeis guineensis*. Used in manufacture of soap, candles, *etc.*

Palm Sunday, Christian holy day commemorating Jesus' entry into Jerusalem. Celebrated on Sunday before Easter.

Palmyra, ancient city of C Syria. Rose to prominence (AD 130-270) until destroyed by Romans in 273. Has ruins of temple devoted to sun worship.

Palomar, Mount, mountain of S California, US; near San Diego. Height 1867 m (6126 ft). Has world's largest reflecting telescope, 508 cm (200 in.) in diameter.

Pamirs, mountainous region of C Asia, mainly in USSR, E Tadzhik SSR, but extending into Afghanistan and China. Consists of high mountain valleys bordered by mountain ranges; peaks incl. Mt. Communism.

Pampas, large grassy plain of NC Argentina, mainly given over to cattle raising, dairy farming; wealth from related industs., *eg* meat packing.

pampas grass, several giant perennial South American grasses of genera *Cortaderia* and *Gynerium*. Grown as ornamentals.

Pamplona, city of N Spain, at foot of Pyrenees, cap. of Navarra prov. Pop. 147,000. Agric. market, iron, lead-smelting. Annual festival when bulls run through streets. Basque kingdom founded 824, was cap. of kingdom of Navarre until union with Castile (1515). Cathedral (14th cent.).

Pan, in Greek myth, god of flocks and shepherds. Represented as partly goat-like in form. Played musical pipes in memory of nymph Syrinx, who had been changed into a reed when he was pursuing her. Worshipped originally in Arcadia, believed to inspire lonely travellers with terror (panic). Identified with Faunus by Romans.

Panama, republic of Central America, enclosing Panama Canal Zone. Area 75,650 sq km (29,210 sq mi); pop. 1,719,000; cap. Panama City. Language: Spanish. Religion: RC. Volcanic mountains in W and E; fertile lowlands in C (bananas, coffee, mahogany exports). Also important fishing industs., esp. shrimps. Pop. mainly mestizo (mixed). Explored by Balboa (1513); became part of Colombia after break with Spain (1821); independence after Colombia's refusal to allow US to build Canal (1903).

Panama Canal, waterway across Isthmus of Panama, connecting Caribbean and Pacific; 64 km (40 mi) long. Incl. artificial Gatun L. (area 422 sq km/163 sq mi). Built by US (1904-14), admin. as part of Panama Canal Zone.

Panama Canal Zone, admin. region of US comprising c 16 km (10 mi) wide canal strip in C Panama. Area 1432 sq km (553 sq mi). Admin. hq. Balboa. Incl. ports Cristóbal (Atlantic), Balboa (Pacific).

Panama City, cap. of Panama, on Gulf of Panama. Pop. 420,000. Prosperous from building of Panama Canal. Clothing, shoes, beer mfg. Founded 1519; rebuilt 1673 after destruction by pirates under Henry Morgan. Became cap. 1903.

Pan-Americanism, movement for economic and political cooperation among countries of North and South America. Sporadic 19th cent. attempts to formulate policy frustrated by suspicions of US imperialism. Series of 20th cent. meetings culminated in formation of ORGANIZATION OF AMERICAN STATES.

Panay, isl. of Philippines, S of Luzon. Area c 11,500 sq km (4450 sq mi). Lowlands in E produce rice, corn, copra.

pancreas, gland found in mesentery, near duodenum, of vertebrates. Secretes alkaline mixture of digestive enzymes through a duct into duodenum. Cell groups (islets of Langerhans) also secrete hormones insulin and glucagon.

panda, arboreal, mainly vegetarian mammal of order Carnivora. Giant panda, *Ailuropoda melanoleuca*, found in Tibet and SW China, feeds mostly on bamboo shoots; black and white, resembles bear. Lesser panda, *Ailurus fulgens*, of Himalayas, resembles raccoon; reddish-brown fur, long bushy tail.

Pandora, in Greek myth, first woman on earth. Fashioned from clay by Hephaestus at command of Zeus as vengeance on man because of Prometheus' stealing of fire from the gods. Endowed with charm and deceit by the gods. Sent to Epimetheus, brother of Prometheus, carrying box which she opened, releasing all evils on world, while hope alone remained in box.

pangolin or **scaly anteater,** any of order Pholidota of toothless mammals of Africa and tropical Asia. Body and tail protected by horny scales; feeds on ants, termites caught by sticky tongue. Species incl. giant pangolin, *Manis gigantea*.

Pankhurst, Emmeline, née Goulden (1858-1928), English suffragette. Founded Women's Social and Political Union (1905), whose members used militant methods in cause of women's suffrage. Imprisoned (1912-13) and released after hunger strikes. Supported by daughters, **Christabel Pankhurst** (1880-1958) and **Sylvia Pankhurst** (1882-1960).

panpipes, ancient musical instrument made of several pipes of different length bound together and played by blowing across open upper ends. Used in folk music, *eg* that of Romania.

Pan-Slavism, doctrine of 19th cent. urging political and cultural unity of all Slavs. First Pan-Slav conference, held (1848) in Prague, favoured Austrian protection of Slavs. Russia later seen as champion of Pan-Slavism, but widely believed to use doctrine for expansion into Austrian and Turkish empires.

pansy, *see* VIOLET.

pantheism, system of belief which identifies God in all things. Found in all periods, *eg* in Brahmanism and philosophy of Xenophanes, and in much nature poetry, *eg* Wordsworth's.

pantheon, originally building for worship of all gods. Pantheon at Rome was built by Agrippa (27 BC) and rebuilt *c* AD 120 by Hadrian. Preserved almost intact, it has great hemispherical dome. Term also denotes building in which illustrious men are buried, *eg* Panthéon, Paris.

panther, *see* LEOPARD.

pantomime, originally type of drama without speech. In 18th cent.

term used for mimed scenes, spectacles, based on Italian *commedia dell'arte*. Now a typically British Christmas entertainment, with comedy, songs, dancing.

Panzer (Ger., = armour), a mechanized unit of the German army, organized for rapid attack, Panzer divisions were highly successful in WWII, esp. in N Africa.

papacy, office of the pope as bishop of Rome and head of RC church. Estab., according to RC doctrine, when Jesus gave Peter primacy of Church.

Papadopoulos, George (1919-   ), Greek political leader. Became premier after leading 1967 military coup. Abolished monarchy (1973) and became president. Overthrown by military coup amidst popular unrest (1973). Sentenced to death for treason (1975); sentence commuted.

Papal States, former independent territ. of C Italy, cap. Rome. Originated in 'Patrimony of St Peter' given to popes in 4th cent.; grew to max. extent 16th cent. (incl. Latium, Umbria, the Marches, E Emilia-Romagna). Italian unification (1861) absorbed all but Rome (annexed 1870). Also *see* VATICAN CITY.

papaw, *see* PAWPAW

papaya, *Carica papaya,* tropical American tree. Large, edible melon-like fruit.

Papen, Franz von (1879-1969), German politician. Member of Catholic Centre Party, made chancellor by Hindenburg (1932). On resignation, helped secure Hitler's chancellorship and served as his deputy (1933-4). Acquitted of war crimes at Nuremberg.

paper, thin material consisting of

sheets of cellulose derived from vegetable fibres. Most paper is made from wood pulp freed from non-cellulose material; higher grade made from cotton rags. Invented in China c AD 105, it was spread to rest of world by the Arabs in 8th cent.; paper mfg. in Europe began in Spain in 12th cent. Leading producers incl. Canada, USSR, Scandinavia.

Papineau, Louis Joseph (1786-1871), French-Canadian insurgent. Helped precipitate Rebellion of 1837 after British failures to implement financial and constitutional reform in Lower Canada. Fled to US, then lived in France; returned after general amnesty (1845).

paprika, *see* PEPPER.

Papua New Guinea, country of SW Pacific, member of British Commonwealth. Area 463,000 sq km (178,000 sq mi); pop. 2,829,000; cap. Port Moresby. Consists of E part of New Guinea isl., Bismarck Archipelago, Bougainville and other isls. Timber exports; minerals incl. gold, copper. Country formed from Australian territ. of Papua and former German colony of New Guinea, mandated to Australia by League of Nations in 1920. Became independent 1975.

papyrus, *Cyperus papyrus,* tall sedge of Africa and Asia. Ancient Egyptians used stem for boats, cloth and to make sheets of writing material, also called papyrus.

Pará, river of N Brazil, wide arm of Amazon delta. Separates Marajó Isl. from mainland. Length 320 km (c 200 mi).

parable, term used in Gospels for brief narrative illustrating a religious teaching, esp. those of Jesus.

parabola, in geometry, curve described by a point which moves so that its distance from a fixed point (focus) equals its distance from fixed line (directrix). Also described by intersection of cone with plane parallel to one side.

Paracelsus, Philippus, orig. Theophrastus von Hohenheim (c 1493-1541), Swiss physician, alchemist, chemist. Forerunner of scientific medicine, advocated use of experiment, study of anatomy, specific drugs. Wrote many medical and occult works.

parachute, umbrella-shaped nylon or silk canopy (developed 18th cent.) reducing speed of falling body through air. Used in military and sporting activity; also as brake for aircraft and spacecraft during landing.

Paraclete, in Christian theology, the Holy Spirit, considered as comforter, intercessor or advocate.

Paradise, term denoting Garden of Eden before the Fall; also used to denote heaven or intermediate stage for righteous souls between death and final judgement.

paraffins, hydrocarbons of general formula C_nH_{2n+2}; chemically inactive. First 4 members of paraffin series, incl. methane, are gases, used as fuels. Next 11 are liquids which form principal constituents of paraffin oil (kerosene), a fuel obtained in distillation of petroleum. Other members are wax-like solids, chief constituents of paraffin wax.

Paraguay, republic of SC South America. Area 406,752 sq km (157,047 sq mi); pop. 2,724,000; cap. Asunción. Languages: Spanish, Guaraní. Religion: RC. Unexploited

Chaco in W; concentration of pop. and indust. between Paraguay, Paraná rivers. Cotton, maté growing; cattle rearing (meat packing). Settled in 16th cent. by Spanish; gained independence 1811. Extended Chaco frontier in war (1932-5) with Bolivia; political instability, economic under-development from late 1940s.

Paraguay, river of SC South America. Rises in E Mato Grosso (W Brazil), flows S 2100 km (c 1300 mi) through Paraguay to join Paraná R. Forms part of Argentina-Brazil border.

parakeet, any of several small parrots with long tails. BUDGERIGAR is common species.

parallax, in astronomy, apparent difference in position of heavenly body with reference to some point on surface of Earth and some other point, eg centre of Earth (diurnal parallax) or centre of Sun (annual parallax). Caused by Earth's rotation and revolution about Sun. Used to measure distance from Earth to heavenly body.

parallel, in mapping, see LATITUDE.

paralysis, loss of voluntary movement, usually caused by disorders of nervous system. Damage to spinal cord or brain, stroke, poliomyelitis may result in paralysis.

paramagnetism, property of certain materials, eg platinum and aluminium, of being weakly attracted by magnets (magnetic permeability of such material is slightly greater than 1). Degree of paramagnetism may be increased in some substances by decrease of temperature.

Paramaribo, cap. of Surinam, port near mouth of Surinam R. Pop. 111,000. Rum, bauxite, coffee exports. Many canals give it a Dutch appearance.

Paraná, port of EC Argentina, cap. of Entre Ríos prov. on Paraná R. Pop. 190,000. Grain, cattle produce. Cap. of Argentina 1853-62. Has cathedral; famous Urquiza Park.

Paraná, river of S Brazil. Formed by Paranaíba-Rio Grande rivers, flows SW 3200 km (c 2000 mi) along Paraguay border, through Argentina to Uruguay R. at La Plata estuary.

paranoia, in psychiatry, mental disorder associated with delusions of persecution or grandeur. Often occurs with schizophrenia; true paranoia, in which personality remains intact, is rare.

parasite, plant or animal that lives on or in an organism of another species from which it derives nourishment or protection without benefiting the host and usually harming it. Ectoparasites, eg lice, live on surface of host; endoparasites, eg tapeworms, inside host's body.

parathyroid, one of usually four small glands on or near the thyroid gland. They secrete a hormone, parathormone, which regulates calcium and phosphate concentration of blood.

Parcae, see FATES.

parchment, writing material prepared from stretched untanned animal skins. First used in Pergamum (c 150 BC).

Paris, in Greek myth, son of Priam of Troy. Exposed on Mt. Ida when it was prophesied that he would cause fall of Troy. Brought up by shepherds and returned to the city.

Chosen to settle dispute over APPLE OF DISCORD thus instigating Trojan War. In war, killed Achilles and was killed by Philoctetes.

Paris, Matthew (d. 1259), English monk and historian. His *Chronica majora* is major source of knowledge on European history from 1235 to 1259. Used his influential friends, eg Henry III, to supply him with information.

Paris (anc. *Lutetia*), cap. and dept. of France, on R. Seine. Pop. 2,591,000, greater Paris 8,187,000. River port, transport focus; admin., commercial, indust. centre (esp. luxury goods, clothing); ˙tourism. Dominates France culturally and economically. Gaulish, then Roman settlement; made cap. of France in 987 by Capet. Medieval scholastic, religious centre; *fl* as literary, artistic centre 17th-18th cent. Focus of revolutions in 1789, 1830, 1848, 1871. Places of interest incl. Ile de la Cité (site of 1st settlement) with Notre Dame Cathedral (12th - 13th cent.), Palais de Justice, Sainte-Chapelle; Arc de Triomphe, Eiffel Tower (300 m/984 ft), Montmartre (artistic quarter), Palais d'Elysée (president's residence), Sorbonne univ. (12th cent.), Louvre art gallery. Modern Paris planned (19th cent.) by Haussmann.

Paris, Congress of, conference held (1856) to negotiate settlement of Crimean War. Russian-Turkish boundary restored to pre-war status, Black Sea declared neutral, Moldavia and Walachia (later Romania) became auton.

Paris Peace Conference, see VERSAILLES, TREATY OF.

Paris, Treaty of, name of several

treaties signed in Paris. That of 1763, signed by Britain, France and Spain, ended Seven Years War. By treaty of 1783, Britain acknowledged independence of US. Treaty of 1814 gave France favourable settlement of Napoleonic wars after Napoleon's abdication but that of 1815, after French defeat at Waterloo, was much harsher.

Paris, University of, France's largest univ. Dates from 13th cent., but re-estab. (1808) after Revolution in grounds of SORBONNE. General council of faculties estab. 1885. Now occupies many sites around Paris and incl. several specialized institutes.

parity, conservation of, in physics, principle that there is no fundamental difference between left and right; thus laws of physics should be valid for both left-handed and right-handed systems of coordinates. Lee and Yang showed (1956) principle was violated by certain types of beta-decay of atomic nuclei.

Park, Mungo (1771-1806), Scottish explorer. Explored and estab. much of course of R. Niger (1795-6); drowned on 2nd expedition after attack by natives. Wrote *Travels in the Interior of Africa* (1799).

Park Chung Hee (1917-1979), South Korean political leader. Seized power in army coup (1961); became president (1963). Estab. dictatorial powers, ostensibly to withstand threats of North Korean invasion. Suppressed critics of his govt. Assassinated 1979.

Parker, Charlie ('Bird'), orig. Charles Christopher Parker (1920-55), American jazz musician. Noted for his saxophone improvisations, he was a leader in the movement away from swing to the 'bop' style of the late 1940s.

Parker, Matthew (1504-75), English churchman. Archbishop of Canterbury (1559-75). Revised (1562) the Thirty-nine Articles, basic Anglican creed.

Parkinson, Cyril Northcote (1909-), British historian, author. Known for humorous study of business world, *Parkinson's Law* (1958), stating that 'work expands to fill the time available for its completion'.

Parkinson's disease, disturbance of voluntary movements caused by degeneration of the basal ganglia of the brain. Characterized by rhythmic body tremors and muscular rigidity. Usually occurs in later life. First described by English physician James Parkinson (1755-1824).

Parliament, bicameral legislature of UK, consisting of HOUSE OF LORDS, HOUSE OF COMMONS. Executive power rests in sovereign, who in reality acts only on advice of ministers, *ie* PRIME MINISTER and CABINET. Modern development began in 13th cent. with frequent assemblies, influence of DE MONTFORT; MODEL PARLIAMENT esp. important. Its political power grew under Plantagenets, marked by deposition of 2 kings and growth of Parliament's control of national finance. Commons' drafting of statutes replaced petitions (1414). Tudors generally dominated both Houses, but under Charles I traditional conflict between sovereign's prerogative and parliamentary privilege exaggerated into absolutism v

popular govt. Led to CIVIL WAR. Parliament's power affirmed by BILL OF RIGHTS (1689). Party system developed after Civil War, became important in 19th cent. Reform Bill (1832) reconstituted Commons, extended SUFFRAGE. Parliament Acts (1911, 1949) estab. predominance of Commons, esp. with power in finance bills.

Parliament Act (1911), legislation restricting veto power of House of Lords. Arose from rejection of 1909 finance bill by Lords. In case of financial legislation, Lords stripped of rights to amend or reject; right to delay other legislation limited to two years, reduced to one year under 1949 Parliament Act.

Parma, city of Emilia-Romagna, NC Italy, cap. of Parma prov. Pop. 177,000. Agric. market, textiles, Parmesan cheese mfg. Medieval cultural centre; under Farnese family 1545-1731. Romanesque cathedral (11th cent.), univ. (1502), wooden Farnese theatre (1618).

Parmigianino, orig. Francesco Mazzola (1503-40), Italian painter, etcher. An early mannerist, his elegant graceful work is marked by its elongation of figures. Paintings incl. *Madonna with the Long Neck*.

Parnaiba, river of NE Brazil. Flows N 1300 km (c 800 mi) to Atlantic, near town of Parnaiba. Export route for river valley area.

Parnassiens, les, school of French poets (c 1870), incl. Leconte de Lisle, Mallarmé, Verlaine, who published their work in journal *Parnasse Contemporain* (1866-76). They reacted against ROMANTICISM, advocating emotional detachment, 'art for art's sake'.

Parnassus, Mount, peak of Boeotia, C Greece. Height 2456 m (8061 ft). Sacred to Apollo, Dionysus, the Muses. Fountain of Castalia and Delphic oracle lie on slopes.

Parnell, Charles Stewart (1846-91), Irish nationalist leader. Led obstructive tactics of Irish nationalists in Parliament from 1877. Directed campaign for land reform in Ireland; imprisoned (1881) for obstructing provisions of new land act; released (1882). Supported Gladstone's Home Rule bill (1886). Career ruined after involvement in divorce scandal with Katharine O'Shea (1889-90).

Páros, isl. of Greece, in Aegean Sea, one of Cyclades. Area 166 sq km (64 sq mi). Tourism. Famous from ancient times for Parian marble.

Parr, Catherine (1512-48), English queen consort, 6th wife of Henry VIII. Married Henry in 1543; acted as regent during his absence (1544). After Henry's death, married Lord Thomas Seymour (1547).

parrot, hook-billed, often brilliantly coloured bird of Psittacidae family. Widely distributed, esp. in Australasia and South America. Noted for speech mimicry. Species incl. cockatoo, macaw, parakeet, lory.

Parry, Sir Charles Hubert Hastings (1848-1918), English composer. Leader with Stanford of 'English musical renaissance'. Remembered for settings of Milton's *Blest Pair of Sirens* and Blake's *Jerusalem.*

Parry, Sir William Edward (1790-1855), English explorer, naval officer. Led several expeditions (1818-25) in search of Northwest Passage; attempted to reach North Pole by sledge (1827). Wrote valuable records.

Parry Islands, archipelago of C Franklin Dist., Northwest Territs., Canada. Incl. Melville, Bathurst, Devon Isls.

Parseeism, see ZOROASTRIANISM.

Parsifal, figure in ARTHURIAN LEGEND, sometimes called Percival, often identified with Gawain. Story basis of medieval poems, eg *Parzival* by Wolfram von Eschenbach.

parsley, *Petroselinum hortense,* biennial herb with aromatic curled leaves, used as flavouring, yellow umbelliferous flowers. Also see UMBELLIFERAE.

parsnip, *Pastinaca sativa,* biennial plant of parsley family. Long, fleshy edible root.

parthenogenesis, biological reproduction from unfertilized ovum. Occurs naturally in some organisms; male drones of ants, bees and wasps are produced by parthenogenesis. Can be artificially induced in rabbits, frogs, etc, but resulting offspring rarely reach maturity.

Parthenon, temple of Athena on Acropolis, Athens. Built by Callicrates and Ictinus (447-432 BC) in Doric style; Phidias supervised the sculpture. Middle section destroyed by Venetian bombardment 1687. Part of sculptured frieze was acquired by Lord Elgin (1801-3) and is now in British Museum.

Parthia, ancient kingdom of SW Asia, corresponding to Khurasan, NE Iran. Once part of Assyrian and Persian empires, Parthian kingdom founded in 248 BC. Reached greatest power under Mithradates I and II, controlling regions between Euphrates and Indus. Soldiers were noted horsemen and archers.

partita (Ital. = 'division'), musical term originally meaning a variation, but by end of 17th cent. became synonymous with SUITE. Noted examples are Bach's 3 partitas for solo violin.

Partridge, Eric Honeywood (1894-1979), English literary critic, lexicographer, b. New Zealand. Best known for *A Dictionary of Slang and Unconventional English* (1937), and *Dictionary of the Underworld, British and American* (1950).

partridge, medium-sized European game bird with plump body, short tail. Common European partridge, *Perdix perdix*, mottled brown above with grey speckled breast, successfully introduced into North America.

Pasadena, residential town of S California, US; near Los Angeles. Pop. 113,000. Education centre, has California Institute of Technology; annual Tournament of Roses and football game in Rose Bowl stadium.

Pascal, Blaise (1623-62), French philosopher, scientist. Worked on mathematical theory of probability and differential calculus. Developed hydraulic press, formulating law on application of pressure on contained fluids. Religious writings incl. *Lettres provinciales* (1656) defending Jansenism, and famous collection, *Pensées*, stating his belief in inadequacy of reason.

pasha or **pacha**, title formerly used in Turkey and N Africa for military leaders and provincial governors. Abolished in Turkey (1934), in Egypt (1952).

Pasiphaë, see MINOS.

Pasmore, Victor (1908-), English painter. Early figurative painting influenced by fauvism and cubism. In 1940s suddenly turned to pure abstraction; later developed 3-dimensional constructions using projecting geometric planes of wood, perspex *eg Abstract in White, Black, Maroon and Ochre* (1957).

Pasolini, Pier Paolo (1922-75), Italian film director, poet, novelist. Known for films concerned with Marxism, religion, myth, *eg The Gospel according to St Matthew* (1964); later turned to adaptations of story-sequences, *eg The Arabian Nights* (1974).

pasqueflower, see ANEMONE.

passacaglia, type of musical composition in slow 3/4 time, in which series of variations are constructed over a repeated theme. Very similar to chaconne, in which theme occurs in bass.

Passchendaele, village of W Belgium. Scene of battle (1917) forming part of unsuccessful British offensive; many casualties.

passionflower, any of genus *Passiflora* of climbing vines native to tropical America. Showy flowers; small, edible, yellow or purple egglike fruits.

Passion play, dramatic representation of the suffering, death and resurrection of Jesus; a form of miracle play. Most famous staged at Oberammergau, Bavaria, every 10 years from 1634.

Passover, Jewish religious festival commemorating deliverance of Israelites from Egypt (although based on much older festival). Celebrated late March or early April; lasts 7 days. Meals of first 2 evenings known as Seders, observed with traditional foods and ceremonies.

pastel, painting medium consisting of powdered pigment mixed with just enough gum to bind it; usually moulded into sticks. Used in Italy in 15th cent.; major exponents of medium incl. Chardin and Degas.

Pasternak, Boris Leonidovich (1890-1960), Russian author. Wrote lyric, narrative poetry, novel *Dr Zhivago* (pub. in West, 1958). Forced to refuse Nobel Prize for Literature (1958).

Pasteur, Louis (1822-95), French chemist. Showed that fermentation is caused by micro-organisms and that similar micro-organisms present in air are responsible for infection of wounds. Pasteurization process for sterilization of food is based on his work on fermentation of beer and wine. Eliminated disease of silkworms; produced vaccines against rabies and anthrax.

pastoral, in literature, work idealizing rustic life. The supposedly simple life of a shepherd is contrasted with complexity, hypocrisy of court or city life. Form developed by Theocritus. Used by others incl. Vergil, Spenser, Milton, Shelley.

Patagonia, region of S Argentina, from Colorado R. to Tierra del Fuego (incl. S Chile). Mainly semi-arid grassy plateau; sheep rearing, some cattle in W; oil, gas resources, iron ore deposits S of Rio Negro.

Patan, town of SC Nepal. Pop. 195,000 Cap. of Nepali kingdom until capture by Gurkhas (1768).

patent, govt. document conferring MONOPOLY right to produce, sell, or get profit from an invention for a certain number of years. Rights extend only within state granting patent, but since first signing (1883) of International Convention for the Protection of Industrial Property, many countries give rights outside original country.

Pater, Walter [Horatio] (1839-94), English scholar, critic. Support for humanist values in art reflected in *Studies in the History of the Renaissance* (1873), *Marius the Epicurean* (1885), *Plato and Platonism* (1893). Noted prose stylist.

Pater Noster, see LORD'S PRAYER.

Paterson, William (1658-1719), Scottish financier. Advised (1691) foundation of Bank of England, which Parliament approved in 1694. Helped organize Darien trading colony in Panama; accompanied disastrous expedition of 1698, returned home 1699.

Pathans, semi-nomadic Moslem people of W Pakistan and Afghanistan. Noted as fierce fighters. Former occupants of Northwest Frontier Prov.; absorbed within Pakistan but continue to press for autonomy.

pathology, branch of medicine concerned with structural and functional changes in the body, their causes and effects.

Patmore, Coventry [Kersey Dighton] (1823-96), English poet. Associate of Pre-Raphaelites. Works incl. celebration of conjugal love, *The Angel in the House* (1854-62), collection of odes *The Unknown Eros* (1877).

Patmos, isl. of Greece, in Aegean Sea, in the Dodecanese. Area 34 sq km (13 sq mi). St John the Divine wrote the Revelation here. Monastery (11th cent.).

Patna, cap. of Bihar state, NE India. Pop. 490,000. Railway jct.; centre of rice growing region. Dates from 6th cent. BC. Has famous mosques, Sikh temple.

Paton, Alan [Stewart] (1903-), South African novelist. Known for works indicting regime, *eg Cry, the Beloved Country* (1948), *Too Late the Phalarope* (1953).

Patras (*Pátrai*), town of W Greece, in NW Peloponnese, on Gulf of Patras. Pop. 112,000. Cap. of Patras admin. dist. Port; exports currants, olive oil, wine. Greek War of Independence began here (1821).

patriarch, in OT, one of the founders of the ancient Jewish families, *eg* Abraham, Jacob. Also bishops of Eastern Orthodox Church who hold authority over other bishops, *eg* Alexandria, Antioch, Constantinople.

patricians, members of privileged class of ancient Rome, descended from original citizens. Unlike the plebeians, they were entitled to hold public office. By 3rd cent. BC, almost all public offices were open to plebeians, and term patrician became an honourable title.

Patrick, St (c 385-461), patron saint of Ireland. Prob. born in Britain but captured in youth and enslaved in Ireland. Escaped and returned as Christian missionary, effected conversion of country from Tara. Writings incl. *Confessions*. Buried at Downpatrick. Feast day is 17 Mar.

patristic literature, term for Christian writings up to 8th cent. Mainly in Greek and Latin, incl. works of St Clement I, Origen, St Augustine, St John of Damascus.

Patroclus, in Greek legend, intimate friend of Achilles. In Trojan War slain by Hector, thus causing Achilles to be reconciled with Agamemnon and return to battle.

Patton, George Smith (1885-1945), American general. Commanded 3rd Army, playing leading role in liberation of France (1944), C Europe (1945).

Pau, town of SW France, cap. of Pyrénées-Atlantiques dept. Pop. 74,000. Resort, wine trade, textile mfg., univ. (1724). Hist. cap. of Béarn; residence from 1512 of kings of Navarre.

Paul, St, Jewish name Saul (d. *c* AD 67), Christian missionary, b. Tarsus. Jewish nationalist. Was converted while on road to Damascus to help suppress Christianity (prob. *c* AD 35). Became 'Apostle to the Gentiles'; travelled as missionary throughout Greek world and Near East. Prob. martyred in Rome under Nero. Epistles, attributed to him, contain fundamental statements of Christian doctrine.

Paul III, orig. Alessandro Farnese (1468-1549), Italian churchman, pope (1534-49). During his pontificate, Catholic Reformation began. Attempted to introduce reforms into the church; convened Council of TRENT (1545). Approved founding of Jesuit order (1540).

Paul VI, orig. Giovanni Battista Montini (1897-1978), Italian churchman, pope (1963-1978). First pope to leave Italy in 150 years, visited Holy Land, US, India and Far East; improved relations with communist countries. Reconvened 2nd Vatican

Council and implemented its reforms. Reaffirmed Church's ban on contraception in encyclical *Humanae Vitae* (1968).

Pauli, Wolfgang (1900-58), Austro-American physicist. Awarded Nobel Prize for Physics (1945) for discovery of Pauli exclusion principle of quantum theory: no 2 electrons in atom can have same 4 quantum numbers. Principle has been extended to other elementary particles (fermions).

Pauling, Linus Carl (1901-), American chemist. Awarded Nobel Prize for Chemistry (1954) for work on nature of chemical bond; also worked on structure of protein molecules. Widely known for advocacy of vitamin C in treatment of common cold. Awarded Nobel Peace Prize (1962) for opposition to nuclear tests.

Paulist Fathers, American society of RC priests; officially Society of Missionary Priests of St Paul the Apostle. Founded (1858) in New York by Isaac Hecker to convert Americans in ways appropriate to US society.

Pavlov, Ivan Petrovich (1849-1936), Russian physiologist. His experiments on stimulation of salivation in dogs by ringing of bells led to theory of the conditioned reflex. Awarded Nobel Prize for Physiology and Medicine (1904) for work on digestion, esp. secretion of digestive juice in the stomach.

Pavlova, Anna Matveyevna (*c* 1882-1931), Russian ballet dancer. Danced with Diaghilev's Ballets Russes. Famous in *The Dying Swan*, created for her by Fokine, and *Giselle*, among other ballets.

Pawnee, North American Indian tribe of Hokan-Siouan linguistic stock. Moved from Texas to S Nebraska in 16th cent. Warlike tribe but allied to US govt.; moved to reservation in Oklahoma (1876).

pawpaw or **papaw**, *Asimina triloba*, tree native to S US. Oblong, yellowish, edible fruit with many seeds. Name also applied to PAPAYA.

Pax, in Roman religion, goddess of peace. Identified with Greek Irene.

Paxton, Sir Joseph (1803-65), English architect, landscape gardener. His greenhouses built for Duke of Devonshire served as model for his innovatory design of the Crystal Palace, built for 1851 Great Exhibition.

pea, *Pisum sativum*, annual climbing leguminous herb, widely cultivated for edible pod-borne seeds, used as vegetable. Also *see* CHICKPEA, SWEET PEA.

Peace, river of Canada. Rises in N British Columbia, Canada; flows NE 1923 km (1195 mi) through Alberta to join Slave R. near L. Athabaska. Extensive agric. in river valley.

Peace Corps, agency of US govt. Estab. (1961) to send trained workers to Third World with expressed aim of helping in education, health care, agric. and technology.

peach, *Prunus persica*, small tree of rose family with decorative pink blossom and sweet, velvety-skinned, stone fruit. Native to China, now cultivated throughout warm temperate regions. The nectarine, *P. persica nectarina*, is a smooth-skinned variety.

Peacock, Thomas Love (1785-1866), English author. Known for novels satirizing intellectual fashions of his day, eg *Nightmare Abbey* (1818), *Crotchet Castle* (1831), *Gryll Grange* (1861). Also wrote verse parodies, pastiches.

peacock, *Pavo cristatus,* male game bird native to India and SE Asia, introduced elsewhere as ornamental bird. Erects long iridescent tail feathers into fan shape as courtship display.

Peak District, national park of S Pennines, C England, mainly in Derbyshire. Area 1404 sq km (542 sq mi). Limestone in S, many caves.

Peake, Mervyn (1911-68), English author, illustrator, b. China. Known esp. for trilogy of Gothic fantasies, *Titus Groan* (1946), *Gormenghast* (1950), *Titus Alone* (1959).

peanut or **groundnut,** *Arachis hypogaea,* spreading annual vine of Leguminosae family. Yellow flowers, underground seedpods. Native to Brazil but widely cultivated in tropical and subtropical regions for seeds which are eaten raw or roasted and salted, and also used to make oil and peanut butter.

pear, any of genus *Pyrus* of rose family, esp. European *P. communis* and Oriental *P. pyrifolia,* widely cultivated in temperate regions for edible apple-like fruit.

pearl, hard, rounded secretion found in certain shellfish, esp. pearl oyster and pearl mussel; used as a gem. Colours incl. white, pink, black. Formed by layers of calcite or aragonite encircling an irritant, eg grain of sand, parasite; composition same as flat 'mother-of-pearl', or nacre, layer on inside of shell. Major sources of natural pearls incl. Persian Gulf, Pacific isls.; 'cultured' pearls mostly from Japan.

Pearl Harbor, *see* HAWAII.

Pears, Peter (1910-), English tenor. Long associated with Britten, who created many vocal works and operatic roles for him, eg *Peter Grimes, Serenade* and *War Requiem.*

Pearse, Patrick Henry (1879-1916), Irish patriot, educator. Leading figure in revival of Gaelic language, esp. in schools. Led Irish forces in Easter Rebellion (1916); executed after surrendering.

Pearson, Lester Bowles (1897-1972), Canadian statesman, PM (1963-8). Secretary of state for external affairs (1948-57) before becoming Liberal leader. Led Canadian delegation to UN General Assembly (1946-57). Awarded Nobel Peace Prize (1957) for negotiating compromise to Suez crisis.

Peary, Robert Edwin (1856-1920), American explorer, naval officer. Led expeditions (1886-95) to N Greenland, proving it to be an island. From 1898 made several attempts to reach North Pole, became 1st man to succeed (April, 1909).

Peary Land, penin. of N Greenland. Mountainous, terminates at Cape Morris Jesup, world's most N point of land (710 km/440 mi from N Pole).

Peasants' Revolt, rising of English peasants (1381), led by Wat TYLER and John BALL, resulting from low wages, heavy taxes and desire to reform feudal system. Rebels entered London and, after meeting Richard II, were promised end of serfdom. Rebellion quickly suppressed after Tyler's murder.

Peasants' War (1524-5), rising of peasants in S and C Germany against loss of feudal rights and extortionate demands of princes and landowners. Inspired partly by preaching of Luther, who, however, condemned violence and advised peace. Rising ruthlessly suppressed.

peat, partly decomposed vegetable matter, found in marshy lands in temperate zones, mainly where there is no limestone to neutralize the acids formed by decomposition. Early stage in formation of coal. Used dried as fuel in Ireland, W Scotland, Scandinavia, and as mulch in horticulture.

pecan, *Carya illinoensis,* hickory tree of S and C US, producing edible nut similar to walnut.

peccary, small New World wild pig, genus *Tayassu,* with scent glands and sharp tusks. Two species, collared peccary, *T. angulatus,* found from SW US to Argentina, and white-lipped peccary, *T. pecari.*

Pechora, river of USSR, N European RSFSR. Rises in N Urals, flows *c* 1750 km (1100 mi) N and W to enter Gulf of Pechora on Barents Sea by extensive delta. Coal mining in its basin.

Peckinpah, Sam (1926–), American film director. Known for extreme violence of his films, *eg The Wild Bunch* (1969), *Straw Dogs* (1971).

Pecos, river of S US. Rises in N New Mexico, flows SE 1480 km (926 mi) through SW Texas to join Rio Grande. Extensive water supplies for irrigation from dams.

Pécs (Ger. *Fünfkirchen*), city of S Hungary. Pop. 154,000. Indust. centre in coalmining area; leather, tobacco, wine. Cathedral (11th cent.); 1st Hungarian univ. (1367-1526, 1921). Under Turkish rule (1543-1686).

Pedro I (1798-1834), emperor of Brazil (1822-31). Son of John VI of Portugal, escaped with family to Brazil on Napoleon's invasion; remained as regent on father's return to Portugal. Proclaimed Brazil independent (1822); abdicated 1831. Succeeded by his son, **Pedro II** (1825-91), who ruled benevolently (1831-89) until eventually forced to abdicate in favour of republic. Abolished slavery (1888).

Peeblesshire or **Tweeddale,** former county of S Scotland, now in Borders region. In Southern Uplands; sheep rearing; woollen goods mfg. Co. town was Peebles, former royal burgh on R. Tweed. Pop. 6000. Textile mfg. Has 13th cent. Cross Kirk.

Peel, Sir Robert (1788-1850), British statesman, PM (1834-5, 1841-6). As home secretary, secured Catholic Emancipation Act (1829), created London police force (1829); opposed Reform Bill of 1832. Statement of policy in his Tamworth Manifesto (1834) held to mark beginning of Conservative Party. Split party over removal of import duties and repeal of Corn Laws (1846).

Peele, George (*c* 1558-97), English dramatist. Wrote pastoral *The Arraignment of Paris* (1582), comedy *The Old Wives' Tale* (1595), tragedy *David and Bethsabe* (pub. 1599), pamphlets, commemorative verse, lyrics.

peewit, *see* LAPWING.

Pegasus, in Greek myth, winged horse sprung from blood of Medusa when she was slain by Perseus. From imprint of hoof flowed spring, Hippocrene, sacred to Muses. Captured by BELLEROPHON.

pegmatite, very coarse-grained, igneous rock. Composition similar to granite; contains large crystals of quartz, mica, feldspar. Source of rare elements, tin, tungsten, gem-stones. Major sources in Norway, Brazil, India, US.

Pegu, city of S Burma, on R. Pegu. Pop. 125,000. Cap. of united Burma in 16th cent. Many temples incl. Shwe Mawdaw pagoda.

Péguy, Charles Pierre (1873-1914), French author. Wrote po-lemics in defence of Catholicism, socialism, Dreyfus. In poetry, eg Le Mystère de la charité de Jeanne d'Arc (1897), attempted to fuse Catholicism, nationalism.

Peiping, see PEKING.

Peipus, Lake (Chudskoye Ozero), lake of USSR, on Estonian-RSFSR border. Area c 3540 sq km (1360 sq mi). S extension called L. Pskov. Outlet is R. Narova flowing to Gulf of Finland. Scene of Alexander Nevsky's victory (1242) over Liv-onian Knights.

Pekinese or **Pekingese**, Chinese breed of small dog introduced to Europe in 1860. Long silky coat, pug nose; stands 15-23 cm/6-9 in. at shoulder.

Peking or **Peiping**, cap. of China, special municipality (area c 17,000 sq km/6564 sq mi) of Hopeh prov. Pop. 8,000,000. Financial, political hub of country. Indust., transport centre; international airport. Im-perial centre (Forbidden City), cap. 1421-1911; again after Communist victory (1949). Noted Ming and Ching architecture; several univs.

Peking man, fossil remains of proto-human Homo erectus found at Choukoutien near Peking (1927).

Originally dated as 350,000 years old. Recent finds of almost identical fossils in E Africa, dated as 1.5 million years old, have introduced new problems into study of man's evolution.

Pelagius (c 360-c 420), British monk. Rejected predestination; de-nied existence of original sin and individual's need of GRACE. Spread teachings in N Africa, Palestine. These, regarded as heresy (Pela-gianism), were condemned at Coun-cil of Ephesus (431).

Pelasgians, name given by ancient Greeks to aboriginal inhabitants of Greece, Asia Minor and Aegean isls.

Pelé, real name Edson Arantes do Nascimento (1940-), Brazilian footballer. Considered one of the greatest forwards ever, he scored his 1000th first-class goal in 1969. Played major part in Brazil's World Cup wins of 1958, 1962, 1970.

Peleus, in Greek myth, king of the Myrmidons; father of Achilles by nymph Thetis. See APPLE OF DISCORD.

Pelham, Henry (1696-1754), Brit-ish statesman, PM (1743-54). Served in Walpole's govt. from 1721, then headed Whig admin. until his death.

pelican, any of Pelecanidae family of gregarious web-footed water birds. Very large bill with pouch suspended underneath where it stores fish. Species incl. Pelecanus onocrotalus, white pelican of Africa, Asia.

pellagra, disease caused by lack of niacin, vitamin of B group. Symp-toms incl. sore tongue, diarrhoea, skin rash, disturbance of nervous system. Occurs in areas where diet consists mainly of maize.

Peloponnese (Peloponnisos),

penin. of S Greece, joined to C Greece by Isthmus of Corinth. Formerly called Morea. Main towns Patras, Corinth. Largely mountainous; rugged coast. Currants, vines, olives; livestock; tourism. Dominated by Sparta until defeat by Thebes (4th cent. BC).

Peloponnesian War (431-404 BC), struggle between Athens and Peloponnesian Confederacy led by Sparta. Chief events in 1st 10 years were Athenian successes at Pylos and Sphacteria (425) and Spartan victory at Amphipolis (422). Peace was negotiated by Nicias (421) but only partially observed. Spartans gained important victory at Mantinea (418). Athenian expedition against Sicily (415), urged by Alcibiades, ended in disastrous destruction of fleet and army (413). Athenians rebuilt fleet but despite naval victories (411, 410, 406) were finally defeated by Lysander at Aegospotamos (405), and obliged to accept Spartan terms (404). THUCYDIDES wrote famous account of war.

Pelops, in Greek myth, son of Tantalus. Murdered and served as food to the gods by his father. They punished Tantalus and restored Pelops to life. Won Hippodamia in marriage by defeating her father Oenomaus in chariot race. Bribed and murdered Oenomaus' charioteer who cursed house of Pelops. Curse fell on sons ATREUS and THYESTES.

pelota, name for several games played with ball and racket, glove, hand or bat. Originating in the Basque provs. of Spain and France, it is popular in Latin America and Florida.

pelvis, basin-shaped bony structure composed of lower part of backbone and 2 hip bones. Hip bone consists of pubis, ilium and ischium, on which body rests when sitting. Female pelvis is larger to aid childbirth.

Pemba, isl. of Tanzania, in Indian Ocean. Area 980 sq km (380 sq mi); cap. Chake Chake. Exports cloves, copra. Part of sultanate of Zanzibar from 1822; former slave trade.

Pembrokeshire, former county of SW Wales, now in Dyfed. Co. town was Haverfordwest. Hilly NE; rugged coast is national park. Potato growing, dairy farming; fishing; tourism. Early centre of Celtic Christianity. **Pembroke,** with Pembroke Dock, is mun. bor. Pop. 14,000. Has ruined 11th cent. castle priory; WWII naval base.

Penal Laws, legislation enacted after English Reformation banning Roman Catholics from civil office and penalizing them for not conforming to Church of England. Laws were extended to Nonconformists after Restoration. Ended by Catholic Emancipation Act (1829).

penance, in RC and Eastern Orthodox churches, sacrament involving confession of sin, repentance and submission to the satisfaction imposed, followed by absolution by a priest.

Penang or George Town, cap. of Penang state, NW West Malaysia. Pop. 270,000. Leading seaport of Malaysia, on Penang Isl.

penates, see LARES AND PENATES.

Penelope, in Greek myth, wife of Odysseus. Despite many suitors, she remained faithful during Odysseus' absence. Agreed to marry only when she had finished weaving father-in-law Laertes' shroud, which she unravelled nightly.

penguin, any bird of order Sphenisciformes, of S hemisphere. Flightless, wings form strong flippers for swimming and diving; nests in large colonies. Species incl. emperor penguin, *Aptenodytes forsteri*, and king penguin, *A. patagonica*.

penicillin, group of antibiotic substances produced by *Penicillium* moulds, esp. *P. chrysogenum* and *P. notatum*. Anti-bacterial effect noted by A. Fleming (1929); purified and used medicinally (1941).

Peninsular War, campaign fought (1808-14) against French in Iberian penin. by Britain, Portugal and Spanish guerrillas. Began when Napoleon invaded Portugal (1807) and then provoked revolts in Spain by placing his brother Joseph on Spanish throne (1808). British intervened in Portugal, defeated French at Vimeiro and then invaded Spain. Following Sir John Moore's retreat, Sir Arthur Wellesley (later Duke of Wellington) took command in Portugal. After defensive campaign centred on Torres Vedras, he invaded Spain and routed French at Vitoria (1813). Napoleon abdicated after British advanced into France (1814).

penis, in males of higher vertebrates, organ which emits sperm in copulation. In mammals, also provides a urinary outlet. Human penis consists of 3 columns of erectile tissue.

Penn, William (1644-1718), English religious leader, founder of Pennsylvania. Became a Quaker (1667), then preached and wrote in favour of religious toleration. Obtained charter to estab. colony in Penn-

sylvania, (1682). As its governor, drew up liberal constitution and made exemplary treaty with Indians.

Pennine Alps, mountain range of S Switzerland, NW Italy. Peaks incl. Matterhorn, Monte Rosa. Main resort is Zermatt.

Pennine Range or **Pennines,** England. Hills running N-S from Cheviots to Peak Dist. Watershed of N English rivers; rises to 893 m (2930 ft) at Cross Fell. Rough pasture; tourism. 'Pennine Way' footpath 400 km (250 mi) long, opened in 1965.

Pennsylvania, state of NE US. Area 117,412 sq km (45,333 sq mi); pop. 11,794,000; cap. Harrisburg; chief cities Philadelphia, Pittsburgh. Mainly in Appalachian Mts. Drained by Ohio R. in W, Susquehanna R. in E. Agric.; mineral wealth, esp. coal, oil, iron ore (related iron and steel, heavy industs.). Settled by Dutch, Swedish, English colonists. English colony estab. under William Penn (1682). Centre of activity in Revolution, Civil War. One of original 13 colonies of US.

Pennsylvanian period, later of 2 subdivisions of Carboniferous period in North America. Began *c* 325 million years ago, lasted *c* 45 million years. Fauna incl. freshwater lamellibranchs, 1st reptiles, giant dragonflies, spiders. Luxuriant vegetation, formation of vast swamps; development of European, North American coal measures. Also *see* GEOLOGICAL TABLE.

pension, payment made regularly to a person, or dependants, who has fulfilled certain conditions of service or reached a certain age. Pension plan is paid for prior to retirement and can be part of voluntary scheme or compulsory national scheme, connected with SOCIAL SECURITY provisions.

Pentagon, the, building in Arlington, Virginia in which main offices of US Department of Defense are situated. Consists of 5 concentric buildings connected by corridors; completed 1943.

Pentateuch, first five books of OT. Known in Judaism as the Torah.

pentathlon, five-event athletic contest for women comprising 100 m hurdles, shot put, high jump, long jump and 200 m. Olympic event from 1964.

Pentecost (Gk., *pentekoste* = 50th), Jewish religious festival celebrating end of grain harvest which takes place 50 days after Passover. Also Christian festival celebrating descent of the Holy Ghost upon the Disciples on the 50th day after Jesus' resurrection. Sometimes known as Whit Sunday from the white garments of neophytes baptized on this day.

Penthesilea, in Greek myth, queen of the Amazons who fought against Greeks in Trojan War. Killed by Achilles who mourned beauty of her corpse.

Pentland Firth, strait off N Scotland, separating former Caithness from Orkney Isls. Notorious for rough seas.

penumbra, partly lighted area surrounding complete shadow of a body. Observed when light emanates from large source. Term generally used in connection with eclipses.

Penzance, mun. bor. of Cornwall, SW England, on Mount's Bay. Pop. 19,000. Fishing port; resort.

peony or **paeony,** any of genus *Paeonia* of perennial herbs or shrubs of buttercup family. Native to Eurasia and W US. Large scarlet, pink or white flowers.

Pepin the Short (*c* 714-68), king of Franks (751-68). Son of Charles Martel, he deposed last Merovingian king, Childeric III, thus founding Carolingian dynasty. Father of Charlemagne.

pepper, *Piper nigrum,* tropical vine yielding fruit dried as condiment; ground as black pepper or (without seed cover) as white pepper. Also condiments (sometimes known as paprika) prepared in similar way from tropical American *Capsicum frutescens* or chili. See CAYENNE, PIMENTO.

peppermint, see MINT.

pepsin, digestive enzyme produced in the stomach. In presence of hydrochloric acid, converts proteins into peptones, which are absorbed by body.

peptic ulcer, erosion of lining of stomach (gastric ulcer) or duodenum (duodenal ulcer). Aggravated by action of acidic gastric juices. Symptoms incl. stomach ache, nausea, heartburn. Cause unknown; possibly related to stress.

Pepys, Samuel (1633-1703), English diarist, naval official. Famous for his *Diary* (pub. 1825), recording, in cipher, personal life, public affairs of 1660s.

Perceval, Spencer (1762-1812), British statesman, PM (1809-12). Tory chancellor of exchequer (1807-9) before succeeding Portland as PM. Assassinated in lobby of House of Commons.

perch, any of genus *Perca* of

freshwater food fish with spiny dorsal fins. Species incl. yellow perch *P. flavescens* of North America and European *P. fluviatilis*.

percussion instruments, musical instruments struck to produce sound. Most produce no definite notes and their function is chiefly rhythmic, *eg* drum, triangle, cymbals, though some do produce notes of definite pitch, *eg* xylophone, timpani, glockenspiel.

Percy, Henry, 1st Earl of Northumberland (1342-1408), English nobleman. Helped secure throne for Henry IV from Richard II. Later, took part in plot led by his son, Sir Henry Percy (1366-1403) (known as 'Hotspur') and Owen Glendower to overthrow king. Plan to crown Edmund de Mortimer ended with Hotspur's death at Shrewsbury. **Thomas Percy, 7th Earl of Northumberland** (1528-72), plotted release of Mary Queen of Scots and restoration of Roman Catholicism to England; beheaded after revolt failed.

peregrine falcon, *Falco peregrinus,* swift falcon of Europe, Asia, North America; much used in falconry. Male has slate-grey upperparts, buff under-parts. Feeds on birds, *eg* pigeon.

perennial, *see* ANNUAL.

perfume, fragrant essence prepared from essential oils of plants or synthetic compounds, mixed with fixatives such as musk or ambergris. The ingredients are generally dissolved in alcohol. Favoured plant oils are found in flowers of lavender, roses, jasmine, fruit of bergamot and citrus fruit.

Pergamum or **Pergamus** (modern

Bergama), ancient city of Asia Minor, now in W Turkey on R. Caicus. Cap. of kingdom of Pergamum (3rd-2nd cent. BC); under Roman rule (133 BC). Famous remains incl. altar of Zeus, temple of Athena and library. Early Christian centre; one of Seven Churches in Asia.

Pericles (*c* 495-429 BC), Athenian statesman. Dominant figure in Athens from *c* 460, at time of city's political and cultural zenith. Created empire out of Delian league, successfully defending it against Persia, Sparta. Patronized arts and literature; responsible for building of Parthenon. Onset of Peloponnesian War brought his overthrow (430); reinstated before he died.

perigee, in astronomy, point nearest Earth in orbit of celestial bodies, *eg* Moon and artificial satellites. Opposite is apogee.

Périgueux, town of SW France, on R. Isle, cap. of Dordogne dept. Pop. 40,000. Tobacco trade, food processing esp. pâté, truffles. Hist. cap. of Périgord (incorporated into France 1589). Roman remains incl. amphitheatre, tower.

perihelion, in astronomy, point nearest Sun in orbit of celestial bodies, *eg* planets and comets. Opposite is aphelion.

periodical, publication issued regularly, distinct from a newspaper in that it contains authors'/editors' opinions on news, *etc,* rather than factual accounts. Term incl. magazines, scholarly reviews, journals.

periodic table, arrangement of chemical elements according to their atomic numbers to illustrate periodic law: properties of elements are in periodic dependence upon their atomic numbers. Formulated by MENDELEEV (1869-71). Law reflects way in which successive electron shells are filled; elements with same number of electrons in their outer shell have similar properties, eg alkali metals have one such electron. *See* VALENCY.

periscope, optical instrument which enables observer to see objects not directly visible from his position, esp. those above eye level. Consists of long tube at each end of which is a prism or mirror, which reflects light to observer's eye. Used esp. in submarines.

peritoneum, membrane lining abdominal cavity and enclosing in its folds the internal organs. Also forms double-thickness membrane (mesentery) enfolding and supporting small intestine. Peritonitis is inflammation of peritoneum, usually caused by bacteria.

periwinkle, small marine mollusc with conical spiral shell, genus *Littorina*. Species incl. European edible periwinkle, *L. littorea*.

periwinkle, any of genus *Vinca* of mostly trailing, evergreen plants of dogbane family, esp. European *V. minor* with light lilac-blue, pink or white flowers.

Perm, city of USSR, E European RSFSR; railway jct. and port on R. Kama. Pop. 880,000. Centre of Urals indust. area; agric. machinery, timber products. Developed with estab. of copper-smelting plant in 18th cent.

permafrost, permanently frozen subsoil. Found in high latitudes where rainfall is low and mean annual temperature is below 0°C. Topsoil may thaw for part of year.

Permian period, final geological period of Palaeozoic era; began *c* 280 million years ago, lasted *c* 55 million years. Increasing aridity; swamps dried up, salt beds formed, marls, sandstones, evaporites developed. Increasing reptiles, ammonites, more advanced conifers; last trilobites. Also *see* GEOLOGICAL TABLE.

Perón, Juan Domingo (1895-1974), Argentinian political leader. Elected president (1946) after taking part in military coup (1943). Made series of reforms based on nationalism, populism and state socialism (known as *peronismo*). Career aided by popularity of 2nd wife, Eva Duarte Perón (1919-52), who had great political following. Lost support after her death; deposed by army coup (1955), went into exile. Returned 1973, re-elected president. His 3rd wife, Maria Estela ('Isabel') Martinez 'de' Perón (1931-), succeeded him as president on his death. Deposed by military junta (1976).

perpendicular, name given to final phase of English Gothic architecture (late 14th to middle 16th cent.). Characterized by vertical tracery for walls and windows, fan vaulting. King's College Chapel, Cambridge, is example of style.

Perpignan, city of S France, on R. Têt, cap. of Pyrénées-Orientales dept. Pop. 102,000. Wine, fruit trade; tourist centre. Cap. of Spanish Roussillon (17th cent.). Cathedral (14th cent.), castle.

Perry, Fred[erick John] (1909-), English lawn tennis and table tennis player. World table tennis champion (1929). Won Wimbledon title 3 times in succession (1934-6) and lawn tennis titles of US (1933), Australia (1934) and France (1935).

Persephone, in Greek myth, daughter of Zeus and Demeter. Abducted by Pluto to underworld and required to spend winter months of year there. Return symbolized start of vegetative growth. Her cult was celebrated in the Eleusinian mysteries; also worshipped at Rome as Proserpina.

Persepolis, cap. of ancient Persian empire, now ruined, in SC Iran. Has ruined palaces of Darius and his successors. Nearby are royal tombs. Partially destroyed by Alexander the Great in 331 BC. Shiraz nearest modern town.

Perseus, in Greek myth, son of Zeus and Danaë. Slew Medusa, used her head to turn ATLAS into a mountain. Married Andromeda whom he rescued from sea-monster. Accidentally killed his grandfather, Acrisius, in discus contest thus fulfilling a prophecy at his birth.

Pershing, John J[oseph] (1860-1948), American army officer, commander-in-chief of American Expeditionary Force in WWI (1917-8).

Persia, see IRAN.

Persian cat, small domestic cat with long silky hair, originally raised in Persia and Afghanistan.

Persian Gulf, arm of Indian Ocean, between Iran and Arabian penin. Connected to Arabian Sea by Str. of Hormuz and Gulf of Oman.

Persian Gulf States, see UNITED ARAB EMIRATES; BAHRAIN; QATAR.

Persian Wars, struggles (500-449 BC) between Greek city states and Persian Empire. Begun by Greek support for revolt of Ionian cities of Asia Minor against Persian rule. Persian expedition under Darius I was defeated at Marathon (490). Later expedition led by Xerxes I, son of Darius, successfully invaded Greece but Persian fleet was destroyed at Salamis (480) and army crushed at Plataea (479). Wars dragged on but Greek cities later estab. their freedom.

persimmon, see EBONY.

perspective, system of representing 3-dimensional space in spatial recession on flat surface. Geometric system based on converging lines was formulated by Alberti and Brunelleschi in 15th cent. and developed by Uccello, Piero della Francesca, *etc.* Aerial perspective uses changes of tone and colour to suggest distance; used early in Far Eastern art.

perspex [UK] or **plexiglass** [US], trademark for transparent polyacrylic plastic. May be moulded while hot. Tough, unsplinterable; many uses.

perspiration, see SWEAT.

Perth, city of SW Australia, on Swan R., cap. of Western Australia. Pop. 739,000. Admin., commercial centre; W terminus of Trans-Australian Railway; exports (via Fremantle) agric. produce, minerals, esp. gold. Founded 1829; has Univ. of Western Australia (1911), Anglican and RC cathedrals, many parks.

Perthshire, former county of C Scotland, now in Central and Tayside regions. Grampian Mts., Trossachs; lochs incl. Earn, Tay, Katrine; fertile lowland. Agric.; deer forest, sheep rearing; h.e.p. at Pitlochry; tourist industs. Co. town was **Perth**, former royal burgh on R. Tay. Pop. 43,000. Insurance centre; whisky distilling. Cap. of Scotland (12th-15th cents.).

Peru, republic of W South America. Area 1,285,210 sq km (496,220 sq mi); pop. 16,090,000; cap. Lima. Languages: Spanish, Quechua, Aymará (Indian). Religion: RC. Pacific coastal plain in W rises to 2 Andean ranges in interior. Important mineral resources (zinc, silver, copper); subsistence agric. esp. cotton; sheep, llamas, alpacas raised for wool. Anchovy, fish meal industs. Well-organized Inca empire was destroyed by Spanish following Pizarro's invasion (1532); independence obtained under Bolívar, Sucre (1824). S region lost in war with Chile (1879-84).

Perugia, city of Umbria, C Italy, cap. of Perugia prov. Pop. 132,000. Indust. centre, chocolate mfg. Etruscan, Roman remains. Centre of Umbrian school of painting (13th-16th cents.). Univ. (1276).

Perugino, orig. Pietro di Vanucci (c 1445-1523), Italian painter of Umbrian school. Executed fresco *Christ Giving the Keys to St Peter* in Sistine Chapel. His repetitive style caused his reputation to fade. Raphael was his pupil.

Perutz, Max Ferdinand (1914-   ), British biochemist, b. Austria. Shared Nobel Prize for Chemistry (1962) for discovery of structure of haemoglobin using X-ray diffraction.

Pescara, city of Abruzzi e Molise, EC Italy, on Adriatic Sea at mouth of R. Pescara. Cap. of Pescara prov. Pop. 122,000. Port, resort; mfg.

Peshawar, town of N Pakistan, near Khyber Pass. Pop. 273,000. Centre for trade between Pakistan and Afghanistan. Taken by British (1848), was outpost for operations against Afghans.

Pestalozzi, Johann Heinrich (1746-1827), Swiss educational reformer. Laid foundation of modern educational theory, stressing importance of relating words, ideas to concrete things, through pupil activities, instruction tailored to age-groups and individuals.

Pétain, Henri Philippe (1856-1951), French military, political leader. In WWI, halted German advance at Verdun (1916); created marshal of France (1918). Premier at time of France's collapse in WWII, concluded armistice with Germans. Headed Vichy govt., serving as figurehead for LAVAL after 1942. Death sentence for collaboration (1945) commuted to life imprisonment.

Peter, St, orig. Simon (d. c AD 67), leader of Twelve Disciples. He and brother, St Andrew, were fishermen in Galilee when called by Jesus. Given charge of Church by Jesus after resurrection. Prob. martyred during Nero's rule; traditionally buried on site of St Peter's Church, Rome.

Peter [I] the Great (1672-1725), tsar of Russia (1682-1725). Joint tsar with brother Ivan V, became sole ruler on Ivan's -death (1696). Introduced policy of westernizing Russia; toured Europe to gain knowledge of indust. techniques. Reorganized army and civil admin., encouraged trade, indust. and science. Gained access to Baltic through war with Sweden (1700-21). Built new cap. at St Petersburg.

Peter III (1728-62), tsar of Russia (1762). Forced to abdicate in face of plot led by the Orlovs, favourites of his wife and successor, Catherine II. Assassinated, prob. at behest of Aleksey Orlov.

Peter I (1844-1921), king of Serbia (1903-21). Called to throne after assassination of Alexander Obrenovich. Chosen as ruler of new kingdom of Serbs, Croats, Slovenes (later Yugoslavia).

Peter II (1923-70), king of Yugoslavia (1934-45). Succeeded under regency after murder of his father, Alexander. Assumed power after overthrow of regency (1941); fled to England during Nazi invasion. Deposed by Tito; died in 1970.

Peter 1 and 2, epistles of NT, traditionally ascribed to St Peter.

Peterborough, town of SE Ontario, Canada; on Otonabee R., NE of Toronto. Pop. 58,000. Railway and indust. centre. Has Canada's largest cereal and flour mills.

Peterborough, city of Cambridgeshire, E England, on R. Nene. Pop. 70,000. Railway jct; engineering, brick mfg. Has remains of Saxon village; ruined abbey (655); cathedral (12th cent.).

Peterhead, town of Grampian region, NE Scotland, on North Sea. Pop. 14,000. Herring indust.; granite quarries; offshore oil service industs. Former whaling port.

Peter Lombard (c 1100-60), Italian churchman. Parts of his collection of theological opinions, *Sententiarum libri*, became official RC doctrine, esp. on sacraments.

Peterloo Massacre, incident at St Peter's Field, Manchester, England (1819). Large meeting, petitioning for parliamentary reform, dispersed by yeomanry and hussars; 11 people killed. Resulting indignation accelerated reform movement.

Peter's pence, annual tax of one penny paid to papal see by English households before Reformation. Now annual voluntary donation made by Roman Catholics to papal see.

Peter the Hermit (c 1050-1115), French preacher. Induced many to go on 1st Crusade and became one of its leaders. Founded monastery at Liège.

Petition of Right (1628), document containing constitutional demands presented by English Parliament to Charles I. Declared taxation without parliamentary approval illegal, reaffirmed principle of habeas corpus, *etc*. Acceptance by Charles resulted in restoration of subsidies to him.

Petra, ancient city of SW Jordan. Edomite cap. from 4th cent. BC until capture by Romans in AD 106. Ruins, discovered 1812 by Burckhardt, incl. temples and tombs carved in pink rock.

Petrarch or Francesco Petrarca (1304-74), Italian poet. First Renaissance humanist, began revival of spirit of antiquity, profound influence on later European writers. Famous for Italian songs and sonnets expressing love for Laura in *Canzoniere*, also allegorical poem *Trionfi*.

petrel, one of various small seabirds of 2 families: Hydrobatidae, storm petrels; Pelecanoididae, diving petrels. Noted fliers, returning to land only to breed. Species incl. storm petrel, *Hydrobates pelagicus*, of NE Atlantic and Mediterranean.

petroleum, naturally occurring liquid mixture of hydrocarbons, with varying amounts of sulphur and nitrogen compounds. Fractional distillation yields petrol (gasoline), paraffin oil (kerosene), diesel oils, heavy fuel oils and bitumens, *etc.* Formed millions of years ago from remains of animals and plants buried and compressed. Main petroleum producing areas are in Middle East, USSR and US.

petrology, branch of geology dealing with study of all aspects of rocks. Incl. study of origins (petrogenesis), systematic description of rocks (petrography).

Petronius Arbiter, Gaius (d. AD 66), Roman satirist. Author of *Satyricon,* huge picaresque novel, of which only parts of Books XV and XVI are extant. Favourite of Nero.

Petropavlovsk, city of USSR, N Kazakh SSR; jct. on Trans-Siberian railway. Pop. 180,000. Meat packing, flour milling. Centre for caravan trade between Russia and C Asia in 18th cent.

Petropavlovsk (-Kamchatski), city of USSR, E Siberian RSFSR; on SE Kamchatka coast. Pop. 171,000. Naval base; fisheries, shipbuilding, sawmilling.

Petrozavodsk, city of USSR, cap. of Karelian auton. republic, NW European RSFSR; on L. Onega. Pop. 193,000. Shipyards, fisheries, sawmilling. Named after ironworks founded here (1703) by Peter the Great.

petunia, genus of perennial herbs of nightshade family, with funnel-shaped flowers of various colours. Native to tropical America. Esp.

Petunia hybrida, cultivated widely in temperate regions as garden flower.

Pevsner, Antoine (1886-1962), Russian sculptor. Influenced by cubism, collaborated with brother Naum Gabo on manifesto of constructivism (1920). Later developed abstract and constructional sculpture.

pewter, any of several alloys of tin, with lead, copper or antimony added to improve malleability. Used from Roman times to make domestic utensils until replaced by china in 18th and 19th cents.

peyote, *see* MESCAL.

Phaedra, in Greek myth, daughter of Minos and wife of Theseus. Fell in love with stepson Hippolytus, but was rejected by him and hanged herself.

Phaestos, ancient town of Crete. Ruins of Minoan palace equal in sophistication to that at Knossos.

Phaethon, in Greek myth, son of Helios (the sun). Attempted to drive father's chariot, but unable to control horses. Killed by Zeus' thunderbolt.

phagocyte, blood cell, esp. a leucocyte, which engulfs and destroys bacteria, dead cells, foreign particles.

phalanger, arboreal Australasian marsupial of Phalangeridae family. Thick fur, prehensile tail; nocturnal. Flying phalangers use membrane stretched between limbs to glide through trees. Also called possum.

phalarope, small aquatic bird of Phalaropodidae family. Male, smaller and less brightly coloured than female, incubates eggs. Species incl. Wilson's phalarope, *Phalaropus tricolor,* of North American prairies.

phallicism or **phallism,** worship of image of male reproductive organ as symbol of regenerative powers of nature. Occurs in many primitive societies, also in cult of Priapus in classical Greece and of Cybele and Attis in Rome. In India, the deity Siva is often represented as a phallic symbol or lingam. Also *see* FERTILITY RITES.

Phanerozoic eon, all geological time from beginning of the Palaeozoic era to the present. Contrasts with Precambrian times in possessing sedimentary accumulations in which are found abundant remains of plants and animals. Also *see* GEOLOGICAL TABLE.

Pharisees, one of two main Jewish sects which originated in Maccabean age (other being their opponents, SADDUCEES). Insisted on strictest observance of Mosaic Law. Advocated democratization of religious observances.

pharmacy, preparation and dispensing of medicines and drugs. Pharmacology is the scientific study of drugs, their chemistry, effects on the body; it incl. research into new drugs.

Pharos of Alexandria, lighthouse which stood on an isl. off Alexandria, Egypt. Completed c 280 BC under Ptolemy II, it was destroyed in 14th cent. by earthquake. One of the Seven Wonders of the ancient World.

Pharsala, ancient city of Thessaly, EC Greece. Here in 48 BC Caesar defeated Pompey, recorded in Lucan's *Bellum Civile* or *Pharsalia.*

pharynx, muscular cavity of alimentary canal leading from mouth and nasal passages to the oesophagus. Top part, nasopharynx, is concerned only with breathing; middle part, oropharynx, is passage for food and air; lower part, laryngeal pharynx, is for swallowing only.

pheasant, game bird of Phasianidae family. Males brilliantly coloured, with long tapering tail. Mainly terrestrial, building nest on ground. Species incl. ring-necked pheasant, *Phasianus colchicus,* and Lady Amherst's pheasant, *Chrysolophus amherstiae,* of Chinese origin.

phenols, aromatic compounds having hydroxyl (OH) radicals directly attached to benzene ring. Commonest is carbolic acid (C_6H_5OH), white crystalline. solid produced from coal tar; used as disinfectant and in manufacture of plastics.

phenomenology, movement in philosophy founded by HUSSERL. Aims to study objects of consciousness without any preconceptions about the objects themselves and thus apprehend phenomena directly. Influential in early development of EXISTENTIALISM.

Phidias (active c 475-430 BC), Athenian sculptor, architect. Greatly admired by his contemporaries, none of his original work remains. Works incl. colossal statues of Athena on the Parthenon, Athens, and Zeus at Olympia, one of Seven Wonders of the ancient World.

Philadelphia, port of SE Pennsylvania, US; on Delaware R. Pop. 1,950,000, state's largest city. Shipping, commercial centre. Exports coal, grain, timber. Imports raw materials. Varied industs. incl.

oil refining, shipbuilding. Founded 1682 by Quakers. Focus of activity in Revolution; federal state cap. in 18th cent. Has many hist. famous buildings esp. Independence Hall, scene of Constitutional Convention (1787); Philharmonic Orchestra, Univ. of Pennsylvania (1740).

philately, collection and study of postage stamps. Collecting began after issue of first stamps in 1840s; 1st catalogues printed *c* 1861. Important collections in British Museum, London, and Smithsonian Institute, Washington.

Philemon, Epistle to, NT epistle written by St Paul. Consists of request to Philemon asking him to forgive his slave, Onesimus, for escaping.

Philemon and Baucis, in Greek myth, an aged couple of Phrygia. Showed such hospitality to the disguised Zeus and Hermes that their cottage was made a temple. On death, became trees whose branches intertwined.

Philip, St (*fl* AD 1st cent.), one of Twelve Disciples. Possibly preached in Phrygia.

Philip [II] Augustus (1165-1223), king of France (1180-1223). Abandoned 3rd Crusade after quarrel with Richard I of England. Gained English possessions in France at expense of King John (1202-03). Defeated alliance of Germans, Flemings and English formed against him at Bouvines (1214).

Philip [IV] the Fair (1268-1314), king of France (1285-1314). Quarrel with Boniface VIII over right to tax clergy ended in pope's deposition by Philip, who secured Clement V's election (1305) and transfer of see to

Avignon (1309). Supplemented treasury by persecution of KNIGHTS TEMPLARS (1308-14), who held powerful banking role in France.

Philip VI (1293-1350), king of France (1328-50). Elected regent on death of cousin, Charles IV, invoking Salic law to exclude claims of Edward III of England (1328). Crowned first of Valois kings (1328). Disputes with Edward led to Hundred Years War and English victory at Crécy (1346).

Philip II (382-336 BC), king of Macedonia (359-336 BC). Seized throne from his cousin; reorganized army, introducing formidable phalanx formation. Began conquest of Greece, culminating in defeat of Athens and Thebes at Chaeronea (338). Assassinated while preparing for war against Persia. Father of Alexander the Great.

Philip V (238-179 BC), king of Macedonia (221-179 BC). Involved almost continually in wars to establish Macedonian supremacy in Eastern Mediterranean; finally defeated by Romans (197 BC).

Philip II (1527-98), king of Spain (1556-98). Succeeded his father, Emperor Charles V. His dominions incl. Netherlands, Naples, Sicily, and much of New World. Championed orthodox Catholicism, persecuting heretics. His repression and introduction of Inquisition provoked major revolt in Netherlands (1567). Annexed Portugal (1580). Economy drained by wars, Spanish power declined after destruction of Armada (1588). Husband of Mary I of England.

Philip V (1683-1746), king of Spain (1700-46). Grandson of Louis XIV, his accession as 1st Bourbon king of Spain provoked War of Spanish Succession. Policies dominated by his wives and Cardinal ALBERONI.

Philip Mountbatten, see EDINBURGH, PHILIP MOUNTBATTEN, DUKE OF.

Philip the Bold (1342-1404), duke of Burgundy .(1363-1404). Virtual ruler of France during Charles VI's minority. His struggle for power with Louis d'Orléans during period of king's insanity (beginning 1392) was continued by his son, John the Fearless (1371-1419).

Philip the Good (1396-1467), duke of Burgundy (1419-67). Allied with the English during their attempts to secure French throne for Henry V and his heirs, but later supported Charles VII of France. Made Low Countries centre of commerce and culture.

Philippi, ancient city of Macedonia, N Greece. Here Octavian and Antony defeated Brutus and Cassius (42 BC).

Philippians, epistle of NT, written by St Paul from captivity in Rome to Christians at Philippi, Macedonia.

Philippines, republic of SE Asia, isl. group incl. Luzon, Mindanao. Area c 300,000 sq km (115,000 sq mi); pop. 43,751,000; cap. Quezon City. Language: Filipino. Religion: RC. Mountainous, densely forested; tropical monsoon climate on larger isls. Mainly agric. economy; produces rice, corn, hemp, sugar, timber; minerals incl. chromite, gold. Discovered by Magellan (1521); under Spanish control (1564-1898) until ceded to US after Spanish-American War. Total inde-

pendence gained in 1946. Occupied by Japanese in WWII.

Philistines, non-Semitic people, prob. of Cretan origin, who inhabited S Palestine from 12th cent. BC. Constantly at war with Israelites; conquered by David and under Solomon incorporated into kingdom of Israel. Regained independence, finally accepted Assyrian domination (8th cent. BC).

Phillip, Arthur (1738-1814), British colonial administrator. First governor of New South Wales (1786-92), estab. penal settlement at Sydney (1788). Promoted agric., colonization.

philology, see LINGUISTICS.

philosopher's stone, substance sought by alchemists, who believed it would turn base metals into gold.

philosophy (Gk., = love of wisdom), theory or logical analysis of principles underlying the ultimate nature of the universe (ontology, metaphysics) and related fields, incl. conduct (ethics), thought (logic), knowledge (epistemology). In the West, tradition springs from classical Greece (esp. Plato, Aristotle) and was reinterpreted in Christian terms by medieval scholastics mainly from Arabic editions. Modern rationalism begins with Descartes; modern empiricism with Locke. Other disciplines are critically examined for basic principles and concepts, eg philosophy of science, philosophy of history. Eastern philosophy, though often rigorous, tends to be regarded as part of mystical theology.

Phiz, see BROWNE, HABLOT KNIGHT.

phlebitis, inflammation of a vein, usually associated with blockage of vein by blood clots (thrombophlebitis). May occur after childbirth or surgery; use of oral contraceptives sometimes disposes women to thrombophlebitis. Blood clots, usually in leg, may dislodge and travel to lungs.

phloem, vascular tissue of a plant which distributes synthesized foods, eg proteins and sugars.

phlogiston theory, proposition advanced in 17th cent. that all combustible material contained phlogiston which escaped when material was burned, leaving ash or calx that represented true material. Theory refuted by Lavoisier.

phlox, genus of herbs native to North America, esp. various hybrids of *Phlox drummondi*, cultivated for showy flowers.

Phnom Penh or **Pnom Penh**, cap. of Cambodia. Pop. 470,000. Trade centre, port on R. Mekong. Stronghold of government forces during civil war (1970–5). Became cap. of Cambodia 1867.

phobia, irrational fear of a particular thing or situation, creating state of anxiety.

Phoenicians, Semitic people descended from the Canaanites who occupied the coastal areas of modern Syria and Lebanon (Phoenicia). Exercised maritime and commercial power c 1200–600 BC throughout the Mediterranean area, founding colonies in Cyprus, N Africa and Spain. Chief cities were Tyre and Sidon.

Phoenix, cap. of Arizona, US; on Salt R. Pop. 581,000. Commercial centre in irrigated agric. region producing fruit, cotton. Health resort. Has Pueblo Indian ruins, excavated 1927. Became cap. 1889.

phoenix, in ancient Egyptian myth, beautiful lone bird which lived in the Arabian desert for 500 years and then consumed itself in fire, new phoenix arising from ashes. Used in religion as symbol of death, resurrection.

Phoenix Islands, group of 8 coral isls. in C Pacific Ocean. Canton and Enderbury Isls. jointly admin. by US, UK; other 6 part of Gilbert and Ellice Isls. colony.

phonetics, study of system of LANGUAGE sounds. Branches incl. study of speech sounds using written symbols to transcribe accurately their differences, and phonemics, the study of significant differences between groups of roughly similar sounds.

phonograph, see GRAMOPHONE.

phosphates, salts or esters of phosphoric acid (H_3PO_4). Calcium superphosphate used as fertilizer, sodium phosphate (Na_3PO_4) used in detergents.

phosphorescence, property of certain substances of giving off lingering emission of light following excitation by radiation, eg light or X-rays. Causes certain minerals, eg zinc sulphide, to glow in dark.

phosphorus (P), non-metallic element; at. no. 15, at. wt. 30.97. Occurs in various allotropic forms: white form is waxy poisonous solid which ignites spontaneously in air; red form is non-poisonous and less reactive, obtained by heating white form. Occurs widely in phosphate minerals; essential to life, occurs in blood, bones, *etc*. Compounds used in fertilizers, detergents, matches, *etc.*

photochemistry, study of influence of light and other radiant energy on chemical reactions; photochemical effects are utilized in photography and photosynthesis.

photoelectric effect, emission of electrons from surface of certain substances when exposed to light of suitable frequency. Photoelectric cell uses effect to convert light into electrical energy. Commonest type contains electric circuit with 2 electrodes separated by light-sensitive semiconductor; current flow in circuit increases when light strikes semiconductor. Used to open automatic doors, as burglar alarm, *etc.*

photoengraving, photomechanical process used for printing illustrations. Subject to be reproduced is photographed and its image is transferred through the negative to a metal plate coated with light-sensitive chemical. Coating unaffected by light is removed and underlying metal plate etched away. Half-tone is form of photoengraving using dots of varying size to obtain variations in tone.

photography, process of reproducing optical image on light-sensitive substance (silver bromide or chloride) under controlled conditions in camera. Developer produces metallic silver on those parts of photographic plate previously exposed to light. Fixing agent, *eg* 'hypo', dissolves remaining silver salts, leaving negative image. Positive image is obtained by placing negative on light-sensitive paper and then repeating developing and fixing process.

photon, fundamental quantum of electromagnetic energy, the energy of light. Sometimes regarded as uncharged elementary particle of zero rest mass, travelling at speed of light. Its energy is product of Planck's constant and frequency of electromagnetic wave.

photosynthesis, process by which plants make food by transformation of carbon dioxide and water into carbohydrates. Occurs in green part of plants and utilizes energy from sunlight. The green pigment CHLOROPHYLL is necessary for the reaction.

Phrygians, ancient people of Asia Minor. Spoke Indo-European language. Culture *fl* 8th to 6th cents. BC, marked by impressive architecture, geometric ornamentation. Phrygian cap. Gordion destroyed by Cimmerians (676 BC). Later subject to Lydians, Persians.

pH-value, in chemistry, *see* HYDROGEN ION CONCENTRATION.

phylacteries, two small leather cases holding parchment inscribed with passages from Scripture (Exodus and Deuteronomy). One is worn on the forehead, other on left arm by Orthodox Jews during morning prayers as a reminder of God.

physical anthropology, branch of ANTHROPOLOGY concerned with physical characteristics of peoples. Studies evolution of body types and development of racial groups using statistical methods.

physics, science concerned with fundamental relationships between matter and energy. Classical physics, developed in 19th cent., deals with electricity, magnetism, heat, optics, mechanics, *etc.* Quantum physics of 20th cent., which assumes that energy exists in discrete bundles, explains atomic and nuclear phenomena.

physiocrats, group of 18th cent. French economic theoreticians headed by FRANCOIS QUESNAY. Among first to study economics systematically. Saw land and agric. as basis of wealth. Believed in natural economic laws which must be allowed to operate freely. Influenced Adam Smith and other laisser-faire economists.

physiology, study of functions and vital processes of living organisms, both plants and animals.

physiotherapy, method of treating illness and injury by physical means such as massage, exercise, heat and electricity.

pi (π), symbol used to denote ratio of circumference of a circle to its diameter; $\pi = 3.14159$ (to 5 decimal places).

Piaf, Edith, orig. Edith Giovanna Gassion (1915-63), French singer, known as 'the Little Sparrow'. Renowned for her passionate songs of troubles and unhappiness, *eg* 'Je ne regrette rien'.

Piaget, Jean (1896-   ), Swiss psychologist. Known for unique contributions to theories of cognitive development, postulating genetically determined stages through which children pass to reach abstract reasoning ability. Later abandoned these theories for application of structuralism to behavioural sciences.

piano or **pianoforte,** keyboard instrument having compass of 7 octaves, keys of which operate hammers which strike the strings. First appeared mid-18th cent. Many 19th cent. composers were also virtuoso pianists (*eg* Beethoven, Chopin, Liszt, Grieg and Brahms).

Picabia, Francis (1879-1953), French painter. Leading dadaist painter, works incl. *A la memoire de Léonard de Vinci* (1919). Founded magazines *291* (with Duchamp), *391*. Briefly associated with surrealists. Influenced many subsequent trends.

Picardy (*Picardie*), region and former prov. of N France, hist. cap. Amiens. Fertile area, drained by R. Somme; agric., textile indust. Part of France from 1477. Battlefield in WWI.

Picasso, Pablo [Ruiz y] (1881-1973), Spanish artist. Dominant figure in many 20th cent. art movements. In his 'blue' period (1901-4), painted expressive scenes of human poverty and degradation; in 'rose' period (1905-7), painted circus scenes. Influenced by Cézanne and negro sculpture, evolved cubist style with Braque in Paris; *Les Demoiselles d'Avignon* (1907) marks beginning of cubist phase. Later turned to monumental classical nudes, sculptures, pottery. Famous work *Guernica* (1936) expresses his horror at outrages of Spanish Civil War.

Piccard, Auguste (1884-1962), Belgian physicist, b. Switzerland. Made 1st balloon ascents into stratosphere (1931). Constructed bathyscaphe to explore ocean; reached depth of 10,900 m (35,800 ft).

piccolo, small woodwind instrument; pitched an octave higher than FLUTE.

Pickering, Edward Charles (1846-1919), American astronomer, physicist. Devised instruments to measure light of stars and studied stellar spectra. His brother, **William Henry Pickering** (1858-1938), predicted location of planet Pluto before its discovery; discovered 9th satellite of Saturn.

Pickford, Mary, orig. Gladys Smith (1893-1979), American film actress, b. Canada. Became famous as 'America's sweetheart' through silent films, incl. *Pollyanna* (1919), *Little Lord Fauntleroy* (1921). Cofounded United Artists Films.

Pico della Mirandola, Giovanni, Conte (1463-94), Italian philosopher, humanist. Sought to reconcile Platonism and Christianity in series of theses, prefaced by *On the Dignity of Man*. Also wrote *Heptaplus*.

Picts, Iron Age people inhabiting Scotland, N Ireland. First described by Romans in AD 297, they resisted Roman conquest and maintained their independence until absorbed into kingdom of the Scots c 850.

pidgin, lingua franca, not 1st language of speakers, with restricted vocabulary, simple syntax. Originally applied to variety of English spoken by Chinese trading with English, extended to incl. pidgins developed from Portuguese, French, Spanish, Malay *etc*, in Africa, West Indies, as well as Far East.

Piedmont (*Piemonte*), region of NW Italy, cap. Turin. H.e.p., livestock in mountainous W; wheat, rice in fertile Po valley. Ruled by house of Savoy from 13th cent; part of Sardinia from 1720 to unification

(1860). Annexed to France 1798-1814. Battleground in many wars.

piedmont, area of land lying at foot of mountains or upland. May also describe particular feature *eg* piedmont plain, piedmont glacier.

Pierce, Franklin (1804-69), American statesman, president (1853-7). Unexpected Democratic presidential nominee in 1852, elected on policy of appeasing the South on slavery issue. Alienated North by authorizing KANSAS-NEBRASKA BILL (1854).

Piero della Francesca (*c* 1420-92), Italian painter. Known for the geometric perfection of his forms, his mastery of perspective and subtle colour harmonies, work incl. fresco series *The Legend of the True Cross* at Arezzo, and *Flagellation of Christ* at Urbino.

Pierre, cap. of South Dakota, US; on Missouri R. Pop. 10,000. Livestock market, shipping industs. Founded 1880; became cap. 1889.

Pietermaritzburg or **Maritzburg,** cap. of Natal, South Africa. Pop. 113,000. Admin., indust., railway centre in stock rearing area; produces wattle extract for tanning; has part of univ. of Natal (1909). Founded (1838) by Boer leaders. Two cathedrals, Voortrekker museum, many gardens.

Pietism, movement in Lutheran church favouring devotion rather than dogmatism. First leader was German theologian, Philip Jakob Spener (1635-1705), who in *Pia desideria* (1675) stressed study of Bible and participation of lay members in spiritual control of Church. Attacked as unorthodox;

declined in late 18th cent. Influenced Kant, Kierkegaard.

piezoelectric effect, property exhibited by certain crystals of developing electric charge on their surface when subjected to pressure. Crystals also expand and contract in response to alternating current. Piezoelectric crystals are used in microphones, loudspeakers, record player pick-ups, etc.

pig, any of Suidae family of hoofed mammals. Omnivorous, canine teeth often lengthened into tusks. Domestic pig developed from wild boar, Sus scrofa; source of pork, lard. Wild species incl. babirussa, wart hog.

pigeon, bird of Columbidae family, widely distributed in tropical and temperate regions. Wood pigeon or ring dove, Columba palumbus, with greyish plumage, is largest European species. Domesticated breeds derived from rock dove, C. livia; noted for homing ability.

Pigmy, see PYGMY.

Pigs, Bay of, inlet of S Cuba. Scene of unsuccessful invasion by Cuban exiles backed by US forces in attempt to overthrow Communist Castro regime (1961).

pika, small tailless mammal, genus Ochotona, of same order (Lagomorpha) as rabbit. Found in rocky mountains of Asia and North America.

pike, Esox lucius, carnivorous freshwater fish of N temperate regions. Voracious predator, feeding on fish, water birds, etc. Reaches lengths of 1.5 m/5 ft.

pike, obsolete infantry weapon with long shaft and iron point, often used defensively in rows braced against the ground. Superseded by the bayonet.

Pikes Peak, mountain of C Colorado, US. Height 4301 m (14,110 ft). Most famous peak in Rocky Mts. Colorado Springs is at foot. Tourist region.

Pilate, Pontius (fl AD 1st cent.), Roman procurator of Judaea (c 26-36). Fearing Jewish religious and popular recrimination, allowed execution of Jesus. Traditionally, committed suicide in Rome.

pilchard, Sardina pilchardus, small marine food fish of herring family, common in Mediterranean and off Portuguese coast. Sardine is young pilchard. Other species incl. Californian and South African pilchard.

piles, see HAEMORRHOIDS.

pilgrimage, journey made to a shrine or holy place as a religious act. Occurs in many religions, eg in Hinduism to Ganges, in Islam to Mecca, in Judaism to Temple at Jerusalem, in Christianity to Jerusalem, Bethlehem, Nazareth. Important in medieval Europe, with major centres at Canterbury (England), Santiago de Compostela (Spain). In RC church, pilgrimage is still festered with Rome being the major centre.

Pilgrimage of Grace (1536), rising of English Roman Catholics, esp. in Lincolnshire and Yorkshire, protesting against abolition of papal supremacy and suppression of monasteries by Henry VIII. Rebels dispersed peacefully, but many were executed after further rebellion in 1537.

Pilgrim Fathers, name given to those English emigrants who sailed in Mayflower (1620) to found

Plymouth Colony in Massachusetts. About ½ of them had previously migrated to Holland in search of religious freedom.

Pill, the, popular name for oral contraceptive which interferes with menstrual cycle, preventing ovulation by hormone action.

Pillars of Hercules, see GIBRALTAR, STRAIT OF.

Pillnitz, Declaration of, statement (1791) calling on European powers to restore Louis XVI of France to his former power; issued by Prussia and Austria.

pilot fish, *Naucrates ductor*, spiny-finned marine fish, often found accompanying sharks, turtles.

Pilsen see PLZEŇ, Czechoslovakia.

Pilsudski, Joseph (1867-1935), Polish military and political leader. Active in cause of Polish independence from Russia before WWI. Led Polish troops against Russia in support of Austria in WWI. Became head of state of independent Poland (1919). Retired 1922, returned as virtual dictator (1926-35) after coup d'état.

Piltdown man, human skull fragment found with ape-like jaw at Piltdown, Sussex (1912). Believed to be oldest human species found in Europe until proved to be a hoax (1953). Fragments had been tampered with and were of modern origin.

pimento, *Pimenta officinalis*, tree of myrtle family, native to West Indies. Dried fruits used as spice.

pimpernel, any of genus *Anagallis* of annual herbs of primrose family; esp. scarlet pimpernel, *A. arvensis*, with red, white or blue, star-like flowers which close in bad weather.

Pindar (518-438 BC), Greek poet. Wrote choral lyrics, incl. odes celebrating athletic victories, *Epinikia*.

Pindus Mountains (*Pindhos*), range of NC Greece, runs N-S between Epirus (W), Thessaly (E). Highest point Smólikas (2636 m/8652 ft).

pine, any of genus *Pinus* of evergreen conifers, widely distributed in N hemisphere. Needle-shaped leaves. Certain varieties yield timber, turpentine, resin. Species incl. stone pine, · *P. pinea*, Austrian pine, *P. nigra*, pitch pine, *P. rigida* and Scots pine, *P. sylvestris*.

pineal body, small cone-shaped · projection from centre of brain of all vertebrates. In certain amphibians and reptiles, it is sensitive to light and is remnant of central eye. Function in humans unknown, but believed to secrete hormone which influences sexual development.

pineapple, *Ananas comosus*, plant native to tropical America, now grown chiefly in Hawaii. Edible, juicy fruit develops from flower spike.

pine marten, *Martes martes*, nocturnal carnivore of forests of N Europe and W Asia. Omnivorous, often catching squirrels. Has dark brown fur, bushy tail.

Pinero, Sir Arthur Wing (1855-1934), English playwright. Wrote skilful farces, eg *Dandy Dick* (1887), problem plays, eg *The Second Mrs Tanqueray* (1893), sentimental comedies, eg *Trelawny of 'The Wells'* (1898).

Pines, Isle of, isl. off W Cuba. Area 3056 sq km (1180 sq mi). Fishing, agric., marble quarrying; covered by pine forests. Has large prison for political prisoners. Discovered by Columbus (1494). Awarded to Cuba over US claims (1925).

ping-pong, see TABLE TENNIS.

pink, any of genus *Dianthus* of annual or perennial plants native to temperate regions. White or red flowers with ragged edges. Species incl. garden pink, *D. plumarius*, maiden pink, *D. deltoides* and sweet william, *D. barbatus*. See CARNATION.

Pinkie, Battle of, Scottish defeat by English forces under duke of Somerset (1547). Caused Scots to send Mary (later Mary Queen of Scots) to France to avoid marriage to Edward VI. Battle site is near Musselburgh.

Pinochet [Ugarte], Augusto (1916–), Chilean political leader. Took control of govt. after overthrowing Marxist regime of Allende (1973). Suppressed left-wing opposition; declared Marxist parties illegal.

Pinter, Harold (1930–), English dramatist. Known for menacing comedies, eg *The Caretaker* (1959), *The Homecoming* (1964), one-act plays incl. *The Dumb Waiter* (1957), screenplays, eg *Accident* (1967).

pion or **pi-meson,** elementary particle with mass *c* 270 times that of electron. Discovered (1947) in cosmic radiation; plays important role in forces which bind atomic nucleus.

Piozzi, Hester Lynch, neé Salusbury (1741-1821), English writer, b. Wales. Known (as Mrs Thrale) as friend of Dr JOHNSON. Wrote *Anecdotes of the Late Samuel Johnson* (1786), *Letters to and from*

the late *Samuel Johnson LL.D.* (1788).

pipal, see BO TREE.

pipe fish, small elongated marine fish of Syngnathidae family. Long tubular snout, bony plates on skin. Male broods eggs in pouch on body. Species incl. great pipe fish, *Syngnathus acus*, common in E. Atlantic.

Piper, John (1903–), English painter, stage designer. Known for paintings of landscape and architecture eg *Coventry Cathedral* (1940), *Rock Face, Cwm Tryfan* (1950). Designed sets for most of Britten's operas.

pipistrelle, small insectivorous bat of wide distribution, genus *Pipistrellus*. Species incl. eastern pipistrelle, *P. subflavus*, smallest North American bat, and *P. pipistrellus*, smallest British bat.

pipit, small songbird of Motacillidae family, genus *Anthus*. Brown plumage; insectivorous. Species incl. European meadow pipit, *A. pratensis*, and North American Sprague's pipit, *A. spragueii*.

piracy, taking of ship or contents on the high seas, distinct from privateering in that pirate holds no commission, does not fly national flag. Formerly common, esp. in Spanish Main, Barbary coast, Chinese and Malay waters. Famous pirates incl. Henry Morgan, Edward Teach (Blackbeard). See also HIJACKER.

Piraeus, see ATHENS, Greece.

Pirandello, Luigi (1867-1936), Italian author. Known for plays dealing with relationship between illusion, reality incl. *Right You Are If You Think You Are* (1917), *Six Characters in Search of an Author*

(1921), *Henry IV* (1922). Also wrote novels, short stories. Nobel Prize for Literature (1934).

Piranesi, Giovanni Battista (1720-78), Italian architect, engraver. His numerous etchings of Roman antiquities greatly influenced Romantic concept of Rome. Famous for *Carceri d'Invenzione* (reworked 1761), series of fantastic imaginary prisons.

piranha, South American freshwater fish with sharp teeth and powerful jaws. Lives in schools which can attack large animals. Species incl. *Pigocentrus piraya*, up to 60 cm/2 ft in length.

Pisa, city of Tuscany, WC Italy, on R. Arno. Cap. of Pisa prov. Pop. 112,000. Medieval maritime republic, warred with Florence, defeated (1284) by Genoa. Centre of Pisan school of sculpture (13th-14th cent.). Cathedral (12th cent.), leaning tower (1173, height 55m/180 ft). Birthplace of Galileo.

Pisa, Council of, council summoned (1409) to try to end Great Schism. Supporters of Gregory XII and Benedict XIII agreed to depose them both and elect Alexander V pope. Various claims were not finally settled until 1417.

Pisanello, orig. Antonio Pisano (*c* 1395-1455), Italian artist. Leading exponent of International Gothic style in Italy in succession to Gentile da Fabriano, he was an accomplished draughtsman and portraitist. His portrait medals are valuable historical records.

Pisano, Andrea (*c* 1290-1348), Italian sculptor, architect. Continued Giotto's work on cathedral and campanile in Florence; most famous work is bronze doors of Baptistery at Florence, begun 1330.

Pisano, Nicola (*c* 1220-*c* 1280), Italian architect, sculptor. Leading figure in rebirth of sculpture in Italy. His works, incl. pulpits in Baptistery at Pisa and in Siena cathedral, are marked by synthesis of Gothic and classical styles. His son, Giovanni Pisano (*c* 1250-*c* 1314), assisted his father and continued revival of sculpture. Works incl. pulpit of Pisa cathedral.

Pisces, see ZODIAC.

Pisistratus (*c* 605-527 BC), tyrant of Athens. Leader of popular party, he seized power *c* 560. Twice exiled, he returned (541) until his death. Encouraged building, poetry.

Pissarro, Camille (1830-1903), French painter, b. West Indies. A leading member of the impressionists, he participated in all 8 impressionist exhibitions. Enormously prolific, he influenced early work of Cézanne and Gauguin.

pistachio, *Pistacia vera*, small tree native to Mediterranean region and Asia. Fruit contains greenish, edible nut eaten salted or used in cookery and confectionery.

pistol, small, short-barrelled firearm designed to be fired with one hand. Originally made in Italy (16th cent.); REVOLVER made in 19th cent. and 'automatic' repeating pistols in 20th cent.

Pitcairn Island, isl. of SC Pacific Ocean, admin. by UK. Area 5 sq km (2 sq mi). Fruit growing. Colonized (1790) by mutineers from HMS *Bounty* and Tahitian women; pop. removed 1856, some later returned.

pitch, dark sticky substance, liquid

when heated, solid when cold. Obtained as residue from distillation of petroleum, coal tar, wood tar. Used in waterproofing, road construction.

pitch, quality of a musical sound dependent on rate of vibrations producing it. The greater the number of vibrations per second, the higher the note. Instruments are tuned to a standard pitch in which the A above middle C is equal to 440 vibrations per second.

pitchblende, uranium ore mineral, a form of uraninite. Consists of uranium oxide with various impurities. Source of uranium; also radium, lead, thorium, some rare-earth elements. Major sources in US, Canada, Australia, Zaïre.

pitcher plant, any of genus *Sarracenia,* insectivorous bog herbs of North America. Leaves in form of pitcher.

Pitlochry, town of Tayside region, C Scotland, on R. Tummel. Pop. 3000. Control point of Highland h.e.p. system. Annual drama festival; tourism.

Pitman, Sir Isaac (1813-97), English inventor. Developed improved system of phonetic shorthand, expounded in *Stenographic Soundhand* (1837); adapted for use in many languages.

Pitt, William, 1st Earl of Chatham (1708-78), English statesman, known as the 'Great Commoner'. Chief figure in coalition with duke of Newcastle (1757-61), architect of military defeat of French in India and Canada (1759). Forced to resign by George III. Retired because of ill health from 2nd coalition (1766-8). Broke with Whigs over colonial policy in America, favouring conciliation. His son, William Pitt (1759-1806), was Tory PM (1783-1801, 1804-6). Reformed finances to help fund national debt, introduced new taxes. Failed to anticipate war with revolutionary France; his various coalitions had little success on land against French. Took strong measures to suppress political reformers. Solved Irish question by passing Act of Union (1800), but resigned when George III vetoed Catholic emancipation. Second ministry ended with his death soon after defeat of Allies by Napoleon at Austerlitz.

Pitt-Rivers, Augustus Henry Lane-Fox (1827-1900), English soldier, archaeologist. Advanced archaeological technique by recording in detail excavations on his Wiltshire estate; recognized importance of apparently trivial finds. Pub. *Excavations in Cranborne Chase* (1887-98).

Pittsburgh, city of SW Pennsylvania, US; at point where Allegheny and Monongahela rivers form Ohio R. Pop. 520,000. In rich coal mining region. Iron and steel, oil refining, machinery mfg. industs. Settled in 1760 as Fort Pitt (formerly French Fort Duquesne). Has Carnegie Institute of Technology.

pituitary gland, endocrine gland situated at base of brain. Composed of anterior and posterior lobes. Anterior lobe secretes important hormones whose functions incl. maintenance of growth, stimulation of thyroid and sex organs, *etc.* Posterior lobe secretes hormone which regulates flow of urine.

pit viper, any of Crotalidae family of

venomous snakes, incl. rattlesnake, sidewinder, etc, with heat-sensory pits on each side of head. Found in Asia and New World.

Pius V, St, orig. Michele Ghislieri (1504-72), Italian churchman, pope (1566-72). Furthered the Catholic Reformation by implementing the decrees of the Council of Trent. Organized alliance between Venice and Spain against the Turks, which led to victory at Lepanto (1571).

Pius VI, orig. Angelo Braschi (1717-99), Italian churchman, pope (1775-99). Opposed attempts of Emperor Joseph II and subsequently of French Revolution to subject church to state. Taken prisoner (1798) during French occupation of Rome. Died in captivity.

Pius VII, orig. Barnaba Chiaramonti (1740-1823), Italian churchman, pope (1800-23). Signed Concordat (1801) with Napoleon to re-estab. Church in France. Taken prisoner (1809-14) by French on occupation of papal states. Worked to restore Church in Europe on return to Rome.

Pius IX, orig. Giovanni Mastai-Ferretti (1792-1878), Italian churchman, pope (1846-78). Refused to recognize new kingdom of Italy and in 1870 retired to Vatican. Proclaimed dogma of Immaculate Conception (1854); convened 1st Vatican Council which enunciated papal infallibility.

Pius XI, orig. Achille Damiano Ratti (1857-1939), Italian churchman, pope (1922-39). Responsible for Lateran Treaty (1929) estab. Vatican City state. Condemned Nazism in 1937 encyclical.

Pius XII, orig. Eugenio Pacelli (1876-1958), Italian churchman, pope (1939-58). Worked to limit extension of WWII, while taking ambiguous stand towards Axis powers. Attempted to reduce Communist power (excommunicated Hungary, Romania, Poland in 1953).

Piute, see PAIUTE.

Pizarro, Francisco (c 1476-1541), Spanish conquistador. With partner, Almagro, led expedition to Peru (1530) in search of fabulous wealth of Incas. Seized Inca ruler Atahualpa (1532) and had him murdered after receiving his enormous ransom (1533). Captured Cuzco (1533), completing conquest of Peru. Founded Lima (1535). Dispute between Almagro and Pizarro and his brothers led to conflict and execution of Almagro (1538). Almagro's followers later assassinated Pizarro.

Place, Francis (1771-1854), English radical. Successfully campaigned (1814-24) for repeal of Combination Acts, forbidding trade unions. Vigorous organizer of movement for political reform.

placenta, organ consisting of embryonic tissue by which the embryo of viviparous animals is nourished. Attached to lining of mother's uterus. Oxygen and dissolved nutrients are carried to placenta by mother's blood.

plague, contagious disease caused by bacterium *Pasteurella pestis*; carried by fleas from infected rats. Form known as bubonic plague is characterized by swollen lymph nodes (buboes); pneumonic plague infects lungs. Occurred sporadically in Europe, notably in Black Death (1346-9) and Great London Plague (1665).

plaice, *Pleuronectes platessa,* marine flatfish, commercially important in Europe. Light brown body with orange spots.

Plaid Cymru, *see* WELSH NATIONALIST PARTY.

plain, large area of relatively flat land usually at low altitude. Commonest types are glacial plains, flood plains, coastal plains. Often grass-covered *eg* pampas (South America), steppes (USSR), savannah (tropics).

plainsong, religious chant that developed in early Christian church and survives in RC liturgy. Consists of single melodic line sung in unison, usually unaccompanied. Developed into POLYPHONY in late Middle Ages. Also known as Gregorian chant.

Planck, Max Karl Ernst Ludwig (1858-1947), German physicist. Attempts to explain distribution of black-body radiation led to his hypothesis that vibrating atoms absorb or emit radiant energy only in discrete bundles (quanta) whose magnitude. is product of Planck's constant and frequency of radiation. Founder of modern quantum theory. Nobel Prize for Physics (1918).

plane, any of genus *Platanus* of deciduous trees native to temperate regions. Palmate leaves, pendulous burr-like fruit. Species incl. Oriental plane, *P. orientalis,* London plane, *P. acerifolia,* with 3-lobed leaves, and American sycamore or buttonwood, *P. occidentalis.*

planet, heavenly body in orbit round the Sun, which shines by reflected sunlight. Minor planet is called an ASTEROID. *See* SOLAR SYSTEM.

planetarium, arrangement for projecting images of heavenly bodies on inside of large hemispherical dome by means of system of optical projectors which is revolved to show celestial motion. Name also applied to building in which system is housed.

plankton, general term for minute organisms found drifting near surface of sea or lakes. Incl. protozoa, crustacea, algae and other invertebrates.

plant, member of vegetable group of living organisms. Generally manufactures own food by PHOTOSYNTHESIS (but *see* FUNGUS); has an unlimited growth (*ie* old tissue remains in place and new tissue grows away from it); has cells with more or less rigid walls; has no means of independent locomotion. Divided into 4 main divisions: Thallophyta (algae, lichens, fungi); Bryophyta (mosses, liverworts); Pteridophyta (ferns, club mosses, horsetails); Spermophyta (conifers, flowering plants). *See* CLASSIFICATION.

Plantagenet, name applied to English royal house, whose monarchs were Henry II, Richard I, John, Henry III, Edward I, II, III, Richard II. After Richard II's deposition (1399), house divided into houses of York and Lancaster.

plantain, *Musa paradisiaca,* tropical plant. Produces long yellow-green banana-like fruit. Name also applies to any of genus *Plantago* of plants with rosettes of leaves and spikes of greenish flowers.

Plantin, Christophe (1514-89), French printer. Considered greatest printer of his time, he set up his press in Antwerp (1555). Pub. polyglot Bible (8 vols., 1569-73). His printing works continued in op-

eration until 1867, and is now a museum.

plasma, in biology, clear fluid forming 55% of blood. Composed mainly of water, with dissolved proteins, inorganic salts, urea and sugar.

plasma, in physics, high-temperature ionized gas, composed almost entirely of equal numbers of electrons and positive ions. Excellent electrical conductor and responsive to magnetic fields; study of plasma is important to achievement of controlled thermonuclear reactions.

Plassey, village of West Bengal, NE India. Scene of Clive's victory over Nawab of Bengal (1757) giving Britain control of Bengal.

plaster of Paris, fine white powder produced by heating gypsum. When mixed with water, forms paste which sets and hardens. Used for casts, moulds, etc.

plastics, materials which are stable in normal use but are plastic in some part of their production and can be moulded by heat and pressure. Most plastics are synthetic polymers. The 2 main groups are thermoplastic materials, which can be melted and reset many times, and thermosetting materials, which cannot be remoulded.

plastic surgery, surgery dealing with repair of lost or damaged tissue or with making cosmetic improvements. Skin grafting is used to cover extensive burns or other injuries, both to improve final appearance and prevent infection.

Plata, Río de la (River Plate), wide estuary of SE South America, formed at confluence of Uruguay and Paraná rivers. Chief ports Buenos Aires, Montevideo. Explored by Magellan (1520). Scene of naval battle (1939) in which German battleship *Graf Spee* was scuttled.

Plataea, ancient city of Boeotia, SE Greece. Scene of Greek naval victory (479 BC) over Persians. Sacked by Spartans (427 BC), Thebans (373 BC), rebuilt by Alexander the Great.

plateau, elevated area of land with relatively level surface. Causes incl. basalt lava flows (eg Deccan of India), faulting, erosion. Types incl. tableland, bordered by steep sides all around, and dissected plateau, where different rates of erosion eventually leave only isolated peaks.

plate tectonics, study of the main structural features of the Earth's crust, in terms of several great crustal 'regions, or plates, which change their positions through time. Mountain ranges, faults, trenches, mid-oceanic ridges result from plate movements. CONTINENTAL DRIFT theory derives from plate tectonics, continents being embedded in shifting plates.

Plath, Sylvia (1932-63), American poet. Known for intense, highly personal verse, eg in collections *The Colossus* (1960), *Ariel* (1965). Also wrote a novel, *The Bell Jar* (1971), a fictionalized account of her nervous breakdown.

platinum (Pt), metallic element; at. no. 78, at. wt. 195.09. Malleable and ductile; resists corrosion by air and acids; excellent conductor of electricity. Used in electrical apparatus, jewellery and chemical catalysis.

Plato (c 427-c 347 BC), Greek philosopher, pupil of Socrates;

Founded (387 BC) **Academy near** Athens to educate ruling elite. Author of *Republic* advocating ideal state based on rational order, ruled by philosopher kings. Propounded independent reality of universal ideas (esp. idea of the good), and ideal forms which man could come to perceive through dialectic method of inquiry. Held that virtue, reason, happiness were one. Dialogues incl. *Apology, Crito, Protagoras, Phaedo, Timaeus, Laws.* Most noted student was Aristotle.

Plattensee, see BALATON, Hungary.

Platyhelminthes (flatworms), phylum of bilaterally symmetric invertebrates. Reproduction by complex hermaphroditic system. Divided into 3 classes: Cestoda, tapeworms; Trematoda, parasitic flukes; Turbellaria, free-swimming aquatic worms.

platypus, see DUCKBILLED PLATYPUS.

Plautus, Titus Maccius (c 254–184 BC), Roman comic poet. Adapted Greek New Comedy for Roman stage; noted for boisterous humour, gift for dialogue, song, as in *Aulularia, Miles Gloriosus.* Profound influence on later European literature.

Playfair, William Henry (1789–1857), Scottish architect. Particularly active in Edinburgh, where he designed Scottish National Gallery, National Memorial (unfinished copy of Parthenon), parts of New Town.

playing cards, cards used in gaming, divination and conjuring. Originated in the Orient, reaching Europe in 14th cent. Symbols for the 4 suits and 52-card deck were introduced in France in 16th cent.

plebeians, members of unprivileged class of ancient Rome, originally excluded from holding public office. Secured political equality with the patricians in years from c 500–300 BC.

plebiscite, expression of people's will by direct ballot on political issue, as in referendum. Since 18th cent., used for deciding between independent nationhood or affiliation with another nation.

Pléiade, la, group of 16th cent. French poets led by Ronsard, du Bellay. Aimed to enrich, purify French language, create national literature through imitation of classical forms.

Pleiades, in Greek myth, seven daughters of Atlas and nymph Pleione. Pursued by Orion and turned into constellation which bears their name.

Pleiades, star cluster in constellation Taurus. Six stars are readily visible but cluster contains several hundred.

Pleistocene epoch, first geological epoch of Quaternary period. Began c 2 million years ago, lasted until c 11,000 years ago. Incl. 4 major glaciations, or Ice Ages, accompanied in warmer equatorial regions by high rainfall (pluvial) periods. Fauna incl. mastodons, mammoths, sabre-tooth carnivores, wolves, bison. During this epoch, man evolved from primitive ape-like creatures, eg Java, Peking man, to present form; time of Palaeolithic culture. Also see ICE AGES and GEOLOGICAL TABLE.

Plekhanov, Georgi Valentinovich (1857–1918), Russian revolutionary. Influential in introducing Marxist thought to Russia. Broke with Bolsheviks after 1903 split in Social Democratic Party; his view that Russia was not ready for Socialism was adopted by Mensheviks.

plesiosaur, extinct marine reptile of Jurassic period and later, order Plesiosauria. Long thin neck, 4 paddle-like limbs, long tail. Reached lengths of 15 m/50 ft.

pleurisy, inflammation of pleura, the membrane enclosing the lung. Usually caused by infection by bacteria or viruses; often occurs with pneumonia. Characterized by difficulty in breathing and sometimes collection of fluid around lungs.

Pleven or **Plevna,** city of N Bulgaria. Pop. 108,000. Agric. centre; textiles; wine. Taken by Russia from Turks after siege (1877).

plexiglass, see PERSPEX.

Pliny the Elder, full name Gaius Plinius Secundus (AD c 23-79), Roman scholar. Wrote *Historia naturalis*, encyclopedic collection of scientific knowledge in 37 books; some of the fanciful information he relates was long held as scientific fact. His nephew, **Pliny the Younger,** full name Gaius Plinius Caecilius Secundus (AD c 62-c 113), consul. Wrote letters of literary and historical importance.

Pliocene epoch, final geological epoch of Tertiary period. End of Alpine mountain building. Continuing decrease in temperature caused extinction of many mammals, migration of others. Beginning of Lower Palaeolithic culture. Also see GEOLOGICAL TABLE.

Plock, town of NC Poland on R.

Vistula. Pop. 66,000. Oil refining (pipeline from USSR), agric. market. Under Russian rule 1815-1921. Cathedral (12th cent.) contains royal tombs.

Ploeşti, city of SC Romania. Pop. 186,000. Petroleum indust., pipelines to Bucharest, Constanza. Bombed in WWII.

Plotinus (c AD 205-70), Greek philosopher, b. Egypt. Settled (AD 244) in Rome, founding neoplatonist school. Developed concept of creation by Emanation from God rather than directly by God.

plough, farm implement used to cut, break and turn over the soil. First ploughs consisted of wooden wedge tipped with iron, pushed or pulled by men or oxen. Modern plough incorporates: coulter, blade or disc, which makes vertical cuts in soil; share, which cuts horizontally through undersoil; mouldboard, which turns over soil.

Plovdiv (anc. *Philippopolis*), city of C Bulgaria, on R. Maritsa. Pop. 262,000. Agric. centre, esp. cereals, wine, attar of roses; textiles; tobacco. Taken by Philip II of Macedonia, renamed; cap. of Roman Thracia, and of 19th cent. Eastern Rumelia.

plover, wading bird of Charadriidae family. Species incl. golden plover, *Pluvialis dominica*, which breeds in North America and NW Asia, and American KILLDEER.

plum, small tree or shrub of genus *Prunus*, native to Asia Minor. Oval, smooth-skinned, edible fruit with flattened stone. Commercially cultivated species incl. damson, *P. domestica*, and varieties of *P. salicina*.

Plutarch (AD c 46-c 120), Greek biographer, essayist. Best known for *Parallel Lives*, paired biographies of Greeks and Romans, with vivid characterization, anecdotes. Popular in Elizabethan England through translation by Sir Thomas North, source for Shakespeare's Roman plays.

Pluto, in Greek myth, son of Cronus and Rhea; ruler of HADES. Worshipped as god of dead and of earth's fertility. Identified with Roman Orcus or Dis Pater.

Pluto, planet 9th in distance from Sun; mean distance from Sun c 5900 × 10⁶ km; diameter c 5800 km; period of rotation about Sun c 248 years. First detected 1930. Has surface of frozen methane.

plutonic rock, igneous rock formed at great depth below Earth's surface. Commonly occurs as INTRUSIVE ROCK; slow cooling produces coarsely crystalline texture, *eg* granite.

plutonium (Pu), transuranic element; at. no. 94, mass no. of most stable isotope 244. Plutonium 239, produced by irradiating uranium 238 with neutrons, is used as fuel in nuclear reactors and in nuclear weapons.

Plymouth, city of Devon, SW England, at head of Plymouth Sound. Pop. 239,000. Seaport, naval base; boatbuilding, fishing. Medieval *Sutton*, hist. seafaring base (Drake, Raleigh, 'Pilgrim Fathers'). Has RC cathedral. Damaged in WWII air raids.

Plymouth, town of SE Massachusetts, US; on Plymouth Bay. Pop. 19,000. Fishing, tourist indusrs. Site of Pilgrim landing in 1620 after sailing from England on *Mayflower*, marked by Plymouth Rock.

Plymouth Brethren, evangelical sect founded in Dublin by John Nelson Darby (1827). Spread to Europe and North America. Movement follows literal interpretation of Bible, has no ordained ministers.

Plzeň (Ger. *Pilsen*), city of W Czechoslovakia. Pop. 148,000. Agric. market; breweries; metallurgy, munitions.

pneumoconiosis, disease of the lungs resulting from inhalation of mineral dust, esp. asbestos and silica. Usually affects miners, sandblasters, *etc*. Causes lung inflammation and growth of fibrous scar tissue.

pneumonia, inflammation of the air sacs (alveoli) of the lungs, caused by bacterial or viral infection. Bronchial pneumonia is confined to area close to air passages, lobar pneumonia affects whole lobe. Bacterial form characterized by fever, pain in chest, blood-stained sputum; treated by antibiotics.

Pnom Penh, *see* PHNOM PENH.

Po (anc. *Padus*), river of N Italy. Flows c 650 km (405 mi) E from Alps to delta on Adriatic Sea. Po basin is most fertile region of Italy.

Pocahontas (c 1595-1617), American Indian princess, daughter of Powhatan. Said to have saved John Smith, English colonist in Jamestown, Virginia, from execution. Married another colonist, James Rolfe (1614). Died in England.

pochard, *Aythya ferina*, European diving duck found on lakes, *etc*. Male has black chest, grey body, chestnut head and neck. Name also applied to several other diving ducks, incl. CANVASBACK.

Po Chu-i (772-846), Chinese poet. Extremely prolific, known for lucid language use in short, topical poems.

pocket borough, in Great Britain before Reform Bill (1832), borough in which representation in Parliament was controlled by one family or person.

Podgorny, Nikolai Viktorovich (1903-), Soviet politician. Became president (head of state) in 1965, succeeding Mikoyan. Removed from office (1977) to allow constitutional changes redefining role of president.

Poe, Edgar Allan (1809-49), American author. Known for short stories creating atmosphere of suspense, eg in *Tales of the Grotesque and Arabesque* (1840) incl. 'The Fall of the House of Usher'. Poetic works incl. *The Raven and Other Poems* (1845) which influenced Baudelaire. Also wrote detective stories, eg *The Murders in the Rue Morgue* (1841), literary criticism.

poet laureate, office of court poet in Britain. Ben Jonson first held position although Dryden first held title. Poets laureate incl. Wordsworth, Tennyson, Robert Bridges, John Masefield, John Betjeman.

poetry, in literature, term for imaginative, concentrated writing esp. using metrical and figurative language. Verse may be rhymed or un-rhymed (blank).

pogrom, Russian word, originally denoting a riot; later applied to organized attacks on Jews, often carried out with connivance of tsarist govt. Pogroms of 1881-2 and 1903 were esp. severe.

Pohai, Gulf of, arm of Yellow Sea.

Indents NE China coast. Bordered by Hopeh, Liaoning, Shantung provs. Formerly called Gulf of Chihli.

Poincaré, Raymond Nicolas Landry (1860-1934), French statesman, president (1913-20). Demanded strict treatment of Germany after WWI. As premier (1922-4, 1926-9), ordered armed occupation of Ruhr to enforce payment of war reparations (1923). His cousin, Jules Henri Poincaré (1854-1912), was a mathematician. Did pioneering research on topology of surfaces. Anticipated parts of relativity theory.

poinsettia, *Euphorbia pulcherrima*, plant native to Mexico and tropical America. Yellow flowers surrounded by tapering red leaves resembling petals.

pointer, short-haired hunting dog; usually white with brown spots. Hunts by scent and will 'point' to game with tail and muzzle outstretched. Stands c 66 cm/26 in. at shoulder.

pointillism, technique of painting in which a white ground is covered with tiny dots of pure colour which blend together to form intense colour effects when seen at a distance. Developed by the neo-impressionists, incl. Seurat and Signac; they preferred term 'divisionism'.

poison, substance having a dangerous or fatal effect on living things when drunk, absorbed, *etc.* Some are corrosive, eg acids, disinfectants; others interfere with body chemistry, eg cyanide.

poison gas, substance of corrosive or poisonous nature, in form of gas or vapour-forming liquid or solid,

First employed in WWI. Incl. chlorine which affects lungs, mustard gas which affects skin, and nerve gases which attack central nervous system.

poison ivy, any of genus *Toxicodendron* of cashew family. Leaves of 3 leaflets, greenish flowers, ivory-coloured berries. Can cause severe rash on contact with skin.

Poitiers, town of W France, cap. of Vienne dept. Pop. 75,000. Wine and wool trade; metal, chemical industs., univ. (1431). Gaulish religious centre; hist. cap. of Poitou. Scene of victory (1356) of Black Prince over John II of France. Baptistery (4th cent.), cathedral (12th cent.).

poker, card game, with two basic variations, draw and stud poker; usually played for financial stakes. Originated in US, growing popular after 1870.

pokeweed, *Phytolacca americana,* tall, coarse, perennial herb of North America. Dark purple berries contain poisonous seeds and yield emetic and purgative extracts.

Poland (*Polska*), republic of EC Europe. Area *c* 312,600 sq km (120,700 sq mi); pop. 34,362,000; cap. Warsaw. Language: Polish. Religion: RC. Forested N Carpathians in S, elsewhere fertile plain; main rivers Oder, Vistula. Agric. incl. cereals, livestock. Indust. centred in Silesia, Warsaw, Lódź; coal, iron, lead mining, textile mfg., engineering. First united 10th cent., medieval colonization by Teutonic Knights whom the Poles defeated at Tannenberg (1410). Disappeared completely after partitions (1772, 1793, 1795) between Austria, Prussia, Russia; re-formed 1918-21.

Conflict with Germany over Danzig led to WWII; occupied by Germans and Russians, Jewish pop. almost wholly exterminated. Territ. lost to USSR, gained from Germany after WWII. From 1947 ruled by communist govt.; member of COMECON.

Polanski, Roman (1933-), Polish film director. Gained reputation for taut, intense films with touch of macabre, *eg Repulsion* (1965), *Rosemary's Baby* (1968).

polar bear, *Thalarctos maritimus,* large creamy white bear of Arctic Circle. Good swimmer, lives on floating ice; preys on seals, young walruses. Reaches lengths of 2.7 m/9 ft.

Polaris, star of constellation Ursa Minor, less than 1° from the north celestial pole and thus important navigationally. Also called North Star or Pole Star.

polarized light, light whose transverse vibrational pattern is confined to a single plane. Polarizing agents incl. crystals and nicol prism.

polaroid, trade name for transparent material containing embedded crystals which polarizes light passing through it. Used in spectacles to prevent glare.

polder, Dutch term for land reclaimed from sea or fresh water. Normally flat, lying below sea level; protected by dykes, drained by pumps. Makes fertile agric. land, *eg* N Holland polders reclaimed from Zuider Zee.

pole, in geography, extremity of Earth's axis. *See* NORTH POLE, SOUTH POLE, MAGNETIC POLES.

polecat, *Mustela putorius,* carnivorous mammal of N Europe and

Asia, related to weasel. Dark brown outer fur; feeds on rodents, reptiles. Scent glands emit fetid odour for protection. Ferret is domesticated polecat.

Pole Star, *see* POLARIS.

police, force, or body of persons, estab. and maintained for keeping order, enforcing law and preventing, detecting and prosecuting crimes. First instituted as official body in Britain by Peel (1829) with reorganization of SCOTLAND YARD. In UK, police administered by Home Office in England, Scottish Office in Scotland. In US, first local police force estab. in New York (1844).

Polignac, Jules Armand, Prince de (1780-1847), French statesman, premier (1829-30). Leader of ultraroyalists during reigns of Louis XVIII and Charles X. As premier, issued July Ordinances to counter liberal Chamber of Deputies; provoked July Revolution (1830). Imprisoned (1830-6).

poliomyelitis or **infantile paralysis,** virus infection of the grey matter of spinal cord. Affects nerve cells which control muscular contraction, sometimes causing paralysis. Immunity became possible with Salk vaccine (1955) and Sabin vaccine (1961).

Polish Corridor, strip of land, lying between East Prussia and rest of Germany, which gave Poland access to Baltic. Formerly German territ., awarded to Poland (1919). German agitation to recover it led to invasion of Poland, precipitating WWII (1939).

Polish Succession, War of the, war arising out of competition for Polish throne (1733-5). On death of

Augustus II, Stanislaus I sought to recover throne lost in 1709; opposed by Augustus' son, Augustus III. France, with Spain and Sardinia, supported Stanislaus; Russia and Emperor Charles VI supported Augustus III. By Treaty of Vienna, Augustus kept Poland, Stanislaus received Lorraine.

Politburo, policy-making committee of Soviet Communist Party, the effective govt. of USSR. Called presidium of Central Committee (1952-66).

Polk, James Knox (1795-1849), American statesman, president (1845-9). A Democrat, he achieved many of stated aims, incl. reduction of tariffs. Annexation of Texas led to Mexican War (1846-8), by which California and much of SW were acquired.

polka, lively Bohemian dance in 2/4 time, originating *c* 1830. Popular in Europe for about 50 years.

Pollaiuolo, Antonio (*c* 1432-98), Italian artist. Reputedly first to dissect corpses to study anatomy; his anatomical knowledge is displayed in engraving *Battle of the Nude Gods.* Executed statues in bronze and collaborated with his brother, Piero Pollaiuolo (*c* 1443-96), in paintings, *eg* St Sebastian.

pollen, fine, yellowish dust, produced in anthers of flowering plants. Mature grains containing male element unite with female element in ovule to produce embryo which becomes SEED.

pollination, process allowing FERTILIZATION in seed plants. Pollen is transferred to stigma by wind, bees or other insects.

Pollock, Jackson (1912-56), American painter. Leading abstract expressionist; developed 'action painting', influenced by surrealist theories of automatism. Typical works, prepared by dripping paint on large canvases, incl. *Blue Poles*.

pollution, harm caused to environment as a result of man's activities, esp. by emission of substances which are non-biodegradable, or which, when broken down, become dangerous. Became matter of international concern in 1960s, although has been problem since Industrial Revolution. Atmospheric pollutants incl. sulphur gases, hydrocarbons and solid waste from smoke and automobile emissions, which become esp. dangerous in smog; also fluorocarbons, used as aerosol propellants, which reduce OZONOSPHERE's capacity to protect Earth from ultraviolet radiation. Water pollutants incl. sewage, indust. effluent (often containing poisonous heavy metals, *eg* mercury, cadmium, lead), detergents, pesticides (*see* DDT), oil spills. Any may kill living things in water by poisoning or deoxygenation, or be ingested and passed to higher organisms, incl. man, in food-chain. Pollution of seas now one of concerns of UN Environmental Programme which also admins. international monitoring, controls on heavy indust. Pollution protection is responsibility of Environmental Protection Agency in US, Dept. of Environment in UK. Also *see* GREENHOUSE EFFECT.

Pollux, in classical myth, *see* DIOSCURI.

Polo, Marco (*c* 1254–*c* 1324), Venetian traveller. Journeyed with father and uncle to Far East (1271–5). Reached court of Kublai Khan, who later employed him on diplomatic missions. Returned to Venice (1292–5), captured while fighting Genoa. While in prison, dictated valuable accounts of his travels.

polo, outdoor game, prob. originating in Persia, played between teams of 4 on horseback. Long-handled sticks used to hit wooden ball into the opponents' goal. Brought to British army officers from India to England, where it was first played competitively in 1871.

polonaise, stately Polish dance in 3/4 time at a moderately fast tempo. Best known are those by Chopin.

polonium (Po), radioactive element; at. no. 84, mass no. of most stable isotope 209. Formed by decay of radium; discovered (1898) in pitchblende by the Curies. Powerful source of alpha particles.

Poltava, city of USSR, NC Ukrainian SSR. Pop. 239,000. Centre of fertile agric. region producing sugar beet, fruit, grain. Peter the Great defeated Charles XII of Sweden nearby (1709).

poltergeist, name given to force, often supposed to be supernatural, responsible for unexplained rappings, movement of furniture, flying about of small objects in house.

polyanthus, *Primula polyantha*, hardy perennial herb of primrose family. Derived from hybrid of common primrose and cowslip. Grown as garden plant.

Polybius (*c* 201–*c* 120 BC), Greek historian. Taken as a prisoner to Rome (168), he enjoyed patronage of the Scipio family. Wrote history of years 220-146 BC in 40 books, 5 of which survive.

polygamy, state or practice of having 2 or more husbands (polyandry) or wives (polygyny) at same time. Polyandry is found in South Sea Isls. and among some North American Indian and Eskimo tribes. In Tibet, takes form of marriage to several brothers. Often associated with MATRIARCHY. Polygyny is more widespread esp. among hunting peoples, *eg* in Africa. Often confined to ruling caste, as in ancient Egypt. Has occurred in certain Christian sects. Practised by Moslems (limit of 4 wives).

polygon, in geometry, closed plane figure bounded by 3 or more sides; triangle is 3-sided polygon. Designated a regular polygon if all sides have equal length.

polyhedron, solid figure having polygons for its faces. Designated a regular polyhedron if faces are all congruent regular polygons; only those with 4, 6, 8, 12 and 20 faces can exist (formerly called the 'Platonic solids').

polymer, chemical compound consisting of giant molecules formed by linkage of smaller molecules (monomers). In addition polymerization, giant molecules are multiples of monomer molecule; in condensation polymerization, they are formed from monomers by chemical reaction involving elimination of some by-product, *eg* water. Cellulose is natural polymer; nylon and rayon are synthetic.

polymorphism, in zoology, condition in which species has 2 or more different morphological forms, *eg*

various castes of social insects such as ants.

Polynesia, one of three major divisions of Pacific isls., to E of Melanesia and Micronesia. Bounded by New Zealand, Hawaii and Easter Isl., incl. Samoa, Tonga, Line, Cook, Ellice, Phoenix isls. and groups forming French Polynesia.

Polynesians, people of Pacific isls. between Hawaii, New Zealand and Easter Isls., of Malayo-Polynesian linguistic stock. May have come from Malaysia or South America.

Polynices or Polyneices, in Greek myth, son of Oedipus. After banishment of father, agreed to rule Thebes alternately with brother Eteocles. When Eteocles refused to relinquish throne Polynices led 'Seven against Thebes' expedition. All were killed except Adrastus, king of Argos. Story basis of tragedies by Aeschylus, Euripides.

polyp, sedentary form of coelenterate with tube-like body and mouth surrounded by tentacles. Either solitary (*eg* Hydra) or colonial (*eg* coral-forming polyps). Some reproduce asexually, forming free-swimming medusae by budding; others reproduce sexually to form new polyps.

polyp, in medicine, tumour growing from mucous membrane, to which it is attached by a stalk. Found in intestines, uterus, *etc*; removed if malignant. Polyps in nose are swellings caused by allergy or infection.

Polyphemus, in Greek myth, a Cyclops, son of Poseidon. In Homer's *Odyssey*, imprisoned Odysseus and his men in cave. They escaped under Polyphemus' sheep after Odysseus had blinded him with burning stake.

polyphony, style of musical composition in which separate melodic lines are harmonically interrelated *eg* in a round. Developed in West in medieval times, when extra parts were added to plainsong. Reached great heights in music of Bach and Palestrina.

polyptych, set of 2 or more panels bearing pictures, carvings, often hinged for folding together; frequently used as an altarpiece. Two panels form a diptych, three a triptych, *etc.*

polytheism, belief in or worship of more than one god. Usually each god is distinguished by a particular function but is represented in myth as related to other members of cosmic family. Prob. development of primitive ANIMISM.

polythene or **polyethylene,** thermoplastic material made by polymerization of ethylene. Used to make translucent plastic film, moulded objects and in electrical insulation.

polyvinyl chloride (PVC), colourless thermoplastic material formed by polymerization of vinyl chloride. Resistant to water, acid, alcohol. Used for flooring, coated fabrics, cable covering.

pomegranate, *Punica granatum,* small tree native to subtropical Asia. Scarlet flowers followed by many-seeded, pulpy, edible fruit.

Pomerania (Pol. *Pomorze,* Ger. *Pommern*), region of NC Europe, on Baltic coast, extending from Stralsund (East Germany) in W to R. Vistula (Poland) in E; incl. Rügen isl. Flat, low-lying; agric., livestock,

forestry. In 1945, all Pomerania E of R. Oder, incl. Stettin, passed to Poland.

Pomeranian, breed of small dog with long silky hair, erect ears, tail curved over back. Stands *c* 15 cm/6 in. at shoulder.

Pompadour, Antoinette Poisson, Marquise de (1721-64), mistress of Louis XV of France. Her beauty and wit enabled her to rise to great power with Louis; encouraged alliance with Austria, leading to French involvement in Seven Years War. Patron of Voltaire.

Pompeii, ancient city of Campania, S Italy, near Bay of Naples. Roman port, resort; buried (AD 79) with Herculaneum in eruption of Vesuvius. Site discovered 1748. Many public buildings and villas, with well-preserved murals, have been uncovered.

Pompey, full name Gnaeus Pompeius Magnus (106-48 BC), Roman soldier. Made consul (70), he cleared the Mediterranean of pirates (67) and defeated Mithradates in Asia Minor (66). Joined Caesar and Crassus in 1st Triumvirate (60). Later opposed Caesar and championed senatorial party. Defeated by Caesar in civil war at Pharsalus (48); fled to Egypt, where he was murdered.

Pompidou, Georges Jean Raymond (1911-74), French statesman, president (1969-74). Premier (1962-8), dismissed by De Gaulle soon after 1968 student-labour unrest. Elected president after De Gaulle's resignation, pursued similar policies.

Pondicherry, union territ. of S India. Area 474 sq km (183 sq mi); pop. 471,000; cap. Pondicherry.

Comprises former French India (founded 1674); transferred to India (1954). Became union territ. 1962.

pond lily, see LOTUS.

Ponta Delgada, see AZORES, Portugal.

Pontiac (*fl* 18th cent.), American Indian chief. Led uprising (1763-6) against British, who had gained control of Indian lands after defeating French. Besieged Detroit and destroyed British outposts before rebellion was quelled and peace signed.

Pontine Marshes, area of WC Italy, between Tyrrhenian Sea and Apennines. Fertile, populous in Roman times; abandoned due to malaria. Drainage completed 1920s, agric. settlement followed.

Pontius Pilate, see PILATE, PONTIUS.

pontoon, card game. See VINGT-ET-UN.

Pontormo, Jacopo, orig. Jacopo Carrucci (1494-1556), Italian painter. Style represents transition between late classicism and early mannerism. His *Deposition* in Florence is masterpiece of early Florentine mannerism.

Pontus, region of Asia Minor, now in NE Turkey. Became kingdom *c* 300 BC and *fl* under Mithradates until defeat by Romans under Pompey (65 BC).

Pontypool, urban dist. of Gwent, SE Wales. Pop. 37,000. Coalmining; tinplate mfg. (first made here 17th cent.).

Pontypridd, urban dist. of Glamorgan, S Wales, on R. Taff. Pop. 34,000. Coalmining; iron, brass founding.

pony express, mail service running from St Joseph, Missouri to Sacramento, California, US. Riders covered distance of *c* 3200 km (2000 mi) in 8 days. Inaugurated 1860, replaced by telegraph in 1861.

poodle, breed of dog probably developed in Germany. Thick frizzy or curly coat usually trimmed in standard style (introduced in France). Stands over 38 cm/15 in. at shoulder. Miniature poodles are 25-38 cm/10-15 in. at shoulder and toy poodles are under 25 cm/10 in.

pool, see SNOOKER.

Poole, mun. bor. of Dorset, S England, on Poole Harbour. Pop. 107,000. Port, resort; boatbuilding; pottery mfg. (from local clay).

Poona, city of Maharashtra state, W India. Pop. 853,000. Cotton, paper mfg. Military centre. Under British rule was summer residence of Governor of Bombay.

Poor Laws, legislation providing public relief and assistance for poor. English law (1601), 1st state intervention on behalf of destitute, made them responsibility of parish. Poorhouses built, work provided, local levies raised. Workhouses estab. (18th cent). Speenhamland System (1795) attempted to help by subsidizing low wages. Abuses aroused discontent in agric. workers and employers, led to Poor Law amendment (1834). This act granted relief only to able-bodied poor in strictly regulated workhouses, introduced strong central authority. Harsh effects helped rise of CHARTISM. Complete reform finally achieved 1930. Poor Law abolished, replaced by National Assistance Board (1948). In US, states had separate systems until 1930s introduced federal relief, with Social Security Act (1935).

pop art, realistic art style, appearing in late 1950s, which uses subjects and techniques derived from commercial art and popular culture. Subject matter incl. assemblages of cans, replicas of food, enlarged photographs and comic book characters. American exponents incl. Warhol, Oldenburg, Lichtenstein.

Pope, Alexander (1688-1744), English poet. Known for skilled use of heroic couplet, poems incl. discussion of classical values, *An Essay on Criticism* (1711), mock heroic *The Rape of the Lock* (1714), satirical *Dunciad* (1728), deistic *Essay on Man* (1733-4), 'Epistle to Dr Arbuthnot' (1735). Translated *Iliad*, *Odyssey*.

pope, *see* PAPACY.

Popish Plot, name given to story, fabricated (1678) by Titus OATES, of Jesuit-inspired plan to assassinate Charles II and restore Catholicism.

poplar, any of genus *Populus* of trees of willow family. Native to N temperate regions. Soft fibrous wood, flowers in catkins. Species incl. Lombardy poplar, *P. nigra*, North American cottonwood, *P. deltoides*.

Popocatépetl, dormant volcano of C Mexico, overlooking Mexico City. Height 5452 m (17,887 ft). Has unexploited sulphur deposits. Another volcano, Ixtacihuatl, is nearby. Height 5286 m (17,342 ft).

Popper, Sir Karl Raimund (1902-), British philosopher, b. Austria. Wrote classic *The Logic of Scientific Discovery* (1935) on the problem of induction and demarcation of science. Other works

incl. *The Open Society and Its Enemies* (1945) attacking Marxist doctrine, *The Poverty of Historicism* (1961). Settled in UK after 1946.

poppy, any of genus *Papaver* of annual and perennial plants. Showy red, violet, yellow or white flowers. Incl. commercially important OPIUM POPPY. Corn poppy, *P. rhoeas*, is found in Europe; Californian poppy, *P. californium*, is state flower of California.

Popular Front, in French history, term for alliance in 1930s between left-wing political parties. Socialists, Communists, and Radical Socialists united under Léon Blum and formed Popular Front govt. (1936-8) which carried out series of social reforms, incl. introduction of 40-hour working week.

Populism, American agrarian political movement of late 19th cent. Discontent among farmers of Northwest and South led to formation (1891) of Populist Party, whose presidential candidate polled over 1 million votes in 1892 election. Majority of populists had joined Democrats under W.J. Bryan by 1896.

porcelain, hard, white, non-porous variety of pottery which is translucent; made of kaolin, feldspar and quartz or flint. First made by the Chinese during the T'ang period, it was refined during Sung period. European varieties incl. Sèvres and Limoges (France), Chelsea, Bow and Staffordshire (England), Meissen and Dresden (Germany).

Porcupine, river of Canada-US. Rises in C Yukon, flows N, then W 721 km (448 mi) to join Yukon R. in E Alaska.

porcupine, rodent covered with sharp erectile spines in addition to hair. Two families: New World Erethizontidae (partly arboreal) and Old World Hystricidae (mainly terrestrial). Species incl. Canadian porcupine, *Erethizon dorsatum,* and crested porcupine, *Hystrix cristata,* of N Africa and S Europe.

porphyry, igneous rock comprising large crystals, called phenocrysts, embedded in fine-grained groundmass. Term refers to any such texture, not composition. Red porphyry, *ie* feldspar crystals in purplish groundmass, was valued by ancient Egyptians.

porpoise, small toothed whale of Phocaenidae family. Common porpoise, *Phocaena phocaena,* found in N Atlantic, is smallest species, reaching lengths of 1.8 m/6 ft. Feeds on fish, crustaceans.

Porsena, Lars, *see* TARQUINIUS SUPERBUS.

port, sweet fortified wine made in Douro valley of Portugal. May be ruby, tawny or white; genuine port is matured in the bottle after spending 2 or 3 years in casks.

Portadown, town of EC Northern Ireland. Pop. 21,000. In former Co. Armagh. Railway jct., clothing mfg.; rose nurseries.

Port Arthur, China, *see* LU-TA.

Port Arthur, port of SE Texas, US; on Sabine L. Pop. 57,000. Oil refining, exports via canal to Gulf of Mexico.

Port-au-Prince, cap. of Haiti, major port on Gulf of Gonaïves. Pop. 494,000, mostly Negro, mulatto. Rum distilling, sugar refining, brewing. Founded 1749; became cap.

1770. Has Univ. of Haiti (1944); 18th cent. cathedral.

Port Bouet, *see* ABIDJAN, Ivory Coast.

Port Elizabeth, city of S Cape Prov., South Africa, on Algoa Bay. Pop. 469,000. Port, exports minerals, fruit, wool; car assembly works. Founded (1820) by British.

Porter, Cole (1893-1964), American composer of musicals. Songs, of which he wrote both words and music, incl. 'Night and Day', 'Anything Goes'. Renowned for clever internal rhymes in lyrics.

Port Glasgow, town of Strathclyde region, W Scotland, on R. Clyde. Pop. 22,000. Shipbuilding; rope, canvas mfg. Built (1668) as port for Glasgow, declined after Clyde channel deepened.

Port Harcourt, city of SE Nigeria, on Niger delta. Pop. 217,000. Railway terminus and port, exports palm oil, groundnuts, cocoa; commercial and indust. centre, esp. oil refining, metal products, tyre mfg., vehicle assembly. Founded (1912) by British.

Port Kembla, *see* WOLLONGONG, Australia.

Portland, William Bentinck, 1st Earl of (1649-1709), Dutch statesman. Adviser to William of Orange, he came to England after 'Glorious Revolution' (1688). Negotiated Treaty of Ryswick (1697) for French recognition of William as king of England. **William Henry Cavendish Bentinck, 3rd Duke of Portland** (1738-1809), headed coalition govt. of North and Fox in 1783; again PM (1807-9).

Portland, urban dist. on Isle of Portland penin., Dorset, SW England. Pop. 12,000. Limestone quarries; naval base; Portland Bill light-house. Has 16th cent. castle.

Portland, port of NW Oregon, US; on Willamette R. Pop. 381,000; state's largest city. Railway jct.; shipyards. Timber, grain exports, wood industs.

Port Laoighise, co. town of Laoighis, C Irish Republic. Pop. 4000. Formerly called Maryborough.

Port Louis, cap. of Mauritius. Pop. 137,000. Admin. centre; port, exports sugar; international airport. Founded 1735; has citadel, Anglican and RC cathedrals.

Port Moresby, cap. of Papua New Guinea, in SE New Guinea isl. Pop. 66,000. Exports rubber, gold. Air traffic centre.

Pôrto, see OPORTO, Portugal.

Pôrto Alegre, city of S Brazil, cap. of Rio Grande do Sul state; at N end of Lagôa dos Patos. Pop. 886,000. Meat, hides, wool exports. Settled by German, Italian immigrants in 19th cent. Modern city with 2 univs.

Port of Spain, cap. of Trinidad and Tobago, on NW Trinidad isl. Pop. 68,000. Sugar produce, oil refining, rum distilling. Receives iron, bauxite shipments from Venezuela, Guianas. Has many parks; mosque, Anglican, RC cathedrals. Became cap. 1783.

Porto Novo, cap. of Benin, on coastal lagoon near Bight of Benin. Pop. 85,000. Admin. centre; port, exports palm oil, kapok, cotton. Former seat of a kingdom, became colonial cap. 1900.

Port Phillip Bay, inlet of Bass Str., SE Australia. Ports incl. Melbourne and Geelong; resorts on sandy E shores.

Port Said (*Bûr Saîd*), city of NE Egypt, at Mediterranean entrance to Suez Canal. Pop. 313,000. Major port and fuelling station, exports cotton; salt, chemical industs.; railways to Cairo, Suez. Founded 1859, named after Said Pasha. Has statue of Ferdinand de Lesseps, planner of Canal.

Portsmouth, Louise Renée de Kéroualle, Duchess of (1649-1734), mistress of Charles II of England. Encouraged English alliance with France from 1671 until Charles's death (1685). Greatly disliked in England, she fled to France.

Portsmouth, city on Portsea Isl., Hampshire, S England. Pop. 197,-000. Main UK naval base. Has Cathedral of St Thomas (12th cent.); Nelson's flagship *Victory*, Dickens' birthplace, both now museums.

Portsmouth, port of SE Virginia, US; on Hampton Roads (Elizabeth R.). Pop. 111,000. Naval depot; shipyards (has important Norfolk Navy Yard). Exports cotton, tobacco; varied mfg.

Port Sudan, city of NE Sudan, on Red Sea. Pop. 110,000. Sudan's chief port, exports cotton, gum arabic, hides, salt; railway terminus.

Port Talbot, mun. bor. of Glamorgan, S Wales, on Swansea Bay. Pop. 51,000. Ore terminal, new harbour (1970) serve large steelworks. Formed 1921 from union of Aberavon, Margam.

Portugal, republic of SW Europe, on W Iberian penin. Incl. Azores, Madeira Isls. Area 92,000 sq km (35,500 sq mi); pop. 9,449,000; cap. Lisbon. Language: Portuguese. Religion: RC. Mountainous in N, E;

main rivers Minho, Douro, Tagus. Agric., wine, cork, fishing (sardines, tuna). Subtropical in S (tourism). Part of Roman *Lusitania*, fell to Visigoths, Moors. Independent from 12th cent.; acquired overseas empire 15th-16th cent. Under Spanish rule 1580-1668. Suffered in War of Spanish Succession, Peninsular War; lost Brazil 1822. Republic estab. 1910; dictatorships followed, esp. Salazar (1928-68). Political unrest followed military uprising 1974; decolonization policy led to independence of Portuguese Guinea (1974), Angola and Mozambique (1975).

Portuguese, Romance language in Italic branch of Indo-European family. Spoken as 1st language in Portugal, Madeira, the Azores, Brazil. Developed from Latin; displaced but also influenced by Mozarabic language spoken by Christians under Moorish domination.

Portuguese East Africa, see MOZAMBIQUE.

Portuguese Guinea, see GUINEA-BISSAU.

Portuguese man-of-war, *Physalia physalis,* colonial marine coelenterate of open Atlantic. Floating bladder bears medusae and polyps with diverse functions, *eg* reproduction, feeding. Long tentacles with poisonous stinging organs dangerous to swimmers.

Portuguese Timor, see TIMOR.

Portuguese West Africa, see ANGOLA.

Poseidon, in Greek myth, brother of Zeus and god of the sea; sons incl. Pegasus, Polyphemus, Orion. Represented as vengeful god carrying a trident with which he could cause earthquakes. Identified by Romans with Neptune.

Posen, see POZNAŃ, Poland.

positivism, system of philosophy basing knowledge solely on observable scientific facts and their relations to each other. Rejects metaphysics. Founded by Auguste Comte. See LOGICAL POSITIVISM.

positron, anti-particle of electron, possessing same mass but positive electric charge. Positron-electron pairs can be produced by conversion of energy into matter, but the 2 particles annihilate each other.

possum, see OPOSSUM.

postal service, arrangement for delivery of mail to members of public. Early systems estab. in Persian, Roman empires. In Britain, Charles I estab. acceptance of public mail, extending services of royal couriers; flat-rate penny post instituted by Rowland Hill in 1840. In US, penny postage began 1839. Pony express took mail to West (1860-61), rail service then took over, with air mail starting in 1918. Universal Postal Union regulates international harmony (estab. 1875).

post-impressionism, term used to describe work of those French painters who rejected impressionism in favour of greater emphasis on the subject or the formal structure and style of the painting. Most important exponents were Gauguin, van Gogh, Cézanne.

Postojna (Ital. *Postumia*), town of Slovenia, N Yugoslavia, Karst region. Pop. 4000. Has stalagmite/stalactite caves, largest in Europe.

potash or **potassium carbonate**

(K$_2$CO$_3$), compound used as fertilizer and in manufacture of glass and soap.

potassium (K), soft metallic element; at. no. 19, at. wt. 39.10. Highly reactive; combines with water to produce strong alkali potassium hydroxide. Occurs in wide variety of silicate rocks and mineral deposits; essential to life processes. Compounds used in manufacture of soap, glass and fertilizers.

potato, *Solanum tuberosum*, plant of nightshade family. Native to South America but widely cultivated for starchy, edible tubers. Introduced into Europe *c* 1570.

Potemkin, Grigori Aleksandrovich, Prince (1739-91), Russian army officer. Took part in the annexation (1783) of the Crimea, where he governed ably. He reformed the army, built the Black Sea fleet, estab. the port of Sevastopol. Favourite of Catherine II.

Potemkin Mutiny, see RUSSIAN REVOLUTION.

potential, in physics, work done against force exerted by field in bringing unit physical quantity (*eg* mass, electric charge, magnetic pole) from infinity to some specified point. Used as measure of strength of field at any point.

Potomac, river of E US; forms Maryland's S border. Flows E 459 km (285 mi) past Washington DC to Chesapeake Bay. Shenandoah R. (Civil War battleground) is main tributary. George Washington's Mount Vernon estate is on S shore.

Potosí, town of SW Bolivia, cap. of Potosí dept. Alt. 4200 m (c 13,780 ft). Pop. 64,000. Leading mining centre;

tin, copper, tungsten (silver once important). Founded 1545. Has 19th cent. cathedral; univ. (1571).

Potsdam, city of C East Germany, on R. Havel. Pop. 112,000. Produces precision instruments, chemicals. Residence successively of Brandenburg, Prussian, German rulers. Palaces incl. Sans Souci, built 1747 for Frederick II. Scene of Potsdam Conference (1945) on Allied control of post-war Germany.

Potsdam Conference, meeting (July, 1945) of Allied leaders to implement agreement of YALTA CONFERENCE. Estab. American, British, French and Soviet occupation zones in Germany, to be supervised by Allied Control Council. Redistributed German territ. to Poland and USSR; laid economic and political basis of post-WWII Germany.

Potter, [Helen] Beatrix (1866-1943), English author and illustrator of children's books incl. *The Tale of Peter Rabbit* (1902), *The Tale of Jemima Puddle-Duck* (1908).

Potter, Stephen (1900-70), English writer. Known for humorous works, esp. *The Theory and Practice of Gamesmanship* (1947). Also wrote literary criticism.

Potteries, The, area of Staffordshire, NC England, in Trent Valley. Pottery indust. founded 1769 by Wedgwood. Incl. Stoke-on-Trent, Newcastle-under-Lyme.

pottery, general term for objects made of clay and baked hard. Originally hand made, pottery was fashioned on wheels in Egypt before 4000 BC; glazes also developed in Egypt in 2nd millennium BC. Red and black figured vases produced in

Greece c 600-450 BC represent high point of art and provide valuable historic record. Chinese independently developed advanced pottery techniques which inspired potters to emulate them when Chinese pottery was introduced into Europe in 16th cent. Islamic potters of Syria, Persia, Turkey produced brilliantly coloured and glazed work from 9th-16th cents., which also influenced European style.

Poulenc, Francis (1899-1963), French composer, pianist. Member of 'les Six' group of composers. Works, often witty in nature, incl. ballet music, eg Les Biches, and piano, orchestral, chamber works.

Pound, Ezra Loomis (1885-1972), American poet, lived in Europe after 1907. Influenced modern poetry as imagist, vorticist and friend, patron, of younger poets. Works incl. allusive, erudite Hugh Selwyn Mauberley (1920), Cantos (1925-69). Also wrote prose, eg ABC of Reading (1934), Essays (1954, edited by T.S. Eliot). Fascist sympathizer during WWII.

pound, in measurement, British unit of weight; equal to c 0.4536 kilograms.

Poussin, Nicolas (1594-1665), French painter. Dominant influence on French classical painting, he stressed intellectual discipline in art. Developed classical landscape in 1640s, austere and constructed with geometric precision. Works incl. 2 series of Seven Sacraments and Landscape with Diogenes; spent most of his life in Rome.

Powell, Anthony Dymoke (1905-), English novelist. Known for 12 vol. roman-fleuve 'A Dance to the Music of Time' from A Question of Upbringing (1951) to Hearing Secret Harmonies (1975), portraying a comic vision of structure of English social life. Other works incl. Afternoon Men (1931); biog. of John Aubrey (1948).

Powell, Enoch (1912-), British politician. Conservative minister of health (1960-3). Controversial views on immigration, incl. repatriation of non-white immigrants, led to dismissal from shadow cabinet (1968). Re-entered Parliament as an Ulster Unionist (1974).

power, in physics, the rate of doing work. SI unit of power is the watt.

Powys, John Cowper (1872-1963), English novelist. Wrote mystical novels, eg Wolf Solent (1929), A Glastonbury Romance (1932), Porius (1951), expressing highly personal philosophy. Discursive works incl. The Meaning of Culture (1929), In Defence of Sensuality (1930). His brother, **Theodore Francis Powys** (1875-1953), also wrote novels, eg Mr Weston's Good Wine (1927).

Powys, inland county of E Wales. Area 5077 sq km (1960 sq mi); pop. 100,000; co. town Brecon. Created 1974, incl. former Breconshire, Montgomeryshire, Radnorshire.

Poynings' Law, act of Irish Parliament (1494). Stated that approval of English legislature was required for summoning of Irish Parliament and for passing of any legislation. Repealed 1782.

Poznań (Ger. Posen), city of W Poland, on R. Warta, cap. of Poznań prov. Pop. 473,000. Railway jct.; engineering and chemical industs.; univ. (1919). Seat of Polish primate from 1821. Under Prussian rule 1793-1919. Heavily bombed in WWII.

Prado, Spanish national museum of painting and sculpture, in Madrid, opened to the public in 1819. Nucleus of collection derives from royal collections; holdings of Spanish, Flemish and Venetian painting are outstanding.

Praetorians, body guard of Roman emperors, first organized in reign of Augustus. Played important part in accession of certain emperors. Disbanded by Constantine I.

Praetorius, Michael, orig. Michael Schultheiss (1571-1621), German composer. Prolific composer, esp. of choral works. Also wrote on musical instruments and theory of his day in *Syntagma Musicum* (3 vols.).

Pragmatic Sanction, 1) decree issued (1438) by Charles VII of France, limiting papal authority over Church in France; 2) decree issued (1713) by Emperor Charles VI, extending right of succession in Austrian Empire to female line. On death of Charles, led to War of Austrian Succession (1740-8).

pragmatism, movement in philosophy which determines the validity of concepts by their practical results. Opposed to RATIONALISM. Exponents incl. C. S. Peirce, William James, John Dewey.

Prague (*Praha*), cap. of Czechoslovakia, on R. Moldau. Pop. 1,082,000. Admin., commercial centre. Metal working; textiles; food processing; printing, publishing. Univ (1348); Hradčany Palace, St Vitus cathedral. Centre of 15th cent. Hussite movement. Czech cap. from 1918. German occupation 1939-45.

Focus of 1968 liberalization movement, suppressed by Soviet forces.

prairie, area of gently undulating, treeless natural grassland. Applies esp. to such areas in North America between Rockies and Great Lakes, former grazing land now extensively cultivated for cereals.

prairie chicken, brown and white hen-like grouse of North American plains, genus *Tympanuchus*. Species incl. greater prairie chicken, *T. cupido*, and lesser prairie chicken, *T. pallidicinctus*.

prairie dog, *Cynomys ludovicianus*, burrowing squirrel-like rodent of North American plains. Lives in large colonies; barks like a dog.

Prairies, region of WC Canada, incl. Alberta, Saskatchewan, Manitoba provs. Flat agric. region; major wheat, oats, barley growing. Also describes Mississippi valley region of US.

prairie wolf, *see* COYOTE.

Prakrit, languages other than Sanskrit and Vedic of Indic group of Indo-Iranian branch of Indo-European family. Incl. modern vernaculars. Some scholars hold PALI to be a Prakrit. Literature mainly Jainist.

Prasad, Rajendra (1884-1963), Indian statesman. Headed Indian National Congress several times. Followed Gandhi's policy of noncooperation with British; imprisoned (1942-5). Became 1st president of India (1950-62).

praseodymium (Pr), metallic element of lanthanide series; at. no. 59, at. wt. 140.91. Compounds used to colour glass and enamel. First isolated 1904.

Prato, city of Tuscany, NC Italy.

Pop. 143,000. Textiles, hist. centre of woollen indust. Medieval town hall; cathedral contains works by Donatello and Filippo Lippi.

Pravda (Russ., = truth), Russian daily newspaper, founded in 1912. State-controlled since Revolution, represents Communist party line, while *Izvestia* represents govt.

prawn, any of various edible shrimplike crustaceans, widely distributed in fresh and salt waters. Common prawn, *Palaemon serratus*, is 7.5-10 cm/3-4 in. long.

Praxiteles (*fl c* 350 BC), Athenian sculptor. With Phidias, considered greatest sculptor of ancient Greece. Marble *Hermes with the Infant Dionysus* at Olympia is only surviving work. Copies of other statues incl. *Aphrodite of Cnidus*.

Precambrian or **Archaean era,** earliest geological era, incl. all time from consolidation of Earth's crust to beginning of Palaeozoic era. Duration *c* 4000 million years. Sometimes divided into Early and Late Precambrian. Largely metamorphic rock, exposed as continental shields, *eg* Canadian, African, Australian. Rare traces of rudimentary life; forerunners of trilobites, worms, sponges, jelly fish; some algae, fungi. Also *see* GEOLOGICAL TABLE.

precession of the equinoxes, westward movement of equinox along the ecliptic. Caused by gravitational pull of Sun and Moon on Earth's equatorial bulge; Earth's axis describes cone returning to original position every 26,000 years. Noted by Hipparchus (*c* 120 BC); explained by Newton (1687).

precious stone, *see.* GEMSTONE.

predestination, in Christian theology, doctrine that God fore-ordained all events, esp. the salvation of certain souls. Follows from belief in omniscience and omnipotence of God; formulated by St Augustine. RC doctrine allows the co-existence of free will, while Calvin taught absolute predestination of souls. Occurs also in Judaism and Islam.

pregnancy, period of development of fertilized ovum in the uterus. In humans, lasts on average 40 weeks (dated from time of last menstrual period).

prelude, initially an introductory movement in music; later a short piano piece. Preludes of Bach and Chopin use single theme and complete cycle of keys. Other exponents incl. Rachmaninov, Debussy.

premier, *see* PRIME MINISTER.

Preminger, Otto [Ludwig] (1906-), American film producer-director, b. Austria. Known for craftsmanship, serious treatment of intricate stories, as in *Anatomy of a Murder* (1959), *Exodus* (1961), *Advise and Consent* (1961).

Pre-Raphaelite Brotherhood, society, nucleus of which was 3 English artists, D.G. Rossetti, Millais and Holman Hunt, formed 1848 to revive painting with a fidelity to nature they considered characteristic of Italian art before Raphael. Violently attacked by the critics, movement was defended by Ruskin; dissolved by 1853.

Presbyterianism, system of Christian church govt. by elders (presbyters), elected by the congregation rather than by bishops.

Instituted by JOHN CALVIN it is the system of most reformed churches. The Church of Scotland is the only Presbyterian church estab. by law.

president, chief EXECUTIVE of a republic, acting as both head of state and govt. In republic with parliamentary govt. has little or no executive power, head of govt. usually being prime minister or premier. In US, president has substantial powers defined in constitution. In 5th republic of France, president also has substantial executive powers despite having a premier as head of CABINET.

Presley, Elvis (1935-77), American singer. Leading exponent of rock-and-roll in 1950s with such songs as 'Heartbreak Hotel', 'Blue Suede Shoes' and 'Hound Dog'.

press-gang, a naval party empowered by law to force men to serve in British fleet. Initiated by Edward III, it was chief method of naval recruitment from Elizabethan times down to Napoleonic wars, after which it was discontinued though still legal.

pressure, in physics, force per unit area acting on a surface. Atmospheric pressure is pressure due to weight of Earth's atmosphere; at sea level, this pressure supports column of mercury c 76 cm high.

Prester John, legendary Christian priest and ruler of a great empire, originally thought to be in Asia, later associated with Ethiopia. Legend first arose in 12th cent. chronicles.

Preston, co. bor. and co. town of Lancashire, NW England, on R. Ribble. Pop. 97,000. Port; textiles esp. cotton; engineering.

Prestonpans, town of Lothian region, EC Scotland. Pop. 3000. Scene of battle (1745) in which Jacobite forces defeated English.

Prestwick, town of Strathclyde region, SW Scotland. Pop. 13,000. Tourist resort. Has international airport.

Pretender, Old, see STUART, JAMES FRANCIS EDWARD.

Pretender, Young, see STUART, CHARLES EDWARD.

Pretoria, admin. cap. of South Africa and cap. of Transvaal. Pop. 562,000. Admin., indust. centre; railway engineering, large steelworks; univ. (1930). Founded 1855; cap. of Boer confederation from 1860, of Union of South Africa from 1910.

Prévert, Jacques (1900-), French poet. Was member of surrealist group and has maintained anarchic position, attacking the establishment in racy, readable verse. Works incl. *Paroles* (1946), *Histoires* (1963) and screenplay for film *Les enfants du paradis* (1945).

Prévost d'Exiles, Antoine François (1697-1763), French author, known as Abbé Prévost. As gentleman-adventurer, wrote *Mémoires et aventures d'un homme de qualité* (1728-3) incl. *Manon Lescaut* (1731), basis of operas by Massenet, Puccini.

Priam, in Greek legend, king of Troy during Trojan War. Chief wife was Hecuba; among 50 sons and many daughters were Hector, Paris, Cassandra. Slain by Neoptolemus at fall of Troy.

Priapus, in Greek myth, son of Dionysus and Aphrodite. Fertility god of gardens. Statues of him as misshapen little man with enormous phallus were used as scarecrows.

prickly pear, common name for various species of genus *Opuntia* of cacti with flattened, jointed, spiny stems. Native to Mexico. Pear-shaped fruits of several species are edible. Introduced into Australia, has proved to be a pest.

Pride, Thomas (d. 1658), English soldier. Colonel on Parliamentary side during Civil War. Carried out purge (1648) of Presbyterian members of House of Commons (believed to be royalist sympathizers). Resulting Rump Parliament pursued prosecution of Charles I.

Priestley, J[ohn] B[oynton] (1894-), English author, critic. Known for novels incl. *The Good Companions* (1929), *Angel Pavement* (1930). Also wrote plays experimenting with treatment of time, *eg Time and the Conways* (1937).

Priestley, Joseph (1733-1804), English chemist, theologian. Improved methods for studying gases by collecting them over mercury; prepared and studied various gases incl. sulphur dioxide, ammonia and oxygen. Adopted Unitarian views; his sympathy for French Revolution provoked popular resentment and he emigrated to US (1794).

primary school, institution at which children of up to c 11 years old are taught basic subjects, *eg* reading, arithmetic. In US, known as elementary school.

primates, order of mammals, incl. monkeys, apes, man. Primarily arboreal, with 5 digits on hands and feet; well-developed vision and large brain. Order incl. more primitive lemurs and tarsiers.

prime minister or **premier,** chief member of CABINET, responsible to parliament. In UK and Commonwealth, holds executive power; appoints cabinet and is leader of governing party.

prime number, integer that can be evenly divided only by itself and 1. Each integer can be written as a product of prime numbers.

Primo de Rivera, Miguel (1870-1930), Spanish military and political leader. Estab. military dictatorship (1923) with support of Alfonso XIII. Continued as leader of civil admin. from 1925. Resigned 1930. His son, José Antonio Primo de Rivera (d. 1936), founded FALANGE party. Executed by Loyalists.

primrose, *see* PRIMULA.

primula, large genus of perennial herbs with white, yellow and pink flowers, found in temperate regions of N hemisphere. Main European varieties are common primrose, *Primula vulgaris,* COWSLIP, OXLIP and cultivated POLYANTHUS. Himalayan primrose, *P. denticulata,* has lilac- coloured flowers on long stem.

Prince Edward Island, Maritime isl. prov. of SE Canada. Area 5657 sq km (2184 sq mi); pop. 112,000; cap. Charlottetown. Agric.; stock raising, dairy farming; fishing (esp. lobsters). Settled in 17th cent. by French; ceded to Nova Scotia 1763; became separate colony 1769; prov. 1873.

Princeton, residential bor. of W New Jersey, US; on Millstone R. Pop. 13,000. Has Princeton Univ. (1756). Settled 1696 by Quakers.

Principe, *see* SÃO TOMÉ AND PRINCIPE.

printed circuit, electronic circuit in which wiring is printed on an insulating base. May be prepared by attaching copper foil to base, drawing circuit pattern on foil with wax and then etching away untreated foil.

printing, method of reproducing words or illustrations in ink on paper or other material by mechanical means. Block printing was used in China in 8th cent. and movable type was introduced there in 11th cent. GUTENBERG is credited with the European invention of movable type. In England, Caxton set up 1st printing press in London (1476). Modern commercial printing uses such processes as LITHOGRAPHY and PHOTOENGRAVING.

Prior, Matthew (1664-1721), English poet, diplomat. Wrote parodies, *eg The City Mouse and the Country Mouse* (1687) burlesquing Dryden; graceful 'society' verse. Helped draft Treaty of Utrecht (1713).

Pripet Marshes, forested marshland of USSR, C Byelorussian SSR. Formerly natural defence barrier between Poland and Russia. Crossed by R. Pripet, which rises in NW Ukrainian SSR and flows *c* 800 km (500 mi) to join R. Dnepr.

prism, in optics, transparent body whose ends are congruent triangles in parallel planes and whose 3 sides are parallelograms. Glass prisms change direction of light passing through them; triangular prisms disperse white light into colours of spectrum.

prison, place where convicted criminals are confined. Became important in late 18th cent., replacing capital punishment, mutilation, *etc*, in response to Beccaria, JOHN HOWARD. Howard's work influenced reform, esp. in US, where 1st cellular prison estab. (1790), and Pennsylvania system of discipline developed. In UK, Quaker group, esp. ELIZABETH FRY, led reform. Modern prisons seek rehabilitation, *eg* by use of specialist staff, open prisons, although punitive treatment, *eg* chain gangs, solitary confinement still exists. *See* PROBATION.

prisoners of war, members of the regular or irregular armed forces of a nation at war held captive by the enemy. Hague Conference of 1907 and Geneva Conventions of 1929 and 1949 laid down rules governing their treatment.

Pritchett, V[ictor] S[awdon] (1900-), English novelist, short-story writer, critic. Early novels incl. *Shirley Sanz* (1932), followed by more successful volumes of short stories *eg It May Never Happen* (1945). Evocative criticism incl. *The Living Novel* (1946).

privateers, privately owned war vessels having govt. commission to seize enemy shipping (1589-1815). The system was subject to much abuse as a cover for piracy and was abolished by the Declaration of Paris (1856).

privet, any of genus *Ligustrum* of shrubs and small trees of olive family. Widely cultivated for hedges, esp. common privet, *L. vulgare*.

privy council, body of advisors or counsellors appointed by or serving head of state, esp. in UK and Commonwealth. Comprises cabinet, members of judiciary (in UK incl.

archbishops). Acted as executive arm of govt. until 1688, superseded by cabinet.

probability theory, mathematical study of laws of chance. Event whose probability is 0 will never occur, one whose probability is 1 is certain to occur. Probability that tossed coin will fall as a head is ½.

probation, in penology, system whereby sentence on convicted offender is suspended on condition of good behaviour, regular reporting to probation officer. Used first in US (1878).

process engraving, see PHOTOENGRAVING.

Proconsul, extinct primate of Miocene period, known from fossils found in Kenya. Possible ancestor of chimpanzee, gorilla.

Procrustes, in Greek myth, highwayman who forced travellers to lie on either a short or a long bed. Stretched them or cut off their legs to make them fit. Killed in like manner by Theseus.

production, in economics, creation of economic value, eg farming or extraction of raw materials and imparting utility to them. Factors of production are regarded as land, labour, capital.

profit, in economics, return on CAPITAL. Classical economics distinguished between profit of entrepreneur and that of capitalist.

Profumo, John Dennis (1915-), British politician. Conservative secretary of state for war, he resigned after his involvement in prostitution scandal was revealed. 'Profumo affair' prob. contributed to Conservatives' electoral defeat (1964).

programme music, instrumental music intended to portray a scene or a story. Examples incl. Berlioz' *Symphonie fantastique,* Mendelssohn's *Fingal's Cave,* Mussorgsky's *Pictures at an Exhibition,* Strauss's *Till Eulenspiegel.*

progression, in mathematics, series of numbers, each formed by a specific relationship to its predecessor. In arithmetic progression, successive terms differ by a fixed amount (common difference); in geometric series, ratio of successive terms is constant (common ratio).

Progressive party, in US, name of three 20th cent. political organizations, active at different presidential elections. First was 'Bull Moose' party, estab. (1911) by Republicans dissatisfied with W.H. Taft; supported (1912) THEODORE ROOSEVELT. Second had socialist programme, supported LA FOLLETTE in 1924 campaign. Third was again left-wing, challenged Democrats in 1948 election, nominating Henry Wallace.

prohibition, method of legally regulating manufacture, sale and transporting of alcoholic beverages. In US, refers to period (1920-33) of absolute ban on such manufacture and sale by federal law (18th Amendment, 1919). Widespread bootlegging led to repeal (21st Amendment, 1933).

Prokofiev, Sergei Sergeyevich (1891-1953), Russian composer. His music has an individual harmonic quality often allied to great lyricism. Works incl. operas, eg *Love for Three Oranges,* symphonies, satirical film music *Lieutenant Kije,* wrote orchestral fairy tale *Peter and the Wolf.*

proletariat, in socialist theory, term used for class of wage earners existing on their own labour, esp. in indust. environment; derived from word for propertyless class in ancient Rome. In Marxist theory, proletariat is exploited by capitalist class, from which it must take power to achieve classless society.

Prometheus, in Greek myth, stole fire from the gods and gave it to mankind. Chained by Zeus to rock in Caucasus, where his liver was eternally devoured by an eagle. Released by Heracles; in some versions submitted to Zeus. Subject of Aeschylus' *Prometheus Bound.*

promethium (Pm), radioactive element of lanthanide series; at. no. 61, mass no. of most stable isotope 145. Obtained in nuclear reactors from fission of uranium.

pronghorn or **prongbuck,** *Antilocapra americana,* antelope-like North American ruminant, only member of Antilocapridae family. Hollow branched horns cast annually. Long persecuted by man, now protected.

proof spirit, alcoholic spirit containing 49.28% ethanol by weight or 57.1% by volume. Spirit said to be 70° proof or 30° under proof contains $0.7 \times 57.1 = 39.97\%$ ethanol by volume.

propaganda, technique of moulding public opinion by spreading true or false information through all media to gain religious, social or political ends in area of controversy. Important in dissemination of information by political parties in both democratic and totalitarian countries.

Propertius, Sextus (54/48–*c* 16

BC), Roman poet. Friend of Virgil, Ovid. Early poetry dominated by affair with Cynthia, a courtesan; later poetry continued theme of love and women.

prophets, in OT, Jewish religious leaders regarded as chosen by God to guide the people, esp. during kingdom of Palestine and the Captivity. Incl. Isaiah, Jeremiah, Ezekiel and Daniel. Term applied collectively to the books of OT bearing their names.

proportional **representation** (PR), system of voting giving numerical reflection of each party in representative assembly. Advocated by J.S. MILL, in order to allow minorities voice in govt. Best-known system is *single transferable vote,* in which elector has only one vote, but may indicate order of preference on list of candidates. Candidate elected on minimum quota of votes, after which surplus votes go to next on list, *etc.*

Propylaea, portal and entrance to W end of Acropolis, Athens. Built (437-432 BC) by Mnesicles.

prose, ordinary form of spoken or written language, without metrical structure, as opposed to poetry or verse. Usual form of expression in novel, biography, essay. Earliest extant European prose work is Herodotus' *History of the Persian Wars* (5th cent. BC).

Proserpine, see PERSEPHONE.

prostate gland, partially muscular gland surrounding urethra at base of urinary bladder in males. Secretes part of seminal fluid. Enlargement of prostate is common disorder of middle and old age; removal by surgery allows free flow of urine.

prostitution, offering oneself, or another, for sexual intercourse for money, material gain. Legal definitions vary; in UK, only women defined as prostitutes; in some states in US, prostitute is any indiscriminately sexually active woman. In many societies, prostitution was religious act, *eg* in ancient Babylon, W Asia. Tolerated in Middle Ages, became problem with spread of venereal disease (16th cent), and legally suppressed by Protestant reformers. Police regulation, attempt to close or license brothels in 19th cent. Subsequent concern more with suppression of associated crimes, diseases, *eg* West German emphasis on medical checks.

protactinium (Pa), radioactive element of actinide series; at. no. 91, mass no. of most stable isotope 231. Occurs in uranium ores. Discovered 1918 by Hahn and Meitner.

Protectorate, govt. of England (1653-9) estab. by Cromwell after he had dissolved Rump Parliament. Cromwell assumed title of lord protector and, with army support, ruled as dictator. His son, Richard Cromwell, succeeded him as lord protector (1658); resigned 1659.

proteins, large group of complex nitrogen-containing organic substances essential to living organisms. Made up of 20 amino acids, linked together in numerous ways to form large molecules. Synthesis of protein from amino acids is essential to growth and tissue maintenance.

Protestantism, religion of all Christian churches except RC and Eastern

Orthodox, most of which originated during REFORMATION. Stresses individual responsibility to God rather than to ecclesiastical authority.

Proteus, in Greek myth, wise old man of the sea with power of assuming various forms to escape questioning. If caught and held would foretell the future.

proton, stable elementary particle possessing charge equal in magnitude but opposite in sign to that of electron; *c* 1836 times heavier than electron. Occurs in nucleus of all atoms, usually joined with neutrons.

protoplasm, essential living matter of plant and animal cells, consisting of colloidal solution of proteins, lipoids, carbohydrates and inorganic salts. Carries out essential processes of reproduction, absorption of food, waste excretion, *etc.* In cell, differentiated into central nucleoplasm and surrounding cytoplasm.

Protozoa, phylum of all unicellular animals, consisting of naked mass of protoplasm surrounded by membrane. Reproduction often by fission but some parasitic varieties, *eg* malaria parasite, have complicated life cycle involving several hosts.

Proudhon, Pierre Joseph (1809-65), French social theorist. Condemned private property in *What is Property?* (1840) for maintaining inequality and injustice. Favoured theory of mutualism, whereby association of owner-producers cooperate for common good.

Proust, Marcel (1871-1922), French novelist. Influenced by Bergson's theory of subjective nature of time. Known for semi-autobiog. roman-fleuve, *A la recherche du temps perdu* (16 vols., 1913-27), detailing narrator's changing reactions to experience.

Provençal, variety of French. Considered by some to be dialect(s), others a separate language. Spoken in Provence and other areas of S France. Developed as *langue d'oc* of Middle Ages, vehicle of troubadour literature. *Langue d'oc* unsuccessfully revived in 19th cent. by literary movement.

Provence, region and former prov. of SE France, hist. cap. Aix. Largely mountainous, Rhône valley in W, coastal plain (incl. Camargue) in S. Wine, fruit, silk, cattle, h.e.p. Tourism, esp. along Riviera. Settled 7th cent. BC by Greeks, became Roman prov. Part of France from 1486. Provençal language widely used until 16th cent., revived 19th cent.; distinctive culture, esp. literature.

Proverbs, poetic book of OT, collection of moral maxims traditionally attributed to Solomon. Prob. from various sources and collected 9th-2nd cent. BC.

Providence, seaport and cap. of Rhode Isl., US; on arm of Narragansett Bay. Pop. 179,000. Machinery, jewellery, silverware mfg. Founded by Roger Williams on free worship basis (1636). Joint cap. with Newport until 1900. Has famous 18th cent. buildings. Seat of Brown Univ. (1764).

Prud'hon, Pierre-Paul (1758-1823), French painter, interior designer. Patronized by both Napoleon's empresses, he designed bridal suite for Empress Marie Louise. Paintings, *eg Venus and Adonis*, influenced the Romantics.

prune, plum that has been dried

without fermentation taking place. Prepared mainly on Pacific coast of US.

Prussia (Preussen), hist. region and former state of Germany. Comprised much of NE Germany, cap. Berlin. Teutonic Knights conquered heathen Prussians in 13th cent.; their territ. became hereditary duchy in 16th cent. and passed to electors of Brandenburg (1618). Kingdom of Prussia was created from Brandenburg dominions in 1701. Frederick the Great (1740-86) began period of expansion, acquiring Silesia and W parts of Poland. Further territ. gains made after Napoleonic Wars. Under Bismarck, assumed leadership of German states (1860s); William I of Prussia became 1st emperor of Germany (1871). Reduced in size after WWI. Dissolved (1947) after WWII.

prussic acid, see HYDROCYANIC ACID.

Przewalski's horse, *Equus caballus przewalskii*, only surviving wild horse, confined to Mongolia and Sinkiang. Tan coloured with black mane; stands c 1.4m/4.5 ft at shoulders.

Psalms, poetical book of OT, traditionally attributed to David. Prob. by many authors and collected 6th-1st cent. BC.

pseudepigrapha, group of early writings not incl. in Biblical canon or Apocrypha, some of which were falsely ascribed to Biblical characters. Composed c 200 BC-c AD 400 in Hebrew, Aramaic and Greek. Incl. fragments allegedly written by Jesus, most of the Disciples, Pilate among others.

Pskov, city of USSR, W European

RSFSR; near L. Peipus. Pop. 131,000. Centre of flax-growing region; linen mfg. Important medieval town; cap. of powerful commercial city state (1348-1510) until annexed by Moscow. Scene of abdication of Nicholas II (1917).

Psyche, in Greek myth, a beautiful girl and the personification of human soul, loved by Cupid. He forbade her to look at him but she disobeyed and he left her. After a long search, she was made immortal and united with him forever.

psychiatry, medical study and treatment of disorders of the mind, incl. psychosis, neurosis. Gained prominence in late 19th cent., esp. with Freud's development of psychoanalysis.

psychical research, study of supernormal phenomena. Estab. as serious study by British Society for Psychical Research (founded 1882), which investigated mediums, poltergeists, etc. Extra-sensory perception (ESP), ie telepathy, precognition, has been subject of research in 20th cent., eg by J.B. Rhine.

psychoanalysis, term coined by Freud to denote system of psychology and method of treatment of mental disorders (see NEUROSIS). Lays emphasis on importance of unconscious mind, inducing its expression and evading conscious mind's censorship through analytic techniques of free association, dream interpretation.

psychology, science of the mind, more specifically the studies of all interactions between living organisms (esp. humans) and the environment. Allied to biological and sociological sciences, but distinguished by its concentration on individual's behaviour, both through mental and emotional processes. Specific concerns are abnormal behaviour, cognition and cognitive development, etc; modes of approach incl. PSYCHO-ANALYSIS, BEHAVIOURISM, GESTALT.

psychosis, name given to certain severe mental disorders which involve loss of contact with reality. Functional psychoses, without apparent organic cause, are mainly of schizophrenic or manic-depressive type; organic psychoses are caused by brain damage or disease.

psychosomatic disease, physical disorder of body resulting from disturbance of the mind. Asthma, duodenal ulcers, high blood pressure, certain heart disorders, etc, are considered partly psychosomatic in origin.

psychotherapy, treatment of mental disorder by psychological means, involving communication between trained person and patient. Methods incl. suggestion, hypnosis and psychoanalysis.

ptarmigan, bird of grouse family, genus Lagopus, of mountains of N hemisphere. Toes and legs feathered; winter plumage is white. Species incl. willow ptarmigan, L. lagopus, and rock ptarmigan, L. mutus.

Pteridophyta, division of plants comprising fern, horsetail and club moss groups. Incl. many ancient fossil varieties.

pterodactyl, any of order Pterosauria of extinct flying reptiles of Mesozoic era. Membranous wings stretched between hind limb and greatly elongated fourth digit of forelimb.

Ptolemy I [Soter] (d. 284 BC), Macedonian general under Alexander the Great. Given control of Egypt during partition of Alexander's empire, he held it against rival DIADOCHI (305). Estab. new Egyptian dynasty. Descendant, **Ptolemy XII** (d. 47 BC), ruled Egypt jointly with sister (and wife) Cleopatra. Forced by Caesar to accept her reinstatement after he had deprived her of power. Drowned in Nile. His brother, **Ptolemy XIII** (d. 44 BC), was then made joint ruler with Cleopatra by Caesar. She had him murdered.

Ptolemy or **Claudius Ptolemaus** (fl AD 140), Greco-Egyptian astronomer, geographer. Systematized work of Greek astronomers, esp. Hipparchus, in his *Almagest*. Described geocentric solar system in which Sun and planets revolved in circular orbits about stationary Earth; influential until superseded by works of Copernicus. Also wrote *Geography* incl. atlas of maps of known world.

puberty, stage of child's development when sexual maturity begins. Generally, age 11-14 in girls and 12-16 in boys. Hormones from pituitary gland stimulate gonads to form fertile sperm or ova and to secrete hormones which control secondary sex characteristics. In girls, 1st menstrual period signifies onset of puberty.

public ownership, another term for NATIONALIZATION.

public school, in UK, secondary school, run on fee-paying (private) basis and having academic curriculum. Famous examples incl. boys' boarding schools Eton, Harrow, Winchester. Elsewhere, public schools are free to all pupils at primary or secondary levels. Financed usually by public taxes and supervised by local authorities.

publishing, trade concerned with creation and distribution of books and other reading matter. Closely allied to printing and bookselling. Narrowly defined, involves preparation of author's work for chosen market. Introduction of movable type (15th cent.) facilitated large-scale distribution of reading material.

Puccini, Giacomo (1858-1924), Italian composer. Renowned for operas *Manon Lescaut*, *La Bohème*, *Tosca*, *Madame Butterfly* and *Turandot*. Combined great dramatic expression with strong melody to create some of the most moving operas ever written.

Puebla, city of C Mexico, cap. of Puebla state. Pop. 522,000. Onyx quarrying, cotton milling, pottery industs. Has one of finest cathedrals in Mexico (1649); Teatro Principal (one of oldest Latin American theatres); univ. (1537).

Pueblo, group of North American Indian tribes of various language families, living in SW US. Distinguished by custom of living in adobe communal longhouses (*pueblos*). Reached highest level of civilization N of Mexico, esp. in agric., sand paintings, pottery etc. Successfully resisted Spanish colonization in 17th cent. Groups incl. Hopi, Zuni. Some 20,000 still live on reservations in Arizona, New Mexico.

puerperal fever, infection by bacteria of womb after childbirth. Caused many deaths in 19th cent.

until Ignaz Semmelweis introduced disinfection of midwives' hands.

Puerto Rico, isl. territ. of US, E West Indies, in Greater Antilles. Area 8871 sq km (3425 sq mi); pop. 3,213,000, one of highest pop. densities in world; cap. San Juan. Languages: Spanish, English. Religion: RC. Mainly mountainous; tropical climate. Fertile agric. soil (sugar cane, tobacco growing). Settled by Spanish (1508), ceded to US after 1898 war. Became 'Commonwealth' 1952. Much emigration to US because of unemployment.

puff adder, *Bitis arietans*, highly poisonous viper common in tropical Africa. Short tail, yellow markings on body; reaches lengths of *c* 1.2 m/4 ft.

puffball or **smokeball**, spherical fungus which breaks open when ripe to emit dust-like spores. Common puffball is *Lycoperdon perlatum*.

puffer, tropical fish of Tetraodontidae family. Skin covered with small prickles erected when body is inflated with air or water. Edible if expertly prepared; otherwise poisonous.

puffin, *Fratercula arctica*, small marine bird with black and white plumage. Triangular beak banded with blue, red and yellow. Breeds colonially on Atlantic coasts, nesting in burrows.

pug, breed of small dog, probably of Chinese origin. Broad flat nose, curled tail; stands *c* 28 cm/11 in. at shoulder.

Pugin, Augustus Welby Northmore (1812-52), English architect, writer. Influential advocate of Gothic revival in writings, *eg Contrasts* (1836). Designed fittings

and ornamental details for Barry's Houses of Parliament.

Puglia, *see* APULIA, Italy.

Pulitzer, Joseph (1847-1911), American newspaper owner, b. Hungary. Acquired and built up New York *World*, owned *Post-Dispatch*, which was maintained by his son and grandson in liberal tradition. Founded (1903) the School of Journalism at Columbia Univ., left funds for the Pulitzer Prizes, awarded each year since 1917 for achievements in journalism, letters and musical compositions.

Pullman dispute, strike over wage cuts (1894) by railway sleeping car workers at Pullman model community (now a Chicago suburb). Union leader Eugene Debs jailed; President Cleveland sent federal troops to quell strike despite opposition from Illinois govt.

pulsar, heavenly body which emits short pulses of radio waves at regular intervals. First detected 1967. An optical pulsar is in Crab nebula. Believed to be a rotating neutron star, remnant of supernova explosion.

pulse, in physiology, wave of arterial expansion caused by beating of heart. Normal rate in adults is *c* 60-70 beats per min.

puma, *Felis concolor*, large member of cat family, ranging from Argentina to Canada. Yellowish-brown short fur, slender build. Called cougar or mountain lion in North America.

pumice, *see* LAVA.

pump, machine for raising, transferring or increasing the pressure of water or other fluids (incl. gases). In ancient times the screw type was used for irrigation purposes. Various types exist now, incl. reciprocating, gear and centrifugal pumps.

pumpkin or squash, *Cucurbita pepo,* annual vine with large, round, edible fruit. Native to North America, widely cultivated. Name also given to similar plants of genus *Cucurbita,* eg *C. maxima* and musk pumpkin, *C. moschata.*

Punch and Judy, puppet play introduced to England in 17th cent., prob. derived from Italian *commedia dell'arte.* Characters incl. murderous hunchback, Punch, and nagging wife, Judy.

Punic Wars, series of conflicts between Rome and Carthage for dominance of Mediterranean. First Punic War (264-241 BC) resulted in acquisition of Sicily by Rome. During 2nd Punic War (218-201 BC), Hannibal invaded Italy but could not capture Rome. Forced to return to Carthage, he was defeated at Zama by Scipio Africanus Major (202). Third Punic War (149-146 BC), instigated by Roman fears of Carthaginian commercial power, led to total destruction of Carthage by Scipio Africanus Minor.

Punjab, state of N India. Area *c* 75,600 sq km (29,200 sq mi); pop; 13,473,000; cap. Chandigarh. Hist. region of Punjab dominated by Sikhs in 19th cent.; annexed by Britain after Sikh Wars (1845-9). At partition, W Punjab became Pakistani prov. Indian prov. of E Punjab later divided (1966) into states of Haryana (Hindi-speaking) and Punjab (Punjabi-speaking).

Punjabi, Indic language in Indo-Iranian branch of Indo-European family. Spoken in NW India and Pakistan. Close to W Hindi, Urdu.

Punta Arenas, port of S Chile, on Magellan Str. Pop. 65,000. World's most S city. Wool, lamb exports. Coal mining nearby.

pupa, third stage of development of insect undergoing complete metamorphosis. Involves anatomical changes, often occurring in cocoon or cell. Adult emerges after pupa stage.

pupil, in anatomy, circular opening in centre of iris of eye. Size of pupil varies with intensity of light and is affected by adrenaline in the blood and drugs such as belladonna.

puppet, small figure of human or animal made to perform on miniature stage by unseen operator who speaks dialogue. Types incl. marionette, controlled by wires, and 'glove' puppet. Puppet shows have great antiquity, being familiar in 5th cent. BC Greece. Now mainly restricted to performances for children.

Purbeck, Isle of, penin. of Dorset, S England. Purbeck marble (limestone) quarried.

Purcell, Henry (1659-95), English composer, organist of Chapel Royal. Works incl. opera *Dido and Aeneas,* music for *The Fairy Queen, King Arthur,* as well as songs, instrumental and church music (esp. anthems).

purgative, drug given to induce bowel movement. Vegetable purgatives incl. senna, rhubarb, bran; mineral salts used incl. magnesium sulphate (Epsom salts).

purgatory, in RC and Eastern Orthodox theology, place where those who have died in grace of God expiate their unatoned sins by suffering. Suffering can be lessened by prayers of living. Protestants reject this doctrine.

Purim, Jewish festival commemorating deliverance of Jews by Esther from a massacre. Celebrated on 14 Adar (usually mid-March) with carnivals and feasting.

Puritanism, social and theological movement in Protestantism in Britain and America. Arose out of pressure for reform of religious establishment (16th cent.). Influenced by Calvinist theory and aimed at less ritualistic forms of worship. By 17th cent., had separated from Church of England, and opposed Charles I, precipitating Civil War (1640s). Puritanism taken by colonists to New England, where it exerted a great influence on society.

Puritan Revolution, conflict (1603-49) between English kings James I, Charles I and predominantly Puritan Parliament. Arose partly out of kings' advocacy of govt. by 'divine right', disputed by Parliament, which itself claimed sovereignty. Culminated in Civil War, execution of Charles I and estab. of Protectorate.

Purple Heart, Order of the, oldest US military award. Instituted in 1782 by George Washington (1782).

purslane, *Portulaca oleracea,* annual herb native to India. Fleshy, succulent leaves sometimes used as salad or pot herb.

Purus, river of NC South America. Rises in E Peru, flows NE 3380 km (*c* 2100 mi) across Brazil through tropical rain forest to the Amazon SW of Manáus,

pus, thick yellowish-white substance produced as result of bacterial inflammation. Composed of white blood cells, tissue fluid, bacteria and dead tissue.

Pusan, seaport of SE South Korea, on Korea Str. Pop. 1,881,000. Largest Korean port; indust., commercial centre; railway engineering, shipbuilding; produces iron and steel, textiles. UN supply base in Korean War.

Pusey, Edward Bouverie (1800-82), English clergyman, leader in OXFORD MOVEMENT. Helped Newman and Keble with *Tracts for the Times* from 1834. Remained Anglican, delivering sermons that checked moves to RC church.

Pushkin, Aleksandr Sergeyevich (1799-1837), Russian author. Best-known works incl. verse-novel *Eugene Onegin* (1831), tragedy *Boris Godunov* (1831). Poetry incl. Byronic lyrics, narrative poem, *The Bronze Horseman* (1833). Also wrote short story cycle, *Tales of Belkin* (1830). Had great influence on subsequent Russian literature.

Putney, see WANDSWORTH, England.

Putumayo, river of NW South America. Rises in Colombian Andes, flows E 1600 km (*c* 1000 mi) forming Colombia-Peru border, then into Brazil to join Amazon as the Içá.

Puvis de Chavannes, Pierre (1824-98), French painter. Developed style of monumental decorative painting. Specialized in allegorical themes or subjects from antiquity. Decorated many public buildings in France; admired by Gauguin, Seurat.

Puy, Le, see LE PUY, France.

Pu-Yi, Henry (1906-67), last Chinese emperor (1908-12). Member of Ch'ing dynasty, he ruled as Hsuan Tung. Later, served as emperor (1934-45) of Japanese puppet state of Manchukuo. Handed over to Chinese Communists (1950), he was imprisoned until 1959.

PVC, see POLYVINYL CHLORIDE.

Pygmalion, in Greek myth, king of Cyprus. Made ivory statue, Galatea. When he fell in love with it Aphrodite brought statue to life and he married her.

Pygmy or **Pigmy,** diminutive, c 1.5 m (5 ft), Negroid people of Africa, Malaysia and New Guinea. Sometimes called Negrillos (Africa) or Negritos (Far East). Generally hunters and food gatherers living in small nomadic bands in scrub regions.

pygmy hippopotamus, see HIPPOPOTAMUS.

Pylos (*Pilos*), town of Greece, in SW Peloponnese. Scene of Athenian victory (425 BC) over Sparta and of battle of Navarino (1827) in which British, French and Russian fleet defeated Turks, Egyptians. Ruined Mycenaean palace (13th cent. BC).

Pym, John (c 1583-1643), English politician. Led Puritan opposition to Charles I in Parliament; instrumental in drawing up Petition of Right (1628). In the Long Parliament, moved impeachment of Strafford and Laud. One of the five members of Commons whom Charles tried to arrest (1642).

Pynchon, Thomas (1937-), American novelist. Works, eg *V.* (1963), *The Crying of Lot 49* (1966), *Gravity's Rainbow* (1973), use wide-ranging erudition to communicate a paranoid fictive world.

Pyongyang, cap. of North Korea. Pop. 1,500,000. Indust. centre of coal, iron region. Mfg., heavy engineering. Rebuilt after destruction of Korean War.

pyorrhoea, any discharge of pus. Name usually applies to *Pyorrhoea alveolaris,* infection of gums and teeth sockets, usually leading to loosening of teeth.

pyramid, in ancient Egypt, monumental stone structure with square base and triangular sides, meeting at an apex. Erected as tombs for kings of Egypt, great period of pyramid building was c 2700-2300 BC. Three famous pyramids at Giza incl. Great Pyramid of Khufu (Cheops), one of Seven Wonders of the ancient World.

Pyramids, Battle of the, defeat by Napoleon (July, 1798) soon after his invasion of Egypt, of an army of 60,000 Mamelukes. Briefly gave him control of the area until Nelson destroyed his fleet at Aboukir.

Pyramus and **Thisbe,** in classical myth, Babylonian lovers. Pyramus, mistakenly thinking Thisbe had been killed by a lion, killed himself. When Thisbe found his body, she took her own life with his sword.

Pyrenees (Sp. *Pirineos*), mountain range of SW France, NE Spain. Extend from Bay of Biscay to Mediterranean. Higher in C, E, rise to 3403 m (11,168 ft) at Pico de Aneto. Passes incl. Roncesvalles. Incl. Andorra enclave. Tourism, mining.

Pyrenees, Peace of the, treaty ending fighting between France and Spain (1659). By its terms, Louis XIV was to marry daughter of Philip IV of Spain; Spain gave Roussillon and parts of Flanders to France. Franco-Spanish border estab. at Pyrenees.

pyrethrum, *Chrysanthemum coccineum,* perennial plant native to Persia and Caucasus. Widely cultivated in temperate regions for red, pink or white flowers and commercially for insecticide pyrethrum powder extracted from dried flower heads.

pyrite or **iron pyrites** (FeS_2), yellow mineral, consisting of iron sulphide. Most widespread sulphide mineral; often mistaken for gold (nicknamed 'fool's gold'). Source of iron and sulphur.

pyroclastic rock, fragmented volcanic material thrown into atmosphere by explosive activity. May be solid when ejected or liquid solidified by contact with air. Size ranges from dust to large blocks; incl. pumice.

pyrometer, instrument used to measure temperatures beyond range of normal thermometers. Various types incl. platinum resistance thermometer which utilizes change in resistance with temperature.

pyroxenes, group of rock-forming minerals, composed mainly of silicates of calcium, iron and magnesium.

Pyrrho (*c* 365-270 BC), Greek philosopher. Founder of SCEPTICISM. Taught that every proposition could be maintained or contradicted with equal plausibility, thus knowledge must always be in question.

Pyrrhus (*c* 318-272 BC), king of Epirus (295-272 BC). Invaded Italy (281) to aid Tarentum against Rome. Sustained heavy losses in 2 victories over Romans (hence term 'Pyrrhic victory') before defeat at Beneventum (275).

Pythagoras (*c* 582-*c* 507 BC), Greek philosopher, b. Samos. Founded religious brotherhood at Crotona. Held that all relationships could be expressed in numbers. Made discoveries in musical intonations. Influenced subsequent work of Euclid. Believed Earth revolved around fixed point ('hearth') of universe.

Pytheas (*fl* 4th cent. BC), Greek navigator. Explored W coast of Europe, travelled through Britain, visiting 'Thule', prob. Shetlands.

Pythia, in Greek religion, priestess and oracular prophetess of Apollo at Delphi. Uttered prophecies in a trance. These were interpreted to the questioner by a priest.

Pythian games, in ancient Greece, games held at Delphi every 4 years in honour of Apollo. Incl. athletic, literary and musical contests.

python, any of Pythonidae family of constrictor snakes, of Old World tropics. Reaches lengths of 9.1 m/30 ft. Lays eggs, unlike boas.

Q

'Q', *see* QUILLER-COUCH, SIR ARTHUR THOMAS.

Qaddhafi or **Gadafy, Muammar al-** (1942-), Libyan political leader. Gained power after military coup overthrowing King Idris (1969). Fostered Arab unity; failed in attempt to unite Egypt and Libya (1973). Used Libyan oil wealth to support revolutionary movements, esp. Palestinian guerrillas.

Qâhira, El, *see* CAIRO, Egypt.

Qatar, penin. of E Arabia, in Persian Gulf. Area *c* 11,400 sq km (4400 sq mi); pop. 180,000; cap. Doha (pop. 130,000). Oil reserves. Sheikdom under British protection until 1971. Allied with United Arab Emirates.

Qattara Depression, arid region of N Egypt, in Libyan Desert. Area *c* 18,130 sq km (7000 sq mi); falls to 133 m (436 ft) below sea level, lowest point in Africa. Has extensive salt marsh. Formed S part of Allied defence line at El Alamein (1942).

Quadruple Alliance, (1) league formed (1718) by Britain, France, Austria and Netherlands to prevent Spain from nullifying terms of Peace of Utrecht. Spain renounced claims to Austrian territ. in Italy in settlement of 1720. (2) alliance formed (1814) by Austria, Britain, Prussia and Russia to strengthen coalition against Napoleon.

quagga, *Equus quagga,* extinct South African zebra. Excessively hunted for hide in 19th cent.

quail, any of various small migratory game birds. Only European species is *Coturnix coturnix,* which winters in Africa. North American species incl. BOBWHITE.

Quakers, *see* SOCIETY OF FRIENDS.

Quant, Mary (1934-), English fashion and cosmetic designer. Revolutionized fashion in 1960s, making London a leading fashion centre. Popular lines, made for a youthful market, incl. 'mini' skirt.

quantum theory, physical theory introduced by Planck that radiation is emitted and absorbed not continuously but only in multiples of indivisible units (quanta). Extended by Einstein to explain photoelectric effect and by Bohr to explain atomic spectra. In 1920s, developed into mathematical theory of wave mechanics which explains many phenomena of atomic physics.

quarantine, restriction of movements on people and animals who may have been exposed to infectious diseases. Arose in 14th cent. Europe as an attempt to control spread of plague through ports such as Venice and Rhodes. Often applied to animals to prevent spread of foot-and-mouth disease, rabies, *etc.*

quarks, hypothetical elementary particles, introduced by M. Gell-Mann and G. Zweig, which serve as building blocks for all strongly-interacting elementary particles (hadrons). Originally **3** quarks, bearing charges which are fractions of that on electron, were introduced; more may be needed to explain new phenomena.

quarrying, removal of building stone, granite, marble, slate, *etc,* from surface deposits. Stone in broken or crushed form, used for cement, road making and concrete aggregate, is removed by drilling and blasting. Blocks of stone suitable for building and ornamental work are machine cut.

quartz, commonest mineral, consisting of silicon dioxide (SiO_2). Hard, normally colourless and transparent; coloured by impurities. Varieties incl. agate, amethyst, chalcedony, onyx. Used in jewellery, electronics, lenses and prisms.

quartzite, hard metamorphic rock, consisting of firmly cemented quartz grains. Normally light-coloured; may be darker due to mineral impurities. Formed by metamorphism of pure quartz sandstone.

quasars (quasi stellar radio sources), extragalactic sources of immense quantities of light or radio waves. Observed red shift of their spectral lines suggests they are receding at velocity close to that of light.

Quasimodo, Salvatore (1901-68), Italian poet. Early works, *eg Waters and Land* (1929), reflect occult, hermetic interests. *The Promised Land and Other Poems* (1958) marks preoccupation with social, political issues. Nobel Prize for Literature (1959).

Quaternary period, second and current geological period of Cenozoic era. Began c 2 million years ago. Comprises Pleistocene and Holocene (or Recent) epochs. Deterioration of climate, begun in Tertiary, led to extensive glaciations; followed by warmer climate, formation of modern landscape *eg* lakes, deserts. Development of man from primitive ape-like creature to present form. Also *see* GEOLOGICAL TABLE.

Quathlamba, see DRAKENSBERG MOUNTAINS.

Québec or **Quebec,** prov. of E Canada, incl. Anticosti, Magdalen isls. in Gulf of St Lawrence. Area 1,553,640 sq km (594,860 sq mi); pop. 6,028,000; cap. Québec; largest city Montréal. Bounded in N by Hudson, Ungava bays. Resources in Laurentians (timber, asbestos, aluminium, iron ore, h.e.p.). St Lawrence R. valley is agric., indust. base. French landed 1534; settled region as New France in 17th cent.; British gained control 1763; named Lower Canada 1791; became one of original 4 provs. of Canada (1867). French language and customs retained. Separatist movement grew from 1960s.

Québec or **Quebec City,** cap. and major port of Québec prov., Canada; on St Lawrence R. Pop. 186,000, mainly French speaking. Timber produce and exports, shipbuilding, clothing mfg. Port icebound in winter. French settlement under Champlain (1608); cap. of New France until British defeat of French on Plains of Abraham (1759); cap. of Lower Canada (1791). Has Citadel, Laval Univ. (1852).

Quebec Act, legislation passed

(1774) by British parliament. Extended W boundaries of Québec, estab. French civil law in Québec and granted religious freedom to French-Canadians. Intended to estab. permanent British admin. in Canada; opposed by American colonies.

Québecois, Parti, see LÉVESQUE, RENÉ.

Queen Anne's lace, see CARROT.

Queen Charlotte Islands, archipelago of W British Columbia, Canada; separated from mainland by Hecate Str. Timber, fishing insducts. Haida Indian pop. Largest of group is Graham Isl.; area 6436 sq km (2485 sq mi).

Queen Maud Land, see NORWEGIAN ANTARCTIC TERRITORY.

Queen's, see NEW YORK CITY.

Queensberry, John Sholto Douglas, 9th Marquess of (1844-1900), Scottish nobleman. Patron of the rules of modern gloved boxing drafted by John Chambers (1867).

Queen's Counsel, see BARRISTER.

Queensland, state of NE Australia. Area 1,727,500 sq km (667,000 sq mi); pop. 1,823,000; cap. Brisbane. Great Dividing Range parallels coast, incl. Darling Downs (S), Atherton Tableland (N); Great Artesian Basin in SW; Barrier Reef off shore. Sugar cane, fruit growing; timber indust.; beef cattle raising; mining, esp. copper, lead, bauxite, oil. Penal settlement estab. 1824 at Moreton Bay; Queensland became colony (1859), federal state (1901).

Queenston Heights, Battle of, decisive confrontation in War of 1812 in which American invasion force was defeated by British on Niagara frontier, Canada. British

commander, Isaac Brock, was killed in action.

Queneau, Raymond (1903-76), French author. Known for humorous novels, *Skin of Dreams* (1944), *Zazie* (1959); surrealist-inspired verse, *eg Petite cosmogonie portative* (1950).

Quesnay, François (1694-1774), French economist. Founder of the PHYSIOCRATS. Wrote *Tableau économique* (1758).

quetzal, crested bird of Trogonidae family, of forests of Central America. Green and red plumage, with long tail feathers. Species incl. resplendent quetzal, *Pharomachrus mocino*.

Quetzalcoatl, principal god of Toltecs, and subsequently, Aztecs. Credited with discovery of arts and sciences. Represented as plumed serpent.

Quevedo [y Villegas], Francisco Gómez de (1580-1645), Spanish author. Known for cynical picaresque novel *Vida del Buscón*, (1626), satires in *Los Sueños* (1627). Also wrote many short verse satires.

Quezon City, cap. of Philippines, C Luzon isl. Pop. 896,000. Replaced nearby Manila as cap. 1948. Largely residential; textile mfg.

quicksand, deposit of loose, fine-grained saturated sand particles. May engulf heavy object. Often found near river mouths, along sea shores.

quicksilver, see MERCURY.

quietism, form of Christian mysticism which holds that union with God is achieved through complete passivity of soul, annihilation of will and cessation of self-consciousness. Founded (1675) by Spanish priest,

MOLINOS. Condemned (1687) by Pope Innocent XI.

Quiller-Couch, Sir Arthur Thomas (1863-1944), English author. Wrote short stories, novels, *eg The Ship of Stars* (1899), under pseud. 'Q'. Edited *Oxford Book of English Verse* (1900). Known for literary criticism, *eg On the Art of Reading* (1920).

Quimper, town of Brittany, NW France, cap. of Finistère dept. Pop. 58,000. Pottery (Quimper or Brittany ware), tourism. Cathedral (13th cent.).

quince, *Cydonia oblongata*, small tree native to Asia. Bears bitter, yellow, pear-shaped fruit used in preserves.

quinine, crystalline alkaloid extracted from cinchona bark. Introduced into Europe from South America, it was formerly used in treatment of malaria.

Quintilian, full name Marcus Fabius Quintilianus (c AD 35-c 95), Roman rhetorician, b. Spain. Author of instruction course on public speaking, *Institutio oratoria*, in 12 books. First 2 books give much information on Roman education.

Quisling, Vidkun (1887-1945), Norwegian fascist leader. Collaborated in German invasion of Norway (1940); headed subsequent puppet govt. after 1942. Shot for treason after War. Name became synonymous with traitor.

Quito, cap. of Ecuador at foot of Pichincha volcano, near the equator. Alt. 2850 m (9350 ft). Pop. 528,000. Brewing, flour milling, major textile mfg. Indian settlement before Spanish conquest (1534). Has univ. (1787); many famous churches.

Qumran, W Jordan, site of discovery of Dead Sea Scrolls (1947). Originally iron-age fort, occupied (2nd cent. BC) by monastic community until AD 68. Dead Sea Scrolls comprise their library.

quoits, outdoor game in which an iron ring is thrown at a peg in an attempt to encircle it. Known in England since 14th cent. Horseshoe pitching, popular in US, is a similar game.

R

Ra, ancient Egyptian sun god. Represented as hawk, lion. Sailed across sky in barge during day. Early Egyptian kings claimed descent from him.

Rabat, cap. of Morocco, at mouth of Bou Regreg. Pop., incl. nearby Salé, 534,000. Admin. centre; textile, carpet industs. Ancient walled town with 12th cent. Hassan Tower. Former cap. of French Morocco (1912-56).

rabbi (Heb.,=my master), originally a scholar and teacher of the Jewish law. Now refers to those trained and ordained as spiritual heads of congregations. Duties incl. deciding matters pertaining to marriage and kosher laws.

rabbit, *Oryctolagus cuniculus,* burrowing European mammal of hare family, order Lagomorpha. Smaller and less swift than hare; lives in large groups. Serious pest of farmland, its great fertility makes control difficult. Domestic varieties sometimes bred for fur.

Rabelais, François (c 1494-1553), French author. Wrote satirical romance, *Gargantua and Pantagruel* (5 vol., 1532-64, last 2 vol. perhaps not by Rabelais), narrating adventures of giant and son in search of wisdom, experience. Also contain passages on education, politics, philosophy.

rabies or **hydrophobia,** infectious virus disease of mammals, affecting brain and spinal cord. Transmitted in saliva of infected animals, usually by biting; symptoms incl. fever, delirium, muscle spasms, inability to drink, paralysis. Incubation period 10 days to several months. No known treatment; early administration of vaccine usually effective.

Rabin, Yitzhak (1922-), Israeli political leader, soldier. Premier (1974-77). Resigned from premiership and leadership of Labour party over financial scandal.

raccoon, *Procyon lotor,* medium-sized North American mammal, with mask-like facial markings and black ringed tail. Nocturnal, largely arboreal; classed as carnivore, it is omnivorous, immersing all food in water before eating.

race, in biology, term used to denote subspecies or variety of species, differing slightly in characteristics from typical species member.

Rachmaninov, Sergei Vasilyevich (1873-1943), Russian composer, pianist. Works, highly romantic in style, incl. symphonies, concertos, piano music, eg *Preludes.* The *Rhapsody on a Theme of Paganini* for piano and orchestra is esp. popular. Lived mainly in US after 1917.

Racine, Jean (1639-99), French dramatist. Famous for classical tragedies of passion, *Andromaque* (1667), *Iphigénie en Aulide* (1674),

Phèdre (1677). Also wrote comedy satirizing legal system, *Les Plaideurs* (1668).

rackets or **racquets**, ball-and-racket game played on enclosed court by 2 or 4 persons. Ball is struck against end-wall. Modern form developed in England in 19th cent.; SQUASH RACKETS is variant played on smaller court.

Rackham, Arthur (1867-1939), English watercolour painter and illustrator. Known for his illustrations of books, esp. children's books, eg *Peter Pan* (1906), *Alice in Wonderland* (1907).

radar, system employing transmitted and reflected radio waves to detect presence of objects and determine their position, distance, height or speed. Also used for navigation in ships, aircraft.

Radcliffe, Ann, née Ward (1764-1823), English novelist. Known for 'gothick' romances, esp. *The Mysteries of Udolpho* (1794).

Radcliffe-Brown, Alfred Reginald (1881-1955), British social anthropologist. Attempted to develop general laws for social investigation using concept of 'function'. Wrote *The Andaman Islanders* (1922).

radiant energy, energy which is transmitted in form of electromagnetic energy, eg heat, light, X-rays. Radiant heat can be communicated from source to observer through a vacuum or intervening medium without heating it.

radiation, see ELECTROMAGNETIC RADIATION.

radiation sickness, disease resulting from exposure to uncontrolled radiation, esp. X-rays or that resulting from nuclear explosions. Effects incl. genetic damage, cancer of skin and blood cells, etc.

radical, in chemistry, group of 2 or more atoms that acts as single unit and maintains its identity in chemical reactions; usually incapable of independent existence.

radio, transmission of electric signals by means of electromagnetic radiation generated by high-frequency alternating current. Maxwell postulated existence of radio waves (1873) and Hertz demonstrated their existence (1888); Marconi demonstrated their use in communication (1895).

radioactive dating, determination of age of objects or materials by estimation of its content of radioactive isotopes. Radioactive carbon 14, produced in the atmosphere by action of cosmic rays and absorbed into living tissue, is used to estimate age of archaeological specimens.

radioactivity, spontaneous disintegration of atomic nuclei of certain elements said to be radioactive, eg radium, uranium, thorium. Accompanied by emission of alpha or beta particles and possibly gamma rays. Radioactivity can be induced in elements not naturally radioactive by neutron bombardment in nuclear reactor.

radio astronomy, study of heavenly bodies by analysis of radio waves which they emit. These radio waves were first detected by Jansky (1932). Emission sources incl. bodies too distant for optical observation as well as non-luminous or dark stars, and larger bodies in Solar System, eg Sun, Jupiter.

radiography, use of X-rays to produce images on photographic material. Used in medicine and industry.

radiology, use of radiation in diagnosis and treatment of disease. X-rays are used to photograph living bone and tissue and also to destroy abnormal cells (eg cancer cells). Gamma rays from cobalt 60 also used to cure cancer.

radio range, system of application of radio to marine and air navigation. Usually consists of unattended 'beacons' emitting ʃ a constant, identifiable radio signal. Ships and aircraft may take bearings on the beacon (using a receiver with a directionally sensitive antenna) and plot their position.

radish, *Raphanus sativus,* annual plant of mustard family, native to Europe and Asia. Pungent, fleshy root eaten raw as relish.

Radisson, Pierre Esprit (c 1632-1710), French fur trader in North America. Explored Lake Superior and Minnesota. Later worked for the English, voyaging to Hudson Bay for furs (1668). His successful mission led to formation of Hudson's Bay Co. (chartered 1670).

radium (Ra), naturally occurring radioactive element; at. no. 88, mass no. of most stable isotope 226. Occurs in pitchblende and other uranium ores; formed by disintegration of uranium 238. Discovered (1898) by the Curies. Used to treat cancer and in luminous paints.

Radnorshire, former county of EC Wales, now in Powys. Mountainous, incl. Radnor Forest. Sheep rearing; reservoirs. Co. town was Presteigne.

Radom, city of EC Poland. Pop. 161,000. Railway jct., agric. machinery mfg. Ancient settlement. New Radom founded 14th cent. by Casimir the Great; seat of Polish diets 14th-16th cent. Under Russian rule 1815-1919.

radon (Rn), radioactive gaseous element; at. no. 86, mass no. of most stable isotope 222. Formed as immediate disintegration product of radium; one of the inert gases.

Raeburn, Sir Henry (1756-1823), Scottish painter. Influenced by Reynolds, he portrayed many of the leading personalities of Scotland. Works incl. *The Macnab* (1803-13).

Raffles, Sir Thomas Stamford (1781-1826), British colonial official. Served with East India Co.; masterminded capture of Java from the Dutch (1811). As lieutenant governor of Java (1811-16), reorganized its admin. and commerce. Acquired Singapore (1819) and began its settlement.

ragged robin, *Lychnis flos-cuculi,* slender perennial herb native to Europe and N Asia. Pink flowers with ragged-looking petals. Also called cuckoo flower.

Raglan, Fitzroy James Henry Somerset, 1st Baron (1788-1855), British army officer. Served on Wellington's staff at Waterloo (1815). Commanded the British expeditionary force in the Crimea, where he won the battle of Inkerman (1854); blamed for the failure to take Sevastopol.

Ragnarok, in Norse myth, destruction of world in last great battle between the Gods and forces of chaos led by Loki and giants. Would start with ice age and lead to new golden age.

ragtime, style of piano music using syncopated melodic lines over rigid march-like bass. Introduced in 1890s, became widely popular; lost popularity to jazz in 1920s. Principal composer of rags was Scott Joplin.

ragweed, any of genus *Ambrosia* of plants of daisy family, native to North America. Pollen of common ragweed or hogweed, *A. artemisiifolia*, and great ragweed, *A. trifida,* is a major cause of hay fever.

ragworm, annelid worm of Nereidae family, order Polychaeta. Largely marine, living under stones or burrowing in mud and sand. Commonly used for bait.

ragwort, *see* GROUNDSEL.

Rahman [Putra], Tunku Abdul (1903-), Malaysian politician, PM (1963-70). First PM of Malaya at independence (1957). Advised formation of Malaysia federation (created 1963).

rail, marsh bird of Rallidae family, with short wings and tail. Species incl. water rail, *Rallus aquaticus,* of Europe and Asia, noted for piercing cry.

railway, transport system running on fixed rails. Early railways were developed for use in mines. Important innovations incl. introduction of iron rails in 18th cent. and building of 1st locomotive to run on rails (Trevithick, 1804). Stockton-Darlington line (1825) was 1st to carry passengers regularly, and Liverpool-Manchester line (1830) was 1st to use steam locomotives exclusively. In US, Baltimore and Ohio Railroad (1830), operated at first by horses, was 1st public

railway. Railway had important part in development of W North America. In 20th cent., steam gave way to electric and diesel power. Modern developments incl. high-speed trains, *eg* those running between Tokyo and Osaka in Japan, and between Edinburgh and London in UK.

rain, drops of condensed atmospheric water vapour brought to earth by force of gravity. Varieties incl.: orographic, found in mountain areas; cyclonic, associated with depressions; convectional, common in equatorial regions. Rain can be artificially produced by 'seeding' clouds with silver iodide crystals.

rainbow, arc of colours of SPECTRUM seen in sky during rainy weather. Caused by reflection and refraction of sunlight through raindrops. Primary rainbow has red on outside, violet on inside. Secondary rainbow, in which colours are reversed, formed by 2 internal reflections.

Raine, Kathleen Jessie (1908-), English poet. Works, *eg Stone and Flower* (1943), *The Pythoness* (1949), reflect belief in poetry as spiritual mythology. Also known for Blake criticism.

Rainier III, orig. Rainier de Grimaldi (1923-), ruling prince of Monaco (1949-). Married American film actress Grace Kelly (1956).

Rainier, Mount, peak of W Washington, US; highest in Cascade Range, at 4392 m (14,410 ft). In Mt. Rainier National Park.

Rainy Lake, on Ontario-Minnesota border, C Canada-US. Area 890 sq km (345 sq mi). Drained by Rainy R. into Lake of the Woods. Has many isls. Tourist resort.

Rais or **Retz, Gilles de Laval, Seigneur de** (1404-40), French soldier. Fought with distinction against English, accompanying Joan of Arc in her campaigns. Confessed in ecclesiastical court to abusing and murdering about 100 children. Hanged on witchcraft charge. Thought to be original Bluebeard.

raised beach, strip of flat land, formerly beach, raised above sea level by land rising or sea level falling. May be several, producing step-like landscape near coast.

raisin, sun-dried fruit of certain varieties of sweet white grape. Varieties incl. sultana and currant. California, Australia and Mediterranean region are main production centres.

Rajasthan, state of NW India. Area c 342,000 sq km (132,000 sq mi); pop. 25,724,000; cap. Jaipur. Thar Desert in W borders on Pakistan. Mainly agric. economy; grain, cotton.

Rajputs, land-owning warrior caste, formerly dominant in Rajputana (roughly coextensive with Rajasthan, N India). After British conquest of India, many Rajput princes retained independent states.

Raleigh or **Ralegh, Sir Walter** (c 1552-1618), English courtier, navigator, writer; favourite of Elizabeth I. Made unsuccessful attempt to estab. 'Virginia' colony in North America. Introduced tobacco, potatoes into Britain. Under James I, convicted of treason and imprisoned in the Tower (1603), where he began his *History of the World.* Beheaded on original treason charge after failure of voyage to the Orinoco in search of gold (1616).

Raleigh, cap. of North Carolina, US. Pop. 124,000. Tobacco trade; electrical and textile industs. Cap. from 1788.

Ramadan, ninth month of Moslem year; period of daily fasting from sunrise to sunset. Commemorates first revelation of the Koran.

Ramayana, Indian epic. Written c 3rd cent. BC, tells story of Rama in 7 books. Immense popularity in India caused adaptation in most vernacular languages, incl. 2 famous medieval versions in Hindi and Tamil.

Rameau, Jean Philippe (1683-1764), French composer. Wrote pioneering treatises on theory of harmony. Began career as opera writer with *Hippolyte et Aricie* (1733), but his style was later considered obsolete. Noted for harpsichord pieces.

Rameses or **Ramses II** (d. 1225 BC), Egyptian king (1292-1225 BC). Fought for 15 years against Hittites, concluding peace treaty with them in 1272. Splendour of his reign marked by building of temples at Karnak and Thebes; temple at Abu Simbel bears 4 colossal figures of him.

Ramillies, village of C Belgium. Scene of French defeat (1706) by British, Dutch and Danish (under Marlborough) in War of Spanish Succession.

Ramsay, Allan (c 1685-1758), Scottish poet. Known for pastoral comedy, *The Gentle Shepherd* (1725), collections of Scots songs, ballads, eg *The Tea Table Miscellany* (1724-37). His son, **Allan Ramsay** (1713-1784) was a noted portrait painter.

Ramsey, [Arthur] Michael (1904-   ), English churchman, archbishop of Canterbury (1961-74). A leading advocate of ECUMENISM.

Ramsgate, mun. bor. of Isle of Thanet, Kent, SE England. Pop. 39,000. Resort; fishing, yachting.

Rand, The, see WITWATERSRAND, South Africa.

Rangoon, cap. and main port of Burma, near mouth of R. Rangoon. Pop. 3,187,000. Exports rice, teak, petroleum. Dominated by gold-spired Shwe Dagon pagoda, major Buddhist shrine. Cap. of region from 1753. Taken by British (1824, 1852); cap. of united Burma (1886). Severely damaged during WWII Japanese occupation.

Rank, Otto (1884-1939), Austrian psychoanalyst. Early disciple of Freud, but held birth trauma, rather than Oedipus complex, to be source of neurosis. Used Freudian analysis to interpret myth.

Ranke, Leopold von (1795-1886), German historian. First to employ objective technique in historical analysis; made extensive use of contemporary material in official archives. Works incl. histories of Germany, France, also world history *Weltgeschichte* (1881-8).

Ransom, John Crowe (1888-1974), American critic, poet. Founded influential *Kenyon Review*. Wrote philosophical literary criticism, eg *The New Criticism* (1941). Poetry in *Selected Poems* (1945).

Ransome, Arthur Mitchell (1884-1967), English author. Known for realistic children's adventure stories, eg *Swallows and Amazons* (1931), usually with Lake District,

Norfolk Broads setting. Also wrote criticism, travel books.

Ranunculaceae, family of dicotyledonous plants with characteristic divided leaves. Incl. buttercup, anemone, delphinium.

Raoult, François Marie (1830-1901), French chemist. Formulated law stating that in liquid, change in vapour pressure in a solution is proportional to ratio of number of solvent molecules to solute molecules; law useful in finding molecular weights.

Rapallo, town of Liguria, NW Italy. Pop. 21,000. Port, resort on Riviera di Levante. Treaties between Italy and Yugoslavia (1920), Russia and Germany (1922) signed here.

rape, several plants of genus *Brassica,* esp. *B. napus* and *B. campestris.* Widespread in N hemisphere. Grown extensively for forage. Seeds yield edible oil and mustard substitute.

Raphael, archangel in Apocryphal OT book of Tobit.

Raphael, real name Raffaello Sanzio (1483-1520), Italian painter. One of the creators of the High Renaissance, his works are known for their calm perfection of line and colour. Works incl. *The Betrothal of the Virgin, Sistine Madonna.* Executed Vatican murals, notably *The School of Athens* and the *Disputa.*

rare earths, oxides of the lanthanide series of elements; much alike in physical and chemical properties. Name also applied to LANTHANIDES themselves.

Rarotonga, main isl. of Cook Isls., SC Pacific Ocean. Area 67 sq km (26 sq mi); main town Avarua. Produces fruit, copra. Discovered 1823, admin. by New Zealand from 1901.

Ras Addar, see BON, CAPE, Tunisia.

raspberry, various shrubs of genus *Rubus* of rose family. Grown in temperate regions for soft, edible berries. European *R. idaeus* and North American and Asian *M. strigosus* yield red fruit, North American *R. occidentalis* yields black.

Rasputin, Grigori Yefimovich (1872-1916), Russian monk. Gained power over the tsarina who believed he could cure her son, Alexis, of haemophilia. His corrupting influence over state affairs led to his murder by a group of noblemen.

rat, one of many long-tailed rodents of Muridae family, of worldwide distribution. Species incl. BLACK RAT, BROWN RAT.

ratel, nocturnal carnivorous mammal, genus *Mellivora*, with grey pelt above and black below. Resembles badger, but larger. Species incl. African *M. capensis* and Indian *M. indica*. Also called honey badger.

Rathlin, isl. off N Northern Ireland, in former Co. Antrim. Has 6th cent. church founded by St Columba. Traditional scene of Robert the Bruce's encounter with spider (1306).

rationalism, in philosophy, doctrine that truth comes wholly from reason without aid from senses or intuition. Opposed to EMPIRICISM. Implies belief in mind's ability to read the true order of the outside world. Exponents incl. Descartes, Leibnitz, Spinoza.

rational number, number expressed as a quotient of 2 integers; integers are rational numbers whose denominators are 1. Also called fraction.

Ratisbon, see REGENSBURG, West Germany.

rattan, climbing palms of genera *Calamus* and *Daemonorops* native to tropical Asia. Long stems used for Malacca canes and in wickerwork.

Rattigan, Terence Mervyn (1911-1977), English playwright. Known for popular narrative dramas, eg *French without Tears* (1936), *The Winslow Boy* (1946), *Separate Tables* (1954), film scripts.

rattlesnake, venomous New World snake of pit viper family. Loose horny tail segments produce characteristic rattle when shaken. Diamondback, *Crotalus adamanteus*, is largest and most dangerous.

Rauschenberg, Robert (1925-), American artist. A formative influence on pop art; has used collage, silk screen printing, and combinations of disparate objects. Works incl. *Monogram*, a stuffed goat encircled by a tyre.

Ravel, Maurice (1875-1937), French composer. His early works are often poetic and atmospheric. Master of orchestration; works incl. ballet *Daphnis et Chloé*, orchestral pieces, eg *Bolero*, *Rhapsodie espagnole*, chamber music, piano pieces, eg *Miroirs*.

raven, *Corvus corax*, large bird of crow family, found on cliffs and mountains of N hemisphere. Glossy black plumage, large pointed bill.

Ravenna, city of Emilia-Romagna, NC Italy, cap. of Ravenna prov. Pop. 133,000. Indust. centre, agric. market. Cap. of Western Empire from AD 402, Ostrogothic cap. under Odoacer, Theodoric. Many Byzantine buildings, mosaics, *eg* church of St Vitale. Tomb of Dante.

Rawalpindi, city of N Pakistan. Pop. 615,000. Railway engineering, chemical mfg; Pakistani army hq. Interim cap. of Pakistan from 1959 until completion of nearby Islamabad.

Rawlinson, Sir Henry Creswicke (1810-95), English orientalist. Copied (1835) cuneiform inscription at Behistun (in modern Iran) making possible decipherment of Assyrian text.

Ray, Man (1890-1976), American painter, photographer, film-maker. Involved in dada, surrealist, De Stijl movements. Invented (1922) 'Rayogram', form of art using photographic techniques. Paintings, *eg A Woman and her Fish* (1938), juxtapose unexpected objects. Surrealist films incl. *L'Etoile de Mer* (1928).

Ray, Satyajit (1921-), Indian film director. First known for 'Apu' trilogy, incl. *Pather Panchali* (1954); continued to experiment with story, technique, as in *The Adventures of Goopy and Bagha* (1968), *Distant Thunder* (1973).

ray, any of various cartilaginous fish of order Hypotremata, with flattened body, huge pectoral fins and whip-like tail. Many species carry stinging organs. Families incl. sting rays, eagle rays and mantas or devil rays.

ray, in physics, straight line along which light or other radiation is regarded as propagating from its source. Name also applied to streams of particles emitted by radioactive substances or of electrons in vacuum tubes.

rayon, synthetic fibre made from cellulose, usually obtained from wood pulp. Two most important forms are made either by forcing cellulose acetate through fine holes and allowing solvent to evaporate in warm air or by VISCOSE PROCESS.

razorbill, *Alca torda,* seabird of auk family. Plumage black above, white below; bill crossed by white band. Nests colonially on Atlantic coasts.

razorshell, marine bivalve mollusc with long razor-shaped shell. Burrows rapidly in sand when disturbed. Species incl. *Solen marginatus.*

Read, Sir Herbert Edward (1893-1968), English critic. Known for essays on art, poetry incl. *Reason and Romanticism* (1926), *To Hell with Culture* (1963). Also wrote poetry, novel reflecting anarchist beliefs, *The Green Child* (1935).

Reade, Charles (1814-84), English author. Known for historical romance of Reformation, *The Cloister and the Hearth* (1861). Also wrote social propaganda novels, *eg Hard Cash* (1863) on corrupt asylums.

Reading, co. bor. and co. town of Berkshire, S England, at confluence of Thames, Kennet rivers. Pop. 132,000. Railway jct.; biscuits; seed nurseries. Noted agric. work at univ. (1926).

Reagan, Ronald Wilson (1911-), American politician. Film actor before entering politics. Governor of California (1967-75), narrowly defeated by Ford for Republican presidential candidacy (1976).

realism, in medieval philosophy, theory that universal concepts have a real existence and are not merely conveniences of classification. Opposed to NOMINALISM. In scholasticism, St Thomas Aquinas is main exponent. Also has specialized use in modern epistemology to denote theory that objects exist independently of our perception, ie opposite of IDEALISM.

real number, any number expressible as a possibly infinite decimal. Those expressed by non-repeating decimal are called irrational (eg π); those expressed by repeating decimal are called rational (eg ⅓ = 0.333....).

Réaumur, René Antoine Ferchault de (1683-1757), French scientist. Invented alcohol thermometer and devised temperature scale in which boiling point of water is 80°. Worked on methods of making steel and wrote on insect natural history.

Rebellion of 1837, short-lived uprising in Upper and Lower Canada protesting against British admin. policies in Canada. Insurgents advocated that office holders be elected rather than appointed by Crown. Most of leaders, incl. W.L. MACKENZIE and L. J. PAPINEAU, escaped to US.

recall, type of referendum, device intended to give electorate direct control over its representative by voting for his resignation. Used first in Switzerland, adopted by some states in US.

Récamier, Jeanne Françoise Julie, née Bernard (1777-1849), French literary hostess. Her circle incl. Mme de Staël, Sainte-Beuve, Chateaubriand.

Recife, Atlantic port of NE Brazil, cap. of Pernambuco state. Pop. 1,061,000. Sugar, coffee, cotton exports. Canals link 3 parts of city (named 'Venice of Brazil'). Founded 1548, has many notable churches, naval station, airport.

Recklinghausen, city of W West Germany, in Ruhr. Pop. 125,000. Coalmining, iron founding, brewing.

reclamation of land, conversion of unproductive land into land suitable for human settlement, cultivation or indust. development. Methods incl. drainage (eg Dutch polders), irrigation and flood control (eg Al Jazirah scheme, Sudan), control of soil erosion.

Reconstruction, term applied to US post-Civil War era, during which programme to reorganize defeated states and reintegrate them into Union was adopted. To enforce Negro enfranchisement in South, Reconstruction Act (1867) passed by Congress estab. 5 military districts. Structure broke down as South was overrun by CARPETBAGGERS. Civil govt. restored by 1876.

recorder, wind instrument of flute type. Blown from end through whistle mouthpiece; usual sizes are descant or soprano, treble or alto, tenor and bass. Developed in medieval times and popular in 16th-18th cents. until replaced by flute. Revived in 20th cent.

rectifier, in electronics, device for converting alternating current into direct current. Types in use incl. thermionic valve and semiconductors.

rector, in Church of England, clergyman in charge of parish who formerly held rights to all its tithes, unlike a vicar who is paid a stipend.

rectum, in anatomy, terminal part of

large intestine, opening into the anal canal.

Red, river of SC US. Flows 1967 km (1222 mi) from N Texas to Oklahoma border, then SE through Arkansas, Louisiana to join Mississippi R.

red algae, any of division Rhodophyta of ALGAE that contain a red pigment which masks the . green chlorophyll. Distinguished by their sexual reproduction. Mostly found as shrubby masses in depths of warm oceans.

Red Army [Worker-Peasant Red Army], official name (1918-45) of Soviet Army. Set up to combat White Armies of counter-revolutionary forces after Bolshevik seizure of power (1917).

red blood cell, see BLOOD.

Redbridge, bor. of NE Greater London, England. Pop. 239,000. Created 1965 from Ilford, Wanstead, Woodford, part of Dagenham (all in Essex).

redbud or **Judas tree,** any of genus Cercis of mainly North American trees of Leguminosae family. Species incl. common redbud, *C. canadensis.* Traditionally, Judas hanged himself on Old World species.

Red Cross, international society for relief of suffering in time of war or disaster. International Committee of Red Cross founded (1863) on advocacy of J.H. Dunant (1828-1910). Delegates from 14 countries adopted Geneva Convention (1864), providing for neutrality of personnel treating wounded, *etc.* Over 100 national Red Cross societies now exist. Awarded Nobel Peace Prize (1917, 1944, 1963).

red deer, *Cervus elaphus,* deer of temperate Europe and Asia. Branched antlers shed annually, reddish coat; fairly common game animal.

red giant, large star with relatively low surface temperature, between 10 and 100 times larger than Sun and *c* 100 times brighter. Most normal stars are believed to evolve into red giants as their hydrogen fuel is consumed.

Redgrave, Sir Michael Scudamore (1908-), English actor. Played at Old Vic, notably in Shakespearian roles. Has also appeared in films. His daughter, **Vanessa Redgrave** (1937-), actress, known for stage, film roles.

Red Guard, in China, Communist youth organization mobilized 1966-7 by Mao Tse-tung to enforce CULTURAL REVOLUTION. Declined following indust. strikes opposing their violent methods.

red-hot poker, herb of genus *Kniphofia,* native to S Africa. Bright red or orange poker-shaped flowers. *K. uvaria* is garden species.

Red Indians, see AMERICAN INDIANS.

Redmond, John Edward (1856-1918), Irish political leader. Leader of Irish Nationalists in Parliament after 1900. Supported Home Rule bill (1912). Opposed Easter Rebellion (1916); lost power to more radical Sinn Fein.

Redon, Odilon (1840-1916), French painter, lithographer, etcher. Leading symbolist, produced many lithographs of strange creatures *eg* series *Dans le Rêve* (1879). Later turned to pastels, oils. Regarded as precursor of surrealism.

redpoll, *Acanthis flammea*, small grey-brown finch with crimson forehead. Found throughout N temperate areas.

Red River Rebellion (1869-70), revolt of Métis (French-Canadian halfbreeds) and Indians after transfer of Red River Settlement from Hudson's Bay Co. to Canada. Provisional govt. set up under RIEL. Revolt collapsed when troops sent against it.

Red Sea, narrow sea between NE Africa and SW Arabia, in Great Rift Valley. Length c 2400 km (1500 mi). Linked to Mediterranean by Gulf of Suez and Suez Canal; to Gulf of Aden by Str. of Bab-el-Mandeb.

redshank, *Tringa totanus*, wading bird, related to sandpiper, of Eurasia and N Africa. Long red legs.

red shift, in astronomy, displacement of spectral lines towards longer wavelengths at red end of spectrum of light from distant galaxies. Explained as a DOPPLER effect due to recession of galaxies; leads to Hubble's law that velocity is proportional to distance of source.

redstart, *Phoenicurus phoenicurus*, European bird of Turdinae family, with red tail and black throat. Name also applied to American warbler, *Setophaga ruticilla*; male black and orange above, white below.

reduction, in chemistry, reaction opposite to oxidation. Originally denoted removal of oxygen from a substance or addition of hydrogen; now incl. reactions adding one or more electrons to atom or ion.

redwood, see SEQUOIA.

Reed, Sir Carol (1906-76), British film director. Best known for films in 1940s using screenplays by Graham Greene, eg *The Third Man* (1949).

reed, several grasses, esp. of genus *Phragmites*. Cosmopolitan common reed, *P. communis*, is tall, stout aquatic grass. Dried stems used in thatching.

reed instrument, musical instrument in which sound derives from vibrating reed. In double reed instruments, eg oboe, bassoon, wind is blown between 2 reeds. Clarinet has single reed laid against wind aperture.

reed mace, see CATTAIL.

re-entry, return of missile or space vehicle into Earth's atmosphere. Enormous quantities of heat are generated by friction between molecules of air and speeding vehicle; a heat shield is designed to give protection from this heat.

Reeves, William Pember (1857-1932), New Zealand politician, writer. Minister for education and justice in Liberal govt. (1891-6). Estab. 1st compulsory state arbitration system · in world. Wrote classic study of New Zealand, *The Long White Cloud* (1898).

referendum, see INITIATIVE.

refining, process by which impurities are removed from metals, petroleum, sugar, etc. Petroleum is refined by fractional distillation and catalytic cracking; metals by electrolysis (eg for copper), amalgamation with mercury (eg for silver), leaching with cyanide (eg for gold).

reflex, in physiology, involuntary response to a stimulus, eg a sneeze, determined by nervous impulses. Stimulated receptor area causes sensory neurons to transmit nervous impulses to nerve cells in brain and spinal cord; these in turn transmit impulses to motor neurons which determine action of muscles, glands, *etc.*

Reformation, religious revolution in W Europe in 16th cent. Began as reform movement in RC church, evolved into doctrines of Protestantism. Begun in Germany by LUTHER and in Geneva by CALVIN. KNOX introduced Calvinism to Scotland. Spread of Reformation also implemented by church-state political conflict and rise of middle class, commerce. In England, Henry VIII rejected papal control and formed Church of England.

Reformation, Catholic, reform movement in RC church in 16th cent. as response to Protestant REFORMATION; popularly known as Counter-Reformation. Attempted to reform abuses within Church in order to protect traditional Roman Catholicism against Lutheranism. Implemented by Council of Trent (1545).

Reform Bills, in British history, legislation passed to liberalize House of Commons' representation. Whigs' 1832 bill enfranchised large indust. towns previously unrepresented, abolished numerous 'rotten boroughs' and extended vote to middle-class men. Derby-Disraeli's **1867** bill more than doubled franchise by giving vote to working men in towns. Gladstone's **1884** bill relaxed rural qualifications.

Reformed Church in America, founded by Dutch Protestant settlers in New Netherland colony; formerly known as Dutch Reformed Church. Gave civil allegiance to England after her conquest of colony (1664). Remains a major denomination.

refraction, in physics, change in direction of ray of light passing from one medium to another; caused by light travelling at different velocities in different media. Snell's law states that ratio of sine of angle of incidence to sine of angle of refraction is a constant called refractive index of that pair of media. The refractive index of a medium is usually given in relation to a vacuum.

refrigeration, process of reducing temperature of substances. In refrigerators, vaporized refrigerant, usually ammonia or Freon, is compressed and forced through a condenser, where it loses heat and liquefies. It vaporizes in · coils of refrigeration compartment and draws heat from materials placed there. Refrigerant returns to compressor and cycle is repeated.

Regency, in British history, last 9 years (1811-20) of reign of George III. Because of king's periodic insanity, govt. conducted in name of Prince of Wales, later George IV. Period of social unrest, much literary and artistic activity.

regeneration, regrowth or restoration of damaged tissue. In higher mammals, incl. man, regeneration is limited to healing of wounds, production of blood cells and scar tissue. In lower animals, entire new limbs, tails, *etc,* can be grown.

Regensburg or **Ratisbon,** city of SE West Germany, at confluence of Danube and Regen. Pop. 132,000. River port, railway jct. Roman *Castra Regina;* episcopal see from 739. Prosperous medieval centre until 15th cent. Armaments mfg. during WWII, heavily bombed.

Reggio di Calabria (anc. *Rhegium*), city of SW Italy, on Str. of Messina, cap. of Reggio di Calabria prov. Pop. 162,000. Port, resort, agric. market. Scene of riots (1970) following removal of Calabrian cap. to Catanzaro. Badly damaged by earthquakes 1783, 1908.

Reggio nell'Emilia, city of Emilia-Romagna, NC Italy, cap. of Reggio nell'Emilia prov. Pop. 130,000. Agric., indust. centre, aero engines. Renaissance buildings.

Regina, prov. cap. of Saskatchewan, Canada; on Wascana Creek. Pop. 139,000. Railway jct., wheat trade centre; agric. machinery, car mfg., oil refining. Founded 1882. Cap. of Northwest Territs. (1883-1905). HQ of Royal Canadian Mounted Police.

Regulus, Marcus Atilius (d. *c* 250 BC), Roman soldier. In 1st Punic War, invaded Africa, but was defeated and captured by Carthaginians (255). Sent to Rome to propose peace, but advised continuing war. Returned to Carthage as promised, where he was put to death.

Rehoboam, Hebrew king (*c* 931-*c* 914 BC), son of Solomon. During his reign, N tribes rebelled and formed new kingdom of Israel under Jeroboam I. He remained king of Judah in S.

Reich, Wilhelm (1897-1957), Austrian psychiatrist, resident in US after 1939. Works, incl. *The Function of the Orgasm* (1927), stress the importance of frequent sexual release to avoid neurosis. Ideas on therapeutic properties of all-pervading orgone energy led fo imprisonment, in which state he died.

Reichstag, name given to lower chamber of federal German legislature (1871-1945). Grew in power after 1919, but could be dissolved by the president. Under Hitler's regime, only National Socialist party was represented. Fire in Reichstag building (1933) gave Hitler pretext to suppress Communists.

Reid, Sir George Houston (1845-1918), Australian statesman, b. Scotland, PM (1904-5). Leader of Free Trade Party. First Australian high commissioner to London (1910-16).

Reid, Thomas (1710-96), Scottish philosopher. Sought to escape Hume's scepticism by positing self-evident knowledge. Founder of common sense or Scottish school. Works incl. *An Inquiry into the Human Mind* (1764).

Reign of Terror (1793-4), final period of French Revolution. Committee of Public Safety, led by Robespierre, controlled France; effected ruthless elimination of counter-revolutionaries (*c* 2500 guillotined). Ended with overthrow of Robespierre by National Convention.

Reims, *see* RHEIMS, France.

reincarnation or **metempsychosis**, belief common to several religions that, after death, soul of human being enters another body, human or animal. In Hinduism and Buddhism, moral conduct determines quality of subsequent incarnations. Also occurs in Greek thought, *eg* in Pythagoras, Plato.

reindeer, *Rangifer tarandus*, large deer of Arctic regions of Europe and

Asia. Both sexes have long branched antlers. Can be domesticated: milk, flesh and skin valued. Caribou is related species. Numbers greatly reduced by hunting.

reindeer moss, LICHEN of genus *Cladonia*. Grey, tufted *C. rangiferina* of Arctic regions is eaten by reindeer and caribou.

Reinhardt, Max, pseud. of Max Goldmann (1873-1943), Austrian stage director. Pioneered several theatrical techniques, incl. mechanical effects, lighting. Settled in US (1933).

Reith, John Charles Walsham, 1st Baron Reith of Stonehaven (1889-1971), British public official. First director-general of British Broadcasting Corporation, creating and developing radio services and world's first regular TV transmissions. Stamped BBC with own personality, ideals.

relative humidity, measure of moisture of atmosphere. Equals ratio of mass of water vapour per unit volume of air to maximum mass of water vapour same volume of air could contain at same temperature; usually expressed as percentage.

relativity theory, physical theory of space, time, energy and gravitation formulated by Einstein. Special theory of 1905 is limited to observers in state of uniform motion relative to each other. It assumes that the laws of physics take same form for all observers and that speed of light is same for all observers, irrespective of their own motion. Its consequences incl. principle that mass and energy are interchangeable, that it is impossible to travel at speed faster than that of light and that measurement of time depends on observer's motion (there is no absolute time). General theory of 1916 deals with observers not in state of uniform motion and is a geometric interpretation of gravitation. Its consequences incl. fact that light rays are deflected towards large gravitating bodies.

relay, electrical, device by which variations in one electric circuit control switching on and off of current in another circuit. May be mechanical switch operated by electromagnet; used in telegraphy and electrical control.

relics, objects associated with Jesus or saint, venerated in RC and Eastern Orthodox churches. Notable examples incl. pieces of the True Cross, Holy Nails of the iron crown of Lombardy, relics of St Edward the Confessor in Westminster Abbey. Medieval traffic in relics led to their cult being condemned by Protestant reformers.

religion, expression of belief in powers higher than man. Often involves attempts to explain origin and nature of universe, evolution of techniques to make the inexplicable more acceptable. Ethical concepts were introduced by BUDDHISM, JUDAISM, CHRISTIANITY, ISLAM. Religions are divided into 'revealed' *eg* Christianity where Jesus revealed word of God, and 'natural' *eg* Buddhism which is result of human speculation alone. *See* POLYTHEISM, MONOTHEISM.

Religion, Wars of, general term for series of civil wars in France (1562-98), fought between Huguenots (Protestants) and Catholics. After Huguenot leader, Henry of

Navarre, became king of France (1589) and was converted to Catholicism, wars ended with Edict of NANTES (1598).

Rembrandt [Harmensz van Rijn], (1606-69) Dutch painter, etcher. Estab. himself as successful portrait painter with *Anatomy Lesson of Dr Tulp*. Business declined with death of his wife in 1642; declared bankrupt 1656. His later series of portraits, esp. self-portraits, are masterpieces of psychological insight. Best known for *Night Watch* (1642). Enormous output incl. over 300 etchings, of which form he was a great master.

Remonstrants, followers of ARMINIUS who presented a remonstrance in 1610 setting forth their differences from the Calvinism of the Dutch Reformed Church. Originally suppressed, recognized as independent church in 1795.

Remus, see ROMULUS.

Renaissance (Fr., = rebirth), period of cultural and intellectual revival in W Europe (14th-16th cent.). Originated in Italy, where scholarship was stimulated by classical manuscripts, foundation of libraries and academies. Under patronage of popes and nobles, *eg* Medici, men of genius were encouraged to create works of an individuality and humanism unknown in Middle Ages. Study of classical models influenced architecture of Alberti, Brunelleschi; discoveries of laws of perspective by Donatello, Masaccio, *etc*, made painting, sculpture more realistic. Later masters incl. Leonardo da Vinci, Michelangelo, Raphael. Learning spread to other countries in 15th cent., hastened by invention of printing. Other major Renaissance figures incl. Josquin Des Prés in music, Erasmus in humanism, Machiavelli in politics, Cervantes and Shakespeare in literature.

Renault, Mary, pseud. of Mary Challans (1905-), English historical novelist. Known for novels on legend of Theseus *The King Must Die* (1958), *The Bull From the Sea* (1962). Other works incl. *The Charioteer* (1953), *The Last of the Wine* (1956).

Renfrewshire, former county of WC Scotland, now in Strathclyde region. Hilly in W, SE; elsewhere lowland. Dairying; oats, potatoes. Industs. incl. engineering, chemicals, textile mfg., whisky distilling, centred in Paisley, Greenock (shipbuilding). Co. town was Renfrew, port and former royal burgh on R. Clyde. Pop. 19,000. Engineering indust.

Reni, Guido (1575-1642), Italian painter of Bolognese school. Early exponent of Classicism, his sentimentalized religious works were highly regarded in 17th and 18th cents. Best-known work is fresco *Aurora* in Rome. Opened an academy in Bologna.

Rennes, city of NW France, at confluence of Ille and Vilaine, cap. of Ille-et-Vilaine dept. Pop. 181,000. Agric. trade centre, textile mfg.; univ. (1735). Hist. cap. of Brittany. Law courts were scene of Dreyfus case. Badly damaged by fire (1720) and during WWII.

rennet, substance extracted from membrane lining stomach of unweaned mammals, esp. calves. Contains enzyme rennin which

curdles milk; used to make cheese and junkets.

Reno, resort of W Nevada, transport route on Truckee R. Pop. 73,000. Cattle, mining centre. Famous for legal gambling, quick divorces.

Renoir, Pierre Auguste (1841-1919), French artist. Leading impressionist, he was a noted figure painter, specializing in children and beautiful young women. Later returned to more classical style, devoting himself to well-rounded nudes. His son, **Jean Renoir** (1894-1979), was film director. Works incl. *La Grande Illusion* and *La Règle du jeu.*

reparations, payment made by defeated nation to victorious, to compensate for material losses incurred in war. After WWI, Dawes Plan (1924) awarded loan to Germany which had fallen behind in payments to Allies. Young Plan (1929) sought to ensure payment by mortgaging German railways and estab. Bank for International Settlements. After WWII, payment by Germany to Allies was to be effected by confiscation of assets and equipment.

Representatives, House of, *see* HOUSE OF REPRESENTATIVES.

repression, *see* DEFENCE MECHANISM.

reprieve, legal postponement of penalty, esp. death. In UK, prerogative of Crown, which acts on home secretary's advice. In US, prerogative of state governors, or president in federal cases, *eg* treason.

reproduction, process by which all living organisms produce new individuals. May be sexual or asexual.

Asexual reproduction found in plants and lower animals; simplest form is by division of single cell (fission). Sexual reproduction involves union of male and female gamete to form a zygote.

Reptilia (reptiles), class of cold-blooded scaly-skinned vertebrates. Mainly terrestrial, with some aquatic varieties; oviparous. Dominant animal group in Mesozoic period; fossils show links between birds, mammals. Incl. turtles, tortoises, lizards, snakes, crocodiles, tuatara.

republic, state or nation in which supreme power rests in electorate and is exercised by elected representatives. Govt. of republic may be centralized (*eg* France), or federated (*eg* US).

Republican Party, in US, one of the two major political parties. Hist. linked with Hamilton's Federalists. Founded (1854) in opposition to slavery, consolidated with Lincoln's election (1860). Held power during RECONSTRUCTION, became party of business interest in late 19th cent.; T. ROOSEVELT split party (1912). Conservative policies resulted in blame for Depression (1929), after which held presidency twice (1953-61, 1969-77) and dominated by Democrats in Congress.

Requiem, in RC church, Mass for the repose of the souls of the dead. Consists of 8 sections, derived in part from ordinary Mass. Performed on All Souls' Day and at funerals. Has inspired notable musical settings, *eg* by Mozart; Verdi, Fauré, Brahms.

resin, substance exuded from various plants, esp. pines and firs. Used in varnish, lacquer and medicines.

Synthetic resins are used extensively in plastics indust.

resistance, electrical, property of conductor by which it resists flow of electric current, and converts part of the electrical energy into heat. From Ohm's law, resistance is measured by ratio of potential difference between ends of conductor to size of current flowing.

Resnais, Alain (1922-), French film director. Best known for *nouvelle vague* approach; experimented with time in *Last Year at Marienbad* (1961), also made *Hiroshima Mon Amour* (1959).

resolving power, in optics, measure of smallest distance between 2 points in image of an optical system (microscope or telescope) when the 2 points can be distinguished as separate.

resonance, in physics, sympathetic vibration of body in response to vibrations of some external source. Effect is greatest when natural frequency of body is reached by the exciting source. .

Respighi, Ottorino (1879-1936), Italian composer. Produced bright, lyrical music, *eg Fountains of Rome*, *The Birds*, but best known for arranging Rossini's music for the ballet *La boutique fantasque*.

respiration, process by which living organisms take in oxygen from air or water, use it to oxidize carbohydrates, fats, *etc*, with subsequent release of energy, and give off products of oxidation, esp. carbon dioxide. Process describing taking in of oxygen and giving out of carbon dioxide is more properly called breathing.

Restoration, in English history,

name given to re-estab. of monarchy on accession in 1660 of Charles II following collapse of Protectorate. Name also applies to entire period of Charles' reign.

Restoration, in French history, period of Bourbon rule, under Louis XVIII and Charles X, from abdication of Napoleon I (1814) to July Revolution (1830). Excluded return of Napoleon (Hundred Days) in 1815.

Restoration drama, name given to 2 types of play popular in England in late 17th cent.: the heroic play, partly inspired by French classical tragedy, *eg* Dryden's *Conquest of Granada,* and witty, often immoral comedies of manners, *eg* Congreve's *The Way of the World.*

resurrection, rising from death to life. Used esp. for rising of Jesus from the tomb and for rising of all dead at Last Judgment. Belief in resurrection of body also a tenet of Moslem belief.

retina, membrane lining back cavity of eyeball. Light-sensitive nerve endings (rods and cones) convey impulses to the brain via the optic nerve. Visual purple in rods makes them sensitive to dim light, but it is inactivated by bright light. Cones function in bright light and are responsible for colour vision and detailed vision.

Retz, Gilles de, *see* RAIS, GILLES DE.

Réunion, isl. in WC Indian Ocean, overseas dept. of France. Area *c* 2510 sq km (970 sq mi); pop. 510,000; cap. St Denis. Of volcanic origin, with one active volcano; rises to 3069 m (10,069 ft) at Piton des Neiges. Sugar cane leading crop; exports sugar, rum. Settled by French in 1642.

Reuter, Paul Julius, Baron de, orig. Israel Beer Josaphat (1816-99) British news agency founder-owner, b. Germany. Founded Reuters, world news agency based in London.

Reuther, Walter Philip (1907-70), American labour leader. Instrumental in organizing United Automobile Workers of America (UAW) in 1930s, became president (1946). Vice-president of AFL-CIO (1955-68), led UAW dispute with GEORGE MEANY.

Reval, *see* TALLINN.

Revelation, Apocalyptic book of NT, traditionally written by St John the Divine. Consists of prophetic vision of triumph of God and martyrs over evil.

Revere, Paul (1735-1818), American silversmith. Famous for ride (1775) from Charlestown to Lexington to warn Massachusetts patriots of advance by British troops at outbreak of American Revolution.

Revolution of 1848, series of revolts in Europe provoked by February Revolution in France, in which Louis Philippe was overthrown and republic estab. In Germany, popular uprising for united country quelled by Prussian army. In Hungary, attempts to estab. independence from Austria were unsuccessful; led to overthrow of Metternich. In Italy, 1st attempts to expel Austrians and unite country (*see* RISORGIMENTO) were defeated.

revolver, PISTOL with cylindrical breech rotated mechanically and bored with chambers for bullets which are fired in succession. Developed by Samuel Colt (1836).

revue, type of stage show consisting of loosely connected sketches, songs, often with satirical content.

Reykjavik, cap. of Iceland, on Faxa Bay. Pop. 82,000. Admin., cultural centre. Port, fishing indust. (esp. cod, herring), textiles, publishing; univ. (1911). Founded 874. Natural hot water supply from nearby springs. Lutheran, RC cathedrals.

Reymont, Wladyslaw Stanislaw (1868-1925), Polish novelist. Best known for prose epic of village life, *The Peasants* (1902-9). Nobel Prize for Literature (1924).

Reynolds, Sir Joshua (1723-92), English painter. Historically the most important British painter, he did much to raise status of artists in Britain. First president of the Royal Academy (1769); his *Discourses* delivered to the Academy enshrine his advocacy of the Grand Manner, style of history painting practised in 17th cent. academies. Painted numerous portraits.

Rhadamanthus, in Greek myth, son of Zeus and Europa, so renowned for his justice that he was made judge of dead in Hades.

Rhaeto-Romanic, Romance group of dialects in Italic branch of Indo-European family. Incl. Romansh, Ladin, Friulian. Former is one of four official languages of Switzerland, latter two spoken in Italian Tyrol, NE Italy.

Rhea, in Greek myth, a Titan; wife and sister of CRONUS. Helped Zeus overthrow Cronus.

rhea, any of Rheidae family of flightless South American birds, similar to ostrich. Three-toed feet, partially feathered head and neck. Species incl. common rhea, *Rhea americana.*

Rhee, Syngman (1875-1965), Korean statesman. Leader of drive for independence during Chinese, Japanese occupations. President of South Korea (1948-60) until exiled. Rule noted for corruption and repression.

Rheims (*Reims*), city of Champagne, NE France, on R. Vesle. Pop. 153,000. Centre of Champagne wine indust. (nearby caves provide storage), textile mfg.; univ. (1547). Clovis baptized here (496); coronation place of many French kings. Scene of surrender (1945) of Germany. Cathedral (13th cent.) badly damaged in WWI.

rhenium (Re), hard metallic element; at. no. 75, at. wt. 186.2. Very rare; found in molybdenum ores. Used in thermocouples and as a catalyst. Discovered 1925.

rheostat, instrument introduced into electric circuit to vary its resistance and control flow of current. Used to regulate brightness of electric lights, *etc.*

rhesus factor (Rh factor), protein present in red blood cells of 85% of people. Those having factor are said to be Rh positive, those without Rh negative. Transfusion of blood from Rh positive person to Rh negative person causes antibodies to form in latter's blood, resulting in agglutination of red blood cells. An Rh negative mother who has a positive baby may experience problems with later pregnancies, unless suitably treated.

rhesus monkey, *Macaca mulatta*, light brown long-haired macaque of SE Asia. Much used in medical and biological research.

rhetoric, see ORATORY.

rheumatic fever, acute inflammatory disease of lining and valves of the heart and of larger joints. Usually affects children and adolescents. Cause unknown, but is always preceded by infection with haemolytic streptococci.

rheumatoid arthritis, see ARTHRITIS.

Rh factor, see RHESUS FACTOR.

Rhine (Ger. *Rhein*, Dutch *Rijn*), river of WC Europe. Flows 1320 km (820 mi) from SE Switzerland through W West Germany, Netherlands, joining R. Meuse before entering North Sea at Hook of Holland. Tributaries incl. Main, Moselle, Neckar. Forms parts of several national borders, esp. Franco-German. W Europe's main waterway, navigable below Basle; heavy barge traffic; linked to Ruhr indust. area. Vineyards; tourism in Rhine Gorge (Bingen to Bonn; incl. Lorelei). Former E frontier of Roman Gaul; picturesque medieval castles.

Rhine, Confederation of the, league of German princes formed (1806) under Napoleon. Disintegrated after Napoleon's retreat from Russia (1812-13).

Rhineland, area of W West Germany, on both sides of R. Rhine. Incl. parts of North Rhine-Westphalia, Rhineland-Palatinate, Hessen, Baden Württemberg. Occupied by Allies after WWI; demilitarized under treaty of Locarno within 50 km E of Rhine. Refortified by Hitler from 1936.

Rhineland-Palatinate, see PALATINATE, West Germany.

rhinoceros, any of Rhinocerotidae family of massive thick-skinned herbivorous mammals of tropical Africa and Asia. One or two upright horns composed of matted hair on snout. Species incl. Indian rhinoceros, *Rhinoceros unicornis*, with 1 horn and black African rhinoceros, *Diceros bicornis*, with 2 horns. Numbers greatly reduced by hunting.

rhinoceros beetle, beetle of Dynastinae subfamily, male of which has rhinoceros-like horn on head. Species incl. *Dynastes tityus* of E US.

rhizome, creeping stem lying at or under the surface of soil. Differs from root in having scale leaves and leaves or shoots near tip. Produces roots from underside. Unlike root, does not die if cut and may become new plant. Rhizomatous plants incl. common iris, ginger.

Rhode Island, New England state of US. Area 3144 sq km (1214 sq mi); pop. 950,000; cap. Providence. Smallest US state, named after isl. in Narragansett Bay. Mainly low-lying; important farming esp. poultry; fishing, tourist, textile industs. Hist. rum, slave, molasses trade. Last of original 13 colonies to ratify US Constitution (1790).

Rhodes, Cecil John (1853-1902), British capitalist, colonial administrator. Acquired fortune through control of Kimberley diamond mines. As part of plan to estab. British rule in Africa from Cape to Cairo, advised annexation of Bechuanaland (1885), then formed British South Africa Co. (1889) to exploit area known later as Rhodesia. PM of Cape Colony (1890-5), supported British in Transvaal. Resigned over complicity in JAMESON Raid.

Rhodes (*Rhodos*), isl. of Greece, in SE Aegean Sea, largest of Dode-

canese. Area 1404 sq km (542 sq mi); main town Rhodes. Ancient Rhodes *fl* 4th-3rd cent. BC, built 'Colossus of Rhodes' (destroyed by earthquake 224 BC). Held by Knights Hospitallers (1309-1523), ceded to Greece by Italy 1947.

Rhodesia, republic of SC Africa. Area 391,000 sq km (151,000 sq mi); pop. 6,530,000; cap. Salisbury. Languages: Bantu, English. Religions: native, Christianity. Largely plateau, drained by Limpopo, Zambezi river systems. Tobacco growing, stock raising; rich in gold, asbestos, chrome, coal; h.e.p. from Kariba Dam. Admin. by British South Africa Co. (estab. by Rhodes) from 1889; became colony of Southern Rhodesia 1923. United federally (1953-63) with Northern Rhodesia (now ZAMBIA), Nyasaland (now MALAWI). Declared independence (UDI) 1965, republic from 1970. Regime not recognized by UN; increasing political and military pressure in 1970s to allow black majority rule. Now called Zimbabwe-Rhodesia.

rhodium (Rh), hard metallic element of the platinum group; at. no. 45, at. wt. 102.91. Occurs with and resembles platinum. Resists corrosion; used in alloys, electrical contacts, thermocouples and as a catalyst.

rhododendron, genus of trees and shrubs of heath family, native to Asia but widely cultivated in N temperate regions. Mainly evergreen with red, purple or white flowers. *See* AZALEA.

Rhodope Mountains, range of N Greece and S Bulgaria. Runs NW-

SE, rising to 2924 m (9596 ft) in Rila Mts., Bulgaria.

Rhondda, mun. bor. of Glamorgan, S Wales. Pop. 89,000. Coalmining; light industs. Severely hit by Depression (1930s).

Rhône, river of W Switzerland and SE France. Flows c 810 km (505 mi) from Rhône glacier (Switzerland) via L. Geneva, Lyons, Avignon to delta (Camargue) on Gulf of Lions. H.e.p. from Génissiat Dam (1948). Vine, fruit, olive growing in fertile valley. Canal link with Rhine. Rhône-Saône corridor a hist. route between N and S France.

rhubarb, any of genus *Rheum* of perennial, large-leaved plants of edible reddish stalks, esp. *R. rhaponticum* and *R. hybridum*. Leaves of all varieties contain poisonous oxalic acid, stalks yield cathartic extract.

Rhum or **Rum**, isl. of Inner Hebrides, W Scotland. Area 109 sq km (42 sq mi). Mainly mountainous. Nature reserve.

rhyme or **rime**, identity or similarity of sound of final accented syllables of words, esp. in vowels and succeeding consonants. Used in poetry esp. at line endings to form audible patterns. First became popular in medieval Latin poetry.

rhyolite, fine-grained acid volcanic rock. Composition similar to granite, but richer in silica. Occurs as highly viscous lava, explosively ejected through Earth's surface.

rhythm, in music, pattern produced by relative stress and duration of notes. Its use to produce a sense of uplift in both performer and listener is very important.

rib, any of the arched bones attached to the vertebral column and enclosing the chest cavity. In man, there are 12 pairs of ribs, attached to the thoracic vertebrae.

Ribbentrop, Joachim von (1893-1946), German diplomat. As Hitler's foreign minister (1938-45), helped negotiate Russo-German Non-aggression Pact (1939). Hanged as war criminal.

Ribble, river of NW England. Flows 121 km (75 mi) from Pennines via Preston to Irish Sea.

ribbon fish, marine fish of Trachipteridae family, with long laterally-compressed body resembling ribbon. Species incl. deal fish, *Trachipterus arcticus*, of N Atlantic.

ribbon worm, see NEMERTEA.

Ribeirão Prêto, town of SC Brazil, in São Paulo state. Pop. 212,000. Agric. market (esp. coffee); cotton -milling, distilling; agric. machinery mfg.

Ribera, José or **Jusepe** (1591-1652), Spanish painter. Spent his working life in Naples; influenced by Caravaggio, his work is characterized by dramatic contrasts in light and shade and an often gruesome naturalism. Works incl. *The Martyrdom of St Bartholomew*.

riboflavin or **vitamin B₂**, vitamin of B group found in yeast, liver, milk, *etc*. Lack of riboflavin in diet causes stunted growth, loss of hair, skin lesions, *etc*.

Ricardo, David (1772-1823), English economist. Having amassed fortune as stockbroker, wrote influential *Principles of Political Economy and Taxation* (1817) setting out theory correlating rent, profit, wages, taxation.

Rice, Elmer (1892-1967), American

dramatist. Known for portrayal of social injustice, eg *The Adding Machine* (1923), *Street Scene* (1929). Also wrote novels, eg utopian satire *A Voyage to Purilia* (1930).

rice, grain of cereal grass *Oryza sativa*. Grown extensively in tropical and subtropical regions of China, India, Japan, Indonesia and SE Asia, which produce c 90% of world's rice. Also cultivated in US and Europe. Rich in carbohydrate; brown rice, retaining outer husk, has more protein and vitamin value than polished white rice.

Richard [I] the Lion Heart (1157-99), king of England (1189-99). Twice rebelled against father, Henry II, before accession. Leader of 3rd Crusade with PHILIP II of France (1190); helped capture Acre (1191). Captured in Austria during return to England; turned over to custody of Emperor Henry VI and released on payment of great ransom (1194). Killed while fighting Philip in France.

Richard II (1367-1400), king of England (1377-99). Son of Edward the Black Prince, effectively quelled PEASANTS' REVOLT (1381). Power threatened by nobles led by Gloucester until John of Gaunt returned from Spain (1389). Had Gloucester murdered (1397). Deposed after rebellion led by Henry Bolingbroke (HENRY IV). Imprisoned at Pontefract where he died.

Richard III (1452-85), king of England (1483-5). On death of Edward IV, he seized Edward's heir, Edward V, and assumed the crown when Parliament declared Edward illegitimate. Suspected of arranging Edward's murder after he had him imprisoned in the Tower. Defeated

and killed at Bosworth by Henry Tudor (HENRY VII).

Richards, I[vor] A[rmstrong] (1893-1979), English critic. Known for study of relationship of language, thought, *The Meaning of Meaning* (1923, with OGDEN), theoretical works on criticism, eg *Principles of Literary Criticism* (1925), *Practical Criticism* (1929).

Richardson, Sir Ralph David (1902-), English actor. Actor-director of Old Vic (1944-7). Noted roles incl. Sir Toby Belch in *Twelfth Night*, in *Flowering Cherry*, *Home*; film *Oh! What a Lovely War!*

Richardson, Samuel (1689-1761), English novelist. Helped develop novel form with epistolary works, eg *Pamela* (1740), *Clarissa* (1748), *Sir Charles Grandison* (1754). Deals with moral struggles in sentimental terms.

Richelieu, Armand Jean du Plessis, Duc de (1585-1642), French statesman, churchman. Created cardinal 1622. With help of regent Marie de' Medici, became chief minister to Louis XIII (1624) and virtual ruler of France. Sought to reduce Habsburg power by aiding Protestants in Thirty Years War, then brought France into war as ally of Sweden (1635). In France, strengthened royal power to detriment of Huguenots and nobility; captured Huguenot stronghold of La Rochelle (1628).

Richmond, cap. of Virginia, US; at head of navigation on James R. Pop. 249,000. Financial, cultural, shipping centre. Tobacco, grain, coal exports; tobacco processing. Settled 1637; cap. from 1779. Strategic as cap. of Confederacy during Civil War.

Richmond-upon-Thames, bor. of SW Greater London, England, on R. Thames. Pop. 174,000. Formerly Sheen, created 1965 from Barnes, Twickenham mun. bors. Has Richmond Park, Kew Gardens; Hampton Court Palace.

Richter, Johann Paul Friedrich, pseud. Jean Paul (1763-1825), German author. Wrote formally experimental novels, eg *Life of the Complacent Little Schoolmaster Maria Wuz* (1790), *Quintus Fixlein* (1796). Other works incl. theoretical *Introduction to Aesthetics* (1804).

Richthofen, Manfred, Baron von (1892-1918), German airman, known as the 'Red Baron'. Credited with shooting down 80 aircraft during WWI. Died in action.

Rickenbacker, Edward Vernon (1890-1973), American airman. US and French hero during WWI.

rickets, disease resulting from vitamin D deficiency, affecting calcium metabolism and causing softening and bending of bones. Caused by insufficient exposure to sunlight or inadequate diet.

Rideau Canal, SE Ontario, Canada; connects Ottawa with L. Ontario (at Kingston). Length 203 km (126 mi).

Ridley, Nicholas (c 1500-55), English clergyman. Worked with Cranmer on Book of Common Prayer; became bishop of London (1550). After accession of Mary I, burned at stake with Latimer.

Riefenstahl, Leni (1902-), German film director. Best known for her brilliant propaganda films for Nazis, *Triumph of the Will* (1934), *Olympische Spiele 1936.*

Riel, Louis (1844-85), Canadian rebel. Led unsuccessful RED RIVER REBELLION (1869-70). In 1884, led revolt of Indians and Métis in Saskatchewan. Defeated and executed for treason.

Riemann, Georg Friedrich Bernhard (1826-66), German mathematician. Developed theory of analytic functions of complex variable and their representation by Riemann surfaces. Riemannian geometry, which describes non-uniform space, has important applications in relativity theory.

Rienzi, Cola di (c 1313-54), Italian political leader. Used popular support to estab. short-lived Roman republic, but was soon expelled under papal pressure. Sponsored by new pope, Innocent VI, returned (1353) to Rome, but his dictatorial rule ended in his murder.

Rif or **Riff, Er,** mountain region of N Morocco; extends from Ceuta (W) to Melilla (E). Rises to over 2450 m/8000 ft. Stronghold of Berber tribes who revolted against French and Spanish rule (1921-6).

rifle, FIREARM with spiral-grooved barrel which imparts spin to bullet. Usually fired from shoulder.

rift valley or **graben,** natural trough formed by sinking of land between two approximately parallel faults. Associated with volcanic activity. Examples incl. Great Rift Valley of E Africa, Rhine valley, Scottish central lowland valley.

Riga, city of WC USSR, cap. of Latvian SSR; on Gulf of Riga. Pop. 755,000. Port; exports timber, flax, paper; indust. centre. Founded 12th cent., became centre of Livonian Knights and prosperous Hanseatic trading town. Held by Poland, Sweden and finally Russia (1710). Cap. of independent Latvia (1919-40) until Soviet occupation.

Rights, Bill of, in British history, statute (1689) confirming rights of Parliament and the people previously violated during reign of James II. Estab. political supremacy of Parliament. Embodied terms by which William and Mary succeeded to throne and provided for Protestant succession.

Rights, Bill of, in American history, see CONSTITUTION OF THE UNITED STATES.

Rights of Man, Declaration of the, hist. French document, drafted by Sieyès (1789); became preamble of French Constitution of 1791. Influenced by Rousseau and American Declaration of Independence, it asserted equality of all men, sovereignty of the people, inalienable rights of the individual to 'liberty, property, security'.

right whale, whalebone whale of Balaenidae family, found in polar waters. Toothless, with large head. Species incl. Greenland whale, *Balaena mysticetus*, reaching lengths of 21 m/70 ft. Now very rare, due to uncontrolled hunting.

rigor mortis, progressive stiffening of muscles of body which occurs several hours after death (depending on atmospheric conditions and state of body). Ended by onset of decomposition after *c* 24 hrs.

Rig-Veda, see VEDA.

Rijeka-Sušak (Ital. *Fiume*), town of Croatia, NW Yugoslavia, on the Adriatic. Pop. 133,000. Country's largest port; indust. centre, oil refining; shipbuilding; tourism. Hungarian from 1779, seized (1919) by D'Annunzio; annexed (1924) by Italy, ceded (1947) to Yugoslavia. Sušak, E suburb, Yugoslav from 1919. Roman arch, cathedral (14th cent.).

Rijksmuseum, Dutch national museum in Amsterdam, founded 1808 by Louis Napoleon Bonaparte; present building opened 1885. Collection of Dutch art particularly good, esp. of 17th cent. masters.

Rijswijk or **Ryswick,** town of W Netherlands, near The Hague. Pop. 49,000. Treaty of Ryswick (1697) ended War of Grand Alliance against France.

Riley, Bridget (1931-), English painter. Leading exponent of op art, early work, eg *Fall* (1963), was confined to repetitive geometric patterns in black and white. More colour introduced into later work.

Rilke, Rainer Maria (1875-1926), German poet, b. Prague. Early lyrics subjective, eg *Book of Hours* (1905), later works more philosophical, eg *Duino Elegies* (1923) recounting reactions to existentialism, *The Sonnets to Orpheus* (1923). Also wrote novel based on parable of Prodigal Son, *The Notebooks of Malte Laurids Brigge* (1910).

Rimbaud, [Jean Nicolas] Arthur (1854-91), French poet. Known for decadent verse written between 15 and 19. Intimate of VERLAINE. Works incl. 'Le bateau ivre' (1871), prose piece detailing his spiritual development *Une saison en enfer* (1873).

Rimini (anc. *Ariminum*), city of Emilia-Romagna, EC Italy, on Adriatic Sea. Pop. 120,000. Port, resort, railway jct. Founded 3rd cent. BC, donated (AD 754) to Papacy. Siezed (13th cent.) by Malatesta family. Arch of Augustus (27 BC); Renaissance church, designed by Alberti.

Rimsky-Korsakov, Nikolai Andreyevich (1844-1908), Russian composer, one of 'the Five'. Music, strongly influenced by folk tunes, displays brilliant orchestration. Works incl. orchestral piece *Scheherazade*, opera *Le Coq d'or*. Revised Borodin's *Prince Igor*, Mussorgsky's *Boris Godunov*.

rinderpest or **cattle plague**, acute infectious disease of cattle, sheep, *etc*. Characterized by fever and lesions of skin and mucous membrane. Common in C Africa, SE Asia, India.

Ring of the Nibelung, see NIBELUNGENLIED.

ring ouzel, *Turdus torquatus*, European bird of thrush family. Male has black plumage with white band on chest.

ringworm, contagious skin disease caused by infection with certain microscopic fungi. Characterized by formation of ring-shaped eruptive patches and itching. Common sites are between the toes (athlete's foot), scalp and groin.

Rio Bravo, Mexican name for RIO GRANDE.

Rio de Janeiro, major port of Brazil, cap. of Guanabara state, on SW shore of Guanabara Bay. Pop. 4,252,000. Transport and communication centre. Coffee, sugar, iron ore exports; flour milling, sugar refining, railway engineering. Tourist attractions incl. Sugar Loaf Mt., Corcovado peak (with statue of Christ), Copacabana beach, botani-

cal gardens. Has shanty towns on adjacent hills. First settled by French; Portuguese occupation 1567; cap. of Brazil (1763-1960). Seat of Univ. of Brazil (1920).

Rio de la Plata, *see* PLATA, RÍO DE LA.

Rio Grande (Mex. *Río Bravo*), river of S US. Flows S 3000 km (1885 mi) from SW Colorado through New Mexico, then SE along Texas-Mexico border to Gulf of Mexico.

Rio Muni, mainland area of Equatorial Guinea. Area 26,000 sq km (10,040 sq mi); main town Bata. Narrow coastal plain, interior plateau. Hot, wet climate; main products coffee, hardwoods.

Rio Negro, *see* NEGRO.

Riopelle, Jean Paul (1924-), Canadian artist. Known for his dense abstract paintings in rich blobs of paint, worked with palette knife into interlocking bars.

Riot Act, legislation passed (1714) in face of widespread rioting over accession of George I. Under its terms, if an unlawful assembly of 12 or more persons fails to disperse within an hour of reading of prescribed proclamation by a magistrate, those present are guilty of felony and may be dispersed by force.

Río Tinto or **Minas de Riotinto**, town of Andalusia, SW Spain, in Sierra de Aracena. Pop. 9000. Rich copper mines, also iron and manganese deposits.

Riouw Islands, group of isls. off E coast of Sumatra, Indonesia, at S entrance of Str. of Malacca. Area *c* 5900 sq km (2300 sq mi). Largest isl., Bintan, has tin and bauxite mines.

Ripon, town of North Yorkshire, N

England. Pop. 11,000. Tanning, brewing; paint mfg. Has cathedral (12th-16th cent.); Fountains Abbey ruins nearby.

Risorgimento (Ital., = resurgence), movement in 19th cent. Italy for liberation and national unification. Despite failure of 1848-9 insurrections under MAZZINI and CAVOUR, French military intervention against Austria and Garibaldi's conquest of Naples and Sicily enabled Victor Emmanuel of Sardinia to become 1st king of Italy (1861). Unification completed with acquisition of Venetia (1866) and Papal States (1870).

Ritter, Karl (1779-1859), German geographer. A founder of modern geography; emphasized relationships between nature and man's development. Wrote *Die Erdkunde* (1817-18).

river, natural stream of fresh water draining into sea, lake, inland depression or another river. May flow only intermittently in arid regions. Rising at a source, river normally possesses 'youth', 'maturity' and 'old age' stages in upper, middle and lower courses respectively.

Rivera, Diego (1886-1957), Mexican artist. Influenced by Communism while in Europe. Depicted Mexican social problems on large fresco murals commissioned for decoration of public buildings in Mexico.

Riverina, area of S New South Wales, Australia, between Murray, Murrumbidgee and Lachlan rivers. Fertile, irrigated; produces wheat, sheep, fruit, rice.

Rivers, William Halse Rivers

(1864-1922), English anthropologist, psychologist. Wrote *Kinship and Social Organization* (1914) after expeditions to Australasia. Fused ethnological data and psychoanalytic theory. Other works incl. *Medicine, Magic and Religion* (1924), *History of Melanesian Society* (1914).

Riviera, narrow coastal strip extending from Hyères (SE France) to La Spezia (NW Italy). Italian Riviera divided by Genoa into E and W sections; French Riviera also called 'Côte d'Azur'. Many fashionable resorts *eg* Cannes, Monte Carlo. Vine, flower, fruit growing; fishing.

Riyadh, cap. of Saudi Arabia. Pop. 300,000. Oasis trade centre of Nejd region. Centre of Wahabi Islam since 19th cent. Many modern buildings date from oil boom.

Rizzio, David (*c* 1533-66), Italian musician, favourite of Mary Queen of Scots. Became Mary's personal secretary. Influence with Mary aroused enmity of group of nobles, incl. her husband, Darnley; stabbed to death at their command.

RNA or **ribonucleic acid,** fundamental genetic material found esp. in protein-making ribosomes in cytoplasm of cells. Molecule consists of long chains of ribose sugar, phosphate groups and nitrogenous bases. One form, messenger RNA, whose synthesis is controlled by DNA in cell nucleus, migrates to ribosomes where it builds up protein molecules. Another form, transfer RNA, arranges sequence of amino acids which determine structure of a particular protein to be built by messenger RNA.

roach, *Rutilus rutilus,* freshwater

fish of carp family, found in N Europe. Silvery white with reddish fins.

road, man-made semi-permanent route for wheeled vehicles. Constructed in ancient Persia c 500 BC; art developed by Romans, many of whose examples still exist. European road-building neglected from fall of Roman Empire until 19th cent. when TELFORD and McADAM improved surfaces. See MOTORWAY.

roadrunner, Geococcyx californianus, long-tailed, crested desert bird, related to cuckoo, found in SW US. Poor flier, runs with great speed. Also called chaparral cock.

Roanoke, river of E US. Formed in S Virginia, flows SE 660 km (410 mi) through N Carolina to Albemarle Sound. Roanoke Island, off coast of North Carolina, was site of Raleigh's unsuccessful colonies (1585, 1587).

Robbe-Grillet, Alain (1922-), French author. Formulated critical theory of nouveau roman dispensing with many familiar devices of novel. Works incl. Les Gommes (1953), Dans le Labyrinthe (1959), film scenario L'Année dernière à Marienbad (1960).

robbery, in law, illegal taking of another's property from his person or in his immediate presence by use of violence or intimidation.

Robbia, Luca della (c 1399-1482), Florentine sculptor. Head of family workshop which produced glazed terracotta sculpture; specialized in small figures in white set against a blue background.

Robbins, Jerome (1918-), American choreographer, director, dancer. Staged ballets, musicals, eg The King and I, West Side Story.

Robert [I] the Bruce (1274-1329), king of Scotland (1306-29). Fought to recover Scottish territ. from English after assuming throne. Forced to flee after defeat at Methven (1307). His courage allegedly derived from watching a spider spinning its web. Successfully resumed campaign after death of Edward I, ultimately defeating Edward II at Bannockburn (1314). Treaty of Northampton (1328) acknowledged Scottish independence.

Robert II (1316-90), king of Scotland (1371-90). Grandson of Robert the Bruce. Founder of the house of Stuart. Regent during uncle David II's minority, later rebelled (1363) when David named Edward III of England his successor (Robert had been granted succession by decree of 1318). Imprisoned, but released to succeed David.

Robert III (c 1340-1406), king of Scotland (1390-1406). Succeeded father Robert II. During reign, real power was in hands of brother Robert, earl of Fife, later Duke of Albany. English invasion (1399) followed by quarrel between Albany and Robert's son David, Duke of Rothesay; ended with David's mysterious death (1402). Succeeded by other son James I.

Robert II [Curthose] (c 1054-1134), duke of Normandy. Eldest son of William the Conqueror, on whose death he inherited Normandy (1087). Claimed English throne from brother Henry I but was defeated at Tinchebrai (1106) and imprisoned for rest of life.

Roberts of Kandahar, Frederick Sleigh Roberts, 1st Earl (1832-1914), British field marshal. Successful campaign in Afghanistan (1879) incl. relief of Kandahar. Commander-in-chief (1899-1900) against Boers in South Africa.

Robeson, Paul (1898-1976), American singer, leading exponent of Negro spirituals. Also an actor, his roles incl. Othello. His left-wing political views aroused hostility in US and he lived abroad for some years.

Robespierre, Maximilien François Marie Isidore de (1758-94), French revolutionary. Jacobin leader, member of Committee of Public Safety, which instituted Reign of Terror (1793-4). Ousted rivals Hébert and Danton, exercised dictatorial power through Revolutionary Tribunal. Overthrown by the Convention, tried and guillotined. Had reputation of incorruptibility.

robin, *Erithacus rubecula,* songbird of thrush family found in Europe and W Asia. Brownish plumage with orange-red face and breast. American robin, *Turdus migratorius,* is larger thrush with dull-red breast.

Robin Hood, legendary hero of medieval England. Idealized outlaw, lived in Sherwood Forest with Little John, Friar Tuck, Maid Marian and his band. Robbed the rich to help the poor.

Robinson, Edward G., orig. Emanuel Goldenberg (1893-1972), American film actor. Films, often in gangster roles, incl. *Little Caesar* (1930), *A Slight Case of Murder* (1938).

Robinson, Edwin Arlington (1869-1935), American poet. Known for melancholy, ironic verse, *eg The Children of Night* (1897), *Man against the Sky* (1916), verse novels 'Tristram' (1927), 'King Jasper' (1935), often reflecting small-town gloom.

Robinson, [William] Heath (1872-1944), English graphic artist. Known for his book illustrations and humorous drawings of complex machinery which performed simple tasks.

Robinson, ('Sugar') Ray, real name Walker Smith (1920-), American boxer. Rated as one of the best boxers ever, he became middleweight champion (1951). Retired 1952; returned to boxing and won title 3 more times (1955, 1957, 1958).

robot, mechanical device constructed to perform human tasks. Term popularized by Karel Capek in play, *RUR* (*Rossum's Universal Robots*) in 1921. *See* AUTOMATION.

Rob Roy, real name Robert Macgregor (1671-1734), Scottish outlaw. Member of proscribed Macgregor clan, led cattle-stealing raids against duke of Montrose. Submitted voluntarily; sentenced to transportation, was pardoned (1727).

Robson, Dame Flora (1902-), English actress. Roles incl. Mary Paterson in *The Anatomist,* Miss Tina in *The Aspern Papers.*

Rochdale, bor. of Greater Manchester met. county, NW England. Pop. 91,000. Cotton mfg. (esp. spinning). English co-operative movement founded here (1844).

Rochefort, (-sur-Mer), town of W France, on R. Charente. Pop. 35,000. Port, fishing indust. Formerly important naval base, built 17th cent. Napoleon surrendered nearby (1815).

Rochelle, La, *see* LA ROCHELLE, France.

roches moutonnées, in geology, mounds of rock with gradual, smooth slope on one side, steeper, rougher slope on other. Formed by action of advancing ice.

Rochester, John Wilmot, 2nd Earl of (1647-80), English poet, courtier. Known mainly for satires incl. sceptical *A Satyr against Mankind* (1675). Also wrote scurrilous epigrams.

Rochester, city of Kent, SE England, on Medway estuary. Pop. 55,000. Indust. centre; engineering. Has Roman *Durobrivae* (fort); cathedral (11th cent.); Norman castle (12th cent.); Dickens' home nearby.

Rochester, port of NW New York, US; on L. Ontario. Pop. 296,000. Fruit, market gardening, flower nurseries. Optical, photographic equipment. H.e.p. supplies from Genesee R.

rock, naturally occurring substance forming Earth's crust. Consists of one or more types of mineral; may also contain natural glass, decayed organic material, *etc.* Basic types are IGNEOUS, METAMORPHIC and SEDIMENTARY.

Rockefeller, John D[avison] (1839-1937), American industrialist, philanthropist. Ruthlessly built his Standard Oil Co. into largest refining company in US. Philanthropies incl. founding Univ. of Chicago (1892), and Rockefeller Foundation (1913). His son, John D[avison] Rockefeller, Jr (1874-1960), carried on father's businesses and philanthropies, estab. Rockefeller Center. His son, Nelson Aldrich Rockefeller (1908-79), entered public service (1940).

Governor of New York (1958-73); vice-president (1974-7).

rocket, popular name for several biennial or perennial plants of mustard family. Esp. dame's violet, *Hesperis matronalis,* with white or purple flowers and rocket salad, *Eruca sativa,* with leaves eaten in salads.

rocket, projectile driven by its reaction to stream of hot gases it produces by burning propellant. By carrying its own source of oxygen, it operates independently of Earth's atmosphere and can be used in outer space. Propellants used incl. liquid hydrogen and liquid oxygen.

Rockingham, Charles Watson-Wentworth, 2nd Marquess of (1730-82), British Whig statesman, PM (1765-6, 1782). Headed coalition that repealed Stamp Act (1766). Favoured independence of American colonies.

rock music, form of music popular from mid-1950s. Derives in part from American rhythm and blues, gospel, and country and western music. Early exponents incl. Bill Haley, Elvis Presley, Chuck Berry. Status of rock music as vehicle for artistic expression was enhanced by such performers as the Beatles, Rolling Stones and Bob Dylan in mid-1960s. Modern rock music has absorbed such influences as Eastern music, jazz, electronic and classical music.

Rocky Mountain goat, *Oreamnos americanus,* ruminant mammal intermediate between goat and antelope, found in remote mountains of NW North America. Thick white coat, short black horns in both sexes.

Rocky Mountains, extensive

mountain system of W North America, from Alaska to SW US, E of Coast Ranges. Canadian Rockies form British Columbia-Alberta border (glaciers, resorts). In US incl. scenic Grand Teton Range; Sawatch Mts. rise to Mt. Elbert (4399 m/14,431 ft). Many national parks, eg Banff (Canada), Glacier (US).

Rocky Mountain sheep, see BIGHORN.

rococo, style of architecture and decoration developed in early 18th cent. France from the Baroque. Characterized by elaborate and profuse ornamentation imitating foliage, shell work, scrolls, etc. Became popular in Germany, Austria and Italy.

Rodentia (rodents), order of gnawing mammals with large chisel-like incisors which grow continuously. Incl. mouse, rat, squirrel, beaver, porcupine, guinea pig.

rodeo, competitive exhibition of the skills of cowboys. Events incl. bronco-riding (saddled or bareback), bull-riding, calf-roping and steer-wrestling. First rodeo charging admission money took place in Arizona (1888). Most famous is annual Calgary Stampede.

Rodgers, Richard Charles (1902-), American composer. Collaborated with Lorenz Hart on musicals eg Pal Joey, and with Oscar Hammerstein on Carousel, South Pacific, The King and I, The Sound of Music.

Rodin, Auguste (1840-1917), French sculptor. Most famous sculptor of late 19th cent., his powerful realistic sculpture was influenced by Michelangelo and Gothic art. Works incl. The Age of Bronze, The Thinker, The Kiss, The Burghers of Calais.

Rodney, George Brydges Rodney, 1st Baron (1718-92), British admiral. Captured Martinique (1762) in Seven Years War. Famous for victory (1782) over French fleet under de Grasse in American Revolution.

Rodrigo, Joaquin (1902-), Spanish composer. Blind from age of 3. Best known for Concerto d'Aranjuez for guitar and orchestra.

Rodriguez, isl. of Mascarene Isls., W Indian Ocean, a dependency of Mauritius. Area 104 sq km (40 sq mi); main town Port Mathurin. Produces fruit, tobacco, maize. Discovered (1645) by Portuguese; taken (1810) by British.

Roebling, John Augustus (1806-69), American engineer, b. Germany. One of first to manufacture steel cable. Built suspension bridges, notably Brooklyn Bridge (completed by son, 1883), during which project he lost his life.

roe deer, Capreolus capreolus, small Eurasian deer found in woodland. Male has short 3-tined antlers.

Roethke, Theodore (1908-63), American poet. Poetry, involved with unconscious and nature, incl. Words for the Wind (1958), The Far Field (1964).

Rogation Days, in RC calendar, 4 days (25th April and 3 days preceding Ascension Day) observed by processions asking God's mercy. Adaptation of Roman pagan ceremony seeking blessing for crops.

Rogers, Ginger (1911-), American film actress, dancer. See ASTAIRE, FRED.

Roget, Peter Mark (1779-1869), English physician, lexicographer. One of founders of Univ. of London. Best known for *Thesaurus of English Words and Phrases* (1852, constantly revised).

Röhm, Ernst (1887-1934), German political leader. Organized Nazi storm troops (SA), who enabled him to rival Hitler for political power in 1930s. Executed in Hitler's purge.

Roland (d. 778), French national hero. His death at hands of Basques while commanding rearguard of Charlemagne's retreating army at Roncesvalles became subject of legend, notably in *Chanson de Roland* (11th cent.).

Roland, Chanson de, 11th cent. French epic. Oldest and most famous of extant CHANSONS DE GESTE. Poem, part of Charlemagne cycle, describes Roland's heroic death. Noted for characterization, eg contrast of Roland and Oliver, and simple, evocative style.

Roland de la Platière, Manon Jeanne, née Philpon (1754-93), French revolutionary. Made her home intellectual centre of the Girondists during French Revolution; guillotined after their fall. Her husband, Jean Marie Roland de la Platière (1734-93), achieved prominence with Girondists through her influence. Killed himself after her execution.

Rolland, Romain (1866-1944), French author, musicologist. Known for novel series *Jean Christophe* (1904-12, 10 vol.) satirizing modern society. Also wrote plays on revolutionary heroism, eg *Les Loups* (1898), *Robespierre* (1938), music

criticism. Nobel Prize for Literature (1915).

roller, jay-like bird of Coraciidae family, found esp. in S Europe and Africa. Noted for tumbling flight in nuptial display. Species incl. Eurasian common roller, *Coracias garrulus.*

roller skating, see SKATING.

Rolling Stones, English rock music group formed in early 1960s. Estab. wide following in Europe, North America with songs displaying aggressive rhythm eg 'Satisfaction'. Group featured personality of Mick Jagger, music of Jagger and Keith Richard.

Rolls, Charles Stewart (1877-1910), English pioneer motorist, aviator. Drove in many of the European classic races. First to fly across English channel and back non-stop (1910). Killed in flying accident. With Sir [Frederick] Henry Royce (1863-1933), English engineer, formed Rolls-Royce Ltd. (1906), automobile and aeroplane engine manufacturers.

Romains, Jules, pseud. of Louis Farigoule (1885-1972), French author. Founded Unanimism, doctrine that artist can find significance only within group. Wrote novel cycle *Les Hommes de bonne volonté* (1932-47, 27 vol.), prose poems *Puissance de Paris* (1911), verse. See ABBAYE.

Roman Catholicism, major division of Christianity. Main tenets incl. recognition of pope as spiritual leader of the church, belief in apostolic succession, conveyance of God's grace through sacraments. Largest Christian denomination with hundreds of millions of adherents around the world. Centre of

RC community is Vatican City, Rome.

romance, in Middle Ages, narrative poem (*roman*) on chivalry, love, adventure, derived from short episodes from epics, condensed *chansons de geste*.

Romance languages, only surviving group of Italic branch of Indo-European language family. Spoken mainly in Europe, present and past European colonies. Incl. French, Italian, Portuguese, Romanian, Spanish. Developed from Latin vernacular (Vulgar Latin), after fall of Roman Empire.

Romanesque, style of architecture prevalent throughout Europe from mid-11th to mid-12th cents. Based on Roman forms, style is characterized by rounded arches, massive walls, interior square bays. Church of St Etienne at Nevers is representative example.

Romania or **Rumania,** republic of SE Europe. Area 237,428 sq km (91,671 sq mi); pop. 21,446,000; cap. Bucharest. Language: Romanian. Religion: Eastern Orthodox. Crossed N-S by Carpathians, E-W by Transylvanian Alps. Incl. lower Danube. Agric. mainly grain (lowlands), livestock (highlands), vines. Indust. development rapid, esp. petroleum. Corresponds to Roman *Dacia;* formed by union of MOLDAVIA, WALACHIA (1859); independent from 1878. Gained Transylvania (1920); internal strife, lost territ. (1940). Communist govt. estab. 1948. Large minorities in pop., esp. Hungarian, German, Jewish.

Romanian or **Rumanian,** Romance language in Italic branch of Indo-European family. Official language of Romania used in USSR, Albania, Greece, *etc.*

Roman law, code of laws of ancient Rome, basis for modern legal system of many countries. Formulated first (*c* 450 BC) as 12 Tables, achieved final form in Tribonian's *Corpus juris civilis,* compiled (AD 528-34) under Justinian I. Outstanding in clarity, comprehensiveness; incl. *jus gentium,* code of international law, and is basis of all European civil law.

Romanov, ruling house of Russia (1613-1917). Dynasty estab. by Michael, descendant of Ivan IV. Ceased to rule with enforced abdication of Nicholas II.

Roman religion, religious beliefs and practices of Roman state. Derived from animistic cults of indigenous Italic tribes. These were associated with family, home and harvests. During development of republic (from *c* 500 BC) many foreign elements were absorbed, *eg* from Etruscans, Greeks and various Oriental cults. Old Roman gods became identified with Greek equivalents. By end of republic 3 religions existed: old rural cults, upper-class Greco-Roman religion, new Oriental cults of people. New cults reflected demand for more emotionally satisfying beliefs, later shown in spread of Christianity.

Romans, epistle of NT, written by St Paul to Christians at Rome (*c* AD 58). Fundamental statement of Pauline theology; stresses justification by faith and universality of God's love.

Romansh, *see* RHAETO-ROMANIC.

Romanticism, in the arts, movement emphasizing imagination, emotions rather than intellect and formal restraint. Romantic characteristics incl. philosophic idealism, interest in primitive cultures, revolt against social and cultural conventions esp. in treatment of love. Grew in Europe as revolt against 18th cent. NEO-CLASSICISM.

Romany, see GYPSY.

Rome (*Roma*), cap. of Italy and of Latium, on R. Tiber. Pop. 2,843,000. Admin., indust., commercial, transport centre; film-making; tourism. Traditionally founded (753 BC) on 7 hills by Romulus. Etruscan rulers overthrown *c* 500 BC; republic estab., expanded *eg* by Punic Wars. Empire estab. (31 BC) by Octavian; declined after AD 2nd cent., divided (last Western emperor deposed 476), overrun by Goths, Vandals. Cap. of Papal States throughout Middle Ages; annexed to Italy 1870. Ancient ruins incl. Forum, Colosseum. Many churches, incl. St Peter's, St John in the Lateran. Also see VATICAN CITY.

Rome, Treaty of (1957), see EUROPEAN COMMUNITIES.

Romford, see HAVERING, England.

Rommel, Erwin (1891-1944), German army officer. Commanded a panzer division in the invasion of France (1940); as leader of the Afrika Corps (1941-3) showed brilliant qualities in desert warfare. Suspected of implication in the plot to kill Hitler (1944), he was forced to commit suicide by the Nazis.

Romney, George (1734-1802), English painter. With Gainsborough and Reynolds, one of the leading portraitists of his time. Known for his fashionable portraits of women and children, notably Lady Hamilton.

Romney Marsh, low-lying drained coastal marshland of Kent, SE England. Sheep pasturage. Reclamation from Roman times.

Romulus, legendary founder of Rome; son of Mars and Rhea Silvia, daughter of Numitor, king of Alba Longa. With his twin brother Remus, cast into R. Tiber by Amulius, usurper of Numitor's throne. Survived and suckled by she-wolf. Killed Remus in quarrel when building walls of Rome. Procured wives for Roman citizens by rape of Sabine women. Vanished in thunderstorm, worshipped as god Quirinus.

Romulus Augustulus, last Roman emperor in West (475-6). Proclaimed emperor by his father Orestes, who had deposed Julius Nepos. Deposed by German mercenary ODOVACAR.

Roncesvalles (Fr. *Roncevaux*), village of Navarre, NE Spain, in Pyrenees. Mountain pass, height 1056 m (3468 ft), is traditionally scene of defeat of Charlemagne and death of Roland (778).

rondo, form of instrumental music with a recurring section. May be single piece, or last movement of sonata, symphony, concerto.

Ronsard, Pierre de (*c* 1524-85), French poet. Leader of Pléiade group who sought to revitalize French poetry by imitating classical models. Works incl. patriotic *Discours des misères de ce temps* (1562), melancholic love poetry *Sonnets pour Hélène* (1578).

Röntgen or **Roentgen, Wilhelm Konrad** (1845-1923), German physicist. Discovered X-rays while experimenting with cathode rays; showed that these rays affect photographic plates and pass through substances opaque to light.

Awarded Nobel Prize for Physics (1901).

Roodepoort-Maraisburg, city of S Transvaal, South Africa. Pop. 114,000. Goldmining and residential centre in Witwatersrand.

rood screen, in medieval church architecture, ornamental screen serving as partition between nave and chancel. Above it was rood beam which bore wooden crucifix (rood) flanked by figures of St John and the Virgin.

rook, Corvus frugilegus, gregarious European bird of crow family. Glossy black plumage with bare whitish face.

Roon, Albrecht Theodor Emil, Graf von (1803-79), Prussian army officer. As war minister (1859-73) reorganized army, facilitating victories over Austria (1866), and France (1870-1).

Roosevelt, Franklin Delano (1882-1945), American statesman, president (1933-45). Partially crippled by poliomyelitis 1921. Governor of New York (1929-33), successful Democratic presidential candidate (1932). Countered Depression with NEW DEAL legislation to aid labour, agriculture, unemployed. Attempted to reorganize Supreme Court which had invalidated several New Deal measures. Elected for unprecedented 3rd term (1940), kept US out of WWII until Japan attacked Pearl Harbor (Dec. 1941). Laid basis for post-war Europe in meetings with Churchill, Stalin. Died after election for 4th term. Wife, **[Anna] Eleanor Roosevelt** (1884-1962), served as US delegate at UN (1945-53, 1961), worked for social reform.

Roosevelt, Theodore (1858-1919),

American statesman, president (1901-9). Popular hero after serving in Cuba, elected (1898) governor of New York. Republican vice-president (1901), succeeded McKinley at latter's death. Vigorously regulated big business by 'trust busting' under Sherman Anti-Trust Act. Pursued militant Latin American policy; secured independence of Panama (1903) to allow building of Panama Canal. Re-elected 1904, awarded Nobel Peace Prize (1906) after mediating to end Russo-Japanese War. Picked successor, W.H. TAFT, whom he later ran against as Progressive candidate (1912).

root, that part of a plant which absorbs moisture and food, provides anchorage and support. May store food. Usually penetrates soil but can grow in air or water.

root, in mathematics, solution of an algebraic equation. Square root of a number is that number which when multiplied by itself gives original number, eg 3 and -3 are square roots of 9.

rorqual, toothless whale of world-wide distribution, · genus Balaenoptera. Small pointed head, well-developed dorsal fin. Species incl. common rorqual, B. physalus, and blue whale, B. musculus.

Rorschach, Hermann (1884-1922), Swiss psychiatrist. Devised test to analyze personality, in which patient describes his interpretations of 10 standardized ink blot designs. His responses are then analyzed and interpreted.

Rosaceae, large family of flowering herbs, shrubs and small trees. Incl.

rose, bramble, apple, plum and cherry.

Rosario, port of EC Argentina, on Paraná R. Pop. 798,000. Large railway jct., export depot for wheat, beef from Pampas; sugar refining, meat packing, flour milling industs.

rosary, in RC church, series of prayers, counted as they are said on a string of beads. Usually 5 or 15 sets (decades) of 1 large and 10 small beads. Prayers used are Lord's Prayer, Gloria Patri and Ave Maria.

Roscommon, county of Connacht prov., WC Irish Republic. Area 2463 sq km (951 sq mi); pop. 53,000. Bounded in E by R. Shannon; lakes, bogland. Cattle, sheep pasture. Co. town Roscommon, pop. 2000. Agric. market; castle (1269), priory.

rose, any of genus *Rosa* of shrubs native to N temperate regions. Spiny stems, five-parted, usually fragrant flowers of various colours. Many varieties, widely cultivated, are derived from wild sweetbriar, *R. rubiginosa* and dog-rose, *R. canina*.

Rosebery, Archibald Philip Primrose, 5th Earl of (1847-1929), British statesman, PM (1894-5). Succeeded Gladstone as PM. His advocacy of imperialist policies in Africa estranged him from much of Liberal Party.

rosemary, *Rosmarinus officinalis,* evergreen shrub of mint family, native to Mediterranean region. Used as culinary herb and in cosmetics.

Rosenberg, Alfred (1893-1946), German Nazi ideologist. Wrote *Der Mythus des 20 Jahrhunderts* (1930) to provide quasi-scientific basis for Hitler's racist policies. Convicted, hanged as war criminal.

Rosenberg, Isaac (1890-1918), English poet. Poetry initially influenced by Blake and Hebrew mythology. Best known poems deal with experiences in WWI, in which he was killed. *Collected Works* issued 1937.

Rosenberg, Julius (1917-53), American spy. With his wife Ethel, was executed for passing atomic secrets to USSR during WWII. Their accomplices, Ethel's brother David Greenglass and Harry Gold, received long prison sentences.

rose of Sharon, *Hibiscus syriacus,* Asian ornamental plant, and *Hypericum calycinum,* evergreen European shrub with large yellow flowers.

Roses, Wars of the, civil wars (1455-85) fought between Houses of Lancaster and York for the English throne. Their badges were red rose and white rose, respectively. Lancastrian king Henry VI was forced to recognize duke of York as his heir but York's claims were set aside on birth of king's son (1454). Fighting began at 1st battle of St Albans (1455). York was defeated and killed at Wakefield (1460) but his son deposed Henry after 2nd battle of St Albans (1461), becoming Edward IV. Henry was briefly restored (1470-1) but was defeated by Edward at Barnet and Tewkesbury. Wars ended when Henry Tudor, a Lancastrian, assumed power as Henry VII after defeating Richard III at Bosworth (1485).

Rosetta Stone, ancient Egyptian basalt slab, now in the British Museum, discovered during Napoleon's occupation of Egypt. Bears a decree of Ptolemy V (196 BC) written in hieroglyphics, demotic and Greek. Knowledge of Greek version enabled CHAMPOLLION to decipher hieroglyphics.

rose window, in ecclesiastical architecture, circular window divided by mullions radiating from centre or filled with tracery, suggesting rose form. Famous example at Notre Dame, Paris.

rosewood, hard reddish wood obtained from various tropical trees, esp. Brazilian rosewood or jacaranda, *Dalbergia nigra.* Used for cabinet-making, veneering.

Rosicrucians, members of 17th and 18th cent. occult groups claiming ancient Egyptian origins for their movement. Symbols incl. rose, cross, swastika, pyramid. Prob. derives from works of Johan Andreä (1586-1654) who took pseud. Christian Rosenkreuz. Modern US movement adheres to theosophical doctrines.

rosin, residue from distillation of crude turpentine. Hard, brittle resin, usually light-yellow or amber. Used in making varnishes, soaps, and for treating violin bows, *etc.*

Ross, Sir John (1777-1856), Scottish explorer, naval officer. In search of Northwest Passage, discovered Boothia Penin. and King William Land (1829-33). His nephew, **Sir James Clark Ross** (1800-62), made several Arctic expeditions from 1818; located N magnetic pole (1831). Led Antarctic voyage (1839-43), discovered Ross Sea, Ross Isl., Victoria Land.

Ross, Sir Ronald (1857-1932), British physician, b. India. Awarded Nobel Prize for Physiology and Medicine (1902) for discovery of the malaria-causing parasite in the *Anopheles* mosquito.

Ross and Cromarty, former county of N Scotland, incl. some of Hebrides, now in Highland region. Mountains, moorland, lochs (incl. Broom, Carron, Maree); lowland in E (Black Isle). Agric., crofting, sheep farming, deer forests; fishing, tourism. Co. town was Dingwall.

Ross Dependency, New Zealand Antarctic territ., lying S of 60°S and between 160°E and 150°W. Incl. Ross Sea, coastal areas of Victoria, Edward VII and Marie Byrd lands, Ross Isl. (site of Mt. Erebus).

Rossellini, Roberto (1906-77), Italian film director. Became known for film on post-war Rome, *Open City* (1945), went on to make other classic neo-realist films.

Rossetti, Dante Gabriel (1828-82), English painter, poet. Founded Pre-Raphaelite Brotherhood (1848) with Millais and Hunt; pub. journal *Germ* in which appeared poem 'The Blessed Damozel'. Subjects of paintings were taken from Dante and medieval romance; works incl. *Girlhood of Mary Virgin.* His poems were attacked on grounds of morality. His sister, **Christina Georgina Rossetti** (1830-94), was also a poet. Wrote religious, often melancholy poetry; works incl. *Goblin Market and Other Poems* (1862).

Rossini, Gioacchino Antonio (1792-1868), Italian composer. Noted for melodic and humorous qualities. Wrote 36 operas from 1810-29, incl. *The Barber of Seville, William Tell.* Then virtually abandoned composition, although producing *Stabat Mater.*

Ross Sea, inlet of S Pacific Ocean, E

of Victoria Land, Antarctica. Ross Ice Shelf forms S section. Explored c 1841 by Sir James Ross.

Rostand, Edmond (1868-1918), French poet, dramatist. Best known for *Cyrano de Bergerac* (1897), drama of rhetoric, high adventure, lyrical feeling. Also wrote allegory *Chantecler* (1910).

Rostock, town of N East Germany, at head of Warnow estuary. Pop. 201,000. Port; fisheries, shipbuilding, machinery. Hanseatic League member (14th cent.); univ. (1418). Aircraft works bombed in WWII.

Rostov-on-Don, city of USSR, SW European RSFSR; near mouth of Don on Sea of Azov. Pop. 823,000. Port, exports grain, wool; shipbuilding, agric. machinery mfg. Founded 1761, grew in 19th cent. as grain centre. Damaged in WWII.

Rotary International, organization of business, professional men, founded 1905 (US), 1914 (UK). Professed aim to promote standards in business, professions. Supports charities.

Roth, Philip (1933-), American author. Novels, eg *Goodbye Columbus* (1959), *When She Was Good* (1967), *Portnoy's Complaint* (1969), frequently deal with the tension between Jewish and Gentile cultures in middle-class America.

Rotherham, bor. of South Yorkshire met. county, N England. Pop. 85,000. Iron and steel indust. 15th cent. bridge over R. Don (rebuilt 1930).

Rothermere, Harold Sidney Harmsworth, 1st Viscount (1868-1940), English publisher. Provided financial direction in his brother NORTHCLIFFE's publishing firm, at whose death he took control. Founded (1915) *Sunday Pictorial*.

Rothesay, town and small port of Strathclyde region, W Scotland, on Isle of Bute. Pop. 7000. Tourist resort.

Rothko, Mark (1903-70), American painter, b. Russia. Known for his large abstract works which consist of rectangles of luminous colour merging into each other. Committed suicide.

Rothschild, Mayer Amschel (1743-1812), German banker. Founded family fortune as financial agent in Frankfurt. His sons opened branches in Paris, Vienna and London, where **Nathan Meyer Rothschild** (1777-1836) estab. family branch (1798), supplying British govt. with finances in struggle against Napoleon and making loans to European and South American countries. His son, **Baron Lionel Nathan de Rothschild** (1808-79), further extended family's influence. First Jewish MP.

Rotorua, town of NC North Isl., New Zealand, on L. Rotorua. Pop. 31,000. Major health and tourist centre based on hot springs, geysers; Maori culture; also timber, fishing industs.

rotten borough, in English history, parliamentary constituencies which continued to return representatives to Parliament despite virtual disappearance of electorate. Most notorious was Old Sarum. Abolished by 1832 Reform Act.

Rotterdam, city of W Netherlands, on R. Nieuwe Maas. Pop. 670,000. Chief European seaport, canal links via R. Rhine with NW Germany; entrepôt trade. Indust. centre, incl. shipbuilding, oil refining. Chartered

1328, expanded 19th cent. Development of Europoort (1960s), massive port, indust. complex. City centre destroyed in WWII. Birthplace of Erasmus.

Rouault, Georges (1871-1958), French painter. Trained as a stained glass maker; his early paintings, employing heavy black outlines, depict injustice and suffering; subjects incl. prostitutes, clowns, judges. Later turned to religious painting.

Roubaix, city of Nord, N France. Pop. 113,000. Textile centre, esp. woollens, carpets. Forms conurbation with Lille and Tourcoing.

Rouen, city of N France, on R. Seine, cap. of Seine-Maritime dept. Pop. 120,000. Major port, indust. centre (esp. metals, chemicals, textiles); univ. (1966). Hist. cap. of Normandy. Held by English (1419-49); Joan of Arc burned here (1431). Notable Gothic architecture, esp. 13th cent. cathedral. Birthplace of Corneille, Flaubert. Badly damaged in WWII.

roulette, gambling game played by rolling a small ball around a shallow bowl with an inner disc revolving in the opposite direction. Ball comes to rest in one of 36 numbered compartments, coloured alternately red and black, determining winning bets.

rounders, nine-a-side English outdoor game played with bat and ball. Similar to baseball, which is prob. derived from it.

Roundheads, name given to members of Parliamentary or Puritan party during English Civil War. So called because of their close-cropped hair.

Round Table, *see* ARTHURIAN LEGEND.

roundworm, *see* NEMATODA.

Rousseau, Henri (1844-1910), French painter, known as 'le Douanier'. Employed a seemingly naive, but direct, imaginative style to depict jungle scenes, exotic subjects, *etc.* Works incl. *The Sleeping Gypsy.*

Rousseau, Jean Jacques (1712-78), French philosopher, b. Geneva. Wrote *Discours sur l'origine de l'inégalité des hommes* (1754), an attack on property and the state as causes of inequality. His *Contrat social* (1762) describes ideal state with sovereignty held inalienably by people as a whole; individual retains freedom by submitting to 'general will'. Other works incl. novel on education, *Emile* (1762), autobiog. *Confessions.* Had great influence on later thinkers and 19th cent. Romanticism.

Rousseau, [Pierre Etienne] Théodore (1812-67), French painter. Leading member of Barbizon school of landscape painters, work noted for its handling of atmospheric effects.

Roussel, Albert (1869-1937), French composer. Music developed from late romanticism through period of impressionism. Works incl. operas, ballets, symphonies, chamber music, songs, piano pieces.

rowan, *see* MOUNTAIN ASH.

rowing, sport of propelling a boat by means of oars. Competitive rowing dates from early 19th cent. in England; Leander Club, London, was formed in 1818, similar clubs formed in US in 1830s. Annual boat races between Oxford and Cambridge (estab. 1829) and Harvard and Yale (estab. 1852) are major rowing events in UK and US. Olympic sport since 1908.

Rowlandson, Thomas (1756-1827), English caricaturist. Known for satires on the social scene; his *Tours of Dr Syntax* was very popular.

Rowley, William (c 1585-1642), English actor, dramatist. Best known for collaboration with Thomas Middleton on *The Changeling* (presented 1621). Also worked with Dekker and Ford (*The Witch of, Edmonton*, 1621).

Roxana (d. 311 BC), Bactrian princess, wife of Alexander the Great. Gave birth to son after Alexander's death (323). Imprisoned in Macedonia by CASSANDER, who had her and her son murdered.

Roxburghshire, former county of SE Scotland, now in Borders region. Mainly hilly, Cheviots in S. Teviot, Tweed rivers. Sheep rearing; woollens, tweed mfg. Co. town was Jedburgh.

Royal Academy [of Arts], institution founded (1768) in London by George III to encourage painting, sculpture and architecture; moved to present site at Burlington House in 1867. Holds annual summer exhibition of contemporary art and maintains a free school.

Royal Air Force, junior of 3 fighting services in UK, formed (1918) by merging Royal Flying Corps and Royal Naval Air Service.

Royal Canadian Mounted Police, federal law-enforcement agency of Canada. Estab. (1873) as North West Mounted Police, early duties incl. protecting settlers, preventing Indian risings. Renamed 1920.

Royal Marines, see MARINES.

Royal Navy, see NAVY.

royal prerogative, see CROWN.

Royal Society (Royal Society of London for Improving Natural Knowledge), British scientific society, founded (1660) to encourage scientific research. Eminent scientists are elected as fellows (FRS).

Royal Society for the Prevention of Cruelty to Animals (RSPCA), British organization founded (1824) in London to promote humane treatment of animals and provide free veterinary treatment. Founder, Richard Martin (1754-1834), was Irish landowner, known as 'Humanity' Martin. American SPCA was founded in 1866.

Royce, Sir [Frederick] Henry, see ROLLS, CHARLES STEWART.

RSFSR, see RUSSIAN SOVIET FEDERATED SOCIALIST REPUBLIC.

Ruanda-Urundi, see RWANDA; BURUNDI.

Ruapehu, Mount, active volcano of New Zealand, in Tongariro National Park. Highest peak of North Isl. (2975 m/9175 ft); has warm crater lake. Tourist area; timber on lower slopes.

Rub-al-Khali, desert region of S Arabia, mainly in Saudi Arabia. Area c 582,750 sq km (225,000 sq mi). Also known as 'empty quarter'.

rubber, elastic substance produced from latex, esp. of *Hevea brasiliensis* tree. Most rubber articles are made by treating latex chemically, eg by mixing with sulphur and heating (vulcanization). Rubber can be produced synthetically as polymer of isoprene.

rubber plant, *Ficus elastica,* Asian tree of mulberry family. Large, glossy, leathery leaves. Often grown indoors as ornamental where it may reach height of 3 m (10 ft). Also called India rubber tree.

rubber tree, various tropical and subtropical trees producing LATEX. Chief source is *Hevea brasiliensis,* native to Amazon but cultivated in SE Asia. Latex is collected from cuts made in bark.

Rubbra, Charles Edmund (1901-), English composer. His music is influenced by early English polyphonic music and is often traditional in form. Works incl. 9 symphonies, vocal music.

rubella or **German measles,** infectious virus disease, common in childhood. Characterized by pink rash, swelling of lymph nodes behind the ears. In pregnant women, may cause damage to the embryo if contracted before 4th month of pregnancy.

Rubens, Sir Peter Paul (1577-1640), Flemish painter. Court painter to duke of Mantua, then to Archduke Albert in Antwerp. Travelled widely as diplomat and painter, carrying out commissions in Madrid, London and Paris. Work in exuberant Baroque style is fluent in colour and texture; paintings incl. *Descent from the Cross, Peace and War* and series *Life of Marie de' Medici.*

Rubicon, small river of EC Italy, flowing into Adriatic Sea N of Rimini. In ancient times marked border of Italy and Cisalpine Gaul; crossing (49 BC) by Julius Caesar represented declaration of war on Pompey and Senate.

rubidium (Rb), soft metallic element; at. no. 37, at. wt. 85.47. Extremely reactive member of alkali metal group; ignites spontaneously in air and reacts vigorously with water. Used in photocells.

Rubinstein, Artur (1887-), American pianist, b. Poland. Noted for interpretation of Chopin, Beethoven, Schubert. Has performed worldwide into his old age.

Rublev, Andrei (c 1360-c 1430), Russian painter. Considered greatest Russian religious painter. Broke with Byzantine tradition of teacher Theophanes, developed simple linear style. Masterpiece is icon of OT Trinity.

ruby, precious gemstone, a variety of CORUNDUM. Deep red and transparent; used in jewellery. Finest rubies come from Burma, Thailand.

Rudolf, lake, lake of NW Kenya and SW Ethiopia, in Great Rift Valley. Length c 275 km (170 mi). Has no outlet; gradually diminishing. Now called L. Turkana.

Rudolf I (1218-91), Holy Roman emperor (1273-91). Originally count of HABSBURG, he was founder of the imperial dynasty. Defeated Bohemians (1278) and made his sons dukes of Austria and Syria, thus strengthening empire.

Rudolph (1858-89), crown prince of Austria, only son of Emperor Francis Joseph. Found dead at Mayerling with mistress, Maria Vetsera, in mysterious circumstances.

rue, *Ruta graveolens,* European perennial herb. Yellow flowers, blue-green leaves with pungent taste formerly used in medicine.

ruff, *Philomachus pugnax,* Eurasian

sandpiper, related to plover, male of which has ruff of erectile feathers during breeding season.

Rugby, mun. bor. of Warwickshire, C England. Pop. 59,000. Railway jct.; engineering; cattle market, cement mfg. Public school (1567), where rugby football originated (1823). Major radio communications centre nearby.

rugby football, fifteen-a-side team game, played with oval leather ball which may be kicked and handled. Said to have originated at Rugby School, England, in 1823; 1st rules drawn up in 1871. Differences over payment of players led to formation of professional Rugby League (1895), whose members play thirteen-a-side variation of game.

Ruhr, major indust. area of NW West Germany, based on R. Ruhr (length c 230 km/145 mi). Duisburg, Essen, Gelsenkirchen, Bochum, Dortmund form vast conurbation served by extensive system of canals, roads, railways. Major industs. incl. coalmining, iron and steel, chemicals. Developed in 19th cent. Heavily bombed in WWII, but rapid recovery aided post-war revival of German economy.

Ruisdael or **Ruysdael, Jacob van** (c 1628-82), Dutch painter. Major landscape painter of 17th cent., his realist work influenced 19th cent. artists. Frequently depicted overcast skies with light breaking through the clouds; works in more romantic later style incl. *The Jewish Cemetery*.

Rum, see RHUM, Scotland.

rum, spirit distilled from fermented cane sugar by-products, chiefly molasses. Naturally colourless; brown colour results from storage in casks or addition of caramel. Most export rums are produced in West Indies.

Rumania, see ROMANIA.

Rumelia, area of S Balkan Penin. Incl. Thrace, Macedonia. Hist. part of Ottoman Empire; Eastern Rumelia (cap. Plovdiv) autonomous from 1878, annexed by Bulgaria (1885).

Rumford, Benjamin Thompson, Count (1753-1814), British scientist, administrator, b. US. Known for investigations into mechanical production of heat; his belief that heat is produced by motion of particles helped undermine earlier caloric theory of heat.

ruminant, cloven-hoofed cud-chewing mammal. Four-chambered stomach; food passes first 2 chambers, then is re-chewed and passes to last 2 chambers. Incl. cattle, sheep, goats, deer, giraffes.

rummy, card game played by two to six players. Variations incl. gin rummy and CANASTA.

Rump Parliament, name given to members of Long Parliament remaining after exclusion of army's opponents, carried out in Pride's Purge (1648). Dissolved by Cromwell (1653), who later instituted PROTECTORATE.

Rundstedt, [Karl Rudolf] Gerd von (1875-1953), German field marshal. Commanded in Polish (1939) and French (1940) campaigns. Commanded all German occupation forces in Europe from 1942 until Allied invasion (1944), when he was superseded; reinstated to organize Ardennes offensive.

runes, ancient alphabet, prob. derived from Greek script; used by Scandinavians and other early Germanic peoples from c AD 300. Letters consist of oblique, perpendicular and a few curved lines. Carved on wood or stone.

Runnymede, meadow of Egham, Surrey, S England, on S bank of R. Thames. Probable site of sealing of MAGNA CARTA (1215) by King John. National Memorial to President Kennedy (1965).

Runyon, Damon (1884-1946), American short story writer. Known for humorous works, eg Guys and Dolls (1932), detailing lives of Broadway characters in racy vernacular.

Rupert (1619-82), German prince in military service of uncle, Charles I of England. Commanded Royalist cavalry in Civil War; defeated by Cromwell at Marston Moor (1644). Returned to England after Charles II's Restoration, sponsored founding of Hudson's Bay Co. (1670).

Rupert's Land, hist. territ. of N Canada, held by Hudson's Bay Co. (1670-1869). Comprised drainage basin of Hudson Bay, embracing large areas of many modern Canadian provs. Sold to Canada (1869).

rupture, in medicine, see HERNIA.

Rurik (d. 879), traditional founder of first Russian dynasty. Leader of a band of Scandinavian traders (Varangians), he estab. himself as prince of Novgorod (c 862). His heirs eventually ruled all Russia.

Ruse (Turk. Ruschuk), city of N Bulgaria, on R. Danube. Pop. 163,000. Indust., commercial centre, exports cereals. Fortified Roman town; developed as port by Turks. Ceded to Bulgaria (1877).

rush, any of genus Juncus of long-stemmed plants with small, greenish flowers. Found in marshes of temperate and cold regions. Stems used for making mats, baskets, etc. Name also applied to similar plants, eg BULRUSH, CATTAIL.

Rush-Bagot Convention, settlement (1817) of US-Canadian border negotiated by US secretary of state, Richard Rush, and British minister in Washington, Charles Bagot. Limited armaments along border and estab. precedent of peaceful relations between US and Canada.

Rushmore, Mount, see BLACK HILLS.

Rusk, Dean (1909-), American public official. As Assistant Secretary of State for Far Eastern Affairs (1950-2), Secretary of State (1961-9), played prominent part in US involvement in Korean, Vietnam wars.

Ruskin, John (1819-1900), English critic. His Modern Painters (1843-60) started as a defence of Turner but later dealt with politics, social reform, architecture; his Stones of Venice (1851-3) reflects advocacy of Gothic architecture as an uncorrupted style. Believed in possibility of reviving artistic standards by a return to freedom of medieval craftsmanship.

Russell, Bertrand Arthur William, 3rd Earl Russell (1872-1970), English philosopher, mathematician, b. Wales. Collaborated with A.N. Whitehead on Principia Mathematica (1910-13) attempting to estab. logical basis of mathematics. Developed symbolic logic. Other works incl. The ABC of Relativity (1925), History of Wes-

tern Philosophy (1945). Leading pacifist spokesman. Nobel Prize for Literature (1950).

Russell, Charles Taze (1852-1916), American clergyman. Founded (1872) evangelical Jehovah's Witnesses (originally called Russellites). Doctrine centres on belief in imminent 2nd coming of Christ and a millennial period when repentent sinners may be redeemed. Members refuse to participate in warfare or govt. Publications incl. *The Watch Tower.*

Russell, George William (1867-1935), Irish poet, patriot. Known for mystical verse under pseud. 'AE', *eg The Earth Breath* (1897), *House of the Titans* (1934). Also wrote prose work on mysticism *The Candle of Vision* (1918). Associated with Abbey Theatre, Dublin, editor of *The Irish Statesman.*

Russell, John Russell, 1st Earl (1792-1878), British statesman, PM (1846-52, 1865-6). Supported Catholic Emancipation (1829) and helped draft Reform Bill of 1832. As foreign secretary under Palmerston (1859-65), advocated British neutrality in American Civil War.

Russell, Ken (1927-), English film director. Films, often intended to shock, incl. *Women in Love* (1969), *The Music Lovers* (1970).

Russell, Sir William Howard (1821-1907), British journalist, b. Ireland. As *The Times* correspondent covering Crimean War, exposed mismanagement of campaign. Subsequent sensation contributed to fall of Aberdeen's government.

Russia, see UNION OF SOVIET SOCIALIST REPUBLICS.

Russian, language in E Slavic branch of Indo-European family. Spoken by *c* 140 million as 1st language in USSR, one of official languages of UN. Uses Cyrillic alphabet.

Russian Orthodox Church, branch of EASTERN ORTHODOX CHURCH. Originally headed by patriarch of Constantinople, patriarchate of Moscow estab. 1589. National church of Tsarist Russia, power and influence declined after Russian Revolution, esp. 1925-43 (when new patriarch appointed).

Russian Revolution, national uprisings (1905, 1917) against tsarist autocracy. Discontent with agric. and indust. conditions resulted in series (1905) of strikes, mutinies (*eg* battleship *Potemkin* at Odessa); led to limited concessions, such as estab. of *duma* parliament. Further opposition arose after continued Russian losses during WWI. February Revolution (1917) led to estab. of provisional govt. in defiance of tsar, who then abdicated. Socialist opposition to War, led by LENIN and BOLSHEVIKS, culminated in October Revolution. Communist Party estab.; private ownership abolished, Russia withdrew from WWI. Ensuing civil war (1918-20) between Red Army, organized by TROTSKY, and White Army, supported by European nations, ended with Communist consolidation of power and founding (1921) of USSR.

Russian Soviet Federated Socialist Republic (RSFSR), largest constituent republic of USSR. Area *c* 17,070,000 sq km (6,590,000 sq mi); pop. 130,090,000; cap. Moscow. Admin. subdivisions incl.

16 auton. republics and 5 auton. regions. Stretches from Baltic in W to Pacific in E and N to Arctic. Mountain ranges incl. Urals, which divide European plain from Siberia. Economy, history and culture is that of USSR.

Russo-Japanese War (1904-5), conflict provoked by Russian penetration into Manchuria and Korea. Japan attacked and captured Port Arthur, destroyed Russian fleet at Tsushima. Peace settlement reduced Russian role in E Asia.

Russo-Turkish Wars, series of wars (18th-19th cent.) in which Russia sought to control Black Sea and gain access to Mediterranean at expense of Ottoman Empire. Russian expansion checked by European allies during Crimean War (1853-6). Final settlement dictated at Congress of Berlin (1878).

rust, reddish-brown coating formed on surface of iron or steel exposed to atmosphere. Consists mainly of ferric oxide (Fe_2O_3) and hydroxide. Caused by action of oxygen and moisture.

Ruth, George Herman ('Babe') (1895-1948), American baseball player. Member of New York Yankees team, he dominated the sport with his colourful personality and many records incl. 60 home runs in 1927. His career total of 714 home runs was not beaten until 1974 (by Henry Aaron).

Ruth, book of OT. Relates story of Ruth, Moabite widow who accompanied her Jewish mother-in-law to Bethlehem and married Boaz. Ancestress of David.

Ruthenia, region of C Europe, in S Carpathian Mts.; now largely in

USSR (Ukraine). Part of Austro-Hungarian empire until 1918, then held by Czechoslovakia until 1939. Ceded to USSR in 1945.

ruthenium (Ru), hard brittle metallic element of platinum group; at. no. 44, at. wt. 101.07. Used to make hard alloys with platinum and palladium and as a catalyst.

Rutherford, Ernest Rutherford, 1st Baron (1871-1937), British physicist, b. New Zealand. Estab. existence of alpha and beta particles given off during radioactive decay and developed theory of radioactivity with F. Soddy; awarded Nobel Prize for Chemistry (1908). Work with alpha particles led to his description of atom as central positively charged nucleus surrounded by orbiting electrons. Experimented in nuclear transmutation of elements induced by alpha particle bombardment.

Rutherford, Dame Margaret (1892-1972), English actress. Noted in comedy roles, eg Mme Arcati in *Blithe Spirit*, Miss Prism (1939), later Lady Bracknell (1947) in *The Importance of Being Earnest*.

Rutland, former county (smallest) of England, now part of Leicestershire. Co. town was Oakham. Agric., esp. wheat, barley market.

Ruwenzori, mountain range of Uganda and Zaïre, between lakes Albert and Edward. Peaks incl. Stanley, Margherita, Alexandra, all c 5120 m (16,800 ft). Discovered (1889) by Stanley. Possibly the ancient 'Mountains of the Moon', once supposed to be source of Nile.

Rwanda, republic of EC Africa. Area 26,400 sq km (10,200 sq mi); pop. 4,289,000; cap. Kigali. Languages: Bantu, **French.** Religions: native, Christian. Mainly high plateau, L. Kivu in W. Cattle rearing, tin mining, exports coffee. Former kingdom, part of German East Africa from 1899; part of Belgian colony of Ruanda-Urundi after WWI; independent as republic from 1962. Invasion by Tutsi émigrés from Burundi ended in massacre of Tutsi pop. 1964.

Ryazan, city of USSR, C European RSFSR. Pop. 378,000. Trade in agric. produce; agric. machinery mfg. Old town, c 50 km (30 mi) distant, was cap. of principality from 11th cent. until destroyed by Mongols 1237.

Rye, mun. bor. of East Sussex, SE England, on R. Rother. Pop. 4000. Resort; market town. Has Ypres Tower (12th cent.); former Cinque Port.

rye, *Secale cereale,* tall Eurasian annual grass grown extensively in Eurasia and North America. Black grain used in making black rye bread, rye whiskey and for livestock feed.

Rye House Plot, conspiracy (1683) to assassinate King Charles II and brother James on London road in Hertfordshire. Plot uncovered, used as excuse to execute several of Charles' opponents.

Rykov, Aleksei Ivanovich (1881-

1938), Soviet political leader. Supported Stalin against Trotsky after death of Lenin; premier (1924-30). Politically suspect after opposing Stalin's collectivization policy. Executed during party purges.

Ryle, Gilbert (1900-76), English philosopher. Known for influential *The Concept of Mind* (1949), attempting to show that the Cartesian distinction between inner and outer world is false.

Ryle, Sir Martin (1918-), British radioastronomer. astronomer royal (1972). Shared Nobel Prize for Physics (1974) with Antony Hewish for work on detection of pulsars.

Ryswick, Treaty of, settlement of War of Grand Alliance (1688-97) thwarting French territ. ambitions; signed (1697) at Ryswick, Netherlands. Dutch gained commercial concessions. Savoy's independence and William III's rule of England acknowledged.

Ryukyu Islands, archipelago of W Pacific Ocean, between Taiwan and Japan. Area 2200 sq km (850 sq mi); pop. 1,235,000; main isl. Okinawa. Sweet potatoes, sugar cane, pineapples, fishing. Part of Japan from 1879, under US jurisdiction from 1945. N group returned to Japan (1953), remainder returned (1972).

S

SA, *see* BROWNSHIRTS.

Saale or **Thuringian (Saxonian) Saale,** river of Germany. Flows *c* 425 km (265 mi) from NE Bavaria (West Germany) to R. Elbe near Magdeburg (East Germany).

Saarbrücken (Fr. *Sarrebruck*), city of W West Germany, on R. Saar; cap. of Saarland. Pop. 128,000. Coalmining; machinery; instrument mfg. Site of Roman bridge. Ceded to Prussia by France 1815.

Saarland, state of West Germany. Area 2567 sq km (991 sq mi); cap. Saarbrücken. Mainly hilly and forested, incl. R. Saar valley. Rich coalfield, major iron and steel indust. Returned after plebiscites to Germany (1935, 1957) following French occupation.

Saavedra Lamas, Carlos (1880-1959), Argentinian lawyer, diplomat, statesman. Expert in international law, presided over Buenos Aires conference (1935) ending Gran Chaco War. Awarded Nobel Peace Prize (1936).

Sabadell, city of Catalonia, NE Spain. Pop. 159,000. Textile mfg. from medieval times; also timber, dye industs.

Sabah, state of East Malaysia. Area *c* 76,500 sq km (29,500 sq mi); pop. 656,000; cap. Kota Kinabulu. Largely mountainous, rising 4100 m (13,455 ft) at Mt. Kinabulu; densely forested. Produces rubber, copra, timber. Was British protect. of North Borneo (1882-1963) until it joined Malaysia.

Sabbatai Zevi (1626-76), Jewish cabalist, b. Smyrna. Proclaimed himself messiah (1648); proclaimed year 1666 as date of millennium. Eventually embraced Islam to escape death.

Sabbath (Heb., = rest), day of rest and worship. Observed by Jews from sunset on Friday to sunset on Saturday, by most Christian denominations on Sunday (except ADVENTISTS). Friday is Islamic day of public worship.

Sabines, ancient people of C Italy, from earliest times connected with Rome. According to legend, wives were taken from the Sabines for unmarried followers of Romulus ('rape of Sabine women'). Constantly warred with Romans, but by 3rd cent. BC had amalgamated with them.

sable, *Martes zibellina,* carnivorous mammal of marten family, found in N Asia. Cultivated for valuable fur.

sable antelope, *Hippotragus niger,* large dark-coloured antelope of S Africa. Long ringed backward-curving horns.

sabre-toothed tiger, extinct cat of Machairodontidae subfamily, with tusk-like canine teeth in upper jaw. Existed between Oligocene and Pleistocene epochs.

25

saccharin, white crystalline powder produced synthetically from toluene. Slightly soluble in water; c 500 times sweeter than sugar. Used as sugar substitute in diabetic diets and as calorie-free sweetener.

Sacco, Nicola (1891-1927) and **Bartolomeo Vanzetti** (1888-1927), Italian anarchists. Tried and convicted (1921) for murder in Massachusetts; case became *cause célèbre* in US, many believing conviction resulted from their reputation as radicals. Decision upheld despite appeals, both were executed.

Sacher-Masoch, Leopold von (1836-95), Austrian novelist. Famous as source of term 'masochism', the sexual abnormality portrayed in his novels, eg *False Ermine* (1873), *The Legacy of Cain* (1877).

Sacheverell, Henry (c 1674-1724), English clergyman. Accused Whig govt. of neglecting Anglican church and tolerating religious dissenters. His suspension (1710) from preaching led to downfall of Whigs.

Sachs, Hans (1494-1576), German poet, cobbler. Prolific writer, known as Meistersinger portrayed by Wagner in *The Mastersingers of Nuremberg*, but best works in *Schwänk, Fastnachtspiel* forms, producing realistic scenes of everyday life.

Sachs, Nelly (1891-1970), Swedish poet, b. Berlin. Wrote expressionist lyrics, poetic drama often concerned with suffering of Jews. Shared Nobel Prize for Literature (1966) with Shmuel Agnon.

Sackville, Thomas, 1st Earl of Dorset (1536-1608), English poet, statesman. Collaborated with Thomas Norton on *Gorboduc* (1561),

regarded as 1st English tragedy. Also wrote famous 'induction' to 1563 edition of *The Mirror for Magistrates.*

Sackville-West, Victoria Mary (1892-1962), English author. Known for novels, eg *The Edwardians* (1930), poetry, eg *The Land* (1927). Model for hero/heroine of Virginia Woolf's *Orlando.*

sacrament, in Christianity, religious act or ceremony considered esp. sacred and distinct from other rites through institution by Jesus. In RC and Eastern Orthodox churches, 7 sacraments (Eucharist, baptism, penance, confirmation, ordination, matrimony, extreme unction) held to bestow God's grace on man. Most Protestant denominations observe Holy Communion (EUCHARIST) and baptism, but only as symbols of God's grace.

Sacramento, cap. of California, US; on Sacramento R. Pop. 257,000. Railway jct.; food processing, packing. First settled 1839; expanded with 1848 gold rush; became cap. 1854. Terminus of 1st transcontinental railway, Pony Express.

sacrifice, the offering of a person, animal or object in homage to a deity. In Bible, occurs in OT, eg in story of Cain and Abel; in Greek and Roman religion, among Maya and Aztecs, and many primitive cultures. In NT, Jesus is symbolized as sacrificial lamb. Eucharist is regarded as a form of commemorative sacrifice.

Sadat, Anwar el- (1918-), Egyptian political leader. Succeeded Nasser as president (1970); favoured American diplomacy to gain concessions from Israel after 1973 war.

Reduced Soviet influence in country. Visited Jerusalem (1977) to initiate peace negotiations. Nobel Peace Prize (1978).

Sadducees, smaller of two main Jewish sects which originated in Maccabean age (other being opponents, PHARISEES). Opposed all doctrines not taught in Torah, *eg* resurrection and immortality.

Sade, Donatien Alphonse François, Comte de, known as Marquis de Sade (1740-1814), French author. Cruel sexual practices reflected in novels, *eg Justine* (1791), *La philosophie dans le boudoir* (1795), *Juliette* (1797). Gave name to sadism.

Sadowa, village of N Czechoslovakia, near Hradec Králové. Scene of battle (1866) in which Prussians defeated Austrians.

safety lamp, oil lamp for use in mines, designed not to explode firedamp (methane). First successful type usually attributed to Humphrey Davy (c 1816). Uses metal-gauze screen to dissipate heat of flame. Also indicates presence of methane when flame has blue halo. Largely replaced by electric lighting and gas sensing equipment.

saffron, see CROCUS.

saga, in Old Norse literature, long prose narrative written 11th-13th cent., usually relating story of historical or legendary hero or important family, incl. battles, legends, *etc, eg Sturlunga Saga, Heimskringla, Njala, Volsungsaga.*

Sagan, Françoise, pseud. of Françoise Quoirez (1935-   ), French author. Known for novels, esp. *Bonjour Tristesse* (1954), dealing with feminine psychology. Plays incl. *Château en Suède* (1960).

sage, *Salvia officinalis,* aromatic herb of worldwide distribution. Grey-green leaves used as seasoning in cookery.

sagebrush, several bushy, deciduous plants of genus *Artemisia,* common in arid regions of W US. Big sagebrush, *A. tridentata,* is used as forage plant.

Sagittarius, see ZODIAC.

sago, edible starch extracted from pith of various palms esp. *Metroxylon* sago found mainly in Far East. Important food source.

Saguenay, river of C Québec, Canada. Flows S 200 km (125 mi) through L. St John to St Lawrence R. at Tadoussac. Main tributary Peribonca R. Navigable to Chicoutimi. H.e.p.

Sahara, desert of N Africa. Largest in world, area *c* 9,065,000 sq km (3,500,000 sq mi); extends from Atlantic Ocean to Red Sea. Largely stony with some sandy areas; interior ranges incl. Ahaggar, Tibesti Mts. Extremely arid climate; inhabited by Sudanese, Negroes, Berbers, Tuaregs. Oases produce dates, fruit; mineral resources incl. salt, iron ore, phosphates, oil and gas.

Saida, seaport of S Lebanon, on Mediterranean. Pop. 22,000. Ancient Sidon of Phoenicia. Famous for its purple dyes and glassware; excavations have revealed many sarcophagi.

Saigon, see HO CHI MINH CITY.

sail, area of strong material spread from ship's mast to harness force of the wind as means of propulsion. Sails of papyrus used by ancient

Egyptians. Flax and cotton, formerly used in sailmaking, have been replaced by synthetics. Square-rig sail arrangement largely replaced by fore-and-aft rig.

sailfish, any of genus *Istiophorus* of large marine fish. Related to swordfish, has sail-shaped dorsal fin and spear-like upper jaw. Popular as game fish.

sailing, sport, see YACHTING.

sailing ships, wind-propelled vessels prob. first used by ancient Egyptians, later by Greeks and Romans. With introduction of mariner's compass, use of sails in place of oars became general. Rivalry between Britain and America in Chinese and Indian tea trade led to the construction of the clippers, most famous being the British *Cutty Sark* and American *Ann McKim.* Introduction of steamship (19th cent.) led to gradual disappearance of sailing ships, both as commercial and naval vessels.

Saimaa, lake system of SE Finland, comprising *c* 120 lakes draining into L. Ladoga. Area *c* 4790 sq km (1850 sq mi). Connected to Gulf of Finland at Vyborg, USSR by Saimaa Canal (length 58 km/36 mi; built 1856, reconstructed 1968).

saint, see CANONIZATION.

St Albans, mun. bor. of Hertfordshire, EC England. Pop. 52,000. Printing; electronics. Roman *Verulamium,* many remains; St Alban martyred here (*c* 3rd cent.); has 8th cent. abbey; Norman cathedral. Rothamsted agric. station nearby.

St Andrews, town and resort of Fife region, E Scotland. Pop. 12,000. Woollens mfg. Has Royal and Ancient Golf Club (1754); 12th cent.

ruined cathedral; 13th cent. castle; oldest Scottish univ. (1411).

Saint Bartholomew's Day Massacre, massacre of French Huguenots, instigated by Henri de Guise and Catherine de'Medici; began in Paris on 24th Aug. 1572. Number killed est. at 50,000, incl. Huguenot leader Admiral Coligny. Led to resumption of French Wars of Religion.

St Bernard, breed of large dog with dense short hair. Once kept by monks of St Bernard's Hospice in Swiss Alps to rescue travellers. Stands *c* 71 cm/28 in. at shoulder.

St Bernard Passes, two Alpine passes. Great St Bernard (height 2471 m/8110 ft) links Valais canton (Switzerland) with Valle d'Aosta (Italy). Road tunnel, 5.6 km (3.5 mi) long, opened 1964. Little St Bernard (height 2187 m/7178 ft) links Valle d'Aosta with French Savoy. Each pass has hospice founded (11th cent.) by St Bernard of Menthon to aid travellers.

St Boniface, town of SE Manitoba, Canada; on Red R. opposite Winnipeg. Pop. 47,000, mainly French-Canadian. Oil refineries, stockyards, meat packing. Founded by missionaries (1818).

St Catharines, town of S Ontario, Canada; on Welland Ship Canal. Pop. 110,000. In important fruit-growing region. Engineering, food canning industs. Founded 1790.

St Christopher, see KITTS.

St Clair, Lake, on EC US-Canada border, N of Detroit. Area 1270 sq km (490 sq mi). Connects rivers between L. Huron and L. Erie. St Clair R. has deepened shipping channel.

St Cloud, suburb of W Paris, France. Horse racing, porcelain mfg. Palace (17th cent., destroyed 1870).

St Cyr, town of N France, near Versailles. Pop. 17,000. Site of military school, founded 1808 by Napoleon, destroyed in WWII.

St Denis, suburb of N Paris, France. Engineering, chemical industs. Site of Benedictine abbey (626). First Gothic cathedral built here (12th cent.), contains many royal tombs.

Sainte-Beuve, Charles Augustin (1804-69), French literary critic. Wrote criticism stressing biog. detail of author, historical, social background. Criticism collected in *Causeries du Lundi* (1851-62).

Sainte Chapelle, former chapel in Paris, built by Louis IX (1243-8) to house relics brought from Holy Land. Richly decorated with stained glass windows, it is a masterpiece of Gothic art. Now part of Palais de Justice.

Saint Elmo's fire, visible electric discharge seen at wingtips of aircraft or masts of ships. Caused by static electricity in atmosphere; often observed during electric storms.

St Etienne, city of EC France, cap. of Loire dept. Pop. 213,000. Coal-mining centre, iron and steel mfg. Hist. armaments and textiles (esp. silk) industs. School of mining (1816).

Saint-Exupéry, Antoine de (1900-44), French author, aviator. Novels, *eg Vol de nuit* (1931), *Terre des hommes* (1939, *Wind, Sand and Stars*), reflect humanistic philosophy of endeavour. Also wrote whimsical fantasy *Le Petit Prince* (1943).

St Gall (Ger. *Sankt Gallen*), town of NE Switzerland, cap. of St Gall canton. Pop. 81,000. Indust. centre, esp. silk, cotton. Medieval centre of learning; abbey (8th cent.) library has valuable documents.

St George's Channel, British Isles; between Irish Sea and Atlantic, separating Wales from Ireland. Width 74 km (46 mi) at narrowest point.

Saint-Germain, Treaty of, post-WWI settlement (1919) between Austria and Allies. Austro-Hungarian empire dissolved, Austria gave up parts of its German-speaking territ. to Italy and Czechoslovakia. Independence of Hungary, Yugoslavia, Poland and Czechoslovakia recognized.

St Germain (-en-Laye), suburb of W Paris, France, on R. Seine. Residential area with forest park. Renaissance château; scene of treaty (1919) between Allies and Austria.

St Gotthard Pass, mountain pass of S Switzerland, height 2107 m (6916 ft). Road built 1830; railway tunnel (length 14.9 km/9.25 mi; height 1153 m/3786 ft) built 1880.

St Helena, isl. of S Atlantic, British crown colony. Area 122 sq km (47 sq mi); pop. 6000; cap. Jamestown. Napoleon's final place of exile (1815-21). Became crown colony 1834.

St Helens, bor. of Merseyside met. county, NW England. Pop. 105,000. Major glass indust.; iron; chemicals mfg.

St Helier, town of Jersey, Channel Isls., UK. Pop. 28,000. Resort; agric. market. Elizabeth Castle (16th cent.) nearby.

St Ives, mun. bor. of Cornwall, SW

England, on St Ives Bay. Pop. 10,000. Fishing port; resort long favoured by artists.

St James's Palace, in Pall Mall, London, was built by Henry VIII and served as royal residence 1698-1837. Foreign ambassadors are still accredited to Court of St James's.

St John, ice-free port on S New Brunswick, Canada; on Bay of Fundy at mouth of St John R. Pop. 89,000. Railway terminus; has large dry docks. Major timber exports, pulp and paper industs. Estab. as fort. in 17th cent.

St John, river of E Canada-US. Rises in N Maine, flows SE 673 km (418 mi) through New Brunswick to Bay of Fundy. Transport link to coast; navigable to Fredericton. In fertile valley. Strong tides of Bay cause river to reverse its flow at Reversing Falls during high tides.

St John, Henry, see BOLINGBROKE, HENRY ST JOHN, VISCOUNT.

St John's, cap. of ANTIGUA.

St John's, cap. and seaport of Newfoundland, Canada; on Avalon penin. Pop. 88,000. Railway terminus; naval and fishing base; cod, herring industs. One of oldest settlements in North America. Starting point of first transatlantic flight (1919).

St John's wort, any of genus *Hypericum* of plants native to Asia and Europe. Speckled leaves, yellow flowers.

Saint-Just, Louis Antoine de (1767-94), French revolutionary. Leading member of Committee of Public Safety during Reign of Terror (1793-4). Arrested and guillotined with his close associate, Robespierre.

St Kilda, small isl. of Outer Hebrides, W Scotland. Uninhabited from 1930; bird sanctuary.

St Kitts or **St Christopher**, isl. of E West Indies, in Leeward Isls. Area 176 sq km (68 sq mi); pop. 46,000 (with Nevis); cap. Basseterre (pop. 14,000). Former British colony with Nevis, Anguilla from 1783; became associate state (1967).

St Laurent, Louis Stephen (1882-1973), Canadian statesman. Liberal PM (1948-57), succeeding Mackenzie King.

St Lawrence, river of E Canada. Flows NE 1197 km (744 mi) from L. Ontario to Gulf of St Lawrence. Main tributaries incl. Ottawa, Saguenay, St Maurice rivers. Forms numerous lakes along course. Major shipping route. Canal system (St Lawrence Seaway) links Great Lakes to Atlantic. Has wide estuary.

St Lawrence, Gulf of, extension of Atlantic, SE Canada; between Québec and Newfoundland. At mouth of St Lawrence R. Has important fishing grounds (esp. cod).

St Louis, city of E Missouri, US; on Mississippi near mouth of Missouri R. Pop. 622,000; state's largest city. Commercial, trade, transport centre. Furs, livestock, grain market, meat packing; motor vehicles, aircraft, chemical mfg. Estab. 1764 by French; became river port in 19th cent. Boomed with Mississippi steamship traffic.

St Lucia, isl. of SE West Indies, in Windward Isls. Area 616 sq km (238 sq mi); pop. 110,000; cap. Castries (pop. 40,000). Scenic mountains with forest covered slopes. Fruit, coconut exports. Former British colony; became associate state 1967. Independent 1979.

St Malo, town of Brittany, NW France, at mouth of R. Rance. Pop. 44,000. Port, exports agric. produce to England; fishing, tourism. *Fl* 15th-18th cent. as base for privateers. Badly damaged in WWII.

St Martin (*Sint Maarten*), isl. of N Leeward Isls., divided between French (Guadeloupe dependency) and Dutch (Netherlands Antilles). Area 96 sq km (37 sq mi). Has little agric. land. Main export is salt from coastal lagoons.

St Maurice, river of SC Québec, Canada. Rises in Laurentian Mts., flows S 520 km (325 mi) to St Lawrence R. at Trois Rivières. Lumber transportation.

St Moritz, town of SE Switzerland, on R. Inn in Engadine Valley. Pop. 3000. Spa from 16th cent.; winter sports.

St Nazaire, town of W France, at mouth of R. Loire. Pop. 63,000. Port, outport of Nantes; shipbuilding, food processing. German submarine base in WWII, heavily bombed.

St Paul, cap. of Minnesota, US; contiguous with Minneapolis ('Twin Cities') on Mississippi R. Pop. 310,000. Commercial, indust. centre in agric. region. Livestock trade; automobile, tapes, computers, electronic instrument mfg. Has RC cathedral.

Saint Paul's Cathedral, London, was built (1675-1710) by Sir Christopher Wren on site of old St Paul's which had been severely damaged in Great Fire (1666). Has famous classical dome.

Saint Peter's, Rome, patriarchal basilica of St Peter, in Vatican City. Built mainly between 1506 and 1626, it replaced 4th cent. basilica built by Constantine over supposed tomb of St Peter. Designed chiefly by Bramante and Michelangelo, with piazza added by Bernini (1629-62). Largest Christian church in world.

St Petersburg, see LENINGRAD.

St Petersburg, winter resort of W Florida, US; on Tampa Bay. Pop. 216,000. Important recreation centre with associated tourist industs.

St Pierre and Miquelon, overseas isl. dept. of France; off S Newfoundland, Canada. Area 241 sq km (93 sq mi). Pop. 5000, cap. St Pierre. Has ice-free harbour; important fishing industs. (esp. cod). Suffers from fogs. Settled by French in 17th cent.

St Quentin, town of N France, on R. Somme. Pop. 66,000. Textile mfg. (esp. muslin, lace, curtains), engineering. Scene of French defeat by Prussians (1871), and of German counter-offensive (1918).

Saint-Saëns, [Charles] Camille (1835-1921), French composer. Best known for *The Carnival of the Animals* for 2 pianos and orchestra. Also wrote symphonies, piano concertos.

Saint-Simon, Claude Henri, Comte de (1760-1825), French social theorist. Advocated indust. state directed by science and universal association for common good. Writings incl. *Du système industriel* (1821), *Nouveau christianisme* (1825). Followers continued his theories in system called Saint-Simonianism.

Saint-Simon, Louis de Rouvroy, Duc de (1675-1755), French courtier, author. Wrote bitter account of personalities of Louis XIV's court, pub. as *Mémoires* (1829).

St Tropez, town of Provence, SE France, on Côte d'Azur. Pop. 6000. Fishing port, fashionable resort.

St Vincent, isl. of SE West Indies, in Windward Isls. Area 388 sq km (150 sq mi); pop. 100,000; cap. Kingstown (pop. 17,000). Mountainous, well forested. Cotton growing, banana exports. British colony from 1763; became associate state 1969. Independent 1979.

St Vincent, Cape, headland of SW Portugal. Scene of naval battle (1797) when British under Jervis defeated Spanish fleet.

St Vincent Gulf, shallow inlet of Indian Ocean, South Australia, between Yorke Penin. and Adelaide. Many resorts; fishing.

Saint Vitus' dance or chorea, condition characterized by irregular involuntary movements of any part of the body. Most common among children. Cause unknown but closely associated with rheumatic fever.

Saipan, main isl. of Mariana Isls., W Pacific Ocean. Admin. hq. of US trust territ. of the Pacific Isls. Major WWII air base after taken by US (1944).

Sakai, indust. city of Japan, on Osaka Bay in SW Honshu isl. Pop. 594,000. Machinery, chemical and textile mfg. Major port in 15th and 16th cents.; declined when harbour silted up.

saké, alcoholic beverage made from fermented rice. National drink of Japan, where it is served warm.

Sakhalin, isl. of USSR, off E coast of Siberian RSFSR. Area *c* 76,400 sq km (29,500 sq mi). Mountainous, with cold climate; fishing and

lumbering main occupations; oil and coal fields. Settled by Russians in 19th cent.; S half, called Karafuto, occupied by Japan (1905-45).

Sakharov, Andrei Dmitriyevich (1921-), Soviet physicist, dissident. Leader in development of Soviet hydrogen bomb. Vigorous advocate of civil liberty and democratic reform in USSR. Awarded Nobel Peace Prize (1975), but refused permission to receive award.

Saki, pseud. of H[ector] H[ugh] Munro (1870-1916), British author, b. Burma. Known for humorous, often macabre short stories in *The Chronicles of Clovis* (1912), novel *The Unbearable Bassington* (1912). Killed in WWI.

Sakkara or Saqqâra, village of N Egypt, SW of Cairo. Site of main necropolis of ancient MEMPHIS; step pyramids.

Saladin (c 1137-93), Moslem military and political leader, b. Mesopotamia. Gained prominence in conquest of Egypt from Fatimid dynasty (1164-74); became sultan of Egypt (1175). Extended control over Syria (1174-86); led Saracen capture of Jerusalem after defeating Christians at Hattin (1187). Repelled 3rd Crusade led by Richard I of England (1190-2).

Salamanca, city of W Spain, on R. Tormes, cap. of Salamanca prov. Pop. 125,000. Transport jct.; univ. (c 1230) was centre of Arabic learning. Taken from Moors 1085; medieval cultural, religious centre. Scene of Wellington's victory (1812) over French in Peninsular War. Two cathedrals (12th, 16th cent.); colonnaded Plaza Mayor.

salamander, tailed amphibian of

order Urodela. Scaleless with soft, moist skin; teeth in both jaws, no gills. Regenerates lost limbs or tail. Species incl. giant salamander of Japan, *Megalobatrachus japonicus*, reaching length of 1.5 m/5 ft.

Salamis, isl. of Greece, in Saronic Gulf. Area 93 sq km (36 sq mi). Scene of naval battle (480 BC) in which Greeks under Themistocles defeated Persians under Xerxes.

Salazar, António de Oliveira (1889-1970), Portuguese statesman. Stabilized country's economy as finance minister before becoming premier (1932-68). Exercised dictatorial power after introducing (1933) new constitution, *Novo Estado*. Suppressed political opposition in Portugal and independence movements in colonies.

Salé (Arab. *Sla*), suburb of Rabat, NW Morocco, on Atlantic Ocean. Port; carpets, pottery mfg. Base of Barbary pirates ('Sallee Rovers') in 17th cent.

Salem, port of NE Massachusetts, US. Pop. 41,000. Settled 1626. Notorious for witchcraft trials of 1692. Important in sailing clipper era. Hist. buildings incl. Custom House (1819).

Salem, cap. of Oregon, US; on Willamette R. Pop. 68,000. In farming, cattle region; varied agric. related industs., metal goods, paper mfg. Cap. from 1851.

Salerno, city of Campania, SW Italy, on Gulf of Salerno. Cap. of Salerno prov. Pop. 158,000. Port, agric., commercial centre. Medical school founded 9th cent., cathedral (11th cent.). Scene of Allied landings (1943).

Salford, bor. of Greater Manchester

met. county, NW England, on R. Irwell and Manchester Ship Canal. Pop. 131,000. Extensive docks; indust. centre; RC cathedral (1848).

Salic law, law adopted in Middle Ages by certain noble and royal European families, excluding female succession to offices and titles. Name derives from erroneous supposition that it was part of 6th cent. *Lex Salica* of Salian Franks, which excluded women from inheriting land. Applied mainly in France and Spain.

salicylic acid, white crystalline solid obtained from willow bark or phenol. Used in manufacture of aspirin, in food preservation, and as an antiseptic.

Salinger, J[erome] D[avid] (1919-), American novelist. Known for *The Catcher in the Rye* (1951) dealing with adolescent hero's resistance to adult 'phoniness'; novels dealing with Glass family, *eg Franny and Zooey* (1961).

Salisbury, Robert Arthur Talbot Gascoyne-Cecil, 3rd Marquess of (1830-1903), British statesman, PM (1885, 1886-92, 1895-1902). Pursued cautious imperialist policy, trying to arrange territ. expansion in Africa by agreement with European powers; retired at end of Boer war.

Salisbury, Robert Cecil, 1st Earl of (1563-1612), English statesman. Succeeded father, Lord Burghley, as Elizabeth's chief minister (1598); arranged James I's accession to throne and admin. his govt.

Salisbury, town of Wiltshire, SW England, on R. Avon. Pop. 35,000. Market town. Built as 'New Sarum' (near ancient 'Old Sarum' fortress).

Famous cathedral (13th cent.) has highest spire in England (123 m/ 404 ft).

Salisbury, cap. of Rhodesia. Pop. 490,000. Admin., commercial, transport centre in agric. and gold mining region; tobacco indust.; univ. Founded 1890 as Fort Salisbury; cap. of Federation of Rhodesia and Nyasaland 1953-63.

Salisbury Plain, chalk downs of Wiltshire, SW England. Military training area. Incl. STONEHENGE.

saliva, watery secretion of 3 pairs of salivary glands situated around mouth. Contains enzyme ptyalin which begins process of breaking down starch into sugar. Also cleanses mouth and makes sense of taste possible.

Sallust, full name Gaius Sallustius Crispus (86-c 34 BC), Roman historian. After retiring from public office, he wrote histories of the Catiline conspiracy and the wars against JUGURTHA.

salmon, food and game fish, genus Salmo or Oncorhynchus, which breeds in fresh water. After feeding period of up to 6 years, young migrate to open sea, remaining up to 4 years. Adults return to birthplace to spawn. All Pacific salmon, Oncorhynchus, die after spawning but some females of Atlantic salmon, Salmo salar, survive.

salmonella, genus of bacteria which incl. causes of typhoid fever and various forms of food poisoning in man and domestic animals.

Salome, traditional name for the daughter of Herodias. In NT, story of how her dancing pleased Herod so much that he granted her request for the head of John the Baptist.

Salonika (Thessaloniki), town of NE Greece, on Gulf of Salonika, cap. of Macedonia. Pop. 346,000. Founded 4th cent. BC. St Paul addressed 2 epistles to the Thessalonians. Taken by Turks 1430; Greek from 1912. Base for Allied campaigns against Bulgaria in WWII. Has Byzantine churches. Birthplace of Kemal Ataturk.

Salop, county of W England. Area 3490 sq km (1347 sq mi); pop. 348,000; co. town Shrewsbury. Hilly in SW (cattle, sheep); flat in N, E (agric., dairying). Formerly known as Shropshire; reconstituted 1974.

salsify, **vegetable oyster** or **oyster plant**, Tragopogon porrifolius, plant native to S Europe, also grown in North America. Purple flowers, white roots with oyster-like flavour used as vegetable.

SALT, see STRATEGIC ARMS LIMITATION TALKS.

salt, in chemistry, compound formed when hydrogen of an acid is wholly or partly replaced by a metal. Salts are formed by reaction of bases with acids. Common salt, sodium chloride (NaCl), occurs in sea water and mineral deposits; used in manufacture of chlorine and sodium compounds.

Salta, town of NW Argentina, in Lerma valley; cap. of Salta prov. Pop. 183,000. In rich agric. region; meat packing, tanning industs. On railway to Antofagasta (Chile). Founded 1582.

Salt Lake City, cap. of Utah, US; SE of Great Salt L. at foot of Wasatch Range. Pop. 176,000. Transport, commercial, indust. centre. Oil refining, copper smelting; textile, food mfg. Founded 1847 by

Brigham Young; Mormon Temple (1893).

saltpetre or potassium nitrate (KNO₃), white crystalline salt. Used in fertilizers, gunpowder, glass manufacture, *etc.* Chile saltpetre is sodium nitrate.

saluki, breed of slender hound of ancient origin. Long ears, silky coat; stands up to 71 cm/28 in. at shoulder.

Salut, Iles du, small isl. group off French Guiana. Had notorious penal colony on Devil's Isl. (1854-1938).

Salvador, Atlantic port of E Brazil, cap. of Bahia state. Pop. 1,008,000. Cocoa, sugar, tobacco exports; sugar refining, flour milling. Founded 1549, cap. of Portuguese territ. until 1763. Formerly named Bahia.

Salvador, see EL SALVADOR.

salvage, in maritime law, term used either for act of rescuing life or property from destruction at sea, or for reward to which rescuers are entitled.

Salvation Army, international evangelical and philanthropic movement. Estab. (1865) in London, UK, by WILLIAM BOOTH, given present name in 1878. Aims to bring Christian religion to those it does not normally reach, as well as bringing practical relief to poor, *eg* soup kitchens, hostels for homeless. Organized on military lines, with uniforms, ranks.

Salween, river of S China and Burma. Rises in Tibet, flows through deep gorges *c* 2800 km (1750 mi) to Gulf of Martaban. Navigable only 120 km (75 mi) upstream.

Salzburg, city of NC Austria, on R. Salzach, cap. of Salzburg prov. Pop.

129,000. Cultural, tourist centre. Annual music festival (birthplace of Mozart). Archbishopric from 8th cent.; monastery (8th cent.), medieval castle, cathedral (17th cent.). Univ. (1623), opera house (1960).

Samar, isl. of Philippines, SE of Luzon. Area *c* 13,100 sq km (5050 sq mi). Produces bananas, hemp, coconuts. Subject to typhoons.

Samara, see KUIBYSHEV.

Samaria, hist. cap. of kingdom of Israel, during 10th-8th cent. BC. Excavations begun in 1908 have revealed extensive ruins.

Samaritans, descendants of non-Jewish colonists from Babylonia, Syria and elsewhere who were settled in Samaria when Israelites were deported (722 BC). Small number remain in Israel at Nablus and Jaffa. Traditional enemies of Jews; recognized only the Pentateuch.

Samaritans, the, in UK, voluntary organization estab. (1953) by Chad Varah to help potential suicides. Members man telephones to offer counselling, friendship.

samarium (Sm), metallic element of lanthanide series; at. no. 62, at. wt. 150.35. Discovered 1879 by spectroscopy; isolated 1901.

Samarkand, city of USSR, E Uzbek SSR. Pop. 278,000. Silk and cotton centre. Ancient city, destroyed by Alexander the Great (329 BC); centre of Arab culture in 8th cent. AD, on trade route between Europe and China. Cap. of Tamerlane's empire 14th cent.; its buildings incl. his mausoleum. Later held by emirs of Bukhara until taken by Russia (1868).

Samoa, isl. group of C Pacific.

Mainly volcanic and mountainous. Discovered (1722) by Dutch; formerly called Navigators Isls. Divided (1899) between US and Germany. **American Samoa** is overseas territ. Area 200 sq km (77 sq mi); pop. 31,000; cap. Pago Pago. Fruit growing, tuna fishing. **Western Samoa**, comprising Savaii, Upolu, and smaller isls. is independent state. Area 2850 sq km (1100 sq mi); pop. 151,000; cap. Apia. Produces fruit, copra, cocoa. Taken from Germans by New Zealand in WWI, held by them as UN trust territ. until independence 1962.

Sámos, isl. of Greece, in E Aegean Sea. Area 492 sq km (190 sq mi); cap. Vathi. Mountainous; wine, fruit, tobacco. Ancient Sámos *fl* 6th cent. BC under Polycrates. Birthplace of Pythagoras.

Samothrace (*Samothráki*), isl. of Greece, in NE Aegean Sea. Area 181 sq km (70 sq mi). Sponge fishing, goats. Famous *Nike* or *Winged Victory of Samothrace* statue (306 BC) found here 1863.

Samoyed, breed of Siberian dog with thick white or cream coat. Used to pull sleds; stands up to 60 cm/23.5 in. at shoulder.

samphire, *Crithmum maritimum*, European seashore plant of parsley family. Yellowish flowers, pointed, aromatic leaves used in salads.

Samson, one of judges who ruled Israel before estab. of monarchy. Renowned for great strength which depended on his unshorn hair, symbolizing his vows to God. Story of his betrayal to Philistines by Delilah in OT book of Judges.

Samsun, port of N Turkey, on Black Sea. Pop. 151,000. Situated in major

tobacco growing region; exports tobacco. Founded as Greek colony of *Amisus*; important in Pontic and Roman empires.

Samuel 1 and **2**, books of OT dealing with estab. of Israel as monarchy and its struggle against Philistines. Covers lives of Samuel, Saul, David. Samuel was last of judges who ruled Israelites; Saul and David were 1st kings.

Samuelson, Paul Anthony (1915-), American economist. Advocate of Keynesian theory; presidential adviser in 1960s. Wrote standard introductory textbook *Economics* (1948); awarded Nobel Prize for Economics (1970).

samurai, aristocratic warrior class of feudal Japan with a strict code (BUSHIDO) of chivalry. Rose to power in 12th cent. during period of weak govt. and held influence until the Meiji restoration (1868).

Sana, cap. of Yemen. Pop. 125,000. Marketing centre. Noted buildings, esp. Great Mosque; palace of former Imam.

San Antonio, city of SC Texas, US; on San Antonio R. Pop. 654,000. Railway jct., commercial, indust. centre. Cattle, cotton market, oil refining, food processing, brewing. Spanish mission estab. 1718. Taken by Texas (1835); heroic Alamo defence 1836.

sanctions, in international politics, coercive measures adopted in an attempt to enforce a country's fulfilment of its treaty obligations or compliance with international law. Usually economic measures are applied, esp. partial or complete trade boycott. UN banned trade with

Rhodesia after unilateral declaration of independence (1965).

Sand, George, pseud. of Amandine Lucile Aurore Dudevant, Baronne de, née Dupin (1804-76), French novelist. Left husband, formed liaisons with Musset, Chopin and others. Novels advocating free love incl. *Indiana* (1832), *Lélia* (1833), *Elle et lui* (1859).

sand, sediment composed of rock particles, precisely defined in geology as having particle size between 1/16 mm and 2 mm. Major constituent is quartz; used in production of glass, building materials, abrasives.

sandalwood, several trees of genus *Santalum* incl. Indian *S. album*, white sandalwood. Hard, fragrant wood used for ornamental carving and burned as incense. East Indian red sandalwood, *Pterocarpus santalinus*, yields dye.

Sandburg, Carl (1878-1967), American poet. Known for free verse celebrating common man, *eg Chicago Poems* (1916), *The People, Yes* (1936), *Honey and Salt* (1965). Also wrote *Life of Abraham Lincoln* (1926-39).

sand fly, small 2-winged fly, genus *Phlebotomus*, whose bite spreads diseases, *eg* oriental sore, sand fly fever.

sandhopper, small crustacean with body modified for hopping. Common sandhopper, *Talitrus saltator*, abundant in tidal seaweeds.

Sandhurst, village of Berkshire, S England. Has Royal Military Academy (1799); National Army Museum.

San Diego, seaport of S California, US; on San Diego Bay. Pop. 697,000.

Naval base, defence industs.; fish, cotton, agric. exports. Tuna fishing and canning; aerospace and electronic industs. Spanish mission estab. 1769.

sandpiper, small long-billed shore bird of Scolopacidae family. Species incl. common sandpiper *Tringa hypoleucos*, of Old World, and spotted sandpiper *T. macularia* of North America.

Sandringham, village of Norfolk, E England. Sandringham Hall is a private residence of royal family (acquired 1863).

sandstone, porous sedimentary rock composed mainly of sand grains cemented together. Sand grains usually composed of quartz; cementing material may be calcium carbonate, silica, or iron oxides. Widely distributed; used as building stone.

sandstorm, strong, dry wind carrying clouds of coarse sand. Sand particles rarely raised above 30 m/100 ft or transported far from source, but may obscure sun. Common in desert areas, esp. N Africa, Arabia, SW US.

Sandwich, John Montagu, 4th Earl of (1718-92), British politician. Maintained corrupt ministry as first lord of the Admiralty (1771-82); generally blamed for British naval failures of American Revolution. Sandwich Isls. named after him, as are sandwiches (which he invented so meals would not interrupt gambling sessions).

Sandwich Islands, see HAWAII.

San Francisco, seaport of W California, US; on penin. between San Francisco Bay and Pacific. Pop. 716,000. Financial, cultural centre.

Exports iron and steel, agric. produce; shipbuilding, oil refining, printing and publishing industs. Founded 1776; grew after 1849 gold rush; destroyed by 1906 earthquake. Known for Golden Gate Bridge, Latin quarter, Chinatown, cablecars. Has parts of Univ. of California.

Sanger, Frederick (1918-), English biochemist. Awarded Nobel Prize for Chemistry (1958) for research on amino acid sequence in protein structure of insulin.

Sanhedrin, highest court and council of the ancient Jewish nation, with religious and civil functions. Ended with destruction of Temple (AD 70).

San Jacinto, see HOUSTON, Texas.

San José, cap. of Costa Rica, on C plateau. Pop. 199,000. Commercial, indust. centre; coffee, cacao industs., flour milling, fruit canning. Founded 1738. Has univ. (1843); cathedral; National Museum.

San José, city of W California, US. Pop. 446,000. In fruit-growing area; dried fruit processing, packing; varied agric. industs. Founded 1777; prospered during gold rush.

San Juan, cap. of Puerto Rico, seaport on NE coast. Pop. 453,000. Sugar refining; cigar, textile, drug mfg. Founded 1521. Has govt. residence La Fortaleza (built 1529), cathedral (1512).

San Marino, independent republic of S Europe, enclave within E Italy. Area 62 sq km (24 sq mi); pop. 20,000; cap. San Marino. Silk mfg.; agric. (exports wine, cattle). Quarrying on Mt. Titano. World's smallest republic; claims to be oldest in Europe; traditionally founded 4th cent.

San Martín, José de (1778-1850),

Argentinian revolutionary. Organized army in struggle for Argentinian independence from Spain (1812-16). Invaded Chile and defeated Spanish at Chacabuco (1817), securing Chilean independence. Broke off advance into Peru after meeting with Bolívar at Guayaquil (1822).

San Miguel de Tucumán, city of NW Argentina, cap. of Tucumán prov. Pop. 326,000. Railway jct.; in irrigated agric. region in Andean foothills, producing sugar, rice, grain. Cathedral and many colonial buildings.

San Remo, town of Liguria, NW Italy, on Riviera. Pop. 63,000. Resort; fruit, flower growing. Cathedral (13th cent.). Damaged in WWII.

San Salvador, small isl. of Bahamas. First sighted by Columbus in discovering Americas (1492). Also known as Watling or Watlings Island.

San Salvador, cap. of El Salvador. Pop. 359,000. Commercial, indust. centre; meat packing, flour milling, textile industs. Founded 1521; cap. of Central American Federation (1831-8). Has National Univ. Has suffered repeated earthquakes.

sans-culottes, term applied during French Revolution to poorer classes, who wore trousers instead of knee breeches worn by aristocracy and bourgeoisie; by extension name was given to extreme republicans.

San Sebastián, city of N Spain, on Bay of Biscay, cap. of Guipúzcoa prov. Pop. 166,000. Port, resort, fishing indust. Former royal summer residence.

Sanskrit, ancient Indic language in

Indo-Iranian branch of Indo-European family. Oldest known form is Vedic Sanskrit, language of the Veda (c 1500 BC). Became (c 400 BC) court language as well as literary, religious language. Used for Hindu literature until AD 1100, still used in liturgy. Many modern Indic languages developed from it. Comparison of Sanskrit with European languages in 18th cent., esp. by Sir William Jones, initiated scientific study of languages.

San Stefano, Treaty of, settlement (1878) ending war between Russia and Turkey. Concessions to Russia amounting to virtual disintegration of Turkish empire led to treaty's revision at Congress of BERLIN.

Santa Anna, Antonio López de (1794-1876), Mexican military, political leader; president (1833-6, 1841-4, 1846-7, 1853-5). Helped overthrow Iturbide (1823); gained power in lengthy struggle. Attempt to suppress Texas revolt ended in his capture (1836). Defeated in Mexican War (1848). In exile 1848-53, 1855-74.

Santa Barbara, resort town of S California, US; on the Pacific. Pop. 70,000. Centre of citrus fruit growing region. Founded by Spanish (1782); buildings, incl. historic Santa Barbara Mission (1820), retain a Spanish air.

Santa Cruz, town of C Bolivia, cap. of Santa Cruz dept. Pop. 135,000. Agric., commercial centre; trade in rice, sugar cane. Development boosted by transport links. Settled in 1590s.

Santa Cruz de Tenerife, city of Tenerife isl., Canary Isls., Spain; cap. of Santa Cruz de Tenerife prov. Pop. 151,000. Port, exports agric. produce; resort, refuelling station.

Santa Fé, town of EC Argentina, cap. of Santa Fé prov. Pop. 312,000. Linked by canal to Paraná R., transport jct. for · grain, livestock trade. Founded 1573. Has cathedral.

Santa Fé, cap. and tourist resort of New Mexico, US. Pop. 41,000. Commercial centre in agric. region. Founded by Spanish (1609); noted buildings incl. 17th cent. Palace of Governors. W terminus of Santa Fé trail, important 19th cent. caravan route. Los Alamos atomic research centre is c 40 km (25 mi) away.

Santa Isabel, see MALABO.

Santa Marta, port of N Colombia, on Caribbean. Pop. 129,000. Has deep harbour; banana, coffee exports. Founded 1525, frequently sacked in colonial period.

Santander, city of N Spain, on Bay of Biscay, cap. of Santander prov. Pop. 150,000. Port, resort; iron works, shipbuilding. Largely rebuilt after fire (1941). Nearby is ALTAMIRA.

Santayana, George (1863-1952), American philosopher, poet, b. Spain. Lived in Europe from 1912 to escape American Puritanism. Philosophy reflects scepticism, materialism, eg *The Life of Reason* (1905-6), *The Realms of Being* (1940). Also wrote novel *The Last Puritan* (1935), sonnets.

Santiago, cap. of Chile, at foot of Andes; alt. 520 m (c 1700 ft). Pop. 2,662,000 (with suburbs). Commercial, indust. centre; textile, clothing, iron and steel, chemical mfg. Has railway link with Valparaíso. Founded 1541. Chilean independence achieved under San Martín nearby at Maipu. Has National Univ. (1842); cathedral (1619).

Santiago (de Compostela), town of Galicia, NW Spain. Pop. 71,000. Tourist resort, pilgrimage centre from 9th cent.; univ. (1501). Cathedral (11th cent.) contains relics claimed to be those of St James.

Santiago de Cuba, major port of SE Cuba. Pop. 292,000. Sugar, tobacco produce; mineral exports. Founded 1514. Has cathedral.

Santo Domingo, cap. of Dominican Republic, port on S coast. Pop. 671,000. Sugar, coffee, cacao exports; distilling, brewing, soap mfg. Founded 1496; called Ciudad Trujillo (1936-61). Has univ. (1538); 16th cent. cathedral (reputed tomb of Columbus). Badly damaged in 1930 hurricane.

Santos, Atlantic port of SE Brazil, in São Paulo state. Pop. 346,000. Major coffee, sugar, fruit exports. Ocean access for São Paulo.

São Francisco, river of E Brazil. Rises in SW Minas Gerais plateau, flows NE 2900 km (c 1800 mi) to enter Atlantic ocean NE of Aracajú. H.e.p. supplies from Afonso Falls.

São Luis, seaport of N Brazil, cap. of Maranhão state; on São Luis Isl. Pop. 266,000. Cotton, sugar industs. Founded by French (1612).

Saône, river of E France. Flows c 450 km (280 mi) from Vosges via Chalon, Mâcon to R. Rhône at Lyons. Rhône-Saône corridor is hist. route between N and S France; canal links with many rivers, eg Rhine, Seine.

São Paulo, city of SE Brazil, cap. of São Paulo state. Pop. 5,922,000 (with suburbs). Leading commercial,

transport centre. Exports farm produce via port of Santos. Heavy machinery, motor vehicles, chemicals, textiles mfg. Founded by Jesuits (1554). Has many notable modern buildings, 4 univs., law school; Butanta Institute (snake serum). Underwent rapid growth in late 19th cent.

São Tomé and Principe, republic off W coast of Africa, comprising 2 isls. in Gulf of Guinea. Area 964 sq km (372 sq mi); pop. 81,000; cap. São Tomé (pop. 8000). Exports coffee, cacao, coconut products. Prov. of Portugal from 1522, became independent 1975.

sap, fluid in plants consisting of inorganic salts from soil and carbohydrates manufactured by plant in an aqueous solution. See TRANSPIRATION.

Sapir, Edward (1884-1939), American anthropologist and linguist, b. Pomerania. Known for ethnological and linguistic studies of Indians of NW US. Wrote Language, *an Introduction to the Study of Speech* (1921).

sapphire, precious gemstone, a variety of CORUNDUM. Deep blue and transparent; used in jewellery and gramophone styli. Major sources in Burma, Thailand, India (esp. Kashmir), Australia.

Sappho (fl 6th cent. BC), Greek poetess. Famous from own period as lyric poet of love, poems are intensely personal, passionate, metrically versatile. Began tradition of subjective love lyric. Verse survives only in fragments.

Sapporo, city of Japan, indust. centre of SW Hokkaido isl. Pop. 1,010,000. Flour milling, woodworking and printing indusdts. Tourist centre; site of 1972 Winter Olympics.

Saracens, name applied by the Christians during the Middle Ages to their Moslem enemies. Name originally applied to nomadic Arabs inhabiting frontier land between Roman and Persian empires.

Saragossa (*Zaragoza*), city of NE Spain, on R. Ebro, cap. of Saragossa prov. Pop. 480,000. Agric. market; indust., commercial centre; univ. (1587). Roman *Caesarea Augusta*; held by Moors until 1118; cap. of Aragón 12th-15th cent. Surrendered to French after heroic defence (1808-9) in Peninsular War. Moorish castle, 2 cathedrals (12th, 17th cent.).

Sarajevo, city of C Yugoslavia; cap. of Bosnia and Hercegovina. Pop. 244,000. Railway jct.; indust. centre, esp. carpets, tobacco, chemicals. Under Turkish rule 15th-19th cent. Scene of assassination (June 1914) of Archduke Francis Ferdinand, led to WWI. Has mosques (Islamic centre); RC, Orthodox cathedrals.

Saratoga Springs, health resort of E New York, US. Pop. 19,000. Has spa, horse racecourse. Scene of heavy fighting in American Revolution (1777).

Saratov, city of USSR, SC European RSFSR; on Volga. Pop. 790,000. Indust. centre, producing agric. machinery, chemicals, locomotives. Oil refining; natural gas fields nearby.

Sarawak, state of East Malaysia. Area c 125,000 sq km (48,000 sq mi); pop. 977,000; cap. Kuching. Produces oil, bauxite, rubber. Ceded to James Brooke (1841), whose family

ruled as rajahs until 1946; British protect. 1888; joined Malaysia 1963.

sarcoma, malignant tumour arising in the connective tissue, bones or muscles. Spreads by extension into neighbouring tissue or by way of bloodstream.

sarcophagus, stone or terracotta coffin, often elaborately carved and inscribed. Oldest known examples are Egyptian; famous example is that of Tutankhamen (from 14th cent. BC). Well-preserved Greek examples were found at Sidon in Phoenicia.

sardine, see PILCHARD.

Sardinia (*Sardegna*), isl. of Italy, separated from mainland by Tyrrhenian Sea, from Corsica by Str. of Bonifacio. Area 24,092 sq km (9302 sq mi); cap. Cagliari. Mountainous, rising to over 1830 m (6000 ft); pasturage, fishing; zinc, lead mining. Carthaginian, taken by Rome 238 BC; contested by Pisa, Genoa from 11th cent.; papal award to Spain 14th cent. Ruled as Kingdom of Sardinia by Savoy from 1720 until it led move to Italian unification (1861).

Sardis or **Sardes**, ancient city of W Asia Minor, now village in Turkey. Cap. of kingdom of Lydia in 7th cent. BC. Early Christian centre; one of Seven Churches in Asia. Sacked by Tamerlane (1402).

Sargasso Sea, area of still water at centre of ocean currents in N Atlantic between West Indies and Azores. Abundant seaweed covers its surface. Of great biological interest.

Sargent, John Singer (1856-1925), American painter, b. Florence. Resident in London after 1884, he painted fashionable society portraits with brilliant virtuosity. Also painted impressionistic watercolour landscapes.

Sargent, Sir [Harold] Malcolm (1895-1967), English conductor. Conducted BBC Symphony Orchestra (1951-7). Achieved great popularity as conductor-in-chief of Promenade Concerts (1951-67).

Sargon II (772-705 BC), king of Assyria (722-705 BC). Extended and consolidated Assyrian empire. Conquered N kingdom of Israel, carrying Jews into captivity. Subdued Babylon (710).

Sark (Fr. *Sercq*), one of Channel Isls., UK. Area 5sq km (2sq mi); comprises Great and Little Sark connected by isthmus. Isl. governed by hereditary 'seigneur' or 'dame'.

Sarnia, port of SW Ontario, Canada; on St Clair R. at S end of L. Huron. Pop. 58,000. Connected by pipeline to Alberta oil fields, has major oil refineries. Synthetic rubber mfg.

Saronic Gulf or **Gulf of Aegina**, inlet of Aegean Sea, SE Greece. Chief port Piraeus. Joined to Gulf of Corinth by canal (1881-93). .

Saroyan, William (1908-), American author. Known for short story collections, eg *The Daring Young Man on the Flying Trapeze* (1934), plays, eg *The Time of Your Life* (1939). Also wrote novels incl. *Boys and Girls Together* (1963), an indictment of American marriage.

sarsaparilla, several climbing or trailing tropical American vines of genus *Smilax*. Large, heart-shaped leaves; large, fragrant roots used as flavouring in a soft drink and formerly in medicine.

Sarto, Andrea del (1486-1531),

Florentine painter. Noted for his rich colour and painterly qualities, he specialized in religious subjects; works incl. fresco *Nativity of the Virgin* and painting *Madonna of the Harpies*.

Sartre, Jean-Paul (1905-), French philosopher. Leading figure in EXISTENTIALISM. Works incl. novels eg *La Nausée* (1938), trilogy *Les Chemins de la liberté* (1945-9), plays *Les Mouches* (1943), *Huis Clos* (1944), philosophical *L'Etre et le néant* (1943), *Critique de la raison dialectique* (1960). Declined Nobel Prize for Literature (1964).

Sarum, Old and New, *see* SALISBURY, England.

Saskatchewan, Prairie prov. of WC Canada. Area 651,903 sq km (251,700 sq mi); pop. 926,000; cap. Regina; other major city Saskatoon. Drained in N by Churchill R. Forests, lakeland in N, prairies in S. Mineral resources in N (esp. uranium at Athabasca); timber in C parkland; major wheat production in S. Fur trading area purchased by Canada from Hudson's Bay Co. (1869). Became prov. in 1905.

Saskatchewan, river of C Saskatchewan, Canada; formed by confluence of N Saskatchewan and S Saskatchewan rivers. Flows E 550 km (340 mi) through Cedar L. to L. Winnipeg. Provides h.e.p., irrigation for large area.

Saskatoon, city of SC Saskatchewan, Canada; on S Saskatchewan R. Pop. 126,000. Agric. distribution centre; meat packing, oil refining.

sassafras, *Sassafras albidum*, North American tree of laurel family with yellow flowers, dark blue fruits and aromatic bark and foliage. Various extracts formerly used in manufacture of medicines, foods, drinks (root beer) but now regarded as possible carcinogen.

Sassoon, Siegfried Lorraine (1886-1967), English author. Experiences in WWI inspired anti-war *Counter-attack and Other Poems* (1918). Wrote semi-autobiog. novels, *Memoirs of a Fox-Hunting Man* (1928), *Memoirs of an Infantry Officer* (1930).

Satan, in Judaism, Christianity and Islam, the enemy of God and humanity, *ie* a unified personification of evil as opposed to that of good. Also called the Devil. NT developed idea of Satan as prince of demons, enemy of Christ, and describes war in heaven. Central figure of many popular legends, in literature appears as Mephistopheles (*eg* Goethe's *Faust*), Lucifer (*eg* Milton's *Paradise Lost*). During medieval and early modern period, conceived of as everpresent enemy of Christians, esp. saints.

satellite, in astronomy, celestial body in orbit about larger · body, usually a planet; Moon is a satellite of the Earth. Russians placed 1st artifical satellite (sputnik) in orbit about Earth (1957). Many have been launched since for communication purposes and to study upper atmosphere, radiation from outer space, *etc*.

Satie, Erik (1866-1925), French composer. Produced clear and simple music, often ironic or satirical in character. Works incl. ballets, *eg Parade*, songs, and many piano pieces, *eg Gymnopédies*.

satin, silk or rayon fabric having a smooth finish, glossy on the face and dull on the back. First made in China, popularized in Europe during Middle Ages.

satinwood, close-grained, hard, yellow wood of East Indian tree *Chloroxylon swietenia* and West Indian *Zanthoxylum flavum*. Used in veneers, marquetry, *etc*.

satire, literary work, in prose or poetry, or work of art, *etc*, which ridicules individuals, situations, ideas, esp. with aim of correcting vice. Uses mockery, wit, parody or irony; may be humorous or serious.

Sato, Eisaku (1901-75), Japanese statesman. Premier (1964-72) at head of Liberal Democratic ·govt. Negotiated treaty normalizing relations between South Korea and Japan (1965). Awarded Nobel Peace Prize (1974).

Satsuma, penin. of SW Kyushu isl., Japan. Famous porcelain made in area from 16th cent. Scene of revolt against imperial govt. in 1877.

Saturn, in Roman religion, god of harvests, later identified with Greek Cronus. Husband of Ops, father of Jupiter, Juno, Ceres, Pluto, Neptune. His festival, Saturnalia, was celebrated near the winter solstice with feasting, revelry and licence for slaves, and was prototype for modern Christmas.

Saturn, in astronomy, 2nd largest planet of Solar System, 6th in distance from Sun; mean distance from Sun *c* 1427 million km; diameter 119,300 km; revolves about Sun in period of *c* 29½ years. Has 10 natural ·satellites and system of 3 concentric rings of small particles. Has dense atmosphere containing hydrogen, ammonia and methane.

satyr, in Greek myth, minor woodland deity; attendant of Dionysus. Represented with pointed ears, short horns, head and body of man, legs of a goat. Given to riotous merriment and lechery. Similar to Roman faun.

Saudi Arabia, kingdom of SW Asia, occupying most of ARABIA. Area *c* 2,149,690 (830,000 sq mi); pop. 9,240,000; cap. Riyadh. Language: Arabic. Religion: Sunnite Islam. Mainly desert; agric., pastoral economy; great wealth derived from rich oil deposits in E. Has Islamic holy cities Mecca, Medina in Hejaz. State formed 1932 following unification of Nejd and Hejaz under Ibn Saud in 1925.

Saul (d. *c* 1012 BC), first king of Israel. The Bible relates how he was consumed by jealousy for his rival David, whose patron he had previously been. Killed himself after defeat by Philistines at Mt. Gilboa.

Sault Ste Marie, port of SC Ontario, Canada; on international canal link between L. Superior and L. Huron. Pop. 80,000. Timber, steel industs. Estab. as French mission in 17th cent.; became fur trade post. Opposite is **Sault Ste Marie,** town of Michigan, US; on St Mary's R. Pop. 15,000.

Saussure, Ferdinand de (1857-1913), Swiss linguist, regarded as father of structural LINGUISTICS. Clearly demarcated synchronic and diachronic ways of studying language. Held that language must be studied as social phenomenon. Distinguished between total structure of a language (*langue*) and individual acts of speaking (*parole*).

Theories contained in *Cours de linguistique générale* (pub. 1916).

Saussure, Horace Benedict de (1740-99), Swiss physicist and geologist. Studied meteorology, botany, geology of Alpine regions. Wrote *Voyages dans les Alpes* (1779-96).

Sava or **Save,** river of N Yugoslavia. Flows *c* 940 km (585 mi) from Julian Alps via Zagreb to Danube at Belgrade. Fertile basin used for agric.

Savage, Michael Joseph (1872-1940), New Zealand statesman, b. Australia. First Labour PM (1935-40). Term notable for social legislation, *eg* Social Security Act (1938).

savanna or **savannah,** natural grassland containing scattered trees and bushes. Found in tropical and subtropical areas with distinct rainy season. Most extensive in Africa; occurs also in *llanos* and *campos* of South America.

Savannah, port of E Georgia, US; near mouth of Savannah R. Pop. 118,000. Naval supplies, cotton exports; shipbuilding, sugar refining, varied mfg. industs. Strategic in American Revolution and Civil War.

Savoie, see SAVOY, France.

Savonarola, Girolamo (1452-98), Italian Dominican monk. Gained power in Florence through his powerful sermons and prophetic visions. Inspired expulsion of Pietro de' Medici from Florence (1494) and ruled as virtual dictator, advocating a return to ascetic Christian values. Denounced corruption of papal court but was excommunicated by Alexander VI (1497). Ordered to stop preaching by city govt., he was arrested, convicted of heresy and executed.

savory, any of genus *Satureia* of aromatic herbs of mint family. Species incl. summer savory, *S. hortensis,* and winter savory, *S. montana,* both native to Europe and used in cooking.

Savoy (*Savoie*), region of SE France, hist. cap. Chambéry. Incl. Savoy Alps, Graian Alps, Mont Blanc massif. Agric., esp. dairying, tourism, h.e.p. Medieval county; duchy from 1416. Ruled by House of Savoy, lost much territ. to France, Switzerland in early 16th cent. Part of Kingdom of Sardinia from 1720; ceded to France (1860).

Savoy, House of, European royal family, sometime rulers of Piedmont, Valois, Bresse, Nice. Acquired Sicily under Peace of Utrecht (1714) and exchanged it for Sardinia (1720). Reign of CHARLES ALBERT, king of Sardinia, saw beginnings of RISORGIMENTO; his son VICTOR EMMANUEL II was 1st king of united Italy. Ruling Italian dynasty lasted from 1861 until abdication of Humbert II (1946).

sawfish, cartilaginous fish with flattened shark-like body, genus *Pristis,* common in tropical seas. Elongated flattened snout with pointed teeth on side used to dig for food.

Saxe, Maurice, Comte de (1696-1750), German soldier in French service. In the War of the Austrian Succession, gained a brilliant victory over European Allies at Fontenoy (1745).

Saxe-Coburg-Gotha (*Sachsen-Coburg-Gotha*), region of West Germany, former duchy created 1826 by union of Saxe-Coburg and Gotha under Ernest I. Ernest's house came to rule Belgium (under his brother, Leopold) and England (under his son, Albert, consort of Victoria). Duchy dispersed (1920) into Thuringia and Bavaria.

Saxe-Weimar (*Sachsen-Weimar*), region of C Germany. Former duchy, cap. Weimar, ruled by Wettin dynasty from 15th cent. United 1741 with Eisenach, became rich cultural centre in 18th cent. Grand duchy from 1815, incorporated (1920) into Thuringia.

saxhorn, family of conical-bore brass wind instruments with valves. Designed in 1840s by Adolphe Sax; played in brass bands.

saxifrage, any of genus *Saxifraga* of mainly perennial plants of N temperate and Arctic regions. Most species grow wild as low, rock plants. Garden varieties incl. London pride, *S. umbrosa,* and rockery variety, *S. aizoon.*

Saxons, Teutonic people originally inhabiting what is now Schleswig (S Jutland). Spread during 5th-6th cent. through NW Germany, N coast of Gaul, S England (in area of later kingdoms of Sussex, Wessex and Essex). Continental Saxons became known as Old Saxons; fought periodically with Franks until subjugation and conversion by Charlemagne (9th cent.).

Saxony (Ger. *Sachsen*), region of East Germany, hist. cap. Dresden. Main cities Chemnitz, Leipzig. Duchy from 9th cent.; electorate from 14th cent.; kingdom from 1806, joined German empire 1871. Became East German prov. after WWII (dissolved 1952). Name also applied to region of West Germany, corresponding to state of Lower Saxony (Niedersachsen).

saxophone, family of musical wind instruments, varying in range and size but all having single reed and conical tube of brass. Used in military bands, jazz groups and orchestras. Developed by Adolphe Sax in 1840s.

Say, Jean Baptiste (1767-1832), French economist. Recognizing work of Adam Smith, evolved theory of markets (supply creates demand) in *Treatise on Political Economy* (1803).

Sayers, Dorothy L[eigh] (1893-1957), English author. Known for detective novels featuring erudite hero, Lord Peter Wimsey, *eg Clouds of Witness* (1926). Also wrote religious radio play, *The Man Born to be King* (1941), translations of Dante.

scabies, skin disease caused by parasitic mite *Sarcoptes scabiei*. Female burrows under skin, esp. around elbows and groin, to lay eggs. Main symptom is intense itch.

scabious, any of genus *Scabiosa* of annual or perennial herbs native to Europe, Asia and Africa. Species incl. sweet scabious, *S. atropurpurea*, with white, pink or purple flowers and field scabious, *S. arvensis*, with purple flowers.

Scafell Pike, mountain of Lake Dist., Cumbria, NW England. Highest in England (978 m/3210 ft); part of Scafell mountain group. Tourist area.

Scala, Teatro alla, famous opera house in Milan, Italy, usually known as La Scala. Opened 1778; built on site of church Santa Maria della Scala.

scalawags, term used in South after US Civil War to refer to white Southern Republicans who aided RECONSTRUCTION programme.

scale, in music, progression in ascending or descending order of related groups of notes. Most pieces of music are based on specific scale, the key of any piece being given by starting note (tonic note) of scale.

scale insect, small insect of Coccidae family. Female body covered with 'scale' made of cast-off skin and glutinous secretion. Many parasitic on plants, poisoning them with saliva. Others commercially useful, yielding shellac or carmine dye.

scallop, any of Pectinidae family of bivalve molluscs. Two fan-shaped, radially-ribbed shells with wavy outer edge; swims by snapping shells together. Adductor muscle is edible.

scalp, skin covering top and back of head. Attached to an underlying muscle (occipitofrontalis) which in turn covers a layer of loose tissue and blood vessels.

Scandinavia, penin. of NW Europe, comprising Norway, Sweden; bounded by Arctic Ocean, Atlantic, Baltic, Gulf of Bothnia. Culturally and hist. also incl. Denmark, Finland, Iceland, Faeroe Isls.

Scandinavian, see GERMANIC LANGUAGES.

scandium (Sc), rare metallic element; at. no. 21, at. wt. 44.96. Occurs in several minerals; discovered (1879) by spectroscopic analysis.

Scapa Flow, sea area of Orkney Isls., N Scotland. UK naval base in WWI and II. Interned German fleet scuttled (1919).

scarab beetle, any of Scarabaeidae family of large beetles with club-ended antennae. Incl. dung beetles and chafers. Name particularly applies to Egyptian sacred dung beetle *Scarabaeus sacer* whose image appears on seals or charms.

Scaramouche, stock character in COMMEDIA DELL'ARTE, a cowardly braggart.

Scarborough, mun. bor. of North Yorkshire, NE England. Pop. 44,000. Spa, resort; fishing port. Has remains of 12th cent. castle.

Scarlatti, Alessandro (c 1660-1725), Italian composer. Pioneer of Italian opera, developed *aria da capo*; wrote masses, cantatas, oratorios. His son, **[Giuseppe] Domenico Scarlatti** (1685-1757), was also a composer. His harpsichord sonatas, over 500 in number, show great originality in use of the keyboard.

scarlet fever or **scarlatina**, contagious disease, esp. of children, caused by bacterium *Streptococcus pyogenes*. Characterized by fever, sore throat, and a scarlet rash. Treated by antibiotics, *eg* penicillin.

scepticism or **skepticism**, in philosophy, theory contending that range of knowledge is limited by capacity of mind or inaccessibility of object. Exponents incl. Democritus, Pyrrho, Kant.

Schaffhausen, town of N Switzerland, on R. Rhine, cap. of Schaffhausen canton. Pop. 37,000. Indust. centre using h.e.p. from Schaffhausen Falls. Romanesque minster (11th cent.).

Scheldt (Fr. *Escaut*; Dutch, Flem. *Schelde*), river of W Europe. Flows 435 km (270 mi) from N France via Belgium (Tournai, Antwerp) to estuary in Netherlands. Connected to many canals.

Schelling, Friedrich Wilhelm Joseph von (1775-1854), German philosopher. Influential in German Romanticism. Sought to solve problem of knowledge by positing unity of mind and nature. Works incl. *The Ages of the World* (1854).

scherzo (Ital. = 'joke'), lively musical composition, usually as movement in symphony, sonata, *etc*; usually in triple time. Haydn and Beethoven were noted exponents.

Schiehallion, mountain of Tayside region, C Scotland. Almost conical in shape; height 1081 m (3547 ft). Density of Earth calculated here in 1774.

Schiele, Egon (1890-1918), Austrian painter. Influenced by Klimt and Freudian psychology, he is known for his expressionist linear style of depicting figures.

Schiller, [Johann Christoph] Friedrich von (1759-1805), German poet, dramatist, historian. Associate of Goethe, began with STURM UND DRANG prose dramas, *eg The Robbers* (1781). Later works more realistic, classical in form, *eg Wallenstein* (1798-9), *Maria Stuart* (1800), *The Maid of Orleans* (1801), *Wilhelm Tell* (1804). Also wrote didactic poems, *eg* 'The Artists' (1789), scholarly *History of the Thirty Years' War* (1791-3).

Schism, Great, split in RC church (1378-1417) after death of Gregory XI, resulting in rival lines of popes in Avignon and Rome. Following Council of PISA (1409), there were 3 rival claimants to papacy, Gregory XII, Benedict XIII and John XXIII.

Concluded by Council of Constance, when Martin V was elected pope.

schist, metamorphic rock, composed of thin, parallel layers of constituent minerals. Mineral crystals are finer than gneiss, coarser than slate. Types distinguished by dominant mineral eg mica schist, hornblende schist, talc schist.

schistosomiasis, *see* BILHARZIA.

schizophrenia, severe mental disorder characterized by separation of thought processes from reality, fragmentation of personality, withdrawal from human contact, bizarre behaviour, delusions and hallucinations. Treated by electric shocks, tranquillizer drugs such as chlorpromazine, psychotherapy.

Schlegel, August Wilhelm von (1767-1845), German scholar. Known for translations of Shakespeare (1797-1810, completed by others). Edited periodical *Athenaeum* with brother, Friedrich. Critical works influenced German Romantic movement.

Schlesinger, John (1926-), British film director. Became known in early 1960s, esp. for *Billy Liar* (1963); later made *Midnight Cowboy* (1969) in US.

Schleswig-Holstein, state of N West Germany, in S Jutland penin. Area 15,656 sq km (6045 sq mi); cap. Kiel. Low-lying; main rivers Elbe, Eider, crossed by Kiel Canal. Cereals, potatoes, livestock production; industs. centred in Kiel, Lübeck, Flensburg. Duchies associated with Denmark from 15th cent.; annexed by Prussia (1866) after Austro-Prussian War. N Schleswig returned (1920) to Denmark after plebiscite.

Schlieffen, Alfred, Graf von (1833-1913), German army officer. As chief of general staff (1891-1906), devised the 'Schlieffen plan' for a hinge-like flanking movement across Holland and France; used in modified form in WWI.

Schliemann, Heinrich (1822-1890), German archaeologist. Amassed a fortune in business, then devoted himself to locating Homer's Troy. Began excavating (1871) at Hissarlik near Dardanelles and discovered 9 superimposed sites which he identified as Troy. His excavations at Mycenae (1874-6) revealed remarkable MYCENAEAN CIVILIZATION.

Schmidt, Helmut (1918-), West German politician. Posts in Social Democratic govt. incl. finance minister from 1972 until succeeding Brandt as chancellor (1974).

schnauzer, breed of short-haired German terrier with blunt nose, erect ears. Standard schnauzer, used as guard dog, stands 43-51 cm/17-20 in. at shoulder.

Schoenberg, Arnold (1874-1951), Austrian composer. Early music was romantic, eg *Transfigured Night* (1899). Later developed ATONALITY of composition, which dispensed need for a key, as in *Pierrot Lunaire* (1912). From 1921, organized this into system of 12-note composition based on manipulation of rows of notes of the chromatic scale. Lived in US from 1933.

scholasticism, philosophical system of medieval European theologians, esp. Robert Grosseteste, St Thomas Aquinas and Albertus Magnus. Constituted synthesis of Aristotelian philosophy and Christian revelation, influenced by neo-platonism. Central problem that of universal concepts (*see* NOMINALISM, REALISM). Major scholastic works incl. Peter Lombard's *Sentences*, Aquinas' *Summa Theologica*.

Schopenhauer, Arthur (1788-1860), German philosopher. Influenced by Kant. Believed man's irrational will to be the only reality, and release from suffering and discord to be achieved only by negation of will. Works incl. *The World as Will and Representation* (1818), *Will in Nature* (1836). Influenced Nietzsche, Wagner.

Schrödinger, Erwin (1887-1961), Austrian physicist. Following work of de Broglie on wave nature of matter, he developed mathematical form of quantum theory as wave mechanics. Shared Nobel Prize for Physics with Dirac (1933).

Schubert, Franz Peter (1797-1828), Austrian composer. Noted for his lyrical melody, his work is often underlaid by melancholy. Foremost exponent of German *Lieder*, famous song cycles incl. *Die schöne Müllerin* and *Die Winterreise*. Wrote masterly string quartets, piano pieces. Best-known symphonies are 9th ('Great C major') and 8th ('The Unfinished').

Schuman, Robert (1886-1963), French statesman, premier (1947-8). As foreign minister (1948-53), evolved plan (1950) for European Coal and Steel Community, basis of later European Community.

Schumann, Robert Alexander (1810-56), German composer. Works incl. collections of piano pieces, *Carnaval* and *Kreisleriana*, Piano Concerto in A Minor, and *Spring* and *Rhenish* symphonies.

Encouraged appreciation of works of Chopin and Brahms. His wife, Clara Schumann, née Wieck (1819-96), was renowned pianist and leading interpreter of her husband's work.

Schuschnigg, Kurt von (1897-), Austrian statesman. Succeeded Dollfuss as chancellor (1934). Resisted Hitler's attempts to incorporate Austria into Germany; forced to resign after Nazis had occupied Austria (March, 1938). Imprisoned 1938-45.

Schütz, Heinrich (1585-1672), German composer. Studied in Italy, where he was influenced by Giovanni Gabrieli and Monteverdi. Introduced Italian techniques of vocal writing into Germany. Works incl. madrigals, series of *Symphoniae Sacrae*, *Christmas Oratorio*.

Schwarzkopf, Elisabeth (1915-), German singer. Formerly principal soprano at Vienna State Opera and Royal Opera House, Covent Garden. Excelled in Mozart and Richard Strauss. Noted interpreter of *Lieder*.

Schwarzwald, *see* BLACK FOREST, West Germany.

Schweitzer, Albert (1875-1965), Alsatian physician, missionary, theologian. From 1913, devoted himself to medical mission at Lambaréné, Gabon. Noted organist; wrote biog. of Bach and edited his organ music. In philosophy, believed in 'reverence for life', respecting all living creatures. Awarded Nobel Peace Prize (1952).

Schwerin, town of NW East Germany, on L. Schwerin. Pop. 91,000. Chemicals, pharmaceuticals mfg. Founded 1160; hist. cap. of Mecklenburg.

Schwitters, Kurt (1887-1948), German artist. Invented *Merz*, collage form using bits of paper and rubbish. Made large constructions (*Merzbau*) of scrap metal, wood, *etc*.

Schwyz, town of C Switzerland, cap. of Schwyz canton. Pop. 12,000. Tourist centre near L. Lucerne.

sciatica, pain along the course of the sciatic nerve, esp. affecting back of thigh, calf and foot. Often caused by pressure exerted on spinal nerves by invertebral discs.

science, system of knowledge, founded on formal axioms or theories constructed from observation and experiment. Sciences such as · physics and chemistry, which try to describe and account for natural phenomena, are often studied by theories which express mathematically a principle underlying 'numerous observations. Ideally, such theories encompass all previous knowledge on the phenomena and can be used to make testable predictions; they · are discarded or suitably modified if they are found to be too inaccurate or at a variance with experimental evidence.

science fiction, literary genre drawing on scientific knowledge or speculation to present fantasy. Typical motifs incl. interplanetary travel, artificial intelligence, global cataclysm. Early exponents incl. Jules Verne, H.G. Wells; developed by Isaac Asimov, Ray Bradbury, Arthur C. Clarke.

scientology, religio-scientific movement estab. in US (*c* 1950) by Lafayette Ronald Hubbard (1911-

). From 1959 world hq. at East Grinstead, England. Members use process similar to psychoanalysis to release energy of subconscious drives. Controversial practices have led to official inquiries in some countries.

Scilly Isles, archipelago off Cornwall, SW England. Incl. *c* 140 granite isls., 5 inhabited (St Mary's, Tresco, St Martin's, St Agnes, Bryher). Area 16 sq km (6 sq mi); pop. 2000; cap. Hugh Town. Mild climate; tourism; early flowers indust. Prehist. barrow on Samson Isl.

Scipio, Publius Cornelius ('Africanus Major') (*c* 234-183 BC), Roman soldier. Routed Carthaginian armies in Spain (210-206). Invaded Carthage (204), forcing Hannibal to return from Italy. Defeated Hannibal at Zama (202). His son's adopted son, **Publius Cornelius Scipio ('Africanus Minor')** (*c* 185-129 BC), commanded destruction of Carthage, ending 3rd Punic War (146).

Scone, village of Tayside region, C Scotland. Old Scone was site of Scottish coronations. Coronation Stone ('Stone of Destiny') moved (1297) to Westminster Abbey.

Scopes trial, in US legal history, trial (1925) of school teacher John T. Scopes for teaching Darwinian theory of evolution, then contrary to Tennessee state law. He was convicted but later released on a technicality.

Scorpio, see ZODIAC.

scorpion, any of order Scorpionida of arachnids of warm and tropical regions. Two large pincers in front, long segmented tail with venomous sting.

Scotland, constituent country of

UK, in N part of GREAT BRITAIN. Area 78,749 sq km (30,405 sq mi); pop. 5,228,000; cap. Edinburgh; largest city Glasgow. Comprises 9 regions, 3 isl. authorities. Main rivers Clyde, Forth, Tay, Dee. Highlands, isls. in N, W (crofting, fishing, forestry, tourism); uplands in S (sheep rearing). Pop. and industs. mainly concentrated in C lowlands, incl. coalmining, shipbuilding, engineering industs. Offshore oil, gas in E. Christianity spread from 6th cent.; hist. warring with England until union of Crowns under James VI (1603), politically united with England from 1707; Jacobite rebellions in 1715, 1745. Resurgence of nationalism in 20th cent.

Scotland, Church of, established national church in Scotland, presbyterian in govt. Jurisdiction of RC church abolished by Parliament in act of 1560. Under influence of KNOX, reformed church created on self-governing units after Geneva models. Two *Books of Discipline* (1560, 1581) laid out church organization. Development complicated by periods of episcopacy under Stuart rulers leading to National Covenant (see COVENANTERS). Established status confirmed in Act of Settlement (1690) and Act of Union (1707). Secessionary groups incl. Free Church of Scotland (1843).

Scotland Yard, hq. of Metropolitan London police, UK. Name derives from original site in street near Whitehall. Used esp. for Criminal Investigation Dept. (CID) which it houses.

Scott, Sir George Gilbert (1811-78), English architect. Active in Gothic revival, his numerous works incl. St Pancras Station and Albert Memorial, London. Carried out controversial restorations to many churches, eg Westminster Abbey. His grandson, **Sir Giles Gilbert Scott** (1880-1960), designed Liverpool Cathedral.

Scott, Robert Falcon (1868-1912), English naval officer, explorer. Led expedition (1901-4) in *Discovery* to explore Ross Sea; discovered King Edward VII Land. Led 2nd expedition in *Terra Nova*, reached South Pole (Jan. 1912) 35 days after Amundsen. He and 4 companions died on return journey.

Scott, Sir Walter (1771-1832), Scottish author. Kindled interest in Scots folklore in ballad collection *The Minstrelsy of the Scottish Border* (1802-3), narrative poems, eg *Lay of the Last Minstrel* (1805), *Lady of the Lake* (1810). Romantic historical novels incl. *Waverley* (1814), *Old Mortality* (1816), *Rob Roy* (1818), *The Heart of Midlothian* (1818), *Ivanhoe* (1820), *Kenilworth* (1821).

Scott, Winfield (1786-1866), American general. Supreme army commander (1841-61), he headed the push into Mexico, ending Mexican War (1846-8) with the capture of Mexico City.

Scottish Gaelic, see GAELIC.

Scottish Nationalist Party (SNP), political party evolved from Scottish Home Rule Association (formed 1886). Advocates self-govt. for Scotland. Made significant electoral gains in 1970s.

Scottish terrier, breed of dog developed in Scotland in 19th cent.

to hunt game. Stands *c* 25 cm/10 in. at shoulder.

Scotus, *see* DUNS SCOTUS, JOHN.

screamer, any of Anhimidae family of long-legged birds of South American forests and rivers. Two sharp spurs on each wing. Species incl. horned screamer, *Anhima cornuta,* with large bony horn on head.

scree, *see* TALUS.

screech owl, New World owl, genus *Otus.* Species incl. North American *O. asio* with grey or reddish brown body, ear tufts, and wailing cry.

Scriabin, Aleksandr Nikolayevich (1872-1915), Russian composer and pianist. Works, often mystical, incl. tone poems *Prometheus, Divine Poem, Poem of Ecstasy.* Used personal harmony based on a special 'mystic chord'.

scribes, term for officials learned in Jewish law. First applied to Ezra (*c* 444 BC); last to Simeon the Just (4th-3rd cent. BC). Work developed into Oral Law of TALMUD.

scrofula, tuberculosis of lymph nodes of neck. Characterized by swelling of nodes and ulceration of overlying skin. Formerly called the King's evil, it was believed to be cured by royal touch.

scrub, thick, stunted vegetation found on tracts of poor, semi-arid land. Types incl. maquis of W Mediterranean area, mallee and mulga scrub of Australia, cactus scrub of E Africa.

Scudéry, Madeleine de (1607-1701), French author, also known as 'Sapho'. Wrote discursive sentimental romances, *eg Artamène, ou le Grand Cyrus* (1649-53), *Clélie*

(1654-60), containing portraits of her circle.

Scullin, James Henry (1876-1953), Australian statesman, PM (1929-31). United Labor Party (1928), and was its leader (1928-35). Advocated public spending cuts, deflation to deal with Depression.

sculling, sport of propelling a boat by means of sculls (light oars) held in each hand. Competitive sculling races date from 1840s. Single and double sculling are Olympic events.

sculpture, art of producing 3-dimensional representations of forms. Techniques used incl. carving in wood or stone and modelling in wax or clay for eventual casting in plaster, lead or bronze. Field of sculpture has expanded in 20th cent. to incl. kinetic sculpture, assemblages, welded structures, *etc.*

Scunthorpe, mun. bor. of Humberside, E England. Pop. 71,000. Iron and steel indust., developed from local iron ore deposits.

scurvy, disease resulting from deficiency of vitamin C in diet. Characterized by weakening of capillaries, haemorrhages in tissue, bleeding from gums. Formerly a problem on long sea voyages when fresh fruit was unavailable, it was treated in 18th cent. by issuing of lime juice.

Scutari (*Shkodër*), town of NW Albania, on L. Sartari. Pop. 50,000. Wool, grain, tobacco. RC cathedral; Venetian citadel. Cap. of ancient Illyria until 168 BC.

Scutari, Turkey, *see* ISTANBUL.

Scylla, in Greek myth, daughter of Hecate, loved by Poseidon and turned into a monster by Amphitrite. Devoured sailors who passed her cave in Straits of Messina, S Italy. Opposite was **Charybdis**, a monster who had been thrown into sea by Zeus for stealing Hercules' cattle. A whirlpool was created as she sucked and spewed water.

Scythians, nomadic tribe inhabiting the steppes N of Black Sea between the Danube and Don. (7th-2nd cents. BC). Known from their trading contacts with the Greeks. Their expansion was resisted by Persians under Darius (*c* 512 BC). By 4th cent. BC, a declining power and by 2nd cent. BC, had been overwhelmed by Sarmatians.

sea anemone, sedentary marine coelenterate of class Actinozoa. Columnar body without skeleton; mouth surrounded by circles of petal-like tentacles. Found attached to rocks, weeds.

Seaborg, Glenn Theodore (1912-), American chemist. Shared Nobel Prize for Chemistry (1951) with E.M. McMillan for discoveries in chemistry of transuranic elements; co-discoverer of americium, curium, berkelium and several other elements.

sea cow, name applied to DUGONG or MANATEE.

sea elephant, *Mirounga leonina*, large seal, largest of pinnipeds; reaches lengths of 6 m/20 ft. Male has inflatable proboscis.

seagull, common name for many species of GULL.

sea hare, slug-like marine gastropod mollusc, genus *Aplysia*, with small internal shell. Moves by beating 2 lateral lobes (parapodia).

seahorse, small fish of Syngnathidae family, esp. genus *Hippocampus*. Elongated snout and pre-

hensile tail; male has pouch for brooding eggs. *H. ramulosus* is commonest European species.

seal, carnivorous marine mammal, order Pinnipedia. True seal (Phocidae family) has no external ears and rudimentary hind limbs united to tail. Seals of Otariidae family, incl. sea lion, have external ears and hind limbs used for locomotion. Hunted for skins and oil-yielding blubber.

sea leopard, *Hydrurga leptonyx*, large earless seal of Antarctic. Aggressive predator, feeding on penguins and young seals.

sea lion, eared seal of Otariidae family with smooth coat and no under-fur. Californian sea lion, *Zalophus californianus*, noted for agility, is commonest; lives in colonies on N Pacific coast and Galapagos.

Sealyham, breed of terrier developed in Wales in 19th cent. Coat mainly white; stands 25 cm/ 10 in. at shoulder.

séance, see SPIRITUALISM.

sea otter, *Enhydra lutris*, webfooted marine carnivore of N Pacific coast. Larger than common otter, with long tail; dark brown fur valued commercially.

sea sickness, see MOTION SICKNESS.

sea snake, any of Hydrophidae family of poisonous snakes of Indian and Pacific oceans. Flattened oarlike body, small eyes.

sea squirt, any of class Ascidiacea of sedentary marine tunicates. Cylindrical or globular body enclosed in skin of cellulose-like material, Contracts body and squirts water when disturbed.

Seattle, seaport of W Washington, US; on Puget Sound between

Olympic and Cascade Mts. Pop. 531,000. Indust., commercial centre; timber, fish, fruit exports; shipbuilding, aircraft mfg. Settled in 1850s. Boomed in Alaska gold rush (1899) and after opening of Panama Canal (1914).

sea-urchin, any echinoderm of class Echinoidea. Globular or discshaped; body covered with calcareous plates studded with spines.

seaweed, common name for all types of marine ALGAE, esp. BROWN ALGAE.

Sebastian, St (*fl* c 3rd cent.), Roman martyr. Traditionally, a favourite of Diocletian whom he antagonized by embracing Christianity. Shot with arrows and left for dead; wounds healed but he was eventually battered to death. Frequently represented in Renaissance art.

Sebastopol, see SEVASTOPOL.

secondary school, institution providing for the education of children over the age of 11 years; attendance normally compulsory until age of 14-16 years. Types incl. GRAMMAR SCHOOL and secondary modern for less academic pupils, both of these being superseded by COMPREHENSIVE EDUCATION. In US, secondary school also known as high school, divided into junior and senior, offering academic or vocational subjects.

Second Empire (1852-70), period in French history when Louis Napoleon, after overthrowing Second Republic, ruled as emperor NAPOLEON III. Terminated by Franco-Prussian War.

secretary bird, *Sagittarius serpentarius,* long-legged S African bird of prey with head crest resembling -quill pens. Feeds on snakes, insects.

securities, evidence of property, eg bonds or stock certificates.

Security Council, see UNITED NATIONS ORGANIZATION.

Sedan, town of NE France, on R. Meuse. Pop. 24,000. Textile mfg., metal goods. Huguenot stronghold in 16th-17th cent., passed to France (1642). Scene of decisive Prussian victory (1870) over France; German breakthrough (1940) in WWII.

sedative, drug administered to diminish excitement, nervousness or irritation. Among widely used types are barbiturates. Large doses induce sleep, making patient drowsy.

Seddon, Richard John, known as 'King Dick' (1845-1906), New Zealand statesman, PM (1893-1906), b. England. Minister in John Balliance's Liberal govt., succeeding him as PM. Continued social reforms, eg factory acts, old age pensions.

sedge, any of family Cyperaceae of grass-like plants found on wet ground or in water. Genera incl. Carex, Cyperus and Scirpus, used in making paper.

Sedgemoor, former marsh of Somerset, SW England. Scene of James II's victory over Duke of Monmouth (1685).

sedimentary rocks, rocks formed by deposition and compaction of sediments. Consist of sand, gravel etc, laid down by seas, lakes, rivers, glaciers or wind, and compressed into layers, or strata, of varying thickness. Types incl. limestone, sandstone, shale.

sedum, genus of mainly perennial herbs native to N temperate regions. Found on rocks and walls; fleshy stalks and leaves, white, yellow or pink flowers. Species incl. wall pepper, *Sedum acre*, insipid stonecrop, *S. sexangulare*.

Seebeck effect, in physics, production of current in a circuit when junctions of unlike metals have different temperatures. Also called thermoelectric effect.

seed, fertilized ovule which forms reproductive structure of seed plants. Consists of embryo, stored food and protective covering.

Segovia, Andrés . (1893-), Spanish virtuoso guitarist. Pioneered use of guitar as concert instrument. Author of many arrangements of classical pieces for guitar.

Segovia, town of NC Spain, cap. of Segovia prov. Pop. 42,000. Tourist centre, pottery mfg. Roman aqueduct still supplies water; Moorish alcazar, Gothic cathedral (16th cent.).

segregation, policy or practice of compelling different racial groups to live apart from each other, go to separate schools, use separate social facilities, *etc*. In Southern states of US, segregation was extensively enforced by 1920; Supreme Court rulings and legislation in 1950s and 60s banned most forms of segregation. Known as APARTHEID in South Africa.

Seine, river of N France. Flows c 770 km (480 mi) from Langres Plateau via Troyes, Paris, Rouen to English Channel at Le Havre. With tributaries (incl. Aube, Marne, Oise), drains most of Paris Basin; navigable by ocean-going vessels to Rouen.

seismology, study of earthquakes and related phenomena. Occurrence and severity of tremors are recorded on a seismograph. Seismological techniques are also used in eg mineral prospecting, measuring thickness of ice sheets, depth and shape of ocean floors.

Sekondi-Takoradi, city of SW Ghana, on Gulf of Guinea, cap. of Western Region. Pop. 161,000. Port, exports cocoa, timber, manganese, bauxite. Sekondi was Gold Coast's chief port, superseded by Takoradi deepwater harbour (completed 1928). Towns merged 1946.

Selene, in Greek myth, moon goddess; daughter of Titans Hyperion and Theia, sister of Helios (the sun). Sometimes identified with Hecate and Artemis.

selenium (Se), non-metallic element of sulphur group; at. no. 34, at. wt. 78.96. Occurs in several allotropic forms; obtained from flue dust produced by burning sulphide ores. Grey metallic form used in photoelectric cells as its conductivity varies with intensity of light. Used in glass and ceramic indust. to impart red colour.

Seleucus I (c 358-280 BC), one of Alexander the Great's generals. Ruler of Babylonia (312 BC) after Alexander's death. Extended empire to include much of Asia Minor, Syria, Bactria. Founded Seleucid dynasty, line of kings, incl. ANTIOCHUS THE GREAT, who reigned in nearer Asia till 65 BC.

Selfridge, Harry Gordon (1857-1947), American businessman. After career in retailing in US, founded (1909) Selfridges Store, London, 1st big dept. store in Britain.

Selim I (1467-1520), Ottoman sultan (1512-20). Conquered parts of Persia

(1514), Egypt and Syria (1517). Succeeded to Islamic caliphate, gaining control of holy cities of Islam.

Seljuks, Turkish ruling dynasty, who conquered and controlled most of Near East (11th–13th cents.). Power decayed in 13th cent. and Mongols captured most of their territs.

Selkirk, Alexander (1676–1721), Scottish sailor. Marooned on Juan Fernández isl. for 4 years. Episode suggested Defoe's *Robinson Crusoe*.

Selkirkshire, former county of SE Scotland, now in Borders region. In Southern Uplands; sheep rearing; woollens, tweed mfg. Co. town was Selkirk, former royal burgh. Pop. 6000. Tweed mfg. Once famous for 'souters' (shoemakers).

Selznick, David O[liver] (1902–65), American film producer. Formed (1936) Selznick International Pictures after working for RKO and MGM. Films incl. *A Star is Born* (1937), *Gone with the Wind* (1939).

semantics, study of the relations between words and meaning. Divided into empirical study of how words are used, philosophic study of nature of meaning itself and the generation of symbolic formal languages. *See* SEMIOTICS.

Semarang, city of Indonesia, cap. of Central Java prov., on Java Sea. Pop. 647,000. Shipbuilding and mfg. centre. Exports sugar, tobacco, copra.

Semele, in Greek myth, daughter of Cadmus and Harmonia. Loved by Zeus in human form, whom she asked to appear as a god, but was consumed by lightning when he did.

Zeus took her unborn son, Dionysus, from ashes and nurtured him in his thigh.

semiconductor, substance whose electrical conductivity is low at normal temperatures but which increases with rising temperature. Conductivity also increases by addition of minute quantities of special impurities. Those in use incl. germanium, silicon and gallium arsenide; important in transistors, rectifiers and photoelectric cells.

semiotics or **semiology**, science of signs in general, incl. SEMANTICS and pragmatics, the study of relationship of signs to their users.

Semiramis, legendary queen of Assyria. Reputedly founded Babylon. Noted for her beauty, wisdom, sexual excesses. Changed into dove after death.

Semite, etymologically a descendant of Shem, son of Noah in Old Testament. Term now used for a linguistic category which incl. Hebrews, Arabs, Syrians, Ethiopians and ancient peoples of Babylon, Assyria, Canaan, Phoenicia.

Semitic, one of two major language groups making up Afro-Asiatic family. Divided into E and W branches, incl. Aramaic, Hebrew, Arabic, Ethiopic.

Semmering Pass, E Austria, between Lower Austria and Styria. Height 980 m (3215 ft); site of oldest mountain railway in the world (1848–55).

semolina, cereal food consisting of coarsely ground particles of durum wheat produced during making of fine flour. Used in making macaroni, puddings, *etc.*

Senanayake, Don Stephen (1884–

1952), Ceylonese statesman. First PM (1947-52) of independent Ceylon (now Sri Lanka). Succeeded by his son, Dudley Shelton Senanayake (1911-73), who was PM (1952-3, 1960, 1965-70).

Senate, in US, upper house of CONGRESS. Composed of senators (2 from each state) serving 6-year terms; presided over by vice-president. Senators were chosen by state legislatures until 17th Amendment (1913) estab. direct popular election. In addition to passing legislation, Senate must ratify treaties and confirm presidential appointments.

senate, governing body in ancient Rome. In early years of republic, censors chose its members, usually from ex-magistrates. During 3rd and 2nd cent. BC, it controlled foreign affairs, the army, finances, *etc.* Power first challenged by the Gracchi, resulting in division into senatorial and popular parties, and by military leaders, *eg* Sulla, Pompey, Julius Caesar. Its authority diminished after Caesar's death, lessening still further during empire.

Sendai, city of Japan, N Honshu isl. Pop. 545,000. Produces chemicals, metal goods, silk. Seat of Tohoku Univ. (1907).

Seneca, [Lucius Annaeus] (*c* 4 BC-AD 65), Roman philosopher, dramatist, statesman. Tutor to Nero, briefly virtual ruler of Rome; later ordered to commit suicide, doing so in manner suited to his philosophy, Stoicism. Best known as writer of tragedies, incl. *Medea, Phaedra, Oedipus,* which greatly influenced Renaissance and later literature.

Senegal, republic of W Africa. Area 196,000 sq km (76,000 sq mi); pop. 5,115,000; cap. Dakar. Language: French. Religion: Islam. Mainly low-lying savannah; stock rearing; exports groundnuts, phosphates. Coastal settlements disputed by France, Portugal 18th-19th cents.; centre of slave trade. Part of French West Africa from 1895; part of Mali Federation 1959-60; independent 1960. Member of French Community.

Senegal, river of W Africa. Flows c 1690 km (1050 mi) NW from Fouta Djallon highlands to Atlantic at St Louis. Forms Senegal-Mauritania border; provides irrigation.

senility, mental deterioration associated with old age. Characterized by loss of memory, confusion, *etc.* Causes incl. degeneration of brain cells and inadequate blood flow to the brain resulting from hardened arteries.

Sennacherib (d. 681 BC), king of Assyria (705-681 BC), son of Sargon II. Captured and destroyed Babylon (689). Restored Nineveh as his cap. and built splendid palace there. Murdered, prob. by his sons.

Sennett, Mack, orig. Michael Sinnott (1888-1960), American film director. Famous for slapstick silents of 1920s, creating the Keystone Kops, using Charlie Chaplin, Fred Mace.

sensationalism, in philosophy, belief that all knowledge is acquired through the senses. Central to the philosophies of *eg* Hobbes, Locke, Hume.

sensitive plant or **humble plant,** *see* MIMOSA.

Seoul, cap. of South Korea. Pop. 5,536,000. Indust. centre on R. Han;

railway engineering, textile mfg. Historical cap. of Korea from 14th cent. Seat of Japanese occupation govt. (1910-45). UN hq. (severely damaged) during Korean War, it was rebuilt on modern lines.

separation of powers, in political theory, principle that executive, legislative and judicial functions of govt. should be independent of each other. Principle formulated by Montesquieu, served as basis for framers of US Constitution.

sepia, dark brown pigment, originally prepared from inky secretion of cuttlefish.

Sepoy Rebellion, see INDIAN MUTINY.

Septuagint (Lat., = seventy), most ancient and celebrated Greek version of the Hebrew Scriptures. Traditionally written in 72 days by 72 translators employed by Ptolemy II. Prob. made c 250-100 BC from versions of texts now lost.

Sepulchre, Holy, site NW of Calvary, Jerusalem. Traditional site of Jesus' tomb, now covered by Church of the Resurrection, shared by Orthodox, Coptic, Syrian, Armenian and RC churches.

sequoia, two species of large coniferous trees of W US coast. Redwood, *Sequoia sempervirens,* and big tree *Sequoiadendron giganteum.* Both grow to c 100 m (300 ft). Some big trees are c 4000 years old.

seraphim, see ANGEL.

Serbia (*Srbija*), autonomous republic of E Yugoslavia, incl. Vojvodina autonomous prov., Kosovo autonomous region. Area 88,337 sq km (34,107 sq mi); cap. Belgrade. Mountainous in S; fertile Danubian plain in N (wheat, flax, fruit growing). Medieval kingdom, defeated (1389) by Turks. Independent from 1878, kingdom 1882. Expansionist policy led to Balkan Wars (1912-13), conflict with Austria led to WWI. Nucleus of Yugoslavia 1918, reorganized as republic 1946.

Serbo-Croat, language in S Slavic branch of Indo-European family. Chief official tongue of Yugoslavia.

serenade, in music, a set of movements for chamber orchestra or wind instruments, lighter than orchestral suite.

Serengeti National Park, area of N Tanzania, E of Victoria Nyanza. Game reserve, mainly grass-covered plain; area 13,000 sq km (5000 sq mi).

serfdom, condition of hereditary semi-bondage characteristic of most peasants under FEUDALISM. Serf usually worked on land of his master, but unlike a slave, retained certain rights and could not be sold. Widespread practice developed throughout Europe during Middle Ages. Disappeared in England towards end of Middle Ages; abolished in France by French Revolution; remained in Russia until Edict of Emancipation (1861).

serialism, theory of time posited by philosopher John William Dunne (1875-1949) to account for telepathic phenomena; argues that all time exists simultaneously.

Seringapatam, town of S India. Pop. 14,000. On isl. in R. Cauvery. Former cap. of Mysore (Karnataka). Has mausoleum of Tippoo Sahib and his father. Fortress captured and Tippoo killed by British (1799).

serpent, ancient bass wind musical instrument shaped like coiled snake. Usually made of wood with fingerholes and sometimes keys, and played with a cup mouthpiece like that of brass instruments.

serpentine, green or brownish-green mineral, consisting of hydrous magnesium silicate. Chrysotile, a fibrous variety, is major source of asbestos. Name also applied to rock, a mixture of serpentine and other minerals, which may be cut and polished for ornaments.

serum, clear yellowish liquid which separates from blood after clotting. Name also applies to blood fluid containing antibodies of immunity taken from an animal immunized against a specific disease; used as an antitoxin.

Servetus, Michael (1511-53), Spanish theologian. Gained renown as physician in Vienne, France. Entered into correspondence with Calvin over radical religious views; denied doctrine of Trinity. Fled from Inquisition to Geneva after pub. of *Christianismi Restitutio* (1553), arrested on Calvin's orders and burnt at stake.

Service, Robert William (1874-1958), Canadian poet, b. England. Known for popular ballads of Yukon gold rush, eg 'The Shooting of Dan McGrew'. Also wrote novels.

servomechanism, automatic device in which small input power controls much larger output power. Output is compared with input through feedback so that difference between the 2 quantities can be used to achieve desired amount of control. Used in aircraft and mfg. machinery.

sesame, *Sesamum indicum,* Asian plant whose flat seeds are used in flavouring and yield edible oil.

Set or **Seth,** in ancient Egyptian religion, god of evil and darkness. Brother and murderer of OSIRIS.

set, in mathematics, collection of objects, eg numbers, with some defining property to tell whether a particular object is member of this collection. Operations with sets and their study are important in modern mathematics and logic.

Sète, town of Languedoc, S France, on Gulf of Lions. Pop. 41,000. Port (terminus of Canal du Midi) with wine, salt, fish trade, oil refining; tourist resort. Formerly called Cette.

Sétif, town of NE Algeria. Pop. 98,000. Grain and livestock market, on Algiers-Tunis railway. Roman *Sitifis,* remains incl. mausoleum.

setter, large gun dog trained to find game and point its position. Breeds incl. English, Irish and Gordon setter.

Settlement, Act of, act of English Parliament (1701) regulating succession to throne. Provided that succession should pass to house of Hanover (which it did in 1714) if William III and Anne died without heir. Also declared that only Protestants can succeed to throne.

Setúbal, town of S Portugal, on Bay of Setúbal. Pop. 45,000. Port, exports oranges, wine, cork; fishing. Castle (16th cent.).

Seurat, Georges (1859-91), French painter. Devised divisionist (pointillist) technique of painting in small dots of colour; his works have a classical rigour of draughtsmanship and composition. Works incl. *Un Dimanche à la Grande Jatte,* most complete exposition of his theories.

Sevastopol or **Sebastopol,** seaport of USSR, Ukrainian SSR; on S Crimea coast. Pop. 246,000. Naval base and shipbuilding centre; seaside resort. Site of 5th cent. BC Greek colony. Captured after 11 month siege (1854-5) by French, British and Turkish troops in Crimean War. Fell to Germans after 8 month siege (1942).

Seven, Group of, group of Canadian landscape painters, incl. A.Y. Jackson and J.E.H. MacDonald, formed in Toronto · c 1913. Inaugurated nationalist movement in Canadian painting. Renderings of N Canadian landscape characterized by brilliant colour and bold form.

Seven against Thebes, see POLY-NICES.

seven deadly sins, in RC theology, capital sins (pride, covetousness, lust, anger, gluttony, envy, sloth). Frequently portrayed by artists, writers.

Seventh Day Adventists, see ADVENTISTS.

Seven Weeks War, name for AUSTRO-PRUSSIAN WAR.

Seven Wonders of the World, in antiquity, held to be Great Pyramid of Khufu, Hanging Gardens of Babylon, Statue of Zeus at Olympia, Temple of Artemis at Ephesus, Mausoleum at Halicarnassus, Colossus of Rhodes, Pharos (lighthouse) at Alexandria.

Seven Years War, conflict (1756-63) resulting from formation of coalition by France, Austria, Russia and allies to reduce · power of Prussia. Also involved French-British colonial wars in North America (called French and Indian Wars) and India. Campaigns by Frederick II of Prussia in Bohemia, Saxony and Silesia · thwarted by Austria and Russia. Peace treaty of Hubertusburg, although restoring status quo, marked emergence of Prussia as European power. Britain's colonial supremacy settled by Treaty of Paris after victories at Québec (1759) and Plassey (1757).

Severn, river of SW UK. Flows *c* 338 km (210 mi) from C Wales via Worcester, Gloucester to Bristol Channel. Has tidal bore as far as Tewkesbury. Road suspension bridge (1966).

Severus, Septimius (146-211), Roman emperor (193-211), b. Africa. Seized throne after murder of emperor Pertinax, overthrowing rival claimants in Rome (193), Syria (194) and Gaul (197). Built famous triumphal arch in Old Forum at Rome.

Sévigné, Marquise de, née Marie de Rabutin-Chantal (1626-96), French noblewoman. Letters to her daughter and intimates survive as lively account of Louis XIV's reign.

Seville (*Sevilla*), city of SW Spain, on R. Guadalquivir, cap. of Seville prov. Pop. 548,000. River port, fruit, wine trade, mfg. industs.; univ. (1502). Chief city of S Spain under Romans (anc. *Hispalis*), Visigoths; *fl* under Moorish rule 712-1248; New World trade centre (15th-17th cents.). School of painting (Murillo, Velázquez). Moorish tower and palace, 15th cent. cathedral contains tomb of Columbus.

Sèvres, suburb of SW Paris, on R. Seine. Porcelain works (Sèvres ware) estab. 1756. Treaty of Sèvres (1920) between Allies and Turkey signed here.

Sèvres, Treaty of, peace settlement (1920) signed at Sèvres, N France, between Turkey and Allies.

Abolished Ottoman Empire, created new Turkish frontiers. Rejection of treaty by Kemal Ataturk led to LAUSANNE CONFERENCE.

sewage disposal, system for removal and disposal of (mainly liquid) indust. and domestic wastes and excess rainwater. Frequently, toxic indust. wastes are disposed of separately. Domestic sewage treatment is dependent on aerobic bacteria feeding on organic material. Sludge may be processed as plant fertilizer. Early sewers incl. Cloaca Maxima in Rome (c 6th cent. BC), but most effective systems date from 19th cent.

Sewell, Anna (1820-78), English author. Known for children's story *Black Beauty, the Autobiography of a Horse* (1877).

sewing machine, device with mechanically driven needle for sewing of cloth, leather, .etc. First successful model built (1846) by Elias Howe; developed by Isaac Singer. Two basic types; chain stitch uses single thread, lock stitch has second thread fed to underside of cloth.

sex, either of 2 divisions, male and female, into which animals are divided, depending on their reproductive functions.

sex chromosome, chromosome present in germ cells of most animals and some plants. Such chromosomes are usually designated by letters X and Y. In humans, ova carry an X chromosome, spermatozoa either an X or a Y. An ovum receiving an X chromosome at fertilization develops into a female, and into a male if it receives a Y. Inherited characteristics, *eg* colour

blindness, determined by genes on the X chromosome are said to be sex-linked.

sextant, instrument for measuring angular distance of celestial bodies from the horizon. Used in navigation, surveying. Developed independently by John Hadley in England and Thomas Godfrey in US during 18th cent.

sexton beetle, *Necrophorus humator,* bluish-black burying beetle. Larvae feed on corpses of buried vertebrates.

Seychelles, volcanic isl. group (c 90) in W Indian Ocean; member of British Commonwealth. Area c 380 sq km (150 sq mi); pop 59,000; cap. Victoria (pop. 12,000) on Mahé Isl. Coconuts, fish, copra, cinnamon, guano exports. French territ. 18th cent., ceded to British 1814. Became independent 1976.

Seymour, Jane (c 1509-37), English noblewoman, 3rd wife of Henry VIII. Died after birth of son, Edward VI. Her brother, **Edward Seymour, Duke of Somerset** (c 1506-52), became Edward's protector (1547). Sponsored Protestant reforms of Cranmer. Beheaded after losing power to NORTHUMBERLAND. **Thomas Seymour,** Baron Seymour of Sudeley (c 1508-49), secretly married Catherine Parr (1547). Rivalled brother for king's favour before execution for treason.

Sfax, city of E Tunisia, on Gulf of Gabès. Pop. 215,000. Port, exports phosphates, olive oil, sponges; fishing. Former Phoenician then Roman colony; stronghold of Barbary pirates.

Sforza, Ludovico (1451-1508), Italian nobleman. Succeeded to duchy of Milan (1494). Driven from power (1499) by Louis XII of France, he died in captivity. Famous for his lavish expenditure on arts and sciences. Patron of Leonardo da Vinci.

's Gravenhage, see HAGUE, THE, Netherlands.

Shaba, see KATANGA.

Shackleton, Sir Ernest Henry (1874-1922), British explorer, b. Ireland. Accompanied Scott to Antarctic (1901-4); led expedition (1907-9) which located S magnetic pole. Lost ship *Endurance* on expedition (1914-16), journeyed *c* 1300 km (800 mi) overland to safety. Died on expedition to Enderby Land.

Shadwell, Thomas (c 1642-92), English dramatist. Wrote comedies incl. *Epsom Wells* (1672), *The Squire of Alsatia* (1688). Now remembered as butt of Dryden's satire 'Mac-Flecknoe'. Succeeded Dryden as poet laureate (1689).

Shaftesbury, Anthony Ashley Cooper, 1st Earl of (1621-83), English statesman. Gained favour of Charles II after supporting Restoration. Member of CABAL cabinet; opposed to king's pro-Catholic policy. Dismissed as lord chancellor after supporting anti-Catholic Test Act (1673). Sought to exclude James II from succession, backing claims of Monmouth instead; forced to flee to Holland (1682). His grandson, **Anthony Ashley Cooper, 3rd Earl of Shaftesbury** (1671-1713), wrote philosophical essays, many collected in *Characteristics of Men, Manners, Opinions and Times* (1711). **Anthony Ashley Cooper, 7th Earl of Shaftesbury** (1801-85), was social reformer. Tory MP from 1826,

promoted factory legislation forbidding employment of women and children in coal mines (1842), introducing 10-hour working day (1847).

shag, *Phalacrocorax aristotelis,* green-black seabird of cormorant family, found in Europe and N Africa. Nests on cliffs in colonies.

Shah of Iran, see PAHLAVI.

Shah Jehan (c 1592-1666), Mogul emperor (1628-58). Conquered much of the Deccan. Reign considered golden age of Mogul architecture; built TAJ MAHAL at Agra. Deposed and imprisoned by his son Aurangzeb until his death.

Shahn, Ben (1898-1969), American artist, b. Lithuania. Early works were realistic and politically engaged, eg *The Passion of Sacco and Vanzetti* (1931); at others interest in life of poor people and uses photographs, advertisements, *etc.*

Shakers, popular name for ecstatic religious sect, United Society of Believers in Christ's Second Appearing. Originated among Quakers in England c 1747, taken to US (1774) by group under Ann Lee. Practised separation from society in closed, communal group. Now largely extinct.

Shakespeare, William (1564-1616), English dramatist, poet, b. Stratford-upon-Avon. Spent early years in London as actor, becoming a partner in Globe Theatre (1599). Early plays (written before 1596) incl. histories, *Henry VI* (parts I, II, III), *Richard III;* comedies, eg *Two Gentlemen of Verona, A Midsummer Night's Dream;* tragedy, *Titus Andronicus.* Tragedy, *Romeo and Juliet* (c 1595), indicates more developed treatment of character as in later comedies, eg *The Merchant of Venice* (1596), *Much Ado About Nothing* (1598), *As You Like It* (1599), *Twelfth Night* (1599); histories *Henry IV* (parts I, II, 1597), *Henry V* (1598). The 4 great tragedies, *Hamlet* (1600), *Othello* (1602), *King Lear* (1605), *Macbeth* (1606) and classical plays, eg *Julius Caesar* (1599), *Coriolanus* (1608), represent the height of his work. Last period incl. problematic *Measure for Measure* and *The Tempest* (1611). Verse incl. sonnets, narrative poems, eg *Venus and Adonis* (1593), *The Rape of Lucrece* (1594). The 'First Folio' of 1625 is the first reliable text of his work.

shale, fine-grained, sedimentary rock. Consists mainly of clay compressed or cemented into thin, parallel layers which readily separate. Some shales are sources of oil eg in Scotland, US.

shallot, *Allium ascalonicum,* small edible onion with violet-coloured roots and green leaves used as flavouring.

shamanism, religious beliefs and practices of Siberian tribes of N Asia; term also applied to similar practices among Eskimos and North American Indians. Central figure is shaman (priest-magician) who is held to have innate ability to communicate with spirit world and thus protect the tribe from any destructive influences.

Shamash, Assyrian and Babylonian sun god. Responsible for success of crops, symbol of justice.

shamrock, common name for several trifoliate plants, esp. a clover, *Trifolium dubium.* National emblem

of Ireland and symbol of Trinity in Christianity.

Shang, Chinese imperial dynasty (c 1700 or 1500 - c 1000 BC). First historical dynasty, followed semi-legendary Hsia. Period marked by skilled use of bronze, sophisticated system of divination, ancestor worship.

Shanghai, seaport and largest city of China, special municipality of Kiangsu prov. Pop. 11,000,000. Steel mfg., shipbuilding, heavy engineering, textiles. International airport. Open port (1843-1946) with European, American concessions; International Settlement now in modern section. Univs. incl. Futan (1905). Japanese occupation (1937-45).

Shannon, river of Irish Republic, longest in British Isles. Flows 360 km (224 mi) from Cavan via Lough Derg to Limerick. Long estuary to Atlantic. Provides h.e.p. Shannon airport is in Co. Clare.

Shansi, prov. of NC China. Area c 155,000 sq km (60,000 sq mi); pop. (est.) 18,000,000; cap. Taiyuan. High plateau region; low rainfall limits agric. Lumber; coal, iron deposits.

Shantung, prov. of E China on Yellow Sea. Area c 140,000 sq km (54,000 sq mi); pop. (est.) 57,000,000; cap. Tsinan. Mountainous in E and C, Hwang Ho delta in W. Agric. limited by low rainfall; wheat, cotton grown. Coal, iron, oil, silk mfg., fishing.

shanty, work song of sailors dating from days of sailing ships. Verse sung by shantyman gave rhythm, chorus was sung by group hauling on rope, or performing other task.

shares, in finance, capital holdings in business enterprise, ownership of which certified by possession of stocks. Bonds are similar certification of ownership but with guaranteed payment if company is liquidated.

Shari (Fr. *Chari*), river of NC Africa. Flows *c* 960 km (600 mi) from N Central African Republic via Ndjamena (Chad) to L. Chad, entering by broad delta. Floods over wide area in rainy season.

shark, cartilaginous marine fish with slender torpedo-shaped body. Crescent-shaped mouth with numerous pointed teeth. Several families incl. dogfish, whale sharks (largest known fish) and hammerhead sharks. Mainly fish-eating, some species will attack man.

Sharp, Cecil James (1859-1924), English collector of folk music. Revived English folk song and dance after collecting material in England and Appalachian Mts. of US.

Sharp, James (1613-79), Scottish churchman. Sent to London (1660), he was converted to supporting restoration of episcopacy in Scotland. As reward, created archbishop of St Andrews (1661). Persecuted the Covenanters, a group of whom murdered him.

Sharpville, town of S Transvaal, South Africa, near Vereeniging. Scene of civic disturbances (1960) after police fired shots into black African crowd demonstrating against 'Pass Laws', *c* 70 killed.

Shastri, Lal Bahadur (1904-66), Indian statesman, PM (1964-6). Took office as PM after Nehru's death. Died in Tashkent after signing peace agreement with Pakistan.

Shaw, George Bernard (1856-1950), British dramatist, critic, b.

Dublin. Prominent member of Fabian Society. Early work attacks intellectually complacent London theatre, eg *Plays Pleasant and Unpleasant* (1898) incl. *Candida, Mrs Warren's Profession*. Notable plays with recurring theme of social satire incl. *The Devil's Disciple* (1896), *Caesar and Cleopatra* (1899), *Man and Superman* (1903), *Major Barbara* (1905), *Pygmalion* (1912), *Saint Joan* (1924). Also wrote many socialist polemics in prefaces to plays and in longer works, eg *The Intelligent Woman's Guide to Socialism and Capitalism* (1928). Nobel Prize for Literature (1925).

Shawnee, North American Indian tribe of Algonquian linguistic stock. Settled in Ohio in 18th cent. Warrior tribe. Now settled in Oklahoma.

shearwater, any of genus *Puffinus* of oceanic birds, related to petrel. Slender bill, tube-like external nostrils. Species incl. Cory's shearwater, *P. diomedea,* found mainly in Mediterranean.

Sheba, OT name for region of S Arabia, incl. Yemen and the Hadramaut. Inhabitants, Sabaeans, estab. highly developed culture *c* 6th-5th cents. BC. The Queen of Sheba who visited Solomon (1 Kings) *fl* 10th cent. BC.

sheep, ruminant mammal of Bovidae family, esp. genus *Ovis*. Domestic sheep, *O. aries*, reared for wool, leather, mutton. Breeds incl. Cotswold and Merino, known for wool; Southdown and Shropshire, kept for wool, mutton. Wild species incl. bighorn, moufflon.

sheepdog, dog trained to herd and guard sheep. Popular breeds incl. old English sheepdog with shaggy blue-grey and white coat; stands 53-64 cm/21-25 in. at shoulder.

Sheffield, city of South Yorkshire met. county, N England, at confluence of Don and Sheaf rivers. Pop. 520,000. Iron and steel indust. (1st to use Bessemer process), long estab. stainless steel cutlery mfg. Has 15th cent. church now cathedral; univ. (1905).

Shelburne, William Petty Fitzmaurice, 2nd Earl of (1737-1805), British statesman, PM (1783). Tory foreign secretary under both Pitts. Headed ministry that granted US independence at Treaty of Paris.

Shelley, Percy Bysshe (1792-1822), English poet. Romantic works, reflecting radical views on society and religion, incl. *Queen Mab* (1813), *Prometheus Unbound* (1820), *Adonais* (1821, elegy on death of Keats). Now best known for short lyrics, eg 'Ozymandias', 'To a Skylark', 'Ode to the West Wind', 'The Cloud'. Drowned while sailing in Italy. His 2nd wife, Mary [Wollstonecraft] Shelley, née Godwin (1797-1851), wrote Gothic novel *Frankenstein* (1818).

shell shock, obsolete term for severe form of anxiety neurosis which occurred among soldiers in WWI after prolonged exposure to attack.

Shenandoah, see POTOMAC, US.

Shensi, prov. of NC China. Area *c* 197,000 sq km (76,000 sq mi); pop. (est.) 21,000,000; cap. Sian. Wheat, cotton grown; rich coal and iron deposits, oil. Seat of Communists (1935-49).

Shenyang or **Mukden**, cap. of Liaoning prov., NE China. Pop. 3,750,000. Rail jct.; heavy engineer-

ing; aircraft, machine tools mfg., chemicals. Developed indust. after seizure by Japanese (1931). Taken by Communists (1948) after 10 months' siege.

shepherd's purse, *Capsella bursa-pastoris*, annual plant of mustard family. Wide distribution in temperate zones. White flowers followed by seed pods. Regarded as troublesome weed.

Sheppard, Jack (1702-24), English criminal. Notorious for many robberies, escapes, until hanged. Subject of popular stories, plays.

Sheppey, Isle of, off Kent, SE England, in Thames estuary. Separated from mainland by the Swale. Sheep rearing, cereals, vegetable growing. From 1968 part of Queenborough-in-Sheppey.

Sheraton, Thomas (1751-1806), English furniture designer. Wrote *The Cabinet Maker's and Upholsterer's Drawing Book* (1791-4), an influential source of designs. Work characterized by simplicity, straight vertical lines, neo-Classical motifs, use of inlay.

Sherbrooke, town of SE Québec, Canada; on St Francis R. Pop. 81,000. Agric. market; clothing, machinery mfg.

Sheridan, Richard Brinsley (1751-1816), British dramatist, politician, b. Ireland. Known for satirical comedies of manners, eg *The Rivals* (1775) containing Mrs Malaprop, *The School for Scandal* (1777), *The Critic* (1779). Instrumental in impeachment of Warren HASTINGS.

sheriff, in England, officer appointed by Crown to administer county or shire (now honorary), whereas is legal official in Scotland.

In US, chief law-enforcement officer of county; duties are keeping the peace, executing court orders.

Sheriffmuir, battlefield in Ochil Hills, Tayside Region, C Scotland. Scene of battle (1715) between Jacobites and Hanoverians; both sides claimed victory.

Sherman, William Tecumseh (1820-91), American general. During Civil War, commanded Union push through Georgia (1864); burned Atlanta, devastated countryside. Early advocate of 'total' warfare tactics. His brother, John Sherman (1823-1900), was senator from Ohio. Sponsored Anti-Trust Act (1890).

Sherman Anti-Trust Act (1890), legislation passed by US Congress to regulate interstate, foreign trade. Attempted to outlaw restraints, eg monopolies, on such trade. Theodore Roosevelt was first to use it successfully to break up Standard Oil, American Tobacco Co. in 1911.

Sherrington, Sir Charles Scott (1857-1952), English physiologist. Studied the action of the nervous system, incl. the function of synapses, and introduced a theory of reflex action. Shared Nobel Prize for Physiology and Medicine (1932).

sherry, fortified wine, originating in Jerez de la Frontera region of Spain. Three main types: fino, dry and light yellow; oloroso, richer and darker in colour; amontillado, darker than fino and less rich than oloroso.

's Hertogenbosch or **Den Bosch,** town of SC Netherlands, cap. of North Brabant prov. Pop. 83,000. Railway jct., cattle market. Fortress city until 1876. Birthplace of Hieronymus Bosch.

Sherwood Forest, ancient royal forest of Nottinghamshire, C England, now largely cleared. Traditional home of Robin Hood.

Shetland, isl. authority of N Scotland, comprising Shetland Isls. Formerly Zetland county. Incl. c 100 isls.; area 1429 sq km (552 sq mi); pop. 18,000; main town Lerwick. Main isls. are MAINLAND, Yell, Unst. Sheep rearing, Shetland ponies; fishing, knitwear mfg. Offshore oil service industs. Acquired from Norway 1472.

Shetland pony, small breed of pony with thick, shaggy coat, mane and forelock. Noted for strength and endurance; stands 1 m/40 in. at shoulder.

shibboleth, in OT, test word used by Gileadites to detect the escaping Ephraimites who could only pronounce it as 'sibboleth'. Now means watchword or party phrase.

Shihkiachwang, cap. of Hopeh prov., NE China. Pop. 1,500,000. Rail jct.; produces textiles, pharmaceuticals. Grew rapidly with coming of railway in early 20th cent.

Shiites or **Shiahs,** members of the smaller of the 2 main Moslem sects, who upheld right of ALI to succeed Mohammed as 1st caliph and supported later claims of his sons Hasan and HUSEIN to caliphate. Also reject the Sunna, traditional law based on teachings of Mohammed. Predominate in Iran.

Shikoku, isl. of SW Japan, smallest of the 4 major isls. Area 18,770 sq km (7240 sq mi). Mountainous interior, rising to c 1980 m (6500 ft); heavily forested. Produces rice, tobacco, tea.

Shillong, cap. of Assam, NE India. Pop. 84,000. Resort, trade centre.

Destroyed by earthquake (1897) and rebuilt.

Shiloh, Battle of, US Civil War encounter (April, 1862), fought in S Tennessee, in which the Confederates, at first superior, were defeated after the arrival of Union reinforcements.

shingles, in medicine, *see* HERPES.

Shinto, term used for native Japanese religious beliefs and practices. Based on ancient oral myths (collected in the *Kojiki*, AD 712). Modified under influence of Buddhism and Confucianism, developed as patriotic state Shinto (stressing divinity of emperor, disavowed by Hirohito 1946) and sectarian churches (stressing veneration of ancestors).

shinty, twelve-a-side stick and ball game played in Scottish Highlands. Resembles HURLING, from which it is derived. Revival of game and formulation of rules date from 1880s.

ship, term for large sea-going vessel. Used in ancient times by Egyptians, Greeks, Phoenicians and Chinese (propelled by sails and oars). Discovery of Americas led to increase in ship-building. One of first successful steamships was Fulton's *Clermont* on Hudson R. (1807). Steel replaced wood in construction from *c* 1840s. Subsequent developments incl. steam turbines, diesel engine, nuclear power.

ship money, in English history, tax for upkeep of navy and coastal defences. Legality of writs issued by Charles I, levying ship money in peace time and on inland as well as maritime counties, was challenged by John HAMPDEN. Declared illegal 1641.

shipworm, worm-like marine bivalve mollusc, esp. of genus *Teredo*. Uses its small shell to bore into submerged timber; pest to boats and piers.

Shiraz, city of SC Iran, cap. of Fars prov. Pop. 356,000. Produces wines, brocades, rugs. Cap. of Persia at various times, lastly under Karim Khan in 18th cent.

shire horse, breed of powerful draft horse common on farms. Bred in Middle Ages to carry knight in full armour.

shittim, close-grained, yellowish wood of shittah tree used for the Ark of the Covenant in Old Testament. Now generally identified with several Asian *Acacia, eg A. seyal* and *A. tortilis.* Name also used for North American false buckthorn, *Bumelia lanuginosa.*

Shiva, *see* SIVA.

Shkodër, *see* SCUTARI, Albania.

shock, in medicine, disorder resulting from inadequate blood circulation to the tissues. Symptoms incl. decrease in blood pressure, rapid pulse. Causes may be internal bleeding, widening of blood vessels, heart damage.

shock absorber, device for damping motion of elastic suspension system such as that of a vehicle. Retards sudden motion hydraulically or by friction.

Shockley, William Bradford (1910–), American physicist, b. Britain. His studies in semiconductors led to the invention of the transistor, important development in miniaturization of electronic devices. Shared Nobel Prize for Physics (1956) with W. Brattain and J. Bardeen.

shock therapy, method of treating certain mental disorders by chemical agents, *eg* insulin, or by applying electric currents to the brain. Sometimes effective in treating depression.

shoebill or whale-headed stork, *Balaeniceps rex,* stork-like wading bird with broad shoe-shaped bill. Lives along banks of White Nile; feeds on marsh animals, lungfish.

shogun, title given to hereditary military rulers who controlled Japanese feudal system (12th-19th cent.). Held real power under nominal rule of emperors. Shogunate system of govt. displaced by Meiji restoration (1868).

Sholokhov, Mikhail Aleksandrovich (1905-), Russian novelist. Known for stories of native region *Don Stories* (1926) and masterpiece *And Quiet Flows the Don* (1928-40). Nobel Prize for Literature (1965).

shooting, sport of firing with pistol, rifle or shotgun at moving or stationary targets. Organizations such as British National Rifle Association (formed 1860) and American NRA (formed 1871) standardized rules and held competitions in 19th cent. Olympic sport since 1896; events incl. trap or clay pigeon, skeet and small-bore rifle shooting.

shooting star, *see* METEOR.

short circuit, connection, either accidental or deliberate, between 2 points in electrical circuit by path of low resistance, instead of normal high resistance path. Excessive current flow may cause permanent damage to circuit; fuses are designed to avoid effects of short circuit.

shorthand, method of rapid handwriting using strokes, abbreviations or symbols to denote letters, words, phrases. Early systems were orthographic (*ie* using abbreviations for groups of letters but retaining standard spelling and usually applicable to a single language). Phonetic system developed (1837) by Isaac PITMAN allows *c* 280 words per minute to be recorded.

short sight, *see* MYOPIA.

Shoshone, North American Indian tribe of Uto-Aztecan linguistic stock. Spread across NW US in 19th cent. E group were buffalo hunters of N Great Plains, in W tribe were settled food gatherers. Now *c* 4000 live on reservations in California, Idaho, Wyoming.

Shostakovich, Dmitri (1906-75), Russian composer. Works employ modern musical devices, often in traditional forms, and incl. 15 symphonies, string quartets. Twice encountered official disapproval of his music, tried to recover favour with 5th symphony (1937).

shoulder, in man, joint connecting the head of the humerus (bone of upper arm) with the scapula or shoulder blade.

shoveler, freshwater duck with large broad bill, genus *Anas.* Species incl. *A. clypeata* of N hemisphere; male has green-glossed head, white and brown underparts.

show jumping, *see* EQUESTRIANISM.

Shrapnel, Henry (1761-1842), British general. Developed shot-filled shell with bursting charge, adopted by British army in 1803.

shrew, any of Soricidae family of small, solitary, insectivorous mammals, widely distributed in N hemisphere and Africa. Long snout, musk glands; some species secrete poison. Species incl. WATER SHREW and common shrew, *Sorex araneus*, of Europe and N Asia.

Shrewsbury, mun. bor. and co. town of Salop, WC England, on R. Severn. Pop. 56,000. Market town; tanning, brewing. Strategic site in medieval Welsh border conflict. Has public school (1552).

shrike, any of Laniidae family of largely Old World birds. Strong hooked bill; feeds on insects and small animals, impaling bodies on thorns. Species incl. great grey shrike, *Lanius excubitor*, called northern shrike in North America.

shrimp, small free-swimming marine crustacean. Slender elongated body with 5 pairs of legs; many species edible. Species incl. common European brown shrimp, *Crangon vulgaris*.

Shropshire, former county of WC England. Now known as SALOP; scene of hist. English-Welsh border conflict.

Shrove Tuesday, in Christian calendar, day before Lent begins. Named after practice of receiving absolution (shriving). In England, celebrated by eating pancakes. See MARDI GRAS.

shrub, low, perennial woody plant, smaller than TREE and with several permanent stems branching from or near ground rather than single trunk. Usually less than 6 m (20 ft) high at maturity.

Shute, Nevil, pseud. of Nevil Shute Norway (1899-1960), English novelist. Wrote popular novels, *eg A Town Like Alice* (1950), *On the Beach* (1957).

Si or **Si-kiang**, river of S China. Length c 2000 km (1250 mi). Rises in Yunnan prov., flows E to South China Sea near Kwangchow, forming fertile delta. Navigable most of its length.

sial, in geology, upper, discontinuous layer of Earth's crust underlying the continents. Consists of relatively light rocks, *eg* granite; named from silica and aluminium, the main constituents. Also *see* SIMA.

Siam, *see* THAILAND.

Siam, Gulf of, arm of South China Sea, between Malay penin. and Indo-China.

Siamese cat, breed of short-haired cat with slanting blue eyes. Fawn-coloured coat with darker colour at face and legs.

Siamese twins, twins born with bodies joined by tissue in some way. Term derived from male twins, Chang and Eng, b. 1811 in Siam.

Sian, cap. of Shensi prov., NC China. Pop. 1,900,000. Commercial centre. Iron, steel production, textile mfg. Ancient imperial cap. (3rd cent. BC) and religious centre. Has city wall and numerous pagodas.

Sibelius, Jean Julius Christian (1865-1957), Finnish composer. Music, traditional in form, was often inspired by legends and scenery of Finland. Works incl. tone-poem *Finlandia*, violin concerto, 7 symphonies. Govt. grant enabled him to devote himself to composition from 1897.

Siberia (*Sibir*), region of C and E USSR, approximating Asiatic part of RSFSR. Area c 12,700,000 sq km (4,900,000 sq mi). Plains in W, drained by Ob, Irtysh; plateau in C and S; tundra in N along Arctic

Ocean; mainly mountainous in E, incl. Kamchatka Penin. Agric. concentrated in fertile SW plains (main crop wheat); mineral resources incl. oil, coal, gold, iron. Indust., *eg* Kuznetsk basin, has grown rapidly since 1920s. Russian conquest led by Cossacks (16th-17th cent.). Used as political exile colony under tsars; colonization began with Trans-Siberian railway (1892-1905); economic development began in 20th cent.

Sibylline Books, collection of oracular utterances, written in Greek hexameters, thought to have been brought from Greece to Cumae, then to Rome. Traditionally, 3 volumes bought by Tarquinius Superbus from Sibyl of Cumae. Consulted by Romans in cases of calamities, *eg* earthquakes. Destroyed in burning of capitol, 83 BC.

sibyls, name given by Greeks and Romans to prophetesses of Apollo. Most famous was Sibyl of Cumae, Italy. *See* SIBYLLINE BOOKS.

Sicilian Vespers, rebellion (1282) in Sicily against French rule of Charles of Anjou; began at time of vespers on Easter Tuesday. Most of French were massacred. Resulted in estab. of Peter III of Aragón as king of Sicily.

Sicily (*Sicilia*), isl. of Italy, separated from mainland by Str. of Messina. Largest Mediterranean isl., area 25,708 sq km (9926 sq mi); cap. Palermo. Mountainous, incl. Mt. Etna; agric., fishing, sulphur, oil. Phoenician, then Greek colony, taken by Rome 241 BC. Under Normans (12th-13th cent.) before forming, with Naples, Kingdom of

the Two Sicilies (1815); liberated from Bourbons by Garibaldi (1860).

Sickert, Walter Richard (1860-1942), British artist, b. Munich. His sub-impressionist paintings are sombre in tone; helped introduce French ideas into English art. Painted music hall scenes and views of Venice, Dieppe and London.

Siddons, Sarah Kemble (1755-1831), English actress, daughter of ROGER KEMBLE. Renowned in tragic roles, *eg* Lady Macbeth, Ophelia, Desdemona.

sidewinder, *Crotalus cerastes,* desert rattlesnake of SW US. Moves by sideways spiralling action.

Sidgwick, Henry (1838-1900), English philosopher. Worked on ethics. Formulated system combining intuitionism and utilitarianism. Works incl. *Methods of Ethics* (1874), *The Principles of Political Economy* (1883).

Sidi-bel-Abbès, town of NW Algeria, on R. Mekerra. Pop. 101,000. Agric. market. Walled town, French military post from 1843, hq. of Foreign Legion until 1962.

Sidmouth, Henry Addington, 1st Viscount (1757-1844), English statesman, PM (1801-4). Headed Tory govt. which concluded Treaty of Amiens (1802) with Napoleon. Known for repressive policy as home secretary (1812-21) under Liverpool.

Sidney, Sir Philip (1554-86), soldier, writer, leading figure at Elizabeth I's court. Died in battle of Zutphen. Works incl. romance *Arcadia* (pub. 1590), sonnet sequence *Astrophel and Stella* (1591), critiques, *eg The Defence of Poesie*

(1595). Considered archetype of Renaissance courtier.

Sidon, see SAIDA.

Siegfried or **Sigurd,** hero of N European mythology. Appears in German epics, esp. *Nibelungenlied*, as dragon-killer, lover of Kriemhild, conqueror of Brunhild. Earliest account in Norse Volsungsaga (13th cent.).

Siemens, [Ernst] Werner von (1816-92), German industrialist, inventor. Founded (1847) Siemens und Halske, which became one of most important electrical firms in world. Invented many commonly-used techniques, *eg* Siemens armature. His brother, Sir **William Siemens,** orig. Karl Wilhelm (1823-83), was known for his innovatory work in electricity and application of heat, utilized in British business from 1844 on; estab. (1865) firm of Siemens Bros. Developed Siemens-Martin steel-making process.

Siena, town of Tuscany, WC Italy, cap. of Siena prov. Pop. 69,000. Marble, wine; tourism. Medieval cultural, banking centre. Sienese school of painting (13th-14th cent.). Gothic cathedral, town hall. Horse race held annually in Piazza del Campo.

Sierra Leone, republic of W Africa. Area 71,700 sq km (27,700 sq mi); pop. 3,111,000; cap. Freetown. Official language: English. Religions: native, Christianity, Islam. Coastal swamps, rising inland to wooded plateau. Main food crop rice; exports diamonds, iron ore, bauxite, palm products. Minor slave trade 17th-18th cent. Freetown area became colony (1808); hinterland incl. in

protect. created (1896). Independent from 1961.

Sierra Madre, mountain system of Mexico, dominating much of country except Yucatán penin. Comprises Sierra Madre Oriental in NE, Occidental in W and del Sur in S. Rises to 5700 m (18,700 ft) at highest point, Orizaba.

Sierra Maestra, mountain range of SE Cuba rising to 2000 m (6560 ft). Focus of Castro's revolt in 1950s. Rich in minerals, incl. iron, copper, manganese.

Sierra Morena, mountain range of SC Spain. Extends c 600 km (375 mi) E-W, separating Andalusia from C, N Spain. Rises to c 1310 m (4300 ft). Rich in minerals, esp. copper, lead, mercury.

Sierra Nevada, mountain range of S Spain; extends c 100 km (60 mi) E-W from Granada to Almeria. Incl. Mulhacén, highest peak in Spain at 3479 m (11,420 ft).

Sierra Nevada, mountain range of E California. Incl. Mt. Whitney (highest mountain in US outside Alaska) and Sequoia, Yosemite, Kings' Canyon national parks.

Sieyès, Emmanuel-Joseph (1748-1836), French revolutionary. Originally a priest, grew to prominence with pamphlet *What is the Third Estate?* (1788). Became a leader in Estates-General of 1789. Supported Napoleon in coup d'état (1799) which estab. Consulate.

Sigismund (1368-1437), Holy Roman emperor (1433-7). Became king of Hungary (1387), Germany (1411). Persuaded the pope to call Council of Constance (1414) to end Great Schism. Granted safe conduct for Jan Hus to attend Council, but

Hus was condemned to death there for heresy. Led crusade against Hussites in Bohemia (1420) but was defeated.

Sigismund [II] Augustus (1520-72), king of Poland (1548-72). United Poland and Lithuania by Union of Lublin (1569). Reign saw Reformation, which he opposed, at its height in Poland.

Sigismund III (1566-1632), king of Poland (1587-1632). Inherited Swedish throne (1592) from father, John III of Sweden; opposed by Swedish Protestants, deposed (1599) after defeat at Stångebro.

Signac, Paul (1863-1935), French painter. Disciple of Seurat, he adopted the divisionist (pointillist) technique; expounded theories of neo-impressionism in book *De Delacroix au Néo-Impressionisme* (1899).

Sihanouk, Norodom (1922-), Cambodian statesman. Abdicated in favour of father, but continued as premier (1951-70), leading Popular Socialists. Went into exile in China after rightist coup d'état (1970). Returned as head of state in 1975, but resigned and held under house arrest from 1976. Released after overthrow of Khmer Rouge (1979).

sika, *Cervus nippon*, small Japanese deer, introduced into Europe. Chestnut brown coat, white-spotted in summer.

Sikhs, Indian religious community mostly in Punjab. Founded (c 1500) by Nanak. Aiming to unite Hindus and Moslems, taught basic identity of all religions. Developed as military power in early 18th cent. against Mogul empire and Islam.

Today Akali Dal movement seeks to estab. Sikh state in NW India.

Sikh Wars, conflicts (1845-6, 1848-9) between Sikhs and British, resulting in annexation of Punjab. First war resulted from Sikh invasion of British territ. following disorder in Punjab. After British had estab. protect. in Punjab, rioting led to 2nd war.

Si-kiang, river of China, *see* Si.

Sikkim, state of India, in Himalayas between Nepal and Bhutan. Area 7100 sq km (2700 sq mi); pop. 206,000; cap. Gangtok. Constitutional monarchy under British protection until 1947, became Indian protectorate 1950. Independence and power of king virtually ended 1974, when it became Indian associate state. Became 22nd state of India (1975).

Sikorski, Wladyslaw (1881-1943), Polish general, statesman. After German invasion of Poland (1939), became premier of Polish govt. in exile and commander-in-chief of Polish troops fighting with Allies. Killed in air crash.

Sikorsky, Igor Ivanovich (1889-1972), American aeronautical engineer, b. Russia. Built and flew 1st multi-engined plane (1913). Designed, manufactured 1st successful helicopter (1941).

silage, green fodder preserved in airtight silos, used as supplementary feed for cattle, sheep, *etc.* During storage, fermentation processes are set up which generate heat and give off gases.

Silbury Hill, archaeological site in Wiltshire, England. Largest prehistoric mound in Europe (c 2000 BC). Function not yet established.

Silenus, in Greek myth, leader of satyrs and sometimes regarded as foster father and tutor of Dionysus. Represented as inspired, musical and drunken old man. He might be induced to prophesy if caught while asleep.

Silesia (Pol. *Slask,* Ger. *Schlesien,* Czech. *Slezsko*), region of EC Europe, now mainly in Poland; smaller areas in NW Czechoslovakia, SE East Germany. Incl. basin of upper Oder; coal, iron, zinc mining. Chief cities Gliwice, Katowice, Wroclaw. Polish until 14th cent., passed to Bohemia, then to Habsburgs. Annexed by Prussia 1742; divided into Upper, Lower Silesia. Former returned to Poland 1921, latter returned 1945.

silica or **silicon dioxide** (SiO_2), hardy glassy mineral; found free as sand, quartz, flint and as silicates in rocks. Used in manufacture of glass and ceramics.

silicates, salts of silicic acid (H_4SiO_4). Most rocks and many minerals consist of silicates of calcium, magnesium, aluminium and other metals.

silicon (Si), non-metallic element; at. no. 14, at. wt. 28.09. Exists as brown powder and grey crystals; 2nd most abundant element on Earth, occurring in silica and silicate rocks. Obtained by reduction of silica with carbon in electric arc furnaces. Used in alloys, glass making, semiconductor devices.

silicon chip, tiny slice of silicon processed to form miniature INTEGRATED CIRCUIT. Used in electronic circuitry, esp. computers. *See* MICROPROCESSOR.

silicones, group of polymerized organic compounds containing alternate oxygen and silicon atoms with various organic radicals attached to the chain. Characterized by chemical inertness, resistance to electricity and heat; used as lubricants, polishes, waterproofing compounds.

silk, natural fibre produced by silkworms. Usually obtained from cocoon spun by SILKWORM which feeds on mulberry leaves. Silk production began in ancient China, then in 6th cent. spread throughout Asia into Europe (esp. Italy and France).

silk screen printing, method of stencil printing in which paint is squeezed through a piece of fine silk. Parts of design not to be printed are masked by paper or film of lacquer. Developed for commercial purposes, now used for obtaining large numbers of artists' prints.

silkworm, larva of Chinese silkworm moth, *Bombyx mori.* Spins cocoon of silk fibre, cultivated commercially as source of silk.

Sillanpää, Frans Eemil (1888-1964), Finnish author. Wrote sensitive psychological novels, eg *Meek Heritage* (1919), *The Maid Silja* (1931). Nobel Prize for Literature (1939).

Sillitoe, Allan (1928-), English novelist. Wrote regional workingclass novels, eg *Saturday Night and Sunday Morning* (1958), short story collection *The Loneliness of the Long Distance Runner* (1959).

silt, sediment composed of rock particles, precisely defined in geology as having particle size between 1/256 mm and 1/16 mm. Commonest constituent is quartz.

Silurian period, third geological

period of Palaeozoic era. Began *c* 435 million years ago, lasted *c* 40 million years. Extensive seas; Caledonian mountain building period continued. Typified by graptolites, trilobites, brachiopods, cephalopods; jawless fish, 1st land plants. Also see GEOLOGICAL TABLE.

silver (Ag), white metallic element; at. no. 47, at. wt. 107.87. Malleable and ductile; best-known conductor of electricity; resists corrosion by air. Used in coinage, jewellery, mirrors; halogen compounds used extensively in photography as they are light-sensitive.

silverfish, *Lepisma saccharina*, bristletail insect of silvery-white appearance. Found indoors, often attracted by sugary food.

sima, in geology, lower continuous layer of Earth's crust underlying ocean floors and continental SIAL. Consists of relatively heavy rocks, eg basalt; named from silica and magnesium, the main constituents.

Simcoe, Lake, S Ontario, Canada; forms part of Trent Canal system. Area 1396 sq km (539 sq mi). Resort area.

Simenon, Georges (1903-), French author, b. Belgium. Known for detective novels featuring Inspector Maigret, eg *La maison du canal* (1933). Also wrote psychological novels, eg *La neige était sale* (1948).

Simeon Stylites, St (*c* 390-459), Syrian hermit. Traditionally lived for 36 years on top of pillar from which he taught.

simile, see METAPHOR.

Simla, cap. of Himachal Pradesh state, N India. Pop. 43,000. In Himalayas, at height of 2100 m (7000

ft). Summer residence of viceroy and govt. during British rule.

Simnel, Lambert, (*c* 1477-*c* 1535), English imposter. Supported by Yorkists, claimed to be Edward, Earl of Warwick, Edward IV's nephew. Crowned in Dublin as Edward VI. Defeated by Henry VII at Stoke (1487), put to work in royal kitchens.

Simon, St (*fl* 1st cent. AD), one of Twelve Disciples; also called Cananaean, Zealot. Traditionally martyred with St Jude.

Simonstown, town of SW Cape Prov., South Africa, on False Bay. Pop. 10,000. Resort, port, major naval base. Founded (1741) by Dutch; ceded to UK (1898), to South Africa (1957).

Simplon Pass, Alpine pass between S Switzerland and N Italy, height 2008 m (6592 ft). Road built by Napoleon (1800-7). Railway tunnel, world's longest (19.7 km/12.25 mi), opened 1906.

Simpson, Sir James Young (1811-70), Scottish obstetrician. Pioneered use of anaesthetics (chloroform, ether) in childbirth (1847).

Simpson, N[orman] F[rederick] (1919-), English dramatist. Plays, eg *A Resounding Tinkle* (1957), *One Way Pendulum* (1959), depict the development of logic to level of absurdity.

Simpson, Wallis, see WINDSOR, WALLIS WARFIELD, DUCHESS OF.

sin, in Judaism, Christianity and Islam, any transgression of the will of God. Concept does not occur in religions where there is no personal God, eg Buddhism. In RC theology, sins are mortal if committed with

intent in a serious matter. *See*
ORIGINAL SIN, SEVEN DEADLY SINS.

Sinai, barren penin. between Gulf of
Suez (W) and Gulf of Aqaba (E).
Main town El Arish. Coastal plain in
N, El Tih plateau in C; mountainous
in S. Nomadic pastoralism, oil
drilling, manganese, iron mining.
Jebel Musa (possibly Mt. Sinai) has
famous Greek Orthodox monastery.
Part of Egypt; occupied by Israelis
from 1967 war, partly restored 1974-
5.

Sinatra, Francis Albert
('Frank') (1917-), American
singer, film actor. Rose to fame as
singer with bands of Harry James
and Tommy Dorsey; singing idol of
'bobbysoxers' in 1940s. Films incl.
From Here to Eternity.

Sinclair, Upton [Beall] (1878-
1968), American novelist. Polemic
novels of social protest incl. *The
Jungle* (1906) exposing conditions in
Chicago's stockyards, *Boston* (1928)
on Sacco and Vanzetti case. Also
wrote Lanny Budd adventure stories.

Sind, region of SE Pakistan and
former province of British India.
Mainly flat, arid land lying in lower
Indus valley. Agric. economy. Taken
by British under Sir Charles Napier
(1843).

Singapore, island republic off S end
of Malay penin.; in British Commonwealth. Area 583 sq km (225 sq mi);
pop. 2,278,000, predominantly Chinese. British colony 1824-1963;
joined Malaysia 1963, seceded 1965.
City of Singapore (pop. 1,240,000) is
a major seaport, former British
naval base. Commercial centre;
exports rubber, tin and copra from
Malaysia. Occupied by Japanese
1942-5.

Singer, Isaac Bashevis (1904-),
American writer, b. Poland. Writing,
ironically treating irrational and
grotesque and often set in Jewish
communities in Poland, incl. novels
eg The Magician of Lublin (1960),
short stories. Nobel Prize for
Literature (1978).

Singer, Isaac Merritt (1811-75),
American inventor. Patented (1851)
practical sewing machine; became
leading manufacturer. Later added
many improvements.

Singhalese, Indic language in Indo-
Iranian branch of Indo-European
family. Spoken on Sri Lanka.
Separated from other Indic languages by region of DRAVIDIAN
speakers, which has influenced its
vocabulary.

singing, use of human voice for
production of music with or without
words. Voices range from female or
boy soprano, mezzo-soprano, con-
tralto, male and female alto, to male
countertenor, tenor, baritone and
bass. Classical style of singing,
developed in Italy in 17th-18th cent.,
demands special voice production.

single tax, in economics, doctrine
advanced by PHYSIOCRATS, advocating collection of revenue based
only on land.

Sing Sing, see OSSINING, US.

Sinkiang(-Uighur), auton. region
of NW China, bordering on Mongolia, USSR. Area *c* 1,709,400 sq km
(660,000 sq mi); pop. (est.)
8,000,000; cap. Urumchi. Peopled
mainly by Turkic Uighurs (Moslems). Grazing on Dzungaria plateau
in N. Taklamakan desert covers S.
Low rainfall but irrigation schemes
allow agric. (cereals, cotton).

Mineral, oil resources. Scene of frontier incidents with USSR (1969).

sinking fund, sum of govt. or business income set aside; its accumulation eventually allows repayment of outstanding debts. First estab. in Britain (1786).

Sinn Fein (Irish, = ourselves alone), Irish separatist national movement founded by Arthur Griffith (1899). Gained popular political support under leadership of DE VALÉRA; set up Irish assembly in Dublin (1918) and declared independence. Influence declined with formation of Fianna Fáil (1926). Name now applies to political wing of Irish Republican Army.

Sino-Japanese War, First (1894-5), struggle between China and Japan for control of Korea. Japanese victory consolidated by Treaty of Shimonoseki by which China ceded Taiwan and other islands and Liaotung penin.; Korea awarded nominal independence.

Sino-Japanese War, Second (1937-45), struggle prompted by growing Japanese domination of China. Japan annexed Manchuria (1931), set up puppet state of Manchukuo. Hostilities began 1937; Japanese captured most of large Chinese cities and ports by 1938. Chinese, driven W, continued guerrilla warfare. Allies aided China after Japan's entry into WWII. After Japanese surrender (Sept. 1945), Cairo Declaration restored Taiwan, Manchuria to China.

Sinop (anc. *Sinope*), town of N Turkey, on Black Sea. Founded 8th cent. BC; became important port, exporting cinnabar. Cap. of Pontic empire (2nd cent. BC); prospered under Roman and Byzantine rule.

Sino-Tibetan, major language family with 3 branches, Chinese, Thai, and Tibetan-Burman.

sinus, name given to any of the various air cavities of the skull opening into the nasal passage. Inflammation of mucous membranes of the sinuses (sinusitis) may occur as a result of colds, allergies; blockage of sinuses by mucus causes headache.

Sioux or **Dakota**, seven North American tribes, dominant group of Hokan-Siouan linguistic stock. Gradually driven W, they settled (late 18th cent.) in N Great Plains area. Invasion of their reservation by gold prospectors in 1870s led to uprising in which General Custer perished.

siphon, bent tube used to transfer liquid from higher container to lower one by pressure of atmosphere acting on liquid surface. Tube must be filled with liquid before flow will start.

Siqueiros, David Alfaro (1898-1974), Mexican painter. Works, mainly murals and frescoes, reflect support of revolutionary socialism.

siren, any of Sirenidae family of aquatic eel-like amphibians, found in North American swamps. Retains certain larval characteristics: gills, lidless eyes, no hind limbs.

Sirens, in Greek myth, sea nymphs represented as part woman and part bird who, by their beautiful singing, lured sailors to their death on rocks. Argonauts were saved by the more beautiful music of Orpheus, while Odysseus stopped ears of his crew with wax.

Sirius or **Dog Star,** brightest star in sky, located in constellation Canis Major. In 1862, observed to have a companion, Sirius B, a white dwarf star.

sirocco, hot, dust-laden S wind originating in Sahara Desert and affecting N Africa, Sicily, S Italy. Occurs mainly in spring; withers vegetation. Called *khamsin* in Egypt.

sisal, strong fibre obtained from leaves of an agave, *Agave sisalana,* native to S Mexico, but now grown throughout the tropics. Used for making rope, sacking.

Sisley, Alfred (1839-99), French painter of English descent. Member of the impressionist group, he devoted himself to landscape. Noted for his fine sense of colour and tonal values.

Sistine Chapel, private chapel of the pope in the Vatican. Built (1473) under Sixtus IV, it is renowned for frescoes of the Creation, Deluge and Last Judgment by Michelangelo.

Sisyphus, in Greek myth, king of Corinth, renowned for his cunning. For his disrespect to Zeus, condemned in Tartarus to roll repeatedly a heavy stone to top of hill; when stone reached top, it rolled down again.

Sitter, Willem de (1872-1934), Dutch astronomer, mathematician. Using Einstein's general theory of relativity, he developed idea of an expanding universe containing essentially no matter.

Sitting Bull (c 1831-90), American Indian chief. Led Sioux at battle of Little Bighorn (1875) in which Custer and his troops were wiped out. Later settled on reservation; opposed selling of Sioux land, shot by Indian police.

Sitwell, Dame Edith (1887-1964), English author. Works incl. poetry, eg *Façade* (1922) set to music by William Walton, *Green Song* (1944), essays, eg *A Poet's Notebook* (1943). Her brother, **Sir Osbert Sitwell** (1892-1969), wrote series of family memoirs incl. *Left Hand, Right Hand!* (1944), poetry. Their brother, **Sir Sacheverell Sitwell** (1897-), poet and art critic, wrote histories of art incl. books on Baroque.

SI units (Système International d'Unités), internationally agreed coherent system of units, which has replaced c.g.s. and f.p.s. systems for scientific purposes. Based on 7 units: metre (m), kilogram (kg), second (s), ampère (A), kelvin (K), mole (mol) and candela (cd). Numerous other units incl. newton, joule, watt, volt, ohm, are derived from these.

Siva or **Shiva,** in Hinduism, god of destruction and reproduction; one of the supreme trinity. In destructive role, represented with garland of skulls and surrounded by demons. As Natarajah, regarded as Lord of the Cosmic Dance; consort was KALI. Anciently associated with phallic worship.

Six, les, group of six French composers, said to have been influenced by Satie and Cocteau. Comprised MILHAUD, POULENC, HONEGGER, Georges Auric, Louis Durey and Germaine Tailleferre.

Sjaelland, see ZEALAND, Denmark.

Skagerrak, str. between SE Norway and NW Denmark, linking North Sea and Kattegat. Width c 130 km (80 mi).

Skåne or **Scania,** region of S

Sweden, chief city Malmö. Held by Denmark until conquered by Charles X (1658). Many prehist. and medieval remains.

Skara Brae, Neolithic village in Orkney, Scotland, uncovered from a sand dune by a storm (1851). Comprises stone houses linked by a roofed-over alleyway.

skate, large ray, esp. of genus *Raja*, often used as food. Species incl. European skate, *R. batis*, found in deep water.

skating, sport of gliding on ice by means of specially-designed metal blades fitted to boots. Originally, blades made from bone or wood, and iron by 17th cent. Used in ice HOCKEY. Olympic event since 1924, incl. pair, free, figure and speed skating. Another form, roller skating, uses specially-constructed metal skates bearing 4 small roller wheels to glide on smooth surfaces. James Plympton introduced modern roller skates into US in 1863.

Skegness, urban dist. of Lincolnshire, E England. Pop. 14,000. Seaside resort; extensive beaches.

skeleton, solid framework which supports and protects soft tissue of an animal body. Vertebrates have skeletal structures composed of bone and cartilage entirely within the organism (endoskeleton); other animals, eg arthropods, coelenterates, have skeletons external to living tissue (exoskeletons).

Skelton, John (*c* 1464-1529), English poet. Known for artless verse, eg mock-dirge *Philip Sparrow,* crudely comic *Tunning of Eleanor Rumming;* also wrote verse attacking Scots, lampooning

Wolsey. Used 'Skeltonics', short, usually 3-stressed lines.

skepticism, *see* SCEPTICISM.

Skiddaw, mountain of Lake Dist., Cumbria, NW England. Height 930 m (3054 ft).

skiing, method of gliding over snow using elongated wooden or metal runners fastened to the feet. Sport of skiing is divided into 2 sections: Alpine, in which competitors race down prepared slopes; Nordic, which incl. cross-country and ski-jumping events. Competitive skiing began in 19th cent. and was esp. developed in Norway. Skiing was introduced into 1924 Olympics.

Skikda, town of NE Algeria, on Gulf of Stora. Pop. 85,000. Formerly called Philippeville. Outport for Constantine, exports incl. fruit, wine, iron ore. Founded (1838) by French on site of Carthaginian colony.

skin, flexible external covering of body. In humans, consists of outer epidermis and inner dermis. Former is covered by layer of dead cells which are constantly replaced. Latter contains blood vessels, nerve endings, hair follicles, sweat and sebaceous glands. Main functions are to protect, to regulate body temperature and to serve as organ of sense and excretion.

skink, any of Scincidae family of snake-like lizards, found mainly in desert regions. Elongated body, scaly tongue; limbs reduced or absent. Largest lizard family, with *c* 600 species, incl. common skink, *Scincus scincus,* of African desert.

Skinner, B[urrhus] F[rederick] (1904-), American psychologist. Known for extreme behaviourism, completely rejecting the unobservable; developed theory of programmed and social learning based on conditioning. Books incl. *Science and Human Behavior* (1953), *Beyond Freedom and Dignity* (1971).

Skipper, any of Hesperiidae family of primitive moth-like butterflies. Noted for bursts of swift erratic flight. Larvae feed on grass.

skittles, game played with pins and balls or discs. Nine pins are set up in diamond pattern and missile is hurled at the pins with object of knocking them over.

Skopje, city of S Yugoslavia, on R. Vardar, cap. of Macedonia. Pop. 312,000. Transport, indust. centre (iron, steel), univ. (1946). Cap. of Serbia in 14th cent.; under Turks 1392-1913, called Uskub. Badly damaged by earthquake 1963.

skua, any of Stercorariidae family of large gull-like sea birds. Will chase other birds, stealing their food. Species incl. great skua, *Stercorarius skua*, of both polar regions. Some species called jaeger in US.

skull, bony framework of the head comprising cranium, or brain case, and facial skeleton. Contains more than 20 tightly interlocked bones. Protects brain and sense organs, *ie* nose, eyes and ears.

skunk, bushy-tailed North American carnivore of Mustelidae family. Glossy black fur, usually with white stripe on back; ejects foul-smelling contents of 2 glands at back of tail for defence. Species incl. striped skunk, *Mephitis mephitis.*

skunk cabbage, *Symplocarpus foetidus,* low, fetid, broad-leaved plant of E North America. Grows in moist ground.

skydiving, sport of jumping from an aircraft and executing free-fall manoeuvres before opening the parachute, often as late as possible.

Skye, largest isl. of Inner Hebrides, W Scotland, in Highland region. Area 1665 sq km (643 sq mi); main town Portree (pop. 1000). Hilly in S (Cuillins). Sheep rearing, crofting; tourist centre. Has Dunvegan Castle, home of chief of Clan McLeod, in NW.

Skye terrier, terrier originally bred in Skye for hunting. Long silky coat, short legs, long body; stands 25 cm/10 in. at shoulder.

skylark, see LARK.

Skyros (*Skiros*), isl. of Greece, in Aegean Sea. Area 205 sq km (79 sq mi). Agric., fishing; chromite. In legend, Theseus killed here. Burial place of Rupert Brooke.

skyscraper, popular name for many-storeyed building. Originally designed in the US in order to save space, 1st examples were built in Chicago in 1880s. Tallest is Sears Building, Chicago, with 110 stories (473 m/1472 ft high).

slander, see LIBEL.

slate, dense, fine-grained metamorphic rock. Formed by compression of SHALE over long period; splits readily into thin, smooth plates. Used as roofing material.

slavery, ownership of a human being by another. Fundamental to social system of Greek city states and Roman empire. Largely replaced in Europe by serfdom under feudal system, but large numbers of African slaves were introduced to Americas as agric. labourers. Attempts at abolition on humanitarian grounds date from early 19th cent. (slave trade banned by UK 1807; slavery in British West Indies abolished 1833). Major issue in US Civil War, being basis of South's plantation economy. Lincoln's Emancipation Proclamation (1863) and the North's victory abolished slavery in principle.

Slavic or **Slavonic**, branch of Indo-European family of languages, close to BALTIC. Divided into 3 groups: E Slavic, incl. Russian, Ukrainian; W Slavic, incl. Polish, Czech, Slovak; S Slavic, incl. Serbo-Croat, Slovenian, Bulgarian.

Slavonia, region of N Yugoslavia, between Drava and Sava rivers. Main town Osijek. Low-lying, fertile; cereals, vegetable growing. Passed (1699) from Turkey to Hungary; united with Croatia 1868.

Slavs, Indo-European linguistic group, originally from N Carpathian region. incl. Russians, Poles, Czechs, Slovaks, Bulgars, Slovenes and Serbo-Croats.

sleep, bodily state of rest when there is little or no conscious thought or voluntary movement. Electrical waves recorded from brain show sleep occurs in cycles of c 2 hours; in a cycle there is a period of intense electrical brain activity and rapid movement of eyes under lids (REM) followed by longer periods without REM. Dreaming occurs during REM and appears to be necessary animal process.

sleeping sickness, infectious disease of tropical Africa caused by either of 2 trypanosomes transmitted by bite of tsetse fly. Symptoms incl. fever, swollen lymph nodes; lethargy follows later when trypanosomes invade nervous system, and death may follow.

slide rule, mathematical instrument consisting of a ruler with central sliding piece, both being marked with logarithmic scales; used in making rapid calculations by adding and subtracting logarithms.

Sligo, county of Connacht prov., NW Irish Republic. Area 1797 sq km (694 sq mi); pop. 50,000. Indented Atlantic coast; rugged, Ox Mts. in W. Cattle, potatoes; fishing. Co. town Sligo, pop. 14,000. Port, resort; food processing. Abbey, RC cathedral, megalithic remains nearby.

Slim, William Joseph Slim, 1st Viscount (1891-1970), British field marshal. During WWII, commanded repulse of Japanese in Burma. Governor-general of Australia (1953-60).

slime mould, saprophytic fungus of class Myxomycetes. Widely distributed, living in moist places on wood or other plant material undergoing decomposition.

slipped disc, see VERTEBRA.

Sloane, Sir Hans (1660-1753), British physician. Made extensive collection of plants, discovering over 800 new species in Jamaica. His library and cabinet formed nucleus of British Museum collection (founded 1753).

sloe, see BLACKTHORN.

sloth, slow-moving herbivorous mammal of Bradypodidae family, found in tropical forests of Central and South America. Long coarse hair, often coloured green by algae; lives upside down in trees, using hooked claws to walk along branches. Two genera; *Bradypus,* three-toed sloth; *Choloepus*, two-toed sloth.

sloth bear, *Melursus ursinus*, long-snouted bear of S India and Sri Lanka. Uses long tongue to feed on ants.

Slough, mun. bor. of Buckinghamshire, SC England. Pop. 87,000. Industs. incl. chemicals; vehicle, aircraft parts; radio, television mfg.

Slovakia (*Slovensko*), region of E Czechoslovakia; main town Bratislava. Mountainous, incl. Tatra. Agric., mining. Part of Hungary (10th cent.-1918), became prov. of Czechoslovakia. Independent ally of Axis in WWII, reunited (1945). Distinctive Slovak language, culture.

Slovenia, autonomous republic of NW Yugoslavia. Area 20,246 sq km (7817 sq mi); cap. Ljubljana. Julian Alps in NW, main rivers Drava, Sava. Agric., forestry, mining. Under Habsburgs until became (1918) part of Yugoslavia. Occupied by Axis in WWII; awarded (1947) part of NE Italy.

slow-worm, *Anguis fragilis*, legless snake-like lizard, widely distributed in Europe and Asia. Found in woods, damp meadows; diet of insects, worms. Also called blindworm.

slug, terrestrial gastropod mollusc, order Pulmonata, with reduced plate-like shell enclosed by its mantle. Herbivorous, often destructive of plants; moves on muscular foot leaving trail of slime.

Sluis or **Sluys** (Fr. *L'Ecluse*), town of SW Netherlands, near Belgian border. Port, founded 13th cent. Scene of offshore naval battle (1340) in which Edward III of England defeated French. Held by Spanish 1587-1604.

Sluter, Claus (*c* 1350-*c* 1406), Flemish sculptor. Worked for Philip the Bold of Burgundy in Dijon; his masterpiece, *Well of Moses*, in Dijon, marks transition from International Gothic style towards greater realism.

smallpox, infectious virus disease characterized by prolonged fever and red spots which develop into pus-filled blisters. May cause permanent scarring of the skin. Largely controlled by vaccination, it is now no longer endemic in any part of the world.

smell, one of five senses, less developed in humans than sight, touch, hearing. Perceived through stimulation of olfactory nerves of the nose by particles given off by substances.

smelt, small silvery marine food fish of Osmeridae family; spawns in fresh water. Species incl. common smelt, *Osmerus eperlanus*, of Europe, North America; also found landlocked in lakes.

smelting, process of obtaining metal from its ores by action of heat. Usually involves reduction of metal oxide with carbon.

Smetana, Bedřich or **Frederick** (1824-84), Czech composer. Leader of nationalist Czech music. Works incl. opera *The Bartered Bride*, orchestral cycle *Ma Vlast* ('My Country'), string quartet 'From my Life'. Deaf for last 10 years of his life, continued to compose.

Smiles, Samuel (1812-1904), Scottish writer. Known for didactic, popular work, *Self Help* (1859). Also wrote biogs. of successful industrialists, *eg* Josiah Wedgwood.

Smirke, Sir Robert (1781-1867),

English architect. Noted practitioner of neo-Classical style, his works incl. front façade of British Museum.

Smith, Adam (1723-90), Scottish economist. Formulated theory of division of labour, defined value as labour expended to make object. Advocated free trade, rejecting MERCANTILISM. His influential *Wealth of Nations* (1776) was 1st systematic formulation of economic theory, became basis of 19th cent. LAISSEZ-FAIRE doctrine.

Smith, Frederick Edwin, see BIRKENHEAD, 1ST EARL OF.

Smith, Ian Douglas (1919-), Rhodesian statesman, PM (1964-79). Issued Unilateral Declaration of Independence from Britain (1965). Set up republic under constitution perpetuating white minority rule (1969). Under pressure from US, entered into discussion with nationalist leaders on question of majority rule and transfer of power (1976). Made 'Internal Settlement' (1979), giving form of majority rule but with white veto.

Smith, Jedediah Strong (1799-1831), American explorer. Opened up trapping in West. Led small force on pioneering expedition across Great Salt Desert to San Diego and back (1825-7).

Smith, John (c 1580-1631), English colonist. Leader in settlement (1606-9) of Jamestown, Virginia. Supposedly saved from execution at order of Indian chief, Powhatan, by intervention of Powhatan's daughter, Pocahontas (1607).

Smith, Joseph (1805-44), American religious leader. Claimed to have vision directing him to sacred writings, transcribed as *Book of Mormon* (1829). Founded church (1830) based on revelations. Murdered by mob at Carthage, Illinois. Followers formed MORMONS.

Smith, Sir Mathew Arnold Bracy (1879-1959), English painter. Studied briefly under Matisse, subsequent work shows fauvist influence in exuberant use of colour. Paintings incl. *Nude, Fitzroy Street* (1916).

Smith, William (1769-1839), English geologist. Estab. principle that all geological strata contain characteristic groups of fossils, which aid dating of strata. Constructed geological map of British Isles (1815).

Smithsonian Institution, Washington, DC, US, scientific institution, estab. (1846) by Congressional act. Conducts research in all aspects of science relevant to US. Controls National Gallery of Art, museums of history and natural history.

smoke, suspension of solid particles in a gas, esp. particles of carbon and hydrocarbon in atmosphere derived from combustion of carbonaceous fuels. When combined with fog, forms smog. Considered health risk, therefore controlled by govt. measures advocating clean air and smokeless zones.

smokeball, see PUFFBALL.

Smolensk, town of USSR, railway jct. of W European RSFSR; port on R. Dnepr. Pop. 225,000. Linen and textile mfg. Founded 9th cent.; became commercial centre, trading with Constantinople. Cap. of principality 12th-14th cent.

Smollett, Tobias [George] (1721-71), Scottish writer, surgeon. Known for energetic picaresque novels *Roderick Random* (1748), *Peregrine Pickle* (1751), *Humphrey Clinker* (1771).

'smuggling, offence of importing or exporting goods illegally, esp. those requiring payment of duty. Esp. prevalent in 18th cent. with imposition of duties on. In UK, North America, Europe; goods smuggled incl. spirits, lace, tobacco, tea. Modern smuggling incl. drugs, illegal immigrants.

smut or **bunt,** various parasitic fungi of order Ustilaginales. Appear as black sooty spores on host plant. Serious threat to cereal crops. Treatment with compounds of sulphur and mercury.

Smuts, Jan Christian (1870-1950), South African soldier, statesman, PM (1919-24, 1939-48). Commanded Boer forces (1901-2) in war against UK, later sought cooperation with British. Joined Botha in creating (1910) Union of South Africa. Member of British war councils during both WWs.

Smyrna, see IZMIR.

snail, gastropod mollusc of order Pulmonata with spiral protective shell. Marine, freshwater and terrestrial varieties. Species incl. common garden snail, *Hēlix aspersa,* and edible or Roman snail, *H. pomatia.*

Snake, river of NW US, rising in Yellowstone National Park (Wyoming). Flows SW 1670 km (1038 mi) through Idaho, then NW along Oregon border to Washington to join Columbia R.

snake, any of suborder Ophidia of limbless elongated reptiles. Horny scales on body, forked tongue; mouth opens wide for swallowing large prey. Poisonous snakes carry venom in salivary glands; venom acts either as nerve poison, paralysing victim, or as tissue poison, destroying cells and causing haemorrhages.

snapdragon, any of genus *Antirrhinum* of perennial plants native to Mediterranean region, esp. garden variety *A. majus* with showy white, crimson or yellow flowers.

snapping turtle, any of Chelydridae family of turtles, found in North American swamps and rivers; species incl. *Chelydra serpentina,* aggressive predator with powerful jaws.

snare drum, percussion instrument. Consists of side drum with catgut strings to produce rattling sound.

sneeze, reflex action consisting of brief indrawn breath followed by forcible expulsion of air through nose. Initiated by irritation of lining of nose.

Snellius or **Snell, Willebrord** (1591-1626), Dutch physicist, mathematician. Discovered law governing REFRACTION of light, connecting sines of angles of incidence and refraction.

snipe, wading bird of Scolopacidae family, with long narrow bill used for digging. Species incl. common snipe, *Gallinago gallinago,* of Europe and Asia, and South American noble snipe, *G. nobilis.*

snooker, game played on billiard table with 15 red balls, 6 coloured balls and white cue ball. Derived from BILLIARDS. Similar to US game of pool.

Snorri Sturluson (1179-1241), Icelandic historian, politician. Wrote *Edda* (pre-1223), handbook on poet's art which uses myths as examples; *Heimskringla* (c 1223-35), history of Norwegian kings, incl. *Saga of Saint Olaf, King Harold's Saga*. Writing noted for characterization, dialogue and rhetoric, and narrative skill.

Snow, C[harles] P[ercy], Baron Snow of Leicester (1905-), English author, scientist. Known for long novel sequence incl. *Strangers and Brothers* (1940), *The Light and the Dark* (1947), *The Masters* (1951), *Corridors of Power* (1963), dealing with ethics of power. Wrote controversial essay, *The Two Cultures* (1959).

snow, precipitation consisting of delicate, hexagonal ice crystals, formed in atmosphere at temperatures below freezing point. Lower limit of permanent snow cover is called 'snow-line'; it reaches sea level at poles.

snowball, *see* GUELDER ROSE.

snow bunting, *Plectrophenax nivalis,* small bird of N regions; in spring, male's plumage is white with black back and tail. Breeds in Arctic, migrating to Europe and America in winter.

Snowdon, Anthony Armstrong-Jones, 1st Earl of (1930-), British designer, photographer. Married (1960) Princess Margaret; divorced in 1978. Designs incl. aviary at London Zoo.

Snowdon, mountain of Gwynedd, NW Wales. Highest in England and Wales (1085 m/3560 ft). Rack Railway from Llanberis. Snowdonia national park in surrounding area.

snowdrop, any of genus *Galanthus* of early-blooming, bulbous perennials native to Europe. Garden

varieties incl. common snowdrop, *G. nivalis.*

snow goose, *Anser caerulescens,* white North American goose with black-tipped wings, dark pink bill and legs. Breeds colonially in Arctic.

snow leopard or ounce, *Uncia uncia,* large cat of mountains of C Asia; reaches lengths of 2.1 m/7 ft. Coat whitish with dark blotches in summer, almost pure white in winter. Feeds on sheep, goats, ibex.

Snowy Mountains, range of SE New South Wales, Australia, in Australian Alps. Highest point Mt. KOSCIUSKO. Snowy Mts. scheme estab. 1949 to provide h.e.p., irrigation from Snowy, Tumut, Eucumbene and other rivers.

snowy owl, *Nyctea scandiaca,* large owl of Arctic and subarctic regions. Largely diurnal and solitary; white plumage with dark brown markings. Feeds on hares, lemmings, fish.

snuff, powdered tobacco sniffed into nostrils or rubbed on to teeth and gums. Snuff-taking was widespread in 18th cent. when elaborately decorated snuff boxes were made.

Soane, Sir John (1753-1837), English architect. Evolved individual style, based on neo-Classicism; most important work was at Bank of England (now destroyed). His house in London is now a museum.

soap, mixture of sodium salts of fatty acids (esp. oleic, palmitic and stearic acids) or of potassium salts of these acids (soft soaps). Prepared by boiling fats and oils with alkali. Acts most effectively in soft water; hard water causes scum (precipitated calcium or magnesium salts) to form.

soapstone or **steatite**, soft, grey mineral, composed mainly of TALC with other minerals eg chlorite, mica, quartz. Used in sculpture and electrical insulators.

soapwort or **bouncing Bet**, *Saponaria officinalis*, European annual or perennial herb widely naturalized in North America as garden plant. Clusters of pink flowers; sap forms lather with water.

Soares, Mario (1924-), Portuguese political leader. Imprisoned in 1960s for socialist opposition to Salazar regime, exiled (1970-4). Returned after military coup (1974) to become minister for foreign affairs (1974-5). Became PM after elections (1976); dismissed by president (1978).

Sobers, Sir Garfield St Aubrun ('Gary') (1936-), Barbadian cricketer. Leading West Indies' all-rounder of 1960s, he scored over 8000 runs in test cricket, incl. 26 centuries. Hit record 365 in test match against Pakistan (1957-8).

Sobieski, John, see JOHN III [SOBIESKI], king of Poland.

soccer, see ASSOCIATION FOOTBALL.

social class, category or grouping of people according to economic, occupational or social status. In Marxist terms, refers exclusively to those persons with common relationship to material production. Traditionally, society divided into upper, middle and working (lower) classes, according to socio-economic grouping; its study may involve aspects of health, crime rates, racial, political attitudes, mobility between classes, life styles.

social contract, theory that society originated out of voluntary association, bringing with it mutual obligations. Formulated by Hobbes and Locke, expanded by Rousseau, had great influence on subsequent development of responsible govt. in democracies.

Social Credit, economic programme, developed from theories of economist C.H. DOUGLAS. Calls for redistribution of purchasing power by issuing dividends (based on estimate of nation's wealth) to all persons to counter economic depression. Adopted by Social Credit Party of Alberta, Canada; elected (1935) under William Aberhart. Later achieved power in British Columbia.

social democracy, advocacy of socialism within democratic framework, adhering to evolutionary means of achieving power; esp. important in Europe. Split in German Social Democratic party (SPD) at start of 20th cent. reflected dilemma of all European Socialist parties, whether or not to cooperate with bourgeois govts. to achieve gradual reform; E. BERNSTEIN leading proponent of this 'revisionism', opposing use of violent revolution to gain power for proletariat (see MARXISM). Collapse of Internationals during WWI led to increase of reform-conscious Social Democratic parties in Europe, some forming govts., eg in Scandinavian countries and Britain (see LABOUR PARTY), between WWs. In Germany, SPD revived after WWII; gained power under Brandt (1969). In France, Socialist groups under Blum formed Popular Front govt. in 1930s; formed major opposition party in Fifth Republic.

socialism, any of various economic and political theories or systems advocating transfer of means of production and distribution from private ownership to community as a whole, with all sharing work, produce. In this sense, can incl. SOCIAL DEMOCRACY as well as MARXISM. Early socialist theorists (eg OWEN, SAINT-SIMON) believed in reform of existing society to achieve utopian ideal. Attacked by Marx, who taught inevitability of revolution. By 1870s, Marxist ('scientific') socialism was strong political force in Europe, but internally split into 2 main factions, gradualists and revolutionaries. Schism made permanent with triumph of revolutionary COMMUNISM in Russia (1917).

social realism, in art, depiction of contemporary scene, usually with some social or political content. In Britain, Bratby is an exponent; in US, Ben Shahn. Distinct from socialist realism, official art of Communist countries, which glorifies the worker, peasant and Party.

social security, system by which govt. provides for nation's wage earners and dependants, esp. for their protection in sickness, old age or unemployment. First estab. 1883 in Germany with HEALTH INSURANCE and PENSION schemes. In UK, NATIONAL INSURANCE ACT (1911) added unemployment insurance. In US, Social Security Act (1935) embodied principles.

Society Islands, archipelago of SC Pacific Ocean, part of French Polynesia. Comprise Windward Isls. (incl. Tahiti) and Leeward Isls.

Produce copra, pearl shell, vanilla. Acquired by France (1843).

Society of Friends or **Quakers,** Christian sect founded (c 1650) in England by GEORGE FOX. Hold that understanding and guidance come directly from 'inward light' of Holy Spirit and that sacrament, and formal worship are unnecessary for Christian life. Colony estab. (1682) in Pennsylvania, US, by PENN. American Friends Service Committee and Service Council of the British Society of Friends awarded Nobel Peace Prize (1947).

Society of Jesus, see JESUS, SOCIETY OF.

sociology, study of human society, and of social relations, organization and change; specifically the study of the beliefs, values, interrelationships, etc, of social groups and of the principles and processes governing social phenomena. Systematic discipline since 19th cent., esp. through work of Auguste Comte, and later Durkheim and Max Weber.

Socotra, isl. of Southern Yemen, in Arabian Sea. Area c 3630 sq km (1400 sq mi). Barren plateau with mountainous interior. Part of British protect. of Aden after 1886. Former coaling station.

Socrates (469-399 BC), Greek philosopher. Believed knowledge could be approached by question-and-answer sequence (dialectic method), and wisdom to be based on recognition of one's ignorance. Ideas on weakness of democratic govt. unpopular in Athens. Assembly tried and condemned him on charge of corrupting youth; died by drinking poison. Teachings preserved in writings of disciple Plato, and subsequently Aristotle.

soda, name applied to various sodium compounds, incl. sodium carbonate, bicarbonate and hydroxide. Sodium carbonate, manufactured on large scale from common salt, is used to make soap, glass, paper and to soften water. Sodium bicarbonate is used in baking powder and medicine.

Söderblom, Nathan (1866-1931), Swedish churchman, primate of the Lutheran Church of Sweden. Leading ecumenist, awarded Nobel Peace Prize (1930).

sodium (Na), soft silvery-white metallic element; at. no. 11, at. wt. 22.99. Reacts violently with water to form strong alkali sodium hydroxide. Occurs combined as chloride (common salt), nitrate (Chile saltpetre); prepared by electrolysis of fused chloride. Used in organic syntheses, eg of lead tetraethyl; yellow sodium vapour light used in street lighting.

Sodom and Gomorrah, in OT, two of the cities of the plain, destroyed by God because of their wickedness. Possibly situated SW of Dead Sea.

Sofia (anc. *Sardica*), cap. of Bulgaria. Pop. 928,000. Major route centre in W Balkans. Indust. centre, esp. machinery, textiles. Univ. (1880), Black Mosque. Colonized by Romans; sacked by Huns (447). Cap. of former Turkish Rumelia, cap. of Bulgaria from 1879.

Sogne Fjord, inlet of Atlantic Ocean, SW Norway. Longest (c 180 km/110 mi) and deepest (1220 m/ 4000 ft) fjord in Norway, reaches inland to Jotunheim Mts. Tourist area.

Soho, dist. of City of WESTMINSTER, London, England. Has many foreign restaurants; theatres, nightclubs; film co. offices. Origin of name prob. old hunting cry.

soil, loose accumulation of material forming topmost layer of Earth's land surface. Consists of organic material (humus) and inorganic material (weathered rock, incl. clay, silt, sand) together with air and water. Types incl. BLACK EARTH, LOAM, LOESS. Study of soil is called pedology.

Soissons, town of N France, on R. Aisne. Pop. 28,000. Agric. market for Soissonais. Cathedral (12th cent.); ruined abbey contains tombs of Merovingian kings.

Sokoto, town of NW Nigeria, on R. Kebbi. Pop. 50,000. Trade centre, esp. in groundnuts, hides. Cap. of vast Moslem Fulani empire of Sokoto estab. early 19th cent.; fell to British (1903).

Solanaceae, family of plants native to tropical and temperate regions, esp. tropical America. Incl. deadly nightshade, tobacco, potato. Many species contain poisonous alkaloids.

solan goose, see GANNET.

solar energy, energy liberated by thermonuclear reactions in Sun and radiated in form of radio waves, X-rays and light. May be utilized by solar cells to generate electricity or by solar furnaces to produce high temperatures.

solar flare, short-lived eruption of Sun's surface, usually associated with sunspots. Accompanied by emission of particles, X-rays, etc; causes magnetic and radio disturbances on Earth.

Solar System, name for Sun and

collection of bodies in orbit about it. Comprises Sun, 9 major planets (Mercury, Venus, Earth, Mars, Jupiter, Saturn, Uranus, Neptune, Pluto), their satellites, minor planets, comets and meteors.

solar wind, stream of ionized particles, mainly protons and electrons, emitted from Sun's surface, esp. during solar flares and sunspot activity. Particles reaching Earth are trapped by its magnetic field to form Van Allen radiation belt; others cause auroral displays around the poles.

solder, alloy used in joining metal. Soft solders, which have low melting point, contain lead and tin in varying proportions with some antimony.

sole, edible flatfish of Soleidae family, with worldwide distribution. European *Solea solea* is commercially valuable; sold as Dover sole.

Solent, The, channel between Hampshire, S England, and Isle of Wight. Shipping route to Southampton, Portsmouth; yachting.

sol-fa, tonic, see TONIC SOL-FA.

Solferino, village of N Italy, near Mantua. Scene of indecisive battle (1859) between French and Austrians which inspired Dunant to form Red Cross.

solicitor, in England, member of legal profession who is not member of the bar; may not plead cases in superior courts. Advises clients in legal cases, engages barristers for them, *etc.*

solid, state of matter in which constituent molecules or ions possess no translatory movement. Solids possess definite crystalline structure and retain their shape unless deformed by external forces;

certain amorphous non-crys[...] solids, *eg* glass; may be consid[...] as supercooled fluids.

solid-state physics, branch o[...] physics dealing with matter in solid state. Often refers specifically to study of semiconductors and their use in electronic devices without moving parts or heated filaments.

Solomon (d. c 932 BC), king of Israel, son of David and Bathsheba. His peaceful reign was marked by growth of trade and building of the Temple in Jerusalem. The heavy taxes he imposed led to a revolt in N Israel. Famous for his wisdom.

Solomon Islands, state of SW Pacific, member of British Commonwealth. Area *c* 29,800 sq km (11,500 sq mi); pop. 200,000; cap. Honiara. Consists of all isls. of Solomon Isls. archipelago (incl. Guadalcanal), except Bougainville and Buka, which belong to Papua New Guinea. Formerly known as British Solomon Isls. Protect. (estab. by 1899), independent 1977.

Solon (*c* 639-c 559 BC), Athenian statesman. Revised constitution to create limited form of democracy. Extended basis of membership of the sovereign assembly. Improved the conditions of debtors and poor people.

Solothurn (Fr. *Soleure*), town of NW Switzerland, on R. Aare, cap. of Solothurn canton. Pop. 18,000. Watches, precision instruments. Medieval buildings; cathedral (18th cent.).

solstice, time of year when Sun appears directly overhead at the line marking its furthest distance N or S of the Equator. For N hemisphere, summer solstice (21 June) occurs when Sun reaches Tropic of Cancer, winter solstice (22 Dec.) when Sun reaches Tropic of Capricorn. Day is at max. length at summer solstice, night at winter solstice.

solution, homogeneous molecular mixture of 2 or more substances, *eg* of solid or gas in liquid. Some alloys are solutions of one metal in another.

Solway Firth, inlet of Irish Sea, between SW Scotland and NW England. Fishing.

Solzhenitsyn, Aleksandr Isaye-vich (1918-), Russian author. Known for novels critical of Soviet regime, *eg First Circle* (1964), *Cancer Ward* (1966), *August 1914* (1972), *The Gulag Archipelago* (1974). *One Day in the Life of Ivan Denisovich* (1962) is a short novel detailing conditions in a labour camp. Nobel Prize for Literature (1970). Exiled in 1974.

Somalia or **Somali Democratic Republic,** republic of E Africa. Area 637,700 sq km (246,200 sq mi); pop. 3,261,000; cap. Mogadishu. Language: Somali. Religion: Islam. Coastal lowland, arid interior plateau. Nomadic pastoralism; exports bananas, livestock, hides. Formed 1960 from union of British Somaliland (created 1884, cap. Hargeisa) and Italian Somaliland (created 1889, cap. Mogadishu; from 1950 a UN trust terr.). War with Ethiopia in late 1970s over disputed Ogaden territory.

Somaliland, French, see DJIBOUTI.

Somers, John Somers, Baron (1651-1716), English statesman, jurist. Presided over committee which drafted BILL OF RIGHTS (1689). Gained favour as confidential adviser to William III; lord chancellor (1697-1700). Successfully defended himself against impeachment charge.

Somerset, Edward Seymour, Duke of, see SEYMOUR, JANE.

Somerset, county of SW England. Area 3458 sq km (1335 sq mi); pop. 399,000; co. town Taunton. Exmoor in W; Mendips in NE; plain in C. Dairying (esp. Cheddar cheese), sheep, cider apples.

Somme, river of N France. Flows c 240 km (150 mi) from near St Quentin via Amiens, Abbeville to English Channel. Canal links to Oise, Scheldt. Scene of heavy fighting in WWI (1916).

Somoza, Anastasio (1896-1956), Nicaraguan political leader, president (1937-47, 1950-6). Ruthless rule after gaining dictatorial power in coup (1936). Assassinated.

sonar or **asdic,** method of detecting and locating underwater objects, esp. submarines or shoals of fish, by projecting soundwaves through water and registering the vibrations reflected back. Also used in measuring depths.

sonata, piece of instrumental music so named to distinguish it from a cantata for voices and instruments. Developed from *c* 1600 as a composition for a single instrument, esp. a keyboard one, with or without accompaniment. Usually in several movements, first of which is in sonata form containing 2 themes subjected to statement, development and recipitulation.

song, vocal form of musical expression, normally setting of lyric. Earliest documented European song dates from 10th cent. Early practitioners were TROUBADOURS, MIN-

NESINGER. Developed by such masters as Machaut, DUFAY, LASSUS and English lutanists of 16th-17th cents. Reached peak as vehicle of romantic expression in work of Schubert, Schumann and Brahms in 19th cent. Folk song has survived with little change for centuries.

Song of Solomon, poetical book of OT, traditionally attributed to Solomon, but sometimes dated as late as 3rd cent. BC. Primarily a glorification of pure love or an allegory of God's love for Israel.

songthrush, *Turdus philomelos*, common European songbird with brown back and spotted breast.

sonic boom, noise created by shock waves set up by aircraft travelling faster than sound. Waves are transmitted as variations in atmospheric pressure; when waves touch ground, characteristic double bang is heard.

sonnet, poem of 14 lines, expressing single complete thought or idea, generally written in iambic pentameter. Most common rhyme schemes are the Italian form (*eg* Keats's *On First Looking into Chapman's Homer*) with 8 lines (octave) followed by group of 6 lines (sestet), and Shakespearian form with 3 quatrains followed by couplet.

Soochow or **Wuhsien**, city of Kiangsu prov., E China. Pop. 1,300,000. On Grand Canal; rail jct. Famous silks, weaving. Former treaty port, opened 1896. Has many canals, gardens and pagodas.

Sophists, term applied in Athens (middle 5th cent. BC) to persons giving lessons in rhetoric, politics and mathematics in return for money. Later Sophists emphasized

rhetoric rather than substan. knowledge, becoming known their ability to conduct specio. argument. Condemned by Socrates and Plato. Leading Sophists incl. Protagoras, Gorgias.

Sophocles (c 496-406 BC), Greek tragic poet. One of three great masters of tragedy, other two being contemporaries Aeschylus and Euripides. Known for use of dialogue rather than lyric, introducing 3rd actor to increase dialogue's importance, complexity; also use of dramatic irony. Extant plays are *Oedipus Rex*, *Oedipus at Colonus*, *Antigone*, *Electra*, *Ajax*, *Women of Trachis*, *Philoctetes*.

Sophonias, see ZEPHANIAH.

soprano, highest singing voice in women and boys, latter also known as treble. Term sometimes applied to high-pitched member of a family of instruments, *eg* soprano saxophone.

Sopwith, Sir Thomas Octave Murdoch (1888-), British aircraft designer. Flew across English Channel (1910). Founded (1912) company which built WWI aeroplanes.

Sorbonne, traditional name for Univ. of Paris, France, from 1st college estab. (1253) by Robert de Sorbon; reorganized in 19th cent. Early known for theological studies.

Sorel, Georges (1847-1922), French social philosopher. Introduced Marxist ideas into France, later becoming anarcho-syndicalist, then Leninist, regarding Marxism, like all extremist social doctrines, as world-changing myth, not science. Known for *Reflections on Violence* (1908), defending role of violence in revolution.

sorghum, genus of grasses with solid stems native to Africa; esp. *Sorghum vulgare*, widely cultivated as forage crop. Variously known as Kaffir corn, durra, Guinea corn, Indian millet.

sorrel, see DOCK, OXALIS.

Sorrento, town of Campania, SW Italy, on Bay of Naples. Pop. 29,000. Scenic cliff-top resort; long famous for wine.

Sosnowiec, city of S Poland. Pop. 145,000. Iron and steel industs., engineering. Rapid growth from late 19th cent. based on coalmining. Under Russian rule 1815-1919.

Sotheby, John (1740-1807), English auctioneer, antiquarian. Director of saleroom for prints, manuscripts; developed auction house, Sotheby's of London, which bought Parke-Bernet Gallery, New York City (1964).

soul, concept of non-material, immortal life-essence or spiritual identity of individual. Mind and body conceived as its vehicle. Occurs in most religions either as individual attribute (Christianity, Islam) or as general principle or world soul (Hinduism, Buddhism). Denied by materialists.

Sound, The, see ÖRESUND, Denmark.

sound, vibrations in air or some other medium which stimulate the auditory nerves and give sensation of hearing. Travels at c 330 m/sec (760 mph) in air; velocity varies with temperature and is greater in solids. Pitch of sound depends on number of vibrations per second; lowest normally audible sound has frequency of *c* 20 cycles/sec, highest *c* 20,000.

Sousa, John Philip (1854-1932), American composer, band leader. Best known for marches, eg *The Stars and Stripes Forever*, of which he composed more than 100.

Sousse or **Susa**, town of E Tunisia, on Gulf of Hammamet. Pop. 83,000. Tourist resort; port, exports olive oil. Ancient *Hadrumetum*, founded 9th cent. BC by Phoenicians. Mosque, fortress (both 9th cent.).

South Africa, republic of S Africa. Area 1,221,000 sq km (471,500 sq mi); pop. 26,129,000; caps. Pretoria (admin.), Cape Town (legislative), Bloemfontein (judicial). Languages: Afrikaans, English. Religion: Christianity. Comprises Cape Prov., Natal, Orange Free State, Transvaal; controls South West Africa despite withdrawal of UN mandate (1966). Mainly plateau, fringed by mountains (eg Drakensberg); main rivers Orange, Vaal. Cereals, fruit, sugar cane, vines; great mineral wealth, esp. in Witwatersrand. Dutch settlement estab. 1652 at Table Bay; Cape annexed by UK 1806. Boer dislike of British rule led to 'Great Trek' 1836 to Orange Free State, Transvaal; Boer republics estab. 1850s. Boer War (1899-1902) ended in British victory; Union of South Africa estab. 1910. Republic from 1960, withdrew from British Commonwealth 1961. Follows controversial policy of separate development (*apartheid*) of blacks and whites; incl. 9 Bantu 'homelands' eventually to become partly independent (eg TRANSKEI).

South African War, see BOER WAR.

South America, S continent of W hemisphere, bounded by Pacific in

W and Atlantic in E. Area *c* 17,819,000 sq km (6,880,000 sq mi); pop. 195,000,000. Dominated in W by Andean cordillera; C plateau incl. Mato Grosso, Pampas; drained by Amazon, Plata, Orinoco river systems. Hist. highly developed Indian civilizations (esp. Incas) fl before Spanish, Portuguese exploration and colonization for mineral wealth in 16th cent. Nine Spanish-speaking republics estab. under Bolívar, San Martín in 19th cent.; Brazil is Portuguese-speaking. Guiana Highlands comprise Surinam, Guyana, French Guiana. Much political instability in all republics after independence.

Southampton, Henry Wriothesley, 3rd Earl of (1573-1624), English courtier. Patron of Shakespeare and other poets; Shakespeare's *Venus and Adonis* is dedicated to him. Imprisoned by Elizabeth I for involvement in Essex's rebellion (1601); pardoned by James I.

Southampton, city of Hampshire, S England, on Southampton Water. Pop. 215,000. Chief English passenger seaport; transatlantic services. Also cargo port; large graving dock (1933). Oil refinery at Fawley. Medieval walls, churches; univ. (1952). Damaged in WWII bombing.

Southampton Island, in E Keewatin Dist., Northwest Territs., Canada; at entrance to Hudson Bay. Area 40,700 sq km (15,700 sq mi). Scattered communities, mainly Eskimo.

South Arabia, Federation of, *see* SOUTHERN YEMEN.

South Australia, state of S Australia. Area 984,500 sq km (380,100 sq mi); pop. 1,173,000; cap. Adelaide. Mainly low-lying, incl. Nullarbor Plain in SW, L. Eyre in N; has Musgrave (N), Flinders and Mt. Lofty (SE) ranges. Produces sheep, wheat, fruit, wine; minerals incl. iron ore, salt. First settled 1836; became crown colony 1842, federal state 1901. Controlled Northern Territ. 1863-1911.

South Carolina, state of SE US, on Atlantic coast. Area 80,432 sq km (31,055 sq mi); pop. 2,591,000; cap. Columbia. Low coastal plain, Savannah R. on S border; plateau in NW. Important agric. (tobacco, cotton, soya beans, maize, stock rearing), related industs.; stone, clay mining. First settled by Spanish (1526); then by English (1670). One of original 13 colonies of US. First secessionist state before Civil War (1860).

South China Sea, part of Pacific Ocean enclosed by SE China, Indo-China, Malay penin., Borneo, Philippines and Taiwan.

South Dakota, state of NC US. Area 199,552 sq km (77,047 sq mi); pop. 666,000; cap. Pierre. Mainly agric. (grains, livestock rearing); plains in E divided from Black Hills in SW (gold mines) by Missouri R. Acquired by US as part of Louisiana Purchase (1803). Territ. estab. (1861); Sioux Indians resisted white settlement (1868-90), deprived of land. Admitted to Union, jointly with North Dakota, as 39th state (1889).

Southeast Asia Treaty Organization (SEATO), alliance, estab. 1954 at Manila, Philippines. Charter members incl. Australia, France, New Zealand, UK and US; formed

for collective defence against aggression.

Southend-on-Sea, co. bor. of Essex, SE England, on N side of Thames estuary. Pop. 162,000. Electrical goods mfg. Resort, famous pier (2 km/1.25 mi long).

Southern Alps, mountain range of South Isl., New Zealand. Runs SW-NE, highest point Mt. COOK. May snowfields, glaciers eg Tasman Glacier; source of many rivers, eg Clutha, Waitaki. Tourist area, snow sports.

Southern Cross (Crux), small constellation in S hemisphere whose 4 brightest stars appear to form tips of a cross.

Southern Rhodesia, see RHODESIA.

Southern Yemen, republic of SW Asia. Area c 287,500 sq km (111,000 sq mi); pop. 1,749,000; cap. Aden. Coastal strip in S borders Arabian Sea; mountains and plateau in interior. History dates from 1963 estab. of Federation of South Arabia out of states of Aden protect. Southern Yemen proclaimed 1967.

Southey, Robert (1774-1843), English author. One of 'Lake poets'. Known for short poems, eg 'The Battle of Blenheim', 'Inchcape Rock', and biog. of Nelson (1813). Poet laureate (1813).

South Georgia, see FALKLAND ISLANDS.

South Glamorgan, see GLAMORGAN, Wales.

South Holland, see HOLLAND.

South Island, one of main isls. of New Zealand, separated from North Isl. by Cook Str. Area 150,480 sq km (58,100 sq mi); pop. 810,000; chief cities Christchurch, Dunedin. Plateau in SW; Southern Alps form W backbone. Coastal lowland incl. Canterbury Plains. Grain, sheep farming; timber; h.e.p.

South Korea, see KOREA.

South Orkney Islands, group of isls. in S Atlantic, SE of Cape Horn, forming part of British Antarctic Territ. from 1962. Area c 620 sq km (140 sq mi). Discovered 1821; also claimed by Argentina.

South Pole, point at S end of Earth's axis, latitude 90°S. First reached 1911 by Roald Amundsen.

Southport, co. bor. of Merseyside met. county, NW England. Pop. 84,000. Clothing mfg. Seaside resort. Has Royal Birkdale golf course.

South Sea Bubble, popular name for financial scheme in which South Sea Co. (founded 1711 with monopoly in South American trade) took over British national debt, exchanging its stock for govt. bonds. After widespread speculation, company became bankrupt (1720); resulting investigation revealed govt. corruption.

South Shetland Islands, group of isls. in S Atlantic, NW of Graham Land, forming part of British Antarctic Territ. from 1962. Area c 4700 sq km (1800 sq mi). Discovered 1819; formerly base for sealers and whalers.

South Shields, co. bor. of Tyne and Wear met. county, NE England, on S side of Tyne estuary. Pop. 101,000. Shipbuilding, engineering, chemicals industs.

South Vietnam, see VIETNAM.

Southwark, bor. of SC Greater London, England. Pop. 260,000. Created 1965 from Bermondsey, Camberwell, Southwark met. bors. Hist. famous for inns; has former

Clink prison for heretics; Globe Theatre; Guy's Hospital (1721).

South West Africa or **Namibia,** territ. of SW Africa, admin. by Republic of South Africa. Area 824,000 sq km (318,000 sq mi); pop. 852,000; cap. Windhoek. Languages: Bantu, Afrikaans, English. Religions: native, Christianity. Namib Desert along coast, plateau inland; salt pans in N. Stock raising, rich in minerals; exports skins, diamonds, copper, lead, manganese. German colony from 1892; admin. after WWI by South Africa under League of Nations mandate. Revocation 1966 by UN disputed by South Africa. Independence was due in 1978, but postponed.

South Yorkshire, met. county of NC England. Area 1560 sq km (602 sq mi); pop. 1,319,000; admin. centre Barnsley. Created 1974 from part of former S Riding of Yorkshire.

Soutine, Chaïm (1894-1943), Lithuanian painter, resident in Paris after 1911. Painted tormented, heavily impasted works in violent expressionist style; noted for his portraits of cooks and page-boys, studies of carcasses, and landscapes.

sovereignty, in politics, supreme independent power held by state or other govt. unit. Sovereign state can conduct diplomacy, make treaties, war, peace. Internally, it makes laws, controls finances and the military.

Sovetsk, town of USSR, W European RSFSR; port on R. Neman. Pop. 60,000. Woodworking and cheese mfg. As Tilsit, site of treaty between Russia, Prussia and France (1807), leading to loss of Prussian

SPACE EXPLORATION

territ. Passed to USSR (1945) and renamed.

soviet (Russ., = council), in USSR, any of various governing councils, local, intermediate, national, elected by and representing people. Each forms part of a pyramid govt. structure, with village, town soviets at base, Supreme Soviet at apex. Organized first (1905) as strike committees. Re-estab. 1917 by workers, soldiers, became govt. instruments under Lenin (1918).

Soviet Union, *see* UNION OF SOVIET SOCIALIST REPUBLICS.

sowbug, *see* WOODLOUSE.

Soweto, township of S Transvaal, South Africa, near Johannesburg. Black African pop. Scene of antigovt. riots (1976) following protests against use of Afrikaans language in schools for black African children; *c* 150 killed.

soybean, soyabean or **soja bean,** *Glycine max,* annual plant of Leguminosae family. Native to China and Japan but widely cultivated for seeds which are rich in protein and oil used in glycerine and rubber substitutes.

spacecraft, vehicle designed for travelling in outer space. Pioneered by USSR and US. Early craft were artificial satellites put into orbit round Earth. Subsequent developments incl. manned capsules, docking vehicles steered by rockets, *Skylab* orbiting space station with living quarters for 3 astronauts. Planned developments incl. space shuttle capable of re-landing on Earth and being used many times.

space exploration, navigation in manned spacecraft in regions beyond Earth's atmosphere. Unmanned artificial satellites carried out 1st explorations, relaying to Earth information about atmospheric conditions. Orbital flight by manned vehicle first achieved by YURI GAGARIN. Subsequent extended flights have incl. manned flights to Moon (US), eg that of Apollo XI (1969), and unmanned probes to Venus and Mars sending back data to Earth.

space-time continuum, four-dimensional description of the universe, blending three space dimensions with dimension of time. Necessitated by theory of relativity in which time is no longer absolute but depends on relative motion of the observer. The geometry of space-time continuum is determined by gravitation; large gravitating bodies affect its curvature.

spaghetti, see MACARONI.

Spain (España), kingdom of SW Europe, occupying most of Iberian penin.; incl. Balearic, Canary Isls. Area 505,000 sq km (195,000 sq mi); pop. 35,971,000; cap. Madrid. Language: Spanish. Religion: RC. Distinct languages and cultures in Basque Provs. and Catalonia. Pyrenees in NE; large C plateau between Cantabrian Mts. (N), Sierra Morena (S). Main rivers Douro, Ebro, Tagus. Agric. incl. fruit, olives, wine (S), livestock (N); rich in minerals, tourism. Inhabited from prehist. times, part of Roman Empire after defeat of Carthage. Germanic invasion 5th cent. Moorish conquest 8th cent. Christian reconquest completed 1492, led by Aragón and Castile (united 1479). Exploration led to colonizing Americas, empire fl under Habsburgs, colonies lost 19th cent. Republic proclaimed 1931; Civil War (1936-9) resulted in fascist state under Franco; monarchy restored 1975.

Spalato, see SPLIT, Yugoslavia.

spaniel, one of various breeds of dog with drooping ears and silky coat. Breeds incl. King Charles spaniel, with black and tan coat; stands 25 cm/10 in. at shoulder.

Spanish, Romance language in Italic branch of Indo-European family. Spoken as 1st language in Spain and 18 countries in Central, South America. Developed from Latin, Castilian dialect becoming dominant in early Middle Ages.

Spanish-American War (1898), conflict between US and Spain occasioned by US intervention in Cuban struggle for independence from Spain. Mysterious sinking of US battleship Maine in Havana heightened pro-war sentiments in US. Spanish fleet destroyed in Manila by Dewey; Spanish forces surrendered after defeat at Santiago de Cuba. Treaty of Paris granted Cuba independence under US protection; US acquired Guam, Puerto Rico, Philippines.

Spanish Armada, see ARMADA, SPANISH.

Spanish Civil War, conflict (1936-9) precipitated by military opposition to liberal govt. of Spanish republic (proclaimed 1931). Conservative interests, merged under FRANCO, won early victories over Republican (or loyalist) forces. International non-intervention pact (signed 1936) broken; Germany and Italy supplied arms to Franco's Insurgents, USSR supported Republicans. Triumph by Insurgents

(Madrid captured, Mar. 1939) led to estab. of Franco's dictatorship.

Spanish fly, *see* BLISTER BEETLE.

Spanish Guinea, *see* EQUATORIAL GUINEA.

Spanish Inquisition, *see* INQUISITION; TORQUEMADA.

Spanish Sahara, former overseas prov. of Spain, in NW Africa. Area 266,000 sq km (102,700 sq mi); pop. 128,000; cap. El-Aaiún. Mostly desert, pop. largely nomadic; livestock, dates, fishing, rich phosphate deposits. Spanish colony from 1884, became prov. 1958. In 1975, Spain withdrew, leaving Morocco and Mauritania in joint control until future is decided; territ. also claimed by Algeria. Interim name is Western Sahara.

Spanish Succession, War of the (1701-14), European conflict over succession to Spanish throne; claimants were Philip, grandson of Louis XIV, and Charles, son of Emperor Leopold I of Austria. England, Holland and Austria, seeking to prevent potential union of Spain and France, allied against France, Spain and Bavaria. Hostilities ended by treaties of Utrecht (1713), Rastaat (1714); Philip recognized as king (Philip· V).

Spark, Muriel Sarah (1918-), Scottish novelist. Known for *The Ballad of Peckham Rye* (1960), *The Prime of Miss Jean Brodie* (1961).

sparking plug or **spark plug,** device used in internal combustion engine to ignite fuel-air mixture. Consists of 2 electrodes with a gap of *c* 0.38 mm–1.02 mm between them. When a high voltage is impressed on electrodes a spark is discharged.

sparrow, one of various small short-beaked seed-eating birds, esp. of genus *Passer*. House sparrow, *P. domesticus*, has streaked brown and grey plumage; native of N Europe and Asia, introduced into North America, Australia, New Zealand.

sparrow hawk, *Accipiter nisus,* small Old World hawk with short rounded wings and long tail. Male has slate-grey upper parts, red-brown barred lower parts. American sparrow hawk, *Falco sparverius,* is a falcon.

Sparta (*Spárti*), town of Greece, in SC Peloponnese, on R. Eurotas. Pop. 10,000. Founded 1834; fruit,· olive trade. Nearby are ruins of ancient Sparta (*Lacedaemon*) militaristic city state at zenith after defeating Athens in Peloponnesian War. Defeated by Thebes (371 BC), Philip II of Macedon.

Spartacists, radical German Socialist group, founded 1916. Led by Karl Liebknecht and Rosa Luxemburg. Became (1918) German Communist Party. Uprising (Jan. 1919) ruthlessly suppressed by Berlin govt.

Spartacus (d. 71 BC), Roman gladiator, b. Thrace. Organized revolt of escaped slaves in S Italy and defeated 2 Roman armies sent against him. Defeated and killed in battle with Crassus. Many of his followers were crucified along Rome-Capua road.

spastic paralysis, condition in which certain muscles are kept permanently taut, causing loss of voluntary movement and spasms of affected muscles. Congenital form (cerebral palsy) is caused by brain damage and may be accompanied by mental retardation.

species, in biology, *see* CLASSIFICATION.

specific gravity, ratio of material's density to density of water at 4°C.

specific heat, in physics, quantity of heat required to raise the temperature of unit mass of a substance by one degree. Expressed in calories per gm per °C.

spectacles, lenses worn to correct or help defective vision. Concave lenses correct short sight (myopia), convex lenses long sight (hypermetropia), cylindrical lenses astigmatism. Earliest European spectacles date from 13th cent.

spectroscope, optical instrument designed to study spectrum of light. Light is introduced through a slit, its rays made parallel by a collimator, dispersed by a prism or grating, and viewed through a telescope eyepiece. Used to determine chemical composition of substances by examination of spectral lines in light emitted or absorbed, and in astronomy to determine physical and chemical nature of stars. The spectral lines of a substance are fundamental characteristics of it and thus a means of identification.

spectrum, in physics, originally name for coloured bands produced by white light passing through a prism or diffraction grating. Colours seen are red (longest wavelength), orange, yellow, green, blue and violet (shortest wavelength). Now refers to resolution of any electromagnetic radiation into its constituent wavelengths.

Spee, Maximilian, Graf von (1861-1914), German naval officer. Defeated Cradock at Coronel (Nov. 1914) but lost and was drowned at battle of Falkland Isls. (Dec. 1914).

speedwell, *see* VERONICA.

Speer, Albert (1905-), German architect, Nazi leader. Official architect to Nazi party. Became minister of armaments (1942); organized major indust. output in last months of war. Pleaded guilty to war crimes (1946); sentenced to 20 years' imprisonment.

Speke, John Hanning (1827-64), English soldier, explorer. Accompanied R.F. Burton on 2 African expeditions (1854, 1857-9). Discovered L. Victoria (1858), returning (1862) to confirm it as source of Nile.

Spence, Sir Basil Urwin (1907-76), Scottish architect. Designed Coventry Cathedral, buildings for Sussex Univ., Knightsbridge Cavalry Barracks.

Spencer, Herbert (1820-1903), English philosopher. Stated theory of evolution was of universal application, that all change within any structure was of increasing differentiation and, at same time, of increasing integration. Works incl. *The Principles of Psychology* (1855), *First Principles* (1862).

Spencer, Sir Stanley (1891-1959), English painter. Painted religious scenes set in familiar environment of his native village; work, incl. several interpretations of Resurrection theme.

Spencer Gulf, inlet of Indian Ocean, South Australia, between Eyre and Yorke penins. Ports incl. Port Augusta, Port Pirie, Whyalla.

Spender, Stephen Harold (1909-), English poet, critic. Associated with Auden, Day-Lewis in 1930s. Later poems indicate more liberal than left-wing attitudes. *Collected Poems* pub. 1955.

Spengler, Oswald (1880-1936), German philosopher, historian. Author of *The Decline of the West* (1922); postulated existence of life cycles through which all human cultures pass. Held that Western civilization was in unavoidable decline.

Spenser, Edmund (*c* 1552-99), English poet. Works incl. *Amoretti* (1595) on his courtship, *Epithalamion* (1595) on his marriage, *The Shepheardes Calender* (1579). Developed Spenserian stanza for masterpiece, *The Faerie Queene* (1590, 1596), an allegorical epic of moral development, praising Elizabeth I.

sperm or **spermatozoon**, in biology, male gamete or reproductive cell. When female ovum is fertilized by sperm, union develops into new member of same species.

spermaceti, white wax-like substance solidifying from colourless oil in head of sperm whale; significance unknown, but may assist in diving. Used in making cosmetics, candles, *etc*.

Spermatophyta, in botany, term for seed-bearing plants. Subdivided into GYMNOSPERM and ANGIOSPERM.

sperm whale or **cachalot**, *Physeter catodon*, large whale of worldwide distribution, much hunted by whalers. Enormous head, one cavity of which contains SPERMACETI oil; teeth in lower jaw. Feeds on molluscs; reaches lengths of 18.3 m/60 ft.

Spey, river of NE Scotland, flows 172 km (107 mi) from Highland region to Moray Firth at Spey Bay. Salmon fishing.

Spezia, La, city of Liguria, NW Italy, on Ligurian Sea. Cap. of La Spezia prov. Pop. 128,000. Port, oil refining; main Italian naval base. Shelley drowned nearby. Badly damaged in WWII.

sphagnum, bog moss or **peat moss**, genus of soft mosses. Found mainly on surface of bogs. Used for potting and packing plants and in absorbent dressings.

sphinx, in ancient Egyptian art, sculptural representation of recumbent lion with head of man, ram or hawk. Often taken to symbolize pharaoh as descendant of Ra. Many built, most famous near Giza, Egypt. In Greek myth, destructive agent of gods, represented as winged woman with body of lion or dog. Either killed itself or was slain by Oedipus after he answered its riddle.

spice, aromatic vegetable product, *eg* pepper, ginger, nutmeg, cinnamon, clove, used in cookery to season or flavour food.

Spice Islands, *see* MOLUCCAS.

spider, any of order Araneida of arachnids. Abdomen bears 2 or more pairs of spinnerets; silk thread produced used for web-making and to enclose cocoons. Most species possess poison glands for killing prey; venom of black widow and Australian funnel-web is dangerous to man.

spider crab, sea crab of Majidae family with triangular body and long thin legs. *Macrocheira kaempferi*, found off Japan, is largest crustacean; leg span of *c* 2.4 m/8 ft.

spider monkey, long-legged South American monkey with long prehensile tail, genus *Ateles*. Diet of fruit. Species incl. black-faced spider monkey, *A. ater*.

spin, in nuclear physics, intrinsic angular momentum of an elementary particle or photon, produced by rotation about its own axis. Quantum considerations restrict the value of spin.

spina bifida, congenital defect of the vertebrae in which one or more of the vertebral arches does not develop. Resulting damage to spinal cord causes varying amounts of paralysis. Treated by immediate surgery.

spinach, *Spinacia oleracea*, widely cultivated annual plant, native to SW Asia. Dark-green edible leaves are rich in iron and eaten cooked as vegetable.

spinal column, see VERTEBRA.

spinal cord, portion of central nervous system extending from brain and enclosed in spinal canal formed by vertebral arches. Consists of outer layer of white matter (nerve fibres), inner layer of grey matter (nerve cells) and central canal containing cerebrospinal fluid. Spinal nerves (31 pairs) connected to it convey sensory and motor impulses to and from brain.

spinet, small harpsichord, popular in 17th cent. Usually triangular in shape, with strings at an angle of 45° to keyboard. Replaced rectangular virginals, in which strings are parallel to keyboard.

spinning, process of drawing out and twisting fibre into continuous thread. Simplest tools used were distaff, a rod on which fibre was wrapped, and spindle, a weighted rod on which fibre drawn from distaff was twisted. Later developments incl. spinning wheel, which revolved spindle, often by means of a treadle. In 18th cent. spinning was mechanized by efforts of Hargreaves, Crompton, Arkwright, etc.

Spínola, António Sebastião Ribeiro de (1910-), Portuguese soldier, political leader. Wrote influential *Portugal and the Future* (1974), asserting that Portugal could not win military victory against rebels in its African colonies. Led coup which overthrew Caetano govt. (April, 1974). Headed provisional govt., went into exile 1975.

Spinoza, Benedict or **Baruch** (1632-77), Dutch philosopher. Influenced by Descartes, developed system chiefly contained in *Ethics* (1677), in which all life is embraced by infinite God (or Nature). Excommunicated (1656) from native Jewish sect for unorthodoxy of thought.

spiny anteater, see ECHIDNA.

spiraea, genus of herbs of rose family found in temperate regions. Dense clusters of small pink or white flowers. Species incl. European willow spirea, *Spiraea salicifolia*.

spiral galaxy, galaxy with spiral structure; 2 or more spiral arms, composed mainly of dust, gas and relatively young stars, emerge from central nucleus and swirl round it. Milky Way is spiral galaxy.

spire, steeply pointed tapering structure topping a tower. First examples appeared in Romanesque architecture of 12th cent.; elaborate spires were developed in Gothic period in England, Germany and France.

spiritual, religious folk song of American Negroes. Created by black singers and choirs in 19th cent.

spiritualism, popularly, belief and practice of communication with spirits of the dead. Common to many cultures, *eg* Haiti, North American Indians. Became popular in West during 19th cent., originally in US. Practice usually involves a medium, who (sometimes in trance) acts as intermediary between living and dead, at meeting called séance. Physical phenomena incl. unexplained noises, movement of objects, levitation, *etc*.

Spithead, anchorage in the SOLENT, off Portsmouth, S England. Scene of fleet mutiny (1797).

Spitsbergen (*Svalbard*), isl. group of Norway, in Arctic Ocean. Area *c* 62,150 sq km (24,000 sq mi); main town Longyearbyen. Ceded to Norway 1920. Coalfields shared with USSR. Hist. starting point for polar expeditions, whaling station.

spittle bug, see FROGHOPPER.

Spitz, Mark (1950-), American swimmer. Won record 7 Olympic gold medals (1972) with victories in 100m and 200m freestyle and butterfly events, and 3 relays.

spleen, large lymphatic organ on left hand side of abdominal cavity. Destroys old red blood cells and forms certain white cells; acts as reserve blood supply in emergencies. Removable without risk.

Split (Ital. *Spalato*), town of Croatia, W Yugoslavia, on Adriatic Sea. Pop. 152,000. Port, fishing, resort. Estab. 7th cent. by refugees from nearby Salona. Ruled by Venice from 1420, by Austria 1815-1918. Has cathe-

dral, baptistery, remains of Roman palace.

Spock, Benjamin McLane (1903-), American pediatrician. Best-known for enormously popular *The Common Sense Book of Baby and Child Care* (1945), which influenced parents worldwide.

Spode, Josiah (1754-1827), English potter. Took over pottery firm founded (1770) by his father (of same name) at Stoke-on-Trent. Originated type of bone china, bearing his name, which became standard in England.

Spohr, Ludwig (1784-1859), German composer, violinist, conductor. Wrote over 15 violin concertos and many operas, symphonies now seldom performed. His nonet remains popular. One of 1st conductors to use a baton.

spoils system, practice developed in US of rewarding loyal supporters by appointing them to political offices. First used on large scale by President Jackson. Corruption incurred by system led to civil service reform in late 19th cent.

Spoleto (anc. *Spoletium*), town of Umbria, C Italy. Pop. 40,000. Agric. market, textiles. Cap. of medieval duchy, passed to Papal States (13th cent.). Roman remains; cathedral (12th cent.).

sponge, any of Porifera phylum of sessile aquatic animals. Body-wall usually supported by skeleton of either lime, silica or spongin (used in bath sponges). Sponge feeds by drawing water through pores on body surface.

spontaneous combustion, sudden burning of substance of low ignition point, caused by heat produced through slow oxidation of substance.

spoonbill, wading bird with beak flattened and spoon-shaped at tip, genus *Platalea*. Species incl. roseate spoonbill, *P. ajaja*, of Florida and South America.

Spooner, William Archibald (1844-1930), British scholar. Best known for tendency to transpose initial consonants of adjacent words (*eg* 'town drain' for 'down train') from which term 'spoonerism' was coined.

Sporades, isls. of Greece, in Aegean Sea. N Sporades, NE of Euboea, incl. Skyros. S Sporades, or Dodecanese, incl. Sámos, Ikaria.

spore, in botany, non-sexual reproductive cell produced by flowerless plants. Capable of giving rise to new plant which may or may not resemble parent.

sprat, *Sprattus sprattus*, small European food fish of herring family. Pale green back with silver underside; lives in large coastal shoals, exploited commercially.

spring, natural outlet at ground surface for accumulated underground water. Where WATER TABLE intersects sloping ground surface, 'spring line' occurs; springs also common in limestone areas. Mineral springs may contain sulphur, salt, *etc*; hot springs, *eg* GEYSERS, occur mainly in volcanic areas.

springbok, *Antidorcas marsupialis*, antelope of S Africa, noted for high, stiff-legged leaps in air.

Springfield, cap. of Illinoïs, US; on Sangamon R. Pop. 92,000. Agric. machinery mfg., food products. Home, burial place of Abraham Lincoln.

Springfield, town of SW Massachusetts, US; on Connecticut R. Pop. 164,000. Plastics, chemical mfg.; printing and publishing industs. US armoury here (1794-1966) developed Springfield army rifle.

spruce, any of genus *Picea* of evergreen trees of N temperate zones. Cultivated as ornamentals and for straight-grained, lightweight timber. Varieties incl. Norway spruce, *P. abies*, white spruce, *P. glauca*, Colorado spruce, *P. pungens*. Most species yield pulp for paper-making.

sputnik, *see* SATELLITE.

squash, *see* PUMPKIN.

squash rackets, game similar to RACKETS, played in 4-walled court, normally by 2 people. Originated at Harrow School, England, before 1850.

squid, marine cephalopod mollusc with torpedo-shaped body. Ten tentacles, two being much longer than others, with suckers at ends. Giant squid, genus *Architeuthis*, reaches lengths (incl. tentacles) of 15 m/50 ft.

squill, any of genera *Scilla* and *Urginea* of lily family. Garden varieties incl. Siberian squill, *S. sibirica*. Sea onion, *U. maritima*, yields extract from bulbs used as diuretic and rat poison.

squint, disorder of muscles of eye in which both eyes cannot be focused on same point at same time. Concomitant squint, affecting both eyes equally, is due to muscle imbalance. Treatment incl. corrective glasses and exercise of eye muscles.

squirrel, small, usually arboreal, rodent of Sciuridae family. Species incl. European red squirrel, *Sciurus vulgaris*, which hides food (acorns, nuts) in ground; North American grey squirrel, *S. carolinensis*, now common in Europe.

Sri Lanka, isl. republic, off SE coast of India; member of British Commonwealth. Area 65,600 sq km (25,300 sq mi); pop. 14,270,000; cap. Colombo. Chief language: Sinhalese. Religion: Buddhism. Mountainous centre with broad coastal plain. Agric. economy (rice, rubber, coconuts, tea). Under Dutch control from mid 17th cent. to late 18th cent; annexed by British (1815). Independent as Ceylon (1948), republic (1956); native name adopted in 1972.

Srinagar, summer cap. of Jammu and Kashmir, N India. Pop. 404,000. Resort on R. Jhelum. Many canals and wooden bridges linking different parts of town.

SS, *see* BLACKSHIRTS.

Staël, Madame de, née [Anne Louise] Germaine Necker (1766-1817), French woman of letters, b. Switzerland. Introduced German Romanticism into France in *De l'Allemagne* (1810). Known for influential salons incl. Chateaubriand, Constant. Also wrote novels, *eg Delphine* (1802).

Staël, Nicolas de (1914-55), French painter, b. Russia. Influenced by impressionism, fauvism, developed individual abstract style using bars of thick paint. Works incl. *Marathon* (1948).

Staffordshire, county of WC England. Area 2716 sq km (1049 sq mi); pop. 985,000. POTTERIES in N; BLACK COUNTRY in S; R. Trent plain in C. Large coalfields; iron ore, clay also extracted. Co. town Stafford, on R. Sow. Pop. 55,000. Footwear mfg.

stag beetle, any of Lucanidae family of beetles with branched antler-like mandibles. Larvae feed on rotting wood. *Lucanus cervus* is large European species.

stagecoach, carriage used from 17th to early 19th cent. for conveyance of passengers, mail, luggage. Drawn by 4 to 6 horses, changed at staging points. Declined after building of railways.

stained glass, coloured glass used in making windows. Designs or figures are made from panes of many colours held together by lead strips which themselves form part of design. Art is of Byzantine origin; introduced into W Europe in 11th cent., best work was executed in medieval Gothic cathedrals, *eg* Chartres, Canterbury and York.

stalactite, icicle-shaped deposit hanging from ceiling of cave in limestone area. Consists mainly of calcium carbonate, transported to cave in water solution and left behind as water drips from ceiling to floor. Outstanding examples found *eg* in Carlsbad Caverns, New Mexico, US. Also *see* STALAGMITE.

stalagmite, icicle-shaped deposit rising from floor of cave in limestone area. Consists mainly of calcium carbonate, transported to cave in water solution and left behind as water drips onto floor from ceiling. Also *see* STALACTITE.

Stalin, Joseph, orig. Joseph Vissarionovich Dzhugashvili (1879-1953), Soviet political leader. Returned (1917) from exile during Russian Revolution. Elected Communist Party general secretary·

(1922); shared leadership after Lenin's death (1924) until 1927, when he engineered removal of TROTSKY and Zinoviev. Consolidated power through series of purges in 1930s, becoming· premier 1941. Initiated indust. and agric. collectivization with Five Year Plans. Assumed military leadership after Germany· invaded USSR (1941). Expanded Soviet power in E Europe in meetings with other Allied leaders and by aggressive post-war foreign policy. His tyrannical methods and personality cult were denounced by Khrushchev (1956).

Stalinabad, see DUSHANBE.

Stalingrad, see VOLGOGRAD.

Stalinsk, see NOVOKUZNETSK.

stamen, male organ of flower. Consists of pollen-bearing anther on filament.

Stamitz, Johann (1717-57), German musician, composer, b. Bohemia. Became musical director at court of Mannheim (1745); largely responsible for reputation of Mannheim orchestra. His numerous symphonies helped estab. classical form of symphony.

Stamp Act, measure passed by British Parliament (1765), requiring all legal documents in American colonies to bear a revenue stamp. Violently opposed in America on grounds that Parliament did not have right to impose taxation without corresponding representation. Act repealed 1766.

Stanford, Sir Charles Villiers (1852-1924), Irish composer. One of leaders of 'English musical renaissance'. Work, incl. symphonies, chamber and choral music, often influenced by Irish folk song. Taught Vaughan Williams, Arthur Bliss.

Stanhope, Charles Stanhope, 3rd Earl of (1753-1816), English statesman, inventor. A radical in Parliament, supported French Revolution and parliamentary reform. Invented a printing press and lens. His daughter, **Lady Hester Lucy Stanhope** (1776-1839), was Pitt's private secretary. Settled in Lebanon (1810); gained reputation as prophetess with local tribesmen.

Stanislaus I, surname Leszczynski (1677-1766), king of Poland (1704-9, 1733-5). First elected king with aid of Charles XII of Sweden, on whose defeat at Poltava, Stanislaus lost throne to Augustus II. Return from exile as king precipitated War of POLISH SUCCESSION; defeated, renounced rights to throne. Awarded duchy of Lorraine.

Stanislaus II [Augustus Poniatowski] (1732-98), king of Poland (1764-95). Elected king through Russian influence, which remained strong in Poland throughout his reign. Series of 3 partitions of Poland by Prussia, Russia and Austria (1772, 1793, 1795) led to end of country's separate existence.

Stanislavsky, Konstantin, pseud. of Konstantin Sergeyevich Alekseyev (1863-1938),· Russian actor, producer, dramatic theorist. With Nemirovich-Danchenko, founded (1898) Moscow Art Theatre, where he implemented influential 'method' theory of production, sometimes called 'Stanislavsky system'.

Stanley, Edward George Geoffrey Smith, see DERBY, 14TH EARL OF.

Stanley, Sir Henry Morton, adopted name of John Rowlands (1841-1904), British explorer and journalist, b. Wales. Sent by New York *Herald* to Africa (1871) to find David LIVINGSTONE. In service of Belgium, explored and organized Congo Free State (1879-84).

Stanley Falls, series of cataracts on R. Lualaba, NE Zaïre. Extends c 88 km (55 mi) between Ubundi and Kisangani; river drops c 60 m (200 ft). Interrupts navigation; towns linked by railway. Recently renamed Boyoma Falls.

Stanleyville, see KISANGANI, Zaïre.

staphylococcus, any of the genus *Staphylococcus* of spherical bacteria, usually occurring in clusters. *S. aureus* causes boils, abscesses and infection in wounds. Can cause food poisoning by release of toxins.

star, self-luminous gaseous body similar to the Sun, whose energy is derived from thermonuclear reactions which convert hydrogen into helium. Nearest star, other than Sun, is Proxima Centauri, c 4 light years away. Stars are grouped into galaxies, those visible from Earth being part of Milky Way. They appear to be fixed, but in fact are in motion about the galaxy. See STELLAR EVOLUTION.

Stara-Zagora, city of C Bulgaria. Pop. 118,000. Railway jct., trade centre. Food processing, fertilizers; textiles, attar of roses. Turkish Eski-Zagora until ceded to Bulgaria in 1877.

starch, polymeric carbohydrate derived from glucose, found in grain, potatoes, rice, *etc.* Produced in plants by photosynthesis, it serves as food store. Starch in plants is converted into glucose by animals and is major energy source. Used as stiffener in laundering and in adhesives, foods, *etc.*

Star Chamber, room in king of England's palace, Westminster, so named for stars on ceiling. Name used from 15th cent. for tribunal comprising king's councillors, judges, which met there. Important under Tudors as regular part of law enforcement, became hated when Stuarts used it to enforce unpopular policies, esp. religious. Abolished (1641) by Long Parliament.

starfish, any of class Asteroidea of echinoderms with 5 or more arms radiating from central disc. Skin covered with calcareous plates and spines; moves by tube-feet on underside of arms. Species incl. common *Asterias rubens*, predator of oysters and mussels.

starling, *Sturnus vulgaris,* gregarious European bird with dark metallic plumage. Roosts in woods and city buildings, where it is often regarded as a pest. Introduced into North America, now common in E US.

star-of-Bethlehem, *Ornithogalum umbellatum,* bulbous plant of lily family. Native to Mediterranean region but widely cultivated. Narrow leaves, white star-shaped flowers with green markings.

Star-spangled Banner, national anthem of US from 1931. Words written by Francis Scott Key, after witnessing British assault of Fort McHenry (1814). Music by John Stafford Smith, adapted from an English song.

Staten Island, see NEW YORK CITY.

States-General, see ESTATES-GENERAL.

states' rights, constitutional doctrine advocated by exponents of decentralized govt. in US. Arose over interpretation of 10th Amendment of Constitution. Manifested in KENTUCKY AND VIRGINIA RESOLUTIONS, NULLIFICATION crisis and ultimately in secession of Southern states leading to Civil War (1861-5). Invoked in 20th cent. by states opposed to civil rights programme.

static electricity, electric charge at rest, usually produced by friction or electrostatic induction.

statics, in physics and engineering, branch of mechanics dealing with bodies and forces at rest or in equilibrium.

statistics, science of collecting, classifying and interpreting numerical facts and data. Used as method of analysis in sciences, social science, business, etc. Concerned both with description of actual events and predictions of likelihood of an event occurring.

statute, law passed by legislature and formally placed on record. In UK, statutes make up written law, distinct from COMMON LAW; in Europe, almost all law is statutory. Term used by international jurists to denote whole body of law of a state.

Stavanger, town of SW Norway, on Stavanger Fjord. Pop. 81,000. Port, fishing, shipbuilding, offshore oil service indust. Founded 8th cent., cathedral (12th cent.).

Stavisky affair (1934), French financial and political scandal. Serge Alexander Stavisky (1886-1934), floated fraudulent companies, sold forged bonds, gained control of several newspapers, became associate of public figures. When exposed (1933), he fled and was either shot by police or committed suicide. Scandal caused fall of govt. and riots (Feb. 1934).

steady-state theory, in cosmology, theory that universe is in steady state. Although the universe is expanding, matter is continuously created and so no overall change can be detected. In this theory, universe has no beginning or end. Rival theory is BIG-BANG THEORY.

steam engine, engine using steam under pressure to supply mechanical energy. When water is converted to steam, it expands c1600 times, producing force capable of mechanical work either on piston or in TURBINE. Experiments first recorded (c130 BC) by Hero of Alexandria. James Watt produced 1st practical version (1769) using separate condenser and valves allowing steam to exert force on piston in both directions.

stearic acid, colourless wax-like fatty acid, found in animal and vegetable fats. Used in manufacture of soap, candles, cosmetics and medicine.

steel, iron containing up to 1.5% carbon. Its properties can be varied by changes in quantity of carbon and other metals present and by heat treatment. Manufactured by Bessemer and open-hearth processes, and more recently in oxygen-blowing or electric furnaces. Corrosion-resistant stainless steel contains up to 25% chromium.

Steele, Sir Richard (1672-1729), English author, b. Ireland. Founded *The Tatler* (1709) and, with Ad-

DISON, *The Spectator* (1711-12), writing witty essays, creating character of Sir Roger de Coverley. Plays incl. *The Conscious Lovers* (1722). Became (1714) manager of Drury Lane Theatre.

Steen, Jan (1626-79), Dutch painter. Known for his depiction of peasant life and scenes of merriment in taverns and homes. Works incl. *The Game of Skittles*.

Steer, Philip Wilson (1860-1942), English painter. Founder member of NEW ENGLISH ART CLUB; landscape paintings in tradition of Constable, Turner, influenced by impressionists. Figure paintings show similar detachment.

stegosaurus, genus of extinct vegetarian dinosaurs. Had small head, double row of defensive bony plates along back, spikes on tail. Length c 9 m (30 ft). Lived during Jurassic period.

Stein, Gertrude (1874-1946), American author, settled in Paris (1903). Attempted to create 'cubist' literature, eg *Tender Buttons* (1914). Best known for *Autobiography of Alice B. Toklas* (1933). Leader of American expatriate 'lost generation' in Paris.

Stein, Heinrich Friedrich Karl, Freiherr vom (1757-1831), Prussian statesman. Premier (1807-8), abolished serfdom and opened up occupations to all classes; dismissed on pressure from Napoleon. Helped form Russian alliance against Napoleon (1813).

Steinbeck, John Ernst (1902-68), American author. Concerned with struggle of poor within dehumanized society. Works incl. short stories, eg *The Red Pony*

(1937), novels *Of Mice and Men* (1937), *The Grapes of Wrath* (1939), *Cannery Row* (1944), *East of Eden* (1952), screenplays. Nobel Prize for Literature (1962).

Steiner, Rudolf (1861-1925), German occultist, b. Austria. Originally leading theosophist, subsequently developed own system of 'anthroposophy' attempting to explain world through nature of man. Works incl. *Philosophy of Spiritual Activity* (1922). Schools named after him follow his theories.

stellar evolution, description of life-history of a star. Stars are believed to condense from clouds of gas, mainly hydrogen, which contract under internal gravitational forces. Thermonuclear reactions take place and create energy by fusion of hydrogen into helium; as hydrogen is used up, star expands to become red giant. It then contracts, its final state depending on its size.

Stendhal, pseud. of Marie Henri Beyle (1783-1842), French novelist. Wrote novels treating melodramatic subjects with intense realism, eg *Le rouge et le noir* (1830), *La Chartreuse de Parme* (1839). Also wrote criticism, eg *Racine et Shakespeare* (1823) dealing with Classicism and Romanticism.

sten gun, light sub-machine gun, working on recoil principle. Used as close-range infantry weapon in WWII.

Stephen, St (d. c AD 36), one of seven deacons of early Church. Stoned to death at Jerusalem, becoming 1st Christian martyr.

Stephen [I], St (c 975-1038), king of Hungary (1001-38). His coronation with crown sent to him by the pope marks beginning of Hungarian kingdom. Continued his father's policy of converting Magyars to Christianity.

Stephen (c 1097-1154), king of England (1135-54). Grandson of William I, usurped throne from Henry I's daughter, MATILDA, whose invasion (1130) of England to regain throne began long period of civil strife. She reigned briefly after Stephen's capture (1141) but regained throne on release. After death of his son (1153), forced to name Matilda's son, Henry II, as successor.

Stephen, Sir Leslie (1832-1904), English man of letters. First editor of *Dictionary of National Biography* from 1882. Wrote studies of rationalist thinkers, eg *English Thought in the Eighteenth Century* (1876-81), biogs. incl. *Pope* (1880), *Swift* (1882). Father of Virginia Woolf. Also noted alpinist.

Stephens, James (1882-1950), Irish author. Helped found *Irish Review* (1911). Works incl. poetry, eg *Insurrections* (1909), prose fantasy *The Crock of Gold* (1912), mythological romances, eg *Deirdre* (1923).

Stephenson, George (1781-1848), English engineer. Built his 1st locomotive (1814) and 1st locomotive to use steam blast (1815). His famous *Rocket* (1829) was used for Liverpool-Manchester railway. Devised a type of miner's safety lamp.

Stepney, *see* TOWER HAMLETS, England.

steppe, level, treeless grasslands extending from SE Europe to C Asiatic USSR. Used for grazing, extensive wheat growing. Term also applied to similar mid-latitude grasslands in other continents and to semi-arid areas bordering hot deserts.

stereochemistry, branch of chemistry dealing with arrangement in 3-dimensional space of the atoms which make up a molecule, and the effect of the arrangement on physical and chemical properties of molecule.

stereophonic sound, sound recorded simultaneously by microphones at various distances from sound source. In playback sound emanates from several speakers situated in roughly similar relative positions as original microphones. Gives impression of depth of original sound. Quadrophonic sound uses 4 channels of sound.

sterility, inability to reproduce sexually. Causes in humans incl. glandular imbalance, disease and psychological problems.

sterilization, method of rendering substances free from contamination by bacteria. Immersion in boiling water or alcohol solution, or exposure to radiation are methods used. Term also used for rendering of sexual organs incapable of reproduction; in male, sealing of vas deferens is used, in female, blocking of Fallopian tubes.

Stern, Otto (1888-1969), American physicist, b. Germany. Awarded Nobel Prize for Physics (1943) for developing molecular beam to measure magnetic properties of atom and atomic nuclei.

Sterne, Laurence (1713-68), English author, b. Ireland. Known for idiosyncratic treatment of thought, feeling, time, as in *The Life* and *Opinions of Tristram Shandy* (1759-67). *A Sentimental Journey* (1768) burlesques the cult of sentiment.

steroids, group of organic compounds with 4 carbon rings incl. vitamin D, bile acids, male and female sex hormones, adrenal cortex hormones.

stethoscope, instrument used in medicine to detect sounds made by heart and lungs. Consists of chest piece connected by rubber tubes to 2 ear pieces. Devised (1816) by Laënnec to aid diagnosis.

Stettin, *see* SZCZECIN, Poland.

Stevenage, urban dist. of Hertfordshire, SC England. Pop. 67,000. First 'new town'; furniture mfg.

Stevens, John (1749-1838), American inventor. Helped estab. 1st US patent laws. Built (1806-8) *Phoenix* steamboat, which later shuttled between Philadelphia and Trenton. Developed locomotive after receiving 1st US railroad charter. His son, **Robert Livingston Stevens** (1787-1856), improved design and building of steamboats, railway track. Another son, **Edwin Augustus Stevens** (1795-1868), designed Stevens plough. Built ironclad warships.

Stevens, Wallace (1879-1955), American poet. Known for stylish, philosophically speculative verse, eg *Harmonium* (1923), *The Man with the Blue Guitar* (1937), *Collected Poems* (1954). Also wrote prose essays on aesthetics, *The Necessary Angel* (1951).

Stevenson, Adlai Ewing (1900-65), American politician. Governor of Illinois (1949-53). Defeated by Eisenhower as Democractic presidential candidate (1952, 1956). Ambassador to the UN (1961-5).

Stevenson, Robert Louis [Balfour] (1850-94), Scottish author. Works incl. travel books, eg *Travels with a Donkey in the Cévennes* (1879), popular novels incl. *Treasure Island* (1883), *Kidnapped* (1886), *The Strange Case of Dr Jekyll and Mr Hyde* (1886), poetry in *A Child's Garden of Verses* (1885). Suffered from tuberculosis, spent last years in Samoa.

Stewart, House of, *see* STUART, HOUSE OF.

Stewart, James (1908-), American film actor. Known for drawl; in star roles from 1935. Films incl. *Destry Rides Again* (1939), *Broken Arrow* (1950), *Anatomy of a Murder* (1959).

Stewart, John ('Jackie') (1939-), Scottish motor racing driver. Won 27 world championship Grand Prix victories, taking world championship 3 times. Retired 1973.

Stewart Island or **Rakiura,** volcanic isl. of S New Zealand, separated from . South Isl. by Foveaux Str. Area 1375 sq km (670 sq mi); largely mountainous. Summer resort; fishing, esp. for oysters.

stick insect, insect of Phasmidae family, commonest in tropical forests. Elongated wingless body resembles twig and matches surroundings. Species incl. North American walking stick, *Diapheromera femorata*.

stickleback, any of Gasterosteidae family of small spiny-backed fish; found in fresh and salt water of N hemisphere. Species incl. three-spined stickleback, *Gasterosteus* *aculeatus*; male builds nest for eggs and guards young.

Stieglitz, Alfred (1864-1946), American photographer. Opened (1905) his '291' gallery in New York to exhibit photography as a fine art; made innovations in methods of photography. Helped introduce work of European artists to US by exhibitions at his gallery.

Stijl, De, title of Dutch magazine founded (1917) by MONDRIAN and van Doesberg; also refers to group of contributing artists, architects, designers. Magazine propounded ideas of neo-plasticism, expanding it to aesthetic of purely functional design based on regular shapes without ornament. Influenced BAUHAUS, and much of modern design.

stilt, wading bird of Recurvirostridae family, mainly inhabiting marshes. Black-winged stilt, *Himantopus himantopus*, with black upper-parts, white under-parts, is found in S Europe, Africa, Asia. *H. mexicanus* is American species.

sting ray, *see* RAY.

stinkhorn, *Phallus impudicus*, foul-smelling mushroom. Spores borne in jelly and dispersed by insects attracted by smell.

Stinnes, Hugo (1870-1924), German industrialist. Built up huge combine of coal mines, iron and steel foundries, shipping firms. During WWI, he was chief supplier of war materials to German govt.

Stirling, William Alexander, Earl of (1567-1640), Scottish poet, statesman. Wrote love lyrics, *Aurora* (1604), and *Four Monarchicke Tragedies* (1603-7). Member of court of James I. Founded Nova Scotia (1621).

Stirlingshire, former county of C Scotland, now in Central region. Mountainous in S and W incl. Campsies; fertile lowlands. Agric., coalmining; industs. centred in Falkirk, Grangemouth (oil refining). Scene of many battles in independence wars 13th-14th cents. Co. town was Stirling, former royal burgh and market town on R. Forth. Pop. 30,000. Has univ. (1965); royal castle, Wallace Monument (1869).

stoat, *Mustela erminea*, small carnivore, resembling weasel, with short legs, long body. Reddish-brown coat with black-tipped tail. Found in N Europe, C Asia, North America. Northern varieties turn white in winter, being known as ermine (name also applies to white fur).

stock exchange, organized market for trading in stocks and bonds. Only open to members (brokers) who conduct trade for customers on commission. Board of governors stipulate requirements before stock may be listed for trading. Exists in every major financial centre.

Stockhausen, Karlheinz (1928-), German composer. Early exponent of electronic music, eg *Mikrophonie*. Later work has favoured indeterminacy and oriental mysticism. Compositions incl. *Gruppen* for 3 orchestras, *Stimmung* for 6 voices.

Stockholm, cap. of Sweden, between L. Mälaren and Baltic Sea. Pop. 973,000. Admin., commercial centre; port; engineering; food processing; chemicals. Founded 1255; associated with Hanseatic League; built partly on isls. ('Venice of the North'). Staden Isl. has royal palace

(1754). Mainly modern, planned city, incl. Olympic stadium (1912), city hall (1923).

Stockport, bor. of Greater Manchester met. county, NW England. Pop. 140,000. Textiles, esp. cotton; machinery.

stocks, *see* SHARES.

Stockton-on-Tees, *see* TEESSIDE, England.

Stoicism, school of philosophy founded by Zeno of Citium (*c* 315 BC). Exponents incl. Cleanthes, Chrysippus. Saw world as shaping force. Man's true end is active life in harmony with Nature, *ie* God's will. Universal benevolence and justice conceived of as duty, necessitating control of emotion and passions. Followers of stoic doctrine in Rome incl. Seneca, Epictetus, Marcus Aurelius.

Stoke-on-Trent, city of Staffordshire, WC England, on R. Trent. Pop. 265,000. In POTTERIES dist.; formed 1910 from Burslem, Hanley, Fenton, Longton, Tunstall. Pottery indust. (Wedgwood, Minton, Spode); also coalmining, engineering.

Stoker, 'Bram' (Abraham) (1847-1912), Irish author. Known for horror story of vampires, *Dracula* (1897), which became basis of many films.

Stokowski, Leopold Anton Stanislaw (1882-1977), American conductor, b. England. Conducted Philadelphia Orchestra (1913-36). Orchestrated Bach's organ music. Championed cause of modern music.

stomach, *see* ALIMENTARY CANAL, DIGESTION.

Stomatopoda (stomatopods), order of burrowing marine crus-

taceans, sometimes called mantis shrimps. Strong clasping claws on 2nd pair of legs used to crack shells of crabs, *etc.*

Stone Age, period of human culture when stone implements were first used. Usually divided into PALAEOLITHIC, MESOLITHIC and NEOLITHIC periods.

stonefish, highly venomous tropical fish, genus *Synanceja*. Lies motionless in reefs, camouflaged to resemble stone or coral; dorsal fins inject dangerous poison. *S. trachynis* is common Australian species.

Stonehaven, resort town and small port of Grampian region, NE Scotland, former co. town of Kincardineshire. Pop. 5000.

Stonehenge, prehist. monument on Salisbury Plain, England. Outer circle of sarsen stone blocks connected by lintels surrounds horseshoe formation of 5 trilithons, each trilithon consisting of 2 upright stones connected by a lintel. This structure dates from *c* 1500-1400 BC. Within it is ovoid structure, which surrounds Altar Stone. A circle of bluestone menhirs was later set between outer circle and trilithons. Believed to have religious or astronomical significance.

Stone of Destiny, stone on which Scottish kings were crowned at Scone. Seized by Edward I of England on annexation of Scotland (1296); placed under coronation chair in Westminster abbey.

Stopes, Marie Carmichael (1880-1958), British advocate of birth control. With husband H. V. Roe set up first birth control clinic in Holloway, London (1921).

stork, any of Ciconiidae family of large migratory wading birds. Long legs, neck and bill; tree or roof nesting. Species incl. Old World white stork, *Ciconia ciconia*.

Stormont, parliament of Northern Ireland, formerly responsible ·for internal affairs. Estab. 1920 at Stormont, near Belfast. Suspended 1972 in favour of direct rule by UK Parliament during civil strife.

Stornoway, main town of Lewis with Harris, NW Scotland, in Western Isles. Pop. 5000. Fishing port; Harris tweed mfg.

stout, dark beer made from roasted malt. Similar to porter, but containing higher percentage of hops.

Stowe, Harriet Beecher (1811-96), American novelist. Known for anti-slavery novel, *Uncle Tom's Cabin* (1851-2).

Strabane, town of NW Northern Ireland, at confluence of Finn and Mourne rivers. Pop. 9000. Clothing mfg., salmon fishing.

Strabo (*c* 63 BC-*c* AD 24), Greek geographer and historian, b. Asia Minor. Only surviving work is *Geographia*, survey of known world in 17 vols.

Strachey, [Giles] Lytton (1880-1932), English biographer. Member of BLOOMSBURY GROUP. Rejected panegyrics for psychological, critical biogs., *eg Queen Victoria* (1921), *Eminent Victorians* (1918) debunking Dr Arnold, Florence Nightingale, General Gordon.

Stradivari, Antonio or **Antonius Stradivarius** (1644-1737), Italian violin maker. Studied under Niccolò Amati; founded renowned Cremona workshop continued by sons. Often considered greatest of violin makers.

Strafford, Thomas Wentworth, 1st Earl of (1593-1641), English statesman. Became supporter of king's policy in Parliament in response to royal favour (1628). Took efficient, but repressive, measures as lord deputy of Ireland (1632-9), then became Charles I's chief adviser. Impeached by Parliament after unsuccessful campaign against Scots; convicted and beheaded.

Stralsund, town of N East Germany, on Baltic Sea. Pop. 68,000. Port, fishing, shipbuilding. Causeway to Rügen Isl. Founded 1209, former Hanseatic League member. Many medieval buildings.

strangeness, in nuclear physics, property of certain elementary particles of decaying much more slowly than would be expected. These particles are created in strong nuclear interactions but decay by weak interactions.

Stranraer, market town of Dumfries and Galloway region, SW Scotland. Pop. 10,000. Fishing industs. Ferry service to Larne, Northern Ireland.

Strasberg, Lee (1901-), American theatrical director, b. Austria. Co-founder of influential Group Theatre, New York (1931), where he taught Stanislavsky's acting method. Director of Actor's Studio, New York, from 1948.

Strasbourg (Ger. *Strassburg*), city of E France, at confluence of Ill and Rhine, cap. of Bas-Rhin dept. Pop. 254,000. Indust., commercial centre of Alsace; major river port. Metal goods, oil refining; tanning, wine trade, pâté mfg. Free city from 13th cent., taken by Louis XIV (1681); part of Germany (1871-1919). Cathe-

·dral (11th. cent.) with famous astronomical clock; univ. (1567). Site of European Parliament.

Strassburg, Gottfried von, see GOTTFRIED VON STRASSBURG.

Strategic Arms Limitations Talks (SALT), series of discussions between US and Soviet Union to limit size of defence forces of the 2 countries. Accord reached in 1972 agreed to restrict antiballistic missile systems. Second round of talks in 1974 failed to achieve purpose.

Stratford, town of SW Ontario, Canada; on Avon R. Pop. 25,000. Textiles, food processing. Has annual Stratford Shakespearian festival.

Stratford-upon-Avon, mun. bor. of Warwickshire, WC England, on R. Avon. Pop. 19,000. Tourist centre, associations with Shakespeare (birthplace, grave, etc), annual festival at Memorial Theatre (1932).

Strathclyde, region of W Scotland. ·Area 13,849 sq km (5347 sq mi); pop. 2,578,000; chief city Glasgow. Created 1975, incl. former Argyllshire, Ayrshire, · Dunbartonshire, Lanarkshire, Renfrewshire. Site of ancient kingdom.

Strathcona and Mount Royal, Donald Alexander Smith, 1st Baron (1820-1914), Canadian statesman, financier, b. Scotland. Governor of Hudson's Bay Co. (1889-1914). Instrumental in construction of Canadian Pacific Railway (1880-5). High commissioner in UK (1896-1914).

stratification, in geology, arrangement of SEDIMENTARY ROCKS in strata, or layers. Strata are separated by surfaces called 'bedding

planes'. Strata need not be horizontal; angle determined by earth movements.

stratosphere, second lowest layer of Earth's ATMOSPHERE, immediately above troposphere. Begins between c 9.5 km (6 mi) and 16 km (10 mi) above surface. Temperature low, varies little with height (hence sometimes called 'isothermal layer'); no clouds or dust. Incl. ozone layer.

stratus cloud, see CLOUD.

Strauss, Johann (1804-49), Austrian composer, conductor. Toured many countries with his own orchestra playing Viennese waltzes and other dances. Composed *Radetzky March.* His son, Johann Strauss (1825-99), was also a composer and conductor. Wrote over 400 waltzes, such as *Blue Danube, Emperor Waltz,* and operetta *Die Fledermaus* ('The Bat').

Strauss, Richard Georg (1864-1949), German composer. Continued Romantic style of the 19th cent. well into the 20th cent., but with great dramatic and orchestral gifts. Works incl. symphonic poems *Don Juan, Till Eulenspiegel,* operas *Salomé* and *Der Rosenkavalier.*

Stravinsky, Igor Fedorovich (1882-1971), Russian composer. Music is noted for original use of harmony and rhythm. Worked with· Diaghilev early in career, for whom· he wrote ballets *Rite of Spring, The Firebird, Petrouchka.* In 1920s, wrote such works as *Pulcinella* in neo-Classical style. Took up serial music in 1950s, using this method to compose *Requiem Canticles.* Left Russia in 1914, eventually settling in US (1939).

strawberry, any of genus *Fragaria*

of low perennial herbs of rose family. Native to temperate regions. Valued for fruit. *F. vesca* is the wild strawberry; cultivated strawberry is hybrid between *F. virginiana* of E North America and *F. chiloensis* of Chile.

stream of consciousness, in literature, narrative technique of presenting thoughts and images as they occur to a character rather than in logical external sequence. First used in Edouard Dujardin's *Les Lauriers sont coupés* (1887) which influenced Joyce in writing *Ulysses*. Virginia Woolf adapted technique, *eg* in *Mrs Dalloway*.

Streicher, Julius (1885-1946), German political leader of Nazi era. Edited pornographic periodical *Der Stürmer*, vehicle for his fervent anti-Semitism. *Gauleiter* of Franconia from 1933. Hanged after conviction at Nuremberg trials.

streptococcus, any of the genus *Streptococcus* of spherical bacteria, usually occurring in chains. Some species cause infection, *eg* sore throats, and pus formation in wounds. Also release toxins which can destroy blood cells and tissue.

Stresemann, Gustav (1878-1929), German statesman, chancellor (1923). As foreign minister (1923-9), negotiated LOCARNO PACT (1925) with European powers. Obtained French evacuation of Ruhr (1924). Accepted terms of Dawes and Young plans for payment of reparations. Shared Nobel Peace Prize (1926) with Briand.

strike, total withdrawal of labour by employees. Chief weapon of labour unions, first used in UK in early 19th cent., *eg* by Luddites, and in US in late 19th cent., with first national strike (1877) by rail workers. Strike follows union authorization to make it official. Unofficial strike, often local, also known as 'wildcat' strike. Inter-union demarcation disputes led to passing of TAFT-HARTLEY ACT in US (1947). GENERAL STRIKE weapon of European labour, esp. in Russia (1905), UK (1926), France (1968), Italy (1970s).

Strindberg, [Johan] August (1849-1912), Swedish author. Paranoid sensibility reflected in short stories, novels, naturalistic dramas, incl. *The Father* (1887), *Miss Julie* (1888), *Dance of Death* (1901). Later works, *eg A Dream Play* (1901), reflect interest in inner life, mysticism. Autobiog. *Inferno* (1897) recounts an emotional crisis.

string[ed] instruments or **strings,** group of musical instruments which produce sound from vibrating strings. Strings may be plucked (*eg* harp, guitar, lute), stroked: with horsehair bow (*eg* violin, viola) or struck with hammer (*eg* dulcimer, piano, clavichord).

stroboscope, flashing lamp whose frequency can be synchronized with frequency of a rotating object so that the object will appear at rest when illuminated by stroboscope light. Used to study periodic or varying motion.

stroke, see APOPLEXY.

Stromboli, see LIPARI ISLANDS, Italy.

strong nuclear interaction, nuclear force acting between certain elementary particles, *eg* protons, neutrons and certain mesons, when they are less than 10^{-13} cm apart. It lasts *c* 10^{-23} secs and is the strongest known force in nature.

strontium (Sr), metallic element, resembling calcium in its chemical properties; at. no. 38, at. wt. 87.62. Occurs in strontianite and celestine. Compounds impart crimson colour to flames; used in fireworks. Radioactive strontium 90 occurs in fallout; dangerous as it replaces calcium in bones.

structuralism, methodology, originating in linguistics, whose advocates hold that systems, esp. of myths, language, can be regarded as structures which are stable, whole, self-regulating (by a process of exclusion), and which obey internal 'transformation laws' by which whole structure can be deduced from separate elements. Stemming from work of F. de SAUSSURE, developed .. by LÉVI-STRAUSS, CHOMSKY, Roland Barthes, Michel Foucault. Subsequently extended to other areas incl. biology, mathematics.

Struensee, Johann Friedrich, (1737-72), Danish statesman, b. Germany. As physician to the insane Christian VII, became chief minister (1771) and exercised dictatorial powers. Arrested, confessed to adultery with queen consort; beheaded.

Strutt, Jedediah (1726-97), English inventor, manufacturer. Patented (1759) knitting machines for ribbed fabric. Partner of Arkwright.

strychnine, alkaloid drug obtained from seed of nux vomica tree of genus Strychnos. Small doses used as stimulant. Poisonous in large doses; often used as rat-killer.

Stuart or Stewart, House of, ruling family of Scotland (after 1371) and of England (after 1603)

until death of Anne (?1714). James VI of Scotland succeeded to English throne as James I. Two crowns united by Act of Union (1707). Subsequent Hanoverian rule challenged by JACOBITES.

Stuart, Charles Edward, see STUART, JAMES FRANCIS EDWARD.

Stuart, Gilbert (1755-1828), American painter. Best known for his portraits of George Washington, of which exist in 3 main types and numerous versions.

Stuart or Stewart, James Francis Edward (1688- 1766), son of James II, known as the 'Old Pretender'. Claim to English throne frustrated by Act of Settlement (1701) which guaranteed succession to House of Hanover. Accession of 1st Hanoverian, George I, resulted in series of uprisings by his Jacobite supporters; landed briefly in Scotland during 1715 Jacobite rebellion. His son, Charles Edward Stuart (1720-88), called 'Bonnie Prince Charlie' and the 'Young Pretender', led Jacobite rebellion of 1745. Won victory at Prestonpans; reached Derby in march on London. Retreated into Scotland, defeated at Culloden Moor (1746). Fled to France. His brother, Henry Benedict Maria Stuart (1725-1807), was last direct male Stuart heir. Made RC cardinal (1747).

Stuart, John McDouall (1815-66), Scottish explorer, surveyor. Emigrated to Australia (1838), joined Sturt's expedition to C Australia (1844-6). Made 6 expeditions to interior from 1858, finally reached Van Diemen's Gulf (1862).

Stubbs, George (1724-1806), English painter. Studied human and animal anatomy; pub. *Anatomy of the Horse* (1766) for which he made the engravings. Known for his paintings of animals, esp. horses, and sporting scenes.

stucco, plaster or cement, used for surfacing inside or outside walls or for moulded decoration.

sturgeon, fish of Acipenseridae family found in N hemisphere; usually migratory, feeding in sea and breeding in fresh water. Long pointed head, toothless mouth; rows of spiny plates on body. Valued as source of caviare and isinglass.

Sturm und Drang (Ger., = storm and stress), literary movement originating in late 18th cent. Germany. Name from lyric drama *Die Wirrwarr: oder, Sturm und Drang* (1776) by Maximilian Klinger. Emphasized genius of individual as opposed to rationalist ideal of the Enlightenment. Exponents incl. Goethe, Schiller, Lenz. Great influence in development of Romanticism.

Sturt, Charles (1795-1869), English soldier and explorer, b. India. Explored Murray, Darling, Murrumbidgee river area of SE Australia (1828-30). On 3rd expedition (1844-6), accompanied by J. McD. Stuart, journeyed to interior via L. Eyre and Cooper's Creek.

Stuttgart, city of SW West Germany, on R. Neckar, cap. of Baden-Württemberg. Pop. 633,000. Railway jct.; publishing, precision instruments, motor vehicle mfg. Badly damaged in WWII. Birthplace of Hegel.

Stuyvesant, Peter (d. 1672), Dutch colonial administrator. Governed despotically as director-general (1647-64) in Dutch colony of New Netherlands (New York). Lost colony in surprise attack by English (1664).

Stymphalian birds, in Greek myth, man-eating birds with brazen claws and beaks. Lived in woods around L. Stymphalus in Arcadia. Destroyed by Heracles (6th labour).

styrene, colourless aromatic liquid, which polymerizes to polystyrene, a thermoplastic material used as electrical and heat insulator. Styrene is used to make synthetic rubber.

Styria (*Steiermark*), prov. of SE Austria. Area 16,384 sq km (6326 sq mi); cap. Graz. Largely mountainous, main rivers Mur, Enns. Forestry, mining (lignite, iron ore), tourism. S part ceded to Yugoslavia 1919.

Styx, in Greek myth, *see* HADES.

Suárez, Adolfo (1932-), Spanish politician. Following Franco's death, appointed premier of interim govt. by Juan Carlos (1976). Won 1977 election as head of Centre Democratic Union, forming 1st democratically elected govt. since 1930s. Re-elected 1979.

subconscious, in psychology, term used for processes of same kind as conscious processes, but occurring outside individual's awareness. Often used loosely as synonym of UNCONSCIOUS.

sublimation, in chemistry, process of changing a substance directly from solid to vapour, by-passing liquid stage.

sublimation, in psychology, term employed, originally by Freud, for an unconscious transformation of socially or personally unacceptable impulse, esp. sexual, into acceptable expression.

submarine, warship that submerges and travels under water. Usually equipped with torpedoes or missiles. In use since 19th cent. Latest are nuclear-powered.

submersible, small underwater research vessel, with pressurized hull, self-contained air supply, power system *etc*. Bathysphere is lowered from deck of ship by winch. Largely replaced by bathyscaphe (developed 1954 by A. Piccard) which is free-moving, using petrol for buoyancy, iron shot for ballast. In 1960 a bathyscaphe took 2 men to depth of 35,800 ft (10,900 m) in Mariana trench.

subway, *see* UNDERGROUND.

succubus, *see* INCUBUS.

Suchow, city of Kiangsu prov., E China. Pop. 1,500,000. Rail jct; commercial, indust. centre; produces machine tools, textiles. Called Tungshan (1912-45). Civil war battle (1948).

sucker, freshwater fish of Catostomidae family, of North America and E Asia. Mouth adapted for sucking up food.

Suckling, Sir John (1609-42), English poet. Wrote Cavalier love lyrics, *eg* in *Fragmenta Aurea* (1646), plays, *eg* tragedy *Aglaura* (1637), comedy *The Goblins.*

Sucre, cap. of Bolivia, in Chuquisaca dept. Pop. 49,000. Agric. market. Scene of outbreak of South American independence revolt (1809). Founded 1538. Has cathedral, archbishopric; univ. (1624).

sucrose, sugar obtained from sugar cane, sugar beet, maple syrup, *etc.*

Consists of glucose and fructose joined together in single molecule.

Sudan, republic of NE Africa. Area 2,505,800 sq km (967,500 sq mi); pop. 16,126,000; cap. Khartoum. Language: Arabic. Religions: Islam, native. Nubian Desert in NE; savannah in C; forest, swamps in S. Main rivers Nile and tributaries. Agric. incl. millet, livestock; exports cotton, gum arabic. Unified (1820-2) by Egyptians; scene of Mahdist revolt (1883-5). Taken by Kitchener (1898); ruled as Anglo-Egyptian condominium until independence (1956).

Sudbury, town of EC Ontario, Canada. Pop. 91,000. Railway jct. In world's major nickel mining region; related smelting, refining industs. Also processes lead, silver, gold.

Sudeten (Czech *Sudety*), mountain range of N Czechoslovakia, rising to 1602 m (5258 ft). Minerals; timber; spas. German pop. in NW used to justify Hitler's annexation of region (Munich Pact, 1938). Restored to Czechoslovakia (1945).

Suetonius [Tranquilius], Galus (AD c70-c130), Roman biographer. Extant works are *De vita Caesarum,* describing lives of the Caesars from Julius Caesar to Domitian, and *De viris illustribus.*

Suez (*El Suweis*), city of NE Egypt, at head of Gulf of Suez and S end of Suez Canal. Pop. 315,000. Port; oil refining, pipeline to Cairo; railways to Cairo, Port Said. Damaged in Arab-Israeli wars (1967, 1973).

Suez Canal, waterway linking Mediterranean (at Port Said) with Red Sea (at Suez); 166 km (103 mi) long. Built 1859-69 by Ferdinand de Lesseps; formerly managed by Suez

Canal Co., in which Britain held majority of shares. Nationalization (1956) by Egypt precipitated SUEZ CRISIS. Closed 1967 after Arab-Israeli war; reopened June, 1975. At S end is Gulf of Suez, NW arm of Red Sea.

Suez Crisis, international incident (1956) begun when Egypt nationalized Suez Canal. In combined operation, Israel invaded Egypt and French and British troops occupied canal area. Under US pressure, invading forces withdrew and were replaced by UN emergency force. Disagreement over British role led to resignation of PM, Anthony Eden.

Suffolk, county of E England. Area 3800 sq km (1467 sq mi); pop. 562,000; co. town Ipswich. Flat, lowlying, with marshy coasts. Crops incl. wheat, barley, sugar beet. Racehorse training, breeding at Newmarket.

suffrage, right of voting, or exercising of that right. Universal adult suffrage is system whereby every national has vote on reaching age of majority, usually 18 or 21 years. In UK, achieved with Representation of the People (Equal Franchise) Act (1928), which included women over 21 in franchise; culmination of process begun by REFORM BILL of 1832. In US, 14th-15th Amendments provided for Negro enfranchisement, 19th Amendment for women (1920). *See also* ELECTION; WOMEN'S SUFFRAGE.

suffragettes, name given to those who campaigned for women's right to vote (*see* WOMEN'S SUFFRAGE). Often adopted measures, esp. in UK (early 20th cent.), putting themselves at physical risk.

Sufism, mystical movement of Islam; developed (10th cent.) among Shiites with Neoplatonic, Buddhist and Christian influences. Rejects ritual, emphasizing personal union with God. Influenced many Persian poets, *eg* Omar Khayyam, who developed rich symbolism of soul's relation with God.

sugar, any of class of sweet soluble crystalline carbohydrates, comprising monosaccharides, *eg* fructose, glucose, and disaccharides, *eg* sucrose, lactose, maltose. Name is most commonly applied to sucrose, obtained from juice of sugar beet and sugar cane.

sugar beet, *see* BEET.

sugar cane, *Saccharum officinarum,* tall, perennial, tropical grass. Cultivated as main source of sugar (c 65% of world production). By-products incl. molasses and rum.

Suharto, T.N.J. (1921-), Indonesian military, political leader. Took power after leading army coup that deposed Sukarno (1966). Became president 1968.

suicide, act of voluntary, intentional self-destruction. In UK, until 1961 regarded as crime if committed while of sound mind. In US, rarely so regarded, though assistance in act may be counted as criminal. Many religions count suicide as murder, although considered honourable in India (SUTTEE), Japan (HARA-KIRI).

suite, musical term; before c 1750 meant group of dance-type movements in same key; later, a sequence of instrumental movements, often from music for play or ballet. Examples incl. Bach's 4 *Orchestral Suites,* Grieg's *Pier Gynt.*

Sukarnapura, *see* DJAJAPURA.

Sukarno, Achmed (1901-70), Indonesian political leader, president (1945-66). Active in Indonesian nationalist movement before WWII. Became 1st president of independent republic (1945). His pro-Communist sympathies led to an army coup under Suharto.

Sukhumi (anc. *Dioscurias*), port of USSR, cap. of Abkhazian auton. republic, Georgian SSR. Pop. 107,000. Resort with sulphur baths. Trade in fruit, tobacco. Site of ancient Greek colony.

Sulawesi, see CELEBES.

Suleiman I (1494-1566), Ottoman sultan (1520-66), known as 'the Magnificent'. Brought Ottoman empire to peak of its power; captured Belgrade, Rhodes; annexed much of Hungary. Entered into long-lasting alliance with France (1536). Patronized arts, introduced legal and admin. reforms.

Sulla, Lucius Cornelius (138-78 BC), Roman soldier and political leader. Campaigned successfully against MITHRADATES in Pontus. His return to Italy precipitated civil war with followers of popular party (originally led by MARIUS). Captured Rome and ruled as dictator (82-79). Proscribed members of popular party and had them killed; made constitutional reforms.

Sullivan, Sir Arthur Seymour (1842-1900), English composer. Songs incl. 'Onward Christian Soldiers', 'The Lost Chord'. With W.S. GILBERT, wrote numerous popular light operas.

Sullivan, Louis (1856-1924), American architect. Formative influence in development of modern style; pioneered steel-frame construction,

coined dictum, 'form follows function'. Worked mainly in Chicago.

Sully, Maximilien de Béthune, Duc de (1560-1641), French statesman. A Protestant, he supported Huguenots in French Wars of Religion. Became Henry IV's superintendent of finances (1598), restored country's prosperity by encouraging agric. and extending system of roads, canals.

Sully-Prudhomme, pseud. of René François Armand Prudhomme (1839-1907), French poet. Member of PARNASSIENS. Works incl. *La Justice* (1878), *Le Bonheur* (1888). Nobel Prize for Literature (1901).

sulphates, salts or esters of sulphuric acid. Calcium sulphate in form of gypsum used in building or casting. Magnesium sulphate sold as Epsom salts.

sulphonamides, in medicine, range of drugs derived from amide of a sulphonic acid. Developed in 1930s, used extensively to cure infections (except those by viruses) till advent of antibiotics. Still often used where antibiotics are unsuitable.

sulphur (S), non-metallic element, occurring in several allotropic forms; at. no. 16, at. wt. 32.06. Common form is rhombic sulphur, pale yellow solid; occurs free and as sulphide and sulphate minerals. Burns with blue flame to form sulphur dioxide. Used in manufacture of sulphuric acid, carbon disulphide, gunpowder, matches, in vulcanizing rubber and in medicine.

sulphuric acid (H_2SO_4), oily colourless corrosive liquid. Manufactured by catalytic oxidation of sulphur dioxide. Wide indust. use in manufacture of explosives, fertilizers, detergents, dyes and in land ACCUMULATOR.

sumac or **sumach**, any of genus *Rhus* of subtropical and temperate trees. Pinnate leaves, large, coneshaped clusters of hairy red fruits. Dried bark and leaves yield extract used in tanning. Species incl. staghorn sumac, *R. typhina*, of E US.

Sumatra, isl. of Indonesia, SW of Malay penin. Area *c* 474,000 sq km (183,000 sq mi). Barisan Mts. run parallel to W coast, jungle lowlands in E. Equatorial climate, with heavy rainfall. Produces rice, rubber, tobacco, petroleum. Hindu kingdom estab. 8th cent, Islam introduced by Arab traders in 13th cent. Dutch control started in 17th cent.

Sumerians, people inhabiting S Mesopotamia between 4th and 2nd millennia BC. Began world's 1st urban civilization at such cities as Ur, Lagash and Erech, developed pottery and metalwork. Credited with the invention of cuneiform writing. Eventually conquered by rival Semitic cities.

summer time, *see* DAYLIGHT SAVING TIME.

Sumter, Fort, *see* CHARLESTON, South Carolina, US.

Sun, central body of Solar System around which planets revolve in orbit; it is star nearest Earth, an incandescent sphere composed mainly of hydrogen and helium. Mean distance from Earth *c* 150 million km; diameter *c* 1.4 million km. Temperature at visible surface (photosphere) 6000° C; temperature at its interior, between 10 and 20 million° C, enables fusion of hydrogen into helium to take place and supply Sun's energy. Chromosphere, av. temperature *c* 20,000° C, surrounds the photosphere, and the corona, region of extremely high temperature and low density, forms outermost part of Sun's atmosphere.

sun bear, *Helarctos malayanus*, smallest of bears, found in SE Asia. Harmless; agile tree climber. Also called Malayan bear.

Sundas, Greater, isl. group of Indonesia. Comprises Borneo, Sumatra, Java, Celebes, and adjacent isls. **Lesser Sundas** or **Nusa Tenggara**, E of Java, incl. Bali, Lombok, Sumba, Flores and Timor.

Sunday school, organization for giving religious instruction to children, usually attached to church. Robert Raikes began movement in UK, estab. 1st school in 1780; by 1785 over 1000 schools had been founded. Movement introduced (1786) into US by Francis Asbury; American Sunday-School Union estab. in 1824, using British curriculum *etc*. At height by end of 19th cent., with founding (1889) of World Sunday School Convention, later (1947) World Council of Christian Education. Movement had immense influence on spread of popular education in UK.

Sunderland, bor. of Tyne and Wear met. county, NE England, at mouth of R. Wear. Pop. 217,000. Port (coal exports from 14th cent.); shipbuilding, engineering industs. Has remains of monastery (674).

sundew or **dew plant**, any of genus *Drosera* of INSECTIVOROUS PLANTS. Worldwide distribution. Catches and digests prey by sticky tentacles on cup-shaped leaves.

sundial, instrument indicating time

of day by position of shadow of upright centre pin (gnomen) cast by Sun on graduated surface. Earliest extant example is Egyptian (c 1500 BC).

sunfish, any of various large oceanic fish of Molidae family, esp. ocean sunfish, *Mola mola.* Name also applied to some North American freshwater fish of Centrarchidae family.

sunflower, any of genus *Helianthus* of plants of daisy family. Native to New World. Large, yellow daisy-like flowers with dark central discs containing edible seeds from which oil is extracted. Species incl. common sunflower, *H. annuus,* state flower of Kansas.

Sung, Chinese imperial dynasty (960-1279). Period noted for improvement in commercial facilities, growth of large cities, intensive scholarship and development of fine arts. Overthrown by Mongols.

Sunnites or **Sunnis,** members of the larger and more orthodox of the 2 main Moslem sects. They accept historical order of 1st 4 caliphs as rightful line of succession to Mohammed and admit the authority of the Sunna, law based on Mohammed's traditional teachings (as opposed to SHIITES).

sunspot, dark spot appearing on surface of Sun, caused by solar magnetic fields; its temperature is lower than surrounding points on surface. Periods of sunspot activity usually follow cycles of c 11 years; associated with magnetic storms on Earth.

Sun Yat-sen (1866-1925), Chinese revolutionary, national hero. Worked outside China from 1895 to bring about revolution. Adopted 'Three People's Principles' of nationalism, democracy, people's livelihood, as his political philosophy (basis of KUOMINTANG party which he led). Returned to China (1911) to serve briefly as president (1912). Set up unofficial govt. of S China at Kwangchow (1921) to oppose warlords in N. Agreed to cooperate with Chinese Communists despite misgivings.

superconductivity, phenomenon exhibited by certain pure metals and alloys, *eg* mercury, cadmium, aluminium, of having almost no electrical resistance at temperatures near absolute zero. Current induced in superconductor will flow almost indefinitely after current source is removed.

superego, in psychoanalysis, that part of the mind which acts as a form of conscience, critical of EGO, and causing guilt and anxiety when ego's thoughts and acts oppose it. At UNCONSCIOUS level, censors unacceptable impulses of ID.

superfluidity, phenomenon exhibited by liquid helium at temperatures below 2.18° Kelvin of flowing without friction and having high thermal conductivity. Helium in superfluid state will flow upwards out of a container, along an invisible film of liquid.

Superior, Lake, largest, deepest and most W of Great Lakes, C Canada-US. Area 82,414 sq km (31,820 sq mi). Drained by L. Huron. Important trade route; main cargoes are grain, timber, metal ore. Canals at Sault Ste Marie enable ships to enter and leave US. Commercial fishing.

supernova, exploding star whose brightness suddenly increases by up to 10^8 times and then fades away. Only 3 have been observed in our galaxy recently, in 1054, 1572 (Tycho's nova), 1604 (Kepler's nova). Believed to occur when sufficiently massive star undergoes gravitational collapse as its store of hydrogen becomes depleted.

supply and demand, in classical economics, factors determining price. Supply refers to the amount of a commodity that producers will supply at varying prices (supply falls as prices decreases); demand refers to the desire for the commodity (falls as prices increases). In perfect competition, price will stabilize at equilibrium of these 2 values.

suprematism, movement in abstract art founded by Malevich in 1913; based on the use of squares, circles, triangles, it was earliest form of pure geometric abstract art.

supreme court, highest organ of JUDICIARY in Federal systems of govt. US Supreme Court is composed of 9 judges, of whom one acts as chief justice. Estab. (1789) by Constitution with status independent of Congress. Greatest bulk of work is as appeal court, also rules on disputes between states, between state and central govts. Interprets Constitution, its function as reviewer of acts of Congress estab. by JOHN MARSHALL; later extended to state legislation. Has functioned to regulate economy, civil liberties in 20th cent.

Supreme Soviet, highest legislative body of USSR. Consists of 2 equal chambers, Soviet of the Union (members elected on basis of population), and Soviet of Nationalities (members elected on basis of voting by the various republics and auton. regions).

Surabaya or **Surabaja,** city of E. Java prov., Indonesia. Pop. 1,556,-000. Seaport and major export centre; naval base. Shipbuilding, oil refining, textile mfg.

Surat, city of Gujarat state, W India, on Gulf of Cambay. Pop. 472,000. Important port in 17th cent.; English trading post (1612). Textile, paper mfg.

surface tension, force tending to contract surface area of a liquid, due to unequal cohesive forces between molecules near surface. Causes surface to behave like elastic membrane, capable of supporting light objects; also responsible for shape of water droplets and soap bubbles.

surfing, sport of gliding in towards the shore on the crest of a wave, usually on a surfboard. Prob. originated in Polynesia and Hawaii. Developed in early 20th cent. by Hawaiian Duke Kahanamoku, who introduced sport to Australia in 1915.

surgery, branch of medicine concerned with treatment of injury, deformity and disease by means of manual operations with or without instruments. Although practised from ancient times, major advances in this field were not made until the introduction of aseptic techniques and anaesthetics in 19th cent.

Surinam, republic of NE South America. Area 63,037 sq km (163,266 sq mi); pop. 435,000; cap. Paramaribo. Coastal lowlands rise to forested highlands in S. Coffee, rum, timber, bauxite production, exports. Indian, Negro, Indonesian, European pop. Region disputed by English, Dutch; resolved 1815. Named Dutch Guiana; renamed 1948. Ceased being colony (1954), fully independent 1975.

surrealism, in literature and art, movement (esp. 1920s-30s) attempting to draw symbols and images from subconscious mind, influenced by Freud. Founded (1924) by French author André Breton in his *Manifeste du surréalisme*. In literature, confined almost entirely to France. In painting, international figures incl. Salvador Dali, Max Ernst, Joan Miró; in films, Luis Buñuel.

Surrey, Henry Howard, Earl of, *see* HOWARD, THOMAS.

Surrey, county of SE England. Area 1654 sq km (639 sq mi); pop. 994,000; co. town Kingston-upon-Thames. Crossed E-W by North Downs (sheep rearing); dairying, market gardening. London suburbs in NE.

Surtsey, isl. of Iceland, formed 1963-5 by eruption of underwater volcano. Area *c* 325 ha. (800 acres). Nature reserve.

surveying, science of determining relative position of points on the Earth's surface. Such data may then be presented as maps by techniques of cartography. Land surveying incl. both GEODESY and plane-surveying, latter not taking account of Earth's curvature; other branches incl. hydrographic (*ie* water) surveying, topographic (*ie* relief) surveying. Surveying by use of air photographs is called photogrammetry.

Susa, *see* SOUSSE, Tunisia.

Suslov, Mikhail Andreyevich (1902-), Soviet political leader. Communist Party's principal ideologist; member of Politburo from 1955.

suspension, in chemistry, system in which small solid particles are dispersed, but not dissolved, in a fluid medium. Differs from a COLLOID in that particles are larger.

Sussex, former county of SE England. South Downs in S, ending at Beachy Head; Vale of Sussex in C; Weald in N. Agric., livestock; extensive woodlands. Coastal resorts incl. Brighton, Worthing. From 1974 divided into **East Sussex** (area 1795 sq km/693 sq mi; pop. 658,000; co. town Lewes) and **West Sussex** (area 2016 sq km/778 sq mi; pop. 630,000; co. town Chichester).

Sutherland, Graham Vivian (1903-), English painter. Known for his landscapes and studies of natural forms, *eg* thorns, trees. Works incl. portraits *Maugham* and *Churchill*; also tapestry for Coventry Cathedral.

Sutherland, former county of N Scotland, now in Highland region. Mountains, moorland; rocky indented coast. Cape Wrath in NW. Deer forest, sheep farming, crofting, fishing, tourism. Co. town was Dornoch.

Sutlej, river of SC Asia. Longest of five rivers of Punjab, rises in Tibet. Flows *c* 1450 km (900 mi) SW through Himachal Pradesh and Indian Punjab to join Indus in Pakistan.

suttee, Hindu custom involving voluntary cremation of widow on husband's funeral pyre. Abolished by British colonial govt. (1829).

Suttner, Bertha, Baroness von

(1843-1914), Austrian author. Known for pacifist novel *Lay Down Your Arms* (1889). Influenced Nobel in estab. Nobel Peace Prize which she received (1905).

Sutton, bor. of S Greater London, England. Pop. 169,000. Created 1965 from N Surrey towns, incl. Carshalton.

Sutton Hoo, site in Suffolk, England, of Saxon ship-burial, dating from c AD 650. Excavated in 1939, superb examples of jewellery, coins and weapons were found.

Su Tung-po or **Su Shih** (1036-1101), Chinese poet, essayist, painter. Considered greatest poet of Sung dynasty, although equally famous for prose in own time. Poems typically descriptive or lyrical; also wrote satires.

Suva, cap. of Fiji Isls., on Viti Levu isl. Pop. 63,000. Admin. centre; port, exports fruit, sugar, copra, gold; seat of Univ. of South Pacific (1968).

Svalbard, see SPITSBERGEN, Norway.

Sverdlovsk, city of USSR, W Siberian RSFSR; railway jct. and indust. centre in E Ural foothills. Pop. 1,073,000. Metallurgical plants process iron, gold, copper from Ural Mts.; chemical and machinery mfg. Founded in 1721 as Ekaterinburg; expanded with coming of Trans-Siberian railway (1895). Scene of execution of Tsar Nicholas II and his family (1918).

Svevo, Italo, pseud. of Ettore Schmitz (1861-1928), Italian novelist. Friend of Joyce. Wrote psychological novel *The Confessions of Zeno* (1923). Other works incl. *Senility* (1898).

Swabia (*Schwaben*), hist. region of SW West Germany, now in S Baden-Württemberg and SW Bavaria. Incl. source of Danube, Black Forest, Swabian Jura. Duchy under Hohenstaufens from 1079, divided 1268. Cities, incl. Augsburg, formed several Swabian leagues 14th-16th cent.

Swahili, Bantu language of Niger-Congo branch of Niger-Kordofanian language family. Spoken as native tongue in Tanzania, Kenya, Zaïre, Burundi, Uganda, also used as lingua franca by non-indigenous peoples, *etc.* Since beginning of 18th cent. has been used for literature. Term also used for many inhabitants of EC Africa, not united ethnic group but defined by common cultures, livelihood, esp. trade, use of language.

swallow, small long-winged migrating bird of Hirundinidae family. Long forked tail; weak feet; feeds on insects caught in flight. Species incl. *Hirundo rustica,* summer visitor to Europe; builds mud and straw nest on buildings.

swallowtail butterfly, *Papilio machaon,* yellow and black European butterfly whose rear wings have tail-like points. Related species found worldwide.

swamp, tract of water-saturated land, normally with abundant vegetation. Found in low-lying coastal plains, river flood plains. Temperate swamps contain grasses, rushes, sphagnum moss; tropical swamps contain cypresses, mangroves.

Swan, Sir Joseph Wilson (1828-1914), English inventor. Made electric lamp (1860). In photography, invented carbon printing, a dry plate process and bromide paper.

swan, large web-footed aquatic bird, genus *Cygnus*. Long slender neck, adult plumage generally white. Species incl. European mute swan, *C. olor*, North American trumpeter swan, *C. buccinator*, and Australian black swan, *C. atratus*.

Swansea (*Abertawe*), co. bor. and port of Glamorgan, S Wales, on R. Tawe. Pop. 173,000. Exports coal, metal goods, imports ore for iron, steel industs. Oil refining. Has coll. of Univ. of Wales (1920). Famous blue pottery.

swastika, decorative mystic symbol consisting of cross with right-angle extensions at points. Of great antiquity, occurs in many cultures. Adopted as symbol of German Nazi party and Third Reich.

Swaziland, kingdom of SE Africa. Area 17,350 sq km (6700 sq mi); pop. 497,000; cap. Mbabane. Languages: Swati, English. Religions: Christianity, native. High, middle and low veld areas from W to E; main rivers Komati, Usutu. Crops incl. maize, fruit, sugar, cotton; cattle rearing; iron ore and asbestos mining. Independent from Zulus in 19th cent.; British protect. from 1906 until independence 1968. Member of British Commonwealth.

sweat, weak solution of salt secreted by sweat glands in skin. Heat lost in evaporation of sweat from body helps regulate body temperature.

swede or **rutabaga**, see TURNIP.

Sweden (*Sverige*), kingdom of N Europe, in E part of Scandinavian penin. Incl. Baltic isls., Gotland, Oland. Area 449,748 sq km (173,648 sq mi); pop. 8,222,000; cap. Stockholm. Language: Swedish. Religion: Lutheranism. Mountains in N, W; lakes in S. Mainly agric. (wheat, dairying); timber indust.; iron ore; h.e.p. Settled by Germanic tribes, Christianity estab. by 11th cent. United with Norway, Denmark at Kalmar (1397). Independent kingdom from 1523; *fl* under Gustavus Adolphus (17th cent.). United with Norway 1814-1905; neutral in WWs. Increasingly indust.; advanced social welfare system.

Swedenborg, Emanuel, orig. Emanuel Swedberg (1688-1772), Swedish theologian, mystic. Scientific investigations led him to pursue religious studies, believing Second Coming of the Lord had occurred. After his death NEW CHURCH organized by his followers. Works incl. *Heaven and Hell* (1758).

Swedish, N Germanic language of Indo-European family. Spoken in Sweden, S Finland, Estonia. Descended from Old Norse. Historically divided into Old Swedish (9th-16th cent.), New Swedish (from 16th cent.).

sweetbriar, see BRIAR.

sweet gum, *Liquidambar styraciflua*; tall, pyramidal tree native to North America. Hard, red wood used in furniture. Exudes balsam used in medicine and perfumery.

sweet pea, *Lathyrus odoratus*, climbing annual plant of Leguminosae family, native to Europe. Butterfly-shaped, fragrant flowers.

sweet potato, or **long potato**, *Ipomoea batatas*, tropical American trailing, perennial plant. Widely cultivated for edible, reddish, sweet-tasting tubers. Used as vegetable, dessert or preserved.

sweet william, see PINK.

Sweyn (d. 1014), king of Denmark (c 986-1014). Partitioned Norway with Swedish allies after victory over Olaf I (1000). Led series of raids against England, exacting tribute; accepted as king of England (1013). Succeeded by his son, CANUTE.

Swift, Jonathan (1667-1745), English author, b. Ireland. Tory pamphleteer. Known for political, moral satire *Gulliver's Travels* (1726). Also wrote religious satire *Tale of a Tub* (1704), *The Battle of the Books* (1704) on merits of ancient v modern writers, *The Drapier's Letters* (1724) and *A Modest Proposal* (1729) on Irish question. Dean of St Patrick's, Dublin (1713-45).

swift, any of Apodidae family of migratory swallow-like birds. Long scythe-like wings, short tail; spends most of time in flight. Species incl. common European swift, *Apus apus,* with black plumage and white throat patch, and North American chimney swift, *Chaetura pelagica.*

swimming, recreation and competitive sport of. self-propulsion through water. Four basic swimming styles: front crawl, developed in Australia and US; backstroke; breaststroke; butterfly, classed as new stroke in 1952. Olympic event since 1896.

Swinburne, Algernon Charles (1837-1909), English poet. Works notable for technical skill, radical fervour, sensuality, *eg* classical verse *Atalanta in Calydon* (1865), poetry *Songs before Sunrise* (1871), *Tristram of Lyonesse* (1882).

Swindon, mun. bor. of Wiltshire, S England. Pop. 91,000. British Rail

workshops; has railway museum (1962).

swine, name given to members of Suidae family, esp. domestic pig.

swine fever or hog cholera, infectious, often fatal, virus disease of swine. Characterized by fever, vomiting, diarrhoea.

swing music, style of jazz played by big bands consisting of brass, saxophone and rhythm sections. Originated in US in 1930s and remained popular to 1950s. Exponents incl. Benny Goodman, Count Basie.

Swithin or Swithun, St (d. 862), English churchman, bishop of Winchester. According to tradition, weather on his feast day (15 July) guarantees same weather on succeeding 40 days.

Switzerland (Fr. *Suisse,* Ger. *Schweiz,* Ital. *Svizzera*), federal republic of WC Europe. Area 41,285 sq km (15,940 sq mi); pop. 6,346,000; cap. Bern. Main cities Basle, Geneva, Zürich. Languages: French, German, Italian. Religions: Protestant, RC. Plateau in C (lakes incl. Geneva, Zurich, Constance); Alps in S, E. Dairy produce (cheese, milk), confectionery; watches, optical instruments; banking, tourism. Part of Holy Roman Empire from 1033, Confederation estab. 1291 for defence against Habsburgs, now comprises 22 cantons. Centre of 16th cent. Reformation. Full independence from 1648; French occupation (1798-1815). Neutrality estab. by Treaty of Paris (1815). Hq. of many international agencies, *eg* League of Nations (1920-46), WHO (1946).

swordfish, *Xiphias gladius,* large

food and game fish (up to 4.6 m/15 ft long), related to tunny, widely distributed in warm seas. Upper jaw extended into flat sword-like structure.

sycamore, *Acer pseudoplatanus,* Eurasian maple tree. Large and deciduous with yellow flowers; planted as shade tree. Name also used for several American PLANE trees. *Ficus sycamorus,* a FIG tree, is sycamore of the Bible.

Sydney, city of SE Australia, on Port Jackson inlet, cap. of New South Wales. Pop. 2,800,000. Admin., commercial centre; major port, exports wool, wheat, meat; industs. incl. coalmining, iron and steel mfg., food processing, car assembly. Settled (1788) as penal colony. Has harbour bridge (1932), opera house (1973), 3 univs.

syenite, coarse-grained igneous rock. Consists of feldspars plus any of various ferromagnesian minerals, *eg* augite, hornblende; similar to granite but contains no quartz. Major sources in US, Germany, Norway.

Syktyvkar, city of USSR, cap. of Komi auton. republic, NE European RSFSR. Pop. 136,000. Timber centre; wood pulp and paper mfg; shipyards.

syllogism, in logic, method of argument drawing a conclusion from 2 premises. Described by Aristotle, remains principal instrument of traditional deductive logic. Most common form is categorical, made up of 3 statements of fact, *eg* all dogs have 4 feet; a pug is a dog; therefore a pug has 4 feet. The 2 other types are hypothetical (conditional proposition and 2 statements of fact); and disjunctive (alternative proposition and 2 statements of fact).

symbiosis, in biology, living together of 2 dissimilar organisms by which each benefits, *eg* cellulose-digesting bacteria present in stomach of cows.

symbolists, group of French poets esp. Rimbaud, Verlaine, Mallarmé, active in late 19th cent., who reacted against realism in literature, feeling that poetry should evoke inexpressible subjective states. Doctrine taken up by painters *eg* Redon, Puvis de Chavannes, Moreau, and composer Debussy.

Symons, Arthur (1865-1945), English poet, critic, b. Wales. Known for influential critical work *The Symbolist Movement in Literature* (1899). Also wrote decadent poetry, *eg Silhouettes* (1892), *Images of Good and Evil* (1899).

symphony, orchestral composition generally in similar form to SONATA. Classical symphony was estab. by Haydn and perfected by Mozart in 18th cent. In 19th cent., composers who developed the form incl. Beethoven, Schubert, Berlioz and Mahler. Symphony has been less dominant in 20th cent. music; noted 20th cent. symphonists incl. Sibelius, Shostakovich.

synagogue, in Judaism, building designed for public prayer, religious education and other communal activities. Prob. originated *c* 6th cent. BC among Jews in exile in Babylon, unable to visit TEMPLE in Jerusalem.

synapse, junction between nerve cells where nervous impulses are transmitted from one cell to another.

Impulses usually travel down conducting nerve fibre (axon) of nerve cell and, on reaching end of fibre, stimulate release of ACETYLCHOLINE. This excites dendrites of adjacent cell and passes on the impulses.

synchrotron, particle accelerator used to obtain high energy protons, electrons, etc, by combination of magnetic field, whose intensity is modulated cyclically, and high frequency electric field.

syncopation, in music and poetry, shifting of stress from normal beat. Rhythmic suspension, unaccented beat, rest, or silence on beat are types of syncopation. Characteristic of modern music and of verse using speech rhythms.

syndicalism, revolutionary doctrine and plan for post-revolutionary society. Adherents advocate abolition of central govt., replacement by trade unions as decision-makers on production and distribution. Influenced by Proudhon, SOREL.

Synge, J[ohn] M[illington] (1871-1909), Irish dramatist. A leading figure in Irish Renaissance. Known for controversial presentation of peasant life in plays, eg Riders to the Sea (1904), The Playboy of the Western World (1907).

Synoptic Gospels, see GOSPELS.

synthesis, in chemistry and biology, formation of compounds from their constituent elements or simpler materials.

synthetic fibres, artificial, chemically produced fibres, usually derived from long-chain polymers. Woven as fabrics which are generally quick-drying, resistant to creasing and chemical damage; less pleasant to wear than natural fibres as they absorb less moisture and are not so warm. Incl. nylon, rayon, Dacron and Orlon.

syphilis, infectious disease caused by spirochaete (spiral bacterium) Treponema pallidum. Usually transmitted by sexual intercourse or acquired congenitally. In later stages, can affect almost any organ or tissue of the body, esp. mucous membranes, skin and bone, nervous system. Treatment by penicillin effective if applied early enough.

Syracuse (Siracusa), city of SE Sicily, Italy, cap. of Siracusa prov. Pop. 109,000. Port; fishing, salt, wine. Founded c 734 BC by Greeks, fl 5th-3rd cent. BC; taken by Rome 212 BC. Many remains, esp. on Ortygia Isl. (original site).

Syracuse, town of C New York, US; on Barge Canal. Pop. 197,000. Electrical equipment, typewriter mfg. Hist. salt indust. declined c 1870.

Syr Darya (anc. Jaxartes), river of SC USSR. Rises as R. Naryn in E Kirghiz SSR and joins Kara Darya in Fergana valley, Uzbek SSR; flows c 2100 km (1300 mi) through Kazakh SSR to Aral Sea.

Syria, republic of SW Asia. Area 185,000 sq km (71,000 sq mi); pop. 7,596,000; cap. Damascus. Language: Arabic. Religion: Islam. Bounded by Anti-Lebanon Mts. in W and Syrian desert in S. Agric. in fertile valleys of Euphrates and Orontes; cotton main export; pipelines carrying Iraqi oil provide revenue. Conquered by many peoples, was part of Ottoman Empire (1516-1918). Mandated to France (1920), became completely independent 1944. Joined Egypt in UAR (1958-61).

Syros (*Síros*), isl. of Greece, in Aegean Sea, most populous of Cyclades. Area 85 sq km (33 sq mi); cap. Syros (Hermoupolis), port, pop. 17,000.

Szczecin (Ger. *Stettin*), city of NW Poland, on R. Oder, cap. of Szczecin prov. Pop. 340,000. Port; shipbuilding, indust. centre; formerly port for Berlin. Hanseatic League member from 1360. Part of Prussian Pomerania 1720-1945. Birthplace of Catherine the Great.

Szechwan, prov. of SC China. Area

c 570,000 sq km (220,000 sq mi); pop. (est.) 70,000,000; cap. Chengtu. Isolated region. High mountains in W crossed by Yangtze. Fertile Red basin in C is densely populated and major source of rice, sugar cane, cotton.

Szeged, city of SE Hungary, on R. Tisza. Pop. 130,000. Port in agric. area, food processing; light industs. Partly destroyed by flood (1879).

Szymanowski, Karol (1882-1937), Polish composer. Works incl. operas, *eg King Roger*, symphonies, 2 violin concertos, and much piano music.

T

tabasco, trademark for extremely spicy sauce made from *Capsicum conoides,* a pepper native to Mexico.

Tabernacle, in OT, portable sanctuary carried by the Jews in their wanderings from Egypt to Palestine. Contained Ark of the Covenant.

Tabernacles, Feast of, Jewish festival (Sukkoth), celebrated 15th-22nd of Tishri (late October). Marks end of harvest season and celebrated by taking meals in tents or huts in memory of wanderings during Exodus.

Table Bay, inlet of Atlantic Ocean, SW Cape Prov., South Africa; *c* 9.7 km (6 mi) across. First Dutch settlement in S Africa estab. 1652 on shores. Overlooked by Table Mountain, height 1087 m (3567 ft). Flat-topped; ascended by cable railway (built 1929).

table tennis or **ping-pong,** indoor game played on a rectangular table with hollow celluloid ball and rubber-covered bats. Prob. originated in 1880s and 1890s in England. International Table Tennis Federation was formed (1926) to arrange championships and standardize rules.

taboo or **tabu,** prohibition, common among primitive peoples, of certain words and actions, usually on religious grounds. Also refers to certain objects set aside for religious use. Practice occurs esp. in Polynesia.

Tabriz, city of NW Iran, cap. of E Azerbaijan prov. Pop. 493,000. Market centre for fèrtile agric. area; textile and rug mfg. Often devastated by earthquakes, has ruined 15th cent. Blue Mosque.

Tacitus (AD *c* 55–*c* 120), Roman historian. Author of *Germania,* giving valuable hist. information on Germanic tribes. Wrote biography of Agricola, his father-in-law and governor of Britain. His history of the empire from reign of Galba to Domitian (69-97) gives picture of Roman life.

Tacoma, port of W Washington, US; on Puget Sound, S of Seattle. Pop. 155,000. Exports timber, grain, flour, phosphates; shipyards, lumber, flour mills, copper smelting.

Tadoussac, village of SC Québec, Canada; at confluence of Saguenay and St Lawrence rivers. Pop. *c* 1000. Earliest French settlement in Canada (1600); estab. as fur trading post.

Tadzhik Soviet Socialist Republic, constituent republic of SC USSR. Area *c* 143,000 sq km (55,200 sq mi); pop. 2,900,000; cap. Dushanbe. Largely mountainous, containing Pamir and Alai systems; lowlands in Amu Darya valley. Crops incl. cotton, wheat, fruit; sheep and cattle raising. Region under Russian control by 1895; constituent republic (1929).

Taegu, city of SE South Korea. Pop. 1,083,000. Commercial centre of agric. region (grains, tobacco); textiles produced.

Tafawa Balewa, Alhaji Sir Abu-bakar (1912-66), Nigerian statesman, 1st PM (1957-66). Assassinated in military coup.

taffeta, light plain-weave fabric with high sheen, originally made of silk. Used in ribbons and umbrellas.

Tafilelt or **Tafilalet,** oasis of SE Morocco. Largest in Sahara, area *c* 1375 sq km (530 sq mi). Produces dates, leather. Rich independent kingdom 8th-10th cent.; original home of Morocco's ruling dynasty.

Taft, William Howard (1857-1930), American statesman, president (1909-13). Republican secretary of war under T. Roosevelt, whom he succeeded. Defeated in 1912 election after Roosevelt split Republican vote by running as Progressive candidate. His son, **Robert Alphonso Taft** (1889-1953), was Senator from Ohio. Sponsored TAFT-HARTLEY LABOR ACT.

Taft-Hartley Labor Act, common name for Labor-Management Relations Act (1947). Attempted to regulate labour disputes in US, with sanctions against 'wildcat' (unofficial) and demarcation strikes, extended govt. mediation, and prohibited CLOSED SHOP. Also *see* INDUSTRIAL RELATIONS ACT.

Taglioni, Maria (1804-84), Italian ballet dancer. Known esp. 'for *La Sylphide* (Paris, 1832), created for her by her father. May have introduced *sur les pointes* technique.

Tagore, Sir Rabindranath (1861-

1941), Indian author, educator. Founded Santiniketan (1901), forerunner of Visva-Bharati Univ. Wrote love lyrics, *eg* collection *Gitanjali* (1912), and philosophical *Sadhana* (1913). Nobel Prize for Literature (1913).

Tagus (Span. *Tajo,* Port. *Tejo*), river of Spain and Portugal. Flows c 910 km (565 mi) from Teruel prov., EC Spain to Atlantic Ocean by estuary at Lisbon. Forms part of Spain-Portugal border.

Tahiti, main isl. of French Polynesia, in Windward group of Society Isls. Area 1040 sq km (402 sq mi); cap. Papeete. Mountainous; produces fruit, sugar, copra, vanilla. Home of Gauguin for many years.

Taimyr Peninsula, most N projection of USSR mainland, on Arctic coast of Siberian RSFSR. N extremity is Cape Chelyuskin. Covered mainly by tundra; inhabited by nomadic Samoyeds.

Tainan, port of SW Taiwan, on Formosa Str. Pop. 495,000. Agric. centre for rice, sugar cane; produces textiles, machinery. Cap. of isl. in 17th cent., retained political power until 1885.

taipan, *Oxyuranus scutellatus,* large brown dangerously poisonous snake, up to 3 m/10 ft in length. Found in NE Australia and New Guinea.

Taipei, cap. of Taiwan, commercial and indust. centre. Pop. 1,922,000. Founded in 18th cent., replaced Tainan as cap. in 1885. Developed under Japanese rule.

Taiping Rebellion (1850-64), revolt in China against Manchu dynasty. Led by Hung Hsiu-chuan who declared himself leader of

Taiping (Great Peace) dynasty. After initial success, incl. capture of Nanking (1853), crushed with help of Western troops under C. G. GORDON.

Taiwan (*Formosa*), isl. republic of E Asia, separated from China by Formosa Str. Area *c* 36,000 sq km (13,900 sq mi); pop. 15,500,000; cap. Taipei. Language: Mandarin Chinese. Religion: Buddhism. Crossed N-S by mountain range, reaching *c* 4000 m (13,100 ft); tropical climate, with abundant rainfall. Produces rice, timber, sugar. Settled in 17th cent. by Chinese after expulsion of Dutch. Ceded to Japan (1895-1945). Seat of Chiang Kai-shek's nationalist govt. after 1949; under threat of Chinese invasion, has developed under US economic and military aid (latter terminated 1979). Withdrew from UN (1971) on entry of China.

Taiyuan, cap. of Shansi prov., NC China. Pop. 2,725,000. In major iron and coal area; iron and steel plants, heavy machinery and chemical mfg. Ancient walled city.

Taj Mahal, white marble mausoleum beside R. Jumna, near Agra, India. Built 1630-48 by Shah Jehan as tomb for his favourite wife.

Tajo, see TAGUS.

Taklamakan, desert region of Sinkiang, NW China. Area *c* 323,750 sq km (125,000 sq mi).

Takoradi, see SEKONDI-TAKORADI, Ghana.

Talbot, William Henry Fox (1800-77), English photographic pioneer. Patented various processes for making negative and positive prints ('talbotypes'). Wrote *The Pencil of Nature* (1844), illustrated with his own photographs.

talc, softest common mineral; consists of hydrated magnesium silicate. Main constituent of SOAPSTONE. Used in electrical insulators, lubricants, paper mfg., also as talcum powder. Major sources in Austria, Italy, US.

Talcahuano, see CONCEPCIÓN, Chile.

Talien, see LU-TA.

Tallahassee, cap. of Florida, US. Pop. 73,000. Lumber produce. Indian, Spanish settlement prior to territ. cap. (1824).

Talleyrand [-Périgord], Charles Maurice de (1754-1838), French statesman. Bishop of Autun (1789-91), represented clergy in Estates-General (1789); supported moderate reform. Fled abroad on fall of monarchy. Foreign minister under Directory (1797-9) and under Napoleon (1799-1807). On Napoleon's exile to Elba, secured accession of Louis XVIII and favourable peace terms for French at Congress of Vienna (1814-15). Ambassador to London (1830-4) under Louis Philippe.

Tallinn (Ger. *Reval*), city of USSR, cap. of Estonian SSR; on Gulf of Finland. Pop. 378,000. Port; exports timber, paper; shipbuilding; wood products and textile mfg. Founded by Danes (1219); member of Hanseatic League (1285). Taken by Russia from Sweden (1710). Cap. of Estonia (1919-40).

Tallis, Thomas (*c* 1505-1585), English composer. Joint organist with Byrd of Chapel Royal. Compositions, noted for contrapuntal skill, incl. motets, eg *Spem in Alium* and *Cantiones sacrae,* anthems, keyboard music.

tallow, solid fat extracted from animals, esp. cattle and sheep. Used to make candles and soap.

Talmud, collection of writings constituting Jewish civil and religious law. Consists of 2 parts, Mishnah (text), and Gemara (commentary). Passages devoted to law itself are known as Halakah; those which contain illustrative parables, legends, *etc,* as Haggadah. Regarded as Oral Law as distinct from Written Law of the TORAH.

talus or scree, accumulation of rock fragments formed at foot of steep slope. Results from weathering of rock face above.

tamarind, *Tamarindus indica,* large evergreen tree of Leguminosae family, native to tropical Africa. Pod contains seeds enclosed in juicy acid pulp, used in beverages and food.

tamarisk, any of genus *Tamarix* of shrubs and small trees native to Mediterranean region and C Asia. Feathery leaves, pink or white flowers. Often cultivated as windbreak near salt water.

tambourine, hand-held percussion instrument consisting of circular frame and single drumhead, with circular metal plates or jingles in frame.

Tamburlaine, *see* TAMERLANE.

Tamerlane or Timur Leng (*c* 1336–1405), Mongol conqueror. Estab. himself as ruler of Turkestan with his cap. at Samarkand (1369). Conquered Persia, S Russia, India as far as Delhi. Defeated Ottoman Turks at Angora (1402) and captured the sultan Beyazid. Patron of learning; notorious for his cruelty.

Subject of Marlowe's play *Tamburlaine.*

Tamil, *see* DRAVIDIAN.

Tamil Nadu, maritime state of S India; formerly Madras, renamed 1969. Area *c* 130,000 sq km (50,000 sq mi); pop. 41,103,000; cap. Madras. Plain along Coromandel Coast in E; mountainous in W, reaching alt. of 2400 m (8000 ft) in Nilgiri Hills. Agric. economy; rice, cotton, groundnuts. Under British control by 1800 after wars against French and Tippoo Sahib.

Tammany, powerful Democratic political organization of New York City, incorporated 1789. Historically associated with corruption under such leaders as 'Boss' Tweed. Declined in power during La Guardia admin. (1933–45); ceased to exist after 1965.

Tammuz, in Babylonian and Assyrian religion, god of nature, personification of recreative power of spring. Loved by fertility goddess ISHTAR; killed and restored to life by her.

Tampa, resort and port of W Florida, US; on Tampa Bay. Pop. 247,000. Citrus fruit canning indust., phosphates export; breweries, cigar mfg.

Tampere (Swed. *Tammerfors*), city of SW Finland, between Lakes Näsi and Pyhä. Pop. 154,000. Railway jct.; indust. centre, esp. textiles, timber, using h.e.p. from nearby rapids. Has cathedral (20th cent.).

Tamworth Manifesto, election address by ROBERT PEEL at Tamworth, Staffordshire (1834). Considered manifesto for emerging Conservative Party; accepted Reform Bill of 1832 and proposed careful social and economic reform.

Tana or **Tsana, Lake,** largest lake of Ethiopia, in NW. Area 3625 sq km (1400 sq mi); alt. 1830 m (6000 ft). Source of Blue Nile.

tanager, small songbird found mainly in New World tropics; male usually brightly coloured. North American species incl. scarlet tanager, *Piranga olivacea*.

Tanaka, Kakuei (1918-), Japanese politician. Premier of Liberal Democratic govt. (1972-4), resigned in corruption scandal.

Tananarive, cap. of Malagasy Republic, in C Madagascar highlands. Pop. 378,000. Admin., commercial centre; univ.; railway to port at Tamatave. Founded 17th cent., taken (1895) by French.

T'ang, Chinese imperial dynasty (618-907). Under second emperor, T'ai Tsung (627-649), China became strongest and largest empire on earth. Period marked by prosperity, stability, development of bureaucracy. Poetry and painting flourished.

Tanga, town in NE Tanzania, on Indian Ocean. Pop. 61,000. Railway terminus; port, exports sisal, coffee, copra.

Tanganyika, see TANZANIA.

Tanganyika, Lake, lake of EC Africa, in Great Rift Valley. Borders on Burundi (NE), Tanzania (E), Zambia (S), Zaïre (W). Area 32,900 sq km (12,700 sq mi); second deepest (1432 m/4700 ft) in world. Reached 1858 by Burton and Speke.

tangerine, small, thin-skinned variety of ORANGE belonging to mandarin orange species, *Citrus reticulata*. Native to SE Asia, now

widely grown in tropical and subtropical regions.

Tangier (anc. *Tingis*), city of N Morocco, on Str. of Gibraltar. Pop. 186,000. Port, commercial and tourist centre. Focus of dispute over Morocco in 19th cent., estab. (1923) as international zone. Part of Morocco from 1956, declared free port 1961.

tangle, see KELP.

tango, dance of Spanish-American origin, internationally popular since *c* 1915. Tempo is moderately slow, and rhythm similar to Cuban habanera.

Tangshan, city of Hopeh prov., NE China. Pop. (pre 1976) 1,200,000. Coalmining centre. Iron and steel works, motor vehicle and chemical mfg. Devastated by earthquake (1976), est. 500,000 killed.

Tanguy, Yves (1900-55), French surrealist painter. Paintings of sparse dreamlike landscapes filled with strange objects incl. *Sun on Cushion* (1937).

tank, heavily armoured vehicle, moving on tracks, mounting a field gun or smaller armament. First used by the British in the Somme (1916). Became major weapon of land warfare in WWII, esp. in N Africa.

Tannenberg (Pol. *Stebark*), village of Olsztyn prov., NE Poland. Scene of defeat (1410) of Teutonic Knights by Poles and Lithuanians under Ladislaus II, and defeat (1914) of Russians by Germans under Hindenburg.

tannin or **tannic acid,** astringent compound present in many plants, *eg* tea, walnut, gall nuts, hemlock and oak bark. Used in tanning, making of inks, as a fixative in dyeing and for clarifying solutions in medicine.

tanning, process by which animal skins are turned into leather. Skins are usually soaked in tannin obtained from vegetable material. Alum and chrome salts or fats and oils (for chamois leather) are also employed.

tansy, *Tanacetum vulgare,* common European flowering herb of daisy family now naturalized in North America. Formerly used as stimulant in medicine, now cultivated as garden plant.

Tanta, city of N Egypt, on Nile delta. Pop. 254,000. Railway and commercial centre, cotton indust. Noted for Moslem festivals and fairs.

tantalum (Ta), rare metallic element; at. no. 73, at. wt. 180.95. Occurs with niobium in certain minerals. Corrosion resistant, malleable and ductile. Used in surgical instruments, manufacture of hard alloys, and electronic equipment.

Tantalus, in Greek myth, son of Zeus and father of Pelops and Niobe. For angering the gods, eternally punished in Tartarus by being set in pool of water, hungry and thirsty, but unable either to drink from the pool, or to reach fruit trees.

Tantra, group of post-Vedic Sanskrit treatises. Consist of dialogues between SIVA and his consort. Basis of various secret and erotic cults which worshipped female divinities. Influenced Hindu erotic art.

Tanzania, republic of E Africa. Area 945,000 sq km (364,900 sq mi); pop. 15,607,000; cap. Dar-es-Salaam. Languages: Swahili, English. Religions: native, Islam, Christianity. Narrow coastal plain; interior plateau, with volcanic peaks (eg Kilimanjaro), cut by Great Rift Valley. Bordered by L. Tanganyika (W) Victoria Nyanza (N). Exports coffee, cotton, sisal, diamonds; TanZam railway links Zambia with Dar-es-Salaam. Explored 16th cent. by Portuguese; ivory, slave trade under Arabs 18th-19th cent. Part of German East Africa from 1884; mandated to Britain 1916. Independent 1961. Tanzania formed 1964 by union of Tanganyika with Zanzibar.

Taoism, Chinese religion and philosophy. Based on book, *Tao-teh-king,* traditionally ascribed to Lao-tse (6th cent. BC) but prob. written 3rd cent. BC. By AD 5th cent., developed into religious system with influences from Mahayana Buddhism. Emphasized effortless action, cessation of all striving. Condemned social philosophy of Confucius.

Tapajós, river of WC Brazil. Rises in Mato Grosso, flows NE 970 km (c 600 mi) to join Amazon at Santarém.

tape recorder, electromagnetic instrument which records speech and music by interpreting sounds as variations in magnetic field which act on MAGNETIC TAPE. On playback, magnetic patterns reconverted into electrical impulses, in turn converted into audible sound waves.

tapestry, ornamental fabric for covering walls, furniture and for curtains. Made by interweaving of plain warp threads with silk or wool of varying colour and texture. European wool tapestries are extant from 10th cent. Noted centres were Arras (from 14th cent.), Brussels, Aubusson, Beauvais and Gobelins factory, Paris.

tapeworm, long ribbon-shaped segmented parasitic flatworm of class Cestoda. Adults infest intestines of man and other vertebrates, absorbing nutrients through body; life cycle may involve several hosts.

tapioca, *see* CASSAVA.

tapir, nocturnal timid pig-like ungulate of tropical America and SE Asia. Flexible snout, resembling small trunk; herbivorous. Species incl. Malayan tapir, *Tapirus indicus*, with black limbs and forequarters, white hindquarters.

tar, dark brown or black viscous liquid obtained from distillation of wood, coal and similar substances. Pitch is more solid form. Used for road-making, as protective coating for wood, *etc.* Distillation of coal tar yields basels for aniline dyes.

Tara, Hill of, Co. Meath, E Irish Republic. Seat of Irish kings until 6th cent. Earthworks.

Taranaki, region of W North Isl., New Zealand. Area 9710 sq km (3750 sq mi); pop. 101,000; main town New Plymouth. Sheep farming in E hills; dairying (butter, cheese mfg.) on W lowlands.

Taranto (anc. *Tarentum*), town of Apulia, SE Italy, on Gulf of Taranto. Cap. of Ionio prov. Pop. 236,000. Port, naval base; major steelworks. Founded 8th cent. BC by Greeks, taken by Rome 272 BC. Byzantine castle, medieval cathedral.

tarantula, name given to various large hairy spiders of Theraphosidae family, with poisonous but rarely fatal bite. Name originally applied to S European *Lycosa tarantula* whose bite was believed to lead to dancing mania in Middle Ages.

Tarbes, town of SW France, on R. Adour, cap. of Hautes-Pyrénées

dept. Pop. 60,000. Tourist resort; livestock trade. Romanesque cathedral.

tare, *see* VETCH.

tariffs or **customs,** duties on imported goods intended to protect domestic producers by increasing prices of imports in relation to home-produced goods. Used as protectionist policy by most countries, EEC is leading example of international cooperation on tariffs. Opposed to FREE TRADE.

Tarn, river of S France. Flows c 370 km (230 mi) from Cévennes via Albi, Montauban to R. Garonne. Limestone gorges attract tourists.

taro, *Colocasia esculenta,* large, tropical Asiatic plant of arum family. Shield-shaped leaves. Cultivated for edible corms.

tarot, oldest surviving card game, using esoteric designs; now used mainly for fortune-telling.

tarpan, wild horse, once common in Europe and Asia, closely related to Przewalski's horse. Became extinct c 1900; attempts since made in Poland to regenerate species by selective breeding.

tarpon, *Tarpon atlanticus,* large primitive fish found in warm Atlantic waters; reaches lengths of 1.8 m/6 ft. Popular game fish.

Tarquinius Superbus, Lucius (fl 6th cent. BC), last king of Rome. Expelled from Rome (510 BC) because of his despotism; enlisted the aid of Etruscan Lars Porsena to restore himself to throne. Although Porsena captured Rome, Tarquinius was not made king.

tarragon, *Artemisia dracunculus,* European perennial WORMWOOD.

Long, slender aromatic leaves used as seasoning, esp. in vinegar.

Tarragona, town of NE Spain, on Mediterranean Sea, cap. of Tarragona prov. Pop. 78,000. Port, exports wine; Chartreuse liqueur mfg. from 1903. Cap. of Roman *Tarraconensis.* Roman walls, aqueduct. Cathedral (12th cent.).

Tarrasa, city of Catalonia, NE Spain. Pop. 139,000. Major textile centre, esp. woollens, cotton.

tarsier, small arboreal primate of Tarsiidae family, related to lemur; found in Philippines and East Indies. Rat-sized, with large eyes and ears; long feet and hands equipped with sucker-like discs. Nocturnal, feeds on lizards, insects, *etc.*

Tarsus, town of S Turkey. Pop. 57,000. Agric. trade centre. Has extensive ruins of ancient Tarsus, cap. of Cilicia. Birthplace of St Paul.

tartan, woollen cloth woven in pattern of coloured checks. Tartan kilts and plaids were worn by Scottish clans from 15th cent., each clan having distinctive pattern. Illegal (1746-82) after 1745 Jacobite uprising.

tartaric acid, crystalline organic acid, found in vegetable tissue and fruit juices. Salt, potassium hydrogen tartrate, present in grape juice, is deposited as argol in wine casks; used in baking powder (cream of tartar).

Tartars or **Tatars,** name given to peoples who invaded Russia (13th cent.) under Mongol leadership. Known as GOLDEN HORDE, they overran and dominated parts of Eurasia until their empire was lost to Ottomans and dukes of Moscow (15th-16th cents.). In USSR, there are *c* 5 million Tartars, who are Moslems and speak a Turkic language.

Tartarus, in Greek myth, abyss below HADES where Zeus hurled Titans. Place of punishment of wicked after death.

Tartini, Giuseppe (1692-1770), Italian composer, violinist. Founded school of violin-playing at Padua (1728), wrote treatises on violin-playing. Numerous compositions incl. concertos, symphonies, sonatas (incl. *The Devil's Trill*).

Tartu (Ger. *Dorpat*), town of USSR, Estonia SSR. Pop. *c* 84,000. Metalworking, textile, cigarette mfg. Founded in 1030 as Yuryev; Hanseatic town. Disputed by Poland, Sweden and Russia; passed to Russia (1704). Has univ. founded by Gustavus Adolphus of Sweden (1632).

Tashkent, city of USSR, cap. of Uzbek SSR; in oasis of R. Chirchik. Pop. 1,460,000. Cotton textile mfg.; fruit and cotton grown by irrigation. Founded 7th cent.; conquered by Genghis Khan and Tamerlane. Taken by Russia in 1865.

Tasman, Abel Janszoon (1603-59), Dutch navigator. Discovered Tasmania (named it Van Diemen's Land), New Zealand, Friendly Isls. (1642-3); proved Australia . not united to polar continent.

Tasmania, isl. state of Australia, separated from SE mainland by Bass Str. Area incl. King Isl. and Furneaux Isls. 67,900 sq km (26,200 sq mi); pop. 390,000; cap. Hobart. Large forested C plateau with many lakes and valleys; narrow coastal plains. Fruit (esp. apples) and vegetable growing, wool, dairying;

timber indust.; h.e.p.; minerals incl. copper, zinc. Discovered (1642) and named Van Diemen's Land by Tasman. First settled (1803) as penal colony, part of New South Wales until 1825; federal state from 1901.

Tasmanian devil, *Sarcophilus harrisii,* burrowing nocturnal carnivorous marsupial of Tasmania. Much hunted because of attacks on domestic animals, now rare.

Tasmanian wolf or thylacine, *Thylacinus cynocephalus,* wolf-like carnivorous marsupial; red-brown coat with dark stripes on back. Confined to Tasmania, is almost extinct.

Tasman Sea, area of SW Pacific Ocean, between SE Australia and NW New Zealand. Named (1890) after Abel Tasman.

Tasso, Torquato (1544-95), Italian poet, one of most famous of Renaissance. Known for *Gerusalemme Liberata* (*Jerusalem Delivered,* 1575), religious epic on 1st Crusade, and *Aminta* (1573), hedonistic pastoral play. Also wrote lyrics.

taste, sensation caused by stimulation of sensory organs (taste buds) in mucous membranes of tongue and palate. Four basic tastes: bitter, salt, sour and sweet. Flavour depends more on smell than taste.

Tatars, *see* TARTARS.

Tate, Nahum (1652-1715), English author, b. Ireland. Remembered for version of Shakespeare's *King Lear* with happy ending which was generally produced until mid-19th cent. Made poet laureate (1692).

Tate Gallery, art gallery in London, containing British national collection of modern foreign art and British art. Opened 1897 following donation of pictures and money by Sir Henry Tate (1819-99).

Tati, Jacques (1908-), French actor. Originally in music hall, later known for writing, directing and acting in films, incl. *Monsieur Hulot's Holiday* (1952), *Playtime* (1968), *Traffic* (1971).

Tatlin, Vladimir (1885-1953), Russian painter, designer. Influenced by cubism, founded CONSTRUCTIVISM. Most famous work is model of giant spiral tower in wood and glass called *Monument to the 3rd International.*

Tatra Mountains (Czech *Tatry*), range on Czech-Polish border, part of Carpathians. High Tatra (N) reach 2662 m (8737 ft); Low Tatra (S) reach 2044 m (6709 ft). Tourism; winter sports.

Taunton, mun. bor. and co. town of Somerset, SW England. Pop. 37,000. Clothing mfg. Scene of Judge Jeffreys' 'Bloody Assize' after Monmouth's rebellion (1685).

Taupo, Lake, largest lake in New Zealand, in volcanic region of C North Isl. Area 620 sq km (240 sq mi). Used as h.e.p. reservoir; tourist area, with hot springs.

Taurus, *see* ZODIAC.

Taurus Mountains, range of S Turkey, running parallel to Mediterranean. Rises to 3734 m (12,251 ft) at Ala Dag; crossed by Cilician Gates N of Tarsus. Extends NE as Anti-Taurus. Has important mineral deposits (chromium, copper).

tautomerism, in chemistry, existence of certain compounds as a mixture of 2 isomeric forms in equilibrium; each form may be converted into the other but the equilibrium will tend to be maintained in the mixture.

Taverner, John (c 1490-1545), English composer. Wrote polyphonic church music in elaborate Tudor vocal style. Works incl. 8 Masses, 3 Magnificats, motets. Believed to have abandoned music to work as paid agent of Thomas Cromwell.

Tawney, R[ichard] H[enry] (1880-1962), English economic historian, b. India. Best known for *Religion and the Rise of Capitalism* (1926), relating Protestant ethic and early capitalism.

tawny owl, *Strix aluco*, woodland bird of Europe and Asia; black eyes, no ear-tufts, tawny-brown upperparts.

taxation, govt. levy to provide revenue. Oldest form is land tax; other means of taxation developed as scope of govt. responsibilities widened, esp. in 19th-20th cent. Direct taxes, graduated according to individual's ability to pay, incl. INCOME TAX (major source of internal revenue), death duties or inheritance tax, rates, corporation tax. Forms of indirect taxation incl. sales, purchase and value-added taxes, based on stipulated percentage of retail cost. All levels of govt. have designated taxation powers. Income tax is levied by national govt., eg by Inland Revenue in UK and by Internal Revenue in US.

taxidermy, art of skinning and preserving animals in life-like state, mostly for exhibition. Fur or feathers are cleaned with special preservative preparation and hide is stretched over artificial framework.

Tay, longest river of Scotland, flows 193 km (120 mi) from Central region via Loch Tay, Firth of Tay, to North Sea. Estuary crossed by road, rail bridges at Dundee. Salmon fishing.

Taylor, A[lan] J[ohn] P[ercivale] (1906-), English historian. Works incl. *The Origins of the Second World War* (1961). Noted popularizer through his TV lectures and newspaper articles.

Taylor, Zachary (1784-1850), American statesman, president (1849-50). Renowned Indian fighter; won decisive victory at Buena Vista (1847) in Mexican War. Successful Whig presidential candidate (1848). Died in office.

Tayside, region of EC Scotland. Area 7501 sq km (2896 sq mi); pop. 397,000; chief city Dundee. Created 1975, incl. former Angus, Kinrosshire, most of Perthshire.

Tbilisi (Russ. *Tiflis*), city of USSR, cap. of Georgian SSR; route centre on R. Kura. Pop. 927,000; Agric., trade centre; textile, machinery mfg. Founded 4th cent.; prospered on trade route between Europe and Asia. Under Russian rule from 1800. Old section incl. Zion cathedral (5th cent.) and Armenian cathedral (15th cent.).

Tchaikovsky, Piotr Ilich (1840-93), Russian composer. His music is melodious and romantic; orchestral compositions particularly popular. Works incl. *Pathétique* symphony, ballets *Swan Lake*, *The Sleeping Beauty*, and fantasies, eg *Romeo and Juliet*. Also wrote *1812* overture, operas, song cycle *Eugene Onegin*, piano and violin concertos.

tea, *Thea sinensis*, shrub with fragrant white flowers, extensively cultivated in China, Japan, India, Sri

Lanka, etc. Bitter, aromatic beverage is prepared by infusion of dried leaves in boiling water. Tea drinking became popular in Britain in 17th cent.

Teach, Edward (d. 1718), English pirate, called 'Blackbeard'. Gained notoriety through his raids on West Indies and coasts of Virginia and the Carolinas. Killed by force sent by governor of Virginia.

teak, *Tectona grandis*, large East Indian timber tree of family Verbenaceae. Now cultivated in W Africa and tropical America. Hard, yellowish wood used in shipbuilding and furniture.

teal, small freshwater duck, genus *Anas*. Species incl. green-winged teal, *A. crecca*, smallest European duck, and North American blue-winged teal, *A. discors*.

Teapot Dome scandal, incident arising out of lease (1922) of US naval oil reserve, Teapot Dome, in Wyoming. Secretary of Interior, Albert Fall, convicted for accepting bribes to lease land without competitive bidding. Senate investigations led to allegations of govt. corruption.

tear gas, aerosol, usually bromide compound, inducing temporary loss of sight through excessive flow of tears. Used in warfare and civil disturbances.

teasel, any of genus *Dipsacus* of biennial or perennial herbs native to Europe, Asia and N Africa. Fuller's teasel, *D. fullonum*, is cultivated for its prickly flower heads, used for raising the nap on woollen cloth.

technetium (Tc), radioactive metallic element; at. no. 43, mass no. of most stable isotope 97. First

artificially made element, prepared 1937; now obtained as fission product of uranium.

technology, study of methods used in application of science in industry. First technological univ., Ecole Polytechnique, Paris (1794). US institutes incl. Massachusetts (1861) and California (1913).

tectonics, study of the main structural features of the Earth's crust. Current theories on changing formation of Earth's surface centre on PLATE TECTONICS.

Tedder, Arthur William Tedder, 1st Baron (1890-1967), British air force officer. In WWII, organized Middle East air campaign against Rommel. Deputy Supreme Commander, Europe, under Eisenhower (1943-5).

Tees, river of N England. Flows 113 km (70 mi) from Pennines to North Sea at Middlesbrough.

Teesside, bor. of Cleveland, NE England, at mouth of R. Tees. Pop. 395,000. Heavy industs. Formed 1968 from Middlesbrough, Redcar, Stockton-on-Tees, etc.

teeth, in most vertebrates, hard bone-like structures embedded in upper and lower jaws, serving to bite, tear and chew. Tooth consists of pulp-filled central cavity, surrounded by shell of dentine (ivory) which is coated on crown by enamel and on root by softer cement. In man, early set of 20 deciduous (or milk) teeth is replaced by 32 permanent teeth, beginning in c 6th year. On each side of jaw, there are 2 incisors, 1 canine, 2 premolars and 3 molars.

Tegucigalpa, cap. of Honduras, on Choluteca R. Pop. 219,000. Food processing, distilling, cigarette, textile mfg. Founded 1578 as gold, silver mining centre. Became cap. 1880. Has univ. (1847); 18th cent. cathedral.

Tehran or **Teheran, cap.** of Iran, S of Elburz Mts. Pop. 3,858,000. Industrial, commercial and transport centre. Became cap. 1788 under Aga Mohammed Khan. In royal palace is Peacock Throne, brought from India. City centre modernized after 1925 by Riza Shah. Univ (1935). Scene of Allied Conference (1943).

Tehran Conference, meeting (Nov.-Dec. 1943) held at Tehran between Allied leaders Churchill, F.D. Roosevelt and Stalin during WWII. Outlined plans for invasion of Europe and role of UN in peace settlement.

Tehuantepec, isthmus of E Mexico between Campeche and Tehuantepec gulfs. Narrowest part of Mexico.

Teilhard de Chardin, Pierre (1881-1955), French theologian, palaeontologist. A Jesuit, he attempted controversial reconciliation of Christian theology with evolutionary theory. Evolved concept of interaction of psychic and physical energy. Works, pub. posthumously, incl. *The Phenomenon of Man* (1955), *The Divine Milieu* (1957).

Tejo, *see.* TAGUS.

Tel Aviv, city of WC Israel, on Mediterranean. Pop. 362,000. Financial, indust. centre; textiles, metals, chemicals. Incorporated neighbouring Jaffa 1949. Univ. (1953). International airport.

telecommunications, long-distance communication . by radio, TELEGRAPH, TELEPHONE, *etc.* Formerly relied on long distance cables, now increasingly uses microwaves reflected from artificial satellites. First of these was *Telstar* (launched July, 1962).

telegraph, method of sending messages in form of electrical impulses by radio or wire. First practicable system developed by Samuel Morse (c 1837). Traditionally, message carried by opening and closing circuit at a distance; sophistications incl. simultaneous transmission of several messages, reception of messages in printed form (teleprinter), and transmission of photographs (facsimile ·machine).

Tel-el-Amarna or **Tell-el-Amarna,** site of N Egypt, N of Asyût. City of Akhetaton built here c 1365 BC by IKHNATON as new cap. and centre of reformed religion. Ruins, rock tombs; inscribed tablets discovered 1887.

Telemachus, in Greek myth, son of Odysseus and Penelope. Set out to search for his father, returned in time to help in massacre of Penelope's suitors.

Telemann, Georg Philipp (1681-1767), German composer. Director of music for several churches in Hamburg from 1721. Wrote numerous compositions, incl. motets, 44 passions, oratorios, 600 overtures, 40 operas, keyboard and chamber music.

telepathy, *see* PSYCHICAL RESEARCH.

telephone, device for conveying speech over distances by converting sound into electrical impulses. Invented by Alexander Bell (1876).

telephoto lens, combination of convex and concave lenses, used to increase effective focal length of camera and thus magnify images, without increasing distance between film and camera lens.

telescope, optical instrument for viewing distant objects. Refracting telescope uses 2 convex lenses, objective and eyepiece; reflecting telescope uses concave mirror and eyepiece. A further lens or prism is needed for upright image. Invented (c 1608) in Holland, first used for astronomy by Galileo (1609).

television, transmission and reception of visual images using electromagnetic radiation. Pattern of electric impulses from camera reconstructed in receiver to form picture on luminous screen. First developed in UK by John Logie Baird (1926) using mechanical scanning system; later replaced by electronic scanning. TV has become a major form of media communication, profoundly affecting esp. Western lifestyles. Also *see* BROADCASTING.

Telford, Thomas (1757-1834), Scottish civil engineer. Built Caledonian Canal (1803-23), c 1000 miles of roads in Scotland. Constructed (1826) Menai Suspension Bridge, Anglesey.

Tell, William (*fl* c 1300), Swiss hero. Traditionally, forced to shoot apple off son's head as punishment for failure to recognize Austrian authority. After his success, he instigated revolt by shooting Austrian bailiff, Gessler.

Teller, Edward (1908-), American physicist, b. Hungary. Authority in nuclear physics, aided atomic bomb research during WWII. Called 'father of hydrogen bomb' for contributions to development of H-bomb.

tellurium (Te), semi-metallic element, with properties similar to sulphur; at. no. 52, at. wt. 127.6. Appears as brittle white crystalline solid or amorphous powder. Used to colour glass and ceramics, in vulcanizing rubber and in alloys.

Telugu, *see* DRAVIDIAN.

Temesvár, *see* TIMISOARA, Romania.

tempera, method of painting in which pigments are mixed with size, casein or egg, esp. egg yolk. Egg tempera was commonest mode of painting easel paintings until 15th cent.; paint dries quickly to produce dull finish.

temperance movement, movement with aim of persuading people against, or preventing by laws, the consumption of alchoholic beverages. Became powerful in 19th cent., leading to estab. in US of Women's Christian Temperance Union (1874), Anti-Saloon League (1893), Prohibition Party, instrumental in securing PROHIBITION.

temperature, measure of degree of hotness of a body, referred to some scale. Celsius (centigrade) scale takes freezing point of water as $0°$, boiling point of water as $100°$. Fahrenheit scale takes freezing point as $32°$ and boiling point as $212°$. Kelvin or absolute scale takes ABSOLUTE ZERO as its zero point. Kelvin and Celsius degrees are equal, Fahrenheit degree equals 5/9 of Celsius degree.

Temple, Sir William (1628-99), English diplomat, essayist. Negotiated Triple Alliance with Holland and Sweden against France (1668) and William of Orange's marriage to Mary. Devoted himself to writing after 1681. Husband of Dorothy Osborne who wrote him famous series of letters (1652-4).

Temple, William (1881-1944), English churchman. Archbishop of York (1929-42), of Canterbury (1942-4). First president of Workers' Educational Association (1908-24). Works incl. *Nature, Man and God* (1934).

Temple, three centres of worship successively built by the Jews in ancient Jerusalem: Solomon's, destroyed by Nebuchadnezzar; Zerubbabel's, built after exile in Babylon; and Herod's, destroyed by Romans (AD 70). Wailing Wall survives as part of the last.

tempo, in music, indication of speed at which piece should be played. A description is given often in Italian, eg largo, andante, allegro, presto, or a metronome number is given indicating number of beats per minute.

tench, *Tinca tinca,* European freshwater fish of carp family. Bronze-brown with red eyes.

Ten Commandments or **Decalogue,** in OT, summary of law of God as given to Moses in form of 10 statements on Mt. Sinai. Basis of ethical code of Judaism, Christianity and Islam. Divided into 3 groups dealing with duty to God, personal integrity, proper treatment of others.

tendon, cord of tough fibrous tissue which connects muscle with bone. Achilles tendon attaches muscles of the calf to the heel bone.

Tenerife, largest of Canary Isls., Spain. Area 2060 sq km (795 sq mi); cap. Santa Cruz. Rises to 3712 m (12,192 ft) in volcanic Pico de Teide. Tourist resort; banana, tomato growing.

Teng Hsiao-ping (1904-), Chinese political leader. General secretary of Communist Party (1956-67; removed from office during Cultural Revolution. Restored to office (1973), influence declining with death of Chou En-lai (1975) and increasing after death of Mao Tse-tung (1976). Vice-chairman of Communist Party and vice-premier from 1977.

Teniers, David (1610-90), Flemish painter. Court painter to Archduke Leopold Wilhelm, governor of Austrian Netherlands, and curator of his great art collection. Known for his genre scenes of peasant life and paintings of the archduke's collection.

Tennessee, state of EC US. Area 109,412 sq km (42,244 sq mi); pop. 3,924,000; cap. Nashville; largest city Memphis. Mississippi R. forms W border; agric. plain rises to Cumberland Plateau and Appalachians in E. Cotton, tobacco, maize, livestock farming; coal, stone and zinc, phosphate mining; industs. incl. textiles, chemical mfg. Economic development under Tennessee Valley Authority. British estab. claim 1763; admitted to Union as 16th state (1796). Joined Confederacy in Civil War; important battlegrounds.

Tennessee, river of EC US. Formed in E Tennessee, flows 1050 km (650 mi) SW through Tennessee, Kentucky to Ohio R. Series of dams created by Tennessee Valley Authority (estab. 1933) control flooding and provide h.e.p.

Tennessee Valley Authority (TVA), independent, govt.-supported agency, created (1933) by US

Congress, empowered to develop Muscle Shoals, Alabama, and integrate power and irrigation projects of Tennessee R. basin. Widespread programme arrested flood damage, soil erosion, provided stimulus for growth of region.

Tenniel, Sir John (1820-1914), English caricaturist. Cartoonist of *Punch* (1851-1901). Illustrated *Alice in Wonderland* (1866) and *Through the Looking-Glass* (1870).

tennis or **lawn tennis**, ball-and-racket game played by 2 or 4 players on prepared surface, either indoors or outdoors. Descended from royal game (real tennis) played in France and England in 14th cent. Modern game devised by Major Wingfield in England (1873); 1st Wimbledon championships held 1877. International tournaments restricted to amateur players until late 1960s, esp. popular in US, Australia, England, Europe.

Tennyson, Alfred Tennyson, 1st Baron (1809-92), English poet. Shorter poems incl. 'Ulysses', 'Break, Break, Break', elegies incl. *In Memoriam* (1850). Longer narrative poems incl. *The Charge of the Light Brigade* (1855), *Idylls of the King* (1859-88) on Arthurian legends. Created poet laureate (1850).

tenor, in singing, high male voice, below alto but above baritone. Also member of family of instruments of similar range, *eg* tenor trombone.

Tensing Norkay, *see* HILLARY, SIR EDMUND.

tent caterpillar, hairy moth caterpillar, genus *Malacosoma*, that lives colonially in tent-like webs spun in trees. Causes serious defoliation; common in North America.

tepee or **tipi,** *see* WIGWAM.

tequila, Mexican spirit distilled from fermented juice of various agaves.

terbium (Tb), metallic element of lanthanide series; at. no. 65, at. wt. 158.92. Occurs in gadolinite; difficult to isolate.

Ter Borch, Gerard (1617-81), Dutch painter. Known for his small portraits and scenes of prosperous middle-class life. Most famous work is *Peace of Münster.*

terebinth, *Pistacia terebinthus,* small European tree. Bark yields turpentine.

Terence, full name Publius Terentius Afer (*c* 195-159 BC), Roman comic poet. After Plautus, leading adapter of Greek New Comedy for Roman stage. Influenced modern comedy of manners. Works incl. *Andria, Hecyra, Eunuchus* and *Adelphi.*

Teresina, town of N Brazil, cap. of Piauí state; on Parnaíba R. Pop. 221,000. Agric., livestock market, sugar refining; textiles, soap mfg.

termite, any of order Isoptera of soft-bodied social insects. Lives in colonies composed of several castes: fertile winged forms, sterile workers and soldiers, *etc.* Builds or tunnels large nests; feeds on wood, destroying trees and wooden structures. Most species are tropical.

tern, migratory seabird of Laridae family, related to gull. Species incl. common tern, *Sterna hirundo*, of Europe and North America; slender body, forked tail, graceful flight.

Terni, city of Umbria, C Italy, cap. of Terni prov. Pop. 106,000. Railway jct., iron and steel, munitions; h.e.p. from nearby waterfalls. Founded 7th cent. BC. Birthplace of Tacitus.

terpenes, in chemistry, series of unsaturated hydrocarbons, found in resins and essential oils. Used in perfumes and medicine.

Terpsichore, in Greek myth, Muse of dancing. Represented with lyre and plectrum.

terracotta, hard reddish brick-like earthenware, porous and unglazed. Used since antiquity for statues, figures, vases, *etc.*

terrapin, name applied to several species of edible aquatic turtles. Species incl. diamond back terrapin, *Malaclemys terrapin,* found in salt marshes of S and E US.

terrier, breed of dog originally used to dig out burrowing animals. Breeds incl. Boston, bull, cairn, fox, Scottish and Skye terriers.

Territorial Army, British volunteer force. Estab. under Territorial and Reserve Forces Act of 1907. Replaced in 1967 by a smaller Territorial and Army Volunteer Reserve.

Terry, Dame Ellen Alice (1847-1928), English actress. Acted opposite Henry Irving, accompanying him on American tours. Notable in Shakespearian roles.

Tertiary period, first geological period of Cenozoic era; began c 65 million years ago, lasted c 63 million years. Comprises Palaeocene, Eocene, Oligocene, Miocene, Pliocene epochs. Alpine, Himalayan mountain-building period. Evolution of primitive mammals, ancestors of modern fauna, eg mammoths, manlike apes; had modern birds. Deterioration of climate toward end of period. Also *see* GEOLOGICAL TABLE.

Test Act, legislation passed (1673) by English Parliament to exclude from office those who refused to take oaths of supremacy and allegiance and to receive communion according to Church of England. Repealed (1828).

test-ban treaty, see DISARMAMENT.

testis or testicle, either of two oval male sex glands which are suspended in the scrotum. Secretes spermatozoa and sex hormone testosterone.

testosterone, male steroid sex hormone, obtained as white crystalline substance from animal testes. Promotes development of male secondary sex characteristics.

tetanus or lockjaw, acute infectious disease caused by toxin released by bacterium *Clostridium tetani,* which usually enters body through wounds. Toxin disturbs motor nerve cells, causing muscular spasms, esp. in jaw, face and neck. Prevented by vaccination, treated with tetanus antitoxin.

tetracycline, any of group of broad-spectrum antibiotics derived from bacteria of genus *Streptomyces.*

Tetuán or Tétouan, city of N Morocco. Pop. 137,000. Textile, leather industs.; Mediterranean outport at Río Martín exports agric. produce. Former cap. of Spanish Morocco (1912-56).

Teutonic Knights, members of medieval German military and religious order, founded c 1190 in Holy Land. Undertook conquest of pagan E Prussia (13th cent.), where they estab. their rule. Gradually lost power to the Poles after defeat at Tannenberg (1410).

Teutonic mythology, pre-Christian religious mythology of tribes of Germany and Scandinavia. Originally 2 groups of gods: Aesir, Vanir; Vanir was absorbed by Aesir. Chief gods incl. Woden (ODIN), Tiw, Thor, Frey and Freyja; all lived in the palace of Valhalla in ASGARD. Gods were not immortal and most were doomed to die at RAGNAROK. Related stories, with some Christian influence, found in Icelandic Norse myths.

Tewkesbury, mun. bor. of Gloucestershire, SW England, on R. Severn. Pop. 9000. Has Norman abbey (12th cent.). Scene of Yorkist victory during Wars of the Roses (1471).

Texas, state of SC US; on Gulf of Mexico. Area 692,408 sq km (267,339 sq mi); pop. 11,197,000; cap. Austin; main cities Houston, Dallas, San Antonio. Plains in N Panhandle, plains in W, Rio Grande separates Texas from Mexico, Red R. forms NE border. Greatest agric. yield in US. Livestock, major cotton crop, rice, grains; minerals esp. oil, natural gas. Space research indust. Spanish settlement in 18th cent. Americans ousted Mexicans (1835-6). Republic until annexed by US (1845), precipitating Mexican War. Admitted to Union as 28th state (1845). Joined Confederacy in Civil War.

Thackeray, William Makepeace (1811-63), English author, b. India. Masterpiece *Vanity Fair* (1847-8) uses self-seeking adventuress as heroine to expose hypocrisy of social code. Other novels incl. *Pendennis* (1850), *Henry Esmond* (1852), *The Newcomes* (1853-5).

Thailand, kingdom of SE Asia. Area c 514,000 sq km (198,500 sq mi);

pop. 42,960,000; cap. Bangkok. Language: Thai. Religion: Hinayana Buddhism. C plain watered by R. Chao Phraya, major rice producing area; S is narrow strip extending down Malay penin. Mainly agric. economy; produces tin, tungsten, rubber, teak. Siamese kingdom dates from 14th cent.; frequent wars with Burmese; lost territ. to British and French in 19th-20th cent. Constitutional monarchy (1932). Formerly Siam, name changed 1939.

Thales (c 636-c 546 BC), Greek philosopher, mathematician, astronomer. Regarded as first Western philosopher. Believed water to be fundamental matter of Nature.

Thalia, in Greek myth, Muse of comedy. Represented with comic mask, shepherd's staff or wreath of ivy.

thalidomide, drugs used as a sedative in Europe (1958-61). Withdrawn when found to cause defects of limbs in unborn children if taken during 1st 12 weeks of pregnancy. Discovery led to adoption of stricter regulations in testing of new drugs.

thallium (Tl), rare soft metallic element, similar to lead; at. no. 81, at. wt. 204.37. Obtained from flue dust during processing of pyrites ores. Thallium and its compounds are poisonous; used in insecticides, rat poison, and alloys.

Thames, river of S England. Flows 338 km (210 mi) from Cotswolds via Oxford, Reading, London to North Sea. Tidal to Teddington, W London; hist. major waterway, serving port of London. Boating, angling above London.

Thanet, Isle of, Kent, SE England.

True isl. until 16th cent. Resorts incl. Ramsgate, Margate.

Thanksgiving Day, US national holiday. Commemorates 1st harvest of Plymouth Colony and celebration feast held by Pilgrims and neighbouring Indians. Celebrated 4th Thursday in Nov.; also observed in Canada.

Thant, U (1909-74), Burmese diplomat. Succeeded Dag Hammarskjöld as UN secretary-general (1961-72); granted wider emergency powers. Sought to bring stability to Middle East.

Thar Desert, sandy region of NW India; mainly in Rajasthan, extends into Pakistan.

Thásos, isl. of Greece, in N Aegean Sea. Area 399 sq km (154 sq mi). Olives, vines. Famous goldmines, exploited by Phoenicians. Turkish from 1455, passed to Greece 1913.

Thatcher, Margaret Hilda, née Roberts (1925-), British politician. Succeeded Edward Heath as leader of Conservative Party (1975). Became first woman PM in UK (1979-).

theatre, building for presentation of dramatic performances. Originally an outdoor auditorium for Greek drama, first recorded c 5th cent. BC. In Middle Ages, European religious drama performed in churches and in open. Palladio's Teatro Olimpico (1580) was 1st indoor secular theatre. English Elizabethan theatres used courtyard plan, open to the air. By 17th-18th cent., audience separated from performers by raised stage, lights, curtains. 'Theatre in the round', with actors entirely surrounded by audience, is 20th cent. innovation.

Thebes, ancient city of C Egypt, site now occupied by Karnak and Luxor. Fl between XI and XX dynasties (2134-1085 BC) as cap. of Upper Egypt, centre of Amon worship. Many remains, incl. Tutankhamen's tomb (discovered 1922) in nearby Valley of the Kings.

Thebes (mod. *Thívai*), ancient city of Boeotia, SE Greece. Led Boeotian League; fought against Athens in Persian, Peloponnesian Wars. Defeated Sparta at Leuctra (371 BC). Defeated and destroyed (336 BC) by Alexander the Great.

theft, see LARCENY.

Theiss, see TISZA, Hungary.

Themistocles (c 525-c 460 BC), Athenian statesman. Responsible for the building of a strong Athenian navy. During Persian invasion of Greece (480), planned both the evacuation of Athens and Greek naval victory at Salamis. Exiled by his opponents (471), fled to Persia.

Theocritus (fl 270 BC), Greek poet. Regarded as founder of pastoral poetry, using own background of Sicily which, when imitated later, became artificial, set form for genre. Poems known as idylls.

theodolite, portable surveying instrument with telescopic sight. Used to establish horizontal and vertical angles.

Theodorakis, Mikis (1925-), Greek composer. Noted for revival of Greek popular music in 1960s, esp. through his melodious songs. Imprisoned for Communist sympathies; music banned during military dictatorship in Greece.

Theodoric the Great (c 454-526), king of Ostrogoths (c 474-526). Encouraged by Roman emperor of the East, Zeno, to invade Italy (488), he completed his conquest with defeat of ODOVACAR at Ravenna (493). Ruled ably after having Odovacar murdered.

Theodosian Code, Roman legal code issued (AD 438) by Theodosius II, emperor of the East. Was collection of imperial constitutions for benefit of public officials. Used in compiling *Corpus juris civilis.*

Theodosius [I] the Great (c 346-95), Roman emperor in the East (379-95). Proclaimed emperor in the East by Gratian, he defeated the puppet emperor in the West, Eugenius, and replaced him by his own son Honorius. Empire remained split after his death.

theology, the study of God, his attributes and relation with universe. Systematic theology concerns specific doctrine, *eg* Christianity.

Theophanes the Greek (c 1370-c 1405), Byzantine painter. Worked mainly in Russia, teacher of Andrei Rublev. Combined Byzantine, Russian styles. Work incl. frescoes in Church of Transfiguration, Novgorod.

Theophrastus (c 370-c 285 BC), Greek philosopher. Pupil of Aristotle, later took over his school. Wrote extensively on botany, history of philosophy, physics, metaphysics; the *Characters* is collection of 30 sketches of human types.

theosophy, term for various systems which claim direct mystical contact with divine principle. Esp. doctrines of the Theosophical Society founded by Mme BLAVATSKY to promote study of comparative religions and philosophies.

Theresa of Avila, St, orig. Teresa de Cepeda y Ahumada (1515-82), Spanish nun, mystic. Founded (1562) reformed order of (Discalced) Carmelite nuns. Inspired revival and Catholic Reformation. Devotional works incl. *The Way of Perfection* (c 1565).

Theresa of Lisieux, St, orig. Thérèse Martin (1873-97), French Carmelite nun, called 'Little Flower of Jesus'. Spiritual autobiog. *The Story of a Soul* (1897) with account of 'little way' of humble goodness became immensely popular.

thermae, in Roman architecture, public baths, often elaborately decorated and of great architectural splendour. Earliest date from c 25 BC; surviving examples incl. Thermae of Caracalla (AD 217) at Rome.

Thermidor, eleventh month of French Revolutionary calendar. Revolution of 9 Thermidor, year 2, (27 July, 1794) saw overthrow of ROBESPIERRE and end of Reign of Terror; those responsible were called Thermidorians.

thermionic valve, electronic device consisting of heated cathode which emits electrons, an anode which attracts the electrons, and possibly further perforated grids which control electron flow. Arrangement is placed in glass or metal envelope, usually evacuated or containing gas at low pressure. *See* DIODE, TRIODE.

thermit, mixture of aluminium powder and metal oxide (*eg* iron oxide). Emits tremendous heat when ignited by magnesium ribbon. Used esp. in welding and for incendiary bombs.

thermocouple, device used to measure temperature. Consists of pair of different metals joined at each end; one end is kept at fixed temperature, other is placed at point whose temperature is to be found. Temperature difference causes thermoelectric current to flow which is measured by suitably calibrated galvanometer.

thermodynamics, mathematical study of relation between heat and other forms of energy, and the conversion of one form into another. Based on 3 laws, concerning conservation of energy principle and concept of entropy. Applied to theory of heat engines and chemical reactions.

thermometer, instrument used to measure temperature. Common type consists of graduated sealed glass tube with bulb containing mercury or coloured alcohol. Other types used incl. thermocouple, platinum resistance thermometer.

thermonuclear reaction, nuclear fusion reaction between atomic nuclei whose energy is derived from thermal agitation. Principle is employed in hydrogen bomb. Controlled thermonuclear reaction as means of energy production involves problem of containing deuterium and tritium gas at temperatures as high as $5 \times 10^{9}°C$.

Thermopylae, pass of EC Greece. Here Leonidas' 300 Spartans heroically resisted Persians under Xerxes (480 BC).

thermostat, device employing BIMETALLIC STRIP used to regulate temperature automatically or to activate equipment when temperature changes.

Theseus, in Greek myth, son of Aegeus, king of Athens, or of Poseidon. Heroic deeds incl. killing of Minotaur of Crete (with help of ARIADNE). Abducted Queen Hippolyte who bore him Hippolytus. Married Phaedra, sister of Ariadne. Helped Pirithous abduct Persephone; sent to Hades, but rescued by Heracles. Returned to Athens, found his kingdom in rebellion; sailed to Skyros where he was murdered by King Lycomedes.

Thespis (*fl* 6th cent. BC), Greek poet. Traditionally regarded as inventor of tragedy. First to appear in tragedy as actor replying to chorus, thereby introducing dialogue into hitherto choral performance.

Thessalonians, two epistles of NT, written (*c* AD 52) by St Paul from Corinth to church at Thessalonica. Praises faith of Thessalonians but corrects false ideas about general resurrection and the Second Coming.

Thessaloniki, *see* SALONIKA, Greece.

Thessaly (*Thessalia*), region of EC Greece. Mountains flank central fertile lowland drained by R. Peneus. United under Jason (374 BC), fell (344 BC) to Philip II of Macedon; part of Roman Macedonia. Turkish from 1355, passed to Greece 1881.

Thetis, in Greek myth, one of Nereides and mother of Achilles. Loved by Zeus and Poseidon but given by them in marriage to mortal Peleus because of prophecy that her son would be greater than his father.

thiamin or vitamin B₁, vitamin of B group, found in milk, liver, beans, peas, *etc.* Essential to carbohydrate metabolism; deficiency results in beriberi.

Thibault, Jacques Anatole François, see FRANCE, ANATOLE.

Thiers, [Louis] Adolphe (1797-1877), French statesman. Writings in journal *National* helped precipitate July Revolution (1830); held various offices under Louis Philippe. Later, led opposition in legislature to Napoleon III's policies. Negotiated peace after Franco-Prussian War (1871), suppressed Paris Commune. First president of Third Republic (1871-3). Written works incl. *History of the French Revolution* (1823-7).

Thieu, Nguyen van (1923-), South Vietnamese political leader, president (1967-75). Rose to prominence in army, helped overthrow Diem (1963). Nominal president (1965), exercised near-dictatorial powers after official election. Fled country shortly before capitulation of South Vietnam to Communist forces (April, 1975).

Thimbu, see BHUTAN.

Third Reich, name given by Hitler to German state under his dictatorship (1933-45). Supposed to last 1000 years.

Third World, name given to those technologically underdeveloped nations of Africa, Asia and Latin America. Distinguished from technologically advanced Western nations and those of Soviet bloc. China not usually considered Third World country.

Thirteen Colonies, name applied to British colonies in North America that fought American Revolution and founded United States. They were Massachusetts, New Hampshire, Rhode Island, Connecticut, New York, New Jersey, Pennsylvania, Delaware, Maryland, Virginia, North Carolina, South Carolina and Georgia.

Thirty-nine Articles, basic CREED of Church of England. Originally drawn up (1551-3), revised and adopted by Convocation (1562). Estab. by Act of Parliament (1571).

Thirty Years War, European conflict (1618-48), fought mainly in Germany, involving religious and territ. struggle between German princes, variously supported by external powers, and Holy Roman Empire. War precipitated by refusal of Protestant nobles in Bohemia to elect Emperor Ferdinand II king; revolt crushed (1620). War continued in Palatinate; imperial victories led to Danish intervention (1625), effectively crushed by WALLENSTEIN and TILLY (1626-9). Victories of Gustavus Adolphus of Sweden (1631-2) recovered N Germany for Protestants; imperial cause improved with death of Gustavus (1632). War spread beyond Germany after France allied with Sweden (1635). Eventual settlement came with PEACE OF WESTPHALIA, which broke power of Empire and confirmed French ascendancy.

Thisbe, see PYRAMUS AND THISBE.

thistle, any of genera *Onopordum, Cirsium* and *Cnicus* of spiny-leaved plants of composite family. Heads consist of many small, purple, yellow, pink or white flowers followed by wind-borne seeds (thistledown). Species incl. Scotch thistle, *O. acanthium,* the emblem of Scotland, bull thistle, *Cirsium lanceolatum,* and Canada thistle, *Cirsium arvense.*

Thistlewood, Arthur (1770-1820), English conspirator. Active in trying to bring about revolution in Britain. Leader in Cato Street conspiracy to assassinate cabinet ministers; after plot failed, he and 4 others hanged for treason.

Thomas, St (*fl* 1st cent. AD), one of the Twelve Disciples, also known as Didymus (Gk., = Twin). Doubted Resurrection of Christ until he saw Jesus, touched his side. Tradition-ally, went to S India or Parthia.

Thomas, Dylan Marlais (1914-53), Welsh poet. Wrote intricate life-affirming verse, *eg Deaths and Entrances* (1946), radio play *Under Milk Wood* (1954). Also wrote prose autobiog. *Portrait of the Artist as a Young Dog* (1940).

Thomas, R[onald] S[tuart] (1913-), Welsh poet and clergyman. Poetry, handling rural themes with-out sentimentality, incl. *Song at the Year's Turning* (1955), *Tares* (1961).

Thomas à Becket, St (c 1118-70), English churchman, martyr. Be-friended by Henry II, appointed chancellor (1155) and archbishop of Canterbury (1162). Opposed king over taxation. Henry's attempt in Constitutions of Clarendon (1164) to secure jurisdiction over clergy ended in Becket's flight to Rome. Quarrel after return led to murder of Becket in Canterbury Cathedral. Henry did public penance (1174), built shrine.

Thomas à Kempis (c 1380-1471), German monk. Augustinian. Re-puted author of famous devotional work, *The Imitation of Christ*.

Thomas Aquinas, St (1225-74), Italian philosopher. Major figure of SCHOLASTICISM. Member of Domini-can order; pupil of Albertus Magnus. Taught at Paris. His system, known as Thomism, became official Catholic theology in 1879. Major work is *Summa theologica* (1267-73).

Thompson, Francis (1859-1907), English poet. Wrote mystic, re-ligious verse, *eg* 'The Hound of Heaven' in *Poems* (1893).

Thompson, John Taliaferro (1860-1940), American army officer. Invented (1920) .45 calibre sub-machine gun, known as 'tommy-gun', used in WWII.

Thomson, Alexander ['Greek'] (1817-75), Scottish architect. Parti-cularly active in Glasgow, designed many churches, commercial build-ings, terraces, *etc*. Employed indi-vidual Greek style, later incor-porating Egyptian and 'early mod-ern' elements.

Thomson, Roy Herbert, 1st Baron Thomson of Fleet (1894-1976), British newspaper owner, b. Canada. Controlled newspapers, radio and TV stations in Britain and Canada. Acquired *Times* News-papers Ltd. (1966).

Thomson, Virgil (1896-), American composer and music critic. Influenced by Satie, Les Six; Stravinsky. Compositions incl. 2 operas, 2 symphonies, cello concerto, a ballet, film and theatre music, choral and chamber music. Books incl. *The Art of Judging Music* (1948).

Thonburi, city of SC Thailand, on R. Chao Phraya opposite Bangkok. Pop. 628,000. Rice milling and saw-milling. Has Wat Arun temple. Cap. of Siam (1767-82).

Thor, in Norse and Teutonic myth, god of thunder, patron of peasants and warriors. Attributes incl. hammer which returned when he threw it and belt of strength. Sometimes identified with Roman Jupiter, thus Jove's day became Thor's day (Thursday).

thorax, in higher vertebrates, part of body between neck and abdomen, containing heart and lungs, protected by ribs. In mammals, diaphragm separates it from abdomen. In insects, thorax consists of 3 segments bearing legs and wings.

Thoreau, Henry David (1817-62), American poet, naturalist. Associate of EMERSON. Wrote *Walden* (1854) recording observations of nature, thoughts about society, after 2 years spent in isolated cabin. Other works incl. essay 'Civil Disobedience' (1849) which influenced Gandhi.

thorium (Th), radioactive metallic element; at. no. 90, at. wt. 232.04. Occurs in monazite sands. Used in filaments and as nuclear fuel; oxide used in gas mantles.

Thorndike, Dame [Agnes] Sybil (1882-1976), English actress. Known for leading roles in works of Shakespeare, Shaw.

Thorshavn, see FAEROES.

Thoth, ancient Egyptian god of wisdom and magic. Credited with invention of hieroglyphics, geometry, *etc.* Represented as human with ibis head. Identified by Greeks with HERMES TRISMEGISTUS.

Thousand and One Nights, see ARABIAN NIGHTS.

Thousand Islands, group of c 1800 isls. on Canada-US border in St Lawrence R., at E end of L. Ontario. Popular summer resort area.

Thrace (*Thráki*), region of NE Greece. Main town Komotíni. Tobacco, wheat, cotton. Formerly much larger, incl. S Bulgaria to R. Danube, European Turkey. Did not accept Greek culture; Greek colonies traded gold, silver. Subdued (342 BC) by Philip II of Macedon; *fl* under Romans. Hist. battleground; present borders fixed after Balkan Wars, WWI.

Thrale, Hester Lynch, see PIOZZI.

thrasher, North American songbird of Mimidae family. Species incl. thrush-like brown thrasher, *Toxostoma rufum*, with long tail, curved bill, chestnut upper-parts.

Three Age system, scheme devised (1816-19) by Danish archaeologist C. Thomsen for dividing prehist. into Stone, Bronze and Iron Ages, which followed each other in this order. Scheme was gradually elaborated by further subdivisions of the 3 ages.

Three Emperors' League, informal agreement (1872) between Germany, Russia and Austria-Hungary to maintain social order and ensure peace between Russia and Austria-Hungary. Superseded by TRIPLE ALLIANCE.

Three Rivers, see TROIS RIVIÈRES, Canada.

thrift, any of genus *Armeria,* esp. *A. maritima,* common thrift or sea pink found on sea cliffs and salt marshes. Cultivated for globe-shaped, papery flowers which may be dried as EVERLASTING FLOWERS.

throat, passage leading from arch of the palate to upper openings of trachea and oesophagus. Incl. PHARYNX.

Throgmorton or **Throckmorton, Francis** (1554-84), English conspirator. In 1583 became involved in conspiracy ('Throgmorton's Plot') planning French invasion of England to free Mary Queen of Scots and restore papal authority. Govt. suspicion led to arrest and execution. Confession led to expulsion of Spanish ambassador and war with Spain.

thrombosis, clotting of blood in an artery or vein. In coronary thrombosis, clot forms in coronary artery or its branches; loss of blood supply may cause death (infarction) of heart tissue. Also *see* APOPLEXY.

thrush, widely distributed songbird of Turdidae family, with dark spots on light breast. Species incl. European mistle thrush, *Turdus viscivorus*, which feeds on mistletoe berries, and American robin, *T. migratorius*.

Thucydides (*c* 460–400 BC), Greek historian. After an unsuccessful command against the Spartans in the Peloponnesian War, he went into exile from Athens (424–404). During his exile, wrote *History of the Peloponnesian War*, an objective and analytical account of war until 411.

Thugs or **Phansigars**, secret Indian religious sect, incl. both Hindus and Moslems. Worshipped Hindu goddess Kali, strangling victims as sacrifices to her. Suppressed by British (1829–48).

Thule, name given by ancients to most N land of Europe, variously identified as Norway, Iceland, Shetland Isls. Modern Thule is settlement (pop. *c* 550) of NW Greenland, founded 1910. Major US air base nearby.

thulium (Tm), metallic element, rarest of lanthanide series; at. no. 69, at. wt. 168.93.

Thun, town of WC Switzerland. Pop. 37,000. Metal goods, pottery; castle (12th cent.). On R. Aare at NW end of L. Thun (Ger. *Thunersee*), length 18 km (11 mi); boating, tourist area.

thunder, sound following lightning flash. Caused by rapid expansion of air produced by heat of lightning.

Thunder Bay, port of SW Ontario, Canada; on NW shore of L. Superior. Pop. 108,000. Shipping terminus of Great Lakes; exports grain, iron ore. Has many grain elevators; pulp and paper, flour milling industs. Formed (1970) after amalgamation of Fort William and Port Arthur.

thunderstorm, storm accompanied by thunder, lightning, and often violent gusts of wind, heavy rain or hail. Strong upward currents of moist, rapidly cooling air form deep *cumulonimbus* clouds which produce rain, static electricity. Commonest over land areas of equatorial regions.

Thurber, James [Grover] (1894–1961), American humorist. Known for elegant pieces for *New Yorker*, eg 'The Secret Life of Walter Mitty', illustrated by himself. Collaborated on parody of 'scientific' sex articles, *Is Sex Necessary?* (1929). Collections of work incl. *The Seal in the Bedroom* (1932), *Men, Women, and Dogs* (1943).

Thuringia, region of SW East Germany. Main towns Erfurt, Mühlhausen. Hilly, crossed NW–SE by Thuringian Forest; main rivers Saale, White Elster. Agric., esp. cereals, sugar beet. Divided (1485) into several duchies; part of German empire from 1871. East German prov. after WWII (dissolved 1952).

Thurrock, urban dist. of Essex, SE

England, on Thames estuary. Pop. 125,000. Formed 1936, incl. Port of London docks, Tilbury; oil refineries. Road Tunnel to Dartford (1963).

Thurso, town of Highland region, N Scotland. Pop. 9000. Dounreay nuclear power station nearby.

Thyestes, in Greek myth, son of Pelops and brother of ATREUS. Seduced Atreus' wife, Aerope. Regained throne of Mycenae with help of his son AEGISTHUS.

thyme, any of genus *Thymus* of shrubby plants or aromatic herbs of mint family. White, pink or red flowers used in seasoning. European *T. vulgaris* is a common garden variety.

thymus gland, ductless gland-like body found in base of neck. Shrinks in size after puberty, becoming vestigial. Plays important role in development of infant's immune system.

thyroid gland, ductless gland in front of neck, consisting of 2 lobes on each side of trachea connected by thin tissue. Secretes iodine-containing hormone thyroxine which accelerates carbohydrate metabolism and release of energy.

Tiber (*Tevere*), river of C Italy. Flows 405 km (252 mi) from Tuscan Apennines via Rome to Tyrrhenian Sea at Fiumicino and Ostia.

Tiberias, town on sea of Galilee. Pop. 24,000. Trade centre; holiday resort noted for hot springs.

Tiberias, Lake, see GALILEE, SEA OF.

Tiberius [Claudius Nero] (42 BC-AD 37), Roman emperor (AD 14-37). Succeeded his stepfather Augustus. Improved finances of the empire by reforming taxation system and imposing economies. Lived as recluse in Capri towards end of life, becoming cruel, tyrannical.

Tibesti Mountains, mountain range of Sahara desert, NC Africa, in N Chad and S Libya. Volcanic in origin, rise to Emi Koussi (3412 m/ 11,200 ft).

Tibet, auton. region of SW China. Area *c* 1,221,700 sq km (471,700 sq mi); pop. (est.) 1,400,000; cap. Lhasa. High plateau, *c* 4880 m (16,000 ft), lying between Kunlun Mts. in N and Himalayas in S. Agric. in Tsangpo valley; rough grazing. Largely unexploited mineral resources. Chief religion: Lamaism. Theocratic kingdom under Dalai Lama from 7th cent. Often claimed by China; absorbed 1950. Dalai Lama fled to India after suppression of 1959 revolt.

Tibetan Book of the Dead, collection of Buddhist Tantras, prob. written in 8th cent., intended to give guidance to dying persons,

Tibullus, Albius (*c* 48-19 BC), Roman poet. Known for elegies, esp. on erotic themes.

Ticino (Ger. *Tessin*), canton of S Switzerland. Area 2813 sq km (1086 sq mi); cap. Bellinzona. Mainly mountainous; lakes incl. Maggiore, Lugano. Tourism, vines, tobacco. Pop. is Italian-speaking, RC. Joined Swiss Confederation (1803). Source of R. Ticino, flows 257 km (160 mi) via L. Maggiore to R. Po near Pavia (Italy).

tick, parasitic wingless arachnid of order Acarina. Sucks blood of mammals and birds; may spread diseases, incl. forms of typhus.

tide, alternate rise and fall of surface of oceans, seas, bays, rivers,

Caused by gravitational pull of Moon and Sun; level rises and falls twice per lunar day (24 hrs., 50 mins.). Spring tides occur when Moon and Sun act together, giving higher high tide, lower low tide; neap tides occur when they act in opposition, reducing amplitude.

Tien Shan, mountain range of C Asia, in Kirghiz SSR and Sinkiang auton. region, China. Reaches 7439 m (24,406 ft) at Mt. Pobeda.

Tientsin, city of NE China in Hopeh prov., admin. directly to central govt. Pop. 4,500,000. International port on Grand Canal and Hai Ho. Chemical, metallurgical, textile industs. Has Nankai Univ. (1919). Treaty port for French and British (1860); walls razed by Europeans during Boxer Rebellion (1900). Japanese occupation 1937-43.

Tiepolo, Giovanni Battista (1696-1770), Italian painter. Leading exponent of Venetian rococo style, he is renowned for his fresco decorations, eg in episcopal palace at Würzburg and royal palace in Madrid.

Tierra del Fuego, archipelago of extreme S South America, separated from mainland by Magellan Str. Divided between Chile and Argentina. Main isl. consists of flat tableland (sheep, timber production). Cape Horn is in S. Frequent high winds and heavy rainfall on coast.

Tiffany, Louis Comfort (1848-1933), American artist, designer. Famous for invention of Favrile glass, characterized by iridescent colour and flowing shapes. Founded decorating firm of Tiffany Studios.

Tiflis, see TBILISI.

tiger, *Panthera tigris*, large lion-sized cat, widely distributed in Asia. Coat usually orange-yellow striped with black; no mane. Hunts at night.

tiger moth, any of Arctiidae family of moths with brightly striped or spotted wings. Larvae (woolly bears) are brown hairy caterpillars. Species incl. common tiger moth, *Arctia caia*, of N hemisphere.

Tigris, river of SW Asia. Length *c* 1850 km (1150 mi). Rises in E Turkey, flows through Iraq, merges with Euphrates to form Shatt-al-Arab. Watered ancient Mesopotamia. Large flood control and irrigation scheme near Baghdad. Navigable to Baghdad for shallow draught vessels.

Tijuana, resort of NW Mexico, in Baja California. Pop. 335,000. Varied tourist industs.; gambling casinos, racecourses, bull rings.

Tilburg, city of S Netherlands, in North Brabant. Pop. 155,000. Railway jct.; textile centre, dyeing.

Tilbury, see THURROCK, England.

till, see BOULDER CLAY.

Tillett, Benjamin (1860-1943), English labour organizer. Co-leader, with Tom Mann, John Burns, of 1889 dock strike, important step towards British unionization. Labour MP after WWI.

Tilly, Jan Tserklaes, Count von (1559-1632), Flemish army officer. Commanded Catholic army in Thirty Years War, won victories at White Mt. and Prague (1620), took Magdeburg (1631) but lost to Gustavus Adolphus at Breitenfeld (1631). Died of wounds after defeat at the Lech (1632).

Tilsit, see SOVETSK.

timber wolf, see WOLF.

Timbuktu (Fr. *Tombouctou*), town

of C Mali, near R. Niger. Pop. 10,000. First settled 11th cent.; long famous as centre of caravan trade routes, slave market. *Fl* 14th-16th cent. as Moslem commercial, educational centre. Taken by French (1893).

Times, The, British national daily newspaper. Founded (1785) by John Walter, called *The Times* after 1788. Reputation for serious reporting, comment, as well as letters page. Name also used for renowned *New York Times* founded (1851) by H.J. Raymond.

Timişoara (Hung. *Temesvár*), city of W Romania. Pop. 205,000. Railway jct., indust. centre; univ. (1945), 2 cathedrals. Former cap. of the Banat of Temesvár; annexed by Hungary, Turkey, Savoy; passed to Romania (1920).

Timor, isl. of Malay Archipelago, most E of Lesser Sundas. Indonesian Timor in W part of isl. forms prov. of E Nusa Tenggara. Area *c* 15,000 sq km (5700 sq mi); pop. 823,000. Passed to Indonesia from Dutch 1950. Portuguese Timor comprises E half of isl. and an enclave on NW coast. Area *c* 19,000 sq km (7300 sq mi); pop. 610,000; cap. Dili (pop. 7000). Indonesian intervention in civil war (1975) led to its forcible annexation by Indonesia.

Timor Sea, arm of Indian Ocean between Timor and NW Australia.

timothy or **timothy grass,** *Phleum pratense,* tall European grass with long cylindrical spikes. Grown in N US and Europe for hay.

Timothy, two epistles of NT, traditionally ascribed to St Paul. Prob. addressed to Timothy, bishop of Ephesus. Gives counsel on the safeguarding of Christian faith.

timpani, see DRUM.

tin (Sn), soft metallic element; at. no. 50, at. wt. 118.69. Exists in 3 allotropic forms; malleable, ductile, unaffected by water or air at normal temperatures. Occurs as cassiterite (SnO_2) in Bolivia and Malaysia. Used in tin plating and in alloys (solder, bronze, pewter).

Tinbergen, Nikolaas (1907-), British zoologist, b. Netherlands. Studied animal behaviour, incl. social signals and their ritualization; awarded Nobel Prize for Medicine and Physiology (1973).

Tintagel Head, cape of Cornwall, SW England. Tintagel Castle traditional birthplace of King Arthur. Has ruined Celtic monastery.

Tintoretto, real name Jacopo Robusti (1518-94), Venetian painter. Leading Venetian mannerist, his works are marked by brilliant brushwork and dramatic use of light and colour. Works incl. great religious cycle in Scuola di San Rocco, Venice.

Tipperary, county of Munster prov., SC Irish Republic. Area 4255 sq km (1643 sq mi); co. town Clonmel. Mountains (Galty, Knockmealdowns); fertile Golden Vale. Admin. divisions North Riding (pop. 54,000), South Riding (pop. 69,000). Towns incl. Tipperary, pop. 5000. Dairy produce; lace mfg.

Tippett, Sir Michael Kemp (1905-), English composer. Music combines appreciation of early English music and folk song with that of 20th cent. advances. Works incl. *Fantasia Concertante on a Theme of Corelli,* oratorio *A Child of Our Time,* opera *The Midsummer Marriage.*

Tippoo Sahib (*c* 1750-99), Indian

prince, sultan of Mysore (1782-99). Continued French-backed wars of father, Hyder Ali, against British; eventually defeated by Cornwallis at Travancore (1792). Killed when British stormed Seringapatam.

Tirana (*Tiranë*), cap. of Albania. Pop. 175,000. Cultural indust. (textiles, soap, flour) centre; univ. (1957). Founded by Turks (17th cent.); rebuilt as cap. 1920. Has mosques.

Tiresias, in Greek myth, Theban blinded by Hera and given long life and gift of prophecy by Zeus. Consulted by Odysseus; revealed truth about OEDIPUS and warned Creon of consequences of defiance of divine laws. Appears in many Theban myths.

Tir-nan-Og, in Celtic myth, 'the Land of Youth'. Prob. one of the Azores.

Tirol, see TYROL, Austria.

Tirpitz, Alfred von (1849-1930), German naval officer. As naval secretary (1897-1916), initiated the naval arms race in Europe and advocated unrestricted submarine warfare in WWI.

Tiryns, ancient town of Argolis, Greece. Occupied by Achaens *c* 2000 BC. Stronghold of MYCENAEAN CIVILIZATION.

tissue, in biology, an aggregate of cells similar in form, such as in nerve, connective, muscle and epithelial tissue in animals, and equivalents in plants.

Tisza (Ger. *Theiss*), river of C Europe. Flows *c* 980 km (610 mi) SW from Ukrainian Carpathians through Hungary to R. Danube near Novi Sad in Yugoslavia. Partly navigable; fisheries.

tit or **titmouse**, any of Paridae family of small short-billed songbirds. Species incl. coal tit, *Parus ater*, and blue tit, *P. caeruleus*. Widely distributed, except South America and Australia.

Titanic, English passenger liner (46,000 tons). On maiden voyage, 14th April, 1912, struck iceberg in N Atlantic and sank with loss of 1513 lives of 2224 aboard. Disaster prompted stricter safety regulations and permanent iceberg patrol.

titanium (Ti), metallic element resembling iron; at. no. 22, at. wt. 47.9. Compounds widely distributed in nature, but metal difficult to extract. Corrosion resistant, strong and light. Added to various steel alloys and used in aircraft and missiles because of heat-resisting properties.

Titans, in Greek myth, 6 sons and 6 daughters of Uranus and Gaea. Overthrew their father and ruled universe but defeated by OLYMPIAN GODS.

tithes, in Church of England, originally one tenth of produce of land paid by inhabitants of parish to support parish church and its incumbent. In 1836 commuted to a cash payment. System abolished in 1936.

Titian, real name Tiziano Vecellio (*c* 1487-1576), Venetian painter. Leading Venetian artist of High Renaissance, noted for dramatic use of colour. Worked for Emperor Charles V and Philip II of Spain. Developed esp. free handling of colour and form in late paintings. Works incl. religious subjects, eg *Assumption of the Virgin*, portraits, eg *Paul III and his Nephews*, and

mythological subjects, *eg Rape of Europa.*

Titicaca, Lake, in WC South America, on Peru-Bolivia border. Area 8290 sq km (3200 sq mi). Drained by Desaguadero R. Highest lake in the world, alt. 3810 m (*c* 12,500 ft). Its ameliorating effect on temperature makes agric. possible.

Tito, Josip Broz (1892-), Yugoslav military and political leader, president (1953-). Led partisan resistance to German occupation in WWII. Became premier of new Communist republic (1945). Accused of deviation from orthodox Communist doctrine, withdrew Yugoslavia from Cominform (1948). Favoured policy of nonalignment, resisted Soviet attempts to reimpose hegemony. Sought to maintain national unity in face of Croatian separatists.

titration, process of finding out how much of a certain substance is contained in known volume of solution by measuring how much of a standard solution is required to produce a given reaction.

Titus, epistle of NT, traditionally ascribed to St Paul. Addressed to Titus, bishop in Crete, giving advice on church govt.

Titus [Flavius Sabinus Vespasianus] (AD 39-81), Roman emperor (79-81), son of Vespasian. Completed building of Colosseum in Rome. Captured Jerusalem (70); commemorated by building Arch of Titus by Domitian (81).

Tivoli (anc. *Tibur*), town of Latium, C Italy, on R. Aniene. Pop. 34,000. H.e.p. from nearby waterfalls. Ruins of Hadrian's villa; Villa d'Este (16th cent.).

Tiw or **Tyr,** in Teutonic myth, god of war and athletic events. Identified with Roman Mars, thus Mars' day became Tiw's day (Tuesday).

TNT or **trinitrotoluene,** high explosive solid, prepared by action of sulphuric and nitric acids on toluene.

toad, tailless amphibian, esp. of genus *Bufo*. Frog-like, but with drier, warty skin, from which it secretes noxious white fluid. Largely terrestrial, lays eggs in water. Species incl. giant toad, *B. marinus,* of Australia.

toadflax or **butter-and-eggs,** any of genus *Linaria* of European herbs. Esp. *L. vulgaris* with yellow and orange flowers, naturalized as weed in North America.

toadstool, *see* FUNGUS.

tobacco, any of genus *Nicotiana* of tropical American plants of nightshade family. Now widely cultivated esp. in US, India, China and USSR. Large, sticky leaves, white, greenish or purple flowers. Dried and cured leaves of *N. tabacum* may be rolled into cigars, shredded for cigarettes and pipes, processed for chewing, powdered for snuff. *N. rustica* now grown in Turkey is mainly used for cigarettes.

Tobago, *see* TRINIDAD AND TOBAGO.

tobogganing, sport of sliding down ice-covered slopes on small sleds. Perfected in Switzerland in 1880s using specially prepared runs, *eg* Cresta at St Moritz. Form known as luge tobogganing has been Winter Olympic event since 1964.

Tobruk, town of NE Cyrenaica, Libya, on Mediterranean Sea. Pop. 28,000. Supply base in WWII; scene of heavy fighting, taken by British 1942.

Tocantins, river of C Brazil. Flows N 2640 km (1640 mi) from E plateau to join Pará R. near Belém.

Tocqueville, [Charles] Alexis de (1805-59), French writer, politician. Wrote *Democracy in America* (1835), in which he foresaw triumph of democracy and social equality in Europe. Considered liberty incompatible with equality.

Todd, Alexander Robertus (1907-), Scottish biochemist. Awarded Nobel Prize for Chemistry (1957) for work on structure and synthesis of nucleotides, important contribution in determining structure and function of nucleic acids.

Togo, Heihachiro, Count (1847-1934), Japanese naval officer. As commander-in-chief in Russo-Japanese war, destroyed Russian fleet at Port Arthur and won the decisive battle of Tsushima (1905).

Togo, republic of W Africa. Area 57,000 sq km (22,000 sq mi); pop. 2,283,000; cap. Lomé. Official language: French. Religions: native, RC. Tropical forest in N, savannah in S. Exports cacao, coffee, copra, phosphates. Formerly French Togoland, formed (1922) from part of former German protect. of Togoland under League of Nations mandate. Independent 1960.

Togoland, British; French, *see* GHANA; TOGO.

Tojo, Hideki or Eiki (1884-1948), Japanese military, political leader. Premier (1941-4). Provoked US entry into WWII by bombing of Pearl Harbor (Dec. 1941); resigned after sustained losses. Hanged as war criminal after suicide attempt in 1945.

Tokaj or Tokay, town of NE

Hungary on R. Tisza. Pop. 5000. Centre of vine-growing area, producing famous Tokay wine.

Tokyo, city of Japan, port on Tokyo Bay, SE Honshu isl. Pop. 8,841,000; incl. suburbs, 11,408,000. Major commercial, mfg. (textiles, cars), indust. (shipbuilding, engineering) and publishing centre. Founded 12th cent. as Edo, became cap. of Tokugawa shogunate. Replaced Kyoto as imperial cap. 1868 and renamed as Tokyo ('Eastern Capital'). Rebuilt after extensive damage from 1923 earthquake and bombing in WWII. Site of imperial palace and 4 univs.

Toledo, city of C Spain, on granite hill above R. Tagus, cap. of Toledo prov. Pop. 44,000. Famous from Moorish times for swords; steel; textile mfg. Seat of Spanish primate. Cap. of Visigothic kingdom from 6th cent., fl under Moors from 712. Taken by Castile 1085, cap. of Spain until 1561. Cathedral (13th cent.); home of El Greco, several churches have works by him.

Toledo, port of NE Ohio, US; at W end of L. Erie. Pop. 379,000. Commercial, shipping centre; exports coal, oil, agric. produce; glass, motor vehicle, chemical mfg., oil refining.

Tolkien, J[ohn] R[onald] R[euel] (1892-1973), English author, philologist, b. South Africa. Known for imaginatively complex fantasies *The Hobbit* (1937), *The Lord of the Rings* (3 vol. 1954-5) using knowledge of Germanic, Celtic myths and language.

Toller, Ernst (1893-1939), German dramatist. Leading expressionist. Wrote abstract dramas on problems of maintaining ideals in mass movements, eg *Masses and Man* (1920), *The Machine Wreckers* (1922). Also wrote *Hurray, We're Living!* (1927) a dramatic treatment of politics of post-WWI Europe.

Tolpuddle, village of Dorset, S England. 'Tolpuddle Martyrs' were agric. labourers transported for forming a trade union (1834).

Tolpuddle Martyrs, name given to 6 farm labourers prosecuted and transported (1834) to Australia for organizing trade union branch of fellow workers. Public protest forced pardon (1836).

Tolstoy, Leo Nikolayevich, Count (1828-1910), Russian author. Advocated social reform, passivity in opposition to evil forces. Evolved own theology of universal love, mysticism, personal deity. Best known for great realistic novels, eg *War and Peace* (1865-9), *Anna Karenina* (1875-7). Also wrote plays, eg *The Power of Darkness* (1886), short stories, essays.

Toltec, hist. (c 6th-13th cent.) civilization of Mexico. Associated with archaeological sites at Teotihuacán, Cholula, Tollán. Noted as skilled metal and stoneworkers. Religion centred on deified hero, Quetzalcoatl. Southern expansion (11th-13th cent.) led to domination of MAYA, but eventually supplanted by Aztecs.

toluene (C_7H_8), liquid hydrocarbon of benzene series. Obtained by distillation of coal tar or from petroleum. Used as solvent and in manufacture of TNT, dyes, *etc.*

tomato, *Lycopersicon esculentum*, annual plant of nightshade family. Native to tropical America but widely cultivated for edible, red or yellow, pulpy fruit. Introduced into Europe in 16th cent.

Tombouctou, *see* TIMBUKTU, Mali.

tommy-gun, *see* THOMPSON, J. T.

Tomsk, city of USSR, WC Siberian RSFSR; on R. Tom. Pop. 360,000. Machinery, ball bearing and electrical equipment mfg. Cultural centre; univ. (1888). Founded 1604; developed in 19th cent. with discovery of gold.

Tom Thumb, orig. Charles Sherwood Stratton (1838-83). American dwarf, entertainer. Exhibited first by P.T. BARNUM, later guest of European monarchs; amassed enormous fortune. Height never more than 84 cm (33 in.).

Tone, [Theobald] Wolfe (1763-98), Irish nationalist. A founder of society of United Irishmen (1791), whose members he convinced of necessity of revolution against Britain. Enlisted French aid to invade Ireland and set up independent republic. Captured by British, convicted of treason. Committed suicide.

tone poem or **symphonic poem**, musical composition characteristic of Romantic period, intended as interpretation of literary, dramatic and pictorial elements. Introduced by Liszt.

Tonga or **Friendly Islands**, kingdom of S Pacific Ocean, comprised of Tongatabu, Vavau, Haapai isl. groups. Area 675 sq km (260 sq mi); pop. 90,000; cap. Nuku'alofa. Exports copra, fruit. Discovered (1616) by Dutch; named Friendly Isls. by Cook (1773). Under British protection from 1900, independent

1970. Member of British Commonwealth.

tongue, muscular organ attached to floor of mouth in most vertebrates. Covered by mucous membrane in which the taste buds are embedded. Minute projections (papillae) give it rough texture. Used in mastication and swallowing and, in man, articulation of speech.

tonic sol-fa, in music, notation system adapted from French *solfège* and Italian *solfeggio* systems, designed to simplify sight-reading. Notes are doh, ray, me, fah, soh, lah, te, doh, indicating position in major scale relative to a given key note. Signs mark punctuation marks indicate duration of notes.

Tonkin, hist. region of North Vietnam. Area c 103,600 sq km (40,000 sq mi). Became French protect. of Union of Indo-China in 1887. With parts of ANNAM formed North Vietnam after 1954.

Tonkin, Gulf of, arm of South China Sea bounded by S China and North Vietnam. Here, in 1964, an alleged attack by North Vietnamese torpedo boats on 2 US destroyers precipitated increased US involvement in Vietnam.

Tonlé Sap, lake of C Cambodia. Expands from c 2850 sq km (1100 sq mi) to c 10,360 sq km (4000 sq mi) in wet season. Important fisheries.

tonsil, mass of lymphoid tissue on each side of throat at back of mouth. Tonsillitis is an inflammation of tonsils, usually by streptococci; occurs mostly in childhood.

Toowoomba, city of SE Queensland, Australia. Pop. 58,000. Road and rail jct., trade centre for Darling Downs agric. region; food pro-cessing (meat, dairy produce), agric. machinery.

topaz, hard, colourless to yellow mineral; consists of silicate of aluminium and fluorine. Found among acid igneous rocks. Yellow variety used as a gem. Major sources in USSR, Brazil, Australia.

Topeka, cap. of Kansas, US; on Kansas R. Pop. 125,000. Commercial, indust. centre; wheat, cattle shipping; tyre mfg., railway engineering, printing.

topology, mathematical study of those features of surfaces which remain unchanged under continuous transformations; it is concerned with structure, rather than size.

Torah, see PENTATEUCH.

Torbay, co. bor. of Devon, SW England. Pop. 109,000. Created 1968 from Torquay, Paignton, Brixham.

Tordesillas, town of Valladolid prov., NC Spain, on R. Douro. Pop. 5000. Scene of treaty (1494) signed by Spain and Portugal dividing between them the New World.

Torino, see TURIN, Italy.

tornado, funnel-shaped, rotating column of air extending downward from *cumulonimbus* cloud. Travels at 30-66 kph (20-40 mph); small in area but very destructive. Common E of Rocky Mts., US and Australia.

Toronto, prov. cap. of Ontario, Canada; on N shore of L. Ontario at mouth of Humber R. Pop. 713,000. Natural harbour. Important transport, commercial, education centre. Food processing, printing and publishing, railway industs. Supplied with h.e.p. from Niagara Falls. Founded by French as fort 1749; called York 1793-1834. Has famous City Hall; Univ. of Toronto (1843).

torpedo, name given to various electric rays of genus *Torpedo.* Commonest Atlantic species is *T. nobiliana.*

torpedo, underwater explosive missile first developed by Robert Whitehead (1866). Early types were propelled by compressed air or electric motor, later by jet engines with sophisticated guidance systems. Discharged usually from tubes on ship or submarine, but also from aircraft.

Torquay, town of Devon, SW England, on Tor Bay. Resort, yachting. Torre Abbey (12th cent.). Part of TORBAY.

Torquemada, Tomás de (1420-98), Spanish Dominican monk. Appointed (1483) inquisitor general of Castile and Aragón. Responsible for expulsion of Jews from Spain (1492). Notorious for cruelty during INQUISITION.

Torrens, Lake, salt lake of SC West Australia, W of Flinders Range. Area *c* 5850 sq km (2250 sq mi); rarely contains any water.

Torres Strait, channel between S New Guinea and Cape York Penin., NE Australia. Width *c* 130 km (80 mi); contains many isls.

Tôrres Vedras, town of W Portugal. Pop. 6000. Medieval fortress, royal residence. Centre of Wellington's defence lines in Peninsular War.

Torricelli, Evangelista (1608-47), Italian physicist, mathematician. Invented principle of barometer, using mercury-filled tube, and demonstrated existence of air pressure with it. Obtained 1st man-made vacuum by means of his barometer.

tortoise, name given to various land-dwelling turtles, esp. of genus *Testudo.* Widely distributed in warm regions, may hibernate in cool climates; herbivorous. Giant tortoises live up to 150 years.

Toruń (Ger. *Thorn*), city of NC Poland, on R. Vistula. Pop. 131,000. Railway jct., river port; engineering. Founded 1231 by Teutonic Knights; Hanseatic League member. Under Prussian rule 1793-1919. Birthplace of Copernicus.

Tory Party, British political organization. Began (*c* 1680) as group supporting James II. Discredited for pro-Jacobite leanings after accession of George I, spent much of 18th cent. in opposition to Whigs. Traditionally favoured continued influence of Crown and Church of England; supported by country gentry. Revived under younger Pitt, held almost unbroken power until 1830. Evolved into CONSERVATIVE PARTY in 1830s.

Toscana, see TUSCANY, Italy.

Toscanini Arturo (1867-1957), Italian conductor. Became musical director at La Scala, Milan (1898), then principal conductor of Metropolitan Opera, New York (1908). Also conducted New York Philharmonic and NBC Symphony orchestras. Renowned for concern with detail.

total internal reflection, in optics, reflection of light ray incident at boundary with medium in which it travels faster. Occurs when angle of refraction predicted by Snell's law exceeds 90°.

totalitarianism, system of absolute govt., in which social and economic activity of state organized hierarchically to eliminate opposition. Highly centralized govt. controlled by single official party. Doctrine usually appeals to nationalist and socialist sentiment through aggressive foreign policy. Extreme modern examples incl. Stalinist USSR and Nazi Germany.

otemism, belief of tribe or clan that its distinctive bond is symbolized by a particular animal or plant. This symbol may be represented in tattoos, carvings, *eg* in totem poles of certain North American Indian tribes. Also occurs in Melanesia, Australia.

oucan, any of Ramphastidae family of fruit-eating birds, found in tropical American forests. Black body with bright throat; extremely long brightly coloured beak.

ouch-me-not, any of genus *Impatiens* of Eurasian annual plants, esp. *I. noli-me-tangere.* When ripe, pods burst on being touched, scattering seeds.

ouchstone, hard, black, fine-grained stone, usually basalt or chert. Formerly used to determine purity of gold and silver by examining streaks left on it when rubbed with metal.

Toulon, city of Provence, SE France, on Mediterranean Sea. Pop. 175,000. Port, shipbuilding, armaments mfg. Major naval base from 17th cent.; French fleet scuttled here (1942). Fortifications, Gothic church.

Toulouse, city of Languedoc, S France, on R Garonne. Cap. of Haute-Garonne dept. Pop. 371,000. Agric. trade centre, aeronautics indust., univ. (1230). Cap. of Visigoths; countship from 9th cent. Centre of medieval Provençal culture. Plundered during Albigensian Crusade; part of France from 1271. Romanesque church (11th cent.), Gothic cathedral (13th cent.).

Toulouse-Lautrec, Henri Raymond de (1864-1901), French artist. Influenced by Degas and Japanese prints, he painted ·scenes from cabarets, music halls, circuses, *etc.* Famous for his posters, *eg* Jane Avril and Aristide Bruant.

Touraine, region and former prov. of WC France, hist. cap. Tours. Fertile 'garden of France' (wine and fruit growing) drained by Loire, Indre, Cher. Many châteaux (15th-17th cent.). Under counts of Anjou from 11th cent., passed to France 1204.

Tourcoing, town of Nord, N France. Pop. 99,000. Textile centre (esp. woollens, carpets). Forms conurbation with Lille and Roubaix.

tourmaline, crystalline mineral, consisting of complex silicate of boron and aluminium. Usually black, gem forms are blue, green, yellow; found among granites, gneiss, schist. Major sources in Burma, Sri Lanka, Brazil, US.

Tournai (Flem. *Doornik*), town of W Belgium, on R. Scheldt. Pop. 33,000. Textiles (wool, linen), carpets. Cathedral (11th cent.).

Tournefort, Joseph Pitton de (1656-1708), French botanist. Classified plants on basis of similarity in structure of flowers and fruits. System widely accepted until superseded by Linnaeus'.

Tourneur or **Turner, Cyril** (c 1575-1626), English poet, dramatist. Wrote satire The Transformed Metamorphosis (1600). Known as probable author of typically Jacobean

The Revenger's Tragedy (1607), *The Atheist's Tragedy* (1611).

Tours, city of WC France, on R. Loire, cap. of Indre-et-Loire dept. Pop. 128,000. Agric. market for Touraine; wine, brandy trade. Medieval centre of learning, silk indust. Gothic cathedral (12th cent.). Birthplace of Balzac. Nearby Charles Martel defeated Moors (732).

Toussaint L'Ouverture, François Dominique (c 1744-1803), Haitian revolutionary. Born a slave, he led successful Negro revolt to free slaves (1791-3). Drove British and Spanish from Haiti; achieved complete control of isl. by 1801. Captured by French forces sent to reintroduce slavery; died in prison in France.

Tower Hamlets, bor. of EC Greater London, England. Pop. 165,000. Created 1965 from met. bors. Bethnal Green, Poplar, Stepney. Incl. Tower of London.

Tower of London, fortress in London, England, on N bank of R. Thames. Enclosed by dry moat and double wall. Oldest part, the Keep or White Tower, built (1078) by Gundulf, bishop of Rochester. Formerly used as royal residence and state prison, now an armoury and museum. British Crown Jewels on display in Jewel House.

town planning, process of arranging urban land use pattern to satisfy considerations of health, amenities, communications and attractive appearance. Planned towns often show rectangular 'gridiron' plan. Practised in ancient times, *eg* by Indus Valley, Greek, Roman civilizations; examples of recent plan-

ning incl. Paris (19th cent.), Brasilia, Canberra, Rotterdam (all 20th cent.). Also *see* GARDEN CITY.

Townshend, Charles (1725-67), British statesman. As chancellor of exchequer, introduced Townshend Acts (1767) which imposed duties on tea, glass, *etc*, imported by American colonies. Ensuing colonial unrest led to Boston Massacre (1770), Boston Tea Party (1773).

Townshend, Charles Townshend, 2nd Viscount (1674-1738), English statesman. Whig secretary of state for northern dept. (1715-16) quelled Jacobite uprising (1715). Reappointed (1721-30). Devoted himself to experimental agric. in retirement (hence nickname 'Turnip Townshend).

Townsville, city of NE Queensland Australia, on Cleveland Bay. Pop. 68,000. Port, serving extensive agric., mining hinterland; meat processing, copper refining; tourist resort. Has James Cook Univ. (1970).

toxaemia, see BLOOD POISONING.

toxin, name applied to various unstable poisonous proteins formed by bacteria, which cause disease such as botulism and tetanus. Name also applied to various similar poisons produced by plants on animals, *eg* cobra venom.

Toynbee, Arnold (1852-83), English reformer, historian. Author of *Lectures on the Industrial Revolution of the 18th Century in England* (1884). Worked among the poor of London; 1st social settlement, Toynbee Hall, in E London named after him. His nephew Arnold Joseph Toynbee (1889-1975) was also historian. Wrote *A Study of History* (1934-54), rejecting determinism and attempting to analyse rise and fall of civilizations.

Trabzon or **Trebizond,** port of NE Turkey, on Black Sea. Pop. 66,000. Exports tobacco, nuts. Founded as Greek colony (8th cent. BC). Cap. of Greek empire of Trebizond (1204-1461) until capture by Ottomans; it was renowned for its wealth and beauty.

trace element, chemical element essential in plant and animal nutrition, but only in minute quantities, eg iron, copper, zinc. Some are constituents of vitamins, hormones and enzymes.

tracery, ornamental stonework in upper part of window or panel; sometimes used decoratively in vaults and arches. Characteristic of Gothic architecture from early 13th cent., its basic forms are bar and plate tracery.

trachea or **windpipe,** tube extending from larynx to its division into the 2 main bronchi. Strengthened by rings of cartilage and muscle.

Tractarianism, see OXFORD MOVEMENT.

Tracy, Spencer (1900-1967), American film actor. Known for tough, often humerous roles, eg The Power and the Glory (1933), Father of the Bride (1950), Guess Who's Coming to Dinner (1967).

Trades Union Congress (TUC), voluntary organization of British trade unions. Estab. 1868. Delegates of affiliated unions meet annually, elect General Council to negotiate with govt., international labour bodies.

trade union, see UNION, LABOUR.

trade winds, winds blowing constantly from subtropical high pressure belts (25°-30°N and S) to equatorial low pressure belts (doldrums). Blow from NE in N hemisphere, from SE in S hemisphere.

Trafalgar, Cape, headland of Cádiz prov., SW Spain, on Str. of Gibraltar. Scene of naval battle (1805) in which French were defeated by English under Nelson, who was killed.

tragedy, dramatic form defined by Aristotle as a representation of events in which hero of stature brings unforeseen disaster on himself by error, not accident or wickedness. Definition still used today, but seldom fully achieved even by ancient Greeks. Evolved by them in 6th cent. BC from religious ritual, reached peak in hands of Aeschylus, Sophocles, Euripides. Other conventions, eg violence, revenge, ghosts, transmitted by Seneca, influenced development of English tragedies, eg those by Marlowe, Shakespeare. French tragedy, constrained by unities of time, place and action, as in plays of Corneille, Racine. Modern tragedy much looser category. Concerned more with ordinary people, who may still display heroic attributes in conflicts, eg those of Ibsen, or may be 'anti-heroes', part of meaninglessness, etc, of life, as in Miller's Death of a Salesman.

Traherne, Thomas (c 1638-74), English poet, mystic. Known for metaphysical Poetical Works (first pub. 1903), prose reflections Centuries of Meditations (first pub. 1908). Majority of works only discovered in 1896.

Trajan, full name Marcus Ulpius

Trajanus (AD c 53-117), Roman emperor (98-117), b. Spain. His conquest of Dacia (106) is commemorated by Trajan's Column in Rome (erected 114). Built Forum of Trajan in Rome.

Tralee, co. town of Kerry, SW Irish Republic, on R. Lee. Pop. 12,000. Agric. market; tourism.

tranquillizer, drug used to calm the emotions. Distinct from sedative in that it does not induce sleep. Those used incl. meprobamate, chlorpromazine, rauwolfia.

transcendence, see IMMANENCE.

transcendentalism, in philosophy, mode of thought emphasizing intuitive and spiritual perception beyond mundane thought or experience. First associated with Kant. Developed in America in writings of Emerson, Thoreau.

transducer, device used to transform energy from one form into another, eg loudspeaker or electric generator.

transept, transverse section of cross-shaped church, at right angles to long main section; usually set between nave and chancel.

transformational-generative grammar, see CHOMSKY.

transformer, device used to change voltage of alternating current without changing its frequency. Consists of 2 coils of insulated wire wound on an iron core; current is induced in one coil by variation of magnetic field resulting from current flow in other coil. Ratio of voltages in coils is roughly equal to ratio of number of turns of wire in coils.

transistor, electronic semiconductor device used to amplify voltage and current. Invented 1948,

it is smaller, requires less power and has a longer life than equivalent thermionic valve.

Transjordania, see JORDAN.

Transkei, Bantu homeland of South Africa, between R. Great Kei and Natal. Area 42,750 sq km (16,500 sq mi); pop. 1,751,000; cap. Umtata. Comprises Griqualand East, Pondoland, Transkei, Tembuland territs. Stock rearing; labour source for Witwatersrand mines. Separated from Cape Prov. 1963; autonomous state from 1976.

transmigration of souls, passing of soul into another body on death. See REINCARNATION.

transpiration, loss of water by evaporation from leaves of green plants. Promotes ascent of SAP from roots of plant allowing intake of water and minerals.

transplantation, in surgery, transfer of tissue or organs from one subject to another. Grafting usually refers to tissue transplants from one part of same subject's body to another. Main problem in transplantation is rejection of foreign tissue by action of antibodies. First human kidney transplant was performed 1950, first heart transplant 1967.

Trans-Siberian railway, line in USSR from Leningrad to Vladivostok on Pacific coast. Serves Moscow, Omsk, Novosibirsk, Irkutsk. Begun 1891, completed 1905; originally passed through Manchuria (this part now Chinese Eastern railway); now branches near Chita to remain entirely in USSR. Crucial to development of Siberia.

transubstantiation, see EUCHARIST.

transuranic elements, chemical elements with atomic number greater than 92 (that of uranium). Such elements are radioactive and do not normally occur naturally; prepared by nuclear reactions.

Transvaal, prov. of NE South Africa. Area 286,000 sq km (110,500 sq mi); pop. 8,717,000; cap. Pretoria. Mainly high veld, lies between R. Limpopo (N), R. Vaal (S). Produces grain, fruit; great mineral wealth, esp. in WITWATERSRAND. Boer state estab. 1837 after Great Trek; became South African Republic 1856. Discovery of gold (1886) led to influx of British prospectors, resulting in Boer War (1899-1902). UK colony from 1902; prov. of Union of South Africa from 1910.

Transylvania, region and former prov. of N Romania. Main towns Cluj, Brasov. Mainly forested plateau c 450 m (1500 ft) high, crossed by R. Mureş. Incl. S Carpathians, known as Transylvanian Alps, rising to c 2530 m (8300 ft). Part of Roman *Dacia*; independent (1526-1699). Pop. Romanian, Magyar, German.

trapdoor spider, spider, esp. of Ctenizidae family, which makes silk-lined burrow with tight-fitting hinged lid.

Trappists, in RC church, order of CISTERCIANS of the Stricter Observance. Founded (17th cent.) at La Trappe, France. Monks normally observe silence, are vegetarian.

Trasimeno, Lake, largest lake of central Italy, in Umbria Area 130 sq km (50 sq mi). On N shore Hannibal defeated Romans under Flaminius (217 BC).

travel sickness, see MOTION SICKNESS.

treacle, see MOLASSES.

treason, crime of attacking safety of sovereign state or its head. In US (as declared in Constitution) consists only in levying war against US, or in giving aid, comfort, to its enemies. In UK, Statute of Treasons (1351) distinguished high treason (*eg* killing king, king's law officers, making war on realm) and petty treason (killing one's superior, *eg* master, husband). Reforms in 19th cent. incl. abolition of petty treason, less harsh punishment. Now punishable by death or life imprisonment in US, UK. Famous trials incl. Aaron Burr (1807) in US, and Roger Casement (1916) in UK.

treasury, dept. of state or nation controlling revenue, taxation, public finances. In UK, concerned with major aspects of fiscal policy, esp. annual BUDGET; does not admin. revenue. Main function that of controlling govt. expenditure. Effective chief is chancellor of exchequer. In US, federal dept., estab. 1789, does not prepare budget, but admin. revenue; initiates tax proposals, has close relationship with, although has no legal authority over, Federal Reserve System. Headed by secretary of treasury.

Trebizond, see TRABZON.

treble, in singing, unbroken voice of boy, similar in range to soprano.

Tree, Sir Herbert Beerbohm (1853-1917), English actor-manager. Manager of Haymarket Theatre, London (1887-97) and Her Majesty's Theatre, London (1897-1917). Noted in Shakespearian and modern roles.

tree, perennial plant with permanent

woody, self-supporting main stem or trunk. Usually grows to greater height than shrub, developing branches and foliage. May be either deciduous, with leaves shed at end of growing season, or evergreen.

tree creeper, small insectivorous bird esp. of Certhiidae family. Long slender curved bill, long tongue; uses sharp claws to climb trees. Species incl. common tree creeper, *Certhia familiaris,* of Europe and North America.

tree fern, any of various tropical ferns with tree-like trunk, esp. of genera *Cyathea, Alsophila* and *Hemitelia.* Mainly native to Australia.

tree frog, arboreal frog of Hylidae family. Digits end in adhesive suckers to assist climbing; strong jumpers.

tree shrew, any of Tupaiidae family of squirrel-like primates, found in forests of SE Asia. Solitary, nocturnal; feeds mainly on insects.

trefoil, any of various plants with leaves divided into 3 leaflets, *eg* CLOVER and similar plants of genus *Lotus* of Leguminosae family. Varieties incl. European bird's foot trefoil, *L. corniculatus,* and prairie trefoil, *L. americanus.*

Treitschke, Heinrich von (1834-96), German historian. Supported German unification under Prussian domination. Known for his extreme nationalism and anti-Semitism. Major work was *History of Germany in the Nineteenth Century* (1879-94).

Trek, Great, migration from Cape Colony, South Africa (1835-6) of Boer farmers. In protest against British rule, they moved N to found Transvaal and Orange Free State.

Trematoda, *see* FLUKE.

Trenchard, Hugh Montague Trenchard, 1st Viscount (1873-1956), British air force officer. First commander of Royal Flying Corps in WWI. As chief of air staff (1918-29), shaped offensive strategy used in WWII. Commissioner of metropolitan police (1931-5), instituted many reforms esp. in training.

trench warfare, that in which opposing forces dig systems of defensive earthworks as base for operations, reached most elaborate form in WWI. Outdated by increased mobility of mechanized warfare, esp. with introduction of TANK.

Trent, river of C England. Flows 274 km (170 mi) from Staffordshire via Stoke, Nottingham, to join R. Ouse in forming Humber.

Trent, Council of (1545-63), ecumenical COUNCIL convened by Pope Paul III, continued under Julius III and Pius IV. Discussed concessions to restore religious peace after Reformation. Protestant demands considered impracticable. Council defined RC doctrine and discipline; effected reform of many ecclesiastic abuses.

Trent Affair, diplomatic incident (1861) of American Civil War, involving removal of 2 Southern diplomats from British ship *Trent* by Union ship *San Jacinto.* After British protest, prisoners were released.

Trentino-Alto Adige, region of NE Italy, bordering Austria and Switzerland. Incl. part of Tryolean Alps, Dolomites; main river Adige. Main towns Trento, Bolzano. Forestry, h.e.p., tourism. Alto Adige largely German-speaking.

Trento (Eng. *Trent*), town of

Trentino-Alto Adige, NE Italy, on R. Adige. Cap. of Trento prov. Pop. 95,000. On route to Brenner Pass. Scene of Council of Trent (1545-63). Held by Austria 1803-1919.

Trenton, cap. of New Jersey; on Delaware R. Pop. 105,000. Metal products, cable, rope, pottery mfg. Settled by Quakers (1679). Scene of Revolution battle in which Washington crossed the Delaware and defeated British (1776).

trepan or **trephine,** small crown saw used to remove circular section of bone from the skull. Trepanning is performed to relieve pressure on brain and, in primitive cultures, to release evil spirits. Trepanned skulls dating from prehist. times have been found.

Trevelyan, Sir George Otto (1838-1928), English historian, politician. Wrote *American Revolution* (1899-1907), *George the Third and Charles Fox* (1912), also biog. of his uncle, Lord Macaulay. His son, George Macaulay Trevelyan (1876-1962), wrote *British History in the Nineteenth Century* (1922), *History of England* (1926).

Trèves, see TRIER, West Germany.

Trevithick, Richard (1771-1833), English engineer. Designed high-pressure steam engine (1800) for use in mines. Built (1804) 1st steam locomotive to run on rails.

Trevor-Roper, Hugh Redwald (1914-), British historian. Has written on a wide range of hist. topics; works incl. *The Last Days of Hitler* (1947), researched in Berlin at end of WWII.

Trianon, Treaty of (1920), post-WWI peace treaty between Hungary and Allies. Large amounts of Hungarian territ. ceded to Romania, Yugoslavia, Czechoslovakia, Austria; size of army reduced. Caused much resentment in Hungary.

Triassic period, first geological period of Mesozoic era; began c 225 million years ago, lasted c 30 million years. Extensive arid or semi-arid areas; conifers, ferns, tree ferns. Typified by ammonites, crinoids, lamellibranchs; earliest mammals, dinosaurs. Also see GEOLOGICAL TABLE.

tribune, name assigned to various officers of ancient Rome. Tribunes of plebs were elected defenders of the plebeians rights, protecting them from abuse by the magistrates. Office was begun in 494 BC and its influence was extended (c 130 BC) by the Gracchi.

triceratops, genus of extinct vegetarian dinosaurs of Ceratopsia group. Had two horns on brow, one on nose; neck protected by large bony frill. Length c 6 m (20 ft). Lived during late Cretaceous period.

trichina, *Trichinella spiralis,* parasitic nematode worm often transmitted to man by eating inadequately cooked pork. Larvae may migrate to muscles, forming cysts. Cause of disease trichinosis, characterized by fever, muscular pains, etc.

Trier (Fr. *Trèves*), city of W West Germany, on R. Moselle. Pop. 103,000. Wine trade; textile mfg., tourist centre. Roman remains incl. amphitheatre, gate Porta Nigra; cathedral has 'Holy Coat' of Christ; univ. (1473-1797). Badly damaged in WWII. Birthplace of Karl Marx.

Trieste (Slav *Trst*), city of NE Italy, on Gulf of Venice, cap. of Friuli-

Venezia Giulia and of Trieste prov. Pop. 274,000. Port from Roman times, shipbuilding, oil refining. Held by Austria (1382-1918), as freeport from 1719; passed to Italy 1918. Created Free Territ. 1947; city passed (1954) to Italy, environs to Yugoslavia.

triggerfish, any of Balistidae family of deep-bodied tropical fish. Long spines on dorsal fin used to wedge fish into crevices of coral reefs. Species incl. grey triggerfish, *Balistes capriscus,* of European waters.

trigonometry, branch of mathematics which deals with relations between sides and angles of a triangle. Trigonometric functions, sine, cosine and tangent, express ratios of different sides of right-angled triangle. Applied in navigation, astronomy.

Trilling, Lionel (1905-75), American critic. Essay collections, *eg The Liberal Imagination* (1950), *Beyond Culture* (1965), reflect belief in literature as of primary social value. Other works incl. *E. M. Forster* (1943), novel *The Middle of the Journey* (1947).

trillium, genus of perennial plants of lily family. Native to North America and E Asia. Erect stems have whorl of 3 leaves and large solitary pink or white flower. Species incl. wake robin, *Trillium grandiflorum.*

trilobite, any of class Trilobita of extinct marine arthropods. Flattened oval body divided into 3 segments; fossils found in Cambrian rocks.

Trim, co. town of Meath, E Irish Republic, on R. Boyne. Pop. 2000. Has 12th cent. castle.

Trinidad and Tobago, republic of SE West Indies, member of British Commonwealth. Area 5129 sq km (1980 sq mi); pop. 1,067,000; cap. Port of Spain. Language: English. Religions: Protestant, RC. Hilly in interior; tropical climate. Agric. crops incl. sugar cane, coconuts, citrus fruits. Important asphalt, oil refining industs. Trinidad discovered by Columbus (1498); ceded to Britain (1802). Seat of govt. of Federation of West Indies (1958-62). Joined by Tobago in creation of British crown colony (1888).

Trinity, in Christianity, three aspects of divine being, *ie* God the Father, Son (incarnate in Jesus), Holy Ghost. Doctrine asserted early, estab. in Nicene Creed.

triode, thermionic valve containing three electrodes: cathode, anode and control grid.

Triple Alliance, formed 1882 when Italy joined Germany and Austria-Hungary (united by Dual Alliance of 1879). Growing conflict of interest with other European states (*see* TRIPLE ENTENTE) increased diplomatic tension before WWI.

Triple Entente, diplomatic accord between France, Russia and Britain. Grew out of concern over German commercial, naval and colonial expansion, and alliance of C European powers. Dual Alliance between Russia and France announced 1895. Britain, formerly maintaining isolationist policy in Europe, oriented informal alliance with France (Entente Cordiale) by 1904 and negotiated alliance with Russia in 1907.

Tripoli (Arab. *Tarabulus*), port of N Lebanon, on Mediterranean. Pop.

175,000. Oil refining; terminus of pipeline from Iraq. Founded c 700 BC; cap. of Phoenician federation of Tyre, Sidon and Aradus.

Tripoli, cap. of Libya, on Mediterranean Sea. Pop. 264,000. Admin. centre; port, exports oil, hides, dates, sponges. Founded 7th cent. BC by Phoenicians. Under Turkish rule from 16th cent., stronghold of Barbary pirates. Cap. of Italian colony of Libya (1911-43). Ruins of Roman city *Leptis Magna* nearby.

Tripolitania, region of NW Libya. Fertile coastal strip, interior desert; grain, fruit growing, stock rearing. Name derived from 3 Phoenician cities founded 7th cent. BC. Under Turkish rule from 16th cent.; colonized by Italy 1911-43. Federal prov. (cap. Tripoli) 1951-63.

Tripolitan War, war fought between US and Barbary States of N Africa (1800-15). Arose out of US refusal to pay increased tribute to Pasha of Tripoli to gain immunity from attacks by Barbary pirates on shipping.

Tripura, state of NE India. Area c 10,450 sq km (4030 sq mi); pop. 1,557,000; cap. Agartala. Hilly with dense jungle; timber, rice, jute. Became union territ. 1956, state 1972.

Tristan and Isolde or **Tristram and Yseult**, medieval legend of Celtic origin. Tells of Tristan's journey to Ireland to bring Princess Isolde to Cornwall as bride of uncle, King Mark. On ship while returning, pair drink love potion which causes irresistible, eternal love, leading to death of both. Theme of many French romances, combined with ARTHURIAN LEGEND, eg Malory's

Morte d'Arthur. Used by Tennyson (*Idylls of the King*, 1859-85), Wagner (*Tristan and Isolde.*)

Tristan da Cunha, small group of isls. in S Atlantic, dependency of St Helena since 1938. Only inhabited isl. is Tristan (pop. c 280), formed by volcano rising to 2060 m (6760 ft); eruption in 1961 led to temporary evacuation of pop.

tritium, radioactive isotope of hydrogen, with mass no. 3. Found in minute quantities in natural hydrogen; can be produced from lithium in nuclear reactions. Used as radioactive tracer and in hydrogen bombs.

Triton, in Greek myth, son of Poseidon and Amphitrite. Represented as fish-shaped from waist down, blowing conch shell to calm waves.

Triumvirate, term applied in ancient Rome to govt. carried out by 3 men. First Triumvirate formed by Julius Caesar, Pompey and Crassus (60 BC), Second Triumvirate (43 BC) by Octavian, Mark Antony and Lepidus.

Trivandrum, cap. of Kerala state, S India. Pop. 410,000. Port on Arabian Sea. Coconut products, textile mfg.

Trois Rivières or **Three Rivers**, town of S Québec, Canada; at confluence of St Maurice and St Lawrence rivers. Pop. 56,000. Important newsprint, iron and steel indust. Founded 1634.

Trojan War, in Greek legend, war waged for 10 years by the Greeks on the Trojans to recover HELEN, wife of MENELAUS, abducted by PARIS. Gods fought for both sides. Major events in the war incl.: quarrel between ACHILLES and AGAMEMN-

NON; Achilles' refusal to fight; death of PATROCLUS, Achilles' return to war and death of HECTOR; Trojans reinforced by Amazons and Ethiopians; death of Achilles at hands of Paris; summoning by Greeks of NEOPTOLEMUS and Philoctetes, who slew Paris. Finally, Greeks simulated departure, leaving a huge wooden effigy of a horse outside city gates. Despite warnings by CASSANDRA and LAOCOON, Trojans brought it into city, enabling Greek soldiers hidden inside it to open the gates to their army and destroy the city. War is subject of Homer's ILIAD.

Trollope, Anthony (1815-82), English novelist. Known for 'Barsetshire Chronicles' incl. *The Warden* (1855), *Barchester Towers* (1857), depicting clerical life in imaginary English county. Also wrote political novel series, 'The Pallisers', incl. *Can You Forgive Her?* (1864), *The Eustace Diamonds* (1873).

trombone, brass musical instrument, formerly called sackbut. Known from 15th cent. Fitted with sliding tube which controls pitch or valves. Orchestras today usually have 1 bass and 2 tenor trombones.

Tromp, Maarten Harpertszoon (1597-1653), Dutch naval officer. Defeated Spanish fleet at Downs (1639). Won several skirmishes with English under Blake in the Channel (1652-3), but was finally defeated and killed off the Dutch coast.

Tromsö, town of NW Norway, on Tromsöy Isl. Pop. 36,000. Fishing, sealing industs. Largest town N of Arctic Circle; Arctic museum.

Trondheim, town of WC Norway, on Trondheim Fjord. Pop. 129,000. Port, fishing, shipbuilding. Founded

996 as Nidaros, cap. until 1380. German base in WWII. Cathedral (11th cent.).

tropical fish, name given to aquarium fish requiring controlled water temperature. Varieties incl. angel fish, mollys, gourami, zebra fish.

tropic bird, any of genus *Phaethon* of sea birds which breed on tropical islands. White plumage with black markings; elongated tail feathers.

tropism, natural movement of plants in response to external stimuli, *eg* a sunflower turning to face the light exhibits positive phototropism.

troposphere, lowest layer of Earth's ATMOSPHERE. Extends to c 9.5 km (6 mi) above surface. Temperature falls with increasing height; turbulent layer, containing much water vapour, dust. Separated from stratosphere by tropopause.

Trossachs, scenic glen of Central region, C Scotland, between lochs Achray and Katrine. Incl. Ben Venue.

Trotsky, Leon, orig. Lev Davidovich Bronstein (1879-1940), Russian revolutionary, journalist. In exile for Marxist activities before 1917 Revolution. Following Bolshevik triumph, organized victorious Red Army during civil war (1918-20). After Lenin's death (1924), led opposition to Stalin; expelled from Communist Party (1927), exiled 1929. Founded Communist Fourth INTERNATIONAL (1937). Assassinated in Mexico City, prob. at Stalin's instigation. His political followers (Trotskyists) maintain his policy of continuing world revolution.

trotting, see HARNESS RACING.

troubadours, poets of 11th-13th

cent., who created first cultivated vernacular lyric poetry in Europe. Carefully stylized, poems were written in *langue d'oc* (Provençal) whether poets were French, German, Spanish or Italian. Subjects were love and chivalry, esp. ideals of courtly love. Poems spoken to musical accompaniment.

trout, game and food fish of salmon family, esp. of genera *Salmo* and *Salvelinus*. Found mainly in fresh water, but some varieties migrate to sea to feed. Species incl. European trout *Salmo trutta* (brown trout, sea trout and lake trout are subspecies) and N American rainbow trout *S. gairdneri.*

trouvères, poets of 11th–14th cent., N French counterparts of TROUBADOURS. Poetry incl. CHANSONS DE GESTE.

Troy (*Ilium*), ancient city of Asia Minor, in NW Turkey, near mouth of Dardanelles. Excavations by Schliemann (1871–82) revealed 9 city levels; Homer's Troy, c 1200 BC, believed to lie at 7th level. *See* TROJAN WAR.

Troyes, town of NE France, on R. Seine, cap. of Aube dept. Pop. 75,000. Road and railway jct., textile and hosiery mfg. Cap. of Champagne from 11th cent. Scene of medieval fairs; gave name to 'troy' weight. Gothic cathedral (13th cent.).

Trst, *see* TRIESTE, Italy.

Trucial States, *see* UNITED ARAB EMIRATES.

Trudeau, Pierre Elliott (1919–), Canadian statesman, PM (1968–79). Chosen by Liberals to succeed Pearson. Imposed War Measures Act after political kidnappings by Québec separatists (1970). Ardent federalist, term subsequently marked by rise of PARTI QUÉBECOIS.

Truffaut, François (1932–), French film director, critic. One of first and most popular of *nouvelle vague* directors. Films incl. *Quatre Cents Coups* (1959), *Jules et Jim* (1961).

truffle, any of genus *Tuber* of European edible fungi. Regarded as great delicacy, truffles grow underground and are sought with the aid of pigs or dogs.

Trujillo Molina, Rafael Leonidas (1891–1961), Dominican political leader, president (1930–8, 1942–52). Military coup brought him to power, which he maintained both in and out of office. Used autocratic, repressive measures to improve material welfare of country. Assassinated.

Truman, Harry S. (1884–1972), American statesman, president (1945–53). Democratic vice-president, took office at death of F.D. Roosevelt. Authorized use of 1st atomic bomb (1945) against Japan. Implemented Marshall Plan to aid recovery of post-war Europe and 'Truman Doctrine' of containing Communist expansion. Re-elected in surprise victory over Thomas Dewey (1948); 2nd term dominated by KOREAN WAR.

trumpet, brass wind instrument. A long cylindrical tube bent twice on itself, opening out into bell. Played with cup mouthpiece. Modern trumpet has 3 valves, and is usually pitched in B flat or A.

Truro, co. town of Cornwall, SW England. Pop. 15,000. Tourism; hist. tin mining. Bishopric estab. 1876,

trusteeship, territorial, system of agreed control of non self-governing territs., administered by UN to promote welfare and preparation for self-govt. Supervised by Trusteeship Council of UN members. Replaced mandates operated by League of Nations. Only remaining trust territ. in 1976 was Pacific Isls.

trypsin, enzyme produced by vertebrate pancreas. Converts proteins into amino acids and polypeptides.

Tsana, see TANA, LAKE, Ethiopia.

tsar or **czar,** title of Russian emperors, first adopted (1547) by Ivan IV. Last tsar was Nicholas II.

Tsaritsyn, see VOLGOGRAD.

tsetse fly, blood-sucking fly of genus *Glossina,* of C and S Africa. Bite transmits trypanosomes (flagellate protozoa) which cause sleeping sickness in man and nagana in cattle and other domesticated animals.

Tshombe, Moise Kapenda (1919-69), Congolese political leader. President (1960) of secessionist Katanga. Imprisoned 1961 after Lumumba's murder; later exiled. Returned as premier of Congo (1964-5); fled after MOBUTU's 2nd coup; kidnapped and detained in Algiers (1967), where he died.

Tsinan, cap. of Shantung prov., E China. Pop. 1,500,000. Near Hwang Ho. Railway jct. Machinery, chemicals, textile mfg. Ancient walled city. Japanese occupation 1937-45.

Tsinghai or **Chinghai,** prov. of W China. Area *c* 647,500 sq km (250,000 sq mi); pop. (est.) 2,000,000; cap. Sining. Contains Kunlun and Nan mountains, Koko Nor salt lake, sources of Hwang Ho, Yangtze, Mekong rivers. Mainly high, desolate plateau. Rich coal, oil resources largely unexploited. Hist. part of Tibet.

Tsingtao, port of Shantung prov., E China. Pop. 1,900,000. Naval depot, indust. centre on Yellow Sea. Railway engineering. Former treaty port, leased to Germany (1898).

Tsitsihar, city of Heilungkiang prov., NE China. Pop. 1,500,000. On R. Nen. Food processing; engineering, cement and paper mfg.

Tsushima, isl. group of Japan, in Korea Str. Scene of decisive naval victory of Japanese under Admiral Togo over Russians (1905); most of Russian ships captured or destroyed.

Tuamotu Islands, archipelago of SC Pacific Ocean, part of French Polynesia. Comprise *c* 80 atolls. Produce copra, pearl shell. Acquired by France (1844).

Tuareg, BERBER people of Sahara. Matrilinial culture in which men, rather than women, wear veil. The upper classes are nomadic traders, warriors; the lower group are partly settled farmers.

tuatara, *Sphenodon punctatus,* primitive lizard-like reptile found on islands in Cook Strait of New Zealand. Row of spines along head, back and tail; well-developed pineal eye. Only living representative of order Rhynchocephalia.

tuba, bass brass instrument of SAXHORN type. Used in orchestras and in most brass bands.

tuber, see BULB.

tuberculosis (TB), infectious disease caused by tubercle bacillus *Mycobacterium tuberculosis.* Similar form of disease affects cattle and can be passed to man in milk. Characterized by formation of nodular lesions (tubercles) in various parts of body, esp. lungs, lymph nodes, bones and skin. Treated by drugs such as streptomycin; BCG vaccine provides immunity. Pulmonary form formerly known as consumption.

Tübingen, town of SW West Germany, on R. Neckar. Pop. 55,000. Printing, precision instruments, textile mfg. Famous univ. (1477), scholars incl. Melanchthon.

Tubman, William Vacanarat Shadrach (1895-1971), Liberian statesman, president (1944-71). Suppressed rivalry among native tribesmen. Encouraged economic development of country.

Tubuai or **Austral Islands,** archipelago of SC Pacific Ocean, part of French Polynesia. Produce copra, coffee, tobacco. Acquired by France (1844).

TUC, see TRADES UNION CONGRESS.

Tucson, city of SE Arizona, US. Pop. 263,000. Railway jct.; mining, ranching trade centre; electronics and optics indust.; health resort. Settled by Spanish c 1700.

Tucumán, see SAN MIGUEL DE TUCUMÁN.

Tudor, House of, English ruling family (1485-1603). Estab. by Owen Tudor, a Welsh squire who married widow of Henry V. His grandson took throne as Henry VII, during Wars of the Roses. Succeeded by Henry VIII, Edward VI, Mary I and Elizabeth I.

Tu Fu (712-70), Chinese poet. Considered one of greatest of Tang dynasty, poetry reflects compassion for terrible effects of civil strife. Also wrote satires.

Tuileries, former royal palace, Paris, France. Planned by Catherine de' Medici, begun (1564) in present Tuileries Gardens. Used as residence by Louis XVI and Napoleon I. Destroyed by fire (1871) during Commune of Paris.

Tula, city of USSR, C European RSFSR. Pop. 478,000. Metal goods mfg.; esp. firearms and samovars; sugar refining. First Russian gun factory estab. here (1595) by Boris Godunov.

tulip, any of genus *Tulipa* of bulbous plants of lily family. Large, cup-shaped solitary flowers of various colours. Most garden tulips are varieties of *T. gesneriana* introduced into Europe from Turkey in 16th cent.

Tull, Jethro (1674-1741), English agriculturist. Known for his improvements of British agric., he invented (c 1701) a seed drill which sowed in rows. Wrote *Horse-hoeing Husbandry* (1733).

Tullamore, co. town of Offaly, C Irish Republic, on Grand Canal. Pop. 7000. Brewing, distilling. Nearby Durrow Abbey founded (6th cent.) by St Columba.

Tulsa, city of NE Oklahoma, US; on Arkansas R. Pop. 330,000. Important oil refining; oilfield equipment, aircraft mfg. Settled in 1880s as cattle town.

tumbleweed, any plant which breaks away from its roots in autumn and is blown by the wind, scattering seeds. Abundant in prairie regions as Russian thistle, *Salsola kali*, and amaranth, *Amaranthus graecizans*.

tumour, swelling on some part of the body, esp. a growth of new tissue that is independent of its surrounding structures and serves no useful purpose. Said to be benign if localized and harmless; malignant tumour is a CANCER.

tumulus, in archaeology, tomb covered by mound of earth or stones. Bronze Age BARROW is form of tumulus.

tuna, *see* TUNNY.

Tunbridge Wells, (Royal), mun. bor. of Kent, SE England. Pop. 45,000. Spa, discovered 1606; has 'Pantiles' promenade.

tundra, cold, treeless plains in N Eurasia and N North America. Region of PERMAFROST; mean monthly temperature below freezing point for most of year. Snow and ice cover in winter; topsoil thaws in summer, giving swampy conditions.

tungsten (W), hard metallic element; at. no. 74, at. wt. 183.85. Occurs in tungstite, scheelite, wolframite. Corrosion resistant, ductile. Used in lamp filaments, alloys, electric contact points; tungsten carbide used in drills and grinding tools. Also known as wolfram.

Tunguska, name of 3 rivers of USSR, NC Siberian RSFSR; tributaries of R. Yenisei. They are Lower Tunguska, *c* 2550 km (1600 mi) long; Stony Tunguska *c* 1500 km (950 mi) long; Upper Tunguska, the lower course of R. Angara, all rise in Sayan Mts. near L. Baikal and flow NW into Yenisei.

Tunicata (tunicates), subphylum of marine chordates with bodies enclosed in hard covering. Active tadpole-like larvae have notochord in tail region. *See* SEA SQUIRT.

Tunis, cap. of Tunisia, on L. of Tunis. Pop. 470,000. Canal link with Mediterranean, exports iron ore, phosphates, petroleum, dates, olive oil; textile and carpet mfg. Cap. of Berber state of Tunis from 13th cent.; taken 16th cent. by Turks. Pirate centre until French occupation 1881. Mosques, Bardo museum; nearby are ruins of CARTHAGE.

Tunisia, republic of N Africa. Area 164,200 sq km (63,400 sq mi); pop. 5,737,000; cap. Tunis. Languages: Arabic, French. Religion: Islam. Atlas Mts. in N, Sahara in S. Produces wheat, dates, olives, grapes; exports phosphates, petroleum, iron ore; fishing; growing tourist indust. Ruled by Carthage until 2nd cent. BC; became Roman prov. of 'Africa'. Fl 13th-16th cent. under Berbers; fell to Turks, became Barbary pirate base; occupied (1881) by France. Independent 1956, republic from 1957.

tunnel, passage cut underground to facilitate communications. Longest rail tunnel is Simplon, Switzerland (20 km/12.3 mi, completed 1922); longest road, Mont Blanc, France-Italy (11.5 km/7.2 mi, 1965). Earth tunnels normally cylindrical, lined with rings of cast iron or pre-cast concrete. Shield tunnel driving is method whereby circular ring is pressed forward by hydraulic jacks, first used by M.I. Brunel under R. Thames (1824).

tunny or **tuna,** large marine food fish of Scombridae family. Species incl. bluefin tuna, *Thunnus thynnus,* migratory fish of warm Atlantic, and albacore, *T. alalunga.* Large quantities canned.

Tupolev, Andrei Nikolayevich (1888-1972), Russian aeronautical engineer. First to design all-metal aircraft in USSR. Designed many of foremost military and commercial aircraft.

turbine, rotary engine driven by pressure of a fluid (liquid or gas) against curved vanes of a wheel. Steam turbine, developed by C. PARSONS (1884), widely used in electrical generation and ship propulsion. Gas turbine, in which air is burnt with fuel to provide high pressure flow, used in aircraft propulsion.

turbot, *Scophthalmus maximus,* large flatfish of N Atlantic and Mediterranean. Both eyes on left side of head. Valuable food fish.

Turenne, Henri de la Tour d'Auvergne, Vicomte de (1611-75), French soldier. Hero of French army during Thirty Years War. Defeated Condé in Fronde (1652) and at Battle of the Dunes (1658) in subsequent war against Spain. Killed in Louis XIV's war against Dutch.

Turgenev, Ivan Sergeyevich (1818-83), Russian novelist. Concern about serfdom produced *A Sportsman's Sketches* (1852). Masterpiece *Fathers and Sons* (1862) portrays conflict of traditionalists with new generation of nihilists. Also wrote plays, short stories, *eg First Love* (1860), *Poems in Prose* (1878-82).

Turgot, Anne Robert Jacques (1727-81), French economist, statesman. Comptroller general of finances (1774-6), attempted sweeping economic reform, incl. removal of tax immunities and estab. of free trade.

Turin (*Torino*), city of NW Italy, on R. Po, cap. of Piedmont and of Torino prov. Pop. 1,188,000. Car, aircraft mfg., textiles. Under house

of Savoy from *c* 1280; cap. of Kingdom of Sardinia from 1720 and Italy 1861-4. Cathedral (1492) has shroud reputedly of Christ; univ. (1404). Badly damaged in WWII.

Turkana, Lake, *see* RUDOLF, LAKE.

Turkestan or **Turkistan,** region of C Asia, now divided between USSR, China and Afghanistan. Russian sector comprises Kirghiz, Turkmen, Uzbek SSRs and S Kazakh SSR; conquered by Russia in 19th cent.

Turkey, republic of Asia Minor and SE Europe. Area 781,000 sq km (296,000 sq mi); pop. 40,163,000; cap. Ankara, largest city Istanbul. Language: Turkish. Religion: Islam. Major part consists of Anatolia, an arid plateau crossed by Pontic Mts. in N and Taurus Mts. in S. Separated from European Turkey by Sea of Marmara, Bosporus and Dardanelles. Mainly agric. economy; produces wheat, barley, tobacco, fruit; minerals incl. coal, copper, chromium. Centre of Hittite civilization in 2nd millennium BC; parts colonized by Greeks; has ruins of Troy. Invaded by Seljuk Turks in 11th cent., then by Ottoman Turks. Ottoman Empire grew to incl. Balkans, Egypt, Arabia, *etc*; declined after defeat at Vienna (1683). Empire lost in series of wars, ending with WWI. Became republic (1923) under Ataturk who introduced Westernizing policy.

turkey, *Meleagris gallopavo,* large American game bird introduced into Europe from Mexico in 16th cent. Bronze-coloured plumage with bare head and neck; intensively reared for flesh.

Turkic, language group within W Altaic family. Incl. Kirghiz, Kazakh,

Turkish, Turkoman, Tatar, Uigur, Uzbek.

Turkmen Soviet Socialist Republic, constituent republic of SC USSR, on Iran border. Area *c* 488,000 sq km (188,400 sq mi); pop. 2,160,000; cap. Ashkhabad. Largely arid lowland (Kara Kum desert) in W and C; plateau in E. Agric., esp. cotton, maize and fruit growing, concentrated in oases and river valleys. Fisheries on Caspian Sea; oil fields. Conquered by Russia (1881); incorporated as republic (1924).

Turks and Caicos Islands, two isl. groups E of Bahamas; British crown colony. Area 430 sq km (166 sq mi); pop. 6000; admin. town Grand Turk (on Grand Turk Isl.). Salt, crayfish exports. Settled in 17th cent.; admin. by Jamaica (1873-1962).

Turku (Swed. *Åbo*), city of SW Finland, on Baltic Sea. Pop. 152,000. Port, exports timber, butter; sawmilling, textile industs. Cultural centre; Swedish, Finnish univs., cap. of Finland until 1812. Rebuilt after fire (1827). Has cathedral (13th cent.).

turmeric or **tumeric,** *Curcuma longa,* East Indian perennial herb of ginger family. Large aromatic yellow rhizome which yields spice, colouring and medicinal agents.

Turner, Joseph Mallord William (1775-1851), English painter. Began as topographical painter working in watercolour; early oils were in emulation of Claude, Poussin and Dutch marine painters. His rendering of light and dissolution of form in an attempt to capture atmospheric effects make late works almost abstract. Works

incl. *Rain, Steam and Speed* and *The Fighting Temeraire.*

turnip, plant of genus *Brassica* of mustard family. Cultivated in temperate zones for edible tubers used as cattle food and vegetable. Chief varieties are *B. rapa* with white tubers and rutabaga or Swedish turnip, *B. napobrassica,* with yellow tubers.

turnpike, stretch of road paid for and maintained by fees collected from users at tollgates. Authorized in England in 1346 and in North America in 1785. Now usually stateowned.

turpentine, essential oil obtained by distillation of gum or resin from pine or other trees. Consists mainly of pinene ($C_{10}H_{16}$); used to thin paints and as solvent.

Turpin, Richard ('Dick') (1706-39), English highwayman. His famous overnight ride from London to York was an invention by Harrison Ainsworth in romance *Rockwood* (1834). Hanged at York.

turquoise, semi-precious gemstone, consisting of hydrous phosphate of aluminium plus some copper. Colour varies from sky blue to green; former most valued. Major sources in Iran, US.

turtle, any of order Chelonia of reptiles; name often applied only to aquatic species, terrestrial species being called tortoises. Soft body encased in plates of bone usually covered with horny shields; horny edged toothless jaws; retractile head, limbs and tail. Species incl. snapping turtle, hawksbill turtle, edible green turtle.

turtle dove, see DOVE.

Tuscany (*Toscana*), region of WC

Italy, cap. Florence. Incl. Elba; hilly, main river Arno. Main towns Leghorn, Pisa, Siena. Wheat, olives, wine; iron ore, mercury, Formed most of ancient Etruria; grand duchy (1567-1860). Renaissance cultural centre, esp. under Medici family. Language adopted by united Italy.

Tussaud, Marie (1760-1850), Swiss wax modeller. Imprisoned during French Revolution, later founded (London, 1802) Madame Tussaud's wax museum, containing life-size models of famous hist. and contemporary figures.

Tutankhamen (*fl* 14th cent. BC), Egyptian king. Reversed policies of his father-in-law, IKHNATON, returning to worship of god Amon and restoring Thebes as cap. His tomb in Valley of Kings (excavated 1922 by H. Carter) contained many ancient Egyptian treasures.

Tutuola, Amos (1920-   ), Nigerian author. Known for fantasies which mingle magic, folk mythology with texture of modern life, *eg The Palm-Wine Drinkard* (1952), *Feather Woman of the Jungle* (1962).

Tuvalu, see ELLICE ISLANDS.

TVA, see TENNESSEE VALLEY AUTHORITY.

Tver, see KALININ.

Twain, Mark, pseud. of Samuel Langhorne Clemens (1835-1910), American humorist, novelist. Based classics *Tom Sawyer* (1876), *Huckleberry Finn* (1885) on Mississippi boyhood. Also wrote novels incl. *The Prince and the Pauper* (1881), *A Connecticut Yankee in King Arthur's Court* (1889), autobiog. *Life on the Mississippi* (1883).

Tweed, William Marcy (1823-78), American politician. Leader of

TAMMANY in New York, controlled political appointments and city admin. 'Tweed Ring', consisting of Tweed and 3 others, defrauded city of millions of dollars; exposed in *New York Times* (1870). Died in prison, having been extradited from Spain.

Tweed, river of Scotland and England, flows 156 km (97 mi) from Borders region to North Sea at Berwick, forming part of national border.

tweed, rough-surfaced woollen fabric woven in various shades and patterns. Durable and almost weather-proof. Well-known types are made in Harris, Scotland, and Donegal, Ireland.

Tweedsmuir, 1st Baron, see BUCHAN, JOHN.

Twelfth Night, eve of EPIPHANY. Celebrated as end of Christmas season.

Twelve Disciples, men chosen by Jesus to be his original followers: Andrew, Bartholomew, James (the younger, son of Alphaeus), James (the elder) and John (sons of Zebedee), Jude, Judas Iscariot, Matthew, Philip, Simon the Zealot, Simon (called Peter) and Thomas (Didymus).

twelve-tone system or **twelve-note music,** music composed by system utilizing equally all 12 chromatic notes of octave. Developed by SCHOENBERG and his followers, *eg* Berg, Webern. Also known as dodecaphonic or serial music.

Twickenham, former mun. bor. of SW Greater London, England, now part of RICHMOND-UPON-THAMES.

Incl. English rugby football stadium; Hampton Court Palace.

twins, two offspring born at the same time. Identical twins born from division of a single fertilized ovum are of same sex and closely resemble each other. Fraternal twins born of separately fertilized ova may differ in sex and appearance. In humans, twins occur once every *c* 90 births.

two-stroke (cycle) engine, *see* INTERNAL COMBUSTION ENGINE.

Tyche, in Greek myth, personification of chance. Represented with ship's rudder and cornucopia. *See* FORTUNA.

Tyler, John (1790-1862), American statesman, president (1841-5). Joined Whigs in protest against Democrats' federalist and fiscal policies. His own cabinet resigned after he vetoed Whig bank proposals.

Tyler, Wat (d. 1381), English rebel. Led impoverished serfs in PEASANTS' REVOLT (1381). Captured Canterbury and entered London. After his murder by Lord Mayor of London, uprising was crushed.

Tyndale or **Tindale, William** (*c* 1494-1536), English humanist, reformer. Began translation of NT in England; continued work in exile after meeting Luther. Pub. edition of NT from 1526. Copies denounced and suppressed in England. Convicted of heresy and executed at Antwerp.

Tyne, river of NE England. Formed by union of N, S Tyne rivers near Hexham, flows 48 km (30 mi) in Northumberland to North Sea via indust. Tyneside (Newcastle, South Shields).

Tyne and Wear, met. county of NE England. Area ‘540 sq km (208 sq mi); pop. 1,198,000; admin. centre Newcastle. Created 1974 to incl. area around mouth of R. Tyne.

Tynemouth, co. bor. of Tyne and Wear met. county, NE England. Pop. 69,000. Shipbuilding, engineering industs.

type, rectangular piece of metal used for printing. European invention of movable type is attributed to Gutenberg. Designers of widely-used typefaces incl. Jenson, Aldus Manutius, Caslon, Bodoni, Baskerville. Mechanized methods of typesetting incl. MONOTYPE, LINOTYPE. More recent methods of letterpress typesetting use photocomposition and computer (rather than hot metal).

typewriter, writing machine with a keyboard for reproducing letters, figures, *etc*, that resemble printed ones. When the keys are pressed, raised characters are pressed against an inked ribbon, making an impression on an inserted piece of paper. First practical, commercial machine patented (1868) by C.L. Sholes (1819-90). Subsequent developments incl. electric machines requiring minimum effort (*c* 1935), 'golf-ball head' in which the characters are carried on quickly interchangeable globes (1961).

typhoid fever, acute infectious disease caused by bacillus *Salmonella typhosa*, usually found in contaminated food and water. Affects intestine, spleen and bones. Treated by chloramphenicol, *etc*.

typhoon, *see* HURRICANE.

typhus, acute infectious disease caused by rickettsia, micro-organisms transmitted by bite of lice, fleas. Characterized by eruption of red spots, prostrating fever.

Tyr, see TIW.

tyrannosaur, *Tyrannosaurus rex*, ferocious 2-legged carnivorous dinosaur; *c* 6 m/20 ft tall, with short forelimbs and sharp teeth. Existed in Cretaceous period.

tyrant flycatcher, any of Tyrannidae family of New World flycatchers; *c* 360 species, incl. kingbirds. Usually olive-green or dark with white markings; many species crested.

Tyre (Arab. *Sur*), port of S Lebanon, on Mediterranean. Pop. 12,000. Ancient Phoenician centre, founded *c* 1500 BC on an island. Commercial centre, famous for purple dye. Destroyed 1291 by Arabs, it never recovered.

tyre or **tire,** pneumatic, rubber tube, filled with air, fixed about wheel of vehicle to absorb shocks and provide traction. First invented by R. W. Thomson (1845) but largely ignored until DUNLOP patented bicycle tyre (1888). First fitted to automobiles by Michelin company in France. Recent developments incl. radial ply tyres giving longer life and better handling on road.

Tyrol (*Tirol*), prov. of W Austria. Area 12,650 sq km (4884 sq mi); cap. Innsbruck. Alpine region, highest peak GROSSGLOCKNER; main river Inn. Tourism, dairying, forestry, salt mining. S Tyrol ceded to Italy 1919.

Tyrone, former county · of WC Northern Ireland. Hilly, Sperrin Mts. in N. Agric., dairying. Co. town was Omagh.

Tyrrhenian Sea, part of W Mediterranean Sea, bounded by Italy, Sicily, Sardinia, Corsica. Named after Tyrrhenoi (ancient Etruscans).

Tyumen, city of USSR, W Siberian RSFSR; on R. Tura. Pop. 291,000. Sawmilling, shipyards. Centre of oil and natural gas producing region. Founded 1586, oldest Russian settlement in Siberia.

Tzepo or **Tzupo,** city of Shantung prov., E China. Pop. 850,000. Formed by merger of coalmining towns.

Tzu Hsi or **Tsu Hsi** (1834-1908), dowager empress of China (1861-1908). Served as regent 3 times (1861-73, 1874-89, 1898-1908). Fostered anti-foreign feeling which led to unsuccessful BOXER REBELLION (1898-1900).

U

UAR, see EGYPT.

Ubangi-Shari, see CENTRAL AFRICAN REPUBLIC.

U-boat, abbreviation of German *Unterseeboot*, SUBMARINE.

Ucayali, river of E Peru. Flows N 1600 km (c 1000 mi) to join Marañón R., forming mainstream of Amazon.

Uccello, Paolo, orig. Paolo di Dono (c 1396-1475), Florentine painter. Early exponent of perspective and foreshortening; works incl. fresco *The Flood* and 3 scenes of *Rout of San Romano.*

Udall, Nicholas (1505-56), English dramatist. Known for *Ralph Roister Doister* (c 1553), 1st known English comedy.

udder, mammary gland of cow, goat and other mammals. Mammary tissues manufacture liquids and solids forming milk for feeding of young.

Udine, city of Friuli-Venezia Giulia, NE Italy, cap. of Udine prov. Pop. 110,000. Produces machines, textiles. Gothic town hall, cathedral (13th cent.) in arcaded square. Damaged in earthquake (1976).

Udmurt, auton. republic of E European RSFSR, USSR. Area 42,100 sq km (16,250 sq mi); pop. 1,417,000; cap. Izhevsk. Forested area in W foothills of Urals; grain, flax, potatoes cultivated. Indust. centred on Izhevsk. Udmurts, a

Finno-Ugrian people, colonized by Russia in 16th cent.

Ufa, city of USSR, cap. of Bashkir auton. republic, E European RSFSR; at confluence of Ufa and Belaya rivers. Pop. 821,000. Oil refining centre, connected by pipeline to Volga-Ural oilfield; chemical mfg. Founded 1574.

Uffizi Gallery, art museum in Florence, Italy. Building is 16th cent. palace built by Giorgio Vasari for Cosimo I de' Medici. Nucleus of collection derives from Medici family collection; esp. strong holding of Italian Renaissance painting and sculpture.

Uganda, republic of EC Africa. Area 236,000 sq km (91,100 sq mi); pop. 11,943,000; cap. Kampala. Languages: Bantu, English. Religions: native, Christianity, Islam. Mainly plateau, bordered by lakes Albert, Edward, Victoria, and Ruwenzori Mts. Tropical savannah; cotton, coffee growing, forestry; industs. based on copper ores, Owen Falls Dam h.e.p. Explored by Speke (1862); Buganda (native kingdom) became British protect. (1894), other territ. added (1896). Independent from 1962 under the kabaka of Buganda, who became president. Coups by Obote (1966) and Amin (1971). Asian pop. mostly expelled 1973. Member of British Commonwealth.

Ugarit, ancient cap. of Ugarit kingdom, W Syria, near modern Latakia. Excavated in 1929; remains dating from 5th millennium BC found. Commercial centre in 15th and 14th cent. BC. Finds of cuneiform tablets in Ugaritic language aided study of Semitic culture.

UHF, see VHF.

Uist, North and South, isls. of Outer Hebrides, NW Scotland, in Western Isles. Separated by Benbecula. Main occupations crofting, fishing.

Ujiji, see KIGOMA-UJIJI.

Ujung Pandang, cap. of S Sulawesi prov. (Celebes), Indonesia. Pop. 435,000. Seaport; exports coffee, spices, resins. Formerly known as Makassar.

ukelele, small four-stringed guitar of Portuguese origin. Easy to play, it became popular in Hawaii and spread to Europe and US after WWI.

Ukrainian Soviet Socialist Republic, constituent republic of USSR. Area *c* 601,000 sq km (232,000 sq mi); pop. 47,136,000; cap. Kiev. Largely steppeland covered with fertile black earth soil; major agric. region, producing grain, sugar beet. Indust. based on coal of Donets basin, iron ore of Krivoi Rog, manganese of Nikopol. N and W part of Kievan principality until Tartar conquest in 13th cent.; passed to Poland, then to Russia by 1795. Independent (1918-20) during civil war. Territ. increased after WWII.

Ulan Bator, cap. of Mongolia. Pop. 282,000. Indust., commercial centre; linked to Trans-Siberian railway. Produces woollen goods, leather, footwear. Founded 17th cent.; has residence of Living Buddha, former spiritual leader of Mongolia. Called Urga until 1924.

Ulanova, Galina (1910-), Russian prima ballerina. Became leading ballerina of USSR, known esp. for performances in *Swan Lake, Giselle.*

Ulan-Ude, city of USSR, cap. of Buryat auton. republic, SC Siberian RSFSR; route centre on Trans-Siberian railway. Pop. 269,000. Railway engineering, wood products, textiles. Formerly called Verkhne-Udinsk.

Ulbricht, Walter (1893-1973), East German political leader, head of state (1960-71). In exile in USSR during Nazi regime. First secretary of Communist party (1953-71). Hardline Stalinist, had Berlin Wall built (1961).

ulcer, break in skin or mucous membrane which does not heal. May be caused by infection (*eg* syphilitic ulcer), defective blood supply (*eg* varicose ulcer) or irritation (*eg* peptic ulcer).

Uleåborg, see OULU, Finland.

Ullswater, scenic lake of Lake Dist., Cumbria, NW England. Length 12 km (7.5 mi).

Ulm, town of S West Germany, on R. Danube. Pop. 93,000. Railway jct.; metal goods, food processing. Scene of victory (1805) of Napoleon over Austrians. Cathedral (14th cent.) has tower 161 m (528 ft) high. Birthplace of Einstein.

Ulster, ancient prov. of NE Ireland. Comprises 6 counties of Northern Ireland, with Cavan, Donegal, Monaghan of Irish Republic. Scene of 17th cent. 'Plantations' of English, Scottish settlers.

ultramontanism, term for party in

RC church which advocated doctrine of papal supremacy, *ie* opposed to GALLICANISM.

ultrasonics, science of sound vibrations of frequencies higher than those normally audible to human ear. Used to detect flaws in metals, detect underwater objects, *etc.*

ultraviolet rays, electromagnetic radiation with wavelength ranging from 4×10^{-5} to 5×10^{-7} cm, between visible light and X-rays. Radiation from Sun contains *c* 5% ultraviolet rays; these are mainly absorbed by oxygen and ozone in atmosphere, and glass. Produced by mercury vapour lamp; action on skin produces vitamin D.

Ulyanovsk, town of USSR, EC European RSFSR; Volga port. Pop. 382,000. Motor vehicle and machine tool mfg.; food processing. Formerly Simbirsk, renamed (1924) after Lenin (V. I. Ulyanov), who was born here.

Ulysses, *see* ODYSSEUS.

Umbelliferae, large family of hollow-stemmed, herbaceous plants with compound flowerheads radiating from point at top of stem. Incl. carrot, parsley, hemlock.

umbilical cord, fleshy structure uniting abdomen of foetus with placenta in mother's womb, through which shared blood circulates. Severed at birth, resulting scar is navel.

umbrella tree, *see* MAGNOLIA.

Umbria, region of C Italy, chief cities Perugia, Terni. Mainly mountainous, incl. L. Trasimeno. Cereals, wine, olive oil; h.e.p., chemicals. Many Etruscan, Roman remains. School of painting (15th-16th cent.) incl. Perugino, Raphael.

Umtali, town of E Rhodesia. Pop. 54,000. Commercial centre, on Salisbury-Beira railway. Tobacco indust.; gold mining nearby.

Umtata, cap. of Transkei, S Africa, on R. Umtata. Pop. 25,000. Admin. centre, railway to East London. Anglican cathedral.

Unanimism, *see* ROMAINS, JULES.

uncertainty principle, law of quantum theory stated by Heisenberg, that it is impossible to measure simultaneously and exactly 2 suitably related quantities, *eg* position and momentum of particle such as an electron. This uncertainty may be neglected for measurements other than those on an atomic scale.

'Uncle Sam', popular personification of US. Came into existence during War of 1812, origin uncertain. Depicted as tall, spare man with chin whiskers, dressed in red, white and blue swallow-tailed coat, striped trousers, tall hat with band of stars.

unconscious, in psychology, term used for dynamic elements of personality, both structures and processes, of which individual is temporarily or permanently unaware. According to Freud, unconscious processes are distinct from rational thought, allowing mutually contradictory wishes to co-exist. Jung postulated existence of racial or collective unconscious as well as individual one, from which derive archetypes, or collective symbols.

underground [UK] or **subway** [US], subterranean railway forming part of city rapid transport system. First was in London, England (1863); others incl. Boston (1898), Paris

(1900). Moscow's is famous architecturally.

Underground Railroad, in US history (mid-19th cent.), system enabling Southern slaves to reach Northern states and Canada. Fugitive slaves were guided and sheltered by abolitionists on journey N.

undulant fever or brucellosis, infectious disease of man and animals caused by bacteria of genus *Brucella*. Contracted by handling diseased animals or from milk. Frequently causes recurrent fever in man and abortion in animals.

unemployment, state in which work is unavailable to large number of people requiring it. Called structural if caused by decline or change in processes of given industry. Widespread during period 1918-39. Industrialized nations attempt to control economy in order to balance supply with demand of labour. Supposedly eliminated in China and USSR through public ownership of means of production and distribution. Also *see* SOCIAL SECURITY.

UNESCO *see* UNITED NATIONS EDUCATIONAL, SCIENTIFIC AND CULTURAL ORGANIZATION.

Ungaretti, Giuseppe (1888-1970), Italian poet, b. Egypt. Leading member of hermetic school of occult poets. Works incl. *L'Allegria* (1919), *Il Dolore* (1947), dealing with personal suffering.

Ungava Bay, inlet of NE Québec, Canada; extending S from Hudson Str. Area rich in iron ore deposits.

ungulate, herbivorous hoofed mammal. Two orders: Perissodactyla, odd-toed ungulates incl. horse, rhinoceros; Artiodactyla, even-toed ungulates, incl. sheep, cattle.

UNICEF, *see* UNITED NATIONS INTERNATIONAL CHILDREN'S EMERGENCY FUND.

unicorn, legendary horse-like animal, usually pure white, with a single horn growing from the centre of its forehead. Believed by Greeks to exist in India. In medieval literature and heraldry, symbolizes virginity.

unified field theory, projected mathematical theory which attempts to describe in single set of equations properties and interactions of the 4 fundamental forces of nature: gravitation, electromagnetism, strong and weak nuclear interactions.

uniformitarianism, in geology, theory that features of Earth's crust evolve by means of process unchanged through geological time. Opposes CATASTROPHISM theory. First advanced (1795) by James Hutton; supported by John Playfair (1802) and LYELL (1830-3). Initially caused much controversy, now widely accepted.

Uniformity, Acts of, four acts of English Parliament (1549, 1552, 1559, 1662) aimed at enforcing standard reformed practices. Last act reestab. Church of England rites, prescribed use of Book of Common Prayer.

Union, Acts of, in British history, two acts, first (1707) uniting parliaments of England and Scotland, second (1800) uniting those of Britain and Ireland.

union, labour, employees' association with aims of self-protection, better pay and working conditions. Developed in Britain in 19th cent., achieving guaranteed legal recognition (1871) and joining (1893) Independent Labour Party. British unions organized on craft lines, called therefore 'trade unions'; in US and rest of Europe, unions are based within their indust. Achieve aims by COLLECTIVE BARGAINING and STRIKE.

Unionist Party, British political party formed (1886) to maintain parliamentary union between Britain and Ireland. Consisted of coalition of Liberal Unionists, who seceded from Liberal Party, and Conservatives. Later identified with Conservative Party.

Union of South Africa, see SOUTH AFRICA.

Union of Soviet Socialist Republics (USSR), federal state of E Europe and N Asia, world's largest country. Area, c .22,402,000 sq km (8,649,600 sq mi); pop. 256,670,000; cap. Moscow; other major city Leningrad. Chief language: Russian. Religion: Russian Orthodox. Comprises 15 constituent republics and 20 auton. republics stretching from Baltic to Pacific and N to Arctic. Hist. Russia founded by Rurik at Novgorod (862); Kievan state dominant 10th-12th cent.; Greek form of Christianity estab. 988. Overrun by Mongols in 13th cent.; Muscovite princes became dominant in 14th and 15th cents. after period of disunity. Expansion into Siberia began with first tsar, Ivan the Terrible. Romanov dynasty estab. 1613. Westernization policy introduced by Peter I; under his rule and that of Catherine II, became European power, taking territ. from

Poland, Turkey, Sweden. Desire for reform of reactionary rule led to abolition of serfdom (1861); social unrest and military defeats led to Revolution (1905, 1917) and estab. of USSR under Lenin. Underwent enormous indust. growth under Stalin. Emerged as a dominant world power after WWII.

Union Pacific Railroad, railway system in US. Main line built (1865-9) W from Omaha, Nebraska, joined Central Pacific Railroad at Ogden, Utah, forming 1st US transcontinental railway. Early history marked by financial scandals. Now operates c 16,100 km (10,000 mi) of track in 13 states.

Unitarianism, form of Protestantism which rejects orthodox doctrine of Trinity. Accepts moral teachings of Jesus but denies his divinity. Holds that God exists only in one person. Arose during Reformation; estab. in England by JOHN BIDDLE. Taken to US by JOSEPH PRIESTLEY.

United Arab Emirates, group of 7 sheikdoms, SE Arabia, on Persian Gulf (Abu Dhabi, Ajman, Dubai, Fujairah, Ras al- Khaimah, Sharjah, Umm al-Qaiwain). Area c 84,000 sq km (32,400 sq mi); pop. 229,000; temporary cap. Abu Dhabi. Pearls, dried fish; oil at Abu Dhabi. British protect. (1892-1971), known as Trucial States at independence.

United Arab Republic, see EGYPT.

United Empire Loyalists, name given to colonists who remained loyal to Britain during American Revolution and migrated to Canada, esp. in 1783-4. Extensive settlement in Nova Scotia and Québec led to estab. of new prov. of New

Brunswick (1784) and of Upper Canada (1791).

United Irishmen, see TONE, WOLFE.

United Kingdom (of Great Britain and Northern Ireland), kingdom of NW Europe. Area 244,750 sq km (94,500 sq mi); pop. 55,928,000; cap. London. Language: English. Religions: Anglican, Presbyterian, RC. Incl. England, Scotland, Wales, Northern Ireland, Channel Isls., Isle of Man. Constitutional monarchy (2-chamber parliamentary govt.); member of British Commonwealth, EEC. After 1801 called UK of GREAT BRITAIN and Ireland; present name derived from Irish partition (1921).

United Nations [Organization] (UN), international body (hq. in New York), estab. 1945 to maintain peace and security and to promote cooperation between nations in solving social, economic and cultural problems. Charter, drawn up at San Francisco conference, designated admin. functions to Secretariat (headed by secretary-general), deliberative functions to General Assembly (comprising delegates from all member nations) and policy decision functions to Security Council (15 members, 5 permanent - UK, US, USSR, France, China - 10 non-permanent). Other principal organs are International Court of Justice, Trusteeship Council, Economic and Social Council. Also sponsors special agencies such as UNESCO, World Health Organization, International Monetary Fund, Universal Postal Union. As arbiter of international disputes, UN has had limited success, as in Arab-Israeli wars (1948, 1956, 1967, 1973), Korea (1951-3), Cyprus (1974).

United Nations Educational, Scientific and Cultural Organization (UNESCO), special agency of UN, estab. 1946 to contribute to peace and security by promoting collaboration among nations through education, science and culture. Trains teachers, encourages scientific cooperation.

United Nations High Commissioner for Refugees, office estab. 1951 to protect refugees, seek solution of their problems by repatriation or resettlement and to provide emergency relief. Awarded Nobel Peace Prize (1954).

United Nations International Children's Emergency Fund (UNICEF), agency estab. (1946) to assist child health, nutrition and welfare, esp. in devastated areas and underdeveloped countries. Financed by voluntary contributions. Awarded Nobel Peace Prize (1965).

United Reformed Church, denomination founded 1972 by union of English Presbyterian and Congregational Churches.

United States (of America), federal republic occupying most of S North America. Area 9,363,353 sq km (3,615,191 sq mi); pop. 215,118,000; cap. Washington; major cities New York, Chicago, Los Angeles, Philadelphia, Detroit, Houston. Language: English. Religions: Protestant, RC. Comprises 50 states, incl. outlying Alaska, Hawaii; mainland stretches from Pacific to Atlantic, Great Lakes to Gulf of Mexico. Rocky Mts. divide W interior; grain-producing Great Plains in C, drained by Mississippi system, S of which is oilrich region (esp. Texas). SE US primarily agric. Great Lakes, Atlantic coast, California centres of indust. and pop. Colonial struggle begun in 16th cent., ended with English victory over French (1756-63). Republic estab. by Thirteen Colonies after AMERICAN REVOLUTION (1776-83). W expansion facilitated by Louisiana Purchase (1803), Mexican War (1846-8). South's secession over slavery issue ended with defeat by Union in CIVIL WAR (1861-5). Indigenous Indians almost exterminated by colonists. Leading indust., agric., mineral producer; political power estab. in 20th cent.; challenged by USSR after WWII.

Universal Postal Union, international agency of UN, hq. at Bern, Switzerland. Founded 1875, passed to UN (1947). Facilitates international exchange of mail.

universe, all space and all matter contained in space. Distant galaxies are believed to be moving away from each other at high speeds and thus the universe is expanding. *See* COSMOLOGY.

university, institute of highest level of education. Generally has one or more undergraduate colleges, together with programme of graduate studies and number of professional schools. Has authority to confer degrees, *eg* bachelor's, master's, doctor's. Earliest were in Italy (Salerno, Bologna), France (Paris). In Middle Ages, developed under royal or ecclesiastical patronage, among most famous being Oxford, Cambridge. By late 19th cent., univs. had secular admin. and curricula (UK in 1871); in most Western states, univs. funded either by private endowment or govt. assistance, or both.

Unknown Warrior, body of unidentified soldier buried in Westminster Abbey (1920) as memorial to dead of WWI. Similar tombs exist at Arlington (US), Paris, Berlin.

Unruh, Fritz von (1885-1970), German author. Major figure in expressionism. Known for antimilitaristic works, *eg* prose epic *The Way of Sacrifice* (1916) on Verdun, novel *The End is Not Yet* (1945).

Untouchables, *see* CASTE.

Upanishads, in Hinduism, group of late Vedic metaphysical treatises. *See* VEDANTA.

Updike, John Hoyer (1932-), American author. Works incl. poetry collections, *eg Hoping for a Hoopoe* (1959), short stories, *eg The Same Door* (1959), novels, *eg Rabbit Run* (1960), *Couples* (1968), *Beck: A Book* (1970).

Upper Palatinate, *see* PALATINATE.

Upper Volta (Fr. *Haute-Volta*), republic of W Africa. Area 274,300 sq km (105,900 sq mi); pop. 6,174,000; cap. Ouagadougou. Official language: French. Religions: native, Islam, RC. Landlocked plateau, mainly savannah and semidesert; maize, millet, groundnuts, livestock. French colony from 1919; divided between Ivory Coast, French Sudan, Niger (1933). Recreated (1947) as territ. of French West Africa, until independence (1960).

Uppsala, city of EC Sweden. Pop. 93,000. Cultural centre, incl. Sweden's oldest univ. (1477), library with precious manuscripts (*eg* 6th cent. *Codex Argenteus*). Cathedral

(13th cent.) has tombs of Gustavus Vasa, Linnaeus.

Ur, ruins of SE Iraq. Cap. of ancient Sumerian empire (*fl* 4th millennium BC).

Ural, river of WC USSR. Rises in S Ural Mts., flows S and W *c* 2250 km (1400 mi) to enter Caspian Sea near Guryev. Navigable to Orenburg.

Uralic, family of languages, main groups of which are FINNO-UGRIC and Samoyedic.

Ural Mountains, range of WC USSR, extending from Arctic Ocean to Kirghiz steppe region of Kazakh SSR; part of natural boundary between Europe and Asia. Rise to 1894 m (6214 ft). C part densely forested and rich in minerals (iron, manganese, nickel, copper). Urals indust. area, based on local coal and mineral resources, developed in 1930s; incl. towns of Chelyabinsk, Magnitogorsk and Sverdlovsk.

uranium (U), hard radioactive metallic element; at. no. 92, at. wt. 238.03. Occurs combined in pitchblende, carnotite, *etc.* Uranium 235, capable of sustaining chain reaction, is used in nuclear reactors; more plentiful uranium 238 is used to make plutonium, another nuclear fuel.

Uranus, in Greek myth, personification of heavens; according to Hesiod, son and husband of Gaea, the earth. Father of Titans, incl. Cronus (father of Zeus); emasculated and overthrown by Cronus.

Uranus, in astronomy, planet 7th in distance from Sun. Revolves about Sun at mean distance of *c* 2870 million km in 84 yrs; diameter 47,000 km; mass 14.5 times that of Earth. Has 5 satellites and dense atmosphere containing hydrogen, methane and ammonia. Discovered (1781) by William Herschel.

Urban II, orig. Odo of Lagery (*c* 1042–99), French churchman, pope (1088–99). His sermon (1095) at Clermont urging Christians to fight for Holy Sepulchre helped launch 1st Crusade.

Urbino, town of the Marches, E Italy. Pop. 23,000. Agric. centre; hist. majolica mfg. Cultural centre under Montefeltro family (12th-16th cent.). Has ducal palace (15th cent.), univ. (1506). Birthplace of Raphael.

Urdu, Indic language in Indo-Iranian branch of Indo-European family. Official language of Pakistan. Written variant of Hindustani. Used by Moslems, written in modified Arabic alphabet, contains many Persian, Arabic loan-words.

urea, crystalline organic compound, found in urine, blood, bile, *etc*, of all mammals. First organic compound to be prepared synthetically (by Wöhler 1828). Used in making fertilizers and resins.

Urga, *see* ULAN BATOR.

urial, *Ovis vignei*, reddish-brown wild sheep of mountains of N India and Tibet.

uric acid, crystalline organic acid, found in urine (and excreta of birds and reptiles). Gout is caused by deposits of uric acid salts in the joints.

urinary bladder, flexible muscular sac acting as temporary reservoir for urine.

urine, fluid formed in kidneys of man and some other vertebrates. Composed of water and waste products, incl. urea, uric acid, mineral salts.

Stored in urinary bladder and discharged via the urethra.

Ursa Major or **Great Bear**, constellation of N hemisphere, whose 7 brightest stars form the Plough or Big Dipper.

Ursa Minor or **Little Bear**, constellation of N hemisphere; brightest star is Polaris or North Star, near N celestial pole.

urticaria, skin irritation caused by allergy. Characterized by itching, burning and formation of blotches. Also called nettle rash and hives.

Uruguay, republic of SE South America. Area 177,508 sq km (68,536 sq mi); pop. 3,101,000; cap. Montevideo. Language: Spanish. Religion: RC. Fertile plains (wheat growing) rise to N grasslands (sheep, cattle rearing). Temperate climate. Spanish-Portuguese struggle for possession in 16th, 17th cents.; liberated with Argentina (1810); gained independence under Artigas (1825). Repression under military dictatorships in 20th cent.

Uruguay, river of SC South America. Rises in S Brazil, flows W, then S 1610 km (c 1000 mi) to join Paraná R., together with which it forms Rio de la Plata. ·Forms Argentina-Uruguay, Brazil-Argentina borders. Navigable to Paysandú.

Usedom or **Uznam**, isl. of Bay of Pomerania, Baltic Sea. Area 445 sq km (172 sq mi). Divided from 1945 between Poland and East Germany; chief town Swinoujście (Poland). Agric., fishing, tourism.

Ushant (*Ile d'Ouessant*), rocky isl. off Brittany, NW France. Fishing, sheep raising. Scene of 2 naval battles between French and English (1778, 'Glorious First of June' 1794).

Usküdar, see ISTANBUL.

Uspallata Pass, route 3800 m (c 12,500 ft) high through Andes. Connects Santiago (Chile) and Mendoza (Argentina). 'Christ of the Andes' statue built here (1904).

USSR, see UNION OF SOVIET SOCIALIST REPUBLICS.

Ust Urt, desert plateau of USSR, SW Kazakh SSR and NW Uzbek SSR; between Caspian and Aral seas. Area c 235,000 sq km (90,000 sq mi).

Usumbura, see BUJUMBURA, Burundi.

usury, see INTEREST.

Utah, state of W US. Area 219,932 sq km (84,916 sq mi); pop. 1,059,000; cap. Salt Lake City. Arid Great Basin in W, Great Salt L. in N; scenic Wasatch Range runs N-S. Limited agric. mainly livestock, wheat; rich copper, gold mines. Settled by Mormons in 1847; ceded to US after Mexican War (1848). Admitted to Union as 45th state (1896).

Utamaro, Kitagawa (1753-1806), Japanese colourprint artist. Famous for his depiction of women, distinguished by graceful line and colour. Also produced drawings for book *Insects* (1788), innovatory in naturalism.

uterus or **womb,** hollow muscular organ in female mammals in which the foetus develops. Usually c 7.6 cm (3 in.) long in humans, but greatly enlarged during pregnancy. Situated in pelvis; lower end opens via the cervix into the vagina, upper part opens at each side into a Fallopian tube leading to an ovary.

utilitarianism, philosophical school founded by Jeremy Bentham and later developed by J.S. Mill, who incorporated it into 19th cent. LIBERALISM. Doctrine based on concepts that man's needs are dictated by pleasure and the state's concern should be 'greatest happiness for the greatest number'.

Utrecht, prov. of C Netherlands. Area 1362 sq km (526 sq mi); cap. Utrecht, city on Lower Rhine. Pop. 275,000. Railway jct., indust. centre (chemicals, machinery, clothing). Union of Utrecht (1579) united 7 provs. of N Netherlands against Spanish rule. Peace of Utrecht (1713) ended War of Spanish Succession. RC archiepiscopal see, cathedral (14th cent.); univ. (1636).

Utrecht, Treaty of, settlement (1713) ending WAR OF SPANISH SUCCESSION, supplemented by French-Austrian agreements of 1714. Philip V, having renounced claim to French throne, recognized as king of Spain. Spanish possessions in Low Countries and Italy ceded to Austria. France recognized Hanoverian claim to British throne. Britain received Gibraltar, parts of North America and was granted commercial advantages.

Utrillo, Maurice (1883-1955),

French painter. Known for his Parisian street scenes, often painted from picture postcards. Best work, marked by predominance of white, was done between 1908 and 1916.

Uttar Pradesh, state of N India. Area c 294,000 sq km (113,000 sq mi); pop. 88,365,000; cap. Lucknow. Most of state in Ganges plain, with Himalayas in NW. Agric. economy; grains, sugar cane. Formed (1950) from United Provinces of Agra and Oudh and 3 princely states.

uvula, see PALATE.

Uzbek Soviet Socialist Republic, constituent republic of SC USSR. Area c 449,500 sq km (173,500 sq mi); pop. 11,963,000; cap. Tashkent. Largely plain and desert (Kyzyl Kum), watered by Amu Darya and Syr Darya. Agric. in oases and Fergana valley possible through irrigation; cotton and rice grown; stock raising. Minerals incl. coal, oil. Centre of Tamerlane's 14th cent. empire. Settled by remnants of Golden Horde in 16th cent. Conquered by Russia by 1873; constituent republic of USSR (1924).

Uznam, see USEDOM.

V

Vaal, river of South Africa. Flows *c* 1125 km (700 mi) SW from SE Transvaal to R. Orange in N Cape Prov. Forms most of Transvaal-Orange Free State border. Provides irrigation, h.e.p. for WITWATERS-RAND.

vaccine, preparation of weakened or killed micro-organisms introduced into the body to produce immunity against a specific disease by causing formation of antibodies. Introduced by E. Jenner (1795) to immunize against smallpox.

vacuum, in physical theory, an enclosed space containing no matter. In practice, perfect vacuum unobtainable because of vapour emitted by container itself.

vacuum flask, container with double wall enclosing vacuum to prevent conduction and convection of heat. Used to maintain contents at original temperature.

Vadadara, new name of BARODA, India.

vagina, in female mammals, passage leading from the uterus to the exterior at the vulva.

Valais (Ger. *Wallis*), canton of SW Switzerland. Area 5234 sq km (2021 sq mi); cap. Sion. Mountainous, incl. Matterhorn, Monte Rosa (alpine resorts, h.e.p.), forests on lower slopes); Rhône valley (cereals, vines). Pop. is French-speaking, RC. Joined Swiss Confederation 1813.

Valdivia, Pedro de (*c* 1500-54), Spanish conquistador. Commissioned by Pizarro to conquer Chile (1540); appointed governor (1549). Massacred with his men at Tucapel in Indian revolt.

Valence, town of S France, on R. Rhône, cap. of Drôme dept. Pop. 64,000. Textile (esp. silk, rayon) mfg., agric. market. Romanesque cathedral (11th cent.).

Valencia, region and former kingdom of E Spain. Mountainous in NW (sheep rearing), irrigated fertile coastal plain (fruit growing, esp. oranges). Moorish emirate; held by El Cid 1094-9; part of Aragón from 1238. Hist. cap. Valencia, cap. of modern Valencia prov. Pop. 654,000. Port, exports fruit, wine; shipyards, tobacco mfg., textile indust.; univ. (1501). Cathedral (13th cent.), silk market (15th cent.).

Valencia, town of N Venezuela, W of L. Valencia. Pop. 232,000. In leading agric. region producing sugar cane, cotton. Motor vehicles, chemicals, textile mfg. Founded 1555.

valency or **valence,** in chemistry, capacity of an element or radical to combine with another to form molecules, measured by number of hydrogen atoms which one radical or atom of element will combine with or replace. Valency is explained in terms of electrons in outermost shell of atom which take part in reactions.

Valentine, St (*fl* 3rd cent.), Roman martyr. Traditionally patron saint of lovers; declaration of love on feast day (14 Feb.) originated in medieval times but may derive from earlier pagan festival.

Valentino, Rudolph, orig. Rodolpho d'Antonguolla (1895-1926), American film actor, b. Italy. Idolized in 1920s as great screen lover, sudden death brought personality cult. Films incl. *The Four Horsemen of the Apocalypse* (1921), *The Sheik* (1921), *Blood and Sand* (1922).

Valerian, full name Publius Licinius Valerianus (d. after AD 260), Roman emperor (253-60). Became emperor after assassination of emperor Aemilianus. Continued persecution of Christians. Died in captivity after defeat by Persian king Sapor.

Valéry, [Ambroise] Paul [Toussaint Jules] (1871-1945), French poet. Main themes reflect concern with conflict between detached reason against involved passion, *eg* in dramatic monologues *La Jeune Parque* (1917), *Le Cimetiére marin* (1920). Also wrote prose, essays.

Valhalla, in Norse myth, banqueting hall in ASGARD where Odin received souls of dead heroes.

Valkyries, in Norse and Teutonic myth, warrior hand-maidens of ODIN who fly over field of battle, choosing those to be slain and escorting them to Valhalla.

Valladolid, city of NC Spain, on R. Pisuerga, cap. of Valladolid prov. Pop. 236,000. Textile mfg., agric. market; univ. (1346). Castilian royal residence in 15th cent.; scene of marriage of Ferdinand and Isabella. Cathedral (16th cent.).

Valle d'Aosta, region of NW Italy, bordering France and Switzerland, cap. Aosta. Pop. mainly French-speaking. Main river Dora Baltea; h.e.p., forestry, tourism.

Valletta or **Valetta,** cap. of Malta, NE Malta. Pop. 16,000. Port, indust., commercial centre; univ. (1769). Founded 16th cent. by Knights Hospitallers; former British naval base, heavily bombed in WWII. Cathedral (1577).

valley, elongated depression in Earth's surface, between uplands, hills or mountains. Valleys cut by rivers are typically V-shaped, those cut by glaciers U-shaped. Also see RIFT VALLEY.

Valley Forge, site near Philadelphia, US. In American Civil War main camp of Washington's army during winter of 1777-8; troops suffered terrible hardships.

Valley of the Kings, archaeological site near Thebes, C Egypt. Many tombs of pharaohs of New Kingdom (1580-1090 BC) cut into cliff faces, incl. tombs of Tutankhamen, Rameses II.

Valmy, village of Marne dept., NE France. Scene of French victory (1792) over Austro-Prussian army in Revolutionary Wars.

Valois, dynasty of French kings. Family were counts of Valois in Oise dept. Dynasty founded by Charles de Valois, 3rd son of Philip III. Younger branch of Capetian line, which it succeeded (1328); followed (1589) by Bourbon dynasty.

Valois, Dame Ninette de, orig. Edris Stannus (1898-), British prima ballerina, choreographer, b.

Ireland. Founder of The Royal Ballet School (1931), director of the Royal Ballet (1931-63). Wrote autobiog. *Come Dance with Me* (1957).

Valparaiso, port of C Chile. Pop. 251,000. Indust. centre; sugar, textiles mfg. Settlement began 1554. Resort town of Viña del Mar (pop. 184,000) is suburb. Damaged in earthquake of 1906.

value, in economics, worth of commodity or service in terms of money or goods at a certain time. Depends on scarcity and desirability.

value-added tax, form of indirect sales tax paid on products at each stage of production or distribution, based on value added at that stage and incl. in cost to ultimate consumer. Originally introduced in France (1954), in UK (1973). Important element in tax structure of EEC.

vampire, in folklore, a corpse which becomes reanimated, leaving grave at night to suck blood of sleeping persons. Traditional method of killing vampire is to drive wooden stake through its heart.

vampire bat, small blood-sucking bat of genus *Desmodus* or *Diphylla* found in Central and South America. Feeds nocturnally on vertebrate blood; transmits rabies virus in saliva.

Van, for names not listed thus below, *see* 2nd constituent of surname.

Van, Lake, salt lake of E Turkey. Alt. 1700 m (5600 ft); area 3760 sq km (1450 sq mi). Salt and soda extracted by evaporation.

vanadium (V), rare hard metallic element; at. no. 23, at. wt. 50.94. Used to provide heat resistance, tensile strength and elasticity in steel alloys.

Van Allen radiation belts, 2 layers of charged particles (electrons and protons) trapped in outer atmosphere by Earth's magnetic field. Named after J.A. Van Allen (1914-), who suggested their existence following satellite explorations (1958). Inner belt believed to be caused by cosmic rays, outer belt by solar wind.

Vanbrugh, Sir John (1664-1726), English dramatist, architect. Late Restoration comedies of manners incl. *The Relapse* (1696), *The Provok'd Wife* (1697). Later associated with Wren as an architect; designed Blenheim Palace, Castle Howard.

Van Buren, Martin (1782-1862), American statesman, president (1837-41). Vice-president under Andrew Jackson. Advocated treasury system independent of all banks. Unsuccessful Democratic candidate in 1840 presidential election.

Vancouver, George (1757-98), English naval officer, explorer. Commanded expedition (1791-4) to explore coast of NW North America, reached via Australia. Vancouver Isl. named after him.

Vancouver, chief port of SW British Columbia, W Canada. Pop. 426,000. Natural harbour on Pacific. Transport terminus, commercial centre. Lumber, mineral, sawmilling, fishing, shipbuilding industs. Tourist resort, overlooked by mountains. Has Univ. of British Columbia (1908).

Vancouver Island, SW British Columbia, Canada; largest isl. off W North America. Area 32,137 sq km

(12,408 sq mi). Has rugged coastline, mainly mountainous, forested. Agric. incl. dairy, fruit farming; mining incl. coal, gold, copper; fishing, lumbering, tourism. Pop. concentrated in E. Became crown colony (1849), part of British Columbia (1866).

Vandals, ancient Germanic people who settled in Spain (409). Under their leader Gaiseric, they invaded Africa (429) and conquered most of Roman territ., incl. Carthage. Controlled most of Mediterranean with their powerful fleet; sacked Rome (455). Defeated by Byzantine forces under BELISARIUS (534).

Van de Graaf generator, electrostatic generator, using a moving belt to accumulate charge in hollow metal sphere. Produces potentials of millions of volts; used to accelerate charged particles, eg electrons, to high energies.

Vanderbilt, Cornelius (1794-1877), American railway magnate. Known as 'Commodore' Vanderbilt because of large shipping interests, he amassed a fortune in railways after Civil War. Controlled (1867) New York Central Railroad. Endowed Vanderbilt Univ. (1875), Nashville, Tennessee.

Van der Post, Laurens Jan (1906-), South African novelist. Known for travel books, eg Venture to the Interior (1952), The Lost World of the Kalahari (1958), novels, eg The Heart of the Hunter (1961), short story cycle Seed and the Sower (1963).

Vandyke or **Van Dyck, Sir Anthony** (1599-1641), Flemish painter. Assistant to Rubens in his teens, he later worked in Italy, painting pictures of Genoese nobility. Court painter to Charles I of England from 1632, he profoundly influenced subsequent English portraiture.

Vane, Sir Henry (1613-62), English statesman. Governor of Massachusetts Bay Colony (1636-7). Elected to Parliament (1640); member of council of state (1649-53). Negotiated Solemn League and Covenant with Scotland. Executed for treason after Restoration.

Vänern, largest lake of Sweden, in SW. Area 5545 sq km (2141 sq mi). Drained by R. Göta into Kattegat. Linked to L. Vättern by Göta Canal.

vanilla, genus of climbing tropical American orchids. Fragrant greenish-yellow flowers. Pod-like capsule of some species yields flavouring extract.

Vanir, in Nordic myth, gods preceeding advent of AESIR.

Vanzetti, Bartolomeo, see SACCO, NICOLA.

vapour pressure, pressure of a vapour in equilibrium with its solid or liquid form at . any given temperature.

Varanasi, city of Uttar Pradesh, NC India. Pop. 583,000. On Ganges, in which Hindu pilgrims bathe to gain absolution from sin. Many mosques, incl. Golden Temple, and c 1500 Hindu temples. Formerly known as Benares.

Varèse, Edgard (1885-1965), American composer, b. France. Wrote experimental music, often employing unusual combinations of instruments and powerful rhythmic effects. Compositions incl. Ionisation for percussion instruments and siren, *Déserts* for orchestra and magnetic tape.

Vargas, Getúlio Dornelles (1883-1954), Brazilian statesman, president (1930-45, 1951-4). Seized power, estab. benevolent dictatorship to enact social reform, improve agric., and begin industrialization. Re-elected president (1950), again ·forced to resign; committed suicide.

variable star, star whose brightness varies, either periodically or irregularly. Variation of Cepheid stars follows law relating period and luminosity, enabling their distance to be determined.

varicose veins, abnormal and irregular swelling of veins, usually in the legs. Caused by defects in the valves which keep blood circulating towards heart. Results from ageing, prolonged standing, pregnancy, *etc.*

Varna, city of E Bulgaria, on Black Sea. Pop. 252,000. Port, resort, trade centre (fish, grain). Founded by Greeks in 6th cent. BC; Thracian, Roman centre. Ceded to Bulgaria (1878); known as Stalin (1949-56).

varnish, solution of gum or resin in oil (oil varnish) or in volatile solvent (spirit varnish). On drying, forms hard, usually glossy, protective coating.

Varro, Marcus Terentius (116-27 BC), Roman scholar. A prolific writer, his few surviving works incl. *De re rustica,* on farming, and *De lingua latina,* treatise on Latin grammar.

Vasari, Giorgio (1511-74), Italian artist, biographer. Painted frescoes in Florence and Rome and designed Uffizi Palace in Florence. Fame rests on his *Lives of the Artists,* series of biogs. of artists, which serves as basic source of knowledge about Renaissance art.

vasectomy, method of male sterilization by sealing of vas deferens, the duct which conveys sperm away from the testicle.

Västerås, city of EC Sweden, on Lake Mälaren. Pop. 99,000. Västerås Recess (1527) brought Reformation to Sweden. Gothic cathedral, castle (12th cent.).

Vatican City, independent papal state within Rome, WC Italy. Area 44 ha. (109 acres); pop. 1000. Created 1929 by Lateran Treaty; has own citizenship. Seat of govt. of RC church. Buildings incl. Vatican Palace, St Peter's. Libraries, museums contain priceless collections.

Vatican Councils, two ecumenical councils of RC church. First (1869-70), enunciated doctrine of papal infallibility. Second (1962-5), convened by Pope John XXIII, revised church's role in modern society.

Vättern, picturesque lake of S Sweden. Area 1898 sq km (733 sq mi). Linked to Vänern by Göta Canal; to Baltic Sea by R. Motala.

Vaud (Ger. *Waadt*), canton of W Switzerland. Area 3209 sq km (1239 sq mi); cap. Lausanne. Mountainous in SE; fertile elsewhere. Wine indust.; lakeside resorts. Joined Swiss Confederation 1803.

Vaughan, Henry (*c* 1622-95), Welsh poet. Known as 'Silurist'. Works incl. metaphysical religious verse *Silex Scintillans* (1650-5).

Vaughan Williams, Ralph (1872-1958), English composer. Works were influenced by folk song (which he collected) and Tudor polyphony. Wrote 9 symphonies incl. *London*

Symphony, orchestral works, choral works, *eg Sancta Civitas*, operas.

vault, in architecture, arched ceiling or roof built with stone or brick. Romans developed barrel or tunnel vault, continuous semi-cylinder of masonry, which enabled them to build rigid structures. Medieval vaults, developed from Roman styles, incl. Gothic ribbed ' vault.

Veblen, Thorstein Bunde (1857-1929), American social theorist. Best known for interpretative rather than empirical surveys of social institutions, *eg The Theory of the Leisure Class* (1899), examining roles of businessman, technologist, academic bureaucrats.

vector, physical quantity possessing both magnitude and direction, *eg* velocity, momentum.

Veda, general term for scriptures of Hinduism. Oldest, Rig-Veda, incl. *c* 1000 hymns in praise of gods; Sama-Veda incl. stanzas extracted from the former Yajur-Veda has liturgical formulas and Atharva-Veda incantations to appease demons.

Vedanta, philosophic writings forming commentaries of the VEDA; incl. Upanishads. Hold that ultimate reality is not accessible to experience but only to direct intuition. Term is also applied to this system of thought.

Vedic, *see* SANSKRIT.

Vega [Carpio], Lope [Félix] de (1562-1635), Spanish poet, dramatist. Major poet of 'Golden Age'. Wrote *c* 1800 plays incl. religious dramas, 'cloak and sword' plays. Other works incl. lyrics, prose romance *La Dorotea* (1632).

vegetarianism, practice of restricting diet to foods of vegetable

origin, for religious, humanitarian or health reasons. Strict vegetarians abstain from all food of animal origin, *eg* eggs, milk, butter.

vein, in anatomy, blood vessel which carries de-oxygenated blood from the tissues to the heart. Veins have thinner walls than arteries but greater diameters. Provided with valves to prevent back-flow of blood.

Velasco Ibarra, José Maria (1893-), Ecuadorian statesman. Four times president between 1934 and 1961, encouraged social and economic reforms. Re-elected (1968), became dictator (1970); replaced by military junta (1972).

Velázquez, Diego Rodriguez de Silva y (1599-1660), Spanish painter. Court painter to Philip IV, whom he painted frequently; work is noted for its superb colour values and use of plain grey backgrounds. Famous works incl. *Surrender of Breda, Maids of Honour, Rokeby Venus.*

veld or **veldt,** open grassy plateau of E and S Africa. Types distinguished by height *eg* High, Middle, Low Veld, or by vegetation *eg* bush, grass, karoo veld. Used for potato and maize growing, cattle herding.

Velde, Henri van de (1863-1957), Belgian architect, decorator. A leading exponent of art nouveau; influenced by philosophy of William Morris and English arts and crafts movement, he founded Weimar School of Arts and Crafts (1902) to improve the practical arts.

vellum, fine parchment made from specially treated calf, lamb or kid skins. Used as writing surface and in bookbinding.

velocity, rate of change of position. Velocity is vector quantity, distinct from speed, which is a scalar quantity measuring magnitude of velocity.

velvet, fabric woven with short thick pile on one side, often made of silk or rayon. Used for drapery, furniture upholstery, clothing. Modern grades incl. velveteen and corduroy.

Vendée, region and dept. of Poitou, W France, cap. La Roche-sur-Yon. Agric. (esp. cattle, cereals), forests. Scene of peasant-royalist uprising (1793-6) against Revolutionary govt.

Vendôme, Louis Joseph, Duc de (1654-1712), French army officer. In War of the Spanish Succession, campaigned against the European allies in Italy, Flanders, Spain; was relieved of command after defeat at Oudenarde (1708) but recalled to win victories at Brihuega and Villaviciosa (1710).

venereal disease (VD), infectious disease usually transmitted by sexual contact with infected person. Incl. gonorrhoea, syphilis. Prompt medical treatment with antibiotics and sulphonamides usually effective but delay may cause irreparable damage.

Venetia (Veneto), region of NE Italy, cap. Venice. Hilly, incl. Dolomites in N; fertile plain in S. Wheat, vines, sugar beet, hemp. Conquered by Romans 2nd cent. BC; ruled by Austria 1814-66.

Venezia, see VENICE, Italy.

Venezuela, republic of N South America, on Caribbean. Area 912,050 sq km (352,143 sq mi); pop. 12,361,000; cap. Caracas. Language: Spanish. Religion: RC. Coast (valuable oil production) rises to E Andes (agric., esp. coffee, cacao); cattle raising in Llanos of Orinoco basin; rain- forest on Guiana Highlands. Major oil, gold, diamond exports. Settled by Spanish in 16th cent.; independence struggle (1811-21) under Bolivar. Part of Greater Columbia until secession (1830). Subsequent rule mainly by dictatorship. Influx of immigrants in 20th cent.

Venice (Venezia), city of NE Italy, on Gulf of Venice, cap. of Venetia and of Venezia prov. Pop. 378,000. Port, naval base; oil refining, glass; tourist centre. Built on 118 isls., with 170 canals (incl. Grand Canal), 400 bridges (incl. Rialto, Bridge of Sighs). Rich medieval maritime republic, *fl* 14th-15th cent.; defeated Genoa 1380. St Mark's Sq., Doge's Palace, Academy of Fine Arts are major attractions.

Ventris, Michael George Francis (1922-56), English architect, archaeologist, linguist. Worked on examples of Mycenaean and Minoan scripts, esp. Linear B (found near Pylos, Greece, and at Knossos, Crete), identifying them as primitive form of Greek. With John Chadwick, wrote *Documents in Mycenaean Greek* (1956).

Venus, in Roman religion, perhaps orig. goddess of gardens, but became goddess of love, identified with Greek Aphrodite. Venus Genetrix regarded as mother of Aeneas.

Venus, in astronomy, planet 2nd in distance from Sun; revolves about Sun at mean distance of c 108 million km in 225 days; diameter 12,300 km; mass c 0.8 that of Earth. Has dense cloud layer containing carbon dioxide and surface temperature of 425° C. Seen as 'evening star' in W.

Venus' flytrap, *Dionaea muscipula*, perennial insectivorous herb native to North Carolina and Florida. Hinged leaves close when touched; insects trapped in leaves are digested.

Venus' slipper, *see* LADY'S SLIPPER.

Veracruz, port of EC Mexico. on Gulf of Mexico. Pop. 242,000. Major export centre esp. coffee, vanilla, tobacco; chemicals, textile, soap mfg. Estab. 1599. Tourist resort with fine beaches.

verbena, genus of plants chiefly native to tropical America. Showy spikes or clusters of red, white or purplish flowers. Widely cultivated as ornamental. European version, *Verbena officinalis*, was held sacred by ancient Greeks, Romans and Druids.

Vercingetorix (d. 46 BC), Gallic chieftain. Led revolt in Gaul against Roman occupation (58-51 BC). After initial success, he was besieged in Alesia by Caesar and he and his allies defeated. Put to death in Rome.

Verde, Cape, penin. of Senegal; most W point of Africa. Dakar is on S coast.

Verdi, Giuseppe (1813-1901), Italian composer. Renowned for operas, incl. *Il Trovatore*, *La Traviata*, *Rigoletto*, *Aïda*, *Otello* and *Falstaff*; last two based on Shakespeare's plays. Also wrote *Requiem* and *Stabat Mater*.

verdigris, greenish deposit formed on copper, brass or bronze surfaces exposed to atmosphere. Consists of basic copper carbonate or sulphate.

Verdun, town of Lorraine, NE France, on R. Meuse. Pop. 25,000.

Textile mfg., food processing. Treaty of Verdun (843) divided Charlemagne's empire into 3 parts. Fortified 17th cent.; fortress was scene of long German assault (1916) resisted by French. War cemeteries.

Vereeniging, city of S Transvaal, South Africa, on R. Vaal. Pop. 170,000. Indust. centre in coalmining dist. Treaty ending Boer War signed here (1902).

Vergil *or* **Virgil**, full name Publius Vergilius Maro (70-19 BC), Roman poet. Famous for *Aeneid*, epic in 12 books on wanderings of Aeneas, reflecting preoccupations with greatness of Rome, virtues of a leader, nature of human existence and destiny. Also wrote pastoral poems, *Eclogues* (37 BC), didactic poems on rural life, *Georgics* (30 BC). To early medieval writers he was the supreme poet; influence remained profound up to 17th century.

Verhaeren, Emile (1855-1916), Belgian poet. Pre-WWI verse characterized by faith in human brotherhood, progress. *Les Ailes Rouges de la Guerre* (1917) marks failure of his hopes.

Verlaine, Paul (1844-1896), French poet. Prominent among SYMBOLISTS. Encouraged in free-living by RIMBAUD. Graceful, musical verse collections incl. *Fêtes galantes* (1869), *Romances sans paroles* (1874), *Sagesse* (1881).

Vermeer, Jan (1632-75), Dutch painter, b. Delft. Known for the calm perfection of his subtly-lit interiors, with 1 or 2 figures engaged in domestic or recreational activities. Works incl. *Allegory of Painting* and *Woman with a Water Jug*.

Vermont, New England state of US.

Area 24,887 sq km (9609 sq mi); pop. 445,000; cap. Montpelier; largest town Burlington. Canada on N border; L. Champlain in NW; Green Mts. cross N-S; chief river Connecticut. Agric. incl. dairy farming, fruit, maple syrup; marble quarrying, tourism. Settled in 18th cent.; part of New York until 1777. Admitted to Union as 14th state (1791).

vermouth, fortified white wine flavoured with aromatic herbs. Made chiefly in France and Italy.

Verne, Jules (1828-1905), French author. Early exponent of SCIENCE FICTION in novels, eg *Twenty Thousand Leagues Under the Sea* (1870), *Around the World in Eighty Days* (1873).

Verner, Karl Adolf (1846-96), Danish comparative philologist. Known for Verner's law, explaining sound changes in Germanic languages which had seemed exceptions to Grimm's law.

vernier, graduated scale that slides along longer graduated instrument and is used to indicate fractional parts of divisions.

Verona, city of Venetia, NE Italy, on R. Adige. Cap. of Verona prov. Pop. 264,000. On route to Brenner Pass; agric. market, printing. Joined (1167) Lombard League, *fl* 13th-14th cent. under the Scala family. Austrian fortress 1797-1866. Roman amphitheatre, Gothic town hall.

Veronese, real name Paolo Caliari (*c* 1528-88), Italian painter, b. Verona. Worked in Venice from 1553; specialized in huge allegorical, religious and historical scenes. Works, characterized by splendid colour, incl. *Feast in the House of Levi, Marriage Feast at Cana.*

veronica or speedwell, any of genus *Veronica* of perennial plants native to temperate regions. Many species cultivated as garden flowers incl. blue flowered speedwell, *V. persica.*

Verrocchio, real name Andrea di Cioni (*c* 1435-88), Italian sculptor, painter. Ran large workshop in Florence, where many artists, incl. Leonardo da Vinci, were trained. Executed famous equestrian statue of Bartolomeo Colleoni in Venice.

Versailles, town of N France, W of Paris, cap. of Yvelines dept. Pop. 95,000. Tourist centre, noted for palace and gardens built late 17th cent. for Louis XIV. Site of many treaties, eg between France and Prussia (1871), after WWI (1919).

Versailles, Treaty of, peace treaty at end of WWI signed by Allies (Britain, France, US and Italy) and Germany (1919). Germany, which took no part in negotiations, forced to accept terms, incl. loss of colonies, return of Alsace-Lorraine to France, loss of territ. to Denmark, Poland, Belgium, demilitarization of Rhineland, restrictions on armaments, payment of reparations. Treaty also contained covenant of LEAGUE OF NATIONS.

vertebra, segment of spinal column or backbone of vertebrates. Man has 33 vertebrae: 7 cervical in neck, 12 thoracic (each carrying pair of ribs), 5 lumbar; last 9 are fused to form sacrum and tail-like coccyx. Flexible discs unite the vertebrae; pressure on nerve fibres caused by bulges in discs is condition known as 'slipped disc'.

vertebrate, any of subphylum Vertebrata of chordate animals, with segmented spinal column and skull containing well-developed brain. Incl. mammals, birds, amphibians, reptiles.

vertigo, giddiness with associated feeling of whirling movement. Caused by disturbance in balance mechanism of the inner ear or eyes.

vervain, see VERBENA.

Verwoerd, Hendrik Frensch (1901-66), South African statesman, b. Netherlands. As minister of native affairs (1950-8), enacted harsh APARTHEID laws. As premier (1958-66), took South Africa out of Commonwealth and estab. republic (1961). Assassinated.

Vesalius, Andreas (1514-64), Flemish anatomist. His dissections and experiments on human body mark start of scientific anatomy; his findings overthrew accepted teachings of Galen. Wrote *De humani corporis fabrica* (pub. 1543), illustrated by remarkable file Calcar drawings.

Vespasian, full name Titus Flavius Vespasianus (AD 9-79), Roman emperor (AD 69-79). Fought in Britain where he conquered Isle of Wight. Chosen emperor by his troops while campaigning in Palestine. During his reign, Agricola made major conquest in Britain. Built Colosseum.

Vespucci, Amerigo (1454-1512), Italian navigator, b. Florence. In service of Spain, made many voyages to New World; explored mouth of Amazon (1499). Proved South America not part of Asia; American continent named after him.

Vesta, in Roman religion, goddess of the hearth, worshipped in every house. Sacred fire of state kept ever burning in Temple of Vesta, tended by 6 Vestal Virgins, daughters of noble families. Returned to private life after serving 30 years. Penalty for breaking vow of chastity was burial alive.

Vesterålen Islands, see LOFOTEN ISLANDS.

Vesuvius, SW Italy, on Bay of Naples, only active volcano on European mainland. Height now *c* 1185 m (3890 ft). Vines (for 'Lacrima Christi' wine) on lower slopes. Seismological observatory, chairlift. Many eruptions, incl. AD 79 when Pompeii, Herculaneum buried.

vetch, any of genus *Vicia* of weak-stemmed herbs of Leguminosae family, native to N temperate regions and South America. Common vetch or tare, *V. sativa*, is cultivated for forage and soil improvement.

veterinary science, branch of medicine dealing with diseases of animals, esp. domestic varieties.

veto, order prohibiting proposed act, esp. by person in authority. Term used specifically for constitutional right of ruler or branch of govt. to reject bills passed by another branch of govt. In US, president has power of veto over bill passed by Congress; can be overruled by two-thirds majority vote in Congress. Governors of states have similar power. In UN, any of 5 permanent members of Security Council have power of veto on action other than procedural.

VHF (Very High Frequency), electromagnetic radiation at frequency of 30 × 10^6 - 30 × 10^7 cycles per second. Used in frequency MODULATION radio transmission. UHF (Ultra High Frequency) is from 30×10^7 - 30×10^8 cycles per second.

viaduct, long bridge to carry a road or railway line over a valley or gorge. Usually consists of series of short, concrete or masonry spans supported on piers or towers.

Vian, Boris (1920-59), French author. Influenced by surrealism, used fantasy to pierce through accepted social values and semantic confusion. Novels incl. *L'écume des jours* (1947), *L'herbe rouge* (1950).

vibraphone, percussion instrument having metal bars and resonators with rotating lids driven by an electric motor to simulate a vibrato. Also called vibraharp in US.

viburnum, genus of shrubs and small trees of honeysuckle family. Native to Europe, Asia and N Africa. Species incl. wayfaring tree, *Viburnum lantana*. White flowers used as decoration.

Vicenza, city of Venetia, N Italy, cap. of Vicenza prov. Pop. 121,000. Railway jct., agric. market, machinery. Many buildings by Palladio (born here). Medieval cathedral, damaged in WWII.

Vichy, town of C France, on R. Allier. Pop. 34,000. Spa resort from Roman times; exports Vichy water. Seat of pro-German 'Vichy govt.' of France (1940-4).

Vichy government, govt. of unoccupied France, with seat at Vichy, set up under Pétain after Franco-German armistice (1940). Became tool of Germany under P. LAVAL (1942); powerless after German occupation of all France (Nov. 1942).

Vicksburg, town of W Mississippi,

US; near jct. of Mississippi, Yazoo rivers. Pop. 25,000. Cotton, cattle trade centre. Scene of strategic victory by Union during Civil War after lengthy siege (1863).

Vico, Giovanni Battista (1668-1744), Italian philosopher. Originated scientific approach to history in *Scienza nuova* (1725), developing modified cyclical theory of civilization in place of history viewed as development of God's will. Often seen as 1st modern historian.

Victor Emmanuel II (1820-78), king of Italy (1861-78). Succeeded his father, Charles Albert, as king of Sardinia (1849). Acted as figurehead for policies of Italian unification of his premier, CAVOUR; enlisted support of Britain and France for cause. Proclaimed king of Italy following unification of most of country under Sardinian auspices.

Victor Emmanuel III (1869-1947), king of Italy (1900-46). Asked Mussolini to form govt. after declining to oppose his march on Rome; effectively deprived of power under Fascist regime. Made armistice (1943) with Allies in WWII. Abdicated.

Victoria (1819-1901), queen of Great Britain and Ireland (1837-1901). Married Prince Albert of Saxe-Coburg-Gotha (1840); guided by him in matters of policy. On Albert's death (1861), spent several years in seclusion. Influenced by personal charm of Disraeli; became empress of India (1876) under his guidance. Reign marked by indust. and colonial expansion, domestic reform.

Victoria, Tomás Luis de (c 1548-1611), Spanish composer. Worked in Rome for many years, then served as choirmaster to Empress Maria in Madrid. Compositions, all written for church, show masterly handling of polyphony.

Victoria, state of SE Australia. Area 227,700 sq km (87,900 sq mi); pop. 3,496,000; cap. Melbourne. Narrow coastal lowlands; uplands incl. C plateau, Australian Alps (SE); Murray basin in NW. Agric. (irrigated in NW) incl. wheat, fruit, vegetable growing, sheep and cattle raising; timber indust.; minerals incl. coal, oil, natural gas, gypsum. Industs. incl. petro-chemicals, car assembly, paper mfg. Settled from 1834; independent from New South Wales (1851). Pop. grew rapidly after 1851 gold discoveries. Federal state from 1901.

Victoria, seaport and cap. of British Columbia, Canada; on Vancouver Isl. Pop. 62,000. Timber, fishing, tourist industs. Esquimalt naval base is suburb. Founded 1843 by Hudson's Bay Co. as fur trading post.

Victoria, cap. of Hong Kong, on Hong Kong Isl. Pop. 849,000.

Victoria Cross, highest British military decoration. Instituted by Queen Victoria (1856).

Victoria Falls, massive waterfall of R. Zambezi, on Rhodesia-Zambia border. Width 1.6 km (1 mi); max. height 128 m (420 ft). Tourist centre; h.e.p. Discovered 1855 by Livingstone.

Victoria Island, SW Franklin Dist., Northwest Territs., Canada; part of Arctic archipelago. Area 212,200 sq km (81,930 sq mi). Has weather station at Cambridge in SE.

Victoria Land, region of Antarctica, divided between Ross Dependency and Australian Antarctic Territ.

Victoria Nyanza or **Lake Victoria,** freshwater lake of EC Africa, 2nd largest in world. Borders on Uganda (N), Kenya (E), Tanzania (S). Area 69,490 sq km (26,830 sq mi); source of White Nile. Originally called L. Ukerewe; Speke was 1st European to reach it (1858).

Victory, H.M.S., British warship. Launched 1765, she was Nelson's flagship at Trafalgar. Now preserved in dry dock in Portsmouth.

vicuña, *Lama vicugna,* wild llama found in South American Andes. Hunted by man for wool; numbers much reduced.

Vidal, Gore (1925-), American author. Known for sophisticated satirical novels incl. *Messiah* (1954), *The City and the Pillar* (1948), *Myra Breckinridge* (1968), *Burr* (1974). Also wrote plays, *eg The Best Man* (1960).

Vienna (*Wien*), cap. and prov. of Austria, on R. Danube. Pop. 1,615,000. River port, admin., commercial centre. Cap. and cultural centre of Austria from 12th cent. Home of Beethoven, Mozart, Strauss. Univ. (1365) famous for medicine, psychiatry (Freud). Buildings incl. Hofburg (imperial palace), cathedral of St Stephen, Houses of Parliament, opera house; also museums, parks. Resisted Turkish sieges 1529, 1683. Congress of Vienna (1814-15) rearranged Europe after Napoleon's defeat. German-occupied in WWII, Jewish pop. wiped out. Occupied by Allies 1945-55.

Vienna, Congress of, meeting (1814-15) of European powers (foremost being Austria, Prussia, Russia, Britain and France) to settle problems arising out of defeat of Napoleon. Resolved boundary disputes, reallocated control of many small states, estab. 'balance of power' principle in international politics.

Vienne, town of SE France, on R. Rhône. Pop. 30,000. Agric. market, textiles (esp. silk mfg.), tanning. Hist. seat of kings of Burgundy. Council (1312) suppressed Knights Templar. Roman remains incl. temple, theatre.

Vienne, river of WC France. Flows c 355 km (220 mi) from Corrèze dept. via Limoges to R. Loire.

Vientiane, admin. cap. of Laos. Pop. 174,000. Commercial centre on R. Mekong; timber, textiles. Cap. of kingdom 1707-1827. Became cap. of French protect. of Laos 1899. Noted for houses on stilts, pagodas, palaces.

Vierwaldstättersee, see LUCERNE, LAKE, Switzerland.

Viet Cong, Communist military force engaged in guerrilla warfare in South Vietnam during 1960s and 1970s. Following withdrawal of US troops (1973), Communist offensive of 1975 led to surrender of South Vietnam (April, 1975).

Vietnam, country of SE Asia. Area c 333,000 sq km (128,000 sq mi); pop. c 43,198,000; cap. Hanoi. Language: Vietnamese. Religion: Taoism. Forested mountains and plateau with Mekong delta in S. Rice chief crop. Part of French ruled INDO-CHINA until estab. of republic from Annam, Tonkin, Cochin China; dispute with France over independence led to INDO-CHINESE WAR, ending with

Geneva conference (1954) which divided country into 2 states, North and South Vietnam. North Vietnam, area c 159,000 sq km (61,000 sq mi); pop. 23,244,000; cap. Hanoi. South Vietnam, area c 174,000 sq km (67,000 sq mi); pop. 19,954,000; cap. Ho Chi Minh City (Saigon). North Vietnam's attempts (see Ho CHI MINH) to reunify country under Communist rule led to US military intervention (1960s). US withdrew following 1973 ceasefire. South Vietnam fell to Communist forces in 1975 and gradual political reintegration followed.

Vietnam War, conflict in SE Asia, fought mainly in South Vietnam from 1954 between US-backed govt. forces and VIET CONG guerrillas supported by North Vietnam and Soviet armaments. US support of South with economic, military aid began 1961, and intensified from 1964, when alleged Tonkin gunboat attacks prompted bombing of North. Tet offensive (1968) discredited US reports of ultimate victory. After President Johnson withdrew from 1968 election, peace talks involving both Vietnams, US and NLF began in Paris. Despite formal conclusion of war (1973), guerrilla activities continued in South, which capitulated with capture of Saigon (April, 1975). Length of war, high US casualties, corruption of South Vietnam govt. contributed to opposition of war within US.

Vignola, Giacomo Barozzi da (1507-73), Italian architect. Architect to Pope Julius III, he worked mainly in Rome. His work on Il Gesù (1568), mother-church of Jesuits, greatly influenced church architecture. Wrote *Treatise on the Five Orders of Architecture* (1562).

Vigny, Alfred Victor, Comte de (1797-1863), French author. Leading Romantic. Works incl. restrained, stoical *Poèmes antiques et modernes* (1826), play *Chatterton* (1835), historical novel *Cinq Mars* (1826).

Vigo, city of Galicia, NW Spain, on Bay of Vigo. Pop. 197,000. Port; shipbuilding, oil refining, fishing. Twice attacked by Drake (1585, 1589); scene of naval victory (1702) of British and Dutch over French and Spanish.

Viipuri, see VYBORG.

Vikings, Scandinavian sea-warriors who raided coasts of Europe (9th-11th cents.) in their oar-powered longships. Colonized Iceland, Normandy, parts of Britain and Ireland. Thought to have reached North America (see LEIF ERICSSON). Traded S and E to Persia, Spain, Russia. Also called Norsemen.

Villa, Francisco ('Pancho') (c 1877-1923), Mexican revolutionary. Took part in 1910 revolution. Involved in power struggle with Carranza from 1914. Raided New Mexican border towns in retaliation against US recognition of Carranza (1915); escaped capture in subsequent US incursion into Mexico. Assassinated.

Villa-Lobos, Heitor (1887-1959), Brazilian composer. Works show influence of Brazilian folk song and South American Indians. Compositions incl. *Chôros* (serenades) for various instruments and *Bachianas Brasileiras,* series of pieces intended to invoke spirit of Bach in Brazilian styles.

Villars, Claude Louis Hector,

Duc de (1653-1734), French army officer. Commanded French troops aiding elector of Bavaria in War of the Spanish Succession. Won battle of Friedlingen (1702). In charge of main force confronting Marlborough, lost at Malplaquet (1709) but defeated Albemarle at Denain (1712). Negotiated Peace of Rastatt (1714).

Villehardouin, Geoffroi de (c 1160-c 1212), French soldier. Wrote *La Conquête de Constantinople* (pub. 1585), a chronicle of 4th Crusade.

villein, peasant of W Europe under medieval manorial system. Did not own land, but owed services to lord. Unlike serf, was personally free. Villeinage system declined in England by 14th cent. but survived elsewhere until 19th cent.

Villeneuve, Pierre Charles Jean Baptiste Sylvestre de (1763-1806), French naval officer. Consistently unsuccessful in battles with Nelson, from Nile (1798) to Trafalgar (1805). On his way home after captivity in England he committed suicide.

Villiers, George, see BUCKINGHAM, GEORGE VILLIERS, 1ST DUKE OF.

Villiers de L'Isle-Adam, [Jean Marie Mathias Philippe] Auguste, Comte de (1838-89), French author. Forerunner of SYMBOLISTS. Known for macabre short stories *Contes cruels* (1883), also wrote plays, incl. visionary *Axël* (1890).

Villon, François (1431-after 1463), French poet. Violent, criminal life reflected in verse, expressing compassion for human suffering, piety, alongside biting satire, ribaldry.

Wrote *Lais* or *Petit Testament* (1456), containing lighthearted 'bequests' to friends, *Grand Testament* (1461), review of past life into which are set famous *ballades*, eg 'Ballades des dames du temps 'jadis'' with refrain 'Where are the snows of yester-year?'

Vilnius (Russ. *Vilna*), city of USSR, cap. of Lithuanian SSR. Pop. 395,000. Railway jct.; food processing, sawmilling, agric. machinery mfg. Cap. of Lithuania (1323-1795); passed to Russian control. Intended cap. of independent Lithuania but seized (1920) by Poland and held until 1939. Large Jewish pop. decimated by Germans (1941-4). RC cathedral; univ. (1579).

Vincennes, suburb of E Paris, France. Engineering, chemical industs. Royal residence from 12th cent., château near Bois de Vincennes used as state prison (17th-18th cent.).

Vincent de Paul, St (c 1580-1660), French priest. Founded secular Congregation of the Mission or 'Lazarists' (1625) and Sisters of Charity (1634), dedicated to work in orphanages, schools, hospitals.

vine, climbing or trailing plant, either woody or herbaceous, eg grape vine, ivy, Virginia creeper.

vinegar, sour liquid consisting of dilute and impure acetic acid, obtained by action of bacteria on beer (producing malt vinegar), wine, cider, industrial alcohol, *etc*. Used as preservative in pickling and as a condiment.

vingt-et-un, gambling game at cards, in which each player's aim is to obtain from dealer cards totalling 21 points or as near as possible to

that total without exceeding it. Also known as blackjack and pontoon.

Vinland, hist. portion of North American coast discovered by Leif Ericsson (c AD 1000). Location of his landing disputed, most likely on S coast of New England. Also known as Wineland.

vinyl group, univalent chemical radical $CH_2:CH$ derived from ethylene. Various vinyl compounds, incl. chloride and acetate, may be polymerized to form plastics and resins.

viol, family of six-stringed instruments with fretted fingerboards, played with bow; popular esp. 16th-17th cent. Held on or between player's knees. Superseded by violin family; revived for performances of old music.

viola, member of violin family, between violin and cello in range. Pitched an octave above cello. Held under chin.

viola da gamba, member of viol family with similar range to cello.

violet, any of genus *Viola* of small plants native to N temperate zones. White, blue, purple or yellow irregular flowers with short spurs. Species incl. *V. odorata* with small purple flowers and *V. tricolor* or garden pansy.

violin family, string instruments of which the four strings are bowed or plucked. Strings are stretched across a wooden bridge which transfers their vibrations to a sound chamber forming body of instrument. Fingerboard is fretless. Members are violin, viola and violoncello (CELLO), double bass. Evolved in 16th cent. and perfected by Italian violin makers, eg Amati, Stradivari, in 17th cent.

Viollet-le-Duc, Eugène Emmanuel (1814-79), French architect. Leading exponent of Gothic revival in France, he studied medieval architecture extensively. In *Dictionnaire raisonné de l'architecture française* (1858-74), emphasized engineering aspect of Gothic building. Numerous restorations incl. work on Notre Dame, Paris.

violoncello, see CELLO.

viper, any of Viperidae family of Old World venomous snakes, incl. adder, *Vipera berus,* and asp, *V. aspis.* Name also applied to New World pit vipers, incl. rattlesnake, bushmaster, fer-de-lance.

Virgil, see VERGIL.

virginals, see SPINET.

Virginia, Atlantic state of E US. Area 105,711 sq km (40,815 sq mi); pop. 4,648,000; cap. Richmond; largest city Norfolk. Low coastal plain (partly swamp) rises to Appalachians in W. Chief rivers Potomac, James, Rappahannock. Agric. esp. tobacco growing; fisheries, shipbuilding, mfg. industs. First permanent English colony estab. at Jamestown (1607). One of original 13 colonies of US. Major battleground in Revolution, Civil War.

Virginia bluebell, see BLUEBELL.

Virginia creeper, *Parthenocissus quinquefolia,* North American tendril-climbing vine widely cultivated in Europe as ornamental. Palmate leaves of 5 leaflets, green flowers followed by inedible blue berries.

Virgin Islands, group of c 100 isls. in West Indies, E of Puerto Rico. Discovered and named (1493) by Columbus. **British Virgin Islands** incl. Tortola, Anegada, Virgin Gorda isls. Area 153 sq km (59 sq mi); pop. 12,000; cap. Road Town (on Tortola). Colony from 17th cent. **Virgin Islands of the United States** incl. St Thomas, St Croix, St John isls. Area 345 sq km (133 sq mi); pop. 96,000; cap. Charlotte Amalie (on St Thomas). Purchased (1917) from Denmark.

Virgin Mary, see MARY, THE VIRGIN.

Virgo, see ZODIAC.

virus, disease-producing microorganism, capable of multiplication only within living cells. Essential constituent is a nucleic acid (DNA, RNA), surrounded by a protein coat. Typical virus attaches itself to a cell of host and introduces its nucleic acid. Cell is forced to synthesize further nucleic acid and protein, enabling virus to reproduce itself. Cause of diseases such as measles, influenza, smallpox.

Visconti, Gian Galeazzo (c 1350-1402), Italian nobleman. Bought title of Duke of Milan (1395) from Holy Roman emperor Wenceslaus, then thwarted German imperial ambitions in N Italy with victory in 1401. Campaign to unify Italy ended when he died of plague near Florence. Founded Milan Cathedral.

Visconti [de Modrone], Luchino (1906-76), Italian film writer-director. Known as father of neorealism for *Ossessione* (1942). Later films incl. studies of decadence, eg *The Damned* (1969), and passion in old age, eg *Death in Venice* (1970).

viscose process, method of making rayon from viscose, a brown liquid prepared by treating cellulose with sodium hydroxide and carbon disulphide. Yarn is made by forcing viscose through fine holes into acid solution. Discovered in 1892.

viscosity, internal friction of a fluid, caused by molecular attraction, making it resist tendency to flow. Viscosity of liquids decreases with rising temperature.

Vishinsky, Andrei, *see* VYSHIN-SKY, ANDREI.

Vishnu, in Hinduism, one of three supreme gods. Early myth associates him with solar deities of Rig-Veda. Many incarnations incl. Rama, Krishna, Buddha. Represented as dark blue and holding conch, discus, mace and lotus.

Visigoths or **West Goths,** branch of GOTHS who were driven into Thrace and the Balkans by the Huns (c 375). Under ALARIC, they invaded Italy and sacked Rome (410). Later conquered much of S France and Spain. Forced to retreat into Spain by Clovis (507). Their kingdom in Spain was overrun during Moorish conquest (711).

vision, *see* EYE; RETINA.

Vistula (Pol. *Wisla,* Ger. *Weichsel*), river of Poland. Flows *c* 1080 km (670 mi) from N Carpathians via Kraków, Warsaw, Toruń to Gulf of Gdańsk near Gdańsk. Major trade route; canal links with other rivers eg Oder, Dnepr.

vitamin A, fat-soluble vitamin, found in fish-liver oil, milk, butter, *etc.* Can be synthesized in body from carotene found in green plants and carrots. Deficiency causes night blindness.

vitamin B complex, group of unrelated water-soluble vitamins, found in liver, yeast, wheat-germ, *etc.* Incl. THIAMIN, RIBOFLAVIN and

vitamin B12, a deficiency of which causes pernicious anaemia.

vitamin C, *see* ASCORBIC ACID.

vitamin D, any of group of fat-soluble vitamins, found in fish-liver oil, milk, *etc.* Formed in skin by action of ultraviolet radiation from Sun. Essential to formation of bones and teeth.

vitamin K, fat-soluble vitamin found in certain green leaves of plants and synthesized by bacteria in the intestines. Promotes blood clotting.

vitamins, group of complex organic compounds essential in small amounts to normal body metabolism. Some can be synthesized in body from other substances found in food, eg vitamin A; others, eg vitamin C, must be present in diet. Vitamin deficiencies cause various diseases, which can be cured by taking appropriate vitamin.

Vitebsk, city of USSR, N Byelorussian SSR; on W Dvina. Pop. 250,000. Agric. machinery, textile mfg. Chief town of Polotsk principality before coming under Lithuanian rule in 14th cent. Annexed to Russia in 1772.

Vitoria, city of N Spain, cap. of Alava prov. Pop. 137,000. Agric. market, tanning. Scene of Wellington's decisive victory (1813) over French in Peninsular War. Cathedral (12th cent.).

vitrified fort, in archaeology, term for Iron Age hill-forts with walls changed in character by fire. Stone walls had internal timber supports; if these were burnt (by accident or design), adjacent stonework fused together.

vitriol, name given to various

sulphate salts and sulphuric acid. Green vitriol is ferrous sulphate, blue vitriol copper sulphate, oil of vitriol concentrated sulphuric acid.

Vitruvius [Pollio, Marcus] (*fl* 1st cent. AD), Roman architect, engineer. Author of 10 vol. *De architectura*, treatise dealing with all aspects of building, town planning, *etc*. Source much used by Renaissance architects.

Vivaldi, Antonio (*c* 1675-1741), Italian composer. Known for more than 450 concertos, mainly *concerti grossi* for several instruments, but also for solo instruments, esp. violin, eg *The Four Seasons*. Influenced Bach, who rearranged some of Vivaldi's concertos.

vivisection, use of living animals for medical research into causes and prevention of diseases, esp. of man.

Vladimir, city of USSR, C European RSFSR. Pop. 248,000. Textiles, tractor mfg. Cap. of Vladimir principality (12th-14th cent.) until court removed to Moscow. Kremlin contains restored Uspenski and Demetrius cathedrals (12th cent.).

Vladivostok, city of USSR, SE Siberian RSFSR. Pop. 472,000. Port and naval base (kept ice-free in winter) on Pacific coast. Exports timber, soya bean oil; shipbuilding, sawmilling; fishing, whaling. Settled 1860, developed after completion of Chinese Eastern railway (1903). Terminus of Trans-Siberian railway.

Vlaminck, Maurice de (1876-1958), French painter. One of the original fauves, early work is characterized by exuberant colour. Later specialized in darker, more expressionistic landscapes.

Vlissingen, *see* FLUSHING, Netherlands.

Vltava, *see* MOLDAU, Czechoslovakia.

vodka, unaged colourless spirit distilled from barley, rye, maize, or potatoes. Originally made in Russia, Poland and Baltic states.

voice, sound produced by vibration of vocal cords, 2 pairs of membranous cords in larynx. Air from lungs causes lower pair to vibrate; pitch of sound is controlled by tension of cords and volume by regulation of air·passing through larynx. Sinuses act as resonators, and muscles of the tongue and cheek articulate the sound.

Vojvodina, autonomous prov. of N Yugoslavia, in Serbia. Area 21,500 sq km (8300 sq mi); cap. Novi Sad. Fertile, low-lying, drained by Danube, Sava, Tisza; large amounts of cereals, vegetables, fruit grown. Part of Hungary until 1920.

volcano, vent in Earth's crust through which lavas, gases, etc are ejected. May be on land or submarine. Solidified material around outlet gives conical shape. Volcanoes may be active, *ie* subject to frequent eruption, dormant, *ie* undergoing long period of inactivity, or extinct, *ie* no longer liable to erupt.

Volcano Islands, group of ·3 volcanic isls. in W Pacific, S of Japan. Area 29 sq km (11 sq mi); main isl. Iwo Jima. Annexed by Japan 1887. Captured by US forces in WWII and administered by US until 1968.

vole, small rat-like burrowing rodent with blunt nose and short tail. Species incl. field vole, *Microtus* *agrestis,* and water vole, *Arvicola amphibius.*

Volga, river of USSR, European RSFSR; longest river of Europe. Rises in Valdai hills, flows c 3850 km (2400 mi) generally SE into web Caspian delta. Connected by canals to Moscow, Leningrad and R. Don; major transportation system. Used for irrigation, h.e.p.; fishing in lower course.

Volgograd, city of USSR, SE European RSFSR; port on lower Volga. Pop. 852,000. Transport and indust. centre; oil refining, shipyards, steel and heavy machinery mfg. Founded 1589 as Tsaritsyn; Stalingrad (1925-61). Became commercially important in 19th cent. Scene of decisive Soviet victory in WWII after German siege (1942-3).

volleyball, six-a-side team game played on a rectangular court. Players hit a ball with their hands, attempting to return it over net without its touching ground. Originated (1895) in US by W.G. Morgan. Olympic event since 1964.

Volsung Cycle, in Old Norse literature, part of the Elder EDDA, telling same stories as NIBELUNGENLIED.

volt, SI unit of electric potential, defined as difference in potential between 2 points on a conductor carrying constant current of 1 ampère when power dissipated between points is 1 watt.

Volta, Alessandro, Conte (1745-1827), Italian physicist. Invented electrophorus to produce electric charge. His attempts to refute Galvani's idea of 'animal electricity' led to discovery of voltaic pile (battery) which produced steady electric current. Unit of electromotive force, volt, named after him.

Volta, river of W Africa. Black and White Volta rivers from Upper Volta unite to form Volta in C Ghana; flows S to Gulf of Guinea at Ada. Volta River Scheme provides h.e.p., irrigation; Akosombo Dam (1966) formed L. Volta (area 4920 sq km/1900 sq mi).

Voltaic Republic, see UPPER VOLTA.

Voltaire, pseud. of François Marie Arouet (1694-1778), French philosopher, writer. Attacked organized religion, superstition, intolerance, civil repression. Influenced by English thought esp. by Newton, Locke, ideas influenced movement culminating in French Revolution. Wrote immense number of works, incl. tragedy (inspired by Shakespeare's *Othello*) *Zaïre* (1732), *Letters Concerning the English Nation* (1733). Best known for philosophical novel, *Candide* (1759), satirizing LEIBNITZ. Conducted stormy friendship with Frederick the Great.

voltmeter, instrument for measuring potential difference between 2 points. Usually consists of galvanometer in series with a high resistance.

volvox, genus of small chlorophyll-bearing organisms forming hollow, spherical colonies common in ponds. Regarded by zoologists as flagellate protozoans, by botanists as green algae.

Von Braun, Wernher (1912-77), American rocket expert, b. Germany. Helped develop German V-2 military rocket. Director (from 1960) of Space Flight Center which developed *Apollo* rockets. Administrator of National Aeronautics and Space Administration (NASA) from 1970.

Vonnegut, Kurt (1922-), American author. Novels, eg *Player Piano* (1952), *Cat's Cradle* (1963), *Slaughterhouse Five* (1969), use the apparatus of science fiction and black humour to convey mistrust of human institutions.

Von Neumann, John (1903-57), American mathematician, b. Hungary. Made significant contributions to quantum theory, mathematical logic, continuous groups, *etc.* Founder of game theory; influential in development of high-speed computers, which aided production of the atomic bomb.

Von Sternberg, Josef, orig. Josef Stern (1894-1969), Austrian film director, settled in US in 1920s. Known for creation of Marlene Dietrich's image, as in *The Blue Angel* (1930), *Shanghai Express* (1932).

von Stroheim, Erich, orig. Hans Erich Maria Stroheim von Nordenwall (1885-1957), Austrian film actor, director. Went to US (1909); known as director in 1920s, esp. for *Greed* (1923). As actor, remembered for Prussian officer roles, esp. in *La Grande Illusion* (1937).

voodoo, religious beliefs, practices of West Indian, S US and South American Negroes. Derived from W African snake worship, fetishism. Esp. prevalent in Haiti.

Voronezh, city of USSR, SC European RSFSR; near confluence of Voronezh and Don rivers. Pop. 693,000. Indust. centre of blackearth region; synthetic rubber and machinery mfg. Rebuilt after fires in 18th cent.

Voroshilov, Kliment Yefremovich (1881-1969), Soviet general. Active in October Revolution (1917). Armed forces commissar (1925-40), reorganized Red Army. Commanded defence of Leningrad against Germans (1941). Chairman of presidium (1953-60).

Voroshilovgrad, town of USSR, E Ukrainian SSR; in Donbas mining area. Pop. 404,000. Locomotives, coalmining equipment. Iron foundry estab. here 1795. Formerly Lugansk.

Vorster, Balthazar Johannes (1915-), South African political leader, PM (1966-1978). Succeeded Verwoerd, whose APARTHEID policies he upheld. Having sustained Rhodesia after UDI, later put pressure on it to accept black majority rule.

vortex, term used to describe rapid rotatory movement of a fluid. Used mainly of liquids (whirlpools) and of air (tornadoes, whirlwinds).

vorticism, English art movement founded (1913) by Wyndham Lewis; stimulated by futurism, and influenced by cubism, it sought to revitalize English art by introducing modern industrial forms. Adherents incl. Gaudier-Brzeska, Nevinson, Wadsworth. Journal, *Blast,* published literary work by, eg Ezra Pound, T.S. Eliot.

Vosges, mountain range of E France. Extends c 240 km (150 mi) NE from Belfort Gap, separates Alsace (E) from Lorraine (W), highest peak Ballon de Guebwiller (1423 m/4672 ft). Forests, vineyards, resorts. Source of Moselle, Sarre rivers.

vote, see ELECTION, PROPORTIONAL REPRESENTATION, SUFFRAGE, CIVIL RIGHTS.

Voysey, Charles Francis Annesley (1857-1941), English architect, designer. His country houses, built before WWI, were influential in their small size, simplicity and lack of period imitations.

Vries, Hugo de (1848-1935), Dutch botanist. One of three investigators who independently rediscovered Mendel's work on heredity; he discovered role of mutation in evolution.

Vuillard, Edouard (1868-1940), French painter. Known for intimate interiors, portraits, still lifes, which display his feeling for colour and form. Also active in decorative arts and stage design.

Vulcan, in Roman religion, fire god, perhaps god of the smithy. Became identified with Greek Hephaestus.

Vulgate, Latin version of Bible prepared (late 4th cent.) by St Jerome from Hebrew (OT) and Old Latin (NT) texts. Chosen by Council of Trent (1546) as official version in RC church.

vulture, large carrion-eating bird with hooked beak, strong claws, and featherless neck and head. True vultures, found only in C Europe, Africa and parts of Asia, incl. LAMMERGEIER and griffon vulture, *Gyps fulvus*. New World vultures incl. Andean CONDOR.

Vyborg (Finn. *Viipuri,* Swed. *Viborg*), port of USSR, NW European RSFSR; on Gulf of Finland. Pop..63,000. Exports timber, wood products. Site of Swedish castle (1293); Hanseatic port. Ceded to Russia by Sweden (1721); part of Finland (1812-1947).

Vyshinsky or Vishinsky, Andrei (1883-1954), Soviet diplomat. Chief prosecutor at treason trials following Stalin's purges (1936-8). Foreign minister (1949-53); frequently represented USSR at UN.

W

Wade, George, (1673-1748), British field-marshal. Military governor at home during 1715 Jacobite rebellion. In 1724 sent to Highlands to disarm clans and build system of metalled roads and bridges, many of which survive. In 1744 made Commander-in-chief of home forces; during 1745 Jacobite rebellion replaced by Cumberland.

wadi, watercourse in desert regions of N Africa and Arabia. Normally dry; formed by water torrents which accompany infrequent heavy rainfall.

wages, in economics, share of total product of industry that goes to labour as distinct from share taken by capital. May be in money, goods or services. Real wages determined by amount of goods monetary wages will buy. Wage theorists incl. Ricardo, Marx.

Wagner, Richard (1813-83), German composer. Developed romantic music to great heights, using musical motifs in continuously evolving form to underline drama. Founded festival theatre at Bayreuth where he presented 4-opera cycle *Ring of the Nibelung* (1876); this work embodied his operatic theories. Other operas incl. *Die Meistersinger, Tannhäuser, Tristan und Isolde.*

wagtail, small, chiefly European, bird of Motacillidae family. Slender body with long tail that wags up and down. Species incl. black and white pied wagtail, *Motacilla alba.*

Wahabi, followers of Mohammed ibn Abd al-Wahab (*c* 1703-91), who founded strict Moslem religious sect. Stress austerity in worship and living. Religion of ruling family of Saudi Arabia, where it predominates.

Wain, John Barrington (1925-), English poet, novelist. Works incl. collections of dryly witty verse, *eg A Word Carved on a Sill* (1956), novels, *eg Hurry on Down* (1953), criticism.

Wajda, Andrzej (1926-), Polish film director. Known for trilogy *A Generation* (1954), *Kanal* (1955), *Ashes and Diamonds* (1958), on growing up in war-torn Poland.

Wakamatsu, see KITAKYUSHU.

Wakefield, Edward Gibbon (1796-1862), British statesman. Advocated sale of colonial land to finance further immigration. Helped found South Australia (1836). Managed colonization scheme of New Zealand Land Co. (1839).

Wakefield, city and co. town of West Yorkshire met. county, N England, on R. Calder. Pop. 60,000. Agric. market; woollens; coal-mining. Has 14th cent. cathedral; grammar school (16th cent.). Scene of battle (1460) of Wars of the Roses in which Richard of York killed.

Wake Island, atoll with 3 islets, **C** Pacific Ocean, dependency of US. Area 8 sq km (3 sq mi). US naval, air base. Visited and named (1796) by British, annexed (1898) by US. Occupied by Japanese in WWII.

wake robin, see TRILLIUM.

Waksman, Selman Abraham (1888-1973), American biologist, b. Russia. Awarded Nobel Prize for Physiology and Medicine (1952) for discovery of antibiotic streptomycin.

Walachia or **Wallachia,** region of S Romania. Chief city Bucharest. Comprises hist. provs. of Muntenia (Greater Walachia) in E, Oltenia (Lesser Walachia) in W. Agric., oilfields. Principality founded 1290; Turkish rule from 14th cent. until united with MOLDAVIA (1859) to form Romania.

Walburga, St, see WALPURGIS, ST.

Walcheren, region of SW Netherlands, at mouth of Scheldt estuary. Main towns Middelburg, Flushing. Lowland, protected by North Sea dykes; agric., tourism. German occupation in WWII ended by bombing dykes.

Waldenses or **Waldensians,** Christian sect formed (1170) by Peter Waldo (d. 1217). Dedicated to poverty and meditation, with Bible as sole authority. Forbidden to preach by Pope Alexander III (1179); declared heretical (1215). Persecuted 15th-17th cent.; recognized 1848 by Charles Albert of Savoy.

Waldheim, Kurt (1918-), Austrian govt. official, UN secretary-general (1972-). Led Austria's 1st delegation to UN (1958); served as Austrian foreign minister (1968-70).

Wales (Cymru), principality of UK, in W part of Great Britain. Area 20,761 sq km (8006 sq mi); pop. 2,724,000; cap. Cardiff. Languages: English, Welsh. Religion: Methodist groups. Comprises 8 counties. Main rivers Severn, Wye, Taff. Crossed N-S by Cambrian Mts. (highest point Snowdon). Mainly pastoral; indust. based on S Wales coalfields (Swansea, Merthyr Tydfil, Rhondda). Originally inhabited by Celts. English conquest by Edward I (1282), but fierce fighting continued; politically united from 1536. Resurgence of nationalism in late 20th cent.

Wales, Prince of, title created (1301) by Edward I of England for his eldest son after conquest of Wales; since conferred on eldest son of monarch.

Waley, Arthur (1889-1966), English orientalist. Known for influential translations of Chinese, Japanese works incl. *The Tale of Genji* (6 vols., 1925-32).

wallaby, common name applied to small kangaroo when hind foot of adult is less than 25 cm/10 in. long; widely distributed in Australia and Tasmania. Species incl. agile rock-wallaby, genus *Petrogale,* and rare hare-wallaby, genus *Lagorchestes.*

Wallace, Alfred Russel (1823-1913), English naturalist. Researched on geographical distribution of animals; described imaginary (Wallace) line, running between Borneo, Celebes, Bali and Lombok, which marks division between Asian and Australian animal species. Developed theory of natural selection independently of Darwin.

Wallace, George Corley (1919-), American politician. Known for his espousal of segregationist policies as governor of Alabama (1962-6) which led to federal intervention. Won several states as Independent Party's presidential candidate (1968). Paralysed after assassination attempt (1972); re-elected governor in 1974.

Wallace, Henry Agard (1888-1965), American politician. An authority on farming methods, he was secretary of agric. (1933-4); vice-president under Roosevelt (1941-5). Progressive party presidential candidate (1948) after split with Democrats.

Wallace, Sir William (c 1272-1305), Scottish patriot. Led forces which defeated Edward I's army at Stirling (1297), then drove English across border. Ruled Scotland briefly as guardian of kingdom. Defeated (1298) by English at Falkirk. Captured (1305), executed in London.

Wallachia, see WALACHIA, Romania.

Wallasey, bor. of Merseyside met. county, NW England, on Wirral penin. Pop. 97,000. Resort, residential; ferry to Liverpool.

wallcreeper, *Tichodroma muraria,* small grey-black bird of Sittidae family, with crimson wing patches. Inhabits cliffs and rocky places of S Europe, N Africa and Asia.

Wallenstein, Albrecht von (1583-1634), Bohemian soldier, commander of forces of Emperor Ferdinand II. Fought successfully for Catholic League against the Danes in early years of THIRTY YEARS WAR. Dismissed after failure to capture Stralsund (1628). Recalled to counter Swedish threat,

defeated by Gustavus Adolphus at Lützen (1632). Murdered, prob. for carrying out secret peace negotiations.

Waller, Edmund (1606-87), English poet. Wrote polished occasional poems, love lyrics, *eg* 'On a Girdle', 'Go, Lovely Rose' from *Poems* (1645). Banished from England (1643-52) for involvement in a Royalist plot.

walleye, *Stizostedion vitreum,* North American freshwater food and game fish of perch family, c 90 cm/3 ft long. Large staring eyes.

wallflower, *Cheiranthus cheiri,* European plant with sweet-scented yellow or orange flowers. Many garden varieties cultivated.

Wallis, Sir Barnes Neville (1887-1979), English aeronautical engineer. Designed R 100 airship and bouncing bombs used against Möhne and Eder dams (1943). Invented swingwing aeroplane.

Wallis and Futuna Islands, overseas territ. of France, in SC Pacific Ocean. Area 272 sq km (105 sq mi); pop. 9000; main isl. Uvéa. Produce timber. Acquired by France (1842); dependency of New Caledonia until 1959.

Walloons, people of S provs. of Belgium who speak Walloon, a dialect of French. Walloon regions are centres of mining and heavy indust., unlike Flemish-speaking N provs. Friction between Walloons and Flemings remains element of Belgian politics.

Wall Street, New York street in lower Manhattan. As centre of great financial district, name has become synonymous with American finance.

walnut, any of genus *Juglans* of

deciduous trees of N temperate zones. Edible nut; timber valued for cabinet-making. Species incl. Persian or English walnut, *J. regia*, and black walnut, *J. nigra*, of E US.

Walpole, Horace or **Horatio, 4th Earl of Orford** (1717-97), English author. Wrote prototypical 'gothick' novel, *The Castle of Otranto* (1765). Rebuilt villa, Strawberry Hill, at Twickenham, making 'gothick' taste fashionable. Also known for letters (3000 of them).

Walpole, Sir Hugh Seymour (1884-1941), English novelist, b. New Zealand. Wrote popular novels, *eg Mr Perrin and Mr Traill* (1911), *The Herries Chronicle* (1930-3), criticism.

Walpole, Robert, 1st Earl of Orford (1676-1745), British statesman. Led Whig admin. (1721-42) as first lord of treasury and chancellor of exchequer, effectively acting as 1st PM. Restored economic stability after SOUTH SEA BUBBLE (1720). Encouraged free trade, cooperation with France; tried to keep Britain out of European wars. Estab. principle of CABINET responsibility to Parliament.

Walpurgis or **Walburga, St** (d. 779), English missionary in Germany. *Walpurgisnacht*, eve of her feast on 1 May, is traditional witches' sabbath.

walrus, either of 2 species of seal-like carnivores of Odobenidae family. Large upper canines form tusks used for scraping shellfish from sea bottom. Males up to 4.5 m/15 ft long may weigh over 1000 kg/1 ton. *Odobenus rosmarus* inhabits NW Atlantic, Arctic and *O. divergens* the Bering Sea.

Walsall, bor. of West Midlands met. county, WC England. Pop. 185,000. In BLACK COUNTRY; coal, iron industs.; leather goods.

Walsingham, Sir Francis (*c* 1532-90), English statesman. Employed on diplomatic missions to bring about Anglo-French alliance against Spain. Secretary of state after 1573, directed far-reaching spy ring. Discovered Babington's plot which implicated Mary Queen of Scots (1587).

Walter, Hubert (d. 1205), English churchman, archbishop of Canterbury (1193-1205). As justiciar (1193-8), he was virtual ruler of England during Richard I's absence. Carried out reforms in admin. and taxation.

Waltham Forest, bor. of NE Greater London, England. Pop. 234,000. Created 1965 from Chingford, Leyton, Walthamstow (all in Essex).

Walther von der Vogelweide (*c* 1170-*c* 1230), German poet. Famous for lyric poems, many on courtly love, religion; also moral and political lyrics.

Walton, Izaak (1593-1683), English writer. Wrote *The Compleat Angler* (1653) on pleasures of fishing. Also wrote biogs. of Donne, Wotton and others, *Lives* (1670).

Walton, Sir William Turner (1902-), English composer. Works incl. setting of poems by Edith Sitwell, *Façade*. Also wrote *Viola Concerto*, film scores, *eg Hamlet*, opera *Troilus and Cressida*, 2 symphonies and oratorio *Belshazzar's Feast*.

waltz, dance in triple time developed from German *Ländler*. Popularity spread from Vienna in 19th cent.

through compositions of Strauss family.

Walvis Bay, town of South West Africa, on Atlantic Ocean. Pop. 16,000. Railway terminus, port, fishing and whaling industs. With hinterland (area c 970 sq km/375 sq mi) forms exclave of Cape Prov., Republic of South Africa.

wandering Jew, various trailing or creeping ornamental plants, esp. *Zebrina pendula* and *Tradescantia fluminensis.*

Wandsworth, bor. of SC Greater London, England. Pop. 299,000. Created 1965 from Battersea, Wandsworth met. bors. Incl. Putney area; Wandsworth prison.

Wang Ching-wei (1883-1944), Chinese politician. Leader of left wing of Kuomintang after Sun Yat-sen's death (1925); later turned to right. Split with Chiang Kai-shek's nationalists (1938). Headed pro-Japanese Nanking puppet govt. (1940-1).

Wankel rotary engine, type of INTERNAL COMBUSTION ENGINE invented by Felix Wankel (1902-). Derives power from rotor rather than reciprocating pistons. Successfully adapted to automobile.

Wankie, town of W Rhodesia. Pop. 24,000. Coalmining centre serving Zambian Copperbelt.

wapiti, *Cervus canadensis,* also called American elk; large North American deer, related to European red deer.

Warbeck, Perkin (c 1474-99), pretender to English throne, b. Flanders. Under Yorkist influence, claimed to be Richard, son of Edward IV (who had prob. been murdered in the Tower). Invaded Cornwall and proclaimed himself king (1497); captured and hanged.

warbler, small insectivorous songbird. Old World warblers of the subfamily Sylviinae have mainly grey and brown plumage. Species incl. garden warbler, *Sylvia borin.* American wood warblers of Parulidae family are brightly coloured; species incl. yellow warbler, *Dendroica petechia.*

war crimes, actions which contravene rules of war laid down by Hague Convention (1907), UN War Crimes Commission (1943), *etc.* Crimes incl. mass extermination (as in post-WWII Nuremberg trials of Nazi leaders), slave labour, murder of prisoners.

Warhol, Andy (1930-), American artist, film producer. Leading exponent of pop art, uses silk screen printing techniques to obtain repeated images of familiar objects, *eg* soup cans, and popular personalities, *eg* Marilyn Monroe. Films incl. *Chelsea Girls.*

Warner, Rex (1905-), English author. Works incl. novels portraying evils of capitalist society, *eg The Professor* (1938), *The Aerodrome* (1941); translations of Aeschylus, Euripides.

War of 1812, conflict (1812-15) between US and Britain. US claimed rights of neutral shipping to trade with France, disputed by Britain. Campaign saw early US naval successes, US attempts to capture Canada thwarted by Britain, British naval blockade of US coast and burning of Washington (1814). War ended officially by Treaty of Ghent (1814) before defeat of British forces at New Orleans (1815).

Warren, Earl (1891-1974), American politician, jurist. As chief justice of Supreme Court (1953-69), made many important decisions on civil rights. Headed investigation into President Kennedy's assassination (1964-5); its conclusion that Oswald acted alone has been disputed.

Warren, Robert Penn (1905-), American author. Works incl. poetry, eg *Selected Poems 1923-43* (1944), *Brother to Dragons* (1953), novels, eg *All the King's Men* (1946), *World Enough and Time* (1950), explore problems of the South. Criticism incl. *Understanding Poetry* (1938, with Cleanth Brooks).

Warsaw (*Warszawa*), cap. of Poland and of Warszawa prov., on R. Vistula. Pop. 1,317,000. Admin., indust., cultural centre; engineering, food processing; univ. (1818). Cap. of Poland from 16th cent.; under Russian rule 1815-1917. Occupied in WWII by Germans, severely damaged (incl. destruction of Jewish ghetto 1943); rebuilt on old pattern. Scene of Warsaw Treaty (1955).

Warsaw Treaty Organization, military alliance estab. (1955) through defence pact signed in Warsaw between Albania, Bulgaria, Czechoslovakia, East Germany, Hungary, Poland, Romania, Soviet Union. Diplomatic counter to acceptance of West Germany's entry to NATO.

wart, small, usually hard, tumour on skin, caused by a virus. May disappear spontaneously, only to reappear later; treated by application of acid and cauterization.

wart hog, *Phacochoerus aethiopicus,* wild African pig with large incurved tusks and warty skin on face. Capable of running quickly when alarmed.

Warwick, Richard Neville, Earl of (1428-71), English military, political leader, known as 'Kingmaker'. Supported York's claim to protectorship of Henry VI, then fought on Yorkist side in Wars of the Roses. Virtual ruler of England during early years of Edward IV's reign, but superseded by the Woodvilles. Joined Lancastrians and invaded England from France; defeated Edward and restored Henry as king (1470). Killed at Barnet by Edward's forces.

Warwickshire, county of WC England. Area 1980 sq km (765 sq mi); pop. 468,000. Major indust. area in NW (esp. metal working); coal in NE; agric., fruit in S. Stratford, Forest of Arden associated with Shakespeare. Co. town Warwick, mun. bor. of R. Avon. Pop. 18,000. Castle (14th cent.) has art collection. University of Warwick (1965).

Wash, The, shallow inlet of North Sea, E England. Indents Lincoln-Norfolk coast; subject to silting, increasing reclamation. Two navigable channels (Boston, Lynn Deeps).

Washington, George (1732-99), American statesman, president (1789-97). Given command of Continental Army at outset of American Revolution (1775); after victories at Trenton and Princeton, defeated at Brandywine (1776); survived difficult winter at Valley Forge (1778). With French support, gained victories culminating in British surrender at Yorktown (1781). Presided at Constitutional Convention (1787), later becoming 1st president. Admin. marked by split between HAMILTON and JEFFERSON, latter resigning 1793. Set precedent by refusing 3rd term in office. Warned against foreign entanglements in Farewell Address.

Washington, state of NW US, borders on Pacific and Canada. Area 176,617 sq km (68,192 sq mi); pop. 3,409,000; cap. Olympia; largest city Seattle. Cascade Range divides E plateau from Puget Sound; chief rivers Columbia, Snake. Agric. esp. fruit, vegetables; fishing, timber industs., aircraft mfg. H.e.p. supplies boosted industs. (Grand Coulee, Bonneville dams). Region disputed by British; boundary fixed 1846. Territ. estab. 1853. Admitted to Union as 42nd state (1889).

Washington, cap. of US, in DISTRICT OF COLUMBIA (DC) on Potomac R. Pop. 757,000. Built 1790-1800 as cap. Buildings incl. White House (president's residence), Capitol (Congress), Pentagon (military admin.); Library of Congress, National Gallery, Lincoln memorial.

wasp, winged insect of order Hymenoptera, with worldwide distribution. Social wasps have caste system of queens, workers, and male drones. Colonies make nest of chewed wood pulp; in temperate climates only queen survives winter. Queens and workers have sting which can be used repeatedly. Solitary wasps incl. potter wasp.

Wassermann, August von (1866-1925), German bacteriologist. Devised complement fixation test (Wassermann test) for syphilis which determines presence of

syphilitic antibodies in patient's blood serum.

Wast Water, lake of Lake Dist., Cumbria, NW England. Deepest in England (79 m/258 ft).

water (H_2O), colourless liquid, compound of hydrogen and oxygen. Poor conductor of heat and electricity; important solvent. Reaches its maximum density at c 4° C.

water beetle, name given to various aquatic beetles, esp. of Dytiscidae family. Back legs bearing bristles function as oars.

water boatman, name given to aquatic insects of 2 families: Notonectidae, greater water boatmen or backswimmers; Corixidae, lesser water boatmen. Latter are herbivorous, swimming with back uppermost. Former is voracious predator. Both are strong fliers.

waterbuck, *Kobus ellipsiprymnus*, large shaggy brown antelope, with lyre-shaped horns on male. Found in swamps of S, W and E Africa.

water buffalo, *Bubalus bubalis*, buffalo with large crescent-shaped horns, found wild in S Asia and Borneo. Often wallows in mud. Domesticated varieties widely distributed in Europe and Asia; used as draught animals, source of milk. Also called Indian buffalo.

watercolour, method of painting with pigment ground up with water-soluble gums, *eg* gum arabic.

watercress, *Nasturtium officinale*, white-flowered European herb of mustard family. Naturalized in North America. Found in or around water; pungent leaves used as garnish and in salads.

waterfall, abrupt descent of stream or river. Caused normally by bed of soft rock in river bed being more easily eroded than adjacent hard rock. Waterfalls impede navigation but provide water power. Examples incl. Angel Falls, Victoria Falls, Niagara Falls.

water flea, any of order Cladocera of small freshwater crustaceans. Swims by jerky movement of 2 forked antennae. Genera incl. *Daphnia* and *Leptodora*.

Waterford, county of Munster prov., S Irish Republic. Area 1839 sq km (710 sq mi); pop. 77,000. Mountain ranges incl. Comeragh, Knockmealdowns. Agric., dairying; fishing. Co. town Waterford, on R. Suir. Pop. 32,000. Exports dairy produce; hist. glass indust. Protestant, RC cathedrals.

water gas, mixture of hydrogen and carbon monoxide, formed by action of steam on white hot coke. Used as industrial fuel.

Watergate affair, in US history, scandals involving President Nixon's admin. arising out of break-in (June, 1972) at Democratic Party hq. in Watergate apartments, Washington, DC. Conviction of burglars (Jan. 1973) was followed by revelations of widespread conspiracy in campaign to re-elect Nixon in 1972 election and massive cover-up of those who had known of the break-in. White House counsel John Dean implicated attorney general MITCHELL, and presidential advisers Bob Haldeman. Nixon's involvement gradually became apparent, esp. after tape-recordings of his conversations were made public by Supreme Court order. Faced with impeachment proceedings,

Nixon resigned (Aug. 1974) and was succeeded by Ford.

water glass, sodium silicate (Na₂SiO₃), usually dissolved in water to form syrupy liquid; used in fireproofing, as preservative for eggs, *etc.*

waterhen, name applied to various birds of rail family, incl. grey moorhen, *Gallinula chloropus*.

water hyacinth, *Eichhornia crassipes*, tropical American aquatic plant. Floating leaf stalks, violet funnel-shaped flowers. Troublesome river weed.

water lily, *see* LOTUS.

Waterloo, village of C Belgium, S of Brussels. After actions at Ligny and Quatre Bras, British (under Wellington) and Prussians (under Blücher) here defeated Napoleon (June, 1815); ended Napoleonic Wars.

watermark, design impressed into paper during mfg., usually by means of a rubber roller. Used in banknotes and stamps to prevent forgery.

watermelon, *Citrullus vulgaris*, annual trailing vine native to tropical Africa. Widely cultivated for large globular or elongated fruits with hard green rind and pink, sweet, watery pulp.

water moccasin or **cottonmouth**, *Agkistrodon piscivorus*, large poisonous pit viper of SE US. Olive-brown in colour; found in swamps or by rivers.

water polo, game played with inflated ball by 2 teams of 7 swimmers. Goals scored by forcing ball into opponents' goal net. Originated in Britain in 1870s. Olympic event since 1900.

water rat, name applied to various rodents that live near water, esp.

European water vole, *Arvicola amphibius* and North American muskrat, *Ondatra zibethica*.

watershed, elevated land separating river systems. Headwaters of adjacent CATCHMENT AREAS flow in opposite directions on either side of watershed. Major examples incl. Rocky Mts., US, and Andes Range, South America. Term used in US to mean drainage basin itself.

water shrew, *Neomys fodiens*, largest European shrew; semi-aquatic, found on river banks. Hind feet and long tail fringed with stiff hairs to aid swimming.

water skiing, sport of gliding over water surface on ski-like boards while being pulled by motor boat. Competitions date from 1930s. World Water Ski Union (founded 1949) organizes world championships.

watersnake, name applied to various aquatic or semi-aquatic snakes, esp. of genus *Natrix*. Species incl. *N. sipedon* of E US, similar in habits to European GRASS SNAKE.

water spider, *Argyoneta aquatica*, European freshwater spider. Constructs underwater bell-shaped silk structure filled with air bubbles brought from surface in its body hairs. Only spider known to live under water.

water table, level below which soil and rock are saturated with ground water. Uneven and variable, may rise in wet weather. Where water table intersects ground surface, a SPRING results.

waterweed, various water plants with inconspicuous flowers, *eg* pondweed. Esp. North American

Anacharis canadensis with white flowers. Commonly used in aquaria.

Watford, mun. bor. of Hertfordshire, S England, on R. Colne. Pop. 78,000. Printing, engineering, brewing industs.

Watling Island, *see* SAN SALVADOR.

Watling Street, Roman road running *c* 160 km (100 mi) from London via St Albans to Wroxeter in Shropshire, England. Used throughout Middle Ages; parts still in good condition.

Watson, J[ohn] B[roadus] (1878-1958), American psychologist. First formulator of BEHAVIOURISM, emphasized study of learning, need for operational definition of concepts. Wrote *Behaviorism* (1925).

Watson-Watt, Sir Robert Alexander (1892-1973), Scottish physicist. Evolved method of radiolocation of aircraft (1935), developed into radar prior to WWII.

Watt, James (1736-1819), Scottish engineer. Manufactured an improved form (patented 1769) of Newcomen's steam engine, developed method of converting reciprocating motion into rotary. Unit of power, watt, named after him.

watt, SI unit of power, equal to 1 joule/sec or power developed in a circuit by current of 1 ampère flowing through potential difference of 1 volt.

Watteau, [Jean] Antoine (1684-1721), French painter of Flemish descent. Noted for fanciful yet poignant pastoral scenes featuring courtiers or depiction of sad figures from French and Italian comedies. Works incl. *Gilles* and *Embarkation for Cythera*.

Watts, George Frederick (1817-1904), English artist. Known for his portraits of contemporary celebrities, eg Gladstone, Tennyson, and large allegorical pictures, eg Hope. His sculpture incl. *Physical Energy*, executed for Cecil Rhodes Memorial, Cape Town.

Watts, Isaac (1674-1748), English hymn writer. Nonconformist clergyman, he wrote such popular hymns as 'O God, our help in ages past' and 'When I survey the wondrous cross'.

Waugh, Evelyn Arthur St John (1903-66), English novelist. Known for comic novels satirizing upper-class English manners, eg *Decline and Fall* (1928), *Brideshead Revisited* (1945), war trilogy *Men at Arms* (1952-61).

wave, in physics, periodic disturbance in a medium or space. May involve actual displacement of medium (mechanical waves) or periodic change in some physical quantity, eg strength of electromagnetic field. Distance between peaks of disturbance is called wavelength and number of crests per second is frequency.

Wavell, Archibald Percival Wavell, 1st Earl (1883-1950), British army officer. Commander-in-chief in Middle East (1939-41), defeated Italians in N Africa. Viceroy of India (1943-7).

wave mechanics, branch of quantum theory which associates mathematical function (wave function) with atomic particles. Manipulation of this function gives probability of finding position, momentum, *etc*, of particle at any time.

wax, substance composed mainly of esters of higher fatty acids with alcohols. Beeswax is secreted by bees for building honeycombs; carnauba wax, obtained from Brazilian wax palm, is used in polishes, lipsticks, *etc*. Paraffin wax is mineral wax obtained from petroleum.

waxwing, songbird of forests of North America and Eurasia, genus *Bombycilla*. Brown silky plumage and scarlet wax-like wing tips. Species incl. common or Bohemian waxwing, *B. garrulus*.

wayfaring tree, see VIBURNUM.

Wayne, John, orig. Marion Michael Morrison, (1907-79), American film actor. One of best known Hollywood stars, esp. for roles in Westerns as tough hero. Appeared in films from 1929, typically in *Stagecoach* (1939), *The Alamo* (1960); later more genial films incl. *True Grit* (1969).

Waziristan, mountainous region of Pakistan bordered on W by Afghanistan. Peopled by Waziri and Mahsud tribesmen, given to feuds and banditry. Centre of resistance to British rule in 19th cent.

weak nuclear interaction, nuclear force responsible for decay of all unstable elementary particles, c 10^{12} times weaker than strong nuclear interaction. Predicted by Pauli to explain beta decay of radioactive nuclei.

Weald, The, region of SE England, between North and South Downs. Grazing; hops, fruit, vegetables. Once forested, provided charcoal for 16th-17th cent. iron indust.

Wear, river of NE England. Flows 105 km (65 mi) through Tyne and Wear into North Sea at Sunderland.

weasel, small carnivorous mammal,

genus *Mustela*, found in temperate and cold regions of N hemisphere. Resembles small stoat, similar habits; feeds on voles, mice. *M. nivalis* is European species; reddish-brown above, white below.

weather, local atmospheric conditions at a given time or over short period. Factors incl. atmospheric pressure, temperature, humidity, cloud cover, rainfall, wind. Forms part of subject matter of meteorology. Weather conditions over many years give CLIMATE.

weathering, process of disintegration of rock on Earth's surface by atmospheric forces. With erosion and transportation, forms one of constituent processes of denudation. Rain, frost and temperature changes all gradually destroy rocks, aiding soil formation.

weaverbird, bird of Ploceidae family, found mainly in Africa. Weaves elaborate hanging nest of sticks, grass, *etc*; large numbers often together in one tree.

weaving, interlacing of yarns to form a fabric, usually done on a loom. Warp yarn runs lengthwise and weft crosswise, being carried across the loom by a shuttle. Basic weaves are plain, twill and satin.

Webb, Matthew (1848-1883), English swimmer. First man to swim the English Channel (1875), covering distance from Dover to Calais in 21 hrs 45 mins. Drowned attempting to swim rapids above Niagara Falls.

Webb, Sidney James, Baron Passfield (1859-1947), English economist. With his wife, **Beatrice Webb**, née Potter (1858-1943), and other Socialists formed early nucleus of Fabian Society (founded 1884), influential in development of British labour movement. Their works incl. *History of Trade Unionism* (1894), *English Local Government* (1906); founded *New Statesman* (1913).

Weber, Carl Maria Friedrich Ernst von (1786-1826), German composer, pianist. Developed romantic German opera. Works incl. *Der Freischütz*, *Euryanthe*, *Oberon*, and piano music.

Weber, Max (1864-1920), German sociologist. Set up non-Marxist framework for empirical analysis of institutional bases in Western capitalist society. Best-known work is *Protestant Ethic and the Spirit of Capitalism* (1920), demonstrating connection between Calvinism and capitalism.

Webern, Anton von (1883-1945), Austrian composer. Pupil of Schoenberg, he developed 12-note music with great intellectual rigour while retaining sensitivity to tone colour and expression. Works, *eg Five Orchestral Pieces*, are usually very short but highly concentrated.

Webster, John (c 1580-c 1638), English dramatist. Known for powerful, typically Jacobean revenge tragedies, *The White Devil* (1612), *The Duchess of Malfi* (c 1613).

Webster, Noah (1758-1843), American scholar, lexicographer. Sought to standardize American spelling and pronunciation; compiled *American Dictionary of the English Language* (1828, frequently revised). Advocated centralized govt. in *Sketches of American Policy* (1785).

Weddell Sea, extension of S Atlantic, bordered by Antarctic

Peninsula and Coats Land. Lies within British Antarctic Territ.

Wedekind, Frank (1864-1918), German dramatist. Forerunner of theatrical expressionism. Wrote plays on sexual themes, *eg Spring's Awakening* (1891), *Pandora's Box* (1903), creating heroine Lulu as archetypical amoral woman.

Wedgwood, Josiah (1730-95), English potter. Developed Staffordshire pottery indust. with new cream-coloured earthenware ('queen's ware'), and black basalt, used for reproduction of ancient Greek vases. Pottery most famous for jasper ware, unglazed porcelain in blue, decorated with white relief.

weevil, small beetle of Curculionidae family, with worldwide distribution. Head prolonged into beak-like snout used to bore into grain, fruit, *etc*. Many species, incl. boll weevil, major cotton pest.

weigela, genus of E Asian deciduous shrubs of honeysuckle family. Clusters of bell-shaped white or pink flowers. *Weigela florida* is widely cultivated species with dark crimson flowers.

weight, in physics, gravitational force of attraction of the Earth or other planet on a given MASS.

weightlessness, in physics, state experienced by body in absence of gravitational force or when falling freely.

Weill, Kurt (1900-50), German composer. Worked with BRECHT on satirical, jazz-influenced operas, *eg The Threepenny Opera* (based on Gay's *Beggar's Opera*). Wrote musicals in US from 1935.

Weimar, town of SW East Germany, on R. Ilm. Pop. 64,000. Textiles, printing. Former cap. of grand duchy of Saxe-Weimar-Eisenach. Cultural centre in 18th, 19th cents. (Bach, Goethe, Liszt, Schiller). Scene of declaration (1919) of Weimar Republic. Badly damaged in WWII.

Weimar Republic, name given to German Republic (1919-33). Created by constitutional assembly at Weimar (1919). Dissolved by Hitler.

Weismann, August (1834-1914), German biologist. Formulated continuity of germ plasm theory to explain heredity and natural selection; proposed that germ plasm is transmitted from generation to generation and controls development of organism.

Weiss, Peter (1916-), German author, film director, painter. Best known as author of plays *Marat/Sade* (1964), *The Investigation* (1965).

Weizmann, Chaim (1874-1952), Jewish statesman, chemist, b. Russia. Active in Zionist causes in Britain, helped secure Balfour Declaration favouring estab. of Jewish homeland in Palestine; 1st president of Israel (1949-52). Discovered method of producing acetone for explosives in WWI.

welding, process of joining metal surfaces together by heating sufficiently for them to melt and fuse together. Required temperature is obtained by oxyacetylene flame or electric arc.

Welensky, Sir Roy (1907-), Rhodesian politician, PM of Federation of Rhodesia and Nyasaland (1956-63).

Welkom, city of NC Orange Free State, South Africa. Pop. 132,000.

Commercial centre in goldmining dist. Founded 1947.

well, hole bored into Earth's crust for purpose of bringing substances, usually water or oil, to surface. Such substances may require pumping, or flow upward by underground pressure as in ARTESIAN WELL.

Welland, canal port of S Ontario, Canada. Pop. 44,000. In fruitgrowing area. Steel, agric. machinery mfg. Welland Ship Canal bypasses Niagara Falls, connecting L. Ontario with L. Erie. Length 44 km (28 mi). Part of St Lawrence Seaway canal system.

Welles, [George] Orson (1915-), American film actor, writer, director, producer. After stage and radio experience (in 1938 panicked US with radio version of *The War of the Worlds*), turned to films. Best known for *Citizen Kane* (1941), *The Third Man* (1949).

Wellesley, Richard Colley Wellesley, Marquess of (1760-1842), British colonial administrator. Assisted by his brother (later WELLINGTON), checked power of native princes, notably Tippoo Sahib, as governor in India (1797-1805). Greatly extended British colonial power in India. Later served as foreign secretary (1810-12).

Wellington, Arthur Wellesley, 1st Duke of (1769-1852), British army officer, statesman; PM (1828-30). Aided his brother Richard Wellesley (1796-1805). Commanded British troops in PENINSULAR WAR (1809-13), eventually driving French from Spain; ultimately defeated Napoleon at Waterloo (1815). Although opposed to Catholic Emancipation,

saw necessity of his Tory govt. legislating to avoid conflict in Ireland; govt. fell after his declaration against parliamentary reform.

Wellington, cap. of New Zealand, at S tip of North Isl., on Cook Str. Pop. 136,000. Admin., commercial centre; port, exports dairy produce, wool, meat. Founded 1840; replaced Auckland as cap. 1865. Has Parliament House, National Museum, Victoria Univ. (1897). Chief city of Wellington region. Area 28,150 sq km (10,870 sq mi); pop. 553,000. Largely mountainous; coastal lowlands in W. Dairying, sheep rearing.

Wells, H[erbert] G[eorge] (1866-1946), English author. Early exponent of SCIENCE FICTION in novels, *eg The Time Machine* (1895), *The War of the Worlds* (1898). Other works incl. fictionalized naturalistic social commentary, *eg Kipps* (1905), *The History of Mr Polly* (1910), discursive *The Outline of History* (1919).

Wells, city of Somerset, SW England. Pop. 7000. Cheese; paper mfg. Has medieval city wall, cathedral (12th cent.). Nearby is Wookey Hole limestone cave.

Welsh, see CELTIC.

Welsh Nationalist Party (Plaid Cymru), political organization dedicated to obtaining Welsh independence by constitutional methods.

Welwyn Garden City, urban dist. of Hertfordshire, SE England. Pop. 40,000. Light industs.; food processing, chemicals. Planned (1920) by Howard, designated new town 1954.

Wembley, part of BRENT, W Greater

London, England. Incl. English national soccer stadium.

Wenceslaus, St (d. 929), duke of Bohemia. Promoted spread of Christianity in Bohemia. Murdered by his brother Boleslav. Remembered as 'Good King Wenceslaus' of the Christmas carol.

Wenceslaus (1361-1419), Holy Roman emperor (1378-1400). Succeeded his father Charles IV as emperor, but was never crowned; later deposed by German nobles, who elected Rupert in his place. Wenceslaus was reconciled when his brother SIGISMUND became king of Germany (1411). King of Bohemia (1378-1419), he supported early reforms of JAN HUS.

Wentworth, William Charles (1793-1872), Australian lawyer, politician. Leader in self-govt. movement which achieved Representative Council (1842). Helped draft constitution, (passed 1855).

Weser, river of N West Germany. Formed by union of Fulda and Werra rivers at Münden, flows c 480 km (300 mi) via Minden, Bremen to North Sea at Bremerhaven. Connected by Mittelland canal to Elbe, Ems, Rhine rivers.

Wesker, Arnold (1932-), English playwright. Known for committedly socialist plays, eg *Chicken Soup with Barley* (1958), *Roots* (1959), *Chips With Everything* (1962).

Wesley, John (1703-91), English evangelical preacher. Anglican churchman, founded METHODISM. Visited American colonies (1735). Began to preach (in open air) salvation through faith in Christ alone. Estab. framework for Methodist societies. Sermons became

standard for Wesleyans. His brother, **Charles Wesley** (1707-88), was preacher and founding Methodist. Opposed any movement to separate from Church of England. Wrote c 6500 hymns, incl. 'Hark! the Herald Angels Sing'.

Wessex, see WILTSHIRE, England.

West, Benjamin (1738-1820), American painter, resident in London after 1763. Historical painter to George III after 1772; a founder member of the Royal Academy, became its president in 1792. In his paintings, eg *The Death of Wolfe*, broke convention by clothing figures in contemporary clothes.

West, Mae (1892-), American stage, film actress, writer. Famous for wit, sexual innuendo, in comedies, eg *She Done Him Wrong* (1933), *I'm No Angel* (1933), and in films with W. C. Fields.

West, Nathanael, pseud. of Nathan Wallenstein Weinstein (1904-40), American novelist. Known for blackly comic indictments of American success myth, eg *Miss Lonelyhearts* (1933), *A Cool Million* (1934), *Day of the Locust* (1939).

West, Rebecca, pseud. of Dame Cicily Isabel Fairfield (1892-), British author, b. Ireland. Works incl. psychological novels, eg *The Return of the Soldier* (1918), *The Birds Fall Down* (1966), travel book on Yugoslavia, *Black Lamb and Grey Falcon* (1942), criticism, biogs.

West Bengal, state of NE India. Area c 88,000 sq km (33,000 sq mi); pop. 44,440,000; cap. Calcutta. Heavy indust. based in Ganges delta; coal, petroleum deposits. Formed at

1947 partition of Bengal between India and Pakistan.

West Bromwich, bor. of West Midlands met. county, C England. Pop. 167,000. In BLACK COUNTRY; coalmining, metal industs.

westerlies, prevailing winds of mid-latitude areas in both hemispheres. Normally blow from SW in N hemisphere, from NW in S hemisphere. Bring continual procession of depressions and anticyclones.

Western Australia, state of W Australia. Area 2,537,900 sq km (979,900 sq mi); pop. 1,027,000; cap. Perth. Kimberley plateau in N, Hamersley Range in NW; vast desert tableland, salt lakes in interior; fertile area in SW; Nullarbor Plain in SE. Agric. incl. beef cattle, sheep, wheat, fruit. Minerals incl. gold, iron ore. Industs., incl. oil refining, iron and steel mfg., centred in Perth and Fremantle. Settled from 1826; became federal state (1901).

Western European Union (WEU), economic, social, cultural and defensive association of Belgium, France, West Germany, Italy, Luxembourg, Netherlands and UK. Estab. 1955 as extension of Brussels Treaty Organization (1948).

Western Isles, isl. authority of W Scotland. Area 2898 sq km (1119 sq mi); pop. 31,000. Created 1975; incl. Outer Hebrides isls., formerly part of Inverness-shire and Ross and Cromarty.

Western Sahara, see SPANISH SAHARA.

Western Samoa, see SAMOA.

West Germany, see GERMANY.

West Glamorgan, see GLAMORGAN, Wales.

West Ham, see NEWHAM, England.

West Indies, archipelago between North and South America, separating Caribbean and Atlantic Ocean. Incl. Hispaniola, Cuba, Jamaica, Puerto Rico (Greater Antilles); Barbados, Leeward and Windward Isls., Trinidad and Tobago (Lesser Antilles); also Bahamas, Virgin Isls. Cuba, Haiti, Dominican Republic are independent. Remainder are dependencies of UK, US, France, Netherlands or members of British Commonwealth. European settlement followed Columbus' visit in 1492.

West Indies, Federation of, short-lived union (1958-62) of British Caribbean territs. incl. Jamaica, Trinidad and Tobago, Barbados, most of Leeward and Windward Isls.

West Irian, see IRIAN JAYA.

Westland, region of W South Isl., New Zealand. Area 15,560 sq km (6010 sq mi); pop. 23,000; main town Greymouth. Narrow coastal plain, rising to Southern Alps in E. Coalmining, timber, fishing industs. Pop. rose rapidly during 1860s gold discoveries.

West Lothian, former county of EC Scotland, now in Lothian region. Formerly called Linlithgowshire. Coal, iron, oil shale deposits; rich agric. Co. town was Linlithgow.

Westmeath, county of Leinster prov., C Irish Republic. Area 1764 sq km (681 sq mi); pop. 54,000; co. town Mullingar. Low-lying, extensive bogland, lakes incl. Lough Ree. Livestock, dairying; fishing (esp. trout).

West Midlands, met. county of C England. Area 899 sq km (347 sq mi); pop. 2,785,000. Created 1974, incl. Birmingham and suburbs, Coventry.

Westminster, City of, bor. of C Greater London, England. Pop. 233,000. Created 1965 from Westminster, Paddington, St Marylebone met. bors. Incl. Piccadilly, Soho, West End, Mayfair, Hyde Park, Trafalgar Sq. Buildings incl. Westminster Abbey, palaces (Buckingham, St James's, Westminster), Parliament, Royal Albert Hall, Covent Garden, National Gallery.

Westminster, Statute of (1931), British parliamentary enactment recognizing independence of dominions of British Commonwealth. Implemented decision of previous Imperial Conferences which had met from 1887.

Westminster Abbey, national shrine and scene of coronation of almost all English monarchs since William I. Norman church consecrated under Edward the Confessor (1065); rebuilding in Gothic style begun in 1245 and finished 1528; additions made in 18th cent. by Wren and Hawksmoor.

Westminster Assembly (1643-9), convocation summoned by Long Parliament to estab. liturgy and govt. of the Church in England. Strongly influenced by Presbyterian members. Issued Westminster Confession of Faith, creed of most Presbyterian churches.

Westmorland, former county of NW England, now part of Cumbria. Co. town was Appleby. Incl. much of Lake Dist.

Weston, Edward (1886-1958), American photographer. Work, combining technical perfection, rich pictorial imagination, documentary realism, incl. *Artichoke Halved* (1930).

Weston-super-Mare, mun. bor. of Avon, SW England. Pop. 51,000. Resort on Bristol Channel.

Westphalia (*Westfalen*), region of W West Germany, now part of North Rhine-Westphalia state. Mainly low-lying, chief rivers Ems, Lippe, Ruhr. Incl. RUHR coalfield and indust. region; main cities Dortmund, Cologne, Düsseldorf, Essen. Duchy created 12th cent.; made kingdom (1807) by Napoleon; prov. of Prussia from 1816. Treaty of Westphalia (1648), agreed at Münster and Osnabrück, ended the Thirty Years War.

Westphalia, Peace of (1648), settlement ending THIRTY YEARS WAR. Power of Habsburgs diminished; Holy Roman Empire dissolved into sovereign states, rulers of which could grant religious toleration to their subjects.

West Point, American military academy, near Newburgh, New York, US.

West Riding, *see* YORKSHIRE, England.

West Sussex, *see* SUSSEX, England.

West Virginia, state of E US. Area 62,629 sq km (24,181 sq mi); pop. 1,744,000; cap. Charlestown. In Allegheny plateau, has 2 panhandles in N and E. Chief rivers Ohio, Potomac. Important mining incl. bituminous coal, natural gas; glass and chemical industs. Chief agric. crops hay, maize, fruit. Region settled in 1730s. Part of Virginia until Civil War. Admitted to Union as 35th state (1863).

West Yorkshire, met. county of NC England. Area 2039 sq km (787 sq mi); pop. 2,080,000; admin. centre

Wakefield. Created 1974, incl. most of former W Riding of Yorkshire.

Wexford, county of Leinster prov., SE Irish Republic. Area 2352 sq km (908 sq mi); pop. 86,000. Mainly low-lying (except Mt. Leinster), fertile; drained by R. Barrow (SW). Cereals, dairying; fishing. Co. town Wexford, on Wexford Harbour. Pop. 12,000. Fishing port; agric. market. Sacked by Cromwell (1649).

Weyden, Roger van der (c 1400-64), Flemish artist. Major Flemish painter of mid-15th cent.; his religious works, combining dramatic power and spirituality, incl. The Deposition. His portraits incl. Charles the Bold.

Weygand, Maxime (1867-1965), French general, b. Belgium. Chief of staff to Foch in WWI. Supreme Allied commander (1940); his out-moded tactics failed to halt German BLITZKRIEG. Served Vichy regime until interned by Germans (1942-5).

Weymouth (and Melcombe Regis), mun. bor. of Dorset, S England. Pop. 42,000. Resort; has ferry service to Channel Isls.

whale, large marine fish-like mammal, order Cetacea. Whales divided into 2 groups: toothed whales (Odontoceti), incl. sperm whales, porpoises, dolphins; whalebone or baleen whales (Mystacoceti), in which teeth are replaced by whalebone plates used to strain plankton from water. Whalebone whales incl. blue whale, largest of mammals, rorqual and right whale.

whale shark, Rhincodon typus, largest living fish, reaching lengths of 15 m/50 ft, found in tropical waters. Harmless to man, feeds on plankton and small fish.

whaling, industry of catching whales for food, oil, etc. Organized first by Dutch at Spitsbergen in 17th cent. Developed on large scale with invention of explosive harpoon (c 1856) and building of factory ships for extraction of oil. Decline in whale pop. through over-hunting has led to international controls.

Wharton, Edith Newbold, née Jones (1862-1937), American novelist. Wrote novels of manners depicting New York society, eg The House of Mirth (1905), The Age of Innocence (1920). Became prominent in American expatriate circles in Paris, depicted in autobiog. A Backward Glance (1934).

wheat, any of genus Triticum of cereal grasses with dense, erect spikes. T. aestivum is widely cultivated in temperate regions. Yields grain which is processed into flour or meal and used chiefly in breadmaking. Comprises c 40% of world's cereal acreage. Leading producers are Canada, US, China and USSR.

wheatear, small migratory thrush-like bird with white rump, genus Oenanthe. Species incl. O. oenanthe of North America, N Europe and Asia.

Wheatley, Dennis Yates (1897-1977), English author. Known for occult thrillers, eg The Devil Rides Out (1935). Other works incl. 'Roger Brook' espionage series.

Wheatstone, Sir Charles (1802-75), English scientist. Pioneer of telegraphy, he invented an electric telegraph (1837), following advice of Henry. Popularized 'Wheatstone bridge', device to measure electrical resistance. Credited with invention of concertina.

wheel, name given to any disc-shaped device used as part of machine or vehicle. When fitted to an axle gives mechanical advantage equal to ratio of wheel radius to axle radius. Earliest vehicular wheel dates from Bronze Age (c 3500 BC).

Wheeler, Sir [Robert Eric] Mortimer (1890-1976), English archaeologist. Made excavations at MAIDEN CASTLE, Caerleon; helped reveal the INDUS VALLEY CIVILIZATION. Did much to popularize archaeology by his television appearances.

whelk, marine gastropod mollusc with spiral shell, esp. of genus *Buccinum*. Species incl. common edible whelk, *B. undatum*.

Whig Party, British political party, predecessor of present Liberal Party. Name, originally denoting rebel Scottish Covenanters, applied to upholders of exclusion of James, Duke of York, from throne (1679). Supported Glorious Revolution (1688), held power (1714-60). Disorganized in early years of George III's reign, revived in opposition to newly-dominant Tory Party under Pitt. In early 19th cent., advocated parliamentary reform, culminating in Reform Bill (1832), after which Whigs became known as Liberals.

Whig party, US political party. Composed of groups originally formed (1824) in opposition to Andrew Jackson, *eg* National Republican party, Anti-Masonic party. Leaders incl. Henry Clay, Daniel Webster. Successful in election of W.H. Harrison as president (1840). Break-up began 1848, despite Zachary Taylor's victory in presidential election.

whippet, breed of slender hound developed in England from greyhound in 18th cent. Once used for hare coursing, now mainly for racing; stands 46-57 cm/18-22 in. at shoulder.

whip-poor-will, *Caprimulgus vociferus,* nocturnal North American bird of nightjar family. Brown plumage mottled with black and cream; name derived from its call.

Whipsnade, village of Bedfordshire, SC England. Zoological park (2 sq km/500 acres) opened 1931.

whirligig beetle, any of Gyrinidae family of blue-black aquatic beetles. Whirls in circles about water surface; has broad hair-fringed swimming legs.

whirlpool, circular, revolving eddy in river, lake or sea. Caused by meeting of opposing tides or currents, wind action, irregular formation of river or sea bed, or waterfalls. Examples incl. Maelstrom off Norway.

whirlwind, rotating column of air with low atmospheric pressure at centre. Produced by atmospheric instability; in arid areas may cause dust or sand storms.

whisky or **whiskey,** spirit distilled from fermented mash of grain, esp barley, rye. Flavour of Scotch whisky derives from quality of water used and curing of malt over peat fires. US and Canadian whiskeys are mostly made with rye; some, *eg* bourbon, are made from corn (maize). Whisky is stored for several years in wooden casks where it acquires characteristic golden brown colour.

whist, card game for 4 players. Of English origin, its popularity derives in part from writings of Hoyle (1742) and Cavendish (1862). Gave rise to bridge in 19th cent.

Whistler, James [Abbott] Mc-Neill (1834-1903), American artist, resident in France, England. Influenced by Velazquez and Japanese prints, he was a master of tone and colour, and superb etcher. Works incl. series of *Nocturnes* and *The White Girl*. Fought famous lawsuit against Ruskin following Ruskin's criticism of *The Falling Rocket*.

Whitby, urban dist. of North Yorkshire, N England, at mouth of R. Esk. Pop. 13,000. Resort, fishing port, boatbuilding; jet ornaments mfg. Abbey founded 656. Home of Capt. Cook, his ships built here. Synod of Whitby (664) estab. Roman rather than Celtic forms for English church.

White, Gilbert (1720-93), English clergyman, naturalist. Author of classic *Natural History and Antiquities of Selborne* (1789), based on record of observations.

White, Patrick Victor Martindale (1912-), Australian novelist, b. London. Known for symbolic, poetic novels incl. *The Tree of Man* (1955), *Voss* (1957), *Riders in the Chariot* (1961), *The Solid Mandala* (1966). Nobel Prize for Literature (1973).

White, T[erence] H[anbury] (1906-64), English author, b. India. Known for erudite, idiosyncratic treatment of Arthurian legend in tetralogy *The Once and Future King* (1938-58); basis of musical and film *Camelot*.

whitebait, young of several European herrings, esp. common herring, *Clupea harengus*, and sprat. In US incl. young silverside. Esteemed as food.

white blood cell, *see* BLOOD.

white collar, grouping of workers engaged in non-manual labour. American in origin, term derives from white shirts typically worn by clerical, professional, and managerial employees. Meaning developed esp. by C. Wright Mills in *White Collar* (1951).

white dwarf, small, extremely dense star of low luminosity, typically with mass of Sun but radius no larger than Earth's. Represents stage of star's evolution as its store of hydrogen is used up.

Whitefield, George (1714-70), English evangelist. Joined WESLEY's group. Preached in America contributing to revivalist 'Great Awakening'. Opposed Wesley's view on predestination, estab. (c 1741) independent Calvinistic Methodists.

whitefish, fish of salmon family, esp. genus *Coregonus*, found mainly in lakes and rivers of N Europe and North America. Silvery, with small jaws, minute teeth.

whitefly, any of Aleyrodidae family of minute insects. Wings and body coated with white powdery wax. Many species, incl. cabbage whitefly, *Aleyrodes proletella*, are crop pests.

Whitehead, Alfred North (1861-1947), English philosopher, mathematician. Collaborated with Russell on *Principia Mathematica* (1910-13). Formulated an idealist 'philosophy of organism' holding that universal concepts give a useful interpretation

.of experience. Regarded God as sum of potential and actual events.

Whitehorse, cap. of Yukon territ., Canada; on Lewes (Upper Yukon) R. Pop. 11,000. Copper mining region; hunting centre. Cap. from 1952.

White Horse, Vale of the, valley of R. Ock, Berkshire, SC England. Named after White Horse (114 m/374 ft long) cut into chalk hillside of Berkshire Downs to S. In tradition, commemorates Alfred's victory over Danes (871).

White House, official residence of the President of the US, in Washington, DC. White-painted building, designed by James Hoban (1792); first occupied 1800. Rebuilt after being burnt by British (1814).

White Nile, see NILE.

White Russia, see BYELORUSSIAN SOVIET SOCIALIST REPUBLIC.

White Russians, name given to anti-Communist groups who opposed Bolsheviks in Russian civil war (1918-20). Supported by Allied intervention.

White Sea, inlet of Barents Sea, between Kola and Kanin penins., N European USSR. Connected to Baltic by canal. Chief port Archangel.

white-tailed deer, *Odocoileus virginianus,* common American deer whose tail is white underneath. In summer, has red coat with white spots.

whitethroat, Old World warbler with white throat, genus *Sylvia.* Species incl. lesser whitethroat, *S. curruca.*

whiting, *Merlangus merlangus,* common European marine food fish of cod family. Found in inshore waters, esp. of North Sea. Name also applied to Australian fish of genus *Sillago.*

Whitlam, [Edward] Gough (1916-), Australian statesman, PM (1972-5). Headed 1st Labor govt. in more than 20 years, improving Australia's relations with Communist countries of Far East, until economic crisis led to opposition's refusal to cooperate in Senate. Dismissed by governor-general, Sir John Kerr, who appointed Malcolm Fraser as PM.

Whitman, Walt[er] (1819-92), American poet. Best known for stylistically unconventional collection, *Leaves of Grass* (1855), celebrating fertility, sensuality, comradeship. Other works incl. collection, *Drum Taps* (1865), elegy for Lincoln, 'When Lilacs Last in the Dooryard Bloom'd' (1867), prose collection, *Specimen Days* and *Collect* (1882).

Whitney, Eli (1765-1825), American manufacturer. Invented cotton gin, facilitating separation of fibre and seed. Produced 1st muskets with standard interchangeable parts.

Whitney, Mount, mountain of E California, US; in Sequoia National Park in Sierra Nevada. Second highest peak in US (4418 m/14,494 ft).

Whitsunday, see PENTECOST.

Whittier, John Greenleaf (1807-92), American poet. Wrote anti-slavery poems in *Voices of Freedom* (1846). Other works incl. Civil War verse, *eg* classic 'Barbara Frietchie', 'Yankee pastoral' New England nature poetry, *eg* Snow-Bound (1866).

Whittington, Richard (d. 1423), English merchant, 3 times mayor of

London. Made large fortune as a mercer, which he left to charities at his death. Subject of story of Dick Whittington and his cat.

Whittle, Sir Frank (1907-), English aeronautic engineer. Patented (1930) designs for turbo-jet engine, forerunner of modern jet aircraft engine.

WHO, see WORLD HEALTH ORGANIZATION.

whooping cough or **pertussis,** infectious disease, usually of children, caused by bacillus *Haemophilus pertussis*. Characterized by repeated coughing ending in forced intake of air or whoop.

whortleberry, see BILBERRY.

Whymper, Edward (1840-1911), English mountaineer. First man to climb the Matterhorn (1865), succeeding at his 7th attempt; during descent, 4 of his party fell to their deaths.

Wichita, city of S Kansas, US; at jct. of Arkansas and Little Arkansas rivers. Pop. 277,000; state's largest city. Railway jct., commercial, indust. centre in wheat growing, oil producing region. Livestock, grain trade; aircraft, chemical mfg.

Wick, port of Highland region, E Scotland. Pop. 8000. Whisky distilling, glass mfg. Former co. town of Caithness.

Wicklow, county of Leinster prov., E Irish Republic. Area 2025 sq km (782 sq mi); pop. 66,000. Scenic Wicklow Mts. (Lugnaquillia 926 m/3039 ft), Glendalough. Cattle rearing; h.e.p. on Liffey. Co. town Wicklow, pop. 3000. Port; ruined castle (12th cent.), priory (13th cent.).

widgeon, see WIGEON.

Wieland, Christoph Martin (1733-1813), German poet, novelist. Wrote satirical novels, *eg The Abderites, a Very Probable Story* (1774). Poetic works incl. epic, *Oberon* (1780), basis of Weber's opera.

Wien, see VIENNA, Austria.

Wiener, Norbert (1894-1964), American mathematician. Contributed to probability theory, Fourier transforms, quantum theory, *etc.* Founded science of cybernetics; contributed to development of electronic computers. Wrote *Cybernetics* (1948).

Wiesbaden, city of W West Germany, at foot of Taunus Hills, cap. of Hesse. Pop. 252,000. Wine trade, chemicals, film studios. Spa resort from Roman times. Cap. of duchy of Nassau 1815-66; seat of Allied Rhineland Commission 1918-29.

Wigan, bor. of Greater Manchester met. county, NW England. Pop. 81,000. Food processing, engineering indust.

wigeon or **widgeon,** migratory duck, genus *Anas.* Male of Eurasian wigeon, *A. penelope,* has chestnut head, grey body, pinkish breast.

Wight, Isle of, isl. county of S England. Area 381 sq km (147 sq mi); pop. 109,000; co. town Newport. Separated from mainland by SOLENT. Chalk hills run E-W, end in Needles. Resorts; yachting.

Wigtownshire, former county of SW Scotland, now in Dumfries and Galloway region. Indented coast; incl. Rhinns of Galloway penin. in W. Rich agric., dairy farming, livestock. Co. town was Wigtown, former royal burgh on Wigtown Bay. Pop. 1000.

wigwam, Algonquian name loosely applied to dwellings of E North American Indians. Originally referred to dome-shaped huts made of skins or matting stretched over poles. Now confused with portable, conical tepee of Plains Indians.

Wilberforce, William (1759-1833), British reform politician. Campaigned for abolition of slavery. Sponsored passage (1807) of bill abolishing slave trade. Died month before slavery was abolished throughout British Empire. His son, **Samuel Wilberforce** (1805-73), was a churchman; bishop of Winchester (1869-73). Defended Anglican orthodoxy against Tractarians; known for opposition to Darwinism.

Wilbur, Richard (1921-), American poet, critic. Works, *eg The Beautiful Changes* (1947), *Walking to Sleep* (1969), reflect formal aestheticism, polished manner of academic poet.

wild boar, see BOAR.

wild carrot, *Daucus carota*, common biennial weed. *See* CARROT.

wild cat, *Felis sylvestris*, resembles domestic tabby cat, but larger. Exclusively forest-dwelling and nocturnal, found in N, E Europe, Scottish Highlands, Corsica, parts of France. Untameable.

wildcat, see BOBCAT.

Wilde, Oscar [Fingal O'Flahertie Wills] (1854-1900), British author, b. Dublin. Noted decadent wit, aesthete. Works incl. novels, *eg The Picture of Dorian Grey* (1891), satirical social comedies, *eg Lady Windermere's Fan* (1892), *The Importance of Being Earnest* (1895).

Accused of homosexual practices, imprisoned (1895-7). Wrote most famous poem, *The Ballad of Reading Gaol* (1898), in exile.

wildebeest, see GNU.

Wilder, Samuel ('Billy') (1905-), Austrian film writer-director, in US from 1934. Known for comedies, suspense dramas, incl. *Double Indemnity* (1944), *The Lost Weekend* (1945), *Some Like It Hot* (1959).

Wilder, Thornton Niven (1897-1975), American author. Known for undidactic philosophical novels, *eg The Bridge of San Luis Rey* (1927), plays, *eg Our Town* (1938), *The Skin of Our Teeth* (1942).

Wilhelmina (1880-1962), queen of Netherlands (1890-1948). Lived in England during WWII. Abdicated in favour of daughter Juliana.

Wilhelmshaven, city of NW West Germany, on Jade Bay. Pop. 103,000. Port; oil refining, chemical mfg. Chief German North Sea naval base from opening of harbour (1869). Heavily bombed in WWII; dismantled by Allies, rebuilt.

Wilkes, John (1727-97), English politician. Founded periodical *North Briton*; attacked George III's speech from throne, for which he was briefly imprisoned (1763). Expelled from Parliament on seditious libel charge (1764), fled to France. Re-elected (1768), frequently prevented from taking seat in Commons through royal pressure; gained great popular support. Admitted to Commons (1774), championed parliamentary reform, American colonial cause.

will, in law, legal statement of person's wishes concerning disposal of property after death; document containing this. In UK, US, must be witnessed, testator (person making will) must be of sound mind and not under undue influence of another. Testator usually appoints executor to administer will. In US, wills must be submitted to probate, *ie* to legal validation.

will, in philosophy, inner force motivating a person's conscious actions. Existence denied by some philosophers (eg in DETERMINISM), defined by others (eg Plato, Descartes, Kant) on intuitive grounds as motive force of personality, yet others (eg Leibnitz, Hume) have seen it as the resultant of conflicting elements.

Willemstad, cap. of Netherlands Antilles, on Curaçao Isl. Pop. 44,000. Shipping and tourist centre. Refining of Venezuelan oil.

William I (1797-1888), 1st emperor of Germany (1871-88), king of Prussia (1861-88). Dominated by chancellor BISMARCK, whose policies led to creation of German Empire.

William II (1859-1941), emperor of Germany (1888-1918). Dismissed Bismarck (1890), thereafter pursuing aggressive colonial and military policy. Antagonized Britain by supporting Boers, promoting German naval expansion. Influence declined after outbreak of WWI; fled to Holland day before armistice, abdicated.

William [I] the Conqueror (c 1027-87), king of England (1066-87). Succeeded to duchy of Normandy (1035). Prob. promised succession to English throne by Edward the Confessor; forced HAROLD to swear support for his claim. Pursued claim by invading England and defeating

Harold at Hastings (1066). Consolidated Norman power by building castles, granting land to his followers, introducing foreign clergy; introduced hierarchical FEUDAL SYSTEM. Commissioned survey of England in *Domesday Book*.

William [II] Rufus (c 1058-1100), king of England (1087-1100), b. Normandy. Involved in disputes with brother Robert Curthose over rule of Normandy. His extravagant and covetous rule was unpopular. Found slain by arrow in New Forest.

William III (1650-1702), king of England, Scotland and Ireland (1689-1702), prince of Orange. Became stadholder of Holland (1672), successfully defended country against France. Married (1677) Mary, daughter of duke of York (later JAMES II). Invited to become king of England by opponents of James; proclaimed joint sovereign with Mary after James was deemed to have abdicated (*see* GLORIOUS REVOLUTION). Defeated Catholic force under James at Battle of Boyne (1690).

William IV (1765-1837), king of Great Britain and Ireland (1830-7). Third son of George III; succeeded his brother, George IV. Agreed to create enough peers to assure passage of Reform Bill of 1832.

William I (1772-1843), 1st king of Netherlands (1815-40). Created king after Napoleonic Wars; ceded German possessions to Prussia. Anti-Catholic policies precipitated revolt leading to Belgian independence (1831). Abdicated in favour of his son William II.

William of Malmesbury (d. c 1143), English historian. Author of

Gesta regum Anglorum (c 1125) and *Historia novella*, latter of which describes contemporary events after 1126.

William of Occam or **Ockham** (c 1285-1349), English Franciscan philosopher. Major nominalist (*see* NOMINALISM). Held that thought is not a measurement of reality. Demarcated philosophy and theology. Summoned to answer charges of heresy by Pope John XXII.

William of Tyre (c 1130-c 1185), historian and churchman, b. Palestine. Chancellor of Latin Kingdom of Jerusalem (1174-83) and archbishop of Tyre (1175). Wrote important account of Crusades from 1095 to 1184.

William of Wykeham (1324-1404), English churchman. Bishop of Winchester (1366-1404), he was twice lord chancellor (1367-71, 1389-91). Founded New College, Oxford (1379), and Winchester College school (1378).

Williams, Tennessee, pseud. of Thomas Lanier Williams (c 1914-), American dramatist. Plays frequently centre on insecure, neurotic woman, sustained by illusion, confronted with reality of male violence, *eg The Glass Menagerie* (1945), *A Streetcar Named Desire* (1947), *Cat on a Hot Tin Roof* (1955), *Night of the Iguana* (1961). Also wrote novels, poetry.

Williams, William Carlos (1883-1963), American poet, novelist. Known for poetry which extracts detail from everyday objects, speech patterns, *eg Spring and All* (1923), *Collected Later Poems* (1950). Novels incl. *White Mule* (1937) and sequels.

Williamsburg, town of SE Virginia, US. Pop. 9000. Settled 1632, hist. cap. of Virginia (1699-1779). Yorktown campaign fought nearby ending American Revolution (1781). Has many hist. colonial buildings esp. Colonial Palace, Capitol; restoration began 1927.

William the Lion (1143-1214), king of Scotland (1165-1214). After capture at Alnwick (1174), forced to pay homage to Henry II of England by terms of Treaty of Falaise. Treaty was rescinded (1189) by Richard I in exchange for money.

William the Silent, Prince of Orange (1533-84), Dutch statesman. Appointed stadholder of Holland, Zeeland and Utrecht by Philip II of Spain (1559). Opposed Spanish tyranny and religious intolerance in Netherlands. Led armies in struggle for Dutch independence from Spain (1568-76). Became stadholder of 7 N provs. (1579), which declared their independence from Spain (1581). Assassinated by Catholic fanatic.

will-o'-the-wisp or **jack-o'-lantern,** pale, flickering light seen over marshland at night. Prob. caused by spontaneous combustion of methane.

willow or **osier,** any of genus *Salix* of trees and shrubs in N temperate and subarctic regions. Narrow leaves, male and female catkins borne on separate plants. Tough, pliable twigs used in basketwork, *etc.* Common species incl. *S. viminalis* of Europe. Cricket bats made from white willow, *S. alba*.

willowherb, any of genus *Epilobium* of plants, esp. *E. angustifolium* or fireweed, a North American shrub with narrow leaves, reddish-purple flowers. Grows in fireswept areas.

willow pattern, design in blue and white, incorporating bridge, pagoda, willow trees and figures, used to decorate chinaware. Developed after 1780 in Staffordshire, England; design is attributed to Thomas Minton.

Wilson, Angus Frank Johnstone (1913-), English novelist, critic, b. Scotland. Satirical works incl. *Such Darling Dodos* (1950), *Hemlock and After* (1952), *Anglo-Saxon Attitudes* (1956), *No Laughing Matter* (1967).

Wilson, Charles Thomson Rees (1869-1959), Scottish physicist. Developed CLOUD CHAMBER to study ionized subatomic particles by making their paths visible (1911). Awarded Nobel Prize for Physics (1927).

Wilson, Edmund (1895-1972), American author, critic. Known for erudite cultural study, *To the Finland Station* (1940), classic work on symbolism, *Axel's Castle* (1931).

Wilson, Sir [James] Harold (1916-), British statesman, PM (1964-70, 1974-6). Elected Labour Party leader (1963), succeeding Gaitskell. First term highlighted by Rhodesia's UDI (1965); both admins. dominated by serious inflation, civil strife in Northern Ireland. Resigned from office.

Wilson, Henry Maitland Wilson, 1st Baron (1881-1964), British field marshal. In WWII commander-in-chief in Middle East (1943-4); supreme Allied commander in Mediterranean (1944-5). Head of British joint staff mission in Washington (1945-7).

Wilson, [Thomas] Woodrow (1856-1924), American statesman, president (1913-21). Governor of New Jersey (1911-13), successful Democratic presidential candidate (1912). Kept US out of WWI until 1917, then entered to make 'world safe for democracy'. Negotiated armistice of 1918 on basis of his 'Fourteen Points' previously enunciated in Jan. 1918; secured League of Nations covenant at TREATY OF VERSAILLES (1919). Awarded Nobel Peace Prize (1919).

Wiltshire, county of S England. Area 3481 sq km (1344 sq mi); pop. 501,000; co. town Salisbury. Chalk uplands incl. Marlborough Downs (N), Salisbury Plain (S). Fertile vales. Wheat, sheep; military training grounds. Prehist. remains incl. Stonehenge, Avebury. Centre of Saxon kingdom of Wessex.

Wimbledon, see MERTON, England.

Winchester, city and co. town of Hampshire, S England, on R. Itchen. Pop. 31,000. Roman *Venta Belgarum;* Saxon cap. of Wessex. Has cathedral (11th cent.), Norman castle. Famous English public school (1382).

wind, natural current of air parallel to Earth's surface. Caused by differences in air pressure within atmosphere; air flows from. high pressure to low pressure areas. Many sectors of globe have almost continuous prevailing winds, *eg* mid-latitude westerlies, tropical trade winds. Localized winds incl. MISTRAL, SIROCCO. Wind velocity measured by anemometer, classed on BEAUFORT SCALE.

Windermere, Lake, largest lake of England, in Lake Dist., Cumbria.

Length 17 km (10.5 mi). Tourism, steamer service in summer. Resort of Windermere (pop. 7000) on E bank.

windflower, common name for wild varieties of ANEMONE.

Windhoek, cap. of South West Africa. Pop. 61,000. Admin. centre, railways to Walvis Bay and South Africa; trade in skins, minerals. Formerly called Windhuk as cap. of German colony.

wind instruments, name given to woodwind and brass families of instruments. Sound is produced when player sets column of air vibrating inside the instruments. Woodwind instruments incl. clarinet, saxophone, oboe, bassoon, flute. Brass instruments incl. horn, trumpet, trombone, bugle, tuba.

windmill, apparatus which harnesses wind power for pumping water, grinding corn, generating electricity, *etc.* Usually consists of tower with revolving arms at top bearing sails to catch wind. Introduced to Europe prob. during 12th cent, widely used esp. in Holland.

Windsor, House of, name of royal family of Great Britain. Adopted by George V (1917) in place of House of Saxe-Coburg-Gotha. Subsequent monarchs Edward VIII, George VI, Elizabeth II.

Windsor, Wallis Warfield, Duchess of (1896-), American-born wife of Edward, duke of Windsor. Married Edward Simpson (1927), from whom she obtained a divorce (Oct. 1936). Her association with EDWARD VIII led him to abdicate British throne; married him (June, 1937).

Windsor, indust. city of SW Ontario, Canada; on Detroit R. Pop. 203,000. Linked with Detroit (US) by road and rail tunnels. Major auto indust.; salt and chemicals mfg. Settled by French (1749).

Windsor, New, mun. bor. of Berkshire, S England, on R. Thames. Pop. 30,000. ˙ Castle estab. by William I, still royal residence; St George's Chapel, parks. Town hall designed by Wren.

Windward Islands, archipelago of SE West Indies, in S Lesser Antilles. Extends S from Leeward Isls. Incl. Dominica, St Lucia, St Vincent, Grenada; Martinique (French possession). Of volcanic origin; equable tropical climate. French, British contested ownership, resolved 1815.

wine, alcoholic beverage made from fermented grape juice. Fortified wine, *eg* sherry, port, has brandy added to it; sparkling wine, *eg* champagne, is made by inducing secondary process of fermentation in bottle. Dry wine is obtained by allowing all grape sugar to be converted to alcohol, sweet wine by arresting process of fermentation. In red wines, entire grape is used; in white, only juice is used. Leading and best-known wine producers are France, Italy, Germany.

Wingate, Orde Charles (1903-44), British army officer. In WWII, defeated Italians in Ethiopia (1941). Organized Chindits for guerrilla operations against Japanese in Burma (1942-3). Killed in air accident.

winkle, marine snail of genus *Littorina*, found on rocky shores. Destroys oysters by drilling shell and rasping away the flesh. Species incl. common edible winkle, *L. littorea.* Also called periwinkle.

Winnipeg, cap. of Manitoba, Canada; at confluence of Red, Assiniboine rivers. Pop. 246,000. Railway jct., commercial centre. Chief wheat market of Prairie provs. Meat packing, flour milling, agric. machinery mfg. Settled as Fort Rouge; renamed (1873). Seat of Manitoba Univ. (1877).

Winnipeg, Lake, SC Manitoba, Canada. Area 24,514 sq km (9465 sq mi). Receives Red, Winnipeg, Saskatchewan rivers. Drained by Nelson R. to Hudson Bay. In lumbering, fishing, tourist region.

Winters, Yvor (1900-68), American poet, critic. Poetry deals with Western landscape, history, and experience as scholar, teacher. Influential criticism incl. *In Defense of Reason* (1947), attacking romanticism, modernism, *The Function of Criticism* (1957).

Winterthur, town of NE Switzerland. Pop. 93,000. Indust. centre, textiles; railway jct., locomotive mfg.

Winthrop, John (1588-1649), English colonist. Governed Massachusetts Bay Colony, helping to estab. theocratic structure. Banished Anne Hutchinson on charge of heresy.

Wirral Peninsula, area of Merseyside met. county, NW England, between Dee and Mersey estuaries. Birkenhead, Wallasey in NE. Former royal forest.

Wisconsin, state of NC US. Area 145,439 sq km (56,154 sq mi); pop. 4,418,000; cap. Madison; largest city Milwaukee. Bordered by L. Superior in N, L. Michigan in E, Mississippi R. in W. Mainly low-lying. Leading dairy producer, also grains; iron ore mining; industs. incl. meat packing, brewing. Explored in 17th cent. by French; ceded to British 1763. Part of US from 1787. Admitted to Union as 30th state (1830).

wisent, *Bison bonasus,* European bison, almost extinct in wild. Smaller head and less shaggy body than American bison.

Wishart, George (*c* 1513-46), Scottish religious reformer. Achieved conversion of John Knox to Protestantism. Burned for heresy at St Andrews.

wisteria, genus of climbing shrubs of Leguminosae family. Native to E US and E Asia. Showy clusters of white, blue, pink or voilet drooping flowers.

witan, see WITENAGEMOT.

witchcraft, the working of magic. Common to most cultures. In Europe, may be survival of Palaeolithic fertility cults. Features incl: holding of 'Sabbaths' 4 times a year; district groupings into 'covens' of 13; use of spells, charms; supposed transformation into animals, ability to fly, worship of devil. Condemned as heresy (14th cent.) by Christian church; subject of widespread persecution 15th-17th cent. In US, most noted persecution occurred (1692) at Salem.

witch hazel, any of genus *Hamamelis* of small trees and shrubs. Native to North America and Asia. *H. virginiana* of N North America has yellow flowers. Medicinal lotion is derived from bark.

witenagemot or witan, aristocratic assembly of nobles and high churchmen in Anglo-Saxon England. Appointed by king to advise him on questions of law, tax, foreign policy.

Witt, Jan de (1625-72), Dutch statesman. Leader of Republican party and virtual ruler of Holland, he obtained successful conclusion to war with England (1667). Resigned after William of Orange had gained popular support. Killed by mob.

Wittenberg, town of C East Germany, on R. Elbe. Pop. 47,000. Machinery, soap mfg. Here Luther nailed (1517) his 95 Theses to Schlosskirche (which contains his tomb). First Lutheran bible (1534) printed here. Univ. (1502) incorporated into Halle univ. 1817.

Wittgenstein, Ludwig Josef Johann (1889-1951), Austrian philosopher. Worked mainly in England. *Tractatus Logico-Philosophicus* (1919) helped develop LOGICAL POSITIVISM. Later work, in *Philosophical Investigations* (pub. 1953), on the false problems created by the ambiguity of language.

Witwatersrand or The Rand, area of S Transvaal, South Africa, centred on gold-bearing ridge (alt. *c* 1830 m/6000 ft). Gold discovered 1886; now produces 33% world's output. Also coal, manganese deposits. Main cities Johannesburg, Germiston, Benoni.

woad, any of genus *Isatis* of plants of mustard family, esp. *I. tinctoria* with yellow flowers. Leaves yield blue dye used by ancient Britons as body paint; widely used to dye clothes until advent of aniline dyes.

Wodehouse, (Sir) P[elham] G[renville] (1881-1975), English novelist. Known for novels, short stories caricaturing English upperclass world of 1920s in stylized

slang. Created characters Bertie Wooster, his man Jeeves. Settled in US *c* 1920.

Woden, Germanic name for ODIN.

Wöhler, Friedrich (1800-82), German pioneer of organic chemistry. His synthesis of urea (1828) helped refute doctrine of 'vital force' necessary for manufacture of organic compounds. Devised methods of isolating metallic aluminium.

Wolf, Hugo (1860-1903), Austrian composer. Wrote numerous romantic *lieder*, incl. settings of poems by Goethe, *Spanish Songbook* and *Italian Songbook*. Also wrote *Italian Serenade* for string quartet, later orchestrated.

wolf, carnivorous, intelligent, doglike mammal, genus *Canis*, found in remote areas of N hemisphere. Hunts in packs; can attack more powerful animals. North American timber or grey wolf considered subspecies of European *Canis lupus*.

Wolfe, James (1727-59), British army officer. Given command of expedition to take Québec (1759). Victory over French under Montcalm on Plains of Abraham secured Canada for Britain. Fatally wounded.

Wolfe, Thomas Clayton (1900-38), American novelist. Known for vast, intensely realistic, autobiog. cycle, incl. *Look Homeward, Angel* (1929), *Of Time and the River* (1935).

wolfhound, large dog originally used for hunting wolves. Breeds incl. Irish wolfhound and borzoi.

wolfram, *see* TUNGSTEN.

Wolfram von Eschenbach (*fl* early 13th cent.), German poet. Known for Holy Grail epic *Parzival* (basis of Wagner's *Parsifal*), also wrote epics *Titurel, Willehalm,* lyrics. One of greatest of the MINNESINGER.

Wollongong, city of SE New South Wales, Australia, on Tasman Sea. Pop. 250,000. Originally dairying, cedar exporting centre; now major coalmining, iron and steel industs. Coal exported via suburb of Port Kembla.

Wollstonecraft, Mary (1759-97), English miscellaneous writer. Member of group of Radicals which incl. GODWIN, by whom she had daughter who became SHELLEY's second wife. Best-known work, *Vindication of the Rights of Women* (1792).

Wolseley, Garnet Joseph Wolseley, 1st Viscount (1833-1913), British general. Commanded expedition against Red River rebellion in Canada (1870). Known for attempt to relieve Gordon at Khartoum (1884-5). Commander-in-chief of army (1895-1901).

Wolsey, Thomas (c 1473-1530), English churchman, statesman. Created (1515) cardinal and lord chancellor by Henry VIII. Had charge of English foreign and domestic policy; attempted to mediate for peace in Europe. Achieved great personal wealth; founded Cardinal College, Oxford (Christchurch) and had Hampton Court built. Failure to arrange Henry's divorce from Catherine of Aragon led to his dismissal and arrest (1530).

Wolverhampton, bor. of West Midlands met. county, WC England. Pop. 269,000. In BLACK COUNTRY; metal working incl. cars, bicycles, locks; rayon, chemicals. Hist. wool trade, until 16th cent.

wolverine or **glutton,** *Gulo gulo,* carnivorous bear-like mammal,

largest of weasel family, found in Arctic and subarctic regions of Europe, Asia, North America. Short-legged, with bushy tail and shaggy coat; voracious predator, it will attack most animals.

womb, see UTERUS.

wombat, burrowing nocturnal Australian marsupial, esp. of genus *Vombatus*. Rodent-like, with stocky body and continuously growing incisors; herbivorous. Species incl. common wombat, *V. hirsutus*. All species becoming rarer.

women's rights, see CIVIL RIGHTS.

women's services, auxiliary corps of navy, army and air force employing women to release manpower for fighting. In UK and US, women first served in large numbers in WWII, eg Women's Royal Naval Service (UK, 1939), Women's Auxiliary Air Force (UK, 1939), Women's Army Corps (US, 1942). Nursing services, incl. Women's Voluntary Services (UK, 1938), also performed important duties.

women's suffrage, right of women to vote. First proposed by Mary Wollstonecraft in *A Vindication of the Rights of Women* (1792). First women's suffrage committee formed (1865) in Manchester. Local committees united (1897) in National Union of Women's Suffrage Societies. More militant Women's Social and Political Union formed (1903), led by Emmeline Pankhurst and daughters. Used arson, bombing; many arrested, went on hunger strike when imprisoned. Achieved right to vote for married women over 30 (1918); extended to cover all women over 21 (1928). In US, women's participation in Anti-Slavery movement led to women's rights demand; advocates incl. Elizabeth Stanton, Lucretia Mott, Susan B. Anthony. National Woman Suffrage Association formed (1869) to agitate for constitutional amendment. Acquired (1918) equal suffrage in 15 states. WWI accelerated progress, leading to 19th Amendment (1920) making denial of women's right to vote unconstitutional.

Wood, Mrs Henry, née Ellen Price (1814-87), English novelist. Wrote many popular novels of middle-class life. Now known for bestseller *East Lynne* (1861), basis of several melodramas.

Wood, Sir Henry Joseph (1869-1944), English conductor. Began Promenade Concerts in London (1895) and conducted them until his death. Helped introduce many new works to British audiences.

Wood, John (1704-54), English architect, town planner. Influenced by Palladian theories; known as 'Wood of Bath' for work, *eg* the Circus, in planning that city.

wood, hard, fibrous substance which makes up greater part of stems and branches of trees and shrubs beneath the bark. Composed of XYLEM and PHLOEM intersected by transverse vascular rays.

woodbine, name for HONEYSUCKLE and VIRGINIA CREEPER.

woodchuck or **ground hog,** *Marmota monax,* burrowing North American marmot with coarse redbrown hair. Frequents woodland and farms; hibernates underground in winter.

woodcock, woodland game bird, chestnut or brown in colour, genus *Scolopax.* Feeds largely on insect larvae. Species incl. Eurasian woodcock, *S. rusticola,* and American woodcock, *S. minor.*

woodcut and **wood engraving,** terms applied to prints made from wood blocks cut by hand. Earliest dated woodcut is Chinese *Diamond Sutra* of AD 868. Woodcuts appeared in Europe in early 15th cent.; great practitioners of art incl. Dürer and Holbein.

woodlouse, small terrestrial crustacean of suborder Oniscoidea. Flattened elliptical body with 7 pairs of legs; dull brown or grey in colour. Lives in damp places, *eg* under stones. Also called sowbug or slater.

wood mouse, see MOUSE.

woodpecker, widely distributed tree-climbing bird of Picidae family. Wedge-shaped bill used to bore holes, long tongue for catching insects; stiff tail aids climbing. Species incl. European green woodpecker, *Picus viridis,* and American red-headed woodpecker, *Melanerpes erythrocephalus.*

wood pigeon, see PIGEON.

Woods, Lake of the, on Manitoba-Ontario border with Minnesota, C Canada-US. Area 3846 sq km (1485 sq mi). In forested region. Popular tourist area.

wood sorrel, see OXALIS.

Woodville, Elizabeth (c 1437-92), English queen, consort of Edward IV. After her secret marriage to Edward, Woodville family grew powerful at court to detriment of WARWICK. Her sons Edward and Richard were seized by Gloucester (RICHARD III) on her husband's death and declared illegitimate. Daughter married Henry VII.

woodwind, group of musical instruments in which a sound is obtained by blowing through a mouthpiece, and pitch varied by closing keys or holes with fingers.

woodworm, larva of beetles of Anobiidae family. Beetle lays eggs in cracks in wood and larvae burrow into wood; adults emerge leaving holes. Most common is furniture beetle, *Anobium punctatum*. Preservatives have been developed to combat woodworm.

wool, curly fibrous hair of sheep and other animals, eg goat, llama and alpaca. Absorbent, strong, warm, crease resistant and able to hold dye; spun into yarn and used extensively in mfg. of clothing. Major wool producers are Australia, USSR, New Zealand and Argentina.

Woolf, Leonard (1880-1969), English writer, publisher. Early works were stories about Ceylon eg *The Village in the Jungle* (1913). Member of Fabian Society, wrote many works on political theory eg *Imperialism and Civilization* (1928). Set up Hogarth Press (1917) with wife Virginia Woolf.

Woolf, Virginia Adelaine, née Stephen (1882-1941), English novelist, critic. Prominent in BLOOMSBURY GROUP. Known for sensitive novels of inner experience, experimental in form, eg *Mrs Dalloway* (1925), *To the Lighthouse* (1927), *The Waves* (1931), *Between the Acts* (1941). Essays incl. two series, *The Common Reader* (1925, 1932). Committed suicide.

Woolley, Sir [Charles] Leonard (1880-1960), English archaeologist. Led excavations at Ur, where he found treasures in Royal Cemetery

and evidence of a flood similar to that of Genesis and the Gilgamesh epic. Wrote *Ur of the Chaldees* (1929), a popular account of his work.

woolly monkey, monkey of genus *Lagothrix* from Amazon forests. Grey woolly coat, prehensile tail; moves about in troops.

Woolwich, see GREENWICH. England.

Woolworth, Frank Winfield (1852-1919), American merchant. Founded 'dime-store' chain with first (1879) in Pennsylvania. Extended chain to Britain (1910).

Woomera, town of SC South Australia. Pop. 5000. Base for weapons-testing range, rocket launching and tracking facilities; estab. 1947 by Australian, UK govts. on part of aboriginal reserve.

Worcestershire, former county of WC England, now part of Hereford and Worcester. Incl. valleys of Severn and Warwickshire Avon. Vale of Evesham (orchards) in SE; BLACK COUNTRY (indust.) in NE. Worcester, city on R. Severn, co. town of Hereford and Worcester. Pop. 73,000. Gloves, china, 'Worcester Sauce' mfg. Has hospital (11th cent.), cathedral (14th cent.). Scene of battle (1651) in which Cromwell defeated Charles II.

Wordsworth, William (1770-1850), English poet. Romantic lyrics noted for radically new simplicity of language in depicting nature. Wrote *Lyrical Ballads* (1798) with Coleridge, incl. 'Tintern Abbey'. *Poems in Two Volumes* (1807) incl. 'Ode to Duty', 'Intimations of Immortality', 'The Idiot Boy', 'Michael', 'The Daffodils'. Other works incl. verse autobiog. *The Prelude.* Poet laureate from 1843. His sister, **Dorothy Wordsworth** (1771-1835), kept noted journals.

work, in physics, product of a force and displacement in line of action of force. SI unit of work is joule; other units incl. erg.

workers' control, holding of exclusive decision-making rights by workers in an indust. organization, incl. right to hire and dismiss management. In socialist theory, involves total restructuring of relationships with indust. and, in effect, overthrow of capitalism by placing means of production, distribution and exchange in workers' hands.

workhouse, British institution for maintenance of poor. *See* POOR LAW.

works council, consultative body within an indust. organization, in which workers' representatives participate in decisions affecting the work force. Workers' views are taken into account by a board retaining decision-making responsibility. Legal requirement in large companies in West Germany, Netherlands, Sweden, Italy. *See* INDUSTRIAL DEMOCRACY.

World Bank, *see* INTERNATIONAL BANK FOR RECONSTRUCTION AND DEVELOPMENT.

World Council of Churches, organization assembled (1948) at Amsterdam of representatives from 150 Protestant and Orthodox churches. By 1970s had over 260 member churches from *c* 90 countries. Has no legislative power, provides opportunity for practical co-operation and discussion.

World Federation of Trade Unions (WFTU), body formed (1945) to represent trade union organizations in more than 50 countries. All non-Communist trade unions had withdrawn by 1951. Meets every 4 years.

World Health Organization (WHO), agency of UN (estab. 1948) set up with the aim of attaining highest possible level of health for all peoples. Activities incl. medical research and training in care of sick and prevention of disease.

World Meteorological Organization (WMO), agency of UN (estab. 1951), hq. at Geneva. Aims to standardize, coordinate and improve meteorological services around the world.

World War I, conflict (1914-18) precipitated by assassination (June, 1914) of Francis Ferdinand of Austria-Hungary in Serbia. By Aug., Europe was involved in total warfare, opposing alliances being Central Powers (Germany, Austria-Hungary and Turkey) and Allies (Britain, France, Russia, Belgium, Serbia, Montenegro and Japan). Rapid German advance in W thwarted near Paris; followed by prolonged stalemate with concentrated trench warfare. In E, German victories contributed to success of RUSSIAN REVOLUTION (1917) and Russian withdrawal from war. In 1915, Bulgaria joined Central Powers, Italy joined Allies. Unrestricted German submarine attacks (1916-17) led to US entry on Allied side and eventual end to stalemate. Successful counter-attack by Allies in 2nd battle of the Marne followed by surrender of all

Central Powers except Germany. After internal revolt, Germany signed armistice (11 Nov., 1918) at Compiègne. Subsequent peace treaties, esp. TREATY OF VERSAILLES, radically altered political boundaries of Europe at expense of Central Powers. Overwhelming loss of life (est. 10 million dead) led to international search for peace, initially through LEAGUE OF NATIONS.

World War II, conflict (1939-45) climaxing aggressive policies of AXIS powers (Germany, Italy and Japan) and attempts to counter them by W European nations (UK and France). Hitler's success in Bohemia (see MUNICH PACT) and NON-AGGRESSION PACT signed with USSR opened way for attack (Sept., 1939) on Poland. Britain (with Commonwealth) and France declared war on Germany. Hitler's quick victory in Poland followed by occupation of Denmark, Norway and Low Countries; crushed France (surrendered June, 1940) after Allies were forced to evacuate DUNKIRK. Britain, led by W. CHURCHILL, resisted German air offensive in 'Battle of Britain'. German and Italian successes in N Africa and Balkans (1940-1) preceded invasion of USSR (June, 1941). Japanese attack on Pearl Harbor (Dec., 1941) brought US into war; Japan then occupied much of SE Asia. Axis triumphs halted in N Africa (see NORTH AFRICA CAMPAIGN) by Allied landings in Algeria and S Italy, US naval victories in Pacific and USSR's defeat of German forces at Stalingrad (1943). Italy surrendered (Sept., 1943), but Germany continued to resist Allies. Russian drive

through E Europe and Allied invasion of Normandy under EISENHOWER (June, 1944) brought eventual German collapse and surrender (May, 1945). American 'island-hopping' strategy in Pacific and dropping of atomic bombs on Hiroshima and Nagasaki led to Japan's surrender (Sept., 1945). Need to ensure international peace led to formation of UNITED NATIONS; however, problems of post-war Europe remained unresolved, difficulty increasing with development of COLD WAR between East and West.

worm, name given to members of several phyla of elongated creeping animals, esp. common earthworm. See ANNELIDA, NEMATODA.

Worms, town of W West Germany, on R. Rhine. Pop. 77,000. Wine trade. Scene of Synod of Worms (1076) which deposed Pope Gregory VII and of Diet of Worms (1521) which tried and outlawed Luther.

Worms, Diet of (1521), meeting of theologians and officials of RC church called by Emperor Charles V at Worms. Martin Luther appeared under safe conduct to defend his doctrines. On refusal to retract, he was outlawed, together with his followers.

wormwood, *Artemesia absinthium,* Eurasian perennial plant. Silvery-grey leaves, small yellow flowers. Yields intensely bitter oil used in flavouring, eg in absinthe.

Worthing, mun. bor. of West Sussex, S England. Pop. 88,000. Resort; horticulture. Prehist. Cissbury Ring nearby; Roman remains.

Wotan or **Woden,** in Germanic myth, name given to Norse god ODIN.

wrasse, brightly coloured marine fish of Labridae family, found worldwide. Some species pick parasites from bodies of larger fish.

Wrath, Cape, promontory of Highland region, Scotland, most NW point on mainland.

Wren, Sir Christopher (1632-1723), English architect, mathematician. His plan to rebuild London after Great Fire (1666) was not adopted, but he designed St Paul's Cathedral and 51 City churches, noted for their spires. Other buildings incl. parts of Greenwich Hospital, Sheldonian Theatre (Oxford), Trinity College Library (Cambridge). Works characterized by engineering skill, imaginative use of classical orders.

wren, any of Troglodytidae family of small slender-billed, dull-coloured songbirds. Species incl. European Troglodytes troglodytes, with brown plumage and erect tail, and North American house wren, T. aedon.

wrestling, sport in which two contestants struggle hand-to-hand to throw or force one another to the ground. Of ancient origin, wrestling was incl. in Olympics of 704 BC. Two styles are incl. in modern Olympics: freestyle and Graeco-Roman.

Wrexham, mun. bor. of Clwyd, NE Wales. Pop. 39,000. Indust. centre; coalmining; metal goods, chemicals mfg. Seat of RC bishopric.

Wright, Frank Lloyd (1869-1959), American architect. Evolved 'organic' concept to integrate building and environment; innovator in use of industrial materials, eg reinforced concrete. Greatly influenced course of 20th cent. architecture. Works incl. Johnson admin. building, Racine, Wisconsin, and Guggenheim Museum, New York.

Wright, Orville (1871-1948), American aviator. With his brother, Wilbur Wright (1867-1912), developed engine for use in glider and made 1st sustained power-driven aeroplane flight (1903) near Kitty Hawk, North Carolina.

writing, art of forming symbols on surface of some medium to record and communicate ideas. Pictographic writing developed independently in Egypt, China, Mesopotamia and among the Maya. For development of phonemic writing, see ALPHABET.

Wroclaw (Ger. Breslau), city of SW Poland, on R. Oder, cap. of Wroclaw prov. Pop. 528,000. Railway jct.; river port; engineering, food processing; univ. (1702). Cap. of medieval duchy of Silesia, Hanseatic League member; under Habsburgs from 1526, Prussia from 1742; cap. of German Lower Silesia until 1945. Cathedral (13th cent.).

Wuchang, see WUHAN.

Wuhan, cap. of Hupeh prov., EC China. Pop. 4,250,000. Port at jct. of Han and Yangtze rivers. Transport, indust. centre (shipbuilding, cotton mills, major steel complex) formed by union of Hankow, Hanyang, Wuchang. Major road-rail bridge across Yangtze links towns.

Wuhsien, see SOOCHOW.

Wuppertal, city of W West Germany, on R. Wupper. Pop. 417,000. Textile mfg., pharmaceuticals, brewing. Formed 1929 by union of several towns, incl. Elberfeld (noted in 19th cent. for Elberfeld system of poor relief). Badly damaged in WWII.

Württemberg, region of SW West Germany, hist. cap. Stuttgart. Hilly, crossed by Swabian Jura, Black Forest in W; main rivers Danube, Neckar. Duchy from 1495, kingdom 1806-1918. Became part of Baden-Württemberg state 1952.

Würzburg, city of C West Germany, on R. Main. Pop. 116,000. Indust. centre, esp. wine, printing; univ. (1582). Bishopric founded 741; Marienberg fortress was residence of bishops 13th-18th cent. Has cathedral (11th cent.), baroque palace.

Wyatt, Sir Thomas (1503-42), English poet, courtier. With Surrey, introduced sonnet form into English. Works incl. translations of Plutarch, Petrarch, love lyrics posthumously published in *Tottel's Miscellany*.

Wycherley, William (1640-1716), English dramatist. Known for licentious Restoration comedies. eg *The Gentleman Dancing Master* (1672), *The Country Wife* (1675), creating misanthropic picture of society.

Wycliffe, Wyclif or **Wickliffe, John** (c 1328-84), English religious reformer. Gained support of John of Gaunt by denying Church's authority in temporal affairs. Rejected Church doctrine, eg transubstantiation, penances, absolution; held Scriptures to be supreme authority. Condemned as heretic but never sentenced. Made 1st English translation of Bible with help of friends. Followers, called Lollards, spread his teachings, influencing Jan Hus and other reformers.

Wye, river of Wales and England, flows 210 km (130 mi) from C Wales to Severn estuary near Chepstow. Attractive scenery.

Wyoming, state of W US. Area 253,597 sq km (97,914 sq mi); pop. 334,000; cap. Cheyenne. Great Plains in NE, Rocky Mts. dominate W, semi-desert in SW. Chief rivers Yellowstone, Snake, Green. Livestock, wool, grain production; oil, uranium mining. First explored in early 19th cent.; part of Louisiana Purchase (1803). Grew with gold strike (1867) and cattle boom. Became territ. 1869. Admitted to Union as 44th state (1890).

XYZ

Xavier, St Francis, *see* FRANCIS XAVIER, ST.

xenon (Xe), rarest element of inert gas family; at. no. 54, at. wt. 131.3. Found in minute traces in atmosphere (1 part per 170 million); produced commercially from liquid air. Forms compounds with fluorine. Used in bubble chambers, thermionic valves, *etc.*

Xenophon (*c* 430-*c* 355 BC), Greek historian, pupil of Socrates. Joined Greek expedition to aid Cyrus of Persia against his brother Artaxerxes. Wrote *Anabasis*, relating heroic retreat after defeat at Cunaxa (401). Later banished from Athens for siding with Sparta. Other works incl. *Memorabilia* on Socrates and history of Greece.

xerography, commercial process of copying printed material without using light-sensitive paper. Electrostatic image of original is formed by action of light on selenium-coated plate. Oppositely-charged mixture of thermoplastic and carbon powder is dusted on to plate and adheres to charged areas; image formed is transferred to copying paper and fixed by heat.

Xerxes I (d. 465 BC), Persian king (486-465 BC). Succeeded father Darius the Great whose punitive wars against Greece he continued. Defeated Greeks at Thermopylae (480) and razed Athens. Fleet was destroyed at Salamis and army defeated at Plataea after his return to Persia (479). Murdered by one of his guard.

Xingu, river of C Brazil. Rises in Mato Grosso, flows N 1980 km (1230 mi) to Amazon delta. Has rapids in middle course.

X-rays, electromagnetic radiation of short wavelength, varying from *c* 5×10^{-9} m to 10^{-11} m. Produced by bombardment of matter, usually heavy metals, by high-speed electrons (*eg* cathode rays). Detected by ionizing properties or by affecting photographic plates and fluorescent screens. Penetrate substances opaque to light to a varying degree dependent on density and at. wt. of substance; widely used in medicine to photograph internal organs, bones, and to destroy diseased tissue.

xylem, woody vascular tissue of a plant which conducts water and mineral salts in the stem, roots and leaves and gives support to the softer tissues. In mature trees, constitutes majority of trunk.

xylene, or **xylol** (C_6H_{10}), colourless liquid hydrocarbon, existing in 3 isomeric forms. Occurs in coal tar, wood tar; used in manufacture of polyester fibres, dyes and as a solvent.

xylophone, percussion instrument consisting of a set of resonant wooden bars, tuned to different pitches, which are struck with hammers.

yachting or sailing, sport of racing or cruising in yachts. Modern form was developed in Holland in 17th cent. and popularized in England by Charles II. In US organized racing dates from foundation (1844) of New York Yacht Club. Olympic event since 1908. International ocean-racing contests incl. America's Cup, Fastnet Cup.

Yahya Khan, Agha Mohammed (1917–), Pakistani general, president (1969-71). Headed martial law govt. Tried to suppress independence movement in East Pakistan by military intervention, precipitating civil war (1971). Resigned after defeat by combined Indian and East Pakistani forces.

Yahweh, see JEHOVAH.

yak, *Poephagus grunniens,* hardy wild ox of Himalayas and Tibet. Shaggy brown hair, short legs. Domesticated yak is source of milk and meat; also used as beast of burden.

Yakutsk, city of USSR, cap. of Yakut ASSR, E Siberian RSFSR; summer port on R. Lena. Pop. 120,000. Trade in furs and hides; tanning, sawmilling; univ.

Yale University, New Haven, Connecticut, US, privately endowed univ., founded in 1701, becoming univ. in 1887. Incl. Peabody Museum of Natural History, art gallery, large library. Press estab. 1908.

Yalta, town of USSR, S Ukrainian SSR; Black Sea health resort of S Crimea. Pop. 34,000. Scene of Allied conference between Stalin, Roosevelt and Churchill (Feb., 1945), re-solved post-WWII fate of Germany and agreed on founding of UN.

Yalu, river on China-North Korea border. Rises in Kirin prov., flows 800 km (500 mi) SW into Bay of Korea; h.e.p. source. Used to transport timber.

yam, any of genus *Dioscorea* of tropical climbing plants. Edible starchy tuberous roots. Cultivated for human and animal consumption.

yang, see YIN AND YANG.

Yangtze, river of China. At 5550 km (3450 mi), longest in Asia. Rises in Tsinghai prov., flows E into East China Sea near Shanghai. Navigable to ocean-going ships as far as Ichang, 1600 km (1000 mi) upstream. Major commercial waterway.

Yankee or Yank, term used within US for natives of New England, outside, for any American. In Civil War, used for Northerners.

Yaoundé, cap. of Cameroon. Pop. 178,000. Admin., commercial centre; market town on Douala-Chad railway, trades in coffee, cocoa, rubber; univ. of Cameroon (1962). Former cap. of colony of French Cameroons.

Yaqui, American Indian tribe of Uto-Aztecan linguistic stock. Settled agriculturalists on Yaqui R. of Sonora, Mexico. They do not recognize sovereignty of Mexican govt.

Yarmouth, see GREAT YARMOUTH, England.

Yaroslavl, city of USSR, NC European RSFSR; port on upper Volga. Pop. 538,000. Motor vehicles, textiles, synthetic rubber mfg. Founded 1024; cap. of principality until annexed by Moscow in 15th cent.

yarrow or **milfoil**, any of genus *Achillea* of perennial plants of daisy family, esp. *A. millefolium* native to Eurasia but naturalized in North America. Strong-smelling, feathery leaves, clusters of small, pink or white flowers.

Yawata, see KITAKYUSHU.

yaws or **framboesia**, acute infectious tropical disease caused by spirochaete *Treponema pertenue*. Transmitted by insects and direct contagion. Similar to syphilis in early stages; characterized by skin eruptions and later lesions in skin and bone.

year, term used for period taken by Earth to revolve once around the Sun, usually computed at 365 days 5 hrs 48 mins 46 secs. Sidereal year, interval in which Sun appears to complete 1 revolution with respect to fixed stars, is c 20 mins longer; difference is due to precession of equinoxes. Calendar year is fixed at 365 days with an extra day every 4 years (leap year).

yeast, microscopic single-celled fungus, esp. of genus *Saccharomyces*. Lives on sugars, producing alcohol and carbon dioxide. Used in fermentation of alcoholic beverages and industrial alcohol. Also used in baking, as yeast acts upon carbohydrates in dough, producing carbon dioxide and causing mixture to 'rise'.

Yeats, William Butler (1865-1939), Irish poet, dramatist. Prominent in Celtic Revival, helped found ABBEY THEATRE. Poetry draws on mystical, symbolist influences. Works incl. 'The Lake Isle of Innisfree', 'Byzantium', 'Easter 1916', collection *Last Poems* (1940). Plays incl. *Countess Cathleen*

(1899), *Deirdre* (1907). Member of Irish Senate (1922-8). Nobel Prize for Literature (1923).

Yellow, river of China, see HWANG Ho.

'Yellow Book', quarterly magazine pub. in London (1894-7) by John Lane. Contributors incl. Lionel Johnson, Henry James, Arthur Symons and Aubrey Beardsley (illustrations).

yellow fever, infectious tropical disease caused by virus transmitted by *Aedes* mosquito. Characterized by jaundice, vomiting. Prevented by vaccination, mosquito control.

yellowhammer, *Emberiza citrinella*, European bird of bunting family. Male has yellow head and under-parts, chestnut rump. Name also given to yellow flicker, *Colaptes auratus*, woodpecker of E America.

Yellowknife, cap. and admin. centre of Northwest Territs., Canada; on N Great Slave L. in S Mackenzie Dist. Pop. 6000. Gold mining, transport centre. Founded 1935 after discovery of gold in region.

Yellow Sea (*Hwang Hai*), arm of Pacific between China and Korea.

Yellowstone, river of W US. Rises in NW Wyoming, flows N 1080 km (671 mi) through Montana to Missouri R. in W North Dakota. Traverses scenic Yellowstone National Park on high plateau. Wildlife reserve, many hot springs, geysers (incl. Old Faithful).

Yemen, republic of SW Asia, at S end of Arabian penin. Area c 195,000 sq km (75,300 sq mi); pop. 6,870,000; cap. Sana. Language: Arabic. Religion: Sunnite Islam. Coastal strip in W; mountainous, desert in interior;

grains, fruits, **coffee** grown. Historically similar to Arabia. Under Turkish rule (1849-1918); boundaries estab. 1934. Member of UAR (1958-61), became republic 1962.

Yemen, Southern, *see* SOUTHERN YEMEN.

Yenisei, river of USSR, C Siberian RSFSR. Formed by union of 2 headstreams at Kyzyl; flows c 3850 km (2400 mi) W, then N, to enter Arctic Ocean via Yenisei Gulf. Used for timber, grain transport.

yeomen, term in English social history for class of small landowner who worked own farms. Esp. characteristic of period between disintegration of feudal system and beginning of agrarian, Industrial revolutions.

Yeomen of the Guard, royal bodyguard of England, now restricted to ceremonial functions at Tower of London. Instituted (1485) by Henry VII. Also called 'Beefeaters'.

Yerevan (Russ. *Erivan*), city of USSR, cap. of Armenian SSR; on R. Zanga. Pop. 818,000. Textiles, chemical mfg.; h.e.p. derived from Zanga. Founded 8th cent.; alternately Persian and Turkish until ceded to Russia (1828). Buildings incl. Blue Mosque; Armenian state univ. (1921).

Yesenin or **Esenin, Sergei Aleksandrovich** (1895-1925), Russian poet. Wrote lyric poetry, led notoriously debauched life. Other works incl. verse tragedy *Pugachov* (1922). Married dancer Isadora Duncan.

yeti or **abominable snowman,** animal resembling man, said to live in Himalayas. Tracks found have

been ascribed to it. Existence disputed, but believed by some to be a remnant of Neanderthal man.

Yevtushenko, Yevgeny Aleksandrovich (1933-), Russian poet. Known for youthful, rebellious poetry critical of Soviet regime. Works incl. *Stalin's Heirs* (1961), *A Precocious Autobiography* (1963).

yew, any of genus *Taxus* of evergreen coniferous trees and shrubs. Native to Eurasia and North America. Dark green, flattened needles, red, cup-like, waxy cones containing single poisonous seed. Yields fine-grained elastic wood. Species incl. English yew, *T. baccata*, and North American ground hemlock, *T. canadensis*. Wood once used to make longbows.

Yezidis, religious sect living mainly around Mosul, Iraq. Combines elements of Islam and Christianity. Incorporates worship of devil as an agent of God.

Yezo, *see* HOKKAIDO.

Yggdrasill, in Norse myth, tree of universe. Eagle (heaven) at top, serpent (hell) at bottom; squirrel between was symbolic of strife.

Yiddish, language in West Germanic group of Indo-European languages. Non-national but 1st language of Jews all over the world. Vocabulary contains loan-words from HEBREW, Slavic, Romance languages and English. Alphabet Hebrew. Has important literature dating from late 19th cent.

yin and yang, in Chinese philosophy, terms for contrasting and complementary forces or principles of universe. Yin is passive, negative, feminine; yang is active, positive, masculine, source of light and heat.

yoga (Sanskrit, = union), in Hinduism, system of spiritual discipline by which believers seek union with supreme being or ultimate principle through liberation of the self. Involves exercises in self-control, meditation, breathing, posture.

yogurt or **yoghourt**, semi-solid dairy product prepared by curdling action on milk of bacterium *Lactobacillus bulgaricus*. Easily digested, highly nutritious.

Yokohama, seaport of Japan, on Tokyo Bay, SE Honshu isl. Pop. 2,238,000. Exports silk, canned fish; shipbuilding; motor vehicle and textile mfg. Small fishing village when visited by Perry (1854); opened to foreign trade (1859). Rebuilt after extensive damage suffered in 1923 earthquake and bombing in WWII.

Yom Kippur, *see* ATONEMENT, DAY OF.

yoni, representation of the vulva, a symbol used in worship of Hindu god Shakti. *See* LINGAM.

Yonkers, residential town of SE New York; suburb of New York City on Hudson R. Pop. 204,000. Elevators, chemicals, cable mfg. First settled 1646 by Dutch.

York, House of, English royal family. Claimed throne through Edmund of Langley (1341-1402), 5th son of Edward III, who was created (1385) duke of York. Wars of the Roses arose from rivalry between Richard, Duke of York (1411-60) and Lancastrians. Edward IV, Edward V, Richard III were Yorkist kings before 2 houses united under Henry VII.

York, Richard, Duke of (1411-60), English nobleman. Recognized by Henry VI as his heir, York's claims were set aside on birth of Henry's son (1454). Appointed protector (1453-4) during Henry's insanity, his dismissal on Henry's recovery precipitated Wars of the Roses (1455). Reinstated as protector and heir to the throne after Yorkist victories, he was defeated and killed at Wakefield.

Yorke Peninsula, penin. of SE South Australia, between Spencer and St Vincent gulfs. Sheep and grain farming; salt, copper deposits.

Yorkshire, former county of N England. Was divided in 3: East Riding (co. town Beverley); North Riding (co. town Northallerton); West Riding (co. town Wakefield). Pennines, Dales in W; Vale of York in C; Moors, Wolds in E. Iron, steel, woollen industs. based on W coalfield, centres incl. Sheffield, Leeds, Bradford. Fishing at Hull; resorts incl. Harrogate, Scarborough, Whitby. Co. town was York, city on R. Ouse. Pop. 105,000. Railway jct.; confectionery; univ. (1963). Roman *Eboracum*, Constantine proclaimed Emperor here (306); ecclesiastical centre, archbishopric from 7th cent. Cathedral (12th cent.), many medieval buildings.

Yorkshire terrier, English breed of toy terrier. Dark steel blue on back, tan on head, chest and legs; stands 23 cm/9 in. at shoulder.

Yorktown, *see* WILLIAMSBURG, US.

Yoruba, African people within Kwa group of Niger-Congo branch of Niger-Kordofanian language family. Originated in SW Nigeria, spread throughout W Africa. Tend to live in towns. Use as slaves has led to cultural influence being found in Brazil, Cuba.

Yosemite, region of C California, US; in Sierra Nevada. National Park, has mountains, canyons (esp. Yosemite Valley), highest waterfall in North America (739 m/2425 ft), rivers, sequoia groves.

Youghal, town of Co. Cork, S Irish Republic, on Blackwater estuary. Pop. 5000. Port, resort; carpet, lace mfg. Occasional home of Raleigh, who introduced potato, tobacco to Ireland.

Young, Arthur (1741-1820), English agricultural writer. Travelled extensively, recording his observations of farming techniques in series of *Tours.* Founded monthly periodical *Annals of Agriculture* (1784).

Young, Brigham (1801-77), American religious leader. Converted to Mormon faith; became member of Council of Twelve (1835). After assassination (1844) of Joseph Smith, led W migration; settled Salt Lake City as co-operative theocracy.

Young, Owen D. (1874-1962), American public official. Drew up Young Plan for payment of German reparations after WWI. Adopted 1930, Plan was to specify exact debt and reduce annual payments; thwarted by German economic depression.

Young, Thomas (1773-1829), English physicist, physician. Discovered phenomenon of interference of light and revived wave theory to explain it; made calculations of wavelength of light. Conceived 3-colour theory of colour vision, later extended by Helmholtz. Pioneer in decipherment of Egyptian hieroglyphics.

Younghusband, Sir Francis Edward (1863-1942), British explorer, b. India. Explored mountains between China and Kashmir (1886-7), crossing Gobi Desert. Commissioner to Tibet (1902-4), led British expedition into Lhasa (1904).

Young Men's Christian Association (YMCA), international organization providing young men with accommodation, education, recreational facilities. Estab. 1844 in UK by Sir George Williams, spread to North America (1851-4). Originally solely didactic Christian movement. Has Geneva hq. **Young Women's Christian Association (YWCA)** with similar aims founded (1855) in Britain and US.

Young Turks, reformist and nationalist movement of Ottoman Empire in early 20th cent. Organized revolt which deposed Abdul Hamid II (1909). Its leader, ENVER PASHA, became virtual dictator in 1913.

Ypres (Flem. *Ieper*), town of W Belgium. Pop. 18,000. Textile centre from Middle Ages. Gothic cathedral, Cloth Hall (14th cent.), both restored after extensive damage in WWI. Scene of 3 WWI battles, incl. extensive use of gas by Germans.

Ypsilanti, Alexander (1792-1828), Greek revolutionary. Led revolt in Moldavia (1821) and proclaimed Greek independence from Turkey; uprising put down by Turkish overlords. His brother, Demetrios Ypsilanti (1793-1832), was a leader in simultaneous uprising in the Peloponnese (1821). Helped secure Greek independence.

Yseult, *see* TRISTAN AND ISOLDE.

Ysselmeer, *see* IJSSELMEER, Netherlands.

ytterbium (Yb), rare metallic element of lanthanide series; at. no. 70, at. wt. 173.04. Occurs with yttrium and lutetium in gadolinite. Isolated 1907.

yttrium (Y), rare metallic element; at. no. 39, at. wt. 88.91. Occurs with other rare metals in gadolinite, *etc.* Isolated (1843) by C.G. Mosander.

Yucatán, penin. separating Gulf of Mexico from Caribbean. Area 181,000 sq km (*c* 70,000 sq mi). Mainly limestone plateau in E Mexico, incl. N Guatemala, Belize. Forests in S, savannah in NW. Centre of ancient Mayan civilization with many archaeological ruins.

yucca, genus of plants native to Mexico and S US. Pointed, usually rigid leaves, white waxy flowers on erect spike. Species incl. Joshua tree, *Yucca brevifolia*, of desert regions.

Yugoslavia (*Jugoslavija*), federal republic of SE Europe. Area *c* 255,750 sq km (98,750 sq mi); pop. 21,560,000; cap. Belgrade. Main language: Serbo-Croat. Religions: Orthodox, RC, Islam. Comprises Bosnia and Hercegovina, Croatia, Macedonia, Montenegro, Serbia, Slovenia republics. Julian Alps, Karst in NW; Dinaric Alps run NW-SE; fertile lowlands in NE. Drained by Danube and tributaries. Cereals, forestry, livestock; coal, iron, copper; tourism, esp. on Adriatic. Kingdom of Serbs, Croats and Slovenes created 1918, renamed Yugoslavia 1929. Partisans resisted German occupation 1941-5; People's Republic estab. 1945 under Tito, remaining independent from Soviet Communism after 1948. Gained territ. (1947) from Italy.

Yukon, territ. of NW Canada. Area 536,327 sq km (207,076 sq mi); pop. 18,000; cap. Whitehorse. Mainly uninhabited in N Arctic; mountainous in SW with Mt. Logan (Canada's highest peak). Important mining area esp. gold, silver, lead, zinc; fur trading. Dramatic increase in pop. during Klondike gold rush (1896).

Yukon, river of Canada-US. Formed in SC Yukon by jct. of Lewes and Pelly rivers. Flows NW 3220 km (*c* 2000 mi) to Alaska, then SW to Bering Sea. Salmon fishing, h.e.p. resources. Major route to goldfields during Klondike gold rush.

Yunnan, prov. of S China. Area *c* 419,600 sq km (162,000 sq mi); pop. (est.) 23,000,000; cap. Kunming. Mountain ranges in W drained by many rivers incl. Mekong; plateau in E. Great metal resources, esp. tin. Agric. limited by terrain.

Zabrze, city of S Poland. Pop. 197,000. Coalmining, iron and steel indust.; grew rapidly from late 19th cent. Under Prussian rule 1742-1945; known as Hindenburg 1915-45.

Zagorsk, town of USSR, C European RSFSR. Pop. 74,000. Famous for 14th cent. Troitsko-Sergievskaya monastery, containing 15th and 16th cent. cathedrals, bell tower and Boris Godunov tomb; formerly pilgrimage centre; now museum. Called Sergiev until 1930.

Zagreb (Ger. *Agram*), city of NW Yugoslavia, on R. Sava, cap. of Croatia. Pop. 566,000. Transport, indust. centre esp. chemicals, metal goods. Croatian cultural centre, univ. (1669). Old town ('Kaptol') has RC cathedral (11th cent.), palace (18th cent.).

Zagros Mountains, range forming SW edge of Iranian plateau. Rise to 4548 m (14,920 ft) at Zard Kuh.

Zaïre, republic of C Africa. Area 905,400 sq km (345,000 sq mi); pop. 25,629,000; cap. Kinshasa. Languages: Bantu, French. Religions: native, Christian. Occupies most of R. Congo basin; rain forest in N, savannah in S. Produces cotton, coffee, palm oil, timber; cobalt, copper from Katanga; indust. diamonds from Kasai. Source of slaves 17th-19th cent. Explored by Livingstone, Stanley; Congo Free State estab. 1885 by Leopold II of Belgium, became Belgian Congo colony (1908). Independent (1960) as Republic of the Congo; disunity, incl. secession of Katanga, and civil war followed, ended by UN intervention. Renamed Zaïre (1971).

Zaïre, river of C Africa, *see* CONGO.

Zákinthos (Ital. *Zante*), isl. of W Greece, one of Ionian Isls. Area 409 sq km (158 sq mi); cap. Zante. Currants, olive oil. Held by Venice 1482-1797. Site of many earthquakes.

Zama, ancient village of N Tunisia. Scene of defeat (202 BC) of Hannibal of Carthage by Scipio Africanus of Rome, which ended 2nd Punic War.

Zambezi, river of SC and SE Africa. Flows c 2250 km (1700 mi) from NW Zambia via Victoria Falls and Kariba Dam to Mozambique Channel near Chinde. Navigable stretches separated by rapids.

Zambia, republic of SC Africa. Area 753,000 sq km (290,500 sq mi); pop. 5,138,000; cap. Lusaka. Languages: Bantu, English. Religions: native, Christian. Mainly plateau, mountainous in N, NE; main rivers Zambezi, Kafue. Savannah; agric. incl. maize, tobacco, coffee, livestock. Rich copper deposits, h.e.p. from Kariba Dam; 'Tan-Zam' railway to Dar-es-Salaam. Explored 1850s-60s by Livingstone; admin. by British South Africa Co. from 1889. Northern Rhodesia created (1911); part of Federation of Rhodesia and Nyasaland (1953-63). Independent as Zambia (1964). Member of British Commonwealth.

Zamenhof, *see* ESPERANTO.

Zanzibar, isl. of Tanzania, in Indian Ocean. Area 1660 sq km (640 sq mi); cap. Zanzibar. Exports cloves, copra. With PEMBA, under Portuguese rule from 1503; taken by sultan of Oman 1698, became independent sultanate 1856. British protect. from 1890; independent 1963. United 1964 with Tanganyika to form Tanzania.

Zapata, Emiliano (c 1879-1919), Mexican revolutionary. Seeking agrarian reform, led Indian revolt in S (1911-16). Occupied Mexico City 3 times. Killed by agent of CARRANZA.

Zaporozhye, city of USSR, S Ukrainian SSR; on Dnepr. Pop. 697,000. Metallurgical centre; motor vehicle, machinery mfg. Expanded with building of Dneproges dam and h.e.p. station in 1930s. Nearby Khortitsa isl. was home of Zaporozhye Cossacks, important in history of Ukraine (16th-18th cent.).

Zapotec, Indian people of Oaxaca and Isthmus of Tehuantepec, Mexico. Highly-developed civilization c 100 BC. Culturally akin to Maya, but religion different. Conquered by Spanish (1522-6) after resisting Aztec domination. Culture now predominantly Spanish, although strong vestiges of original remain.

Zaragoza, see SARAGOSSA, Spain.

Zarathustra, see ZOROASTER.

Zarqa, city of N Jordan. Pop. 225,000. Rail jct.

Zatopek,. Emil (1922-), Czech runner. Greatest long-distance runner of his time, he won 5000 m, 10,000 m and marathon titles in 1952 Olympics.

Zealand (*Sjaelland*), largest isl. of Denmark, between Kattegat and Baltic, separated from Sweden by Oresund. Area 7016 sq km (2709 sq mi); chief city Copenhagen. Livestock, dairying, fishing. Road, rail bridge to Falster.

Zealots, Jewish party (c 37 BC–AD 70) formed in opposition to idolatrous practices of Herod the Great. Revolted against Romans (AD 6) and continued intermittent violence until Jerusalem was destroyed by Romans (AD 70). Zealots disappeared as Jews left Palestine.

zebra, African mammal of horse genus, *Equus*. White or. buff coloured with dark stripes; attempts to domesticate it have been unsuccessful. Species incl. common or Burchell's zebra, *E. burchelli*, of E and S Africa, and Grévy's zebra, *E. grevyi*, the largest species.

zebra fish, any of various unrelated tropical fish with barred zebra-like markings. Species incl. Indian danio, *Brachydanio rerio*, popular aquarium fish.

zebu, *Bos indicus*, species of domesticated Asiatic cattle, notably resistant to heat and disease. Long pendulous ears, large dewlap, fatty hump over shoulders. Also called humped or brahman cattle.

Zechariah, prophetic book of OT. First part by Zechariah, dated 519–517 BC. Later part, by another author, prob. c 2nd cent. BC. Consists of visions of destruction of Jerusalem and subsequent redemption under Messiah.

Zeebrugge, town of W Belgium, on North Sea. Port, canal to Brugge; produces chemicals, cake and glass. German naval base in WWI.

Zeeland, prov. of SW Netherlands, incl. Walcheren, North and South Beveland isls. Area 1772 sq km (684 sq mi); cap. Middelburg. Chief port Flushing. Mainly agric.; land reclamation in Scheldt estuary. Joined United Provs. 1579.

Zeeman, Pieter (1865-1943), Dutch physicist. Discovered Zeeman effect (1896), involving splitting of single spectral lines into groups of lines when radiation source is placed in magnetic field. Shared Nobel Prize for Physics (1902) with H. A. Lorentz.

Zeiss, Carl (1816-88), German industrialist. With Ernst Abbe, developed outstanding optical instrument factory. Developed many new lenses, heat-resisting glasses. Firm later famous for cameras.

zemstvo, Russian local assemblies estab. (1864) to supervise public services, eg transport, health, education. In spite of land owners' relative majority, achieved liberal reforms. Functions taken over by SOVIET.

Zen Buddhism, form of Buddhism developed in India and widely adopted in Japan from 12th cent. Holds that good works, intellectual effort, etc, are of no value without ultimate insight (*satori*). This is sought through meditation, esp. on paradoxes to throw doubt on conventional logic.

Zend-Avesta, see AVESTA.

zenith, in astronomy, point on celestial sphere vertically above any place on Earth, directly opposite NADIR.

Zenobia, queen of Palmyra from AD 267. Ruled as regent for her son and extended her empire in the East at the expense of Rome. Defeated (272) by Aurelian who took her to Rome as part of his triumph.

Zeno of Citium (c 334-c 262 BC), Greek philosopher, b. Cyprus. In Athens, studied under the Cynics. Taught that logic must serve virtue. Founder of Stoicism.

Zephaniah or **Sophonias,** prophetic book of OT. Dated 7th cent. BC. Denounces sins of the people but ends with prediction of salvation and Jews' return to God's grace.

Zeppelin, Ferdinand, Graf von (1838-1917), German army officer, inventor. Built 1st rigid-frame motordriven airship (1900); subsequent models named after him.

Zermatt, town of S Switzerland. Pop. 3000. Resort, mountaineering centre at foot of Matterhorn. Rackand-pinion railway to summit of the Gornergrat, alt. 3100 m (10,280 ft).

Zetland, see SHETLAND, Scotland.

Zeus, in Greek myth, chief of the OLYMPIAN GODS; son of CRONUS and Rhea. Overthrew Cronus, became ruler of heaven. Husband of Hera who bore him Hebe, Ares; also fathered many children by goddesses, nymphs, mortals. Dispensed good and evil to men, protected law, order, justice. Manifested authority with thunderbolt; made earth fertile

with rain. Identified with Roman Jupiter.

Zhdanov, port of USSR, SE Ukrainian SSR; on Sea of Azov. Pop. 435,000. Exports grain, coal. Steel, machinery, chemical mfg. Formerly Mariupol, renamed 1948 after Soviet statesman.

Zhukov, Georgi Konstantinovich (1896-1974), Soviet army officer. In WWII, led counter-attack at Stalingrad and relief of Leningrad (1943); captured Berlin (1945) and received German surrender. Defence minister (1955-7).

Ziegfeld, Florenz (1869-1932), American theatre manager. His 'Ziegfeld Follies', based on Folies-Bergère of Paris, estab. American theatrical revue.

Ziegler, Karl (1898-1973), German chemist. His work on use of catalysts to control polymerization of chemicals was important in manufacture of plastics. Shared Nobel Prize for Chemistry (1963) with G. Natta.

ziggurat, in archaeology, artifical tower supporting temple, typical of Mesopotamian architecture of Sumerian period. Usually stepped pyramid made of bricks; best-preserved example (c 2000 BC) is at Ur. Regarded as prototype of Tower of Babel.

Zimbabwe, ruined city of EC Rhodesia. Granite ruins of Bantu culture date from 14th-15th cent., incl. temple, acropolis, dwellings; discovered 1868.

Zimbabwe-Rhodesia, name for RHODESIA since 1979.

zinc (Zn), hard metallic element; at. no. 30, at. wt. 65.37. Occurs as zincblende (sulphide), calamine (carbonate, silicate, *etc*; obtained by roasting and reducing- ore. Used as protective coating for iron and steel, in alloys (eg brass) and dry cell batteries.

Zinjanthropus, see AUSTRALO-PITHECUS.

Zinoviev, Grigori Evseyevich (1883-1936), Soviet political leader. President of Comintern after 1919. Opposed Stalin in struggle for Communist Party leadership after Lenin's death. Executed in Stalinist purge. Name linked to forged 'Zinoviev letter' involving alleged Communist uprising in Britain; its publication contributed to Labour govt. defeat (1924).

Zion, originally fortress in Jerusalem captured by David and known as 'City of David'. Later term used for hill in Jerusalem on which Temple was built, and for symbolic centre of Judaism.

Zionism, political and cultural movement seeking to re-estab. Jewish national state in Palestine. First World Zionist Congress, organized by HERZL, convened 1897. Played important part in setting up Israel (1948), esp. by securing BALFOUR DECLARATION. Now promotes emigration to Israel and donations to support Israeli armed forces.

zirconium (Zr), metallic element; at. no. 40, at. wt. 91.22. Occurs in zircon (silicate). Used as structural material in nuclear reactors; compounds used in manufacture of ceramics and refractory materials.

zither, folk musical instrument of Austria and S Germany with 30-45 strings stretched over sounding box. Has 4 or 5 melody strings which are fretted, other strings provide accompaniment. Played with plectrum and the fingertips.

Zodiac (from Gk., *zodiakos kyklos* = circle of animals), in astronomy and astrology, imagined belt in heavens within which lie paths of Sun, Moon, and major planets. Stars in belt arranged in 12 constellations, originally corresponding to 12 equal divisions of the belt. Divisions therefore named after constellations, and distinguished by signs. In order east from vernal equinox, these are Aries (Ram), Taurus (Bull), Gemini (Twins), Cancer (Crab), Leo (Lion), Virgo (Virgin), Libra (Balance), Scorpio (Scorpion), Sagittarius (Archer), Capricorn (Goat), Aquarius (Water Bearer), Pisces (Fish). The 1st 6 lie N of the equator, the 2nd, S. Defined by Babylonians (*c* 2000 BC), precession of equinoxes has since caused misalignments of named divisions and constellations, but astrologers still use Zodiac to predict individual's fate from state of heavens at time of birth.

Zola, Emile (1840-1902), French author. Leader of naturalists, advocating novel of social determinism with close attention to detail, detached narration, in essay *Le Roman expérimental* (1880). Novels incl. *Nana* (1880), *Germinal* (1885), part of 20 vol. series *Les Rougon-Macquart* (1871-93). Advocate of social reform, defended DREYFUS in pamphlet *J'Accuse* (1898); prosecuted for libel, fled to England.

Zollverein, customs union among German states in 19th cent. Began (1818) in Prussia, gradually absorbed other German tariff unions. Contributed to political unity, achieved by creation (1871) of German Empire.

zoology, branch of biology concerned with study of animals. Systematic classification of animals into species, genera, orders, etc, introduced by Linnaeus; later codified by international agreement. Field of zoology expanded by study of embryology, physiology, ecology and genetics.

Zoroaster or **Zarathustra** (c 628-c 551 BC), Persian prophet. Founder of ZOROASTRIANISM. Little known of his life.

Zoroastrianism, dualistic religion derived from Persian pantheism of c 8th cent. instituted by Zoroaster. Doctrines stated in Zend-Avesta scriptures: universe dominated by warring forces of good (Ahura Mazdah or Ormuzd) and evil (Ahriman), in which good will triumph. Ceremony centres on purification rites. Survives in Iran and India (known as Parseeism).

Zouaves, corps of French infantry raised in Algeria in 1831 from like-named Berber tribe; later became purely French. Noted for discipline and colourful uniform.

zucchini, see COURGETTE.

Zug, town of N Switzerland, on L. Zug, cap. of Zug canton. Pop. 23,000. Printing, woodworking, electrical equipment.

Zugspitze, highest mountain of West Germany, in Bavarian Alps. Height 2963 m (9721 ft); ascended by cable railways from Garmisch-Partenkirchen and Ehrwald (Austria).

Zuider Zee, former inlet of North Sea, NW Netherlands. Divided by dam, completed 1932, into Ijssel-

meer (S), Waddenzee (N). Large-scale reclamation since 1920.

Zulu, African people, belonging to BANTU group. Now settled in Zululand (N South Africa). Agric. primarily cattle-raising. Most Zulu live in enclosures (kraals) of beehive huts, each kraal containing community based on close kinship. Ties becoming weaker as many men leave to work in south. Zulu became powerful in early 19th cent. under Chaka; later, chief Dingaan continued clashes with Boers, and later still Cetewayo warred with British, finally defeated in 1879.

Zululand, hist. region of NE Natal, South Africa, cap. Eshowe. Coastal plain (cotton, sugar plantations), interior plateau (cattle raising), several game reserves. Zulus became powerful early in 19th cent., resisted Boer settlers (1830s). Finally defeated (1879) by British; part of Natal from 1897. Partly corresponds to Kwazulu homeland (area 31,000 sq km/12,000 sq mi; cap. Ulundi) estab. 1959.

Zürich, city of N Switzerland, on L. Zürich, cap. of Zürich canton. Pop. 423,000. Cultural, commercial (esp. banking), indust. centre; printing, publishing; univ. (1833). Joined Swiss Confederation 1351. Centre (under Zwingli) of 16th cent. Reformation. Protestant churches, town hall.

Zweig, Stefan (1881-1942), Austrian author. Humanistic view of European culture expressed in biogs., eg Three Masters (1920) on Balzac, Dickens, Dostoyevski, Maria Stuart (1935). Psychological novels incl. Beware of Pity (1938).

Zwickau, town of S East Germany,

on R. Mulde. Pop. 126,000. Coal-mining, textiles, paper mfg. Anabaptist movement founded here by Thomas Münzer (1520).

Zwingli, Ulrich or **Huldreich** (1484-1531), Swiss religious reformer, humanist. Estab. Protestantism in Zürich in 1520s; set forth doctrines opposed to monasticism, worship of images. Believed in republican basis for church, subsequently influenced Calvin. Killed in war with anti-Protestant Swiss cantons.

Zworykin, Vladimir Kosma (1889-), American physicist, b. Russia. Developed cathode-ray tube for television receiver and 1st practical television camera. Perfected electron microscope.

SIGNS & SYMBOLS

ASTRONOMY

Astronomical Bodies

⊙ 1. The Sun   2. Sunday

☾ ☽ 1. The Moon   2. Monday

🌑 New Moon

☽ ☾ First Quarter

○ Full Moon

☾ ☾ Last Quarter

☿ 1. Mercury   2. Wednesday

♀ 1. Venus   2. Friday

⊕ ⊖ ♁ Earth

♂ 1. Mars   2. Tuesday

♃ 1. Jupiter   2. Thursday

♄ 1. Saturn   2. Saturday

♅ ♅ Uranus

♆ Neptune

♇ Pluto

✳ ✳ Star

☄ Comet

① ② ③ ④ Asteroids in chronological order of discovery

Signs of the Zodiac

Spring Signs

    ♈ Aries, the Ram

    ♉ Taurus, the Bull

    ♊ Ⅱ Gemini, the Twins

Summer Signs

    ♋ Cancer, the Crab

    ♌ Leo, the Lion

    ♍ Virgo, the Virgin

Autumn Signs

    ♎ Libra, the Balance

    ♏ Scorpio, the Scorpion

    ♐ Sagittarius, the Archer

Winter Signs

    ♑ ♑ Capricorn, the Goat

    ♒ Aquariùs, the Water Bearer

    ♓ Pisces, the Fish

Aspects and Nodes

    ☌ conjunction; having the same longitude or right ascension

    ✶ sextile; differing by 60° in longitude or right ascension

SIGNS & SYMBOLS

□ quadrature; differing by 90° in longitude or right ascension

△ trine; differing by 120° in longitude or right ascension

․☍ opposition; differing by 180° in longitude or right ascension

☊ ascending node

☋ descending node

Notation Signs

β celestial latitude

Δ distance from Earth

δ declination

θ equation of light

λ longitude

μ proper motion

π parallax

ρ density

$\wp$ mean density

° degree(s) of arc

′ minute(s) of arc

    ″ second(s) of arc
    + North
    — South

BIOLOGY

    ♂ 1. male organism or cell   2. staminate plant or flower
    ♀ 1. female organism or cell   2. pistillate plant or flower
  O,⊙ annual plant
  ⊙⊙ biennial plant
    ♃ perennial herb or plant
    ⊙ monocarpic plant
    △ evergreen plant
    × crossed with: denoting a hybrid
    ∞ numerous or indefinite in number
    ✳ northern hemisphere
    ✳̅ southern hemisphere
    |✳ Old World
    ✳| New World

SIGNS & SYMBOLS

MEDICINE

           * birth

           † death

□, ♂ male

○, ♀ female

       + 1. excess of 2. acid reaction 3. positive reaction

       − 1. deficiency of 2. alkaline reaction 3. negative reaction

     Ⓐ admitted

     Ⓛ left

     Ⓡ right

    ⓜ heart murmur

MATHEMATICS

       + 1. plus, addition sign 2. positive

       − 1. minus, subtraction sign 2. negative

      × times; multiplication sign

      ÷ divided by, division sign; division also indicated by an oblique line (8/2) or a horizontal line between dividend and divisor ($\frac{8}{2}$)

SIGNS & SYMBOLS

=	equals; is equal to
≠	is not equal to
≡	is identical with; is congruent to; is equivalent to
≈	is approximately equal to
>	is greater than
<	is less than
≯	is not greater than
≮	is not less than
≅	is isomorphic to
:	is to; ratio sign
::	as: used between ratios
∞	infinity
∴	therefore
∵	since; because
∠	angle
∟	right angle
⊥	is perpendicular to
∥	is parallel to
O	circle; circumference
⌒	arc of a circle
△	triangle

SIGNS & SYMBOLS

▢	square
▭	rectangle
▱	parallelogram
$\sqrt{}$	radical sign (*i.e.* square root sign)
Σ	sum
$\int$	integral
$\cup$	union
$\cap$	intersection
$\in$	is a member of; is an element of; belongs to
$\subset, \subseteq$	is a subset of
{ }	set braces
ϕ	the empty set
$\|\ \|$	absolute value of; modulus of
$\lhd$	is a normal subgroup of
μ	mean (population)
σ	standard deviation (population)
$\bar{x}$	mean (sample)
s	standard deviation (sample)
π	ratio of circumference of any circle to its diameter
e	base of natural logarithms

MISCELLANEOUS

    & ampersand

   &c. et cetera

    © copyright

    ′ foot, feet; minutes

   ″ inch(es); seconds

   ✕ by: used in quoting dimensions

   < derived from: used in etymology

   ® registered trademark

   ¶ paragraph mark

   § section mark

   ″ ditto

   ° degree(s)

MUSIC

Time values of notes and rests
(Each note has half the value of the preceding note; the note symbol is followed by the equivalent rest symbol.)

‖₫‖	breve (rarely used)
o ⌐	semibreve or whole note
♩ ▬	minim or half note
♩ ᵳ or ₹	crotchet or quarter-note
♪ ੭	quaver or eighth-note
♬ ੭	semiquaver or sixteenth-note
♬ ᵹ	demisemiquaver or thirty-second note

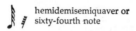 hemidemisemiquaver **or** sixty-fourth note

NB: A dot after a note increases its value by a half.

Clefs in common use (with position of middle C shown)

treble clef

bass clef

alto clef

Accidentals (*i.e.* signs indicating sharpening or flattening of notes)

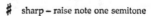 sharp – raise note one semitone

SIGNS & SYMBOLS

✗ double sharp – raise note one tone

♭ flat – lower note one semitone

♭♭ double flat – lower note one tone

♮ natural – after sharp or flat sign, restore note to normal pitch

Time signatures in common use (giving value and quantity of beats in bar)

Simple duple:

$\frac{2}{2}$ *or* **¢**   two minim beats

$\frac{2}{4}$ two crotchet beats

$\frac{2}{8}$ two quaver beats

Compound duple:

$\frac{6}{4}$ two dotted minim beats

$\frac{6}{8}$ two dotted crotchet beats

$\frac{6}{16}$ two dotted quaver beats

Simple triple:

$\frac{3}{2}$ three minim beats

$\frac{3}{4}$ three crotchet beats

$\frac{3}{8}$ three quaver beats

Compound triple:

$\frac{9}{4}$ three dotted minim beats

$\frac{9}{8}$ three dotted crotchet beats

$\frac{9}{16}$ three dotted quaver beats

Simple quadruple:

$\frac{4}{2}$ four minim beats

$\frac{4}{4}$ *or* $\mathbf{C}$ four crotchet beats

$\frac{4}{8}$ four quaver beats

Compound quadruple:

$\frac{12}{4}$ four dotted minim beats

$\frac{12}{8}$ four dotted crotchet beats

$\frac{12}{16}$ four dotted quaver beats

These are the most common time signatures; there are in fact infinite possible combinations.

Miscellaneous

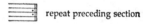 repeat preceding section

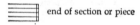 end of section or piece

⌢ pause

8^e play an octave above notes written

Staccato marks and signs of accentuation

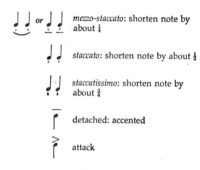

mezzo-staccato: shorten note by about $\frac{1}{4}$

staccato: shorten note by about $\frac{1}{2}$

staccatissimo: shorten note by about $\frac{3}{4}$

detached: accented

attack

Irregular rhythms in common use

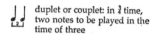 duplet or couplet: in ¾ time, two notes to be played in the time of three

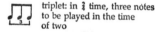 triplet: in ⅔ time, three notes to be played in the time of two

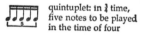 quadruplet: in ¾ time, four notes to be played in the time of three

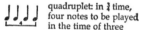 quintuplet: in ¾ time, five notes to be played in the time of four

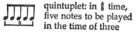 quintuplet: in 6/8 time, five notes to be played in the time of three

SIGNS & SYMBOLS

Ornaments and decorations

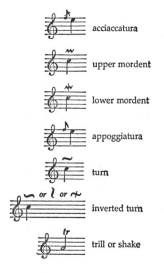

acciaccatura

upper mordent

lower mordent

appoggiatura

turn

inverted turn

trill or shake

SIGNS & SYMBOLS

Dynamics

 *crescendo*

diminuendo

Curved Lines

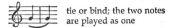 tie or bind; the two notes
are played as one

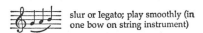 slur or legato; play smoothly (in
one bow on string instrument)

A curved line linking longer passages usually indicates
phrasing.

Pce